GOD'S INSTRUMENTS

Blair Worden is Visiting Professor of History, and Emeritus Fellow of St Edmund Hall, Oxford University.

God's Instruments

'a coherence that sheds so much light on Cromwell's reign that it dazzles . . . quite simply indispensable'

Adrian Tinniswood, *Literary Review*

'one of our finest historians . . . The resulting volume will of course be indispensable for fellow specialists; but it also offers a fine introduction, for the general reader, to some of the best modern historical thinking on the political and mental worlds of the Cromwellian era'

Noel Malcolm, *Standpoint*

'It is a collection which deserves to be and will be . . . treasured, and revisited for its salutary and important wisdom'

Martyn Bennett, *Reviews in History*

'some of the most distinguished writing on the Cromwellian period since the days of Sir Charles Firth'

Keith Thomas, *New York Review of Books*

God's Instruments

Political Conduct in the England
of Oliver Cromwell

BLAIR WORDEN

OXFORD
UNIVERSITY PRESS

OXFORD
UNIVERSITY PRESS

Great Clarendon Street, Oxford, OX2 6DP,
United Kingdom

Oxford University Press is a department of the University of Oxford.
It furthers the University's objective of excellence in research, scholarship,
and education by publishing worldwide. Oxford is a registered trade mark of
Oxford University Press in the UK and in certain other countries

© Blair Worden 2012

The moral rights of the author have been asserted

First published 2012
First published in paperback 2013

Impression: 1

Published in the United States of America by Oxford University Press
198 Madison Avenue, New York, NY 10016, United States of America

British Library Cataloguing in Publication Data
Data available

ISBN 978–0–19–957049–2 (Hbk.)
ISBN 978–0–19–967541–8 (Pbk.)

Printed in Great Britain by
CPI Group (UK) Ltd, Croydon, CR0 4YY

To Chris Jones and to Malcolm Oxley

Contents

A Note to the Reader

My book reproduces, in revised forms, pieces composed on divers occasions. I have tried to bring them together in a way that assists readers who mean to read the volume through, but have also borne in mind ones who may come to it selectively. That second consideration has required occasional moments of near repetition, which anyone in for the long haul is asked to indulge. The essays on which the book draws bore a variety of editorial conventions. I have standardized most of them, but there remain slight inconsistencies which could be repaired only at great labour and to small gain. In quotations the deployment of capital letters has been modernized, but except in Chapter 7 the original spelling has normally been preserved. A word is needed about vocabulary. 'The civil war' means the war of 1642–6; 'the civil wars' the range of the conflicts of 1642–60; 'the Interregnum' the years without a king, 1649 to 1660. There are two little points about the citations. I give the place of publication only of works published outside London since 1900. Secondly, the dates given for weekly newsbooks are those of the last day covered by the issue cited. Thus *Mercurius Politicus* 25 March 1652 means the issue that covered the week 18–25 March.

In this paperback edition I have corrected some typographical slips and other minor errors that appeared in the first impression. I am grateful to Sir Keith Thomas, that most vigilant of readers, for pointing most of them out to me.

Acknowledgements

I thank the publishers and institutions that have allowed or enabled me to reproduce material from earlier writings: Cambridge University Press (Chapters 1, 2, and 6); *Past and Present* (Chapter 2); the Ecclesiastical History Society (Chapter 3); Oxford University Press (Chapters 4 and 9); Boydell and Brewer (Chapter 5); the Royal Historical Society (Chapter 6); Ashgate (Chapter 8); and the British Academy (Chapter 9).

List of Abbreviations

Abbreviations particular to Chapter 4 *are explained in the first citation of each source.*

Abbott	W. C. Abbott, ed., *Writings and Speeches of Oliver Cromwell*, 4 vols (Cambridge, Mass., 1937–47)
BL	British Library
Bodl.	Bodleian Library
Burton	J. T. Rutt, ed., *Diary of Thomas Burton*, 4 vols (1828)
CSPD	*Calendar of State Papers Domestic*
CH	Edward Hyde, Earl of Clarendon, *The History of the Rebellion*, ed. W. D. Macray, 6 vols (1888)
CJ	*Journal of the House of Commons*
CL	*The Life of Edward Earl of Clarendon . . . written by Himself*, 3 vols (1769)
CPW	D. M. Wolfe et al., eds, *Complete Prose Works of John Milton*, 8 vols (New Haven, 1953–82)
CT	*A Collection of Several Tracts of . . . Edward, Earl of Clarendon* (1727)
E	British Library, Thomason Tracts classmark
Firth, *Clarke Papers*	C. H. Firth, ed., *The Clarke Papers*, 4 vols, Camden Society (1891–1901)
Firth and Rait	C. H. Firth and R. S. Rait, eds, *Acts and Ordinances of the Interregnum*, 3 vols (1911)
GD	S. R. Gardiner, ed., *Constitutional Documents of the Puritan Revolution* (Oxford, repr. 1958)
HMC	*Historical Manuscripts Commission Report*
Johnston, *Diary*	G. M. Paul, D. H. Fleming, and J. D. Ogilvie, eds, *Diary of Sir Archibald Johnston of Wariston*, 3 vols, Scottish History Society (Edinburgh, 1911–40)
LP	Blair Worden, *Literature and Politics in Cromwellian England: John Milton, Andrew Marvell, Marchamont Nedham* (Oxford, repr. 2009)
Ludlow, *Voyce*	Edmund Ludlow, *A Voyce from the Watch Tower*, Part V: *1660–1662*, ed. A. B. Worden, Camden, fourth series 21 (1978)
Ludlow's Memoirs	C. H. Firth, ed., *Memoirs of Edmund Ludlow*, 2 vols (1894)
Nickolls	J. Nickolls, ed., *Original Letters and Papers addressed to Oliver Cromwell* (1743) ('Milton State Papers')
ODNB	*Oxford Dictionary of National Biography*

OPH	*The Parliamentary or Constitutional History of England*, 24 vols (1752–63) ('Old Parliamentary History')
Owen, *Works*	W. H. Goold, ed., *The Works of John Owen*, 24 vols (1850–5)
RP	Edward Earl of Clarendon, *Religion and Policy*, 2 vols, continuously paginated (1811)
Somers Tracts	Walter Scott, ed., *A Collection of Scarce and Valuable Tracts selected from . . . Libraries, particularly that of . . . Lord Somers*, 13 vols (1809–15)
SPC	R. Scrope and T. Monkhouse, eds, *State Papers collected by Edward, Earl of Clarendon*, 3 vols (1767–86)
TNA	The National Archives (formerly 'Public Record Office')
TSP	Thomas Birch, ed., *A Collection of State Papers of John Thurloe*, 7 vols (1742)
Whitelocke, *Memorials*	Bulstrode Whitelocke, *Memorials of the English Affairs*, 4 vols (1853)
WJM	*The Works of John Milton*, 18 vols (New York, 1931–8: 'Columbia edition')
Woodhouse	A. S. P. Woodhouse, ed., *Puritanism and Liberty* (1938)

Introduction

No one expected the extent of the Puritan Revolution. Unrevolutionary purposes bore revolutionary results. In 1649 a movement that had aimed to restrain the king, and preserve or restore the ancient constitution, produced his trial and execution for treason, the abolition of the monarchy and the House of Lords, and the establishment of a republic. The initiators of the revolt craved stability in politics and doctrinal uniformity in religion. Instead there came the erratic and abortive constitutional improvisations, and the succession of coups and counter-coups, of the Interregnum, and enduring divisions of faith and worship.

The development that would turn civil war into revolution, and a clash of parties into constitutional upheaval, was the emergence of the new model army in 1647 as a semi-autonomous political force. It had won the civil war of 1642–6, would win the second civil war in 1648, and in 1649–51 would conquer Ireland and Scotland. Though it never aspired to rule alone,[1] it expected and exerted a political influence commensurate with its military achievements. The 'Rump' of the Long Parliament, which ruled the republic, was created by the military purge of December 1648, 'Pride's Purge', and was expelled by the military coup of April 1653, when Oliver Cromwell's musketeers cleared the Commons. 'Barebone's Parliament', the short-lived assembly which followed, was nominated and summoned by the army and then deposed by it. The Cromwellian protectorate was set up by the military coup of December 1653, and was toppled by another in May 1659 after the eight-month rule of Oliver's son and successor, Richard. Over the year thereafter the army, or factions within it, twice restored the Rump; twice deposed it; restored the MPs who had been forcibly purged in 1648; and finally arranged the return of the king.

The politics of the Interregnum have never been lost to historical study. Currently they are attracting fresh and fruitful interest.[2] Even so, professional history has given more attention to the origins and course of the wars of the 1640s than to their aftermath. The broken political landscape of the 1650s is the central territory of this collection of essays, which gives particular attention to the protectorate of Oliver Cromwell. I hope that Oxford University Press, which has honoured me by

---

[1] Austin Woolrych, 'The Cromwellian Protectorate: A Military Dictatorship?', *History* 75 (1990), pp. 207–31.

[2] Notable recent studies are Patrick Little and David L. Smith, *Parliaments and Politics during the Cromwellian Protectorate* (Cambridge, 2007); Patrick Little, ed., *The Cromwellian Protectorate* (Woodbridge, 2007); Patrick Little, ed., *Oliver Cromwell: New Perspectives* (Houndmills, 2009). The role of the army in the Interregnum of 1649–60 will be illuminated in a forthcoming book by Henry Reece.

proposing the book, knows what it is doing, for beside the limitations of the author there are those of the genre. The essays, or chapters, are exploratory in spirit. Addressing the era from a succession of angles, they adopt approaches which, in a rounded narrative or analysis of the period, would need to be integrated into broader discussions. They frequently pay close attention to particularities of events or circumstances. That should never be more than one way of writing history, but it is an indispensable way, for two reasons. First, the microscope may reveal details or patterns of detail that invite the revision of familiar generalizations. Secondly, our comprehension of the words and deeds of the past is shallow, where not misleading, without a knowledge of the immediate pressures or motives that produced them.

The original versions of the chapters were written in two phases, the first four of them in the 1980s, the other six in the last few years. All were commissioned either as lectures or for gatherings of essays by many hands.[3] In bringing the pieces together I have done some embellishing and pruning and adjusting, corrected some slips of fact or expression, and removed some *bêtises*. In half the chapters, numbers 4 to 8, I have done much more. A number of the changes I have made to them expand my material, in some cases extensively, with the result that there are some long essays, now an unfashionable form but one I hope worth preserving. Other alterations bring the book up to date with my thinking or with the findings of others.[4] I have not, however, made extensive changes to the oldest items, the first three chapters, or inserted references to subsequent work into them. The omission needs a word of autobiographical explanation.

When I became a postgraduate student in the later 1960s the predominant issue in analyses of the Puritan Revolution was the social basis of ideological conviction. Studies which in the previous decade had not taken that approach, and which have subsequently achieved a high stature, Brian Wormald's book on the thought of the Earl of Clarendon and J. G. A. Pocock's *The Ancient Constitution and the Feudal Law*,[5] had not been absorbed into the mainstream. Instead, the after-effects of the 'gentry controversy' of the 1950s, and the Marxist interpretations of Christopher Hill, set the agenda of debate. They dominated discussions of Puritanism. Tory, Whiggish, and Marxist judgements, which clashed on other fronts, shared the assumption that religion was the seventeenth century's way of talking about something else: about economic or political aspirations or disappointments, where the real historical interest was taken to lie. The problem with that approach was not its resolve to explain religion, a proper impulse, but the distortion of

---

[3] The essay that is now Chapter 2 is a partial exception. Planned as a contribution to a Festschrift for the historian Owen Chadwick, it outgrew that purpose. It was published instead as 'Providence and Politics in Cromwellian England', *Past and Present* 109 (1985), pp. 55–99. In its place an essay that was written alongside it, now Chapter 1, appeared as 'Oliver Cromwell and the Sin of Achan', in Derek Beales and Geoffrey Best, eds, *History, Society and the Churches: Essays in Honour of Owen Chadwick* (Cambridge, 1985), pp. 125–45.

[4] It is sometimes said that a historian who revises essays when bringing them together ought to particularize the revisions, so that colleagues can trace the development of the author's thinking. In this case, at least, the colleagues must have better things to do.

[5] B. H. G. Wormald, *Clarendon: Politics, History, and Religion 1640–1660* (Cambridge, 1951); J. G. A. Pocock, *The Ancient Constitution and the Feudal Law* (Cambridge, 1957).

religion both by the premises of explanation and by deficiencies of sympathy and observation. The point was brought home to me in the mid-1970s by an accident of research. I learned, from a manuscript by the MP and regicide Edmund Ludlow (or Ludlowe) that had newly come to light, that the work which was known to historians as the *Memoirs of Edmund Ludlow*, and which since its publication in the late seventeenth century had been a main source for Puritan politics, was a posthumous rewriting of his text, whose nimble editor had radically transformed Ludlow's language and beliefs in order to recruit them for a political programme of the editor's own time. The spiritual intensity of Ludlow's Puritanism, and its central place in his narrative and in his explanations of events, had been written out of the script. For by the late seventeenth century Puritan zeal had become an embarrassment to writers and politicians who looked for inspiration to other aspects of the Roundhead cause. It remained embarrassing through the eighteenth century. Some of the consequences of the retreat of Puritan zeal for political and religious thought supply a theme of this volume. The nineteenth century brought a religious revival, which restored public respect for the Puritans' earnestness. Yet it produced more admiration for the moral seriousness of Puritanism than interest in the doctrinal content or impact of the movement.[6] The Victorian trend was in any case reversed by the secularizing forces of the twentieth century.

When Ludlow's manuscript was discovered, the *Memoirs* had been, for nearly half a century, the leading text of a popular undergraduate 'special subject' at Oxford University, which more than anywhere else was the home of sociological debate about the civil wars, and which looked to special subjects to instil a capacity for careful textual analysis. I had first studied and then taught the subject myself, without questioning the judgement of the most knowledgeable historian to have studied Cromwellian England, Sir Charles Firth, the editor of the *Memoirs* in 1894, who vouched for their authenticity. It now struck me that if we had all been taken in, not only by the revision of Ludlow's mentality but by the anachronistic prose in which that mentality had been recast, our habits of textual enquiry must be deficient; and that before we fitted religious experience into sociological frameworks we should look harder at the experience we were framing. I made the point when writing about Ludlow's manuscript in 1977–8.[7] With it again in mind I wrote, in 1983–4, the first three of the essays in this book, two of them on Puritan conceptions of divine providence and on their place in the politics of the time, the third (originally a lecture to the Ecclesiastical History Society in 1983[8]) on the Cromwellian policy of liberty of conscience.

---

[6] Blair Worden, *Roundhead Reputations: The English Civil Wars and the Passions of Posterity* (2001), *q.v.* 'Puritanism'.

[7] 'Who Wrote the *Memoirs* of Edmund Ludlow?', *Times Literary Supplement*, 7 January 1977; and the Introduction to Ludlow, 'Voyce'. I returned to the subject in my *Roundhead Reputations* and in 'Whig History and Puritan Politics: The *Memoirs* of Edmund Ludlow Revisited', *Historical Research* 75 (2002), pp. 209–37.

[8] It appeared as 'Toleration and the Cromwellian Protectorate', in *Studies in Church History* 21 (1984), pp. 199–233.

Since the early 1980s the perspectives of historical enquiry have changed. The mental equipment of the past is no longer accommodated comfortably within sociological explanation or so readily subordinated to it. In those three essays the spirit of protest against the historiographical mood which then prevailed is too ingrained for them to be brought up to date now, when the mood has long passed. In content as distinct from spirit they have, I hope, not dated much. Distinguished work has been produced by a new concern with providentialism[9] and by a revival of interest in arguments about religious toleration,[10] but its findings appear to me to complement rather than contradict mine. Intellectual protest, however, carries a temptation: to underemphasize points which, while compatible with the protesting argument, might obscure the significance the protestor claims for them. In Chapter 3, on toleration, I would now give more attention to two aspects of the subject which I originally hastened by. My main argument was that Cromwell wanted liberty of religious profession not, as previous accounts had often implied, for man's sake, but for Christ's; that he saw it as an indispensable means to the advancement of godliness and the conversion of souls; and that his concern was for the liberty of 'the people of God', not for the unregenerate. I mentioned, but only in the final part of the essay did anything to explore, the commitment of other supporters of the parliamentarian cause to a wider conception of religious liberty than Cromwell's: a commitment which previous and subsequent historians have stressed, but which was not my chief subject. I also mentioned passingly that the protectorate, which officially restricted toleration to beliefs and worship within the Puritan fold and proscribed the practice of 'popery' and 'prelacy', in practice connived at much Catholic and Anglican worship. I hold to the distinction I then made between two incentives: the principle, which was a central preoccupation of Cromwell's career, of liberty for the sake of spiritual fulfilment; and the pragmatic provision of liberty for groups on whose acquiescence in his rule the survival and entrenchment of the protectorate, and thus of his programme of godliness, might depend. Recent research has nonetheless been right to emphasize the extent of the connivance.[11] I hope that Chapter 8, where the angle of approach to Puritanism changes, does something to redress the balance, by giving attention both to latitudinarian arguments for liberty of conscience and to the influence of political needs on Cromwell's language of religious liberty.

My ten chapters can loosely be divided into five successive pairs (though only the pairing of the opening chapters owes anything to intention). If the first and second chapters seek to demonstrate the political power of Puritan beliefs, the third and

---

[9] See especially Alexandra Walsham, *Providence in Early Modern England* (Oxford, 1999). Again because my purpose lay elsewhere, I paid only small attention to providentialism among royalists and Anglicans, on which see John Spurr, 'Virtue, Religion and Government: The Anglican Uses of Providence', in Tim Harris, Paul Seaward, and Mark Goldie, eds, *The Politics of Religion in Restoration England* (Oxford, 1990), pp. 29–47.

[10] For the Puritan period the recent literature is best approached through John Coffey, *Persecution and Toleration in Protestant England, 1558–1689* (2000), and Sarah Mortimer, *Reason and Religion in the English Revolution: The Challenge of Socinianism* (Cambridge, 2010), esp. ch. 8.

[11] The findings of Kenneth Fincham and Stephen Taylor are especially pertinent: below, p. 184.

fourth are about the conversion of beliefs into practical policy: in the first case in the cause of liberty of conscience, in the second of godly reformation. The fourth chapter, the longest of the book, is on the Cromwellian rule of Oxford University, to which Puritans looked to train the future political and spiritual leaders of the nation. I first wrote it in 1986. By that year the spirit of protest was no longer necessary, for the work of John Morrill had brought the subject of religious motivation in the civil wars to the centre of interest.[12] In any case, the story I was commissioned to tell could hardly have been narrated without attention to the content and the resolve of Puritan idealism. The essay appeared as a chapter in the fourth volume of Oxford's *History of the University*.[13] Cromwellians knew that if England were to be Puritanized they must control the universities, where Puritan doctrine could be articulated and be implanted among the young. The chapter studies Cromwell's use of the office of Chancellor of Oxford, to which he was elected in 1651. Readers of the original version, written as it primarily was for students of the university's past, could come to it equipped with the specialized knowledge of the subject imparted by previous chapters of the same volume. Here I have broadened the scope of the essay, which is now intended to illustrate the history not only of Cromwellian Oxford but of Cromwellian England.[14] Though the university, unlike other local communities, was not composed of people who had grown up in it, its dealings with central government have some of the features that the scholarship of recent decades has discerned in the relationship of shires and towns to Whitehall. The rich archival legacy of Puritan Oxford affords unfamiliar views both of the national political aspirations of Puritanism and of its struggle to implement them amid challenging local conditions.

Having moved, in the third and fourth chapters, from the definition of Puritan ideals to their implementation, I turn in the next two to the political setting of that endeavour, and to the mechanisms and the distribution of Cromwellian power. Chapter 5, of which a shorter version appeared in a collection of essays on the protectorate published in 2007,[15] is concerned with the internal politics of the regime. It draws on a voluminous but recalcitrant body of evidence: the records of the executive and advisory council, which in 1657 resumed its regal title the privy council. The powers given to the council were portrayed by the government as a significant political and constitutional development. The essay tests that claim. Chapter 6, which was originally a lecture given to the Royal Historical Society in

---

[12] John Morrill, 'The Religious Context of the English Civil War', *Transactions of the Royal Historical Society*, fifth series 34 (1984), pp. 155–78; idem, 'The Attack on the Church of England in the Long Parliament, 1640–1642', in Beales and Best, *History, Society and the Churches*, pp. 105–24; both reprinted in Morrill's *The Nature of the English Revolution* (1993).

[13] Nicholas Tyacke, ed., *The History of the University of Oxford*, vol. 4: *Seventeenth-Century Oxford* (1997), pp. 733–72.

[14] Amid the revisions there is a statement which I have preserved for quaintness' sake. Of the Visitation sent by the Long Parliament to transform the university, I wrote that 'Never in the history of Oxford has more power been held by its would-be reformers.' The sentence was written before the Higher Education Funding Council set to work.

[15] 'Oliver Cromwell and the Council', in Little, *Cromwellian Protectorate*, pp. 82–104.

2009,[16] discusses the relationship of Cromwell's protectorate with the nation at large, and assesses the strength of the government's power base.

My protesting emphases of the early 1980s have produced some misunderstanding, which I hope Chapters 5 and 6 will rectify. Seeking, in the first three essays, to demonstrate the force of religious conviction in political decision-making, I gave less space to the practical pressures which inevitably made their own impact on Cromwellian politics, and which no realistic observer of them could miss. I was trying to establish a dimension of Puritan rule, not offering a single key to it. It is a point I should have spelled out. In the essay that has become Chapter 1, I wrote (in a passage I have now taken the precaution of adjusting) that Cromwell's alertness to his own and the nation's iniquity, and to the divine displeasure it was bound to provoke, 'may help us to understand' his decision in 1657 to refuse parliament's offer of the Crown. I am taken to have argued that it unilaterally 'caused' it.[17]

It could not have done. No other-worldly figure could have risen to political eminence in Puritan England, let alone to Cromwell's stature. Soul-searching and political calculation were inseparable, as indeed the second essay explains. The prayer-meeting at Putney on 29 October 1647 that turned into the famous debate on the franchise was about a great deal more than prayer. The admonition against betrayals of God's spirit that were made during it, as in countless other prayer-meetings or fasts of soldiers and politicians during the period, were themselves weapons of political contrivance and persuasion. So was the monitoring of souls in Cromwell's own correspondence, as such recipients of his letters as Robert Hammond[18] and Lord Wharton[19] and Oliver's son-in-law Charles Fleetwood[20] might ruefully have testified. The introduction of the protectorate in December 1653 divided the self-styled godly and, in the words of Fleetwood, around whom much of the contention circled, helped set 'saint against saint'.[21] A breach occurred between men who looked to Cromwell for the godly rule, or the liberty of conscience, that the parliamentary governments of 1649–53 had failed to supply, and those who mistrusted his motives or opposed his elevation. How could he win over the doubters?

One way was through the press, which brought conviction and propaganda together. Henry Walker, the editor of the government newsbook *Severall Proceedings of State Affaires*, and long the spokesman for the religious policies and positions of the Puritan regimes, acknowledged in the weeks after the coup that 'some who pretend to godliness' were 'offended with [Walker's] so freely owning and declaring for' Cromwell's rule. Walker's own support for it, he explained, arose not from any motive of reward or favour but from a recognition of God's will.[22] He made a

---

[16] It appeared as 'Oliver Cromwell and the Protectorate', in *Transactions of the Royal Historical Society*, sixth series 20 (2010), pp. 57–83.
[17] See e.g. Little, *Oliver Cromwell*, pp. 218, 236.
[18] Abbott, i. 577, 676–8, 696–9.
[19] Ibid., i. 646, ii.189–90, 328–9, 453, 560–1.
[20] Ibid., iii. 88–9, 756.
[21] *TSP*, iii. 70.
[22] Joseph Frank, *The Beginnings of the English Newspaper 1620–1660* (Cambridge, Mass.), p. 244.

parallel case for the protector's decision to accept the offer of single rule. After 'some days' of pressure to take his new title, wrote Walker, Cromwell had yielded 'as the only means to rescue the people from the danger of ruin; which was made so clear and plain to him, and from God's holy words such satisfactory Scriptures were brought to his mind that he might comfortably expect a blessing in, from some promises, which hath of old been his excellency's recourse unto, who in this had much sought the Lord day and night'.[23] The 'promises', which were contained in Isaiah 1:26 and, behind it, in the Book of Judges, were identified three weeks later in a pamphlet printed by Robert Ibbitson, Walker's collaborator in the production of *Severall Proceeedings*. It presented Cromwell as a divinely appointed English parallel to the virtuous judges who had governed Israel.[24]

In January 1655 the protector's own words aligned his rule with that model, and contrasted it with the selfish principles of unlimited and hereditary kingship that had prevailed until 1649. He had accepted the protectorate, he told parliament, 'well looking, that as God had declared what government he had delivered over to the Jews, and placed it upon such persons as had been instrumental for the conduct and deliverance of his people; and considering that promise in Isaiah, that God would give rulers as at the first, and counsellors as at the beginning'. For 'I did not know but that God might begin, and though at present with a most unworthy person, yet as to the future it might be after this manner, and I thought this might usher it in.'[25] A few days before Cromwell's speech the same parallel had been obligingly drawn, on the government's behalf, in Andrew Marvell's published poem on the 'First Anniversary' of Cromwell's accession.[26]

Cromwell was sensitive to imputations that he cloaked 'carnal' or 'politic' designs in providentialist rhetoric,[27] a charge which to his mind merely confirmed the blindness of his accusers to God's purposes.[28] Yet how congruent divine impulsion and political resourcefulness could be. Who could doubt the place in Cromwell's heart of the cause of European Protestantism? A few hours before his death he 'was distracted, and in those fits he would cry out, "What will they do with the poor Protestants in Piedmont, in Poland and other places," and such kinds of discourse'.[29] Yet his Protestant diplomacy was no less unmistakably designed, as his Secretary of State John Thurloe acknowledged, 'for the support of things at home'.[30] The termination of the Anglo-Dutch war at the outset of the protectorate, and the decision to fight Spain instead, were designed to confront Antichrist—and simultaneously to broaden, through an appeal to the traditional diplomatic objectives of English Protestantism, the basis of his regime's support. Cromwell's

---

[23] *Severall Proceedings of State Affaires* 29 December 1653, p. 3892.
[24] 'Johannes Cornubiensis', *The Grand Catastrophe; or, The Change of Government* (1654).
[25] Abbott, iii. 589.
[26] *LP*, pp. 146–7.
[27] Abbott, ii. 38–9, iii. 592.
[28] Below, p. 53.
[29] Frances Henderson, ed., *The Clarke Papers V*, Camden Society, fifth series 27 (2005), p. 272.
[30] Michael Roberts, ed., *Swedish Diplomats at Cromwell's Court, 1655–6*, Camden Society, fourth series 36 (1988), p. 28n.

programme of religious and moral reform at home was meant to create a common-wealth fit for God's eyes and to avert divine wrath—and simultaneously to reconstruct, as a foundation of his own rule, the Puritan consensus of 1640. It is a mistake to expect the practitioners of ideologies that aspire to transcend the laws of political life to be less likely to be animated or constrained by them than politicians of more mundane outlook. The relationship between the beliefs and actions of politicians is always a jumble, most of all in times of ideological strife and intensity. Cromwellians knew themselves to be 'instruments' of providence, ap-pointed to implement God's will and to follow the directions of his 'outstretched', 'holy arm'. They knew the sinfulness of trusting to their own natural capacities, to 'an arm of flesh'. Yet they also knew that men who do the Lord's work in the world, whether on the battlefield or in politics, must be 'wise as serpents'.[31] The establish-ment and survival of Puritan rule stretched saintly cunning to extremes.

Time and again the direction of events was determined by Cromwell's solitary choices. Whether or not we take his motives at his own valuation, we miss an epic political force, one with decisive consequences for English and British history, if we bypass his unassailably steadfast and defiant service of what he took to be God's purposes, and the exultation and exaltation he drew from it. In January 1655, when he explained the parallel with the judges of the Old Testament to the parliament he was about to dissolve in anger, his regime was to all appearances in disarray. The parliament, to which he had looked to give the protectorate the legal and statutory sanction it desperately needed, had refused to give it. He faced the prospect of financial paralysis and of naked military rule, with not only Cavalier but most Roundhead opinion ranged against him. Yet he had overcome huge odds before. 'Let the difficulties be whatsoever they will,' he told MPs in the same speech, 'we shall in his strength be able to encounter with them. And I bless God I have been inured to difficulties; & I never found God failing when I trusted in him.'[32]

In the two long essays that follow, Chapters 7 and 8, we return from the exercise of political power to beliefs and values that informed it (though Chapter 6, too, makes points about political conviction, which foreshadow the argument of its successor). Chapter 7 was developed from a seminar paper I gave in All Souls College Oxford in February 2011.[33] It addresses a basic problem about the civil wars. No one at the start of the conflict, and hardly anyone before 1649, had argued that England should be governed without a king. How then did the monarchy

---

[31] Matthew 10:16.

[32] Abbott, iii. 590.

[33] The chapter also bears a distant relationship to an essay which began life as a paper for a colloquium in Perugia, arranged by the European Science Foundation, on the history of republicanism. It was published as 'Republicanism, Regicide and Republic: The English Experience', in Martin van Gelderen and Quentin Skinner, eds, *Republicanism: A Shared European Heritage*, 2 vols (Cambridge, 2002), i. 307–27. The seminar at All Souls was one of a series in which speakers were invited to assess the past uses, and the present usefulness, of nouns ending in 'ism'. My allotted noun was 'republicanism'. I have, however, avoided the noun in the rest of this book. As I argued in the paper, such usefulness as it may have had in sixteenth- or seventeenth-century studies has been destroyed by the promiscuity of its recent usage. I have, however, occasionally used 'republican', as a noun or adjective, to denote either an opponent of kingship or opposition to it.

come to be abolished? There is a second part to the problem. The question whether England should have a single ruler became one of the three great divisive issues of the Interregnum. With the other two, liberty of conscience and the army's role in politics, it tore the Puritan cause apart. How did that division emerge?

In offering answers to those questions, the chapter seeks to illustrate general rules of the history of political thought: that ideas which shape politics are also shaped by their course; that their development is steered not by detached contemplation of the world around us but by the impact of events on the way thinkers see it; and that transformations of power can transform or uproot opinion. Chapter 8 makes the same points. It was originally written for a colloquium held at the University of Hull in 2008 to assess, a quarter of a century after its delivery, the lecture in which John Morrill had portrayed the civil wars as 'wars of religion'.[34] He had brought new scholarship to an old problem, the balance of religious and political motives in the conflict. In 1672 Andrew Marvell shrugged his shoulders at the question 'Whether it were a war of religion, or of liberty', and declared the answer 'not worth the labour to enquire. Which-soever was at the top, the other was at the bottom.'[35] Historians must hope that he was wrong about the labour, but there are no good answers to his question that skirt the complexity to which he was alive. Chapter 8 turns to a neglected aspect of the problem. It asks, not which of the two spheres of controversy was the more important, but how the contenders perceived the relationship between them. How had the issues of 'religion' and 'liberty' come together, and how did men come to strive for both of them? At the start of the conflict no innate connection was seen between them, beyond a recognition that God's will must in some way be present in both of them. By its end, there had emerged a vocabulary of 'civil and religious liberty'.

The vocabulary had a long future. In reporting its longevity, the chapter aspires to support another general rule: that a teleological perspective on the past, which a number of historians now seem to expect to distort it, may illuminate it. It is when we explore the durability of the concept of 'civil and religious liberty' that we notice patterns of thought and language in the 1640s and 1650s which studies confined to the horizons of that era have missed. Between us and the conflicts of Stuart politics there lies the long Whig era of English history, which lasted from the Revolution of 1688 to the Great War: the period, that is, when political argument turned on a succession and variety of Whig (or, from the mid-nineteenth century, Liberal) principles and on reactions against them. The defining preoccupation of the era was liberty, though fashions of historical enquiry have obscured its pervasiveness and persistence. In the literature and polemic and political controversies of the period it is everywhere. The cascade of poems and plays and orations and sermons of the eighteenth century that were addressed to liberty by its 'friends', by 'ardent' lovers

---

[34] A shorter version of the chapter appeared as 'Oliver Cromwell and the Cause of Civil and Religious Liberty', in Charles Prior and Glenn Burgess, eds, *England's Wars of Religion, Revisited* (Farnham, Surrey, 2011), pp. 231–51.

[35] Martin Dzelzainis and Annabel Patterson, eds, *The Prose Works of Andrew Marvell*, 2 vols (New Haven, 2003), i. 192.

of its 'sacred flame', by worshippers at its 'altar', was followed in the nineteenth century by unending tributes to the progress of English history towards the liberty that now had been attained, or was being attained, or ought to be attained. Over those two centuries the civil wars were largely viewed from such perspectives.

Modern students of the period have reacted against that approach, in two ways. First there has been an objection of social ethics or preferences. From 1918 the preoccupation with liberty was overtaken, in Britain (though not in the United States, the other main source of modern studies of seventeenth-century England), by one with equality, of which the privileged landed leaders of the parliamentarian cause looked to have been no friends. Whose liberty had they contended for, it was asked, and at whose expense? That question, by bringing the concerns of later centuries to the civil wars, has the anachronistic tendency of which Whig historiography – a capacious term, but useful shorthand here—is itself often accused.[36] The second reaction objected to anachronisms allegedly perpetrated by Whig historians themselves. In Chapters 6, 7, and 8 I suggest that too much has been drained with the Whig bathwater. If the Whig era came after the Puritan revolt, it had roots within it. They did not lie in any practical achievements of the Roundhead movement, which was crushed at the Restoration and removed from the legislative record, and which provoked a profound and enduring reaction against its memory. The Whig indebtedness to the revolt lay, rather, in ways of thinking about both politics and religion.

In politics, Whig historiography dwelled most of all on the history of parliament. It was right to do so. The public esteem for parliament as a guardian of liberty was a powerful force in mid-seventeenth-century politics, not an invention of Whig posterity. MPs acquired new experiences from the civil wars. They governed the country, de facto before 1649, by statute after it. Their claims and activities instilled habits of toughness and confidence and expertise which confronted all future monarchs, and which help to explain the ease of the transition of parliament from a body which in the 1680s the Crown first routed and then neutered to one which from 1689 would become entwined with the executive and meet every year. Parliamentary rule was nonetheless foreign to the aims of the parliamentarians of 1640–2, and was disowned or conveniently forgotten by most of them at the Restoration. It was an exception to a historical norm, produced by a succession of unexpected emergencies. What made it possible was an assumption about the role of parliament in such emergencies, as the great council and representative and arbiter of the realm: the role it was taken to have assumed in 1253, in 1327, in 1399, and in 1422. Parliament's actions of 1640–2, 1649, 1660, and 1689 rested on the same premise. Chapters 6 and 7 draw attention to the esteem of Interregnum politicians for parliamentary authority; to their commitment to the principle of political consent that informed that sentiment; and to the place of those views in the opposition to Cromwell's rule.

---

[36] I have explored the varieties of the Whig tradition in my *Roundhead Reputations*.

On the subject of religion, too, we can learn from Whig perspectives, even as we resist the distortions against which the first three chapters warn. Readers of this book will find allusions to a tension at the heart of all historical enquiry that aims to avoid both present-centredness and mere antiquarianism: between the recovery of the past on its own terms, a pursuit to which hindsight can seem inimical, and the detection of developments over time, to which it is essential. Chapter 8 offers a case for the combination of those goals. If the emphasis of the first three chapters on what we can loosely call Puritan fundamentalism is correct, then Puritanism, which has often been characterized, especially in nineteenth-century Britain but also in twentieth-century America, as a friend to the liberty sought or hailed by later generations, looks like an enemy to it, which is how, down the centuries, opponents of its 'fanaticism' have viewed it.[37] It is simplistic to choose between those perceptions. Puritan conceptions of liberty, in one sense so distant from the liberal values of later ages, prove in another to be a source of them. Oliver Cromwell, whose dissimilarities with subsequent Whig advocates of toleration is emphasized in Chapter 3, and whose deployment of his army against parliaments would be viewed by Whig historiography as an affront to civil liberty, appears in Chapter 8 in a role as inadvertent as it is unexpected: as an anticipator and shaper of what would become a Whig tradition. It is an outcome to add to the unintended consequences of the Puritan Revolution.[38]

The last two chapters offer guides to the minds of two men, John Milton and Edward Hyde, Earl of Clarendon, who were known to their contemporaries mainly for their politics but are familiar to posterity mainly for achievements in literature: in Milton's case the great poems that appeared near the end of his life, in Clarendon's the posthumous *History of the Rebellion*. Both chapters arose from four hundredth anniversaries, the first that of Milton's birth in 1608, the second that of Hyde's in 1609. The two men were born two months apart, and died in 1674, a month apart. The essay on Milton, which arose from a conference at the British Academy held close to his birthday,[39] stands back from, and seeks to make intelligible to a non-specialist reader, some of the findings of a book which I published in 2007 on the literature and politics of the Cromwellian period.[40] The chapter on Clarendon is a revised and expanded version of a lecture arranged by the History Faculty in the Examination Schools at Oxford, the university of which he was a celebrated Chancellor. In converting the lecture into print I have excised its local references and subdued its oral character. The chapter takes us from the Puritan world explored in the rest of the book to the royalist one, that under-examined theme to which historians and literary critics are increasingly turning. It explores religious positions which were distant from Puritanism, but which had no less bearing on the relationship of faith to politics. Between Milton, who gloried in

---

[37] Ibid., *q.v.* 'Puritanism'.
[38] They are a theme of my *The English Civil Wars* (2009).
[39] It was published in Paul Hammond and Blair Worden, eds, *John Milton: Life, Writing, Reputation* (Oxford, 2010), pp. 1–21. In this case I have made only small changes.
[40] *LP*.

the execution of Charles I, and Clarendon, who was devastated by it, there were stark oppositions. Yet there were kindred sentiments too, appalled as both men would have been to be told so. Their conceptions of piety and virtue, and of the government of the world by God's providence, overlapped as well as diverged. Their careers, like Cromwell's and those of many other inhabitants of this book, were struggles, against huge odds, to implement high ideals in a period when the realities of power were abnormally complex and abnormally harsh.

1

Cromwell and the Sin of Achan

Oliver Cromwell knew that God had a special and surpassing purpose in the civil wars. The Lord 'hath been pleased to make choice of these islands wherein to manifest many great and glorious things', 'such things amongst us as have not been known in the world these thousand years'.[1] For 'reasons best known to himself', he had raised up Cromwell, a 'weak instrument', 'not worthy the name of a worm'. Under Cromwell's leadership 'the poor despised people of God', now miraculously delivered from the persecution of the 1630s, and 'by providence having arms', laid low the mighty. Their victories, won by 'an army despised by our enemies, and little less than despaired of by our friends', confounded human calculation.[2] When Cromwell and the self-styled 'saints' sought to comprehend the wonder and meaning of those mercies, they turned to the Old Testament, which they knew so intimately. There they found the figurative models, the 'parallels', which came to dominate their political imaginations and to shape their interpretations of political and military events. In the divine plan of history, they believed, the deliverance of 'God's peculiar' in England might have a place equal in import to the preservation of the people of Israel. The saints had passed out of an Egypt (the captivity of the Church under Archbishop Laud), through a Red Sea (of civil-war blood), towards a promised land.

Their progress constituted in Cromwell's mind a 'remarkable series' or 'chain' of 'providences'. The saints 'were never beaten; wherever they engaged the enemy they beat them continually. And truly this . . . has some instruction in it.'[3] There was Marston Moor, which Cromwell believed to have 'all the evidences of an absolute victory obtained by the Lord's blessing upon the godly party principally'. There was Naseby, where, inspecting the cavalry on the morning of battle, he 'could not . . . but smile out to God in praises, in assurance of victory, because God would, by things that are not, bring to naught things that are'. Then, in 1648, when royalist risings seemed likely to crush the godly cause, the new model army was vouchsafed the spectacular triumphs of the second civil war. Cromwell cried out in astonishment at those 'wonderful works of God, breaking the rod of the oppressor, as in the day of Midian . . . .Wherever anything in this world is exalted,

[1] *A Declaration of his Highness the Lord Protector and the Parliament . . . for a Day of Solemn Fasting and Humiliation in the Three Nations* ([September] 1654); Abbott, iii. 592.
[2] Abbott, i. 697, ii. 483; Stephen Marshall, *A Sacred Record* (1645), p. 30.
[3] Abbott, iv. 471.

or exalts itself, God will put it down, for this is the day wherein he alone will be exalted.'[4]

Still greater mercies were to come. In 1649, when the royalists in Ireland threatened to destroy the infant Commonwealth, God bestowed 'astonishing', 'marvellous great', 'unspeakable mercies' at Dublin and Drogheda and Wexford. Those victories, wrote Cromwell to parliament, were 'seals of God's approbation of your great change of government'. In a private letter he rejoiced that God still prospered

> his own work in our hands; which to us is the more eminent because truly we are a company of poor, weak and worthless creatures. Truly our work is neither from our brains nor from our courage or strength, but that we follow the Lord who goeth before, and gather what he scattereth, that so all may appear to be from him. . . . What can we say to these things? If God be for us, who can be against us? Who can fight against the Lord and prosper? Who can resist his will?

In July 1650, now lord general, Cromwell led his army into Scotland. In September, at Dunbar, the army, and with it the godly cause, seemed doomed to extinction. Instead he could write to parliament on the day after the battle to report 'one of the most signal mercies God hath done for England and his people, this war. . . . It would do you good to see and hear our poor foot go up and down making their boast of God.'[5] The outcome of Dunbar seemed especially revealing of the divine purpose because both sides had 'appealed' to 'the God of battle' to decide between them.[6] 'The Lord hath heard us', proclaimed Cromwell, 'upon as solemn an appeal as any experience can parallel.' A year later the royalists were finally vanquished by that 'crowning mercy', the 'marvellous salvation wrought at Worcester'.[7]

How could the magnitude of those deliverances be measured? How could they be sufficiently praised? Cromwell said a great deal about the central place of providence in his life, in his victories, in the making of his decisions. Yet however much he said, he could never feel that he had done justice to his theme. How, amid the lengthy and autobiographical 'narratives of matter of fact' that he visited upon many audiences, was he to communicate 'those things wherein the life and power of them lay; those strange windings and turnings of providence' which gave a thread of meaning to 'the lowest historical narration . . . there being in very particular . . . a remarkable imprint of providence set upon it, so that he who runs may read it'?[8] He was unmoved when his enemies questioned whether God's will could truly be known from the results of battles; or when they reminded him how unsearchable are God's judgements and that his ways are past finding out; or when they protested that Christ's kingdom is not of this world. His knowledge of God's favour came not only from the victories themselves but from the spiritual 'manifestations of his

---

[4] Ibid., i. 287, 365, 619, 638.
[5] Ibid., ii. 103, 124, 173, 235–6, 324–5.
[6] Nickolls, pp. 19, 25, 73.
[7] Abbott, ii. 335, 463.
[8] Ibid., iii. 53–4.

presence' which they brought to the saints in arms. The Lord declared his 'approbation and acceptance . . . not only by signal outward acts, but to the heart also'.[9]
The experience of victory was an aid to the sanctification of his elect. It strengthened their assurance of faith, and assisted the workings of grace upon their souls.
'I think, through these outward mercies,' Cromwell told his friend Lord Wharton
after the victories of 1648, 'faith, patience, love, all are exercised and perfected, yea,
Christ formed, and grows to a perfect man within us.'[10]

Cromwell's trust in God's providence was the 'rock', the 'sure refuge', the 'sun
and a shield' of his life. Even in adversity 'I can laugh and sing in my heart when I
speak of these things.'[11] Through the fear of God he conquered the fear of men.
When providence led him into unknown political territory he followed unflinch-
ingly, and took his weaker brethren with him. And yet, within all the joy and
confidence of his providentialism, there was always room for anxiety, perhaps even
for doubt. What happened when, as in 1646–8 and again from 1651, peace
afforded no military successes to fortify the saints, or to help them discern God's
will amid the complexities of political manoeuvre? Or what should his elect think
when God 'mingled the cup' of triumph by dividing them among themselves, or by
marking them out for private affliction and grief? There was a further, graver
possibility: that the God of battle, who had brought so many victories, would
one day bring defeat.

Of course, the saints expected setbacks. They expected God to send them
'rebukes', 'trials', and 'corrections', in order to preserve them from the 'security',
the 'drowsiness', the 'sloth', which unbroken prosperity might bring. Although
God loved to melt the soul with mercies, he sometimes needed to scourge it with
judgements. So adversity might be a sign of grace. Yet there might be a very
different explanation. God was known to abandon and exchange his imperfect
'instruments' when they began 'to fail, and fall off like untimely fruit'.[12] Might not
the saints' difficulties signify the withdrawal of his presence from them? Might he
not be angry with them? That a wrathful God providentially punishes sin, and takes
vengeance upon it in order to vindicate his honour, was a seventeenth-century
commonplace, which Cromwell's mentor Thomas Beard wrote a long and famous
book to illustrate. 'Sin causes wrath', that guiding figure of pre-civil-war Puritanism
the minister John Preston explained succinctly; 'sin and wrath are knit together,
they are inseparable'. 'Wrath for sin! Who knows not that?' asked Charles I's civil-
war chaplain Henry Ferne.[13]

God's punishments could visit communities and nations as well as individuals.
The sins which provoked him must be repented collectively as well as individually,
on days of solemn fasting and humiliation. Yet collective sins were the sum of
individual sins. Just as believers looked into their souls to divine the meaning of

---

[9] Ibid., ii. 190.
[10] Ibid., i. 646. Cf. i. 698; John Bond, *Ortus Accidentalis* (1645), p. 34.
[11] Abbott, iii. 590.
[12] *A Briefe Relation* 2 July 1650, p. 30. Cf. *OPH*, xix. 180.
[13] John Preston, *The Saint's Qualification* (1637), p. 252; Henry Ferne, *A Sermon preached at the Publique Fast, the Twelfth Day of April* (1644), p. 15.

military success, so must they search inward to discern God's purpose in public adversity. The Puritan imagination observed a series of God-given correspondences and interactions between external events and the inward motions of faith: between the showers which end drought in the fields and the waters of grace upon the barren soul; or between the trials and deliverances of the traveller and the pilgrim's inner progress towards salvation. To the Puritan, reformation of the world begins with reformation of the soul and heart.

When God was provoked by transgression, he could be appeased only if the offending sin were identified and purged. The force of that conviction is evident in the belief, which was used to explain much killing in the civil wars, that an afflicted land must be cleansed of the blood which has been shed in it (Numbers 35:33). But at least blood-guilt could be laid at the door of the saints' enemies. What if the sin were among the believers themselves? In the fear of that thought, Cromwell and the saints, individually and collectively, devoted many hours and many days to intensive self-examination.

In the dark days of late April 1648, as the second civil war approached, parliament and army reflected on the imminent perils before them. On 25 April parliament ordered a national fast day to be held. For

> whatsoever dangers are threatened or feared, either by divisions amongst ourselves, or practices from enemies abroad, we have assurance, out of the word of God, that we are not in the least danger, if God Almighty be not incensed against us for our sins and wickedness; which our consciences testify that he is exceedingly, against every one of us in particular, and the kingdom in general: yet we believe that, if we do heartily and sincerely humble ourselves, and turn to the Lord, crying mightily to him in fervent prayer, with a lively faith in Christ, we shall certainly be delivered from all evils and dangers, and enjoy all needful blessings and benefit to the whole state and kingdom.

Parliament resolved to suppress the vice and the blasphemy wherewith the land was defiled, so that God's 'heavy judgements' might be 'diverted from us' and the Roundhead cause saved.[14]

Four days later, on 29 April, the new model produced its own response to the crisis. The general council of the army, as the soldier William Allen, who was present, would recall, met at Windsor Castle 'to search out . . . our iniquities, which, we were persuaded, had provoked the Lord against us'. The army leadership often turned to prayer to help restore unity and direction to its counsels. In the Putney debates of 1647 the new model had sought, through a 'seeking of God', or prayer-meeting, to recover the spirit and purpose which had sustained it in battle, but which in the post-war peace had made way for 'carnal' and 'fleshly strivings'. Cromwell spoke for his colleagues at Putney when he dwelt on the necessity 'to recover that presence of God that seems to withdraw from us', to root out 'false deceit', and to reflect that

---

[14] *CJ* 25 April 1648; Keith Thomas, 'The Puritans and Adultery: The Act of 1650 Reconsidered', in Donald Pennington and Keith Thomas, eds., *Puritans and Revolutionaries: Essays Presented to Christopher Hill* (Oxford, 1978), pp. 263, 277; *Severall Proceedings in Parliament* 23 May 1650, pp. 490–2.

'God will discover whether our hearts be not clear in this business'. 'I thinke the maine thinge', concurred Henry Ireton, 'is for everyone to waite uppon God, for the errours, deceits, and weakness of his owne heart.'[15]

The army leaders were still divided and downhearted when they gathered at Windsor in April 1648. A party among them seems to have yielded to political despair, and to have wanted the army to lay down its arms. The Windsor meeting lasted three days. The first of them evidently produced no answer to the army's prayers. On the second day, when 'many spake from the word and prayed', Cromwell

> did press very earnestly on all there present to a thorough consideration of our actions as an army, as well as our ways particularly as private Christians, to see if any iniquity could be found in them; and what it was, that if possible we might find it out, and so remove the cause of such sad rebukes as were upon us by reason of our iniquities.

Allen describes how the council then conducted 'a long search into all our public actions as an army', to enquire why 'the presence of the Lord' was no longer 'amongst us'.[16] At length 'we were, by a gracious hand of the Lord, led to find out the very steps (as we were then all jointly convinced) by which we had departed from the Lord, and provoked him to depart from us'. Those 'steps', it was agreed, were the 'cursed, carnal conferences' which 'our own wisdoms, fears, and want of faith had prompted us in the year before to entertain with the king and his party': in other words the negotiations which Cromwell and Ireton had held with Charles I in 1647, and which had antagonized the army radicals.

At that stage of the meeting a decisive lead was given by lieutenant-colonel William Goffe. It was Goffe who had instigated the 'seeking of God' at Putney, which he hoped would recall the army from 'our wandrings from God'. 'It hath bin our trouble night and day', he had then reminded his hearers, 'that God hath nott bin with us as formerly'.[17] Now he 'made use of that good word, Prov. I, 23, "Turn you at my reproof"'. In that chapter God threatens to 'laugh at your calamity; I will mock when your fear cometh; when your fear cometh as desolation, and your destruction cometh as a whirlwind; when distress and anguish cometh upon you'. But if the elect of Israel—and so of England—will 'turn at my reproof', 'behold, I will pour out my spirit unto you, I will make known my words unto you'. Goffe's speech

> begot in us great sense, shame and loathing our selves for our iniquities, and justifying the Lord as righteous in his proceedings against us. And in this path the Lord led us not

---

[15] Abbott, i. 521, 523, 524; Firth, *Clarke Papers*, i. 253, 256–7.

[16] Allen's account, published in 1659, is reprinted in *Somers Tracts*, vi. 498–504. While we must allow, in reading it, both for the distance of Allen's memory and for his bitterness against what he saw as Cromwell's betrayal of the cause in the 1650s, the outline of his vivid narrative carries conviction. Even if we question it, it is a telling instance of the kind of explanation both of the conduct of Cromwell's entourage, and of the course of political events, to which Cromwellians were drawn. For the date of the Windsor meeting see S. R. Gardiner, *History of the Great Civil War*, 4 vols (1897–8 edn), iv. 117.

[17] Firth, *Clarke Papers*, i. 253–5.

only to see our sin, but also our duty; and this so unanimously set with weight upon each heart, that none was able hardly to speak a word to each other for bitter weeping.

Thus 'we were led and helped to a clear agreement amongst ourselves, not any dissenting'. Two historic decisions—or so Allen recalled—were taken. The army resolved, first, to resume its fight against the royalists. Secondly, 'if ever the Lord brought us back again in peace', it would 'call Charles Stuart . . . to an account for that blood he had shed'.

If Allen's memory on those points is even half-reliable, the Windsor meeting was a critical moment in the Puritan Revolution—and in the career of Oliver Cromwell. His vulnerability to the reproaches of radicals can be glimpsed in the Putney debates, when his advocacy of moderation, and of the practicable, was countered by men ready to match his claims to divine illumination, and to argue that there could be no half measures in the service of the Old Testament God. They claimed that Cromwell's caution on the issue of the electoral franchise betrayed 'a distrust of providence'; or they reported that God had 'providentially' indicated, through the medium of prayer, a liking for the Levellers' tract, against which Cromwell set his face, *The Case of the Army Truly Stated*.[18] Cromwell never supposed that radical programmes were necessarily more pleasing to God than moderate ones. He and his fellows knew that the Lord required his instruments to work through political means and political skill.[19] Yet he also knew God's way of blasting the 'politic contrivances' of men who, professing to serve him but missing the path he had marked for them, stooped to 'carnal' political calculation. Within Cromwell's providentialism, which could lead him in such various political directions, there lay a radical imperative, which asserted itself at times of crisis and uncertainty. In a swift and decisive change of course he would find sudden release from the strains and doubts imposed by negotiation and compromise. So it was in April 1648, when he resolved to 'turn at God's reproof'.[20] In consequence the army recovered its unity and its fire; and the period which followed the Windsor meeting, the time of the second civil war and of the regicide, proved in Cromwell's words 'the most memorable year . . . that ever this nation saw; . . . and this by the very signal appearance of God himself, which, I hope, we shall never forget'.[21]

There were to be many more occasions when the army saints gathered to seek the root of iniquity among themselves.[22] In 1650 God 'mixed' their military successes in Ireland and Scotland with a series of afflictions. The government of the Commonwealth was beset by demoralizing divisions and by despair at its prospects of survival.[23] There were differences within the army about the legitimacy of invading Scotland.[24] There were outbreaks of plague in garrisons in England and

---

[18] Ibid., i. 323, 372–4.

[19] Below, p. 43.

[20] Cf. Abbott, ii. 340 (line 5); *OPH*, xix. 400; *TSP*, vii. 367.

[21] Abbott, iii. 54. Cf. ii. 20, iii. 73; *Somers Tracts*, vi. 501 (lines 32–3, 39–43).

[22] See e.g. Firth, *Clarke Papers*, ii. 58–9; Worcester College Oxford, Clarke MS xxi, fo. 73ᵛ, xxiv, fo. 98ᵛ.

[23] Blair Worden, *The Rump Parliament 1648–1653* (Cambridge, repr. 1977), pp. 224–5.

[24] Nickolls, pp. 21, 29, 58, 73.

Ireland. There were the deaths of 'many choice instruments' of God's work. The Cromwellian forces in Ireland, having earnestly 'enquir[ed] into' the meaning of God's 'chastisements', and of a succession of 'crossings of providence',[25] provoked him by ceasing their practices of self-interrogation after Cromwell's return to England in May, when Ireton took charge of the Irish forces as his deputy. Fresh afflictions duly followed, until 'at last', as Ireton and his colleagues later informed Cromwell,

> by all these sad strokes from heaven we were raised out of that sleepy secure condition to call upon his name, seek his face, and beg to know his mind in these his judgements, which while we were doing he both discovered the sin, which was our departure and backsliding from him, . . . and on a sudden, whilst he was discovering his mind to us, in answer to our desires, he was also pleased to abate . . . that heavy stroke of the pestilence.[26]

As in England in 1648, so in Ireland in 1650, the soldiery was promptly restored by its self-examination to its accustomed course of victory. Meanwhile, army headquarters in England had circulated regiments and garrisons throughout the country to coordinate a day of prayer, when the saints were to seek the cause of their travails. The Lord was besought 'to grant that this may be a cleansing day', and to 'enable us to turn at his reproof'.[27] Even the victory at Dunbar did not wholly assure the chosen of God's contentment with them. Cromwell's cousin and ally Oliver St John, rejoicing in the triumph but remarking too on the present plague and threat of famine, wrote to Cromwell that God, by 'mingling water with his wine, tells us that something is amiss amongst us, and calls upon us to search and try our ways'.[28]

The battle of Worcester in September 1651 brought a reversion to peace—and to its anxieties. Cromwell, who now returned permanently to civilian politics, warned parliament not to permit 'the fatness of these continued mercies' to 'occasion pride and wantonness, as formerly the like hath done to a chosen nation'.[29] The regime must acknowledge its victories to have come from the Lord alone, for 'God will curse that man and his house that dares to think otherwise'.[30] And parliament must 'improve' God's 'mercies' by righteousness and reform. For 'the eyes of the Lord run to and fro; and as he finds out his enemies here, to be avenged on them, so he will not spare them for whom he doth good, if by his loving kindness they become not good'.[31] The nation's want of gratitude for God's glorious dispensations, and its failure to give 'a worthy return of

---

[25] *Briefe Relation* 8 January 1650, pp. 217–18; *A Perfect Diurnall . . . in relation to the Armies* 14 January 1650, pp. 42–3; Whitelocke, *Memorials*, iii. 151.

[26] Nickolls, p. 72.

[27] *Perfect Diurnall* 27 May 1650, pp. 271–4. Cf. 17 June 1650, pp. 304–6; 1 July 1650, pp. 322–4.

[28] Nickolls, p. 26.

[29] Abbott, ii. 463.

[30] Ibid., ii. 173. Cf. i. 621, iii. 583 (lines 4–8), 591 (lines 18–22), iv. 707; Edmund Calamy, *God's Free Mercy to England* (1642), pp. 14–15; Jeremiah 17:5.

[31] Abbott, ii. 130, 433; cf. ii. 215, 325, 506, 588, iii. 56.

all the blessings and mercies [it has] received',[32] were to trouble Cromwell all his days. How often, in his speeches, he would recall the encouragement which, after Worcester, the army gave parliament to reform, and the frustration which had eventually driven him to expel the Commons by force in April 1653. What had gone wrong?

No doubt the immediate blame lay with the notorious 'corruption' and 'self-seeking' of parliament. But might not the failure of reform also be a rebuke to the army saints themselves? Since Worcester, they observed in January 1653, 'the work of the Lord' had 'seemed to stand still, and all the instruments thereof to have been of no might'. In that month they accordingly spent 'several days waiting at the throne of grace', where they 'humbled ourselves at his feet, for those evils which might cause him to withdraw his presence from us, and to manifest tokens of his displeasure against us'. 'Looking after the things of this world', they concluded, they had been 'overtaken with a slothfull spirit'.[33] Once more their self-examination and repentance produced vigorous action. They announced a bold reform programme, and made it clear that parliament's survival depended on its implementation.

In the saints' new-found resolution there lay a challenge not only to parliament but to Cromwell himself. Since September 1651 he had sought to build bridges between parliament and army. The policy had exposed him to suspicion and rebuke from the radicals. As early as December 1651 'the private churches begin to call his excellency an apostate'. By the spring of 1653 he was 'daily railed on by the preaching party, who say they must have a . . . new general before the work be done'.[34] Although such hostility to him was acute only on the political margins, the psychological pressure exerted on Cromwell by the army and the congregations was intense. They kept him informed of their constant prayers on his behalf; instructed him not to 'consult with flesh and blood'[35] or to succumb to the baits of compromise; listed the biblical heroes on whom they expected him to model his conduct; intimated to him his failure to meet their political hopes; and scrutinized his public utterances for statements which might be taken to have indicated approval of their programme, and with which they could confront him when he failed to advance it. In 1651 Ireton and other officers in Ireland urged him to 'remember Hezekiah's fate and judgement' and 'take heed of making it your own'.[36] Hezekiah's fault was to have 'rendered not again according to the benefit done unto him; for his heart was lifted up: therefore there was wrath upon him, and upon Judah and Jerusalem' (2 Chronicles 32:25). The parallel made a point which was to acquire an added force once Cromwell became lord protector in 1653: that a whole people might be punished for the sin of its leader.

Cromwell, whose bond with his radical followers was so important to him, was not well equipped to bear their admonitions. Why, he asked, had the godly cause

---

[32] Ibid., iv. 270; cf. iv. 25.
[33] *The Moderate Publisher* 4 February 1653, pp. 710–12.
[34] Worden, *Rump Parliament*, pp. 291, 379–80.
[35] Nickolls, p. 80. Cf. Owen, *Works*, viii. 349; Galatians 1:16.
[36] Nickolls, pp. 74–5.

become so dependent upon so weak an instrument as himself?[37] Although he had long taken himself to be among the chosen, to have found 'acceptance' among 'the congregation of the firstborn', he retained a sense of spiritual inadequacy which can be glimpsed in his private letters, in his acknowledgements there of 'my corruptions', 'my weaknesses, my inordinate passions, my unskilfulness and every way unfitness to my work'.[38] In 1651–3, as he manoeuvred among the parliamentary factions, he found politics a lonely business. Pride's Purge had divided him from some intimate friends in parliament, who in boycotting the Commonwealth, he alleged, had 'helped one another to stumble at the dispensations of God'.[39] Even among supporters of the new regime he could be visited by a sense of solitariness. In September 1652, when the breach between parliament and army was widening, he wrote to an (unidentifiable) close colleague, 'Have I one friend in our society to whom I can unbowel myself? You absent; [Charles] Fleetwood is gone [to Ireland]; I am left alone ... Lend me one shoulder. Pray for me.'[40]

On 20 April 1653, having 'sought the Lord day and night', he once again cut through 'carnal' politics. He expelled the remnant of the Long Parliament by force, vituperatively attacked its members for their personal and political corruption, and assured his army colleagues after the coup that he had 'consulted not with flesh and blood at all'.[41] His action restored his position among the sectarian churches, which told him that his expulsion of parliament had removed their 'fear of God's presence withdrawing from you'.[42] Yet the new mood did not last. The members of Barebone's, that handpicked assembly of the chosen which met in July 1653, were soon quarrelling among themselves. In August, 'unbowelling myself' to his son-in-law Fleetwood, he confessed that 'I never more needed all helps from my Christian friends than now.'[43]

In December he became lord protector. Repeatedly he and his supporters would claim that God had declared in favour of his elevation, and that the evidence of divine approval obliged the nation to accept the new constitution. Yet he faced persistent accusations by men who had been among his closest and most trusted spiritual counsellors. Ousted from government or favour by his 'usurpation' of supreme authority, they held him to be a traitor who had sacrificed the cause on the altar of his ambition. He was the scapegoat upon whom all political failures and disappointments, past and present, could be blamed. His problems were magnified in January 1655, when the first parliament of the protectorate collapsed without supplying him with the constitutional basis of his rule for which he had looked to it. In the months which followed, a siege mentality is evident in Whitehall. Cromwell's faith in God's approbation was undimmed. He defiantly reaffirmed it in his angry speech at the parliament's dissolution. Testimonies to

---

[37] See Abbott, ii. 421, iv. 872.
[38] Ibid., i. 96–7, 696, ii. 289, 329, 400, 404–5, 483.
[39] Ibid., i. 574–5, 577–8, 646, ii. 189–90, 328–9, 425–6, 453.
[40] Ibid., i. 575–6.
[41] Worden, *Rump Parliament*, p. 356; cf. Abbott, i. 698 (line 21).
[42] Nickolls, pp. 91, 93.
[43] Abbott, iii. 89.

divine approval had not ceased. In March 1655 'the good hand of God going along with us' enabled the government to put down Penruddock's rising. In April the Lord 'was pleased to appear very signally' in the victory of Admiral Blake at Tunis.[44] Three months later, however, there came news of a catastrophe. The expedition which Cromwell had sent to the Caribbean island of Hispaniola (the territory now shared by Haiti and the Dominican Republic), in the hope of launching the conquest of Spanish America, had been abjectly defeated. An ill-prepared, ill-disciplined force had been shamefully routed by a handful of Spaniards. There had been nothing in Cromwell's career to parallel that disaster. When the news came through he shut himself in solitude for a whole day.[45]

Cromwell had sent the expedition to the West Indies because 'God has not brought us hither where we are but to consider the work that we may do in the world as well as at home. . . . Providence seemed to lead us hither, having 160 ships swimming.' Spain, 'the great underpropper' of the papacy, 'that Roman Babylon', was 'providentially' England's enemy. Citing Thessalonians and Revelation, Cromwell told the parliament of 1656 that 'except you will deny the truth of the Scriptures, you must needs see that that state is so described in Scripture to be papal and anti-Christian'. When men questioned the justice of the war he pointed to Genesis 3:15, 'I will put enmity between . . . thy seed and her seed', a text, he averred, 'which goeth but for little among statesmen, but it is more considerable [than] all things'.[46] Yet could Cromwell be certain that God favoured his policy? In October 1656, when news of the capture of Spanish treasure ships had given a needed boost to government morale, the preacher John Rowe told parliament that the exploit had 'silenced the secret thoughts and reasonings of some, touching the engagement in this war; and who are too apt to say, that God never owned you since you undertook this business'.[47] Five months earlier Sir Henry Vane, Cromwell's old ally who had broken with him in 1653, taunted him about the 'great silence in heaven' since 1653.[48]

The debacle at Hispaniola could be blamed partly on 'instruments', on the leaders of the expedition, who were duly punished. But Cromwell knew the need to look deeper. Not only had the invasion force lost a battle. It had been a godless army, untouched by the spirit of the new model. Its cowardice was itself evidence of God's displeasure, for Cromwell knew that in battle God gave and withdrew courage as it pleased him.[49] Sinful armies, the protector understood, were their own worst enemies. The expedition remained spiritually (and militarily) wanting even after it had proceeded to take Jamaica. 'The hand of the Lord hath not been more visible in any part of this rebuke', Cromwell told the commanders of the forces there in

---

[44] Ibid., iii. 672, 745.
[45] S. R. Gardiner, *History of the Commonwealth and Protectorate*, 4 vols (1893), iv. 142–3; cf. Thomas Gumble, *The Life of General Monck* (1671), p. 88.
[46] Firth, *Clarke Papers*, iii. 207; Abbott, iii. 860, 879, iv. 261–2, 264.
[47] John Rowe, *Man's Duty Magnifying God's Work* (1656), p. 20; cf. *A True Narrative of the Late Success . . . upon the Spanish Coast* (1656).
[48] Vane, 'A Healing Question Propounded', *Somers Tracts*, vi. 313; cf. Revelation 8:1.
[49] Abbott, ii. 127, 164, 235, 324.

1656, 'than in taking away the hearts of those who do survive amongst you, and in giving them up to . . . sloth and sluggishness of spirit.'[50] Whatever wickedness had been at work, it would not have been confined to the expeditionary force. For when God humbled soldiers he also punished their rulers, or their countrymen, or both. What had provoked the Lord?

To find out, in November 1655 the government invited the nation to hold a day of solemn fasting and humiliation, when 'we may everyone be searching out the plague of his own heart'. Thus might God's purpose in 'the late rebukes we have received' be discerned. The nation's prayers went unanswered in the months which followed, for in March 1656 the government had to try again. In that month its declaration for a further fast day acknowledged that 'the Lord hath been pleased in a wonderful manner to humble and rebuke us, in that expedition to the West Indies'. The disaster 'gives us just reason to fear, that we may have either failed in the spirit and manner wherewith this business hath been undertaken, or that the Lord sees some abomination, or accursed thing, by which he is provoked thus to appear against us'. In September 1656, after Cromwell's speech at the opening of parliament had lamented the failure of the West Indian expedition, a declaration was passed by protector and parliament for another fast day, on which 'a people laden with iniquity', who had 'provoked the holy one of Israel to anger', was to strive 'to appease his wrath . . . that he will remove whatever accursed thing there is amongst us'.[51]

The Puritan readership of the declarations of March and September 1656 will have recognized, in their allusions to an 'accursed thing', a signpost to the seventh chapter of the Book of Joshua. The story told in it is of the abrupt reversal which afflicted the children of Israel after their triumph at the fall of Jericho. The Cromwellian saints often compared their own 'mercies' of 1642–51 to the fall of Jericho; but they also remembered what followed that victory. For then 'the children of Israel committed a trespass in the accursed thing . . . and the anger of the Lord was kindled against the children of Israel'. The consequence was the shattering defeat of an expedition which had been confidently dispatched by the Israelites from Jericho to the east side of Bethel. The troops 'fled before the men of Ai', who (like the Spaniards on Hispaniola) were 'but few'. Joshua was devastated. He 'rent his clothes, and fell to the earth upon his face before the ark of the Lord until the eventide, he and all the elders of Israel, and put dust upon their heads'. For to what purpose had God brought his people over Jordan, only 'to deliver us into the hand of the Amorites, to destroy us'? What could Joshua say to neighbouring nations 'when Israel turneth their backs before their enemies'?

---

[50] Ibid., iv. 193; cf. iv. 385.
[51] Ibid., iv. 274 (lines 30–1); *A Declaration of his Highness, with the advice of his Council, inviting the People of this Commonwealth to a Day of Solemn Fasting and Humiliation* ([November] 1655); *A Declaration of his Highness, inviting the People of England and Wales to a Day of Solemn Fasting and Humiliation* ([March] 1656: Bodl., Carte MS 70, no. 453); *A Declaration of his Highness the Lord Protector and his Parliament for a Day of Solemn Fasting and Humiliation* ([September] 1656). The declarations will hereafter be cited by their dates.

And the Lord said unto Joshua, Get thee up; wherefore liest thou thus upon thy face? Israel hath sinned, and they have also transgressed my covenant which I commanded them: for they have even taken of the accursed thing, and have also stolen, and dissembled also, and they have put it even among their own stuff. Therefore the children of Israel could not stand before their enemies, but turned their backs before their enemies, because they were accursed: neither will I be with you any more, except ye destroy the accursed from among you. Up, sanctify the people, and say, Sanctify yourselves against tomorrow: for thus saith the Lord God of Israel, There is an accursed thing in the midst of thee, O Israel: thou canst not stand before thine enemies, until ye take away the accursed thing from among you.

One particular man, God intimated, had 'taken of the accursed thing'; and for his wickedness all Israel was punished. He was identified by a ritual process of investigation which revealed the extension of guilt from the sinner to his household, from the household to the tribe, from the tribe to the nation. The sinner was Achan, the son of Carmi, the son of Zabdi, the son of Zerah, of the tribe of Judah. His confession identified the accursed thing:

> When I saw among the spoils a goodly Babylonish garment, and two hundred shekels of silver, and a wedge of gold of fifty shekels weight, then I coveted them, and took them; and, behold, they are hid in the earth in the midst of my tent, and the silver under it. And they took them out of the midst of the tent, and brought them unto Joshua, and unto all the children of Israel, and laid them out before the Lord.

Achan, on God's instructions, was stoned to death and burned in the valley of Achor. Only now that the accursed thing had been found and cast out was the hand of God's blessing laid once more upon his chosen people. The men of Ai were duly smitten, and the conquests of the Israelites resumed.

Puritans did not necessarily expect parallels between Israelite and English history to be exact.[52] But when so many literal and figurative correspondences suggested themselves, divine instruction was clearly visible. There was nothing peculiar to the Cromwellians, or even to the parliamentarian and Puritan movements at large, in turning for political instruction to Joshua 7.[53] Although royalists mocked Puritan invocations of the text, they made their own uses of it. They located the sin of Achan in Roundhead treason, or in the sacrilege of the parliamentarians' destructive steps against the Anglican Church.[54] One royalist thought that the murder of Charles I might be 'an Achan in England'.[55] On the Puritan side, sermons delivered to the Long Parliament on the monthly fast-days of the 1640s

---

[52] See e.g. John Arrowsmith, *England's Eben-ezer* (1645), p. 21.

[53] Sometimes Achan's iniquity was linked to the sins of other Old Testament figures – especially Jonah: Thomas Hodges, *A Glimpse of Gods Glory* (1642), pp. 32–3; John Ley, *The Fury of Warre* (1643), p. 50; William Chillingworth, *A Sermon preached at the Publike Fast before his Majesty at Christ-Church in Oxford* (1644), p. 13; George Gillespie, *A Sermon preached before the Honourable House of Commons* (1644), preface; Thomas Case, *Deliverance-Obstruction* (1646), p. 42.

[54] *Mercurius Aulicus* (Oxford, 1642), p. 41 ('The third Weeke'); *Mercurius Pragmaticus* 21 September 1647, p. 6; 28 December 1647, p. 6; 9 May 1648, p. 1; *King Charles the First, No Man of Blood* (1649), pp. 48–9.

[55] John Paradise, *Hadadrimmon* (1660), p. 13.

were peppered with allusions to Achan's iniquity. MPs were enjoined to 'stone Achan',[56] or were warned that there was some 'Achan unstoned'.[57] Oliver Cromwell, two months before the regicide, intimated that the king himself, or at least the readiness of parliamentarians to reach an accommodation with him, might be England's 'accursed thing'.[58] Other parliamentarian critics of Charles likewise equated Achan with the king himself,[59] or one of the royal advisers: with the Duke of Buckingham,[60] or with Archbishop Laud,[61] or with the Earl of Strafford.[62] Or an MP would discern Achan's sin in the massacre of Protestants in Ireland in 1641,[63] or in the blasphemy of the Quaker James Nayler in 1656.[64] Or Achan's transgression was identified not with individual sinners but with national or general sins. Or it might be located in the peculation, or the mercenary motives, of parliamentarian soldiers and administrators. Puritans found parallels to Achan's iniquity in popish survivals from the pre-war Church, or in Arminianism, or in the lukewarmness and indifference that impeded godly reformation, or in neglect of the Sabbath or of the Solemn League and Covenant, or in the countenancing of heresy and toleration, or in the 'carnall self-love'[65] of politicians. The presence of an Achan, or alternatively of 'many Achans', in the parliamentary armies was repeatedly held to explain the military difficulties of the Roundhead cause in the 1640s.[66] The parallel seemed particularly close in the autumn of 1644. The triumph at Marston Moor in July, and other 'great and gracious things' done by God for parliament, had brought the prospect of outright victory and a speedy end to the war. Instead there had been defeats, despondency, acrimony.[67] 'The case of the children of Israel after their losse' near the city of Ai, observed the pastor John Goodwin, was 'our condition and cause at this very day'.[68] During the winter of 1644–5, parliament identified the problem as the covetousness of MPs. To purge

[56] Edmund Staunton, *Phinehas's Zeal in Execution of Judgement* (1645), p. 10.
[57] Edmund Calamy, *The Noble-Mans Patterne* (1643), p. 37.
[58] Abbott, i. 676–7.
[59] Ludlow, *Voyce*, p. 200.
[60] John Eliot, *The Monarchie of Man*, ed. A. B. Grosart, 2 vols (1879), i. 77.
[61] John Bond, *Salvation in a Mystery* (1644), p. 215; Paul Christianson, *Reformers and Babylon* (Toronto, 1978), p. 190 (cf. pp. 141, 186); cf. William Hunt, *The Puritan Moment* (Cambridge, Mass., 1983), pp. 188–9.
[62] See Conrad Russell in *London Review of Books*, 4–17 October 1984, p. 21.
[63] *Ludlow's Memoirs*, i. 509.
[64] *Burton*, i. 39.
[65] Thomas Hills, *The Militant Church, Triumphant* (1643), p. 28.
[66] George Smith, *Great Britains Misery* (1643), p. 64; *The Scottish Dove* 24 March 1644, pp. 252–3; *Mercurius Civicus* 28 March 1644, p. 451; John Greene, *Nehemiah's Teares and Prayers* (1644), p. 17; Herbert Palmer, *The Glasse of Gods Providence* (1644), p. 60; John Lightfoot, *A Sermon preached before the Honourable the House of Commons* (1645), p. 28; Edward Reyner, *Orders from the Lord of Hosts* (1646), p. 28; Mary Coate, *Cornwall in the Great Civil War and Interregnum 1642–1660* (Oxford, 1933), p. 45. Cf. Stephen Marshall, *A Sermon preached before the Honourable House of Commons...November 17. 1640* (1641), p. 18; and the warning about the presence of 'so many Achans' in the royalist armies offered by William Chillingworth, *Sermon preached...in Oxford*, p. 13.
[67] Matthew Newcomen, *A Sermon tending to set forth the Right Use of the Disasters that befall our Armies* (1644: the preacher took Joshua 7:10–11 as his text); John Goodwin, *Theomachia* (1644), pp. 2–4.
[68] Goodwin, *Theomachia*, p. 2.

that sin it passed the Self-Denying Ordinance. 'Achan the trouble-maker of Israel' having thus been 'discovered', God opened the way to the triumphs of the new model in 1645. 'Never history since Joshua's days', a preacher told the Commons, 'can file up so many glorious victories . . . accomplished by one army in so short a time' as those achieved in that year under the command of Fairfax, 'our Joshua'.[69]

Soldiers and radicals of the decade following the regicide were equally ready to apply the text. In 1649 a sympathizer with the Levellers, the party which Cromwell crushed at Burford in that year, described him as 'one of the Achans that trouble the peace of Israel' and urged the execution of 'justice upon all Achans'.[70] In 1650 the despondent forces in England had explored Joshua 7 when they enquired into God's chastisements of that year.[71] In 1651 Edmund Ludlow, lieutenant-general of the parliamentarian forces in Ireland, rounded on the Catholic leaders there, 'those Achans', on whom he blamed the massacre of Protestants in Ulster a decade earlier.[72] In 1652 the Digger leader Gerrard Winstanley, in identifying covetousness as the root of England's wickedness, called it 'Achan's sin'.[73] But it was after the defeat at Hispaniola that the text reacquired, perhaps in a still sharper form, the potency of political explanation which it had offered in the autumn of 1644.

In his tract of May 1656, *A Healing Question Propounded*,[74] Sir Henry Vane took the declaration for a fast day which the government had issued two months earlier as an invitation to the nation to help identify the 'accursed thing'.[75] That was a strained interpretation of the wording of the declaration. Yet it was not, in itself, a response to which the regime could object. For Achan's sin had itself only come to light through an investigative process.[76] If the iniquity afflicting England were to be identified, there must be investigation now. In the black hour of the parliamentarian cause in 1643, ministers had explained to the Commons that 'the every not inquiring after Achan can lead to divine punishment',[77] and had reminded MPs that 'even Joshua's prayer could not heale, till' Achan's sin 'was laid open and discovered'.[78]

Vane offered his own contribution to the investigation of 1656. The 'accursed thing', he suggested, was the motive of 'self-interest and private gain' that was hidden beneath the protectorate. Cromwell's elevation had sprung from the 'private

---

[69] Thomas Case, *A Sermon preached before the Honourable House of Commons . . . August 22. 1645* (1645), p. 20.

[70] Christopher Cheeseman, *The Lamb Contending with the Lion* (1649), 'epistle' and 'postscript'; Barry Reay, *The Quakers and the English Revolution* (1985), p. 20.

[71] *Perfect Diurnall* 27 May 1650, p. 257.

[72] *Ludlow's Memoirs*, i. 509.

[73] Christopher Hill, ed., *Winstanley. The Law of Freedom and other Writings* (Harmondsworth, 1973), p. 272 (cf. p. 99).

[74] *Somers Tracts*, vi. 303–15.

[75] *Ludlow's Memoirs*, ii. 16.

[76] Cf. Richard Vines, *The Hearse of the Renowned . . . Earle of Essex* (1646), pp. 1–2; J. G. A. Pocock, ed., *The Political Works of James Harrington* (Cambridge, 1977), pp. 629–31.

[77] Herbert Palmer, *The Necessity and Encouragement of Utmost Venturing for the Churches Help* (1643), pp. 13–14; cf. p. 66.

[78] Anthony Tuckney, *The Balme of Gilead* (1643), p. 35.

and selfish interest of a particular spirit . . . which sin (Joshua 7) became a curse in the camp, and withheld the Lord from going any more amongst them, or going out with their forces'. The 'Babylonish garment' which Achan 'saved from destruction' signified the 'tyrannical principles and relics' of rule by an uplifted single person. Cromwell after the civil wars, like Achan after Jericho, 'brought not in the fruit and gain of the Lord's treasure, but covetously went about to convert it to his own use'. 'This', observed Vane, his eye turning to Hispaniola, 'caused the anger of the Lord to be kindled against Israel, and made them unable to stand before their enemies.' So only when England had been purged of Cromwell's selfishness would God again 'become active and powerful in the spirits and hearts of honest men, and in the works of his providences, when . . . they go out to fight by sea or by land'. Vane's *Healing Question* was not the only tract to portray Hispaniola as God's punishment upon the cause for Cromwell's usurpation, and to tell the protector that 'you are not able to bear the reproofs of the Lord',[79] but to Cromwell it must have been the most troubling of them. Vane was brought before Cromwell and the council, and then incarcerated in the Isle of Wight. In 1659, a year after Cromwell's death, Vane's devotee John Milton attributed the disintegration of the godly cause to the 'ambition', 'the Achan among them', of Cromwell and the army officers who had supported his rule.[80] Another exponent of the cause in the same year identified the rule of a 'single person' as the 'accursed thing' that had undone the work of reformation.[81]

Cromwell responded uneasily and defensively to the charges which the defeat at Hispaniola elicited against him. He acknowledged that his own sins had 'justly . . . incurred' the disaster 'and much more'. He professed before the nation his desire 'first to take the shame to himself and find out his provocation'. Yet why, he asked, should the blame be placed on him alone? By what right was the iniquitous nation 'imputing the cause only to the work of the magistrate' and 'charging sad mis-carriages upon instruments . . . when every individual hath helped to fill up the measure of those sins'?[82] Cromwell, belonging in this as in much else to the mainstream of the Puritan tradition, was certain that God punishes nations for vice and blasphemy, sins that were held to be prevalent in the England of the Interregnum.[83] In March 1654 he announced a fast day to implore an end to 'the present rod of an exceeding and unusual drought', an affliction provoked, he ruled, by 'the common and notorious sins so boldly and impenitently practised amongst us'. He was to respond almost identically when God visited the nation

---

[79] *The Proceeds of the Protector (so called) against Sir Henry Vane, Knight* (1656), p. 8; *A Perfect Nocturnall of Several Proceedings, between Hiel the Bethelite, and . . . Madam Policy* (n.p., n.d. [1656]), pp. 4, 6.

[80] *CPW*, vii. 328–9; cf. vi. 385, 387, 689. A tract of 1655 had described a petition to have Cromwell enthroned as 'an accursed thing': *The Protector (so called) in Part Unvailed* (1655), p. 77.

[81] *A Seasonable Word, or, Certain Reasons against a Single Person* (1659), title-page.

[82] Declarations of March and September 1656; cf. Abbott, iii. 858 (line 33).

[83] Abbott, ii. 110, iv. 237 (lines 23–4).

with sickness in 1657 and again in 1658.[84] Why, in 1655–6, should the sin of Achan not be thought to extend across the same broad territory of national transgression?

Of one thing, at least, Cromwell professed himself confident. With other Puritans who contemplated Joshua 7, he interpreted political or military reverses as evidence of divine displeasure but not of divine rejection. At Hispaniola God had punished the English, but had not declared 'in favour of the enemy'. Although England's rulers should, like Joshua, 'lay our mouths in the dust, yet he would not have us despond', for 'undoubtedly it is his cause. . . . Though he hath torn us, yet he will heal us. . . . After two days he will revive us, on the third day he will raise us up.'[85] Did Cromwell remember, when he thus alluded to Hosea 6, how in 1650, after Dunbar, he and his friends had derided the similar biblical explanations of defeat which were then advanced by the Scottish Presbyterians?[86] At all events there are indications that Hispaniola taught Cromwell to think less boldly, and less simply, about the ways in which God reveals his purposes to men. In the days of Cromwell's triumph, providence had been 'clear and unclouded'. In the later protectorate, however, he came to refer to 'the dark paths through the providence and dispensations of God'.[87] Although the Lord might still appear in battle, as in the 'very signal' and 'very wonderful' mercy vouchsafed to Blake off Santa Cruz in 1657, Cromwell's reading of such events became more tentative. 'We have been lately taught', he reminded Blake in April 1656, 'that it is not in man to direct his way. Indeed all the dispensations of God, whether adverse or prosperous, do fully read that lesson.'[88] The dynamic and triumphant providentialism of the civil wars had become a part of Cromwell's past, to be yearned after in the autobiographical passages of his speeches. His reflections on the present or the future now resembled the more conventional and more stoical approach to providence taken by such moderate and court party politicians as John Thurloe and Henry Cromwell. He came to speak, as they did, of the need to become 'submitted' or 'resigned unto' providence.[89]

Did God forgive his people in England for the accursed thing? Cromwell's anxiety on that subject is indicated by his preoccupation, during the last two years of his life, with Psalm 85, which on three occasions he urged upon the consideration of his second parliament of the protectorate. In September 1656 he recited it almost in full before the Commons, whose members he encouraged to 'peruse' that 'very instructive and significant' psalm, which 'I wish . . . might be better written in our hearts'. It seems at first a psalm of wholehearted thankfulness. The Lord 'hast been favourable unto thy land', 'hast forgiven the iniquity of thy people', 'hast taken away all thy wrath', 'hast turned thyself from the fierceness of

---

[84] Ibid., iii. 225 (cf. iii. 290–I); *Mercurius Politicus* 20 August 1657, p. 7994; 17 September 1657, p. 1623; 6 May 1658, p. 500.

[85] Abbott, iii. 859–60, 874. Cf. Edmund Calamy, *Englands Looking-Glasse* (1642), ep. ded.; Nickolls, p. 26.

[86] Nickolls, p. 23; Abbott, ii. 335.

[87] Abbott, i. 697, iv. 472–3.

[88] Ibid., iv. 48, 549; cf. *An Order in Parliament for a Day of Thanksgiving the Third of June next* (1657).

[89] *TSP*, vi. 243, vii. 153, 376, 579, 680; Abbott, iv. 148.

thine anger'. Yet a sudden change of tense and of mood makes the meaning of the psalm ambiguous. The psalmist begs God to 'cause thine anger toward us to cease. Wilt thou be angry with us for ever? Wilt thou draw out thine anger to all generations?' Cromwell is glad to infer from the psalm that 'sometimes God pardons nations'. The protector hopes for a time when Englishmen can 'say as David, thou . . . hast pardoned our sins, thou hast taken away our iniquities'. Even so, he evidently believes the nation to remain under the penalty of its wickedness.[90]

Cromwell's concern with iniquity, his own and the nation's, is a dimension of the political crisis of the spring of 1657 which arose from parliament's proposal that he be crowned king. It can help us to understand—even if, amid the practical calculations he had to make, it could hardly be the sole cause of—his refusal of the offer, which was perhaps the most important (and perhaps the most disastrous) decision he made as protector.

The decision took him three months. His hesitations and delays gave to the opponents of the offer in the army and the churches the chance to mobilize resistance. Soldiers and saints knew that parliament's aim in offering him the Crown was to break the army's hold on him and to surround him with *politique* courtiers who would still the revolutionary momentum of recent years. Yet the prospect of mutiny by the radicals against his authority looked no stronger, and may have been weaker, than opposition which he had withstood before. The title was an attractive prospect. It would give his rule the parliamentary sanction he had long wanted for it, and would boost the hopes of settlement and stability. Those arguments, however, pressing as they were, might be 'carnal'. Had God led his chosen of England through its Red Sea merely in order to effect a change of dynasty? Had not 'the providence of God', asked Cromwell, 'laid this title aside'?[91]

While Cromwell prayed for guidance, the saints 'wearied him with letters, conferences, and monitory petitions'.[92] One missive was from Colonel Thomas Wilkes in Scotland. In the black month of January 1655 Cromwell had written to Wilkes a letter[93] which discloses anxieties often evident at the protector's times of trial: his dismay at his 'wounds' and 'reproaches' from 'such as fear the Lord, for whom I have been ready to lay down my life, and I hope still am';[94] and his concern to convince the saints that in becoming protector he did not 'make myself my aim'.[95] But for the strength which his adherence to God's path gave him, he told Wilkes, 'the comforts of all my friends would not support me, no not one day'.[96] Now, in the kingship crisis, Wilkes urged him to 'stand fast, in these . . . apostatising days', and, rather than yield to parliamentary persuasion, to await 'that crown

---

[90] Abbott, iv. 277–8, 706–7, 720.
[91] Ibid., iv. 473.
[92] Ibid., iv. 448.
[93] Ibid., iii. 572–3.
[94] Cf. ibid., i. 429, iii. 89, 756 (lines 5–6), iv. 272.
[95] Cf. ibid., iii. 289, 452.
[96] Cf. ibid., iv. 146.

which the Lord of righteous judgement gives' in heaven.[97] Congregations in and around Gloucestershire warned Cromwell to keep 'close to God, his cause and his people', and to resist the 'temptations' wherewith 'you are encompassed'. Acceptance of the title, they advised, would 'rejoice the hearts of the profane party', and would expose the saints to the charge 'that they fought not for the exalting of Jesus Christ, as they pretended, but themselves'. The crowning of Cromwell would 'generally sadden, and endanger your losing room in the hearts of, the saints in England'. He should 'search your heart', and beware that 'such as have prayed, wept, fought, followed on with you . . . may never have occasion to sit down by the rivers of bitter waters, lamenting for your sake'. Baptists of London alerted Cromwell to 'the fearful apostasy which is endeavoured by some to be fastened upon you, upon plausible pretences, by such who for the most part had neither heart nor head to engage with you'. They ventured an allusion, which Cromwell would not have missed, to the words of Mordecai to Esther: 'Think not with thyself that thou shalt escape in the king's house, any more than the Jews' (Esther 4: 13).[98]

In his diffuse and anguished speeches to parliament during the kingship crisis, Cromwell recalled the certitudes of civil war: the victories, and the manifest presence of God with his saints. The opponents of the title were eager to keep those memories alive. One of the opponents, Cromwell's former chaplain, John Owen, had once remarked that the rhetorical question 'Where is the God of Marston Moor, and the God of Naseby? is an acceptable expostulation in a gloomy day.'[99] In 1657 the saints expostulated accordingly. 'We beseech you in the bowels of Christ', wrote London Baptists to Cromwell, 'remember what God did for you and us, at Marston Moor, Naseby, Pembroke, Tredah, Dunbar and Worcester, and upon what grounds.' William Bradford, writing as one who as a soldier had 'gone along with you from Edgehill to Dunbar', urged that 'the experiences you have had of God at these two places, and between them, . . . should often make you shrink' from the title. Cromwell should 'remember you are but a man, and must die, and come to judgement. . . . Those that are for a Crown, I fear you have little experience of them: the other, most of them, have attended your greatest hazards.'[100]

The opponents of kingship did not have all the providentialist arguments. On the other side Thurloe and Henry Cromwell encouraged the protector to make his decision as God directed him. It was their hope that God had given him 'the clearest call that any man had' to accept the title.[101] Through the protectorate, Oliver had been described as the instrument of providence by men who welcomed the return to relative political stability under his rule. God had given England 'those lovely twins, peace and plenty (the unexpected issue of cruel

[97] *TSP*, vi. 70–1.
[98] Nickolls, pp. 139–43. John Lilburne had pointedly reminded him of the same text in 1647: Abbott, i. 434.
[99] Owen, *Works*, viii. 88. Cf. Obadiah Sedgwick, *A Thanksgiving Sermon, preached April 9* (1644), p. 21; Mathew Barker, *The Faithful and Wise Servant* (1657), pp. 14–15.
[100] Nickolls, pp. 141–3.
[101] *TSP*, vi. 183, 219, 222–3; cf. Nickolls, p. 144.

wars)'.[102] A part of Cromwell concurred with that view. The arrival of peace seemed to him a 'miracle'. He knew that only if it were preserved, and only under the shelter of stability, could the liberty of conscience won by the war become entrenched. Had not a time come for consolidation rather than advance? In 1655 Cromwell told parliament that, before it had wrecked the protectoral constitution, the Instrument of Government, 'we were arrived . . . at a very safe port, where we might sit down, and contemplate the dispensations of God and our mercies'. Next year he and parliament concurred in lamenting the nation's sin 'in being more dissatisfied that we have not obtained all that we aimed at, than thankful that we have obtained so much as through mercy we now enjoy'.[103]

Images of rest and peace, and the prospect of 'sitting down in quiet under our vines', could also appeal to the army saints.[104] Yet the radicals soon became restless and unhappy when providence 'stood still'. At best, the England of the protectorate was but half reformed. Surely God had not led his people out of bondage on so restricted a mission. The rivalry between that radical perspective and the outlook of the kingship party produced some contrasting biblical allusions. From the regiment of Anthony Morgan, who belonged to that party, the protector learned that 'after our long and troublesome and dangerous pilgrimage through the Red Sea of blood, and wilderness of confusion, we have obtained to some prospect, nay some taste and enjoyment of Canaan, the resting place of God's people'. The Gloucestershire congregations were indignant at such parallels: 'surely he speaks to us (as once to his people in the wilderness), "This is not your rest". It is not for us to call our wilderness Canaan.' The choice before Cromwell in the kingship crisis was between those rival perceptions of the protectorate.[105]

His speeches indicate the difficulty of the decision and the strain which days of fruitless prayer created in him. Acknowledging 'the abundance of difficulty and trouble that lies upon me', he spoke repeatedly of the 'burden', the 'weight', on 'my back'.[106] Though he conceded the political force of parliament's arguments, he asserted that 'I am not able for such a trust and charge'; that 'what may be fit for you to offer, may not be fit for me to undertake. . . . At the best I should do it doubtingly. And certainly what is so [done] is not of faith; and whatsoever . . . is not of faith, is sin to him that doth it.' Cromwell must 'give an account to God' for a decision which, he said again and again, must be taken within his 'conscience'.[107] He must follow the guidance which providence gave him; 'and though a man may impute his own folly and blindness to providence sinfully, yet that must be at my

---

[102] Nickolls, p. 134 (cf. pp. 105–6, 138–9, 147, 150–2). Cf. *TSP*, vi. 431; *Mercurius Politicus* 15 February 1655, pp. 5218–22; 18 March 1658, p. 384; 24 June 1658, p. 623; 15 July 1658, p. 668.

[103] Abbott, iii. 579; Declaration of September 1656.

[104] See e.g. Woodhouse, p. 403.

[105] *Mercurius Politicus* 15 April 1658, p. 456; Nickolls, p. 146. Cf. Richard Vines, *The Happinesse of Israel* (1645), pp. 4–5; Richard Baxter, *True Christianity* (1655), p. 204; George Smith, *God's Unchangeableness . . . wherein is clearly demonstrated and proved that Oliver Cromwell is by the Providence of God Lord Protector* (1655), p. 55; Abbott, iii. 434–5, 442; *TSP*, vi. 401, vii. 57, 295, 402; Owen Watkins, *The Puritan Experience* (1972), p. 167; Deuteronomy 12: 9.

[106] Abbott, iv. 443, 482; cf. iii. 756.

[107] For 'conscience' see Abbott, iv. 446, 454, 470, 472, 473, 513.

peril'. If the title should 'fall upon a person or persons that God takes no pleasure in, that perhaps may be the end of this work': the end of the cause to which Cromwell and the saints had committed their lives.[108]

Was it possible that Cromwell had become 'a person that God takes no pleasure in'? Might the Lord be exchanging his instruments once more? Cromwell's first biographer, Samuel Carrington, writing in 1659, recorded that near the end of his life the protector 'twice a day . . . rehearsed the 71 Psalm of David, which hath so near a relation to his fortune and to his affairs, as that one would believe it to have been a prophecy purposely dictated by the Holy Ghost for him'.[109] What was it that drew Cromwell to psalms which fail to sustain their initial confidence? The opening verses of Psalm 71, like those of Psalm 85, have a message of hope and strength and faith. With the psalmist, Cromwell could call God 'my rock and my fortress', 'my trust from my youth'. Yet a personal application must also have suggested itself in the psalmist's ensuing supplication: 'Cast me not off in the time of old age; forsake me not when my strength faileth. For mine enemies speak against me; and they that lay wait for my soul take counsel together, saying, God hath forsaken him . . . '.

If Cromwell's own salvation was at issue in the kingship crisis, the fate of God's people likewise rested on his choice. Cromwell feared that if he took the Crown wrongfully he might be made 'a captain to lead us back into Egypt'. To take the Crown without the light of God's approval might, in the manner of Achan's iniquity, 'prove even a curse to . . . these three nations'. 'If I undertake anything not in faith, I shall serve you in my own unbelief, and I shall then be the unprofitablest servant that ever a people or nation had.'[110] It was in the knowledge of that peril that he alluded to the warning which Joshua had given to the Israelites between the fall of Jericho and the disaster wrought by the sin of Achan: 'Cursed be the man before the Lord, that riseth up and buildeth this city Jericho' (Joshua 6:26). 'I would not seek', Cromwell told the parliamentary delegation sent to persuade him to take the Crown, 'to set up that that providence hath destroyed and laid in the dust, and I would not build Jericho again.'[111]

---

[108] Ibid., iv. 446, 454, 472–3, 513; cf. iv. 277 (lines 20–3).
[109] R. S. Paul, *The Lord Protector* (1955), pp. 300–1.
[110] Abbott, iv. 263, 446, 472–3, 513, 729. Cf. Owen, *Works*, viii. 448; Numbers 14:4.
[111] Abbott iv. 473.

2

Providence and Politics

Seventeenth-century Englishmen knew that God intervenes continually and continuously in the world he has made. His hand could be seen in every change of the
weather or the wind, in every good crop and every bad one, in every sickness and
recovery, in every misadventure of the traveller and his every safe return. Diaries,
commonplace-books, public speeches, government declarations: all voluminously
testify to the pervasiveness of the belief in providence, and to the anxious vigilance
which attended the detection and interpretation of divine dispensations. So ubiquitous was providentialism indeed, and at times so repetitive in its expression, that
our familiarity with it may breed, if not contempt, then at least neglect. Historians
of politics rarely permit allusions to the workings of God's providence to detain
them. Yet providentialism is to be found at the centre of seventeenth-century
political argument and decision-making.

That is evident even if we stay on the surface of events. For did not Oliver
Cromwell and his soldiers proclaim themselves 'instruments of providence', 'raised
up' by God to re-enact the military history and to implement the political precepts
of the Old Testament? Did they not execute Charles I 'since providence and
necessity had cast them upon it', and then abolish the monarchy because 'the
providence of God has laid this title aside'?[1] When the Commonwealth split the
nation in the winter of 1649–50 by imposing an 'Engagement' of loyalty, the
'straightforward invocation of providence', suggests the historian of the debate,
'remained the most basic argument in favour of "engagement" throughout the
ensuing controversy'.[2] Cromwell, having turned out the Long Parliament in 1653,
exercised 'the power God had most providentially put into my hand'.[3] Time and
again his subsequent speeches to parliament recounted 'the providences of God,
how they have led us hitherto'.[4] His courtiers countered parliamentary criticism
with the statement that 'divine providence' had 'set a stamp and seal upon this
government'.[5] His apologists published tracts 'wherein is clearly demonstrated and
proved that Oliver Cromwell is by the providence of God lord protector of

---

[1] Abbott, i. 719, iv. 473.
[2] Quentin Skinner, 'Conquest and Consent: Thomas Hobbes and the Engagement Controversy',
in G. E. Aylmer (ed.), *The Interregnum: The Quest for Settlement, 1646–1660* (1972), p. 86.
[3] Abbott, ii. 454.
[4] Ibid., iv. 485.
[5] *Burton*, i, xxix.

England, Scotland and Ireland'.[6] Cromwell asserted the right to 'balance this providence, as in the sight of God, with any hereditary interest'.[7] After Oliver's death his son Richard declared himself successor 'by the providence of God'. In parliament Richard's supporters proclaimed that he had been 'set upon the pinnacle by providence'.[8] When he fell from power, the opponents of rule by a single person vied with each other in hailing the restoration of the Rump as 'this opportunity, which the wonderful, and, as they hope, the gracious providence of God hath held forth to them'.[9]

Even if we convinced ourselves that the claims of the Cromwellians and of their Puritan enemies were cynical, we would still confront a sizeable historical problem. For a cynical appeal to providence can seem worth making only if its audience is expected to take notice of it. Cromwell did not merely invoke providence as a sanction of his rule. He lectured parliament at length about the workings of providence on his soul. The spectacle may be puzzling until we reflect that the providentialist language which he spoke was one readily intelligible to Puritan MPs, who themselves employed it habitually in their correspondence and their common-place-books and indeed in their own parliamentary speeches. It was a language of everyday Puritan belief, a language which influenced private lives before public events, and which reinforced conventional authority more often than it challenged it. In his private life, as a landowner and as head of a family, Cromwell spoke of providence in terms that are indistinguishable from those used by countless country gentlemen who were politically neither active nor radical.[10] His appropriation of conventional providentialism for a radical programme aroused anger and provoked logical objections. Yet in the arguments between the Cromwellians and their Puritan opponents—and even their Cavalier ones—about the place of providence in politics, the common ground was broader than the areas of dispute. Beneath that ground there were layers of belief and mental habit which help to explain the character and course of Puritan politics.

The greatest work of Puritan literature begins with the poet's resolve to 'assert eternal providence', and ends with the withdrawal of our first parents from Paradise with 'providence their guide'. But just as Milton's mind and imagination roam beyond Puritanism and across the spectrum of Christian and pagan literature, so there is of course nothing distinctively Puritan or even distinctively Christian, and nothing peculiar to the seventeenth century, about the human propensity to interpret successes and calamities as manifestations of divine intervention or divine order or divine justice. Sometimes we may wonder where, in practice, the difference can have

---

[6] George Smith, *God's Unchangeableness* (1655), title-page and *passim*. Cf. E. M., *Protection Persuading Subjection* (1653), esp. pp. 5–6; [John Hall], *Confusion Confounded* (1654), pp. 20–1; *The Humble Representation and Address to His Highness of Several Churches and Christians in South-Wales* (1656), p. 24.
[7] Abbott, iii. 458.
[8] *Burton*, iii. 8, 25, 116.
[9] *OPH* xxi. 380. Cf. xxi. 378; *CJ* 7 May 1659.
[10] Abbott, i. 585, 590, 592, ii. 8–9, 28, 39, 50, 598, 601–2.

lain between Puritan providentialism and Catholic or pagan beliefs which Puritans scorned as superstitious. Sometimes; but not always. Protestantism, which expelled the intermediaries between God and the soul, and which contrived at once to make God more awesomely distant and to bring him more awesomely close, placed a novel emphasis on providence as the exercise of his power. The Reformation brought what has been called 'a new insistence upon God's sovereignty'.[11] That insistence grew with the advances of zealous Protestantism, and lessened with its eventual retreat. The rise, and the decline, of Puritan providentialism are large questions which lie beyond our present purpose. But while the belief in providence is an essential and prominent feature of the intellectual map both before around 1620 and after around 1660, the providentialism of the period which falls approximately between those dates does seem distinguishable by both the frequency and the intensity of its expression. In those decades the small print of the Protestant doctrine of providence is given fuller and wider attention. It looks as if the civil wars are the time when English providentialism took its most intense forms.

In their teaching on providence, Puritans followed and expanded the statements of John Calvin, who had placed the doctrine at the heart of the true believer's interpretation of the world around him. Calvin was scandalized by his contemporaries' neglect of the subject. They conceived of God, he complained, as 'a momentary Creator, who completed his work once for all, and then left it', 'sitting idly in heaven'. 'It is certain', Calvin ruled, 'that not a drop of rain falls without the express command of God.'[12] The *Heidelberg Catechism*, a large influence on English Puritanism, warned that 'they who deny providence, deny God to be God, and take away all religion'.[13] Richard Sibbes summoned Matthew 10: 29–30, a favourite text of providentialists (Oliver Cromwell among them), when he recalled that God's 'providence extends to the smallest things, to the sparrows and to the hair of our heads; he governs every particular passage of our lives'.[14]

Providence was a large subject, with its own morphology. Contemporaries agreed in distinguishing between God's 'general' and his 'special' providence. The distinction was variously applied. Sometimes the former meant God's government of the natural world, the latter his dealings with humanity.[15] Sometimes God's 'special' providence was taken to be his watch over his church and his elect, while his 'general' providence supervised mankind at large.[16] Sometimes his

---

[11] Keith Thomas, *Religion and the Decline of Magic* (1971), p. 79.

[12] John Calvin, *Institutes of the Christian Religion*, trans. H. Beveridge, 3 vols (1845–6), i. 231, 236, 238.

[13] Zachary Ursinus, *The Summe of Christian Religion* (repr. 1611), p. 329; Joseph Caryl, *An Exposition with Practical Observations upon the Book of Job*, 2 vols (1676), ii. col. 1430.

[14] A. B. Grosart, ed., *The Works of Richard Sibbes, D.D.*, 7 vols (1857–64), v. 35; R. S. Paul, *The Lord Protector* (1955), p. 300.

[15] John Wilkins, *A Discourse concerning the Beauty of Providence* (1649), p. 62; T. Thirlwall, ed., *The Works, Moral and Religious, of Sir Matthew Hale, Knt.*, 2 vols (1805), ii. 256, 266.

[16] Ursinus, *Summe of Christian Religion*, p. 332; Caryl, *Exposition with Practical Observations upon the Book of Job*, i. col. 1189; Owen, *Works*, x. 33, xi. 134; *Articles of Christian Religion Approved and Passed by Both Houses of Parliament* (1648), p. 13; *The Confession of Faith, together with the Larger and Lesser Catechismes, composed by the Reverend Assembly of Divines* (1658), p. 21; Ralph Robinson, *Safe Conduct* (1654), pp. 12, 25.

'general' (or 'ordinary' or 'mediate') providence was his usual operation through second causes, 'when there is a sufficiency in the meanes ordinarily to bring about such an end, as when the greater number doth beat the lesser', or when he cures illness through medicine. By the same token God's 'special' (or 'extraordinary' or 'immediate') providence is made manifest 'when there is not a common, naturall power in the instrumentall causes and meanes, to bring forth such an effect, or to attaine to such an end'.[17] Thus he will enable a weak army to defeat a strong one, or—to show that 'God is not tied to Galen's rules'—will save us after medicine has been shown to fail.[18] God, alas, needs to dispense extraordinary providences because fallen man too often omits to notice his ordinary ones.[19]

Providences were pleasant or unpleasant. Pleasant ones were 'mercies' (or 'deliverances'). Unpleasant ones were 'judgements' (or 'afflictions', 'visitations', 'trials', 'chastisements', 'rebukes', or 'corrections'); they were 'cross providences', 'rugged providences', 'sad', 'black', 'damping', 'frowning', 'louring' providences. Mercies were bestowed, and judgements inflicted, on individuals, on communities, on nations. Mercies were grants of divine favour or clemency, unmerited and unexpected. Judgements, however severe, were never as dreadful as man deserved. They were signals of the wrath provoked in God by sin. Sometimes the offending sins were conspicuous, like the whoredom, adultery, drunkenness, and blasphemy that were held to be rampant in seventeenth-century England, and on which a host of calamities was blamed—not least the civil wars.[20] At other times God sent affliction in order to stir the victim to locate a concealed sin: a mother's miscarriage might point to 'some hidden roote of evill' in her household,[21] while a military setback might prompt the discovery of a sin which had stained an army or a government or a whole nation and impeded its success.[22] Royalists interpreted their defeat in the civil wars, and Puritans interpreted the Restoration, as a punishment for their sins.[23] In the 1640s Puritans wondered at God's mercy in favouring them, even

---

[17] John Bond, *Ortus Occidentalis* (1645), p. 14.

[18] Grosart, *Works of Richard Sibbes*, v. 45.

[19] J. Pratt, ed., *The Works of the Right Reverend Father in God, Joseph Hall, D.D.*, 10 vols (1808), i. 86; Lucy Hutchinson, *Memoirs of the Life of Colonel Hutchinson*, ed. James Sutherland (Oxford, 1973), p. 278; John Rowe, *Man's Duty in Magnifying God's Work* (1656), p. 17. The Earl of Clarendon thought that God 'doth, as it were, more submit the effects to second causes' in peace than in war: *CT*, p. 757.

[20] e.g. *CJ* 2 September 1642; *OPH*, xii. 399; John Taylor, *Mercurius Pacificus* (1650); Humphrey Moseley, *An Healing Leaf* (1658).

[21] Alan Macfarlane, ed., *The Diary of Ralph Josselin, 1616–1683* (1976), p. 371.

[22] Above, ch. 1; George Hakewil, *An Apologie or Declaration of the Power and Providence of God* (1627), preface, sig. C.2ᵛ; R. N. Dore, ed., *The Letter Books of Sir William Brereton*, Record Society of Lancashire and Cheshire (1984–), i. 308; Johnston, *Diary*, ii. 5, 7, iii 23; and compare the discussion of Sir George Booth's rising of 1659 in R. Parkinson, ed., *The Life of Adam Martindale, Written by Himself*, Chetham Society 4 (1845), p. 137, with that in *An Account of the Life and Death of Mr Philip Henry* (1712), p. 49.

[23] Joshua Sprigge, *Anglia Rediviva* (Oxford, 1844), p. 219; Warwickshire Record Office, Warwick, C. R. 1886/unnumbered (Algernon Sidney, 'Court Maxims, Refuted and Refelled'), p. 16; Ludlow, *Voyce*, pp. 114, 115, 149. But as Ludlow shows, it was possible subtly to shift the main burden of guilt on to the sins of one's impure allies.

'though our iniquities testify against us',[24] in battle, where he preserved them from enemy attacks by 'daily and hourly providences'.[25]

The doctrine of providence was not necessarily irrational. There is no logically self-evident boundary beyond which a sovereign Creator can be deemed not to direct events. Providence seemed the friend of reason, even though it transcended it. It gave order and meaning to lives which would otherwise lie at the whim of that most irrational of agencies, chance. Calvin had said succinctly what his Puritan successors said at length: 'nothing cometh by chance, but whatsoever cometh to pass in the world, cometh by the secret providence of God'.[26] Cromwell's chaplain John Owen saw in providence 'a straight line' which 'runs through all the darkness, confusion, and disorder of the world'.[27] Providences were not random or arbitrary displays of the divine sovereignty. They formed a pattern, a 'chain', or 'series', visible to the true believer. Puritans agreed with Francis Bacon that 'while the mind of man looketh upon second causes scattered, it may sometimes rest in them, and go no further; but when it beholdeth the chain of them, confederate and linked together, it must needs fly to providence and deity'.[28] Cromwell, when urging Colonel Robert Hammond to 'look into providences; surely they mean somewhat', impressed upon him that 'they hang so together', and thought Hammond would understand them once he recognized the 'chain' that connected them.[29]

Providence was the thread of divine purpose which drew together the seemingly disparate events of history. Cromwell urged his son Richard to read Sir Walter Raleigh's *History of the World*, a work, it has been observed, in which 'history is the working out of the first cause, God's will, divine providence',[30] because 'it's a body of history, and will add much more to your understanding than fragments of story'.[31] Divines urged the Long Parliament to commission 'an History of Providence' which, by placing the events of the 1640s within the divine scheme of history, would become 'the Magna Charta of miracles'.[32] In biography, as in history, events and dispensations were the vertebrae of a spine of providence. Lucy Hutchinson, widow of the MP and regicide Colonel Hutchinson, recorded apparently small episodes in the life of her

---

[24] T. T. Lewis, ed., *Letters of the Lady Brilliana Harley*, Camden Society, first series 57 (1854), p. 180.

[25] Hutchinson, *Memoirs of the Life of Colonel Hutchinson*, p. 165.

[26] Quoted from Calvin's commentaries on the Book of Daniel by C. A. Patrides, *Milton and the Christian Tradition* (Oxford, 1966), p. 56; cf. Calvin, *Institutes of the Christian Religion*, i. 242–3.

[27] Owen, *Works*, viii. 11.

[28] J. Spedding, R. L. Ellis, and D. D. Heath, eds, *The Works of Francis Bacon*, 14 vols (1857–74), vi. 413. For Puritan approval of Bacon's observation, see BL Add. MS 31984 ('Whitelocke's History of his Forty-Eighth Year'), fo. 43[r–v].

[29] Abbott, i. 696–7.

[30] H. R. Trevor-Roper, reviewing Christopher Hill's *Intellectual Origins of the English Revolution* in *History and Theory* 5 (1966), p. 77.

[31] Abbott, ii. 236.

[32] Obadiah Sedgwick, *A Thanksgiving-Sermon Preached before the Honourable House of Commons at Westminster, 9 April 1644* (1644), ep. ded.; Thomas Coleman, *The Christians Course and Complaint* (1643), p. 66; William Spurstowe, *England's Eminent Judgments Caused by the Abuse of God's Eminent Mercies* (1644), pp. 10–11; Stephen Marshall, *A Sacred Record to be Made of God's Mercies to Zion* (1645), p. 27.

husband, 'since even these little things were linkes in the chaine of providences which measured out his life'.[33] The 'passages' of life were placed within providential patterns. The massive autobiography of the MP and regicide Edmund Ludlow, 'A Voyce from the Watch Tower', was sub-titled 'In Severall Passages of Providence relating to Publiq and Privat Concernes'.[34] The devout scientist Robert Boyle, when he remembered his deliverances from death in childhood,

> would not ascribe any of these rescues unto chance, but would be still industrious to perceive the hand of heaven in all these accidents; and indeed he would profess, that in the passages of his life, he had observed so gracious and so peculiar a conduct of providence, that he should be equally blind and ungrateful, should he not both discern and acknowledge it.[35]

The collection of extraordinary providences into a diary or notebook, a habit which answered to 'the ancient practice of God's people',[36] became common. At regular periods—at the end of the week, at the end of the year—Puritans would record the providences which had been vouchsafed to them in that time, and set them in the larger pattern of their lives.

Puritans paid careful attention to the timing of providences, for if there was no such thing as chance there could equally be no such thing as coincidence. As the minister Adam Martindale had it, 'There is oft much mercie in the timing of mercies'.[37] When parliament learned in October 1641 of the plot to seize the Scottish leaders Argyle and Hamilton, the MP Sir Simonds Dewes told the Commons 'that it was the wonderfull providence of God that this busines should thus breake out just upon the meeting againe of the parliament'.[38] In October 1656 John Rowe, preaching to parliament on a day of thanksgiving for the recent naval triumph, recalled the doubts which the House had experienced before reaching its recent decision to finance the Spanish war, and remarked on

> the season when these tidings [of victory] first came unto you, even at that time, when all the nation was expecting how the Lord would ballance and incline the spirits of the parliament, as to this business. And that the Lord should send you this intelligence immediately after, but not before, you had brought your debates to a resolution, this is that which doth in some measure affect the hearts of all, and there is none that I have met with, but will say, the hand of the Lord appeared in this thing in a more then ordinary manner.[39]

A providential purpose was likewise discerned in the timing of Cromwell's fatal illness, and of his death on the anniversary of Dunbar and Worcester.[40]

[33] Hutchinson, *Memoirs of the Life of Colonel Hutchinson*, p. 86.
[34] Ludlow, *Voyce*, p. 317.
[35] Thomas Birch, ed., *The Works of the Honourable Robert Boyle*, 5 vols (1744), p. 8.
[36] Richard Mayo, *The Life and Death of Edmund Staunton* (1673), p. 33.
[37] Parkinson, *Life of Adam Martindale*, p. 182.
[38] W. H. Coates, ed., *The Journal of Sir Simonds D'Ewes from the First Recess of The Long Parliament to the Withdrawal of King Charles from London* (New Haven, 1942), p. 10.
[39] Rowe, *Man's Duty*, p. 19.
[40] *TSP*, vii. 355, 372; *Mercurius Politicus* 9 September 1658, p. 803; *Somers Tracts*, vi. 479.

Believers must attune themselves to the divine timetable. They might have patiently to 'wait upon God' until the time were ripe for action.[41] In 1647 the Cromwellian army, having resisted Leveller pressure to march prematurely on London, 'to run before hee bids us goe', was gratified when 'God found a better season for us, then if wee had gone att first'.[42] Often God brought deliverance 'in the nick of time', when human helps had been proved wanting.[43] Or he might so time a mercy as to demonstrate the efficacy of prayer. The Essex minister Ralph Josselin noted how God gave the Roundheads victory just when Josselin was praying 'for mercy upon us against our enemies'.[44] In 1648 the preacher John Bond drew parliament's attention to 'a meeting-mercy': 'the articles of [surrender of] Pembrooke Castle, and your order for this thanksgiving, doe both beare the same date and day'.[45] Ten years later, after the taking of Dunkirk, Cromwell's Secretary of State, John Thurloe, summarized a prevalent interpretation of the triumph:

> this mercy is the greater in respect that it was obteyned the very day, whilst his highness and the counsell wer keepinge a day of fasting and prayer, to seeke God for help in that siege . . . it was a mere providence of God, that ordered the fight and the seekinge of the Lord to be upon one day.[46]

The hold of providentialism on mid-seventeenth-century minds may seem more impressive to us than it appeared to Puritan divines. In their eyes the doctrine was imperilled by a massive wave of scepticism and Epicureanism which, in England as in continental Europe, also menaced the Calvinist theory of predestination. Owen connected 'the idol free-will', which challenged predestinarianism, with 'the new goddess contingency', which threatened providentialism. In both evils he recognized that 'strange advancement of the clay against the potter' which to him was a dominant and monstrous tendency of the age. He bemoaned 'that atheistical corruption which depresses the thoughts of men, not permitting them, in the highest products of providence, to look above contingencies and secondary causes'.[47] Indeed the equation of 'atheism' with the refusal to acknowledge providences, or with an inability to look beyond 'secondary causes', was a clerical commonplace.[48] Lay people concurred with it. Lucy Hutchinson wondered at

---

[41] To 'wait upon God' might be to exercise patience in his service, or it might be to pray until he declared himself. For the former meaning, see Thomas Young, *Hope's Encouragement* (1644), pp. 9, 17; Bond, *Ortus Occidentalis*, pp. 7–8; Firth, *Clarke Papers*, i. 87, 374 (cf. i. 256–7); *TSP*, vi. 516; John F. Wilson, *Pulpit in Parliament* (Princeton, 1969), p. 186. Cf. Abbott, i. 453; *MSP*, pp. 7, 10, 25; *Mercurius Politicus* 27 February 1651, p. 609; Abbott, ii. 432, 444.

[42] Firth, *Clarke Papers*, i. 284, 285.

[43] Parkinson, *Life of Adam Martindale*, pp. 103, 184; *A True Relation of Mr John Cook's Passage by Sea from Wexford to Kinsale* (1650), p. 4; Sir William Brereton, *Travels in Holland*, ed. E. Haskins, Chetham Society, 1 (1844), p. 27.

[44] Macfarlane, *Diary of Ralph Josselin*, pp. 13, 15.

[45] John Bond, *Eschol* (1648), p. 36.

[46] *TSP*, vii. 158.

[47] Owen, *Works*, vii. 6, 12, x. 30, 40.

[48] Wilkins, *Discourse concerning the Beauty of Providence*, pp. 74–7; Rowe, *Man's Duty*, pp. 14, 15; Henry Scudder, *God's Warning to England* (1644), pp. 11, 31. Christians often said that pagans could be respected, or might win salvation, only if they believed in divine providence (as well as the immortality of the soul).

the stupidity of blind mortals [who], instead of employing their studies in those admirable books of providence wherein God dayly exhibits to us glorious characters of his love, kindnesse, wisdome and justice . . . ungratefully regard them not, and call the most wonderfull generations of the greate God the common accidents of humane life.[49]

Oliver Cromwell thought that 'he must be a very atheist' who, in his 'blindness', saw 'all those marvellous dispensations which God hath wrought' in the civil wars as 'bare events'.[50] Like ministers, politicians had a special duty to observe the stretching out of God's arm, for, as the minister John Arrowsmith explained to parliament, 'professors eminent for their place in Church or state . . . as being more concerned in the publique welfare than Christians of a more private station, are bound to observe the wheelings of providence more than others'.[51]

Nothing was more certain to provoke divine punishment than man's failure to recognize dispensations. 'Not to see God in such works of his providence', the minister Edmund Calamy warned parliament in 1642, 'is a curse, and will bring a curse'. Like many preachers—and like Cromwell—Calamy pointed to Psalm 28:5: 'Because they regard not the works of the Lord, nor the operations of his hands, he shall destroy them, and not build them up.'[52] After his victory at Pembroke in 1648, Cromwell condemned three royalists, who had earlier 'apostatised' from the parliamentary cause, to the prospect of the death penalty, 'judging their iniquity double because they have sinned against so much light, and against so many evidences of divine presence going along with and prospering a righteous cause'.[53] At Dunbar in 1650, thought Cromwell, the Scots were punished for 'not beholding the glory of God's wonderful dispensations in this series of his providences'.[54] Cromwell's victims in battle discovered that the only way to appease him, and so to avoid further punishment at his hands, was to acknowledge the triumph of his God over theirs. 'Those', he observed, 'whom God hath brought to a sense of his hand upon them, and to amend, submitting thereto and to the power to which he hath subjected them, I cannot but pity and tender.'[55]

Repeatedly after his victories Cromwell urged parliament to 'give God all the glory' for them. Repeatedly he lamented man's tendency to attribute military success not to the Lord himself but to his 'weak instruments', a sin which robbed God of the 'glory' and 'praise' which were his due.[56] 'God is not enough owned' in parliament's victories, complained Cromwell in 1645; 'we look too much to men and visible helps: this hath much hindered our success'.[57] Man's vanity and

---

[49] Hutchinson, *Memoirs of the Life of Colonel Hutchinson*, p. 278.
[50] Abbott, i. 377, ii. 339.
[51] John Arrowsmith, *England's Eben-ezer* (1645), p. 25.
[52] Edmund Calamy, *God's Free Mercy to England* (1642), pp. 14–15; Abbott, iii. 53, iv. 707–8.
[53] Abbott, i. 621.
[54] Ibid., ii. 340.
[55] Ibid., ii. 226.
[56] Ibid., i. 360, 365, 505–6, ii. 38, 124–5, 127, 143, 144, 160, 171, 235, 261, 262, 325, 330, 377, iii. 54, 71, iv. 871.
[57] Ibid., i. 340.

ingratitude in triumph might incite the Lord to limit, even to withdraw, his favour. Jeremiah 17:5, 'Cursed be the man that trusteth in man, and maketh flesh his arm, and whose heart departeth from the Lord', was a favourite text of Puritan and Cromwellian politics.[58] It was God that gave courage and skill to his troops, who were helpless without him.[59] It was God who pierced the enemy's counsels, God who 'infatuated' the royalists and hardened their hearts and lulled them into over-confidence.[60] During the siege of York in 1644, parliamentarians, though invited to be grateful to God for giving their forces there, 'as a meanes', a numerical advantage, were simultaneously warned to 'put not confidence' in it, an error that would 'provoke God'.[61] Sometimes the Lord pointedly placed his forces at an initial disadvantage, in numbers or in the site of battle. After the victory at Preston in 1648, Cromwell requested the Commons to reflect on 'the disparity of forces on both sides; that so you may see, and all the world acknowledge, the great hand of God in this business'.[62] The triumphs of 'our armies' in that year, achieved against all the odds, persuaded John Owen that 'their work was done in heaven before they began it. . . . The work might have been done by children, though he was pleased to employ such worthy instruments. They see, I doubt not, their own nothingness in his all-sufficiency.'[63] Soldiers who won after staring defeat in the face liked to observe that 'our extremity was God's opportunity to magnify his power'.[64] Dunbar, where triumph was snatched from defeat, prompted a spate of such reflections. The Lord, exclaimed the minister Sidrach Simpson to Cromwell,

hath stepped out of heaven to raise those who were even as dead, and to judge his adversaries . . . he is a God mighty in battell, in wisedome going beyond the subtilty of man . . . he hath saved by a few, weake, weaned ones, that the mighty might not glory in their might, but in himself alone. . . . You were before too many, too vigorous when you smote your adversaries. Till you had felt all that the colde earth, and want of provisions in a strange countrey, could doe to you (wherein [the enemy] so much trusted for a conquest) it was not tyme for God to put to his hand.[65]

Cromwell's intimate ally Oliver St John agreed: God had delayed the battle until the enemy, 'relying uppon and bosting in the arme of flesh, [had become too] confident . . . therefore hath the Lord soe ordered the busines, that wee may see it was not our owne sword, nor our owne bow, but his right hand, and his holy arme that hath gotten us the victory.'[66]

A recurrent human failing impaired the saints' relationship with providence. Even when 'we see providence working', 'we will not be satisfied except God bring

---

[58] E.g. Abbott, ii.173; Calamy, *God's Free Mercy to England*, p. 15.
[59] Abbott, ii. 127, 164, 235, 324; Marshall, *Sacred Record to be Made of God's Mercies to Zion*, p. 30.
[60] Dore, *Letter Books of Sir William Brereton*, i. 357; Owen, *Works*, viii. 166; *OPH*, xiii. 286; *Somers Tracts*, vi. 501; *TSP*, vi. 790.
[61] *The Scottish Dove* 17 May 1644, p. 246.
[62] Abbott, i. 637–8.
[63] Owen, *Works*, viii. 97–8.
[64] *OPH*, xiii. 286.
[65] *MSP*, pp. 22–3.
[66] Ibid., p. 25; cf. *OPH*, xx. 37.

his will to our will'. 'Except God will give us the thing we ask in our own way, and by the means we our selves prescribe and set down, we will not own it any other way; we ascribe too much to our selves, therefore we prescribe unto God things, times, men and means.'[67] The less the saints imposed their own conceptions or hopes on the workings of providence, the better the prospects of its assistance. When Cromwell's son Henry viewed gloomily the prospective composition of the second parliamentary chamber created by the Humble Petition and Advice, the protector's son-in-law Charles Fleetwood advised him that 'the lesse we anticipate providence beforehand, and [the more we] in faith and prayer wait upon him, the better will it be for us. He hath most appeared, when we have bin least in expectation.'[68] God liked to demonstrate his sovereignty by confounding the 'reasonable' strategies of his armies—and then bringing them victory nonetheless. After defeating royalist forces in a skirmish of 1645, Cromwell wrote that 'though I have had greater mercies, yet none clearer; because, in the first God brought [the enemy] to our hands when we looked not for them; and delivered them out of our hands, when we laid a reasonable design to surprise them, and which we carefully endeavoured'.[69] Of the 'unspeakable mercy' at Fife in 1651, Cromwell could 'truly say, we were gone as far as we could in our counsel and action, and we did say one to another, we knew not what to do. Wherefore it is sealed up in our hearts, that this, as all the rest, is from the Lord's goodness, and not from man.'[70] Sometimes God intervened when the strategies—or the humanity—of his generals threatened his vengeful purpose. Cromwell informed parliament after the sack of Wexford that it was

> deeply set upon our hearts that, we intending better to this place than so great a ruin, hoping the town might be of more use to you and your army, yet God would not have it so; but, by an unexpected providence, in his righteous justice, brought a just judgment upon them, causing them to become a prey to the soldier, who in their piracies had made preys of so many families, and made with their bloods to answer the cruelties which they had exercised upon the lives of divers poor Protestants ...[71]

Yet, limitless as was God's sovereignty and powerless as men were to alter his purpose, the Lord's servants were not to 'tempt' providence by inaction or inertia. The Presbyterian minister Adam Martindale encapsulated the conventional view: 'Though God can worke by unlikely meanes, or without any, it is ill to tempt him to do soe'.[72] Henry Cromwell, when two of his friends were drowned, observed that 'the hand of God was eminently seen in that dispensation, in that they would not be perswaded to shun the danger that was evident'.[73] To trust wholly in God's providence, while yet not trusting wholly to it, required a balance not easily struck. When plague afflicted the garrison at Shrewsbury in 1650, 'many of the godly' were

---

[67] Smith, *God's Unchangeableness*, p. 43.
[68] *TSP*, vii. 589.
[69] Abbott, i. 340.
[70] Ibid., ii. 433.
[71] Ibid., ii. 142.
[72] Parkinson, *Life of Adam Martindale*, p. 182.
[73] *TSP*, vi. 699.

'blame worthy': some 'for their timerousnesse' in 'dispersing' from the garrison, 'as if they could by it alone escape the hand of God, which argueth a distrust in his providence and preservation', while others 'by their indiscreet over-hardinesse provoke the Almighty by their presumptuous running themselves into danger, when they have no just calling to it'.[74] To avoid 'tempting of God', Cromwell explained to Robert Hammond, the believer must contrive to avoid 'carnal confidence' on one hand and 'diffidence' on the other.[75]

God's servants were obliged to make full use of 'means' in public as in private life. In 1650 a correspondent of Cromwell, describing the government's military preparations in England, explained that 'although wee doe not, nor dare not, rely upon these things, for that wee knowe the arme of our God is not shortened, but that he can save by few as well as many; yet wee dare not but use the meanes, least we should be found tempters of the Lord our God'.[76] In 1655 an apologist for the protectorate declared that while the Lord's manifest approval was the rock of the government's authority,

> God alloweth, nay requireth that we shall use all lawful means; for us to neglect to use the means, or obstinately reject the means, we are self-enemies, and it is just with God to withold the mercy we desire, or to bring the judgements upon us we would avoid. To neglect, slight, or contemn any lawfull means, is a tempting of God; that man that shall cast off all means, and say he will rest upon providence, neither beleeves there is indeed an overruling providence, nor can rest upon providence upon any Scripture ground. . . .

It followed that if Cromwell were to concede to parliament the control of the militia which it had recently demanded, but which 'providence hath put into his hand', 'he should provoke providence and betray his trust to the commonwealth'.[77] Propaganda that stressed the providential sanction of Cromwell's rule was itself a legitimate 'means' through which God's designs were to be accomplished. Cunning and dexterity were qualities as requisite in God's service as courage. Certainly there was a distinction to be made: the one that John Owen drew between 'carnal policy' directed to 'self-ends'—'that cursed policy which God abhors'—and 'civil wisdom, or a sound ability of mind for the management of the affairs of men, in subordination to the providence and righteousness of God'.[78] Nonetheless the wicked must be beaten at their own game. As the preacher William Carter told parliament in 1642, 'the worke of God is such, as must have men of wisdom in it. The enemies of God are crafty.'[79]

There was royalist and Anglican providentialism too. Nonetheless, Puritan teaching on providence had a distinctive character. It lay in its preoccupation with the spiritual processes of grace and election. That 'a special providence watches over the

---

[74] *The Perfect Weekly Account* 17 July 1650, p. 532.
[75] Abbott, i. 698.
[76] *MSP*, p. 18.
[77] Smith, *God's Unchangeableness*, pp. 31, 53.
[78] Owen, *Works*, viii. 348–9.
[79] William Carter, *Israel's Peace with God* (1642), p. 14.

safety of believers', Calvin had written, was 'attested by a vast number of the clearest promises'.[80] As God's instruments on earth, the saints were both specially equipped and specially required to discern providences.[81] The most fundamental of the dispensations which God vouchsafed to a believer was to keep him alive while the process of sanctification was accomplished. Just as God's government of the natural world alone preserved it from its tendency to dissolution, so providence alone preserved the saint from death, the natural consequence of sin, while God's grace worked upon his heart. The average saint was likely in his lifetime to experience a number of 'deliverances' from death. At least some of them probably happened in childhood, and there was a good chance that at least one of them occurred by the fireside, that symbol of the pain of hell.[82] It was a dire offence for men to interfere in each other's progress to salvation. Thus John Goodwin, pleading for liberty of conscience, could portray persecution as soul-murder, and claim that the persecutor, by cutting off his victim from the supply of grace, did 'limit or straiten the providence of God'.[83]

God trained the elect soul by 'mixing' mercies with judgements. The former saved the saints from despair and fortified their faiths. The latter were 'meanes of humbling us and exciteing of us to endeavour a true reformation of what by diligent search and prayer the Lord shall show us to be amisse'.[84] While the joys of the saints might exceed those of the unregenerate, so could their tribulations. God, thought the Puritan MP Sir Gilbert Gerard, made afflictions 'the portion of his dearest children', who 'have found more good in them then in all the pleasures of this world. . . . They be God's rodds to drive into way when we erre, and to weane us from the world which we all love to[o] well'.[85] 'The prosperous state', observed the politician John Jones, 'is the slippery and dangerous state of a Christian, because then the poore creature is apt to have his affections fixed upon outward enjoyments'.[86] Ralph Josselin begged God 'to better me by corrections, for I need it'; and when they came 'I blesse God for divers smitings of heart, in the first budding of temptations'.[87]

Saints must search within themselves to learn why God had favoured or chastised them in particular ways at particular times. Josselin's suspicion that the principal cause of his child's death lay in his own inclination 'to unseasonable playing

---

[80] Calvin, *Institutes of the Christian Religion*, i. 255.

[81] Scudder, *God's Warning to England*, pp. 11–12; *MSP*, p. 25.

[82] Parkinson, *Life of Adam Martindale*, pp. 3–5, 22; Lewis, *Letters of the Lady Brilliana Harley*, pp. 246–7; Macfarlane, *Diary of Ralph Josselin*, p. 1; William Turner, *A Compleat History of the Most Remarkable Providences, Both of Judgment and Mercy, which have Hapned in this Present Age* (1697), p. 100. But Puritans believed that one might die in childhood and still be saved.

[83] John Goodwin, *Theomachia* (1644), pp. 35–6.

[84] Arthur Searle, ed., *Barrington Family Letters, 1628–1632*, Camden Society, fourth series 28 (1983), p. 75. For 'mixture', see also Parkinson, *Life of Adam Martindale*, pp. 43, 121; Macfarlane, *Diary of Ralph Josselin*, pp. 67, 206, 431; Sedgwick, *Thanksgiving-Sermon . . . 1644*, p. 22; *A Third Volume of Sermons Preached by . . . Thomas Manton, D.D.* (1689), pp. 74 ff.

[85] Serle, *Barrington Family Letters*, p. 204.

[86] J. Mayer, ed., 'Inedited Letters of Cromwell, Colonel Jones, Bradshaw and Other Regicides', *Transactions of the Historical Society of Lancashire and Cheshire* 1 (1860–2), p. 201.

[87] Macfarlane, *Diary of Ralph Josselin*, pp. 172, 193.

at chesse' was reached after 'I had seriously considered my heart, and wayes, and compared them with the affliction and sought unto God'.[88] By prompting such self-examination, providences became signposts on the saint's journey to salvation. The godly commonly begged God to 'sanctify' providences, and to 'sanctify the rod' of their afflictions. 'Sanctified providences are the best', pronounced Josselin, 'bee they adversitie or prosperitie.'[89] Mercies on the battlefield were 'improvements to grace' among men whose spirits were properly affected by them.[90] Cromwell repeatedly noticed how the victories of his troops 'seem to strengthen our faith and love' and to help 'perfect' their souls.[91]

In detecting providences, and in opening their souls to their efficacy, saints had two principal aids: the Bible, and prayer. The figurative models of Scripture taught Puritans not only to interpret their providential experiences but to anticipate them. 'The judgements of God which are his rod', explained the preacher Henry Scudder to parliament, 'do second his word. . . . The Lord never smites, but he hath spoken first, and warned by his word.'[92] Prayer is an activity inevitably and tantalizingly beyond historical recovery. Josselin, recording some of the 'hints' and 'intimations' with which God answered his prayers, indicated that the Lord might give concrete guidance, formulated in words and phrases which 'came with power, and commanded my heart'.[93] Did the Cromwellian army derive the political conclusions which emerged from its prayer-meetings from similarly tangible advice? Or did the soldiers rather learn to recognize the moment when a proposal previously formulated among themselves appeared to be at one with the holy spirit present in their counsels? Whatever the experiences of the Cromwellians at prayer, some of the major political decisions of the seventeenth century were taken as a result of them.[94]

So intense was the relationship between God and the elect soul that the distinction between ordinary and extraordinary providences tended to collapse before it. Every state of health or of the weather, even of the most 'ordinary' kind, was a feature of a world whose continuous interaction with the promptings of his own soul the saint must no less continuously observe. When Cromwell's ships went forth on God's behalf, the strength and the direction of the wind, however

[88] Ibid., p. 114. Josselin was gratified when news of a providence found his soul in a healthy state, and dismayed when it did not: ibid., pp. 409, 468. Afflictions might sometimes be rather acts of guidance for the future than rebukes for the past; the believer must discover which: ibid., p. 136.
[89] Macfarlane, *Diary of Ralph Josselin*, p. 657.
[90] Bond, *Ortus Occidentalis*, p. 34.
[91] Abbott, i. 690, ii. 103, 190.
[92] Scudder, *God's Warning to England*, p. 16.
[93] Macfarlane, *Diary of Ralph Josselin*, pp. 114, 205, 236, 297.
[94] See ch. 1. Sometimes God revealed his will through prophecies or visions or dreams—although orthodox Puritans hesitated to travel down those dangerous interpretative paths. For scruples about the interpretation of dreams, see Ludlow, *Voyce*, p. 106; *True Relation of Mr Cook's Passage by Sea*, p. 14; Turner, *Compleat History of the Most Remarkable Providences*, p. 47; Thomas, *Religion and the Decline of Magic*, pp. 128–30; Patricia Caldwell, *The Puritan Conversion Narrative* (Cambridge, 1983), p. 16. Cromwell evidently believed that God might give advance knowledge of military success: Abbott, i. 365, 645.

unexceptionable, were divinely ordained.[95] Any change in the weather at a militarily critical moment must bear a providential significance. Cromwell told parliament how, shortly before Dunbar, a brigade of horse, exposed by night to the advancing Scottish army, was saved when 'the Lord by his good providence put a cloud over the moon, thereby giving us opportunity to draw off those horse to the rest of the army'.[96] Inconveniently, the course of nature could affect the regenerate and the unregenerate indiscriminately. In 1650 the Cromwellian officers in Ireland were distressed when God, by extending to the invaders a plague he had visited upon the natives, 'removes that distinction and difference which formerly he... kept between us and the people of the nation, and by this he sweeps away in that common deluge many precious ones'.[97] In the same year John Cook, the Commonwealth's solicitor at the trial of Charles I, faced death when a huge storm blew up while he and his wife journeyed on the Irish Sea. As they crouched beside their unregenerate fellow passengers, the couple implored God to 'throw the Aegyptians and all thy implacable enemies into the midst of the sea, but let us be preserved that we may prayse thy name'.[98]

That and many other Puritan accounts of the operations of providence may seem to us evidence of self-centredness, or of narrow horizons, or of circularity of reasoning, or simply of a want of common sense. Modern readers are on the side not of William Prynne, who ransacked history for occasions when God had shown his dislike of stage plays by destroying theatres or afflicting spectators, but of Prynne's critic Sir Richard Baker, who asked 'what great wonder is this; if in so many hundred years, in so many thousand places, some few such accidents have sometimes happened?'[99] The same readers may be perplexed by the double thinking of saints who could proclaim God's intervention when things went well but emphasize the inscrutability of providence when they went badly. They may wonder at the apparent self-absorption of Henry Cromwell, who feared that the death of his aristocratic brother-in-law Robert Rich 'may be a reproof particular unto myself, for placing ... too much upon the consequences of this alliance';[100] or of Ralph Josselin, who thanked God for protecting his own household and parish from calamities which had visited his neighbours, and who wrote as if the outcome of the battle of Edgehill had been determined by the prayers of his Essex congregation.[101] Yet such statements are open to misunderstanding. The design of

---

[95] See e.g. Abbott, iii 186. When Edmund Ludlow is 'sure' that the punishment of his cause at the Restoration was 'brought about by the immediate hand of God', or is 'more and more convinced of the hand of the Lord' in Charles II's return, or is 'assured that it was done by the wise disposing hand of God', he invites us to suppose that he has considered, before rejecting, a possibility that God's providence, or at least his special providence, was *not* the cause of the Restoration: Ludlow, *Voyce*, pp. 89, 119, 149. Yet the consuming providentialism of his autobiography makes it hard for its readers to imagine that possibility at work in his mind.

[96] Abbott, ii. 322.

[97] *MSP*, p. 72.

[98] *True Relation of Mr John Cook's Passage by Sea*, p. 6.

[99] Sir Richard Baker, *Theatrum Triumphans* (1670), pp. 71–3.

[100] *TSP*, vi. 821.

[101] Macfarlane, *Diary of Ralph Josselin*, p. 13.

providence, incomprehensible both in its size and in its detail, enabled God's dispensations to interact in a unique manner with the motions of each believing soul. The Puritan could answer only for his own soul, of which he was the steward. Although he loved to learn of the spiritual experiences of his fellow saints, there was a point beyond which he could not hope to share or comprehend them. There, as in so many respects, God's judgements were unsearchable. Writers liked to compare providence to a complicated clock, wherein man, able to glimpse 'onely two or three wheels . . . how they move one against another', could merely see 'contrariety and confusion', while God alone could view the beauty of 'the whole frame'.[102] So 'the greatest statesmen, the wisest polititians . . . cannot discern whether the wheels move forward or backward. . . . The motions of providence are so perplex and various, that it comes not within the compass of the wisdom of man to gather any certain conclusions from them.'[103]

Was there not, therefore, a profound presumption in invocations of divine approval by politicians? Must there not be at least some occasions when God, as Oliver Cromwell liked to say, acted 'for reasons best known to himself'?[104] Milton condemned whomsoever 'without warrant but his own fantastic surmise, takes upon him . . . to unfold the unsearchable mysteries of high providence'.[105] 'Who can look into the bottom of the sea', asked John Owen biblically, 'or know what is done in the depths thereof? God's works in their accomplishment are . . . oftentimes . . . unsuited to the reasons and apprehensions of men', who are too frequently guilty of 'reducing the works of providence to inbred rules of their own'.[106] Yet Puritans who were informed by the clergy of their congenital inability to comprehend providences were also told by them of their inescapable obligation to strive to do so; of the charge of atheism that would be levelled against them if they did not; and of the dreadful wrath and destruction which failure would awaken in the Almighty. In general they were much more alive to their duty than to their incapacity.[107]

When they interpreted dispensations, the saints faced one particularly perilous temptation: the disposition to regard worldly success as evidence of God's favour. Sometimes the temptation proved insuperable—although few slipped as badly as the first Earl of Cork, who adopted the motto 'God's providence is mine inheritance' at the time of his ennoblement, or Sir William Brereton, who detected

---

[102] Wilkins, *Discourse concerning the Beauty of Providence*, p. 52.

[103] William Strong, *A Treatise Shewing the Subordination of the Will of Man unto the Will of God* (1657), pp. 157–8.

[104] Abbott, ii. 177, iii. 874, iv. 473.

[105] Quoted from Milton's *Eikonoklastes* in Michael Fixler, *Milton and the Kingdoms of God* (1964), p. 164.

[106] Owen, *Works*, viii. 142.

[107] Joseph Caryl distinguished between God's 'visible and plain' providences and his 'many invisible works both of mercy and judgment', and wrote of the invisible category that 'we should be, though not curiously, yet seriously searching, as much as possibly we can, even into those ways of God which are unsearchable; we should consider, though we cannot search them out': Caryl, *Exposition with Practical Observations upon the Book of Job*, ii. col. 1430. Allusions to the unsearchable depths of God's purpose were often concessionary preludes to statements which look presumptuous in the light of them: e.g. *MSP*, p. 93; Macfarlane, *Diary of Ralph Josselin*, p. 402.

God's hand when he succeeded in transporting his horses across the Irish Sea without a licence.[108] The fruits of providence were properly to be found in the inward, not the outward man. In any case, not all saints led successful lives, either economically or politically. Indeed, transformative as the joyful and triumphant providentialism of the saints in arms was, it may be that for most believers at most times the doctrine of providence operated principally as a system of consolation and a source of tranquillity.[109] Behind their tribulations there lay the inscrutable but benevolent providence of which Milton, amid the catastrophe of the Restoration, reminded the faithful at the conclusion of *Samson Agonistes*:

> All is best, though we most often doubt,
> What the unsearchable dispose
> Of highest wisdom brings about
> And ever best found in the close.

In its consolatory form the providentialism of the saints bore some resemblance to the neo-stoicism of the late Renaissance, when Justus Lipsius had reinvigorated the tradition of Seneca and Boethius. Puritans and stoics alike spurned the vanity of human wishes, and offered a comforting perspective upon the outward prosperity of the wicked and the outward adversity of the just. John Wilkins, who had been installed by Puritans as Warden of Wadham College Oxford, turned to the stoics in a popular publication of 1649, the title of which indicates the character of mainstream providentialism: *A Discourse concerning the Beauty of Providence in All the Rugged Passages of It: Very Seasonable to Quiet and Support the Heart in these Times of Publick Confusion*.[110] 'To be very solicitous about any particular successe', asked Wilkins, 'what is it but to limit and confine the power of God? nay, to prefer our own policy before the wisedome of providence?' We should 'be carefull of our own duty, to serve providence in the usuall means, and leave the disposal of events to him'.[111]

However sore their adversities might be, saints had more to say about God's loving kindness to them than about the wrath with which he punished them. Judgements were analogous to the Law, mercies to the Gospel; and 'a gracious and godly heart is more wrought upon by mercies than judgements'.[112] It was uncharitable to God to 'enforce' him, by our sins, to 'correct us for our own good', for 'the Lord delights to show mercy'.[113] Miscarriages by Puritan women were endured

---

[108] Nicholas Canny, *The Upstart Earl* (Cambridge, 1982), p. 19; Brereton, *Travels in Holland*, p. 168.

[109] The consolatory properties of providentialism are emphasized by Thomas, *Religion and the Decline of Magic*, ch. 4.

[110] Wilkins, *Discourse concerning the Beauty of Providence*, pp. 79, 95, 106–8.

[111] Ibid., p. 107. Sometimes Puritans, when uncertain how to act, resolved to 'try providence', or 'stay my selfe on God's providence', or 'put my condition to the Lord's providence', or 'cast my self upon providence': e.g. Macfarlane, *Diary of Ralph Josselin*, pp. 8, 199–200; R. Parkinson, ed., *Autobiography of Henry Newcome*, Chetham Society, 2 vols (1852), i. 62; Slingsby Bethel, *The World's Mistake in Oliver Cromwell* (1668), p. 2.

[112] Calamy, *God's Free Mercy to England*, pp. 36–8.

[113] Lewis, *Letters of the Lady Brilliana Harley*, p. 47. (I have not reproduced her unusual spelling.)

without complaint, and instead with acknowledgements of God's mercy, which was manifest in his giving the mother strength to recover—and in his having preserved her previous children through birth.[114] When a child did survive birth but died later, God might be 'wonderfull good' to the parents by protracting the fatal illness and so preparing them for the blow.[115] No doubt Puritans, knowing that 'murmuring against the divine providence' was a 'sin',[116] wrote for the eyes of the God looking over their shoulders. Yet their submission to his will can seem artless enough. Ralph Josselin, whose diary is a haunting testament to the force of Puritan providentialism, was at one point, it is true, almost 'overwhelmed' by the manifold griefs in his life. In 1650, when he lost two children and his closest friend within one week, 'my heart trembled, and was perplexed in the dealings of the Lord so sadly with us'. But Josselin thought his 'sin' to blame; and soon 'my heart is cheered' when 'I eye my God, and thinke on his wisedome in all providences'.[117]

In politics, as in private life, providentialism may have exercised its widest influence as an encouragement to acquiescence and submission. The doctrine of providence may have been summoned to justify regicide in 1649, but alongside that revolutionary usage there persisted the traditional Protestant belief that evil rulers were scourges whom God inflicted as punishments for national sins, and whose tyranny God had commanded his people to endure. There persisted too the habit of resignation to political results which, since providence had determined them, man was powerless to alter. John Thurloe, who amid the troubles of the protectorate seems to have derived strength and comfort from his belief in the overruling wisdom of God's providence, expressed the orthodox position at one crisis when he deemed it 'good to wait upon hym, and to referre all matters to his wise and gratious disposition, without beinge anxious about the event, after wee have done our duty'.[118] Politicians acknowledged the hand of providence, and accordingly fell into line, when their views were overruled by a higher authority or a majority vote. In 1650 Scoutmaster-General William Rowe was hoping to hasten from London to join Cromwell in Scotland when a parliamentary order reached him to stay behind; 'and truly I cannot but submit to it, as that which I reverence as a providence'.[119] In 1657 Thomas Cooper MP initially opposed the passage of the Humble Petition and Advice through parliament, but

haveinge according to what light and understandinge I have receaved from the Lord, discharged my conscience, I can and doe freely acquiesce in the will of God; and though this matter, soe longe as it was in debat, was against my mynde, yet beinge now concluded by the major parte, I can and shall through the assistance of God, I hope,

---

[114] Ibid., p. 78; Serle, *Barrington Family Papers*, p. 220.
[115] Macfarlane, *Diary of Ralph Josselin*, pp. 203–4.
[116] Thirlwall, *Works, Moral and Religious, of Sir Matthew Hale*, ii. 106.
[117] Macfarlane, *Diary of Ralph Josselin*, pp. 205, 207.
[118] *TSP*, vii. 153.
[119] *MSP*, pp. 16–17.

approve myselfe with as much faithfullness to it, as if I had been never soe much for the
thinge in the first promoteinge of it: and this I doe not upon a politick but Christian
account, well knowinge that if a haire of a man's head fall not to the ground without
the Lord's providence, much les doe soe great things as the governments of the world
suffer alteration without special providence.[120]

When Cromwell expelled the Rump in April 1653, 'divers' of its members 'resolv'd
to submitt to this providence of God'—at least for the time being.[121] In March 1659,
as a vote approached, the MP Arthur Annesley resolved to 'rest upon the providence
of God, as to how the question goes'.[122] In May of the same year Richard Cromwell,
'having, I hope, in some degree, learned rather to reverence and submit to the hand of
God, than to be unquiet under it', determined to accept 'the late providences' which
had tumbled him from power; for although 'I could not be active in making a change
in the government of these nations; yet, through the goodness of God, I can freely
acquiesce in it, being made'.[123] When John Desborough, a leading figure in the
toppling of Richard, was himself thwarted by a further restoration of the Rump at the
end of the same year, he declared himself ready 'cheerfully and with much quietnes of
minde' to 'acquiesce in the providence of God therein'.[124]

After the civil wars, providentialism gave the opponents of the new model army a
reason (or pretext) for bowing to their victors. Critics of the Commonwealth's
Engagement conceded that the invocations of providence in government propaganda had proved 'somewhat taking with divers'.[125] The Cromwellians, impressed
by the submissiveness of so many defeated Cavaliers, recalled Deuteronomy 32:31:
'For their rock is not as our rock, even our enemies themselves being judges.' In
1648, the Cromwellian soldiers believed, their 'very enemies were . . . made to say,
God was amongst us of a truth, and therefore they could not stand against us'.[126] In
1653 Cromwell told Barebone's Parliament that 'even our enemies' had confessed
'that God himself was certainly engaged against them, or else they should never
have been disappointed in every engagement'.[127] So perhaps there was truth in the
claim of an apologist for the protectorate who wrote that 'many of the chief
murmurers have acknowledged' that Cromwell 'by the providence of God is
made lord protector', and have 'owned him as our Ioshua'.[128] Certainly Oliver's
own following, and his stature among his critics, had long been strengthened by the
air of providential destiny which surrounded him.

*

---

[120] *TSP*, vi. 157.

[121] Hutchinson, *Memoirs of the Life of Colonel Hutchinson*, p. 206.

[122] *Burton*, iv. 208.

[123] *OPH*, xxi. 419. Cf. Firth, *Clarke Papers*, i. 296; John Morrill, *Cheshire 1630–1660* (Oxford, 1974),
pp. 312–13.

[124] Quoted by C. H. Firth and Godfrey Davies, *The Regimental History of Cromwell's Army*, 2 vols
(Oxford, 1940), i. 208; for Desborough see too *The Publick Intelligencer* 2 February 1660, p. 15.

[125] [Edward Gee], *A Plea for Non-Scribers* (1650), appendix, p. 13.

[126] *Somers Tracts*, vi. 501–2.

[127] Abbott, iii. 54.

[128] Smith, *God's Unchangeableness*, p. 41.

The most conspicuous and clear-cut manifestations of approval which God vouch-safed to the Cromwellians were of course their victories in war. 'The great God of battle', declared the Commonwealth in 1649, 'by a continued series of providences and wonders', had 'determined very much in favour of the parliament'.[129] In the civil wars 'both the then contending parties solemnly appeal[ed] to the great God the Lord of Hosts, to make a just and righteous decision' between them.[130] The Roundhead triumph at Cheriton in 1644, according to the preacher Obadiah Sedgwick, 'was a victory after a mutuall appeal to God': 'the enemy's word was, *God is for us*. Our word was, *God is with us*'; so 'the Lord seemed to decide the great doubt, and to resolve the question which side was right; whose cause was his'.[131] In 1650 men were told of their duty to subscribe to the Engagement, 'especially when God by so many solemne appeales on boath sides have by his divine providence decided the question'.[132] The victory at Dunbar in the same year was viewed as an especially significant declaration of God's favour. Two years earlier Cromwell had reminded the Scots 'what a witness God, being appealed to, hath borne upon the engagement of the two armies', and warned them 'how dangerous a thing it is to...appeal to God the righteous judge in an unjust war'. Now he exclaimed that 'The Lord hath heard us...upon as solemn an appeal as any experience can parallel'.[133] God, concurred Oliver St John, 'takes the umpirage upon him', by answering 'the highest and most solemne appeale that could be made by men; wherein both parties referred the decision to the cause of God, and desyred that he would give his judgment therein at the day of battayle'.[134]

Yet was God's purpose so easily scrutable? Could his will truly be known from the result of battle? The defeated Kirk gave Cromwell's claims short shrift: 'wee have not so learned Christ as to medle with times and seasons which the Father hath keept in his owne hand'.[135] The Cromwellians would not have conceded that detecting God's favour in the outcome of battle was the same as discerning his approval in outward prosperity. The saints, after all, took themselves to be fighting not for their own power or glory but as the weak instruments through whom God was effecting his sovereign purpose. Yet there were logical problems for the victors to face, at least if they wished to convince their critics. For was the Lord necessarily on the victors' side? Had not the Old Testament God often given temporary success to the wicked, in order to make their subsequent fall the greater and the more instructive? Had he not made use of the Israelites' enemies in order to chastise his own people, who, once corrected, had returned to their victorious path? When in 1650 Sir Archibald Johnston of Wariston 'debayted with' Commissary-General Whalley, and was told by him that the Cromwellians' 'successe' was 'an argument

---

[129] *OPH*, xix. 68, 177.
[130] *Mercurius Politicus* 6 January 1659, p. 133.
[131] Sedgwick, *Thanksgiving-Sermon...1644*, p. 24.
[132] J[ohn] G[oodwin] to William Heveningham, 2 January 1650: Bodl., Holkham MS 684 (microfilm), unfoliated.
[133] Abbott, i. 652, ii 335.
[134] *MSP*, p. 25; cf. Ludlow, *Voyce*, pp. 217–18.
[135] Abbott, ii. 304.

of God's approbation', Johnston pointed out 'that God gaive successe to whomsoever he used as instruments of his justice against enemies, or mercy for correction of
his children, and yet without approbation of their course, as Benjamin, Nebuchad-
nezzar, Cyrus . . . '.[136] After Dunbar the minister Sidrach Simpson, describing to
Cromwell how the news of the battle had been received in England, wrote that
although 'some' of the English Presbyterians 'doe reflect upon their appeals to God,
and resolve to sit down under this decision', 'most' of them 'sett not more upon it,
then Israel's being beaten the first and second day against Benjamin, who was
wholly ruined afterwards by them'.[137] In the same year a Presbyterian opponent of
the Engagement made an obvious logical point: 'the argument from providence is
ab eventu or from the issue of a thing; they then that will conclude from this
medium must tarry a while longer, even till the end be seene, and till the winding
up of providence'.[138] Oliver Cromwell's claim, during his negotiations with
parliament over the Humble Petition and Advice in 1657, that God had 'blasted'
the title of king and 'laid' it 'aside'[139] earned him some pointed ripostes from the
parliamentary delegation. 'It may be as truly said', the protector was told, that God
'hath blasted parliaments, for they have undergone and felt the like blasts. The
consequences' of Cromwell's 'position are many, and may be dangerous; for what is
there, by that rule, which is not to be laid aside?'[140] When it was claimed in Richard
Cromwell's parliament that God had 'taken away' the House of Lords 'by a long
series of providence', there were MPs ready to remonstrate that 'No good Christian
can argue from events', and that 'what God doth providentially, he not always
approves'.[141]

   At times, the triumphant Puritans appeared to concede the force of their critics'
arguments. In terms close to the formulations of those critics[142] they acknowledged
that victories could not by themselves be proof of God's favour. Joseph Caryl,
preaching before the Commons in thanksgiving for recent victories in 1644,
allowed that 'successes and events cannot make a bad cause just or good'—
although, he quickly added, 'they make a good cause beautifull, and add lustre to
the justice of it'.[143] Milton agreed: 'Wee measure not our cause by our success, but
our success by our cause. Yet certainly in a good cause success is a good confirmation; for God hath promised it to good men in almost every leafe of Scripture.'[144]
Fairfax and Cromwell concurred with the distinction drawn by Caryl and Milton.[145] The victors, however, wanted it more than one way. In one mood they
could argue that amid the manifold assertions of superior virtue and intention that

---

[136] Johnston, *Diary*, ii. 59.
[137] *MSP*, p. 23.
[138] Gee, *Plea for Non-Scribers*, appendix, p. 15.
[139] Abbott, iv. 473.
[140] *OPH*, xxi. 87, 100–1, 107, 113–16.
[141] *Burton*, iii. 361–2.
[142] e.g. Samuel Gott, *An Essay of the True Happines of Man* (1650), p. 211; D. Parsons, ed.,
The Diary of Sir Henry Slingsby (1836), pp. 29–30.
[143] Joseph Caryl, *The Saints Thankfull Acclamation* (1644), ep. ded.
[144] Fixler, *Milton and the Kingdoms of God*, p. 164 (from *Eikonoklastes*).
[145] Sprigge, *Anglia Rediviva*, p. 222; Abbott, ii. 357.

had been advanced by the contending parties of the 1640s—assertions, they observed, which might all sound equally plausible and which man was not equipped to prove or to test—the unbroken victories of the new model provided clear and objective evidence of God's favour. For

> as the engaging upon such pretences and principles does always imply, and is for the most part accompanied with, appeals to God for judgment, so it is the proper work of God to bear true witness and righteous judgment in such cases; and as he is always engaged to do it sooner or later, clearer or darker; so, in this age and part of the world, he hath seemed both to make haste to judgment in such cases, to give it quickly and speedily, and also to make bare his arm therein, that men may see it . . .

It was with that thesis in mind that the army launched the revolutionary programme of the winter of 1648–9.[146]

Yet on other occasions the Cromwellians were shamelessly, indeed proudly, subjective. They appealed not, or not only, to the 'outward mercies' of the battlefield but to an inward knowledge of God's approval: a knowledge which victory might strengthen, and from which the sensation of victory might at times become indistinguishable in their thinking, but of which victory had not been the originator. Often the army leaders would talk of 'that presence and blessing that God hath afforded this army', the 'blessing' being the outward military success which fortified and interacted with the saints' awareness of the spiritual 'presence' among them.[147] Ultimately the Cromwellians appealed to experience, not to logic: the experience of shared prayer and, in war, of shared tension released by shared triumph. Both the emotional force and the logical deficiency of that position emerge from the long disquisition on providence in the speech with which Cromwell dissolved his first parliament of the protectorate in January 1655. His opponents in the Commons had protested that 'the providences of God are like a two-edged sword, which may be used both ways; . . . and a thief may take as good a title to every purse which he takes by the highways'.[148] Now they paid for that insolent comparison, as Cromwell vented his wrath on men who mocked God's providence, who blasphemously 'call his revolutions human designs' and 'necessities of men's creations'. From such people Cromwell had 'a sure refuge'. They 'are without God in the world, and walk not with him, and know not what it is to pray, or believe, and to receive returns from God, and to be spoken unto by the spirit of God'.[149]

So there was a circular or self-confirming quality to be found in Puritan interpretations both of the public and of the private lives of believers. Edmund Ludlow, without any sense of complication or contradiction,

---

[146] *OPH*, xviii. 161–3. It is my impression that in 1648 the new model, and Cromwell, gave more thought to the problems of interpreting providence than earlier.
[147] Abbott, i. 505, 677, ii. 36–7, 186, 235, 288, 444; *GD*, p. 402; Macfarlane, *Diary of Ralph Josselin*, pp. 78–9.
[148] *Burton*, i. xxx.
[149] Abbott, iii. 591–2.

described 'the unheard-of thunder, lightning and raine' at the coronation dinner of Charles II:

> which though his owne flatterers prophanely applyed to the greatning of their sollemnity, as if heaven itselfe exprest its joy thereat by the dischardge of their cannon, yet others, more understanding in the dispensations of the Lord, supposed it rather a testimony from heaven against the wickedness of those who would not only that he should rule over them, but were willing to make them a captaine to leade them into Egiptian bondage; from which the Lord by his providence plainly spake his desire to have delivered them.[150]

Ludlow was writing of the hour of Puritan defeat, but the saints had reasoned similarly in their time of victory.

For all the logical fallibility of victorious providentialism, and for all the logical objections that were raised against it, its protesting victims found effective criticism hard to sustain. Their own thinking was too often steeped in providentialism to allow them the confidence and detachment with which they might have made nonsense of Cromwellian arguments. One pamphlet of 1650 which came unusually close to doing so, the minister Edward Gee's *A Plea for Non-Scribers*, devoted careful reasoning to a reminder that 'The judgments of God are a great deep, his way is in the sea, and his path in the great waters, and his footsteps are not known'. But when Gee sought to illustrate the dangers of prying into God's secrets, he turned to Thomas Beard's anthology of retributive providences, *The Theatre of God's Judgements*, where he found a 'terrible warning' in a dire physical affliction with which God had once punished a man who had seen divine favour in his present prosperity. Gee appears to have been as oblivious to the contradiction as Beard had been.[151]

Something of the difficulty which confronted Cromwell's critics can be seen too in the influential writings of the minister Richard Baxter. In 1659 Baxter averred that his generation had been too bold in its scrutiny of God's purposes.[152] He had been horrified when soldiers in the new model army told him 'that they thought God's providence would cast the trust of religion and the kingdom upon them as conquerours'.[153] He bemoaned the disastrous lapse of his old friend James Berry, one of the Major-Generals, who had been 'affectionate in religion, and while conversant with humbling providences, doctrines and company, . . . carried himself as a very great enemy to pride', but who had gone to the bad when 'Cromwell made him his favourite, and his extraordinary valour was crowned with extraordinary success. . . . And all this was promoted by the misunderstanding of providence, while he verily thought that God, by their victories, had so called them to look after the government of the land'.[154] Yet Baxter himself noted the 'abundance of strange providences in these times': 'the marvellous preservation of souldiers by bibles in

---

[150] Ludlow, *Voyce*, p. 287.
[151] Gee, *Plea for Non-Scribers*, appendix, pp. 11, 16.
[152] Fixler, *Milton and the Kingdoms of God*, pp. 221–2.
[153] Matthew Sylvester, ed., *Reliquiae Baxterianae* (1696), pt. i, p. 51.
[154] Ibid., pt. i, p. 57.

their pockets which have received the bullets, and such like'.[155] He was as convinced as anyone not only that some cosmic providential design was at work in the civil wars, but that it was 'the duty of his servants to read and study' the 'strange providences in our military affairs and changes of state'. Men, he complained, 'make light' of the immeasurable privilege which God's dispensations conferred upon them; and they neglected the obligation to reform which those providences imposed.[156] They were repeating the sin of the Israelites: 'Who would have thought that a generation that had seen the wonders in Egypt, and had passed through the Sea, and beene maintained in a wildernesse with constant miracles, should yet be so vile idolaters, or murmuring unbelievers . . . ?'.[157]

The inhibitions which forestalled an outright assault on Cromwell's providentialism impeded not only his Puritan critics but his royalist ones. Royalists and Anglicans were sometimes uneasy about the detection of God's purposes. William Laud had complained that 'many things in the works of providence, many men, yea and sometimes the best, are a great deale too busy with'.[158] Royalists frequently derided Puritan appeals to providence as damning evidence of hypocrisy. Yet providentialist assumptions ran deep among them. It was not only Puritans who spoke of 'sanctifying' providences,[159] even if most Cavalier allusions to them lacked the predestinarian dimension of Puritan interpretation. Royalists were torn between two impulses. Should they deny that God's will was visible in the outcomes of war and politics; or should they proclaim that, even if God might temporarily have afflicted them with defeat, in the long term he was on their side? The latter impulse usually prevailed.[160] For royalists to abandon, in defeat and poverty and exile, their belief in God's approval would be to surrender all hope and consolation. Even when their king had been executed, the more committed of the royalists were defiant in their providentialism. 'We make no doubt', their propaganda announced, 'but we have God (the punisher of all perfideous dealers) on our side, and in him is our sole hope.'[161] Although 'these enemies of God prosper, and are mighty . . . and though the divine vengeance be deferred, yet it will surely come, and overtake them in a day when they looke not for it'.[162] That voice was to find echoes on the Puritan side in the 1660s: in the assurances delivered from the 'watch-tower' of Edmund Ludlow that, although God 'permits' the restored royalists to 'smite' the Puritans 'with a rod, yet the staffe of destruction that they lift up against them shall be beaten backe on their owne heads. . . . Yea, it will bee

---

[155] Ibid., pt. i, p. 46.
[156] Richard Baxter, *The Quaker's Catechism* (1655), preface: 'To the Separatists and Anabaptists in England'.
[157] Richard Baxter, *True Christianity* (1655), p. 204.
[158] J. W. Hatherell, ed., *Sermons Preached by William Laud* (1829), p. 149.
[159] Thomas Twittee, *The Art of Salvation* (1643), p. 10; R. Heber, ed., *The Whole Works of the Right Rev. Jeremy Taylor*, 15 vols (1828), xv. 339–40.
[160] *OPH*, xii. 330–1, xiii. 5–6, 72–3.
[161] *The Royall Diurnall* 30 April 1650, p. 7.
[162] *Traytors Deciphered* (1650), p. 84.

but a very little while before . . . the destruction of his enemyes';[163] or in the concluding chorus of *Samson Agonistes*:

> Oft he seems to hide his face,
> But unexpectedly returns
> And to his faithful champion hath in place
> Bore witness gloriously. . . .

Roundhead and Cavalier can sound identical in times of dejection. The lament of Charles Fleetwood in 1659 that 'the Lord had blasted them and spitt in their faces'[164] can be set beside the admission of the royalist divine Henry Hammond after the regicide that 'God hath spit in our face'.[165] And the two sides can sound similar in times of triumph. The royalist Clarendon could be taken for a Puritan in the providentialist explanation of the Restoration in the concluding paragraph of his *History of the Rebellion*. So could another royalist, John Evelyn, when he compares the same event to 'the returne of the Jews from the Babylonish captivity', and declares that 'it was the Lord's doing . . . this hapning when to expect or effect it was past all human policy'.[166] Now at last God's favour had been made clear. 'The court of heaven', declared the Anglican clergyman Gilbert Ironside in 1660, 'hath been solicited this many years *pro* and *con* . . . and now let the world judge whose prayers have been heard.'[167] The manner of the self-destruction of the Puritan cause, noted the returning king, accorded with 'the usual method in which divine providence delighteth itself, to use and sanctify those very means which ill men design for the satisfaction of . . . wicked purposes, to wholesome and publick ends, and to establish that good which is most contrary to the designers'.[168]

If providentialism ran deep among the civil war vanquished, what limits could restrain its application to politics by the victorious saints? When Barebone's Parliament assembled in 1653, Cromwell told it that 'truly God hath called you to this work by, I think, as wonderful providences as ever passed upon the sons of men in so short a time'.[169] Soon his listeners were telling the nation of their

> more than usual expectation of some great and strange changes coming on the world, which we believe can hardly be parallel'd with any times, but those for a while before the birth of our Lord and Saviour Jesus Christ. And we do not know, that any records of all the nations in the world (we scarce except the Jews themselves) can afford such a series of divine providence, or more clear impressions of the goings forth and actings of God in any people, then hath been in these nations.[170]

---

[163] Ludlow, *Voyce*, p. 127.
[164] Firth, *Clarke Papers*, iv. 220.
[165] N. Pocock, ed., 'Illustrations of the State of the Church during the Great Rebellion', *The Theologian and Ecclesiastic*, vi. (July 1848), p. 4.
[166] Quoted by T. Lister, *Life and Administration of Edward, First Earl of Clarendon*, 3 vols (1937–8), i. 516.
[167] Gilbert Ironside, *A Sermon Preached at Dorchester* (1660), p. 13.
[168] *CH*, vi. 203; cf. vi. 206.
[169] Abbott, iii. 60.
[170] Austin Woolrych, *Commonwealth to Protectorate* (Oxford, 1982), p. 155.

Bold as such claims may seem, they were not confined to the heady year 1653. Throughout the Puritan Revolution, political audiences learned that God's recent actings in England had not been surpassed 'since Israel's coming out of Egypt', even 'since the first day of the creation of the world'.[171] Even though Puritans had been distressed by Charles I's refusal to aid the cause of European Protestantism in the Thirty Years War, some of them took the nation's exemption from the conflict as evidence of its providential destiny. England 'hath bin like Noah's arke, safe and secure, when all other nations have been drowned with a sea of bloud';[172] and 'whereas all the nations in Christendome have been in grievous perplexities many yeers round about us: we have bin hitherto kept as another land of Goshen, where light hath still shined, when all others have been in darkness'.[173] That extraordinary mercy seemed to betoken some no less extraordinary divine intention, the more so since England's notorious sins merited a very different return. The glorious privileges which England had been unaccountably vouchsafed, it was recognized, would yield to hideous destruction if the accompanying responsibility to purify the land were not swiftly met. The recognition by godly Englishmen that 'God doth sometimes shew mercy to a nation when it least deserves it, and least expects it'[174] fortified their sense of affinity with the people of Israel, in whose history they detected divinely inspired 'parallels' to their own experience. As Henry Stubbe put it in 1659, 'Our case hath been parallel' to the history of the Old Testament, 'and we may therein read the grounds of our confidence, that thorough a resemblance of events the same providence operateth now in us, which did of old, and we expect the same issue'.[175] It was believed in particular that 'the case of the Israelites opposed by the Benjamites, runs parallel with our present quarrels'.[176] There was nothing new in the detection of parallels between Israelite and English history. They had been almost a Tudor commonplace. But the Puritan Revolution brought them to a higher pitch.

The Old Testament God had smitten and laid waste the Israelites' enemies and obliterated their cities. Cromwell destroyed his enemies in Ireland in 1649 as the self-proclaimed instrument of a vengeful deity. Within England, providentialist language appeared to hold out a comparably obliterative prospect. In his letter to his friend Valentine Walton after Marston Moor, Cromwell reported proudly that 'God made' the royalist forces 'as stubble to our swords', and commended Walton's son for his regret, as he lay dying of his battle wounds, that 'God had . . . suffered him to be no more the executioner of his enemies'.[177] The killing of Charles I is inexplicable without reference to the 'vengeance' breathed by Cromwell after the

---

[171] *Mercurius Politicus* 15 February 1655, p. 5119; Calamy, *God's Free Mercy to England*, p. 10.

[172] Calamy, *God's Free Mercy to England*, p. 17.

[173] William Haller, *Liberty and Reformation in the Puritan Revolution* (repr. New York, 1963), p. 19 (quoting Stephen Marshall).

[174] Calamy, *God's Free Mercy to England*, p. 3.

[175] Henry Stubbe, *Malice Rebuked* (1659), p. 4. Cf. Abbott, iii. 434–5; Jeremiah Burroughes, *An Exposition with Practical Observations continued upon the Fourth . . . Seventh Chapters of . . . Hosea* (1650), preface.

[176] Edmund Staunton, *Phinehas's Zeal* (1644), ep. ded.; cf. Carter, *Israel's Peace with God*.

[177] Abbott, i. 287, 288.

second civil war,[178] and to the biblical theory of blood-guilt which was as potent a force among the regicides in January 1649 as it was to be among Cromwell's soldiers in Ireland later in the year.[179]

Yet there was to be no English equivalent to the scale of the Irish experience. Even the executions of five royalists after the death of Charles I and of two royalist conspirators in 1658 were carried out only after heart-searching. Puritans rarely allowed their providentialism to override the constraints of natural law, still less the moral precepts of Scripture. It was agreed that 'the holy God directs and leads his people onely into the pathes of righteousnesse, that is, into such actions, as agree with his naturall and voluntary divine lawes'.[180] No one would have challenged Ireton when at Putney he reminded the Levellers that, while the saints must follow wherever providence might lead, they could be sure that God 'will soe lead this army that they may not incurre sin, or bring scandall upon the name of God'.[181] The preacher Thomas Jacomb put the conventional view in 1657: 'In the carrying on of God's providentiall will, do not swerve from God's preceptive will, for it is not providence but the word that is your rule; providence without the word is doubt-full, but providence against the word is dangerous'.[182] Providence, agreed a leading MP in the same year, 'is not a rule to walk by without the word'.[183] Even in its most intense forms, Puritan providentialism could be checked by social, mental, and institutional habits.

It nonetheless altered the rules of political conduct. Not least, it devalued political planning. God's sovereignty, which liked to blast the counsels of men, could not be circumscribed by human prediction or calculation. Cromwell thought dispensations especially significant when 'they have not been forecast, but sudden providences'.[184] He and his followers spurned political foresight. They killed the king, or abolished the monarchy, with little idea what to do next. They made a virtue of their own 'irresolution and unpreparedness . . . as to any particular way of settlement' when, four years later, Cromwell expelled the Long Parliament.[185] Politicians and army officers were wont to describe themselves as 'following' providence or as being 'led' (or 'conducted') by it. In the Putney debates of

---

[178] Ibid., i. 653, 669.

[179] Ibid., ii. 127, 142, 199, 349–50. God's wrath had not only to be appeased by the avenging of blood shed in seventeenth-century Britain. It must also be assuaged by repayment of the saints' sacrifices (i) in Mary's reign, whence the blood of the martyrs 'doth lie upon the land, and crieth for vengeance': Calamy, *God's Free Mercy to England*, pp. 49–50; Scudder, *God's Warning to England*, p. 19; (ii) in Europe's wars of religion: Macfarlane, *Diary of Ralph Josselin*, pp. 300–1; *Mercurius Politicus* 22 May 1651, p. 800; *TSP*, vii. 190; and (iii), as readers of Milton's Sonnet XV will remember, in Piedmont. God also demanded vengeance for the blood of the Indians slaughtered by Spaniards in the new world: Abbott, iii. 879–90. On blood-guilt, see also Patricia Crawford, 'Charles Stuart, That Man of Blood', *Journal of British Studies* 16 (1977), pp. 41–61.

[180] *TSP*, vi. 245.

[181] Firth, *Clarke Papers*, i. 296.

[182] Thomas Jacomb, *The Active and Publick Spirit* (1657), p. 45; cf. Robinson, *Safe Conduct*, p. 29.

[183] *OPH*, xxi. 101.

[184] Abbott, iii. 591.

[185] Blair Worden, *The Rump Parliament* (Cambridge, repr. 1977), p. 347.

1647, the officer William Goffe, urging radical courses on his colleagues, reminded them of the saints' duty to 'follow Christ wheresoever hee goes'.[186] Before Pride's Purge the new model leaders ominously announced that 'we are now drawing up with the army to London, there to follow providence as God shall clear our way'.[187] Early in 1650 the Cromwellian officers in Ireland 'thought fit to take the field, and to attempt such things as God by his providence should lead us to upon the enemy'. When they did so they found, as Cromwell told a friend, that 'truly our work is neither from our brains nor from our courage and strength, but we follow the Lord who goeth before, and gather what he scattereth, that so all may appear to be from him'.[188] Later in the same year, when the new model invaded Scotland, its leaders declared their resolution 'to follow [God] in integrity, through difficult paths', and acknowledged their 'fear' lest 'he going before, we should not follow'.[189] Cromwell's reluctance to give his parliaments political guidance, which has been held to have damaged his regime,[190] was characteristic of his providentialism. When Barebones's Parliament met, he announced that he and his fellow officers would behave during its sitting 'as the providence of God shall lead us'. He told the first protectorate parliament, when he dissolved that querulous assembly, that rather than 'intermeddle' in its affairs he had waited to 'see . . . what God would produce by you'.[191] Puritans commonly spoke of following in the 'footsteps' of providence, or of tracing its 'imprint'. In Andrew Marvell's poem on the 'First Anniversary' of Cromwell's assumption of the protectorate, the 'higher force' in Cromwell's life not only 'push'd | Still from behind' but 'before him rush'd'.[192] The protector conceived his expedition to Hispaniola because 'providence seemed to lead us hither'.[193]

The unpredictability of God's providence demanded flexibility and agility of his servants. It dispensed Cromwell from being 'wedded and glued to forms of government'. It entitled him to think of them as 'dross and dung in comparison of Christ',[194] and to move abruptly from one constitutional position to a markedly different one. Ludlow's posthumously revised autobiography tells us, in one of many passages where the providentialism of his own text would have been far more intensive, that in 1648 Cromwell and his fellow 'grandees . . . would not declare themselves either for a monarchical, aristocratical or democratical government: maintaining that any of them might be good in themselves, or for us, as providence should direct us'.[195] Men must adjust to God's will, not prescribe to it by constitutions and documents of their own invention. George Monck, determined to retain his freedom of political manoeuvre as the Restoration approached, said in

---

[186] Firth, *Clarke Papers*, i. 283.
[187] Woodhouse, p. 467.
[188] Abbott, ii 212, 235.
[189] Ibid., ii. 288; cf. *Burton*, ii. 389–90, iii. 110.
[190] H. R. Trevor-Roper, *Religion, the Reformation and Social Change* (1967), ch. 7.
[191] Abbott, iii. 65, 581.
[192] Lines 239–40.
[193] Firth, *Clarke Papers*, iii. 207.
[194] Abbott, i. 527, 540.
[195] *Ludlow's Memoirs*, i. 184–5.

1660 that he 'disliked all promissory oaths; and he entertained scruples shared by many against swearing never to acquiesce in that which divine providence might possibly ordain'.[196] Five years earlier the rumper Edmund Ludlow refused to promise Cromwell to behave peaceably under the protectorate 'because he does not knowe, but that God may give ane opportunity for him to appeare for the libertie of the people'.[197]

With flexibility went courage. Cromwell ventured into the political unknown and took his followers with him. Sometimes his words recall Calvin, who had written that 'when once the light of divine providence has illumined the believer's soul, he is relieved and set free, not only from the extreme fear and anxiety which formerly oppressed him, but from all care'.[198] 'Care we not for tomorrow, nor for anything', proclaimed Cromwell in 1648.[199] Calvin had described 'the exulting confidence of the saints', who said to themselves 'The Lord is on my side; I will not fear: what can man do unto me?'[200] Cromwell warned against the 'bondage spirit' of the man whose 'voice of fear is, If I had done this, if I had avoided that, how well it had been with me!'[201] Cromwell's fearlessness is not to be mistaken for recklessness. Beside the Cromwell whose God exalts every valley and makes every mountain low, there is the Cromwell who insists at Putney that God's servants are obliged 'to consider the probability of the ways and means to accomplish' his ends, 'according to reason and judgment'.[202] There is always a tension between the Cromwell who cuts suddenly through political means to impose the Lord's solution, and the Cromwell who sees conventional political manoeuvre as a divinely approved aid to God's purpose. The first Cromwell is Gideon, triumphing when his followers—God again liking to employ outnumbered forces—have been 'sifted, winnowed and brought to a handful'.[203] There were many such saintly pronouncements in the civil wars. One of the 'providences concerning' the parliamentarian victory at Denbigh Green in 1645 was that 'while our body was entyre we could not breake in upon them, but trifled out the time', whereas when it was 'reduct to a small part', 'that did the worke. When Gideons many thousands are sent away 300 beat the Mideanites. God seldom fights with many.'[204] Preachers reminded the Long Parliament that God would discard lukewarm instruments; that his work would not be done by men who 'runne well a while, and afterwards draw back'; that the children of Israel had failed to prosper when they 'did not drive out the Canaanites from amongst them'.[205] The minister John Bond told parliament in 1648 that 'in our first warre the Lord made it his worke to sift these three nations

---

[196] Quoted by Lister, *Life and Administration of Edward, First Earl of Clarendon*, i. 489.
[197] *TSP*, vi. 744; cf. *Ludlow's Memoirs*, i. 434.
[198] Calvin, *Institutes of the Christian Religion*, i. 261.
[199] Abbott, i. 644.
[200] Calvin, *Institutes of the Christian Religion*, i. 262.
[201] Abbott, ii. 602.
[202] Ibid., i. 518.
[203] Ibid., iii. 54.
[204] *Sir William Breretons Letter* (1646), p. 39.
[205] Carter, *Israel's Peace with God*, p. 11; Scudder, *God's Warning to England*, p. 21.

somewhat generally, and as it were with a wider and courser sieve'. There was, Bond explained,

> a speciall providence in that, for should the first sieve have been too shy and fine, it might have kept back so great a masse and weight on that side, as might have borne and broken out the bottome or floor of the sieve. . . . In this second warre, he is sifting the sifted againe with a much finer rince . . . separating between the faithfull and the formalist.[206]

Yet even in his most revolutionary moments, Cromwell kept open lines of political communication through which he might rebuild the unity of that eclectic godly party whose fracture at Pride's Purge he regretted. The second Cromwell thinks that God will want his instruments to operate from as broad a power base as possible. This is the Cromwell who backs off from needless confrontation; who contemplates the restoration of the ancient constitution; who aims to unite even unregenerate Englishmen behind him against God's enemies in Ireland and Scotland;[207] who appoints ex-royalists to leading positions in the regimes of the Interregnum; who holds out the hope of toleration to Anglicans and Catholics. When he wants to avoid extreme action he remembers the decision of David, taken upon 'prudential grounds', not to attempt revenge for the death of Abner, 'in regard the sons of Zeruiah were too hard for him'.[208] The two Cromwells could conflict. His political instincts could be at odds with his fear of 'fleshly reasonings' which God would punish, of 'thoughts that perhaps may be foolish and carnal'.[209] The tension is caught in the letter of 6 November 1648 in which he described to Robert Hammond his recent diplomatic success in Scotland. He had gone there to effect

> a conquest, or if not, things put in a balance; the first was not very unfeasible, but I think not Christian, and I was commanded to the contrary by the two Houses; as for the latter, by the providence of God it is perfectly come to pass, not by our wisdom, for I durst not design it, I durst not admit of so mixed, so low a consideration; we were led out (to the praise of our God be it spoken) to more sincere, more spiritual considerations. . . .[210]

Cromwell's conscience was clear—and God's purpose had been achieved.

Politicians who appealed to providence often induced scepticism in their enemies. Clarendon described what he took to be the cynical manipulation of providentialist susceptibilities by Sir Henry Vane in his advocacy of the Self-Denying Ordinance.[211] Cromwell, it was maintained, had laid the basis of political absolutism by instilling into his crack army the belief 'that there is no such thing as chance, no

---

[206] Bond, *Eschol*, p. 1. In another favoured metaphor, trials and afflictions were a furnace where those who worked or fought for God were purified and purged.
[207] Abbott, ii. 38–9.
[208] Ibid., i. 551, ii. 273; 2 Samuel 3:39.
[209] Abbott, i. 519, 696, ii. 38.
[210] Ibid., i. 678.
[211] *CH*, iii. 457–8.

mistakes in providence'.[212] Henry Cromwell noted how, in correspondence, politicians could use 'wary' providentialist language to skirt the facts of power.[213] Some politicians paid increased attention to providentialist arguments when addressing colleagues known to be vulnerable to them.[214] The protectoral regime, in the declarations with which it appointed fast days, smuggled vindications of government policy into awed expositions of the workings of providence. In doing so it served God's purpose by strengthening the government he had appointed.[215]

Providentialism was woven into the everyday political thinking of the Puritans. Statesmen who wrote letters concerning urgent matters of state were sometimes so carried away by their reflections on the workings of providence that thoughts on the subject which began as preliminary remarks or as digressions threatened to take over the correspondence. Something of the sort happened to William Steele, the Cromwellian Lord Chancellor of Ireland, in the kingship crisis of 1657, and to John Thurloe after the capture of Dunkirk.[216] Of course, a politician might be more reflective at his writing-desk than amid the turmoil of debate or the detail of committee, where practical challenges had to be faced, or taxes voted or spent. Yet he could not afford to let providence slip from his sight. To do so was the most fundamental of political errors. For whatever calculations the saint might make, there was one perception which dwarfed all others: that to ignore or disobey God's will was to invite the likelihood of retribution and disaster. The voice of political Puritanism is nowhere heard more clearly than in the fear of divine punishment: in the eagerness of MPs to put the Quaker James Nayler to death in order to 'divert the judgement from the nation';[217] in the conviction held by regicides that the execution of Charles I was 'the only way to appease the wrathe of God towards the nation';[218] or in the advice given to his fellow new model officers by William Goffe, when in 1647 they hesitated before the challenge of revolution, to 'tremble att the thought that we should bee standing in a direct opposition against Jesus Christ in the worke that he is about'.[219]

---

[212] Henry Stubbe, *An Account of the Rise and Progress of Mahometanism*, ed. H. M. K. Shairani (1911), pp. 178–9.

[213] *TSP*, vi. 519; cf. *Burton*, iii. 60.

[214] *Somers Tracts*, vi. 499; *TSP*, vii. 669–70, 771–4, 797; *CPW*, vii. 119–20.

[215] e.g. Abbott, iii. 225–8; *A Declaration of His Highness, Inviting the People of England and Wales to a Day of Solemn Fasting and Humiliation* (1656).

[216] *TSP*, vi. 294–5, vii. 192.

[217] Below, p. 83.

[218] Ludlow, *Voyce*, p. 143.

[219] Firth, *Clarke Papers*, i. 283.

3

Toleration and the Protectorate

The study of past English attitudes to religious toleration was brought to life by the Victorians, and bears their legacy. 'To us who have been educated in the nineteenth century', declared F. A. Inderwick in his book on the Interregnum in 1891, 'any declaration inconsistent with religious toleration would be abhorrent and inadmissible'.[1] His sentiment would not have seemed controversial to a generation informed by such works as H. T. Buckle's *History of Civilisation in England* and W. E. H. Lecky's *History of the Rise and Influence of the Spirit of Rationalism*. It may be that the Victorians, enquiring into the origins of the toleration which the nineteenth century had achieved, were prone to congratulate the past on becoming more like the present. Yet in the late nineteenth and early twentieth centuries, when interest in the subject was perhaps at its peak, we can also detect, in the statements on toleration of a Bishop Creighton or a J. N. Figgis, a different sentiment: a fear that the present might become more like the past. Materialism and religious indifference, it was thought, might destroy the moral foundations of toleration and foster a new barbarism which would persecute Christians afresh.[2]

After the First World War the history of toleration, like other subjects attractive to Victorian liberalism, retained its hold not in Britain but in the United States. There the 1930s produced William Haller's edition of *Tracts on Liberty in the Puritan Revolution* and W. K. Jordan's heroic study *The Development of Religious Toleration in England*, a work written under the shadow of European Fascism.[3] Following the completion of Jordan's four volumes, the subject declined. Perhaps there seemed nothing more to say; but perhaps, too, there were changes of intellectual climate which made the moral and evolutionary perspectives of Jordan and his liberal predecessors appear dated or misleading. When, now, we find the late Victorian historian S. R. Gardiner describing the seventeenth-century arguments which led to toleration as 'the lifeblood of future generations',[4] or when we observe the conviction with which Jordan awarded the adjective 'noble' to many of the writers whom he studied, we may wonder at the sense of responsibility shown by those historians to the civilization which sustained them, and at their readiness,

---

[1] F. A. Inderwick, *The Interregnum* (1891), p. 117.

[2] M. Creighton, *Persecution and Tolerance* (1895), e.g. pp. 114–16, 124, 139; J. N. Figgis, 'Toleration', in S. L. Ollard and G. Cross, eds, *A Dictionary of English Church History* (1912), p. 600.

[3] W. K. Jordan, *The Development of Religious Toleration in England*, 4 vols (1932–40). The work covered the period 1558–1660. Jordan's philosophy can be discerned in the prefaces to (and on the dust-jackets of) his four volumes, and on pp. 17, 30, 41, 350 of the first of them.

[4] S. R. Gardiner, *The First Two Stuarts and the Puritan Revolution* (1878), p. 136.

which rebukes the narrow relativism of a later generation, to contemplate the wider significance of the seventeenth-century arguments which they examined. Our difficulty is to dispel the whiff of anachronism. As we try to do so, we discover that relativism has insistent claims to make. We also find that the Victorian legacy, which obscures those claims, runs deeper in modern historical consciousness than we might suppose. Seventeenth-century arguments for religious freedom are still often approved, but are rarely analysed.

As a rule, toleration was a dirty word in Puritan England. It stood not for an edifying principle but for an impious policy. To grant 'a toleration' was to make an expedient concession to wickedness. In the 1640s the Long Parliament consistently used the term pejoratively, when referring to the indulgence of either popery or Protestant sects. The Grand Remonstrance of 1641 lamented that under Charles I 'the popish party enjoyed such exemptions from penal laws as amounted to a toleration'.[5] The Nineteen Propositions of 1642 demanded an end to 'toleration' for 'popish recusants'.[6] Among the 'nationall sins being most agreeable to the nationall judgements under which the land groanes', parliament confessed in 1643, was 'a generall connivance, and almost toleration,' of 'idolatry'.[7] The parliament ordered the books of the separatist Roger Williams 'concerning the tolerating of all sorts of religion' to be publicly burned.[8] Philip Skippon, who would be a councillor of Cromwell in the protectorate', 'always' opposed indulgence to sectaries in 'the Long Parliament', and had 'often been troubled in my thoughts to think of this toleration'.[9] Another of Cromwell's councillors, Nathaniel Fiennes, warned parliament in 1658 that a Stuart restoration would produce 'a toleration of popery'.[10] Most Puritan divines, Congregationalists (or Independents) as well as Presbyterians, spoke the same language. Toleration was 'the whore of Babylon's back door'.[11] It was 'the last and most desperate design of Antichrist', when his stratagems of force and violence had failed, 'to destroy Church and state'.[12] The Presbyterian polemicist Thomas Edwards made a fair point in attacking the sects in 1646: 'if some of those godly ministers who were famous in their time should rise out of their graves and now come among us, as Mr Perkins, Greenham, Hildersham, Dr Preston, Dr Sibs etc., they would wonder to . . . meet with such books for toleration of all religions'. How robustly, Edwards was proud to recall, had Puritans resisted toleration for Arminians in the 1620s.[13] The divines whom he named had refined and inculcated the Puritan scheme of salvation, in which fallen man was clay in the potter's hand, redeemable only through an inexplicable divine clemency and

---

[5] *GD*, p. 219.
[6] Ibid., p. 252.
[7] Firth and Rait, i. 81.
[8] William Haller, *Tracts on Liberty in the Puritan Revolution* (New York, repr. 1963), p. 130.
[9] *Burton*, i. 24–5, 218.
[10] *CJ* 25 January 1658.
[11] Christopher Fowler, *Daemonium Meridianum: Satan at Noon* (1655), p. 167.
[12] Daniel Cawdrey, *Sathan Discovered* (1657), p. 22.
[13] Thomas Edwards, *Gangraena* (1646), p. 145.

through an exacting process of justification and sanctification. In that scheme, 'liberty' could have nothing to do with the individual dignity and self-assertion with which the modern world invests the word. It consisted in freedom from the guilt of sin, and in the release of the will from its bondage to Satan.[14] The only 'true liberty', it was affirmed, was 'a power to do what we ought, not what we will'.[15]

Modern historians view the heresies and the religious diversity of the civil wars as expressions of social protest, and the imposition of orthodoxy as a form of social repression. Yet warnings about the social consequences of toleration were rarely at the centre of debate. More often they were used to reinforce the appeal of an argument from theology. So, on the other side of the controversy, was the claim that freedom of religious profession would be good for trade. For the mid-seventeenth-century discussion about toleration is principally a debate about the salvation not of society, but of souls.[16] Ultimately it is an argument between two positions: the first, that to tolerate heresy is to condemn its converts to eternal torment; the second, that to interpose human authority between God's grace and the soul is to threaten the lifeline of salvation, and to merit damnation 'as accessory to the blood of that soul'.[17] So the stakes were high. 'Thousands might curse you for ever in hell', Richard Baxter warned the parliament of 1654, 'if you grant . . . a liberty to all men to deceive them, and entice them thither.'[18] Heresy was, literally, soul-destroying. It was what in Christian history it always had been, a 'plague', a 'leprosy', a 'deadly poison' from which the faithful must at all costs be protected. The 'false prophets' and 'damnable heresies' against which the Gospel had warned, and which throve upon the collapse of ecclesiastical discipline and the proliferation of sects in the 1640s, were 'a clear indication to us of God's heavy judgement upon this nation', certain to provoke still heavier judgements, in this world and the next, if they were not quickly purged.[19]

To the mainstream Puritan clergy, the civil wars were a demoralizing experience. Members of their flocks, who had shared with them both the persecution of the 1630s and the apocalyptic hopes of the early 1640s, fell away to the sects, lapsed into indifference, or, bewildered by the rapid increase of ecclesiastical options,

---

[14] See e.g. the Westminster Assembly's *Articles of Christian Religion* (1648: a document approved by parliament), pp. 32–3; William Strong (a Congregationalist minister), *A Treatise Showing the Subordination of the Will of Man unto the Will of God* (1657), preface and pp. 45–6.

[15] Richard Vines, *Obedience to Magistrates . . . in Three Sermons* (1655), second sermon, p. 12; cf. e.g. the almost identical words of William Gurnall, *The Magistrate's Portraiture* (1656), p. 10, and Philip Skippon's remark in *Burton*, i. 50.

[16] Of course, the two cannot be so easily separated. Yet it is instructive, say, to ask how many anachronistic assumptions, and how much circular reasoning, we must bring to Thomas Edwards's book *Gangraena* (1646) before we can agree with H. N. Brailsford, who wrote that the passage (on p. 156) in which Edwards claims that toleration would put an end to the 'command of wives, children, servants' is 'more significant than the whole of the rest of his book': Brailsford, *The Levellers and the English Revolution*, ed. Christopher Hill (1961), p. 42. Brailsford's chapter on toleration does make perceptive points about Cromwellian policy.

[17] John Goodwin, in William Haller, ed., *Tracts on Liberty in the Puritan Revolution*, 3 vols (New York, 1934), iii. 42.

[18] *Humble Advice: or the Heads of those Things which were offered to many Members of Parliament by Mr Richard Baxter* (1655), p. 2. Cf. e.g. William Grigge, *The Quaker's Jesus* (1658), preface.

[19] *A Testimony to the Truth of Jesus Christ* (1647), p. 23. The same sentiments can be widely found in the 1650s.

succumbed to tormenting doubts about their own salvation.[20] Toleration seemed the obvious source of those evils. Behind it, Puritans discerned a profoundly subversive movement: Arminianism, the philosophy of free will and free thought. Having been identified with the regime of Charles I, Arminianism was politically defeated in the early 1640s. Yet it infiltrated the civil-war sects, and after 1660 it achieved, within English as well as continental Protestantism, a slow and largely silent triumph. If we favour an evolutionary perspective, and concern ourselves with the seventeenth-century 'development' of toleration, then, as a number of historians have argued—Gardiner, Jordan, and Hugh Trevor-Roper among them—it is to the Arminian reaction against Calvinist dogma that we should look.[21] How could Puritans preserve their intellectual system against that threat? How could they beat off long-term changes in seventeenth-century religion: the weakening of creeds, the 'decline of hell',[22] the retreat of millenarianism,[23] the rise of rational and practical theology?

Arminianism assumed one particularly sinister form. This was Socinianism, a term which, like Arminianism, was used to describe both a doctrine and a frame of mind. The doctrine was anti-Trinitarianism: the frame of mind was rational scepticism. 'The Socinians', it was observed in 1647, 'now begin to appear in great numbers under the title of rationalists'.[24] No heresy was harder to tolerate than anti-Trinitarianism. It was one of the offences that occasioned the last public burnings for heresy in England in 1612, and was excluded from the measure of 1689 that became known as the Toleration Act (though the word 'toleration' nowhere appears in it). Anti-Trinitarianism, in questioning the divinity of Christ and the Holy Ghost, was offensive enough to Christians of most persuasions. In challenging Puritan conceptions of Christ's mediation and of the believer's union with Christ, it struck at the heart of Puritan theology. 'The Trinity', explained Cromwell's chaplain John Owen, was 'the great fundamental article of our profession', 'that mystery the knowledge whereof is the only means to have a right apprehension of all other sacred truths'.[25] Parliament's draft ordinance against blasphemy in 1646, and its fierce legislation against blasphemy in 1648, were responses to the anti-Trinitarian challenge. It was largely in reply to anti-Trinitarian literature that in 1652 John Owen and his allies framed those 'fundamental' articles of faith which were to provide the doctrinal basis of Cromwellian Church policy.

---

[20] For some eloquent complaints, during the protectorate, against that process, see Richard Baxter, *True Christianity* (1655), preface and p. 204; Edward Reynolds, *The Peace of Jerusalem* (1657), p. 34; Stephen Marshall and Giles Firmin, *The Power of the Civil Magistrate in Matters of Religion, Vindicated* (1657), pp. 20, 23–4; Edmund Calamy, *A Patterne for All* (1658), pp. 16–17. It is easy to forget the most obvious characteristic of Puritans: their anxiety about their salvation. For an especially vivid illustration of the widespread and educated nature of that concern, see *Truth's Conflict with Error, or, Universal Redemption Controverted in Three Publike Disputations* (1650).

[21] Gardiner, *First Two Stuarts*, pp. 5–6, 65, 125–6, 135–6; Jordan, *Development of Religious Toleration*, ii. 205, 280; H. R. Trevor-Roper, 'The Religious Origins of the Enlightenment', in his *Religion, The Reformation and Social Change* (1967), pp. 193–236.

[22] D. P. Walker, *The Decline of Hell* (Chicago, 1964).

[23] William Lamont, *Godly Rule; Politics and Religion 1603–1660* (1969), chs 5–6.

[24] *SPC*, ii. 343.

[25] Owen, *Works*, vii. 28–9, xiv. 346.

From 1652 to 1654 alarm mounted at the content and influence of the anti-Trinitarian publications of John Biddle (or Bidle), whose offences inflamed the proceedings of the first parliament of the protectorate.

Socinians, theologically the most subversive of the sects, were socially the least provocative of them. Biddle was the most sober of sectaries. There was nothing in his thinking to match the political or social subversiveness of Fifth Monarchists and Quakers. Biddle's prose, like much Socinian literature, was abstract and knotty. Anti-Trinitarianism was not, at least in any transparent way, a movement of social protest. It was a European intellectual movement, the secret heresy, in England, of Great Tew, of Milton and Newton and Locke.[26] Its biblical case, as Puritans admitted, was embarrassingly 'plausible',[27] based as it was on a Scriptural literalism similar to that which orthodox divines were themselves driven to advocate by the fanciful allegorical readings of other sects.[28] But there was a broader challenge, too, which is conveyed by the sub-title of Biddle's translation (a book condemned as 'very scandalous' before parliament in 1654[29]) of that major work of European Socinianism, *Dissertatio de Pace*: 'wherein is elegantly and acutely argued, that not so much a bad opinion, as a bad life, excludes a Christian out of the kingdom of heaven; and that the things necessary to be known for salvation, are very few and easy; and finally, that those who pass amongst us under the name of heretics, are notwithstanding to be tolerated'. 'Socinians', observed the MP Samuel Gott in 1650, 'suppose him to be a good easy and indulgent God, content with anything'.[30]

In March 1654 the executive council of the protectorate decided to act. John Owen, Vice-Chancellor of Oxford and the chief architect of the Cromwellian Church, accepted the government's invitation to confute Biddle's arguments.[31] The result was one of a series of long works in which Owen, 'the Calvin of England', expounded and defended Puritan orthodoxy. His condemnation of the 'cursed Socinians' was unsparing. Owen defended Calvin's decision to have the Socinian Michael Servetus, Biddle's intellectual ancestor, burned for what Owen called his 'abominations' and 'horrid blasphemies'.[32] Socinianism, declared Owen, was responsible for the 'flood' of 'scepticism, libertinism and atheism' which 'is broken upon the world'. It had advanced until 'nothing certain be left, nothing

---

[26] It can be studied in H. J. McLachlan, *Socinianism in Seventeenth-Century England* (Oxford, 1951) and in McLachlan's *The Religious Opinions of Milton, Locke and Newton* (Manchester, 1941). The broader intellectual significance of Socinianism is discussed by Trevor-Roper, 'Religious Origins of the Enlightenment'. Too much can be made of Owen's warning (Owen, *Works*, xii. 52) that 'there is not a city, a town, scarce a village, in England, wherein some of this poison is not poured forth': Owen was evidently referring to a general Arminian *malaise* of which he saw anti-Trinitarianism as a symptom (cf. ibid., x. 156, xvi. 16). It is true, however, that such evidence as we have of the existence of Socinian congregations suggests that there may have been others which have left no record. See too Keith Thomas, *Religion and the Decline of Magic* (1971), p. 136.
[27] Owen, *Works*, xii. 28; *The Weekly Intelligencer* 3 July 1655, p. '28'.
[28] Cf. *Two Letters of Mr Iohn Biddle* (1655), pp. 2–6; Biddle, *A Twofold Catechism* (1655), preface.
[29] *CJ* 21 December 1654; *Severall Proceedings in Parliament* 28 December 1654, p. 4435.
[30] Samuel Gott, *An Essay of the true Happiness of Man* (1650), p. 267.
[31] *CSPD 1654*, p. 3.
[32] Owen, *Works*, xii. 41.

unshaken'.[33] 'The liberty of men's rational faculties having got the great vogue in the world', people were deciding 'that religion consists solely in moral honesty, and a fancied internal piety of mind towards the deity'.[34]

Here objections might be voiced. If Puritanism was so hostile to toleration, how was it that in the Puritan Revolution so much toleration was achieved? The arrival of liberty of conscience, after all, was proclaimed by Cromwell, attacked by his Presbyterian critics, and acknowledged gratefully by some sects and grudgingly by others. The successive governments of the Interregnum, although they tried to define the boundaries of acceptable doctrine, made no attempt to impose a particular form of worship or of church government or to enforce a solution to the heated controversies of the decade about the sacraments of communion and baptism.

The emergence of religious laissez-faire during the Puritan Revolution might seem to cast doubt on the approach which has been taken here. Ought we really to be dwelling on theological anxieties, especially those of the clergy, who were expected to have them? Should we not instead be studying the facts of political life? The main reason for the wide freedom of religious expression during the civil wars, after all, was the impossibility of stopping it. The Rump Parliament's reluctant repeal of the recusancy laws in 1650[35] gave recognition to practices that no one had both the will and the power to prevent. In any case, the devising of a national statement of theological orthodoxy to which rival religious parties or their political patrons could be brought to agree was a daunting challenge. The Congregationalists and the sects, although ready enough to forget each other's claim to liberty if they saw a chance of imposing their own *iure divino* ecclesiastical solutions,[36] were driven together by the fear of persecution. They developed a common vocabulary of religious freedom. In the new model army, that vocabulary appealed to comradeship and to shared experience. Religious liberty became an integral part of the cause for which, as soldiers and 'saints' persuaded themselves, civil-war blood had been spilt. In the 1650s the army's wishes were not easily disregarded. Orthodox Puritan divines, whatever their theoretical objections to toleration, had their own shaping experiences. They had their own Foxeian martyrology, their own memories of persecution in the 1630s, their own images of the Inquisition.

Even if we insist on the importance of ideas in the subject of toleration, are there not ideas we have been bypassing? Should we not dwell on the pleas for broad

---

[33] Ibid., xii. 12, 48, 61–2, xiv. 277.

[34] Ibid., vii. 5–6, xv. 76.

[35] Blair Worden, *The Rump Parliament 1648–1653* (Cambridge, repr. 1977), pp. 238–9.

[36] That Congregationalists, while they often pleaded for liberty for other groups, were not committed to it in principle became evident at those moments when they sought to make common cause with the Presbyterians against the sects. Owen's priorities are evident from his statement of 1649 that the problem of toleration could not be solved until Independency had been 'rightly established' in England, 'the great disorder of the churches of God amongst us' rectified, and 'the precious distinguished from the vile' (Owen, *Works*, viii. 203). Jordan points out that most Congregationalist pleas for liberty of conscience were made before 1649, when the Congregationalists were more often frightened by Presbyterian (or Anglican) intolerance than by the sects (*Development of Religious Toleration*, iii. 437).

freedom of religious expression voiced by a Sir Henry Vane or a John Milton or a William Walwyn or a Henry Robinson, or on the Erastian anti-clericalism of a John Selden or a Henry Parker?[37] Were there not seventeenth-century intellectual developments, outside theology, to which toleration was the only realistic response? Were not the spread of lay education and of travel, the entrenchment of competition among the creeds on the Continent, and the expanding study of Church history, bound to stimulate religious relativism? Must they not have cast doubt on the likelihood that truth lay where one group of divines in one country at one time said it lay? And were not the philosophical advances of the seventeenth century, which raised in pressing form the question how ideas and beliefs come to settle in the mind, a further stimulus to scepticism? Theology, if it impinged on ideas outside itself, was bound in its turn to be influenced by them, and to absorb something of what it opposed. Thus divines could not be oblivious to, or remain unaffected by, the gradual seventeenth-century elevation of sincerity of intention above correctness of belief. In the words of the Anglican divine Jeremy Taylor, 'an honest error is better than a hypocritical profession of truth'.[38] Milton proclaimed that 'a man may be a heretic in the truth'.[39] Even John Owen implied that what was heresy in one man might not be heresy in another.[40] Owen, in any case, accepted limits to the claims of theology in the government of human affairs. No theocrat, he made use of an argument for liberty of conscience which appealed not to theology but to natural law (though the New Testament supported it): 'that sovereign dictate of nature', 'Do not that unto others which you would not have done to you'.[41] Indeed it may seem perverse to present Owen, politically the most influential clergyman of the 1650s, as an opponent of toleration. After all, he wrote a number of works which appear to defend the principle, among them the treatise *Of Toleration* which he published in 1649.[42]

Yet when we examine the formation of the government's doctrinal policies in the protectorate, we find that Puritan theological conservatism has a central place in the story. We also find, however, that the lessons of Puritan theology did not all point in one direction. It is to the debate within Puritan belief (rather than to a conflict between theological intolerance and lay libertarianism) that we should look for the inspiration of Cromwellian policy. There were some features of Puritan theology, or anyway of Congregationalist theology, which may be said to have pointed towards liberty of conscience. To the Congregationalist, truth lay in the spirit rather than the institution, in the power rather than the form. In this the Congregationalists resembled the Platonists, whom they sometimes addressed amicably

---

[37] The religious positions of Robinson and Parker are studied in W. K. Jordan, *Men of Substance* (Chicago, 1942).

[38] Taylor, *The Liberty of Prophesying* (1647), p. 163.

[39] *CPW*, ii. 543.

[40] Owen, *Works*, viii. 60.

[41] Ibid., viii. 62 (cf. viii. 167, 195); cf. J. C. Davis, 'The Levellers and Christianity', in Brian Manning, ed., *Politics, Religion and the English Civil War* (1973), p. 228.

[42] William Walwyn argued for 'toleration' with less inhibition than Owen: see his *Tolleration Justified* (1646).

across the political and ecclesiastical lines.[43] Like them, they searched for internal unity within an external diversity which might be permissible because it was not of the essence of belief. Peter Sterry, who was both a Congregationalist and a Platonist, and who had influence at Cromwell's court, preached courageously to parliament in defence of the Quakers in 1656, when the Quaker James Nayler was under heavy attack from MPs.[44] For Quaker doctrine, although normally repudiated where not vilified by Congregationalists, could sometimes bear a resemblance to Congregationalist theology similar in one sense to that borne by Platonist teaching. Affinities between the Congregationalists' conception of the holy spirit and the Quakers' notion of the 'inner light'[45] perhaps lie behind a remark of Cromwell's councillor William Sydenham during the parliamentary debates on Nayler: 'that which sticks most with me, is the nearness of this opinion to that which is a most glorious truth, that the spirit is personally in us'.[46] Might not that spirit assume more than one form?

Other characteristics of Puritanism also obliged it to come to terms, in some measure, with diversity of belief. It was a religion of the ear rather than the eye, of conscience rather than ceremony. The pre-war Church of England had demanded conformity to outward forms: to its episcopal structure and its rites of worship. In the civil wars, Presbyterians and sometimes Congregationalists made demands for conformity to their own ecclesiastical systems. Yet by the 1650s those pleas were in retreat. Controversy about compulsion in religion had generally settled on doctrine rather than on worship or ecclesiastical organization. Individual believers, who must answer to God at the day of judgement for the stewardship of their souls, bore their own responsibility for their doctrinal beliefs. Even the stoutest champions of orthodoxy conceded that the conscience could not be forced.[47] Puritan theology, however logically expounded, was verifiable only through the believer's experience, which could not be objectively tested. The journey of the soul towards God was a long and arduous one. Different people might 'grow spiritually' at different paces, 'growing on by parts and piecemeal' according to the various lights God had given them.[48] During the progress of the spiritual pilgrim, truth might, at least temporarily, mingle with error, even among the guardians of orthodoxy. The

---

[43] For the exchanges between them, see e.g. Ralph Cudworth, *A Sermon preached before the House of Commons 31 March 1647* (1647); John Goodwin, *Redemption Redeemed* (1651), ep. ded.

[44] Sterry, *The Way of God with his People* (1656), pp. 14, 28 ff. Sterry had been a client of that influential Platonist advocate of liberty of conscience, Lord Brooke.

[45] Geoffrey F. Nuttall, *The Holy Spirit in Puritan Faith and Experience* (Oxford, 1946).

[46] *Burton*, i. 69; cf. i. 76, 86.

[47] They did, however, think that dissenters could be 'required to attend upon the ministry and dispensation of the Gospel, that they may not presumptuously exempt and deprive themselves of the means of grace and salvation' (Reynolds, *Peace of Jerusalem*, p. 33). Cf. Marshall and Firmin, *Power of the Civil Magistrate*, p. 7; George Petter, *A Briefe and Solid Exercitation concerning the Coercive Power of the Magistrate in Matters of Religion*, in Petter's *A Censure of Mr John Cotton* (1656), pp. 41–2. For the individual's stewardship of his soul, see e.g. Owen, *Works*, xiv. 312; Davis, 'The Levellers and Christianity'.

[48] A. G. Matthews, ed., *The Savoy Declaration of Faith and Order 1658* (1958), p. 161. Cf. e.g. *Works of John Owen*, xiii. 557; Richard Baxter, *The Saints' Everlasting Rest*, ed. William Young (1907), pp. 143–4.

authors of the *Apologeticall Narration* of 1643, virtually the founding document of civil-war Congregationalism, resolved 'not to make our present judgement and practice a binding law unto ourselves for the future'.[49] As the Congregationalist minister Timothy Armitage asked, 'Does all truth come into the world at once? And may not we persecute that which afterwards may appear to be a truth'?[50] Such persecution, risking the murder of souls, would imperil the salvation both of the persecuted and of the persecutors.

The word toleration has so many evaluative and potentially anachronistic connotations that, at least for the particular purpose of exploring Cromwellian policy, it may be an impediment to understanding. For the argument within the Puritan camp was not about toleration: it was about liberty of conscience. Although writers were not consistent in their terminology, there was a basic difference between allowing people to believe what they liked and permitting beliefs which were deemed to be conscionably held.[51] Liberty of conscience would allow doctrines which did not breach fundamental truths whose acceptance was essential to salvation. It would permit error, into which the believer might stumble on the path to salvation, but not heresy, Satan's chief weapon. There were, it is true, men who claimed that God wished heresies to flourish, so that the truths 'which are approved may be made manifest'.[52] But those men were not doctrinal Calvinists (or at least not predestinarians), and they did not shape the ecclesiastical policies of the Interregnum. The same observations may be made about those writers discussed by W. K. Jordan whose arguments are likely to sound most familiar and attractive to a modern ear.

The goal of liberty of conscience was very different from that of modern liberalism. It was religious union, which persecution was held to have destroyed: the union of the believer with Christ, and the union of believers with each other. The former was essential to salvation: the latter was necessary to the creation of a Church and commonwealth fit for God's eyes. Religious division is one of the great anxieties of sixteenth- and seventeenth-century Europe. It could be as keen a stimulus to thought and guilt as class division has been in modern times. Whether we look at Renaissance hermeticism and Platonism, at the international ecumenicalism of the earlier seventeenth century, or at the Association movement of Richard Baxter in the 1650s, always we find the yearning to end the strife in the world and in men's

---

[49] *An Apologeticall Narration, humbly submitted to Parliament. By Tho. Goodwin, Philip Nye, Sidrach Simpson, and Others* (1644), p. 10. Cf. Michael Fixler, *Milton and the Kingdoms of God* (1964), p. 120.

[50] Quoted in Geoffrey F. Nuttall, *Visible Saints: The Congregational Way* (Oxford, 1957) p. 117.

[51] Speakers in the Nayler debates knew the difference between 'liberty of conscience' (or 'liberty to tender consciences'), which in principle they mostly approved, and toleration, of which they disapproved. The Quakers were suspected by MPs of aiming at the latter under colour of the former. Nevertheless there was semantic uncertainty. Often men attacked not 'toleration' but 'universal toleration' or 'toleration of all religions'.

[52] 1 Corinthians 11:19. Sometimes this text was used to justify the permission of error rather than heresy. The parable of the wheat and the tares proved to be similarly ambiguous.

hearts. This was a vision especially compelling to the generation which lived amid the wreckage of the Thirty Years War and the Puritan Revolution.[53]

The religious policy of Oliver Cromwell becomes clearer when we see it as a search not for the toleration for which he is so often commended, but for union: for the unity of the godly party 'in the several forms of it'.[54] The letter which he sent to parliament from Bristol in 1645, a document that is frequently cited to demonstrate his commitment to toleration, observed that 'all that believe have the real unity, which is most glorious, because inward and spiritual, in the body, and to the head'.[55] To Robert Hammond in 1648 he wrote: 'I profess to thee I desire it in my heart, I have prayed for it, I have waited for the day to see union and right understanding between the godly people (Scots, English, Jews, Gentiles, Presbyterians, Independents, Anabaptists, and all).'[56] The Cromwellian plea to the Scots for liberty of conscience in July 1650 was advanced in the hope that God would 'make all Christians of one heart'.[57] Early in 1655 Cromwell longed for 'the several interests of the people of God' to be 'healed and atoned' (that is, 'at-oned').[58] To that end he 'caused to be printed' a pamphlet which looked forward to 'a glorious union of the people of God, made to be of one spirit'.[59] Late in the same year the protector sought the readmission of the Jews to England, for the sake not of tolerating but of converting them, and so of accomplishing the union between Jew and Gentile.[60] The main obstacle to union in the 1650s was the readiness of the sects to persecute each other. Cromwell made the point repeatedly: 'Is it ingenuous to ask for liberty, and not to give it?' 'Where shall we find men of a universal spirit? Everyone desires to have liberty, but none will give it.'[61] When Baptists 'separated [from] love and charity', he alleged, 'it was a cursed Baptisme'.[62] He saw himself as 'a constable to part' the contending religious groups to whom he gave protection, and struggled to preserve the delicate 'posture and balance' which the protectorate secured among them.[63]

Once we see Cromwell's purpose, we can better understand his affinity to Owen, whose own position may now appear less inconsistent. Both men yearned for liberty for 'God's peculiar', not for the unregenerate. Both tolerated error, not heresy. Owen's chief partner in the formation of Cromwellian Church policy, the Congregationalist minister Thomas Goodwin, had assured the House of Commons

---

[53] See H. R. Trevor-Roper, 'Three Foreigners: the Philosophers of the Puritan Revolution', in his *Religion, The Reformation and Social Change*, pp. 237–93.

[54] E828[8] (untitled and undated tract), pp 7–8.

[55] Abbott, i. 376.

[56] Ibid., i. 677.

[57] Ibid., ii. 283–8.

[58] Ibid., iii. 572–3 (cf. iii. 119).

[59] E828[8]; *A True State of the Case of Liberty of Conscience in the Commonwealth of England: Together with a Narrative of . . . Mr John Biddle's Sufferings* (1655), p. 1. Milton sought the 'unity of the spirit' amid diversity of belief: *CPW*, ii. 168, 550, 565.

[60] David S. Katz, *Philo-Semitism and the Readmission of the Jews to England 1603–1655* (Oxford, 1982), esp. p. 224.

[61] Abbott, iii. 459, 547, 586, iv. 271.

[62] David Underdown, 'Cromwell and the Officers', *English Historical Review* 83 (1968), p. 107.

[63] Abbott, iii. 606, iv. 273.

in 1646 that he sought a 'liberty' of conscience not for 'all opinions' but 'onely . . . for saints'.[64] It may be that Cromwell identified the boundary between the godly and the reprobate more through instinct than through theology. Yet we should not underestimate either the theological equipment or the theological orthodoxy of a man who, in conversation, could correct Fifth Monarchists on the identification of Antichrist, and Quakers on the nature of the 'inner light'.[65] Revealing a preoccupation with Christ's mediation that would have pleased Owen, he called for liberty only for those who 'believe the remission of sins through the blood of Christ and free justification by the blood of Christ, and live upon the grace of God'.[66] Repeatedly in the 1650s his words suggest that 'God's peculiar' were to be found exclusively, or almost exclusively, within three groups: Presbyterians, Independents, and Baptists.[67] Like Owen, he was appalled by the newly influential heresies of the 1650s, which he called 'blasphemous' and 'diabolical', the 'height of Satan's wickednesses'.[68] His imagination could not enter the world of the Ranters and Quakers and Socinians, whose principles seemed so different from the biblical and Christocentric radicalism he had known in the new model army in the 1640s. Confident of his ability to distinguish the people of God from 'pretenders and pretences to righteousness' and from 'men that have wonderfully lost their consciences and their wits',[69] he told a Ranter woman in 1651 whose utterances he had 'examined' that 'she was so vile a creature, as he thought her unworthy to live', and had her arrested.[70] It seems that on another occasion he left the room, with Henry Ireton, rather than listen to the heretical statements of 'Doomsday Sedgwick'.[71] Although Cromwell cannot be held directly responsible for the statements of newsbooks friendly to his government, he could, if he had wished, have ended the attacks to which Quakers and Socinians were subjected by the press throughout the protectorate, and which were especially vindictive at moments when leaders of those sects were threatened with the death penalty for their heresies. Quakers, portrayed as thieves and fornicators, were caricatured and diabolized: 'you may commonly know them in the streets by their vizards'.[72]

The Congregationalist, and Cromwellian, preoccupation with the union of the godly people explains the otherwise puzzlingly peripheral role in the debate about

[64] Thomas Goodwin, *The Great Interest of States & Kingdomes* (1646), p. 53.

[65] Abbott, iii. 373, 607–16, iv. 309.

[66] Ibid., iv. 271–2; cf. 586, 592, 756.

[67] Ibid., iii. 586, 607, iv. 272, 496. Cf. Firth, *Clarke Papers*, iii. 92–3; *TSP*, ii. 67; *To the Officers and Souldiers of the Army* (1657: E902[4]), p. 5.

[68] Abbott, iii. 586, 612; iv. 471. Cf. ii. 286; Jordan, *Development of Religious Toleration*, iii. 149.

[69] Abbott, iii. 572, iv. 276, 719.

[70] *Mercurius Politicus* 5 June 1651, p. 831; Abbott, ii. 420 (cf. ii. 353–4).

[71] *Burton*, i. 103–4. Cromwell's old ally Sir Henry Vane, who broke with him in 1653, and who wanted, as Cromwell did not, the separation of Church and state, perhaps has the protector in his sights in describing the Second Beast, who 'mak[es] himself umpire of all controversies in matters of religion, and declarer of heresies, blasphemies and the like': Vane, *The Retired Mans Meditations* (1655), pp. 368–9.

[72] *Certain Passages of Every Dayes Intelligence* 16 February 1655, pp. '24'–'21' (cf. 10 March 1654, p. 61). For evident press fabrication about Socinians, compare the remarks about John Biddle in *The Faithfull Scout* 19 January 1655, p. 1672, with *The Weekly Post* 11 March 1655, p. 1732.

religious liberty of the position of Anglicans and Roman Catholics. Anglicans, as Congregationalists acknowledged and as modern research confirms, retained the loyalty of a large proportion of the population.[73] Yet to the issue of liberty of conscience they could seem scarcely relevant. How could the godly people, who had fought the civil war against popery and prelacy, conceive that their opponents were capable of salvation? Admittedly there were Anglicans whom Cromwell seems to have 'counted godly' and to have hoped to include within the national Church.[74] Within Anglicanism, after all, there were Calvinists as well as Arminians. Even so it is hard to detect, in the connivance which alternated with the repression visited on Anglicans, motives separable from the government's need to broaden its base of support. The leniency of the protectorate towards English Catholicism can likewise be explained in political terms. Like many rulers, or builders of power bases, before him, Cromwell hoped to detach quiescent English Catholics from those who looked to the papacy for the reconversion of the nation. Considerations of foreign policy likewise worked in the Catholics' favour. His attempts to persuade Cardinal Mazarin to secure freedom for Protestant worship in territories under French rule or influence could have a chance of success only if it were complemented by the prospect of a reciprocal indulgence to Catholics in England.[75] At home, Cromwell could not be insensitive to the argument, often pressed on seventeenth-century rulers, that toleration would lead to tranquillity and would foster grateful loyalties that would strengthen the government's authority. Political pressures often blurred the edges, and sometimes obscured the premises, of Cromwell's stance on liberty of conscience. If grounds existed for conciliating Catholics and Anglicans, there were sects which, though their beliefs dismayed him, had followers and sympathizers among a restive soldiery whom he feared to alienate. Yet while reason of state may have influenced or modified his ecclesiastical policies, it was never their foundation.

The extent of officially sanctioned religious freedom in Cromwellian England, even if less great than is sometimes supposed, was incontestably revolutionary. The protector's achievement of 'posture and balance' among the saints created a habit of ecclesiastical diversity in England which was to prove ineradicable after 1660, and which doubtless had a part to play in the subsequent evolution of religious toleration. Not least there was his success in persuading the younger generation of Presbyterians to accept a position as merely one among other religious groups.[76] There is no need to question the eclecticism of Cromwell's conception of the godly party, or the resolve with which, as a 'seeker' after truth who knew that believers

---

[73] For contemporary observation see Jordan, *Development of Religious Toleration*, iv. 46, 173; Jordan, *Men of Substance*, p. 137. For modern research see J. S. Morrill, 'The Church in England, 1642–9', in Morrill, ed., *Reactions to the English Civil War 1642–1649* (1982), pp. 89–114.

[74] Dr Williams's Library, Baxter, Letters, vi. fos 83ᵛ, 90ʳ; cf. Robert S. Bosher, *The Making of the Restoration Settlement: The Influence of the Laudians 1649–1662* (1951), pp. 9–10.

[75] A document purportedly written by Cromwell to Mazarin, and professing a readiness to free English Catholics from 'the raging fire of persecution' (Abbott, iv. 368–9 and n. 109), is surely a forgery. Its reference to Jude probably drew on a printed version of Cromwell's speech to parliament on 4 September 1654: Abbott, iii. 437. Catholics did useful intelligence work for the government: Paul Hardacre, *The Royalists during the Puritan Revolution* (The Hague, 1956), p. 137.

[76] Abbott, iv. 272; Jordan, *Development of Religious Toleration*, iii. 316.

tended to reach it only after painful struggles,[77] he sought to accommodate 'mistaken' godly men who had 'the least of truth' in them.[78] Misunderstanding arises only when we confuse his policy with, or when we measure his achievements against, the principles of Victorian liberalism.

How was Cromwell's conception of liberty of conscience to be translated into practice? Here a number of problems arose, in which theology offered little if any assistance. For example, a familiar distinction was commonly made, which sounded useful and reasonable, between the holding of a belief and the propagation of it. The prominent Puritan minister Stephen Marshall would allow liberty to 'men who hold dissenting opinions in lesser points', provided they were 'content to have their faith, in these, and so be quiet. I can be no advocate for such people, if they judge the spreading of their opinions to be a duty.'[79] Yet how could orthodox Puritans, for whom the spreading of the word was certainly 'a duty'—indeed, the necessary vessel by which grace was imparted—expect the sects to accept Marshall's distinction?[80] The sects themselves asked the question forcefully.[81] Another principle which proved less straightforward than its advocates implied was that liberty should be dependent on peaceable behaviour. Most people would have agreed with Owen that God would not give light to violent men, 'it being a known and received maxim that the Gospel clashes against no righteous ordinance of man'.[82] Yet however peaceable sectaries might be, the hostility to them weakened the regime's political authority, and thus impaired its chances of preserving the nation's peace. Besides, civil disturbance was often caused not by the sects but by mobs who set upon them.[83] It was no less damaging to the regime for that. Likewise, the issue of liberty of religious profession proved hard to separate from questions of political power. Most people, including Cromwell, believed that the chief magistrate had not only a right but a duty to propagate his own beliefs. Was the principle of liberty of conscience threatened if the government removed Quaker JPs from their posts and replaced them with justices of orthodox persuasion? Was it frustrated if the state allowed public maintenance only to ministers who held certain beliefs? Equally, was it offended if men were punished for refusing, on grounds of conscience, to pay tithes?

Those problems, and many like them, dogged the making of religious policy under the protectorate. But the most serious and the most urgent difficulty was to translate into practice the distinction between the godly and the rest, or between

---

[77] Abbott, i. 96–7, 416.

[78] Ibid., iii. 62, 590.

[79] Stephen Marshall, *A Sermon preached to the . . . Lord Mayor . . . tending to heal our Rents and Divisions* (1653), p. 31; Marshall and Firmin, *Power of the Civil Magistrate*, pp. 5, 8–9. Cf. *Humble Advice: or the Heads of those Things which were offered . . . by Mr Richard Baxter*, p. 4; Reynolds, *Peace of Jerusalem*, p. 31; Firth, *Clarke Papers*, iv. 54.

[80] The distinction was likewise made in the Blasphemy Ordinance of 1648, and it exercised the parliament of 1654. Firth and Rait, i. 1133; *CJ* 13–15 December 1654; *Burton*, i. cxvi.

[81] *The Protector (so called) in part Unvailed* (1655), p. 75; James Nayler, *The Power and Glory of the Lord* (1656), p. 6.

[82] Owen, *Works*, viii. 165.

[83] See e.g. *Mercurius Politicus* 9 February 1654, p. 3248; *Weekly Post* 23 January 1655, p. 1672; Ralph Farmer, *Sathan Inthroned* (1656), p. 55; Inderwick, *Interregnum*, p. 134; W. C. Braithwaite *The Beginnings of Quakerism* (Cambridge, 1961), pp. 364–5.

'the precious' and 'the vile' (Jeremiah 15:19). Owen's doctrine of the self-evident truth ('Some things, indeed, are so clearly in the Scripture laid down and determined, that to question or deny them bespeaks a spirit self-condemned'[84]) availed him little in controversy with so acute a biblical scholar as John Biddle. Yet circularity of argument could scarcely be avoided. The 1650s saw a series of attempts to list essential truths, outside which salvation was unattainable and liberty therefore unthinkable. That was the purpose of the 'fundamentals' which Owen drew up, with Cromwell's evident approval, in 1652, and which were to reappear in the protectorate.[85] In their insistence on Calvinist orthodoxy, and particularly in their laboured attempt to define and defeat anti-Trinitarianism, the 'fundamentals' were stiffer and tighter than those alternative models—the Apostles' Creed, the Lord's Prayer, and the less contentious of the Thirty-Nine Articles—which formed the basis of other tests of doctrinal orthodoxy that were proposed during the Puritan Revolution.[86] As we shall now find, the distinction between essentials and inessentials—the Puritan version of the concept of *adiaphora*—played a significant part in the politics of the protectorate.

The Instrument of Government of December 1653 appeared to make generous provision for religious freedom. The 'discovery and confutation of error' were to be left to the spiritual exertions of a godly ministry, and to the influence of 'sound doctrine' and 'the example of a good conversation'. 'Popery', 'prelacy', and 'licentiousness' were exempted from liberty, as was 'the abuse [of] this liberty to the civil injury of others and to the actual disturbance of the public peace'. Otherwise, 'such as profess faith in God by Jesus Christ . . . shall not be restrained from, but shall be protected in, the profession of the faith and the exercise of their religion'. All laws contrary to these provisions were to be 'esteemed as null and void'.[87]

  The document was less straightforward than it looked. Hastily compiled and clumsily worded, it has a prominent place in that trail of ambiguity which attends Cromwell's various attempts to formulate a concrete programme for liberty of conscience.[88] He subsequently acknowledged that the Instrument 'stood in need of mending'.[89] It must be doubted whether he ever had much faith in articles 35 to 38, which contained the ecclesiastical stipulations of the new constitution. The provisions for liberty of conscience were omitted from accounts of the Instrument published or circulated by Cromwell's supporters in the days and weeks which

---

[84] Owen, *Works*, viii. 60.

[85] They can be found in *Proposals for the Furtherance and Propagation of the Gospel* (1653); *The Principles of Faith, presented by Mr Tho. Goodwin, Mr Nye, Mr Sidrach Simpson, and other Ministers* (1654); and Ralph Farmer, *The Great Mysteries of Godliness and Ungodliness* (1655), p. 66.

[86] Matthew Sylvester, ed., *Reliquiae Baxterianae* (1696), pt. 1, p. 198; *Humble Advice . . . by Mr Richard Baxter*, pp. 2–3; Taylor, *Liberty of Prophesying*, p. 40; Jordan, *Development of Religious Toleration*, ii. 147–8 (cf. iii. 395), iii. 91–2, 103. Cf. *The Judgement of the late Lord Chief Justice Sir M[atthew] H[ale] of the Nature of True Religion* (1684), p. 4; Owen, *Works*, xii. 47.

[87] *GD*, p. 416.

[88] For an indication of the uneasiness with which the Instrument was adopted, see Austin Woolrych, *Commonwealth to Protectorate* (Oxford, 1982), p. 358.

[89] Abbott, iv. 417.

followed the inauguration of the protectorate.[90] In February 1654, two months after the adoption of the Instrument, in a passage which Cromwell would endorse in addressing the first parliament of the protectorate, the government apologist Marchamont Nedham approvingly noted that in the wording of articles 36 and 37 'it is intimated or implied' that 'a public profession' of 'doctrine, and worship and discipline' was 'intended to be held forth by the magistrate'. Such an initiative was needed, he explained, because of 'our want of settlement in religious matters', and because of 'the spreading abroad most blasphemous opinions'. The government should 'lay a healing hand to these mortal wounds and breaches, by holding forth the truths of Christ to the nation in some solid establishment, and not quite . . . lay aside or let loose the golden reins of discipline and government in the Church'.[91] In the same month there began a series of meetings between Presbyterian and Congregationalist divines, who were commissioned to agree on a 'confession of faith' or at least on the 'fundamentals' of one, an initiative in which 'my lord protector is very forward'.[92]

Those moves, though bound to offend the vocal but small groups to whom the very idea of a national Church or creed was anathema, were otherwise not in themselves offensive to liberty of conscience, for the Instrument promised the exemption of 'such as profess faith in God by Jesus Christ' from subjection to the 'public profession' which Cromwell evidently envisaged. To saints and congregations within the fold of Calvinist doctrine, who were glad to distance themselves from heterodox groups, the Instrument was 'that excellent instrument the saints' civill Magna Charta, wherein such blessed provision is made for the tender lambs of the Lord Jesus'.[93] In any case the clerical meetings of 1654 may have been concerned more to secure a basis of communion among the people of God than to restrain the unorthodox. Yet in the Interregnum such ecumenical initiatives invariably produced attempts to restrict liberty of profession.[94] This one was certain to do so, for the clergy had noticed a second, more fundamental, uncertainty in the Instrument. What was meant by the words 'such as profess faith in God by Jesus Christ'? In January 1649, when the same wording had been proposed for the *Agreement of the People*, Ireton had asked whether anti-Trinitarians were

---

[90] See e.g. *Mercurius Politicus* 22 December 1653, p. 3053; BL Add. MS 32093, fo. 317[r], Sir Charles Wolseley to Bulstrode Whitelocke, 7 January 1654; cf. Woolrych, *Commonwealth to Protectorate*, p. 362.

[91] Marchamont Nedham, *A True State of the Case of the Commonwealth* (1654), pp. 40–3; Abbott, iii. 587.

[92] Dr Williams's Library, Baxter Letters, v. fo. 199[r-v], vi. fo. 82[r-v]; Johnston, *Diary*, ii. 246; Geoffrey Nuttall, 'Presbyterians and Independents: Some Movements for Unity 300 Years Ago', *Journal of the Presbyterian Historical Society of England* 10 (1952), pp. 11–12; Peter Toon, *God's Statesman: The Life and Work of John Owen* (Exeter, 1971), pp. 91, 95; see too *Certain Passages of Every Dayes Intelligence* 10 March 1654, p. 61.

[93] Nickolls, p. 134. Cf. Whitelocke, *Memorials*, iii. 169; *True State of the Case of Liberty of Conscience*, p. 9.

[94] John Dury reflected ruefully on the same tendency: Dr Williams's Library, Baxter Letters, vi. fo. 77[v].

excluded by it, and had received no satisfactory answer.[95] The looseness of the phrase, which might have seemed to protect dissenters, in reality left them vulnerable to the formulation of explanatory definitions. In August 1654 Richard Baxter, remarking that if the phrase meant anything it 'must comprehend every true fundamental article of our faith', and so must have been designed to suppress 'the intolerably heterodox', urged the forthcoming parliament to set out those articles in a 'confession of faith'.[96]

So when the parliament that assembled in September 1654 was invited by the government to give statutory sanction to the Instrument of Government, a revision of the clauses concerning religion was widely expected. Cromwell did nothing to dampen the expectation. While making it clear to the Commons that 'liberty of conscience' was a 'fundamental' on which he could not compromise, he hinted at his willingness to accept restraints on the 'prodigious blasphemies' and 'heresies' which plagued the nation.[97] It was probably in the autumn of 1654 that an admittedly hostile sectarian source claimed that the protector had 'lately declared, in answer to a peticion, that what he conceaves fundamentall verityes shall be so imposed, as all must suffer gaoles or death, that shall declare their faith and sence of the Scriptures to be otherwayes'.[98] In the speech which he made in dissolving the parliament in January 1655, he dismayed the sects by recalling that he had wished the House to give only 'a just liberty' to 'men who are sound in the faith', 'of the same faith with them that you call the orthodox ministry of England'.[99] His problem in 1654–5 was to persuade parliament to accept the distinction between error and heresy, and to provide protection for the former while it outlawed the latter.

It was a slim hope. The parliament of 1654, like its successor of 1656, was chosen by a new electoral system which favoured the backwoods. Some of its ablest members were making their first political appearances since Pride's Purge had evicted them in 1648. Now, remembering the intervening years of sectarian excess and military rule, they formed an effective alliance with the Presbyterian organization of the city of London. In October 1654, as parliament prepared to take the religious clauses of the Instrument into consideration, the London Presbyterians produced a convenient list of the heresies in circulation, the anti-Trinitarianism of John Biddle being especially emphasized.[100]

Parliament's problem was to weave a verbal net through which Socinians and other heretics could not slip. At first, taking up where the Presbyterians had left off

---

[95] Firth, *Clarke Papers*, ii. 171–2.

[96] Baxter, *True Christianity*, ep. ded.

[97] Abbott, iii. 436, 459.

[98] *TSP*, vi. 246. For the date of the complaint, compare the reference to a speech by Cromwell to parliament at ibid., vi. 244 with Abbott, iii. 455.

[99] Abbott, iii. 586; *The Petition of divers Gathered Churches, and others well affected, in and about the City of London* (1655), p. 4.

[100] *A Second Beacon Fired: Humbly presented to the Protector and Parliament* (1654); and the newsbooks for mid-October 1654. The Presbyterian machine had powerful twin engines: the Stationers Company, and the London Provincial Assembly. Two leaders of the former, Luke Fawne and Samuel Gellibrand, were active officers of the latter, whose minutes can be read in a typed and annotated transcription in Dr Williams's Library.

in 1648, the Commons revived a suggestion made by the Long Parliament to the king in that year. Fourteen of the Thirty-Nine Articles would constitute a 'confession of faith'. After several days' debate, however, they were found to be too broad and imprecise. Owen and the Congregationalist ministers immediately revived their 'fundamentals' of 1652, which were now stiffened by a committee of divines named by parliament and headed by those veterans of the campaign against Socinianism, Owen and Francis Cheynell. Anti-Trinitarianism remained the principal target of the 'fundamentals', which were also aimed at antinomianism, mortalism, and heretical views on the authority of Scripture and on the existence of heaven and hell. When, in December 1654, the House eventually rejected the amended 'fundamentals', it was evidently because they were thought unworkable, not because they were too severe. Indeed they may have been thought not severe enough, for soon the House was proposing to insert into the revised Instrument a sweeping clause against 'damnable heresies'. Some MPs, admittedly, were concerned that so loose a proposal 'might expose the godly party, and people hereafter, to some danger',[101] but that was not an argument to deter the majority. With the army issuing public reminders of its commitment to religious liberty, Cromwell took alarm. He insisted that the 'damnable heresies' should be 'enumerated', and that he should have a share in their enumeration. That was the rock on which agreement between protector and parliament on religion foundered. The breakdown of the discussions was a principal reason for the parliament's premature dissolution.[102]

In the Commons' debates on the Instrument's provisions for religious liberty, there was one moment when the House's determination to crush sectarian radicalism apparently faltered. It came on 12 December, when the articles prepared by the divines were debated. Our sparse parliamentary diary (compiled by Guibon Goddard) informs us that parliament's failing ardour was revived by 'a motion, which had been made often times before, against the books of one Biddle'.[103] The only reason the protracted debates about Biddle which followed are less well known than the parliamentary contest over the punishment of James Nayler in 1656 is that the latter was recorded in the fuller diary of Thomas Burton. Biddle's case was no less significant than Nayler's. He was imprisoned at parliament's behest; his books were burned; and a bill was ordered to be brought in to punish him for his 'horrid, blasphemous and execrable opinions, denying the deity of Christ and the Holy

---

[101] *Burton*, i. cxiv.

[102] The complicated story outlined in this paragraph can be pieced together from: ibid., i. lix–lx, lxxv, cxii–cxix; *CJ* 7–15 December 1654, and 3, 9–12 January 1655; the newsbooks in E236; Vaughan, ed., *The Protectorate of Oliver Cromwell*, 2 vols (1839), i. 70, 77–8, 80, 84, 101–2; Dr Williams's Library, Baxter Letters, v. fo. 169[r]; Sylvester, *Reliquiae Baxterianae*, pt. i, pp. 197–205; *Humble Advice . . . by Mr Richard Baxter, The Principles of Faith* (E 234[5]); and 'A New Confession of Faith' (MS, E826[3], where the revised 'fundamentals' may be found). W. A. Shaw, *A History of the English Church during the Civil Wars and under the Commonwealth 1640–1660*, 2 vols (1900), i. 366, ii. 86–92, has the best (but not an invariably reliable) secondary account.

[103] *Burton*, i. cxiv (i.e. diary of Guibon Goddard, published as an introduction to Burton's diary).

Ghost'.[104] The discussion soon broadened into an attack on the Quakers, and a bill was prepared against them too.[105] Socinians and Quakers, despite great differences between them, were often linked or confused by contemporaries, for Quakers, seeming to deny the historical Christ, threatened the centre of Puritan theology much as Socinians did.[106] 'Convince any of them', wrote Owen of the Quakers, 'of the doctrine of the Trinity, and all the rest of their imaginations vanish into smoke.'[107] The MP Nathaniel Bacon, who had drafted the proposed anti-Trinitarian ordinance of 1646, complained in 1656 that the Quaker James Nayler's offence 'destroys the second person of the Trinity'.[108]

The dissolution of parliament in January 1655 halted its proceedings against Socinians and Quakers. Biddle was released at the end of May 1655.[109] Only weeks later, however, he was in trouble again. Now the City Presbyterians, who supported their moves by skilful propaganda, launched a new and potentially devastating weapon.[110] The Blasphemy Ordinance of 1648 had never been repealed. A narrowly Presbyterian document, it carried the death penalty for anti-Trinitarianism, and enjoined harsh penalties for a range of other beliefs, some of which had found shelter under the protectorate.[111] It had been generally assumed that the Instrument of Government had rendered the ordinance 'null and void'; but if it could be shown that Biddle did not 'profess faith in God by Jesus Christ' (a charge which he and his supporters keenly denied[112]), then it was hard to see how he could be protected by the Instrument, whose authority was in any case under legal challenge in the courts at this time. A chill of fear ran through the congregations, which saw in Biddle's case 'a precedent' which 'prostrateth us all . . . to punishment, and consequently destroys the [Instrument of] Government'.[113] The precedent

[104] Ibid., i. cxv–cxvii, cxxiii–cxxx; *CJ* 15 January 1655.

[105] *Burton*, i. cxxvii; cf. i. 169.

[106] It was widely believed, not always accurately, that Quakers (in what became the standard phrase of their critics) did not believe in 'that Christ that died at Jerusalem'. The objection appeared in Owen's 'fundamentals', and surfaced in the Nayler debates: *Burton*, i. 48, 64.

[107] Owen, *Works*, iii. 66.

[108] *Burton*, i. 132. Cf. (e.g.) *Nayler's Blasphemies Discovered* (1657), p. 13; Jonathan Clapham, *A Full Discovery and Confutation of . . . the Quakers* (1656), pp. 16–19. For Bacon and the ordinance of 1646 see Jordan, *Development of Religious Toleration*, iii. 91.

[109] There is a good account of Biddle's travails in 1654–5 in McLachlan, *Socinianism in Seventeenth-Century England*, pp. 202–11. Cromwell's attitude to Biddle's imprisonment by parliament was closely watched, but is hard to gauge: see *Protector (so called) in part Unvailed*, pp. 26–9, 69–72; cf. *Burton*, i. 161.

[110] For the Presbyterian initiative against Biddle, see: *CSPD 1655*, pp. 224, 393; *The Spirit of Persecution again broken loose . . . against Mr John Biddle and Mr William Kiffin* (1655); *True State of the Case of Liberty of Conscience*. For Presbyterian propaganda see *An Exhortation directed to the Elders of . . . Lancaster* (1655); *An Exhortation to Catechising: the Long Neglect whereof is sadly Lamented* (1655), esp. pp. 4–5, 8, 12; Richard Vines, *The Corruption of Mind Described* (1655), esp. p. 13; Nicholas Estwick, *Mr Biddle's Confession of Faith . . . Examined and Confuted* (1656).

[111] Firth and Rait, i. 1133–6.

[112] *Two Letters of Mr Iohn Biddle* (1655), p. 2; *Spirit of Persecution again Broken Loose*, p. 4; *True State of the Case of Liberty of Conscience*, p. 6; *To the Officers and Souldiers of the Army*, p. 2.

[113] *Ludlow's Memoirs*, i. 412–15; *The Petition of Divers Gathered Churches* (E856[3]), p. 2; *To the Officers and Souldiers of the Army*, p. 4. The fear was widely expressed.

was promptly followed, when the Cromwellian William Kiffin was threatened with imprisonment under the 1648 ordinance 'for preaching that baptism is unlaw-ful'.[114] Well might Biddle urge Henry Lawrence, the Baptist president of the protectoral council, to use his influence against 'these bloodthirsty men, whose malice, if it prevail against me, will not stop there, but extend itself to all other dissenters whatsoever, and consequently even to your lordship'.[115] The Baptists, always torn between the attractions of a respectable political conformism which would secure them liberty of profession, and the claims of a political radicalism which aligned some of them with Fifth Monarchists, were frequently uncertain whether to distance themselves from, or to form a common front with, theologi-cally more adventurous sects whose members, to the Baptists' embarrassment, had often been recruited from their congregations.[116] Biddle himself had Baptist connections.[117] Confronted by the threat to Kiffin, Baptist churches rallied to Biddle's defence.[118] So did the Arminian John Goodwin, who in the previous year had disowned 'J. Biddle's most enormous and hideous notions about the nature of God',[119] but whose own beliefs left him on the periphery of Cromwellian liberty, 'distracted between hope and fear'.[120]

Cromwell's response to the proceedings against Biddle did nothing to allay the anxiety of the sects. He refused to see him,[121] and gave representations on his behalf a cool reception. 'By faith in Jesus Christ', he said when the Instrument was cited on Biddle's behalf, 'we mean such as the generality of the Protestants have'. The Blasphemy Ordinance, he affirmed, was 'in force', and the Instrument 'was never intended to maintain and protect blasphemers' against it.[122] Yet Cromwell could not afford to permit a test case which, if the prosecution were successful, would expose a significant body of the godly people to the ordinance. The only solution he could find offended both Biddle's defenders and his prosecutors. Biddle was hastened away to a long imprisonment in the Scilly Isles.

The status of the Blasphemy Ordinance was to be debated again in the parlia-ment of 1656, when the Quaker James Nayler, who had led his followers into Bristol in the manner of Christ's entry into Jerusalem, was summoned before the

---

[114] *Spirit of Persecution again Broken Loose*, p. 20. For Kiffin's delicately ambivalent political position at this time see: *Perfect Proceedings of State-Affairs* 7 June 1655, p. 4718; *Protector (so called) in part Unvailed*, p. 85; *A Short Discovery of His Highness the Lord Protector's Intentions touching the Anabaptists* (1655), p. 3.

[115] *Two Letters of Mr Iohn Biddle*, p. 6.

[116] Richard Baxter, *The Quaker's Catechism* (1655), preface; *The True Light hath made Manifest Darkness* (1657); Grigge, *Quaker's Jesus*, pp. 37, 39; *The Confession of Faith of Several Churches of Christ in the County of Somerset* (1656); *Protector (so called) in part Unvailed*, p. 72; *Mercurius Politicus* 24 April 1656, p. 6909; cf. *Heart-Bleedings for Professors Abominations* (1650).

[117] *True State of the Case of Liberty of Conscience*, p. 2.

[118] *Short Discovery of the Lord Protector's Intentions*.

[119] Thomas Jackson, *The Life of John Goodwin* (1872), p. 330.

[120] *To the Officers and Souldiers of the Army*, pp. 3–6. Cf. Marchamont Nedham, *The Great Accuser Cast Down: or a Public Trial of Mr John Goodwin* (1657), esp. p. 115; *Exhortation to Catechising*, pp. 12, 15.

[121] *Two Letters of Mr Iohn Biddle*, p. 1.

[122] *Petition of Divers Gathered Churches*, p. 4; *To the Officers and Souldiers of the Army*, p. 2; Abbott, iii. 834.

Commons. Eventually the House decided, as had the parliament of 1654 when Biddle was brought before it, to bypass the statute book and to act on its own authority. Nayler, having been threatened with the death penalty, was subjected instead to brutal and humiliating physical punishment. As in December 1654, so in December 1656, parliament's proceedings against the blasphemer whom it inter- rogated raised and mingled with broader religious questions before the House. For as in September 1654, so in September 1656, men had looked to a new parliament for an authoritative ecclesiastical settlement. The Presbyterians, on the second occasion as on the first, were well prepared with their own solution.[123] Anglicans who saw them as potential allies against ecclesiastical fragmentation sought to join forces with them.[124] 'I know many things will be suggested into you,' John Owen told the parliament at its opening, 'settling of religion, establishing a discipline in the Church, not to tolerate errors, and the like'. Owen did not protest against that prospect: he merely urged parliament to respect the Cromwellian boundary to intolerance. 'It is only the liberty and protection of the people of God as such that we plead for', he explained.[125] Cromwell, addressing the House after Owen's sermon, which his speech carefully endorsed and frequently echoed, made it clear that he too wanted 'liberty of conscience' only for 'the peculiar interest' of the people of God.[126]

In the weeks and months which followed, a series of sermons urged parliament to legislate against the 'fanatical persons' and the 'shoals of libertines, that are every day increasing in numbers, power and malice'.[127] As in the parliament of 1654–5, Quakers and Socinians were the principal targets. The clamour against heresy was supported by frequent demands that MPs exercise their responsibilities as godly magistrates. Dreadful punishments would afflict them, in this world and the next, if they failed to 'exercise religious severity upon the opposers of God's commands'.[128] Those exhortations, conveying a message which MPs will have previously heard in many assize or corporation sermons, appealed to the long-lived Puritan conception of 'ministry and magistracy', which enjoined national and local rulers to join forces with the clergy to suppress vice and heresy and purify the commonwealth.[129] Speech after speech in the Nayler debates shows the continuing strength of that conception. The Old Testament language of the discussion, and the attention paid by MPs to theological problems, cannot be dismissed as decoration. Our only

[123] Dr Williams's Library, Minutes of the London Provincial Assembly (typed transcript), p. 159; cf. Clapham, *Discovery and Confutation of the ... Quakers*, advertisements at the back.
[124] *TSP*, v. 598–601; Bosher, *Making of the Restoration Settlement*, pp. 45–6; cf. Grigge, *Quaker's Jesus*, p. 56.
[125] Owen, *Works*, viii. 421–2.
[126] Abbott, iv. 260, 271.
[127] *A Third Volume of Sermons preached by ... Thomas Manton, D.D.* (1689), pp. 3–4 (for the date of this sermon, see *The Publick Intelligencer* 28 September 1656, p. 853); John Rowe, *Man's Duty in Magnifying God's Work* (1656), pp. 23–6; John Warren, *Man's Fury subservient to God's Glory* (1657), pp. 11–12; Reynolds, *Peace of Jerusalem*, pp. 28–34; Matthew Barker, *The Faithful and Wise Servant* (1657), pp. 15–16, 28–9. Cf. Gurnall, *Magistrate's Portraiture*, pp. 32–3; Clapham, *Discovery and Confutation of the ... Quakers*, ep. ded.
[128] William Jenkyn, *The Policy of Princes* (1656), p. 23.
[129] For the tradition see Patrick Collinson, *The Religion of Protestants* (Oxford, 1983) pp. 141–88.

intimate glimpse of the debates about religious liberty in the parliament of 1654–5 suggests that that assembly had spoken the same language.[130] It may be that the pervasiveness of the language in the parliament of 1656 would be still more evident if the diarist Thomas Burton had shared the theological preoccupations of some of his colleagues, and if he had given members' speeches in full.[131] Pressing biblical issues ran through the arguments. Was the magistrate responsible for both tables of the Commandments? Were the injunctions of Leviticus in force? Was Nayler a blasphemer in the sense for which the Bible enjoined the death penalty? If he was, then MPs had not so much a right to put him to death as a duty. Blasphemy was an offence against the honour of a jealous God. Speaker after speaker urged the House to 'vindicate the honour of God'.[132] To keep the divine wrath at bay, the heresy must be suppressed before the infection spread. 'Such a leper' as Nayler 'ought to be separated from the conversation of all people'. Even MPs who urged leniency towards him agreed that his prison keeper should be 'such a person as is a Quaker already, that those that have not the plague may not be infected by him'.[133]

One indication of God's intentions especially impressed MPs. It was 'a providence' that 'such an indignity to Christ should be done, sitting a parliament'.[134] Yet when we recall the dexterity with which the Biddle case had been slipped into the parliamentary debates of 1654, we wonder whether providence was not acting through politically alert agencies. As the court party, so embarrassed by the Nayler episode, observed, 'two Justices of Peace could have ended it'.[135] The Bristol magistrates who sent Nayler to London had a pair of friends in the House who took a keen interest in parliament's proceedings against him from the start: the experienced Bristol MP Robert Aldworth, and Thomas Bampfield, Recorder of Exeter, a city which had been disturbed, as Bristol had, by the recent Quaker evangelism in the West, indeed by Nayler himself. Bampfield chaired the committee which examined Nayler. In the House he virtually led the prosecution against him. The moves against Nayler were clearly a prelude to a broader attack on the Quakers, against whom petitions and pamphlets and press reports were produced with efficiency and shrewd timing.[136]

The legal position of Quakers, and particularly of the Quaker practice of intervening in church services, had long been unclear. The Bristol magistrates told parliament that they were 'destitute of a law to bound and restrain' Quakers,

[130] *Colonel James Hay's Speech to the Parliament* (1655), pp. 22–3, 31.

[131] Burton's tendency towards abbreviation can be seen from a comparison between *Burton*, i. 128–31 and *State Trials*, 6 vols (1730); ii. 273–6.

[132] *Burton*, i. 25, 26, 34, 48, 50–1, 55, 61, 108, 110, 122, 125, 126, 132, 140, 150, 217.

[133] Ibid., i. 35–6, 39–40, 56, 71, 74, 98, 110, 124; ii. 131.

[134] Ibid., i. 51, 63, 70, 101, 109; cf. Grigge, *Quaker's Jesus*, pp. 13, 35.

[135] *Burton*, i. 146.

[136] *Mercurius Politicus* 6 November 1656, p. 7355; 27 November 1656, p. 7406; 18 December 1656, pp. 7444, 7451–4; 24 December 1656, p. 7460; *Publick Intelligencer* 15 December 1656, pp. 1037–9; 22 December 1656, pp. 1067–8; *CJ* 31 October 1656; Grigge, *Quaker's Jesus*, pp. 11, 13; Farmer, *Sathan Inthroned*; *Burton*, i. 168–9, 171; and BL, the Thomason Tracts for December 1656.

whom they had therefore been 'not able to suppress': 'we have waited long for some directions to this purpose'.[137] Bristol, 'the headquarters of this generation of Quakers',[138] had been reduced to turmoil by their presence since 1654, and its difficulties had been widely publicized. The Quaker presence there had set the garrison against the city government, and the city government against itself.[139] The magistrates' hopes had been briefly raised by the government declaration of February 1655 which prohibited Quakers and Ranters from disturbing services. On inspection it had proved to be worded with paralysing ambiguity.[140]

In 1654 Cromwell had surprised the Bristol magistrates by supporting them against the Quakers' military patrons.[141] What would he do now? Could he afford, any more than in 1654–5, to resolve the ambiguity of government policy? As in the Biddle case, the sects looked anxiously to him for protection. As in the Biddle case they looked in vain. On 25 December 1656, when sentence on Nayler had already been passed and the first of his punishments carried out, Cromwell received representations on Nayler's behalf which argued, what some MPs had already suggested, that parliament's proceedings against him had breached the Instrument of Government. But Cromwell was firm. The councillor Philip Skippon had already heard the protector state that the Instrument 'was never intended to bolster up blasphemies of this nature'.[142] Nayler, Cromwell now told petitioners on his behalf, 'asserts from the letter of the Scriptures such things as are contrary to the common principles written in every man's heart'.[143] The protector did, on the same day, write a mild letter to the Speaker to enquire into the constitutional and legal basis of parliament's proceedings against Nayler, but his question, which parliament correctly believed that it could safely leave unanswered,[144] was accompanied by an assurance that 'we detest and abhor the giving or occasioning the least countenance to persons of such opinions and practices', a view Cromwell later repeated to the army leaders.[145] His concern, as in the Biddle affair, was solely to ensure that the episode would provide no precedent for action against the people of God. As he told the army officers, 'the case of James Nayler might happen to be your own case'.[146] Later in the parliament Cromwell gave his assent to two bills, one against vagrancy and the other for the better observation of the Lord's Day, which provided new

---

[137] Grigge, *Quaker's Jesus*, p. 34; cf. *A True Narrative of the Examination . . . of James Nayler* (1657), p. 56.

[138] Grigge, *Quaker's Jesus*, p. 13.

[139] Henry M. Reece, 'The Military Presence in England, 1649–1660', Univ. of Oxford D. Phil. thesis (1981), pp. 172–6.

[140] Farmer, *Sathan Inthroned*, pp. 54–5; *Severall Proceedings of State Affaires* 15 February 1655, final page; 22 February 1655, pp. 4469–71. Cf. Braithwaite, *Beginnings of Quakerism*, pp. 181, 203, 445–6; Alan MacFarlane, ed., *The Diary of Ralph Josselin 1616–1683* (1976), p. 348 (cf. p. 389); Immanuel Bourne, *A Defence of the Scriptures* (1656), ep. ded.

[141] Farmer, *Great Mysteries of Godliness and Ungodliness*, ep. ded.; Reece, 'Military Presence', p. 175.

[142] *Burton*, i. 50, 63.

[143] *To the Officers and Souldiers of the Army*, p. 3; cf. *TSP*, vi. 246.

[144] *Burton*, i. 246–70.

[145] Abbott, iv. 366, 419; and see *TSP*, vi. 8.

[146] Abbott, iv. 417.

powers against Quaker disturbances.[147] Only when the House tried to combine its sabbatarian legislation with a measure for a compulsory Presbyterian catechism, the antidote to false doctrine for which clergymen were eagerly pressing, did Cromwell demur.[148]

So there is nothing surprising about his grateful acceptance of the religious provisions of the Humble Petition and Advice, the parliamentary constitution of 1657 which is normally regarded as markedly less tolerant than the Instrument of Government, the constitution it replaced. There was to be a confession of faith, which was to be recommended to the nation but not imposed on it, and which it was to be an offence to assail 'by opprobrious words or writing'. The confession was to be compiled not, as the previous parliament had wished, by Cromwell's parliamentary opponents, but in collaboration between Cromwell and the more conciliatory parliament of 1657—although in the event it was never drawn up. The restrictions on liberty imposed or implied by the Instrument were tightened. In place of the capacious term 'profess faith in God by Jesus Christ', the Humble Petition contained a long clause, progressively expanded in debate,[149] which was designed to define and forbid heresy. Anti-Trinitarianism was a particular target. 'Such who publish horrible blasphemies' were also proscribed.[150] The Humble Petition and Advice, which gave parliamentary protection to the people of God, and which at the same time would have proscribed both Biddle and Nayler, delighted Cromwell. The new constitution, he told the House, gave 'all due and just liberty' to 'the people of God': 'you have done that which never was done before'. Indeed it was 'the greatest provision that was ever made': there had not been 'anything since christ's time for such a catholic interest for the people of God'.[151]

Cromwell, then, neither wanted toleration nor provided it, whether we use the noun in its pejorative seventeenth-century sense or its approving modern one. Yet the story is not as simple as that. Although in doctrinal terms he can loosely be called a Calvinist, his entourage was not a fortress of Calvinism. It contained men who wanted a wider liberty of belief than Cromwell allowed. There were politicians around him who, while they could not condone James Nayler's offence, nevertheless sought to comprehend it, and with calm courage pleaded for leniency. The stance of those 'merciful men', as Burton called them, was not sectarian. Among

---

[147] Firth and Rait, ii. 1098–9, 1162–70. Cf. *Burton*, i. 20–4; *CJ* 31 October 1656; *Mercurius Politicus* 6 November 1656, p. 7355.

[148] Shaw, *History of the English Church*, i. 375–6; *Burton*, i. 376; Reynolds, *Peace of Jerusalem*, p. 33; Marshall and Firmin, *Power of the Civil Magistrate*, p. 38. A similar move had been made in 1654 (*Humble Advice . . . by Mr Richard Baxter*, pp. 2–3, 8–10; cf. Baxter's *Catholick Unity* [1660], p. 19). For the background to the initiative of 1657 see e.g. Vines, *Obedience to Magistrates*, third sermon, pp. 14–15; *Exhortation to Catechising*; Dr Williams's Library, Minutes of the London Provincial Assembly, pp. 146, 148; Simon Ford, *A Short Catechism* (1657); Zachary Crofton, *Perjury the Proof of Forgery* (1657), preface; *The Confession of Faith, together with the larger and lesser Catechisms* (1658); Anon., 'An Ecclesiastical Experiment in Cambridgeshire', *English Historical Review* 10 (1895), pp. 744–53; F. J. Powicke, *A Life of the Reverend Richard Baxter 1615–1691* (1924), pp. 128–32.

[149] *CJ* 19 March 1657.

[150] *GD*, pp. 454–5.

[151] Abbott, iv. 445, 454; cf. *TSP*, vi. 94.

them were figures whose influence in the 1650s points to a distinctive feature of Cromwell's civilian patronage: his use for *politiques*, for men who had found it hard—or who had been too young—to choose between king and parliament, and who would be ready to serve either a Cromwell or a Stuart.[152]

Three such men lived into the Restoration to write extensively about the religious problems of their time. The first of them was Bulstrode Whitelocke, one of the most eloquent of the 'merciful men' in the Nayler debates, who in the Puritan Revolution doggedly resisted the repressive instinct of the Presbyterian clergy. Though his relations with the protector were troubled, and though he was hostile to the military basis of its rule, he served the regime as a Commissioner of the Great Seal, as a treasury commissioner, and as head of a major embassy to Sweden; and the protector often turned to him for advice. Whitelocke had 'spoke[n] much' against the harsh ordinance against blasphemy in 1648.[153] In the Rump he had defended the Socinian MP John Fry. He regarded the eviction of Anglican ministers on doctrinal grounds as a breach of liberty of conscience.[154] After 1660 he wrote a series of manuscript treatises intended to fortify the Dissenters under persecution or to persuade the government to tolerate them. They included a characteristically enormous work 'Of the Rise of Persecution', which drew heavily on John Foxe to recount the history of intolerance through recorded time, from Cain to the Stuarts.[155]

The second figure is Whitelocke's fellow lawyer Matthew Hale.[156] Cromwell had raised him from obscurity to chair the commission on law reform of 1652 which bears his name, and on which Anthony Ashley Cooper, another politically pliable advocate of liberty of religious profession who owed his advancement to Cromwell, made his political debut. Like Whitelocke, Hale was no friend to military rule, and like him he had his political differences with the protector. Yet Cromwell continued to look to him as an instrument of law reform.[157] The writings of Hale and Whitelocke, which have much in common, give an instructive impression of the lay Puritanism of the 1650s and beyond: of a generation which withdrew from millenarianism, which preferred family exercises to churchgoing, and which sought, through meditation and the cultivation of a good conscience, to preserve an inward integrity amid the havoc and the bitterness of the civil wars and their aftermath. In both men there is an element of Christian stoicism. They are

---

[152] For the 'merciful men' in the Nayler debate, see Worden, *Rump Parliament*, pp. 129–31.

[153] Whitelocke, *Memorials*, ii. 306.

[154] Worden, *Rump Parliament*, p. 131; Ruth Spalding, *The Improbable Puritan: A Life of Bulstrode Whitelocke 1605–1675* (1975), esp. pp. 96–7, 102, 243, 279; Jordan, *Development of Religious Toleration*, iii. 68–9.

[155] It is at Longleat House (Whitelocke MS xvii), where I have read it by kind permission of the Marquess of Bath.

[156] Hale's posthumous works can be conveniently found in T. Thirlwall, ed., *The Works, Moral and Religious, of Sir Matthew Hale*, 2 vols (1805). Jordan has a section on him: *Development of Religious Toleration*, iv. 61–9.

[157] *Certain Passages of Every Dayes Intelligence* 4 February 1654, p. 27; 17 March 1654, p. 68; *CSPD 1653–4*, p. 407 (cf. 1654, p. 31; Firth and Rait, ii. 845).

mistrustful of a reliance on outward success or fortune, wary of extremes of conduct or outlook, and vigilant monitors of human appetites.[158]

Our third figure is Sir Charles Wolseley, a friend of John Dryden.[159] A much younger man than Whitelocke or Hale, his relationship with Cromwell was smoother and closer than theirs. The son-in-law of Lord Saye and Sele, he came from nowhere in 1653, apparently at the age of twenty-three, to help guide the Cromwellian moderate party in Barebone's Parliament. In the protectorate he was a consistently active member of the council. Left in the cold after the Restoration, he wrote a series of books on religious subjects in the 1660s and 1670s, among them *Liberty of Conscience . . . Asserted and Vindicated.* Whereas Hale and Whitelocke bequeathed manuscripts from the 1650s which express attitudes consistent with those of their later writings, we are left to guess at Wolseley's religious position in that decade. Yet his concern for liberty of conscience after 1660 is unlikely to have been novel.[160]

Wolseley was Whitelocke's closest ally at Cromwell's court, despite the difference in age between them.[161] Both were men of massive—if not always well-digested—learning. Both knew Hebrew and Greek well enough to apply them to biblical scholarship. Wolseley had an impressive knowledge of the by-ways of classical and patristic literature: Whitelocke, like Hale, belonged to one of the most learned of seventeenth-century circles, that of John Selden. After 1660, the careers of Whitelocke and Wolseley can time and again be found in conjunction or in parallel. The two men collaborated with each other and with other Dissenters in writing for liberty of conscience.[162] Wolseley wrote his books for the Whig magnate the Earl of Anglesey,[163] who published Whitelocke's posthumous memoirs in 1681–2. In 1688 one of Whitelocke's treatises on religious liberty was published as a contribution, supposedly written by Anglesey, to the Dissenters' campaign on behalf of James II.[164] Wolseley committed himself to James II in the same year.[165] Perhaps to Wolseley, who had publicly defended de facto political thinking in the 1650s,[166] it seemed as sensible to seek liberty of conscience under

[158] Worden, *Rump Parliament*, pp. 131–2 (for Whitelocke); *Works . . . of Sir Matthew Hale*, i. *passim* (esp. Gilbert Burnet's life of Hale); ii. 12, 25, 138, 159–60, 179, 211, 233, 246, 259, 286–7, 293, 415.

[159] Dryden: Philip Harth, *Contexts of Dryden's Thought* (Chicago, 1968), pp. 108–46, 199–200, 294–7.

[160] Cf. Woolrych, *Commonwealth to Protectorate*, pp. 202–3.

[161] BL Add. MS 31984 (Whitelocke's History of his Forty-Eighth Year), fos 165^v–166^r, 175^v–176^r; BL Add. MS 32093, fo. 317^r.

[162] Compare (e.g.) BL Add. MS 21009 (Whitelocke, 'The King's Right to Grant Indulgence in Matters of Religion'), fos 29^r–33^v, with Wolseley's *Liberty of Conscience upon its true and proper Grounds Asserted and Vindicated* (1668), pp. 52–3, 57–9; and compare both documents with e.g. Owen, *Works*, xiii. 368; Slingsby Bethel, *The Present Interest of England* (1671), pp. 13–17; *Select Works of William Penn*, 3 vols (1825), ii. 295.

[163] Wolseley, *The Unreasonableness of Atheism* (1669), ep. ded. and p. 194; Wolseley, *The Reasonableness of Scripture-Belief* (1672), ep. ded.

[164] *The King's Right of Indulgence in Spiritual Matters* (1688) is an adaptation of BL Add. MS 21009.

[165] G. F. Duckett, *Penal Laws and Test Act*, 2 vols (1882–3), ii. 251.

[166] *Burton*, ii. 40.

James as it had done under Cromwell, whom, like Whitelocke, he had urged to become king. Wolseley may have been lured into support for James by William Penn, with whom he had co-operated during the exclusion crisis.[167] Whitelocke, too, had come under Penn's influence. Penn supervised the publication of much of Whitelocke's posthumous work, including his lay sermons on the text 'Quench not the Spirit' (1 Thessalonians 5:19).[168] They arguably show that Whitelocke had become close to the Quakers in his later years.[169]

In all three men, Whitelocke, Hale, and Wolseley, we find a genuine tolerance of mind, if by that we mean a willingness to understand and permit beliefs based on premises different from their own. They were the kind of people whom Jordan liked. And in all three men we find, in a form suitable to their troubled generation, the old Erasmian spirit of religion: practical, rational, sceptical, tolerant. It is the spirit that had distinguished the Arminian advocates of doctrinal liberty at Great Tew.[170] Whitelocke, the youthful friend of Edward Hyde and, like Hale, the adult friend of moderate bishops, rested much of his case for freedom of conscience on the arguments of the Anglican Jeremy Taylor,[171] much as Wolseley appealed to the authority of that leading influence on Great Tew, Hugo Grotius, and of that key thinker of the Great Tew circle, William Chillingworth.[172]

Whitelocke, for all his learning, was not much interested in doctrinal controversy. To him theology was a guide to behaviour. Wolseley and Hale agreed. Wolseley thought that 'practical sanctity is the great end of religion. . . . When men confine religion to speculation, they turn divinity into metaphysics, where they dispute without end: to reduce it to practice, is to pursue its proper tendency, and to make it (as indeed it is) the great principle of union and peace'.[173] Hale, having said the same thing in very similar words, concluded that 'as the *credenda* are but few and plain, so the *facienda*, or things to be done, are such as do truly ennoble and advance the humane nature'.[174] The advancement and ennoblement of 'the humane nature' had not seemed a legitimate or attainable goal to John Owen.

Whitelocke, Wolseley, and Hale all explored the history of the Church to try to understand the decline of Christianity into dogmatic warfare. All of them found there, in Wolseley's words, 'carnal interests and political concerns . . . twisted into the government of the Church . . . to enable the clergy, under a pretext of the power

---

[167] R. W. Blencowe, ed., *Diary of . . . Henry Sidney*, 2 vols (1834), pp. 114–16.
[168] Whitelocke, *Quench not the Spirit* (1711; 2nd edn 1715); Whitelocke, *Memorials of the English Affairs, from the suppos'd Expedition of Brute . . . to . . . King James the First* (1709), preface.
[169] That suggestion is made by Spalding, *Improbable Puritan*, p. 248.
[170] See H. R. Trevor-Roper, *Edward Hyde Earl of Clarendon* (1975), and his *Religion, The Reformation and Social Change*, pp. 203, 216, 219, 299.
[171] BL Add. MS 21009, fos 46ʳ–56ʳ, 168ᵛ–169ʳ, 190ᵛ. Taylor was sometimes cited by Puritans as an authority on religious liberty in the 1650s: John Reading, *Anabaptism Routed* (1655); Cawdrey, *Sathan Discovered*, pp. 11 ff.; Henry Stubbe, *An Essay in Defence of the Good Old Cause* (1659), p. 42; Jordan, *Development of Religious Toleration in England*, iii. 505.
[172] Wolseley, *Justification Evangelical* (1677), p. 8; Wolseley, *Liberty of Conscience*, pp. 29, 39, 67–8; Wolseley, *Reasonableness of Scripture-Belief*, pp. 47, 300–1.
[173] Wolseley's preface to Henry Newcombe, *A Faithful Narrative of the Life and Death of that Holy and Laborious Preacher Mr John Machin* (1671).
[174] *Judgement of the late Lord Chief Justice Sir Matthew Hale*, pp. 5–6, 8, 16.

of the Gospel, to trample . . . mankind under their feet'.[175] Only blinkered human pride, Hale argued, could explain the enforcement of beliefs about free will and the Trinity, subjects which had been 'as it were industriously kept secret by Almighty God, because they are not of use to mankind to be known'.[176] Hale and Wolseley—both men with a greater capacity and inclination than Whitelocke possessed to reduce a problem to first principles—investigated the claims of conscience from the starting-point not of faith but of 'ratiocination'.[177] To try to force the conscience, said Wolseley, was 'a spiritual rape'.[178] It was likewise pointless to try to enforce the understanding, which could not believe what reason refuted.

In Wolseley's scheme of religion, Calvinist predestination is not so much refuted as forgotten. To attain salvation, he wrote, we need only 'live a sober, righteous, religious life here, such as is rationally best for ourselves, and others, and be gradually preparing for those eternal fruitions that are to come'.[179] Those tenets of Wolseley, as Owen's former mentor at Oxford the Calvinist Thomas Barlow noted reproachfully, were 'opinions very different from the old faith which I and, I think, the generality of our divines have held'.[180] In place of Puritan theology Wolseley provided a 'rational justification' of the Christian religion, which he expounded in a book he called *The Reasonableness of Scripture-Belief.* The title points ahead to John Locke's classic work of 1696, *The Reasonableness of Christianity,* even perhaps to John Toland's more daring tract of the following year, *Christianity not Mysterious.* And from the argument that Christianity is reasonable and not mysterious, it may not be a long step to the view that there are still more reasonable and less mysterious positions than Christianity to adopt.

From an evolutionary perspective, that is no doubt where Wolseley stands. We can hardly miss the dramatic irony of his offer to abandon his claims for 'the reasonableness of Scripture-belief' if anyone could 'palpably disprove any one matter of fact in the history of the Bible'.[181] The evolutionary perspective is valuable and instructive, and without it we may become mere antiquarians, forgetful of those broad human questions about toleration which a historian's audience might fairly ask, and which a Gardiner and a Jordan strove to answer. Can we retain that perspective without succumbing to the opposite danger, of misrepresenting the past by selecting from it those features in which we see our own reflections? The writings of Whitelocke, Hale, and Wolseley indicate the size of the challenge. Those men, like the Arminians and the Erasmians before them—and indeed like Locke (and perhaps Toland) after them—conducted their arguments for religious liberty within Christianity, not in search of emancipation from it. Hale and Wolseley both stated that the Socinians, although they had much to commend

---

[175] Wolseley, *Liberty of Conscience,* pp. 17–18, 20.

[176] *Judgement of the late Lord Chief Justice Sir Matthew Hale,* pp. 5–6, 13, 28; cf. Wolseley, *Liberty of Conscience,* p. 25.

[177] *Ibid.,* p. 38; *Judgement of the late Lord Chief Justice Sir Matthew Hale,* pp. 5–6.

[178] Wolseley, *Liberty of Conscience,* p. 27.

[179] Wolseley, *Justification Evangelical,* pp. 88–9.

[180] See Barlow's notes in his copy of *Justification Evangelical* in Bodl., classmark 8. C. Linc. 345.

[181] Wolseley, *Reasonableness of Scripture-Belief,* p. 195.

them, took their faith in the naked intellect, and their mistrust of revelation, too far.[182] Our three writers were concerned, as the Calvinists were, with the salvation of souls and with the union of believers with Christ and with each other: a salvation and a union which, they believed, theological controversy and clerical intolerance destroyed. They aimed to reconstruct Protestantism on a different base: a base of reason, practice, and Gospel precept.

To those men—no less than to Owen—the most alarming feature of the age was the ubiquitous and pernicious advance of atheism and libertinism. Atheism made converts, they believed, because doctrinal rancour, clerical strife, and confessional dogmatism had discredited religion. 'Love, and charity, and even common human-ity, and mutual conversation between man and man, church and church, party and party,' wrote Hale, 'is broken by the mutual collisions and animosities . . . . And by this means the true life of Christian religion'—what Hale also called 'the true radical vital doctrine and religion of Christ'—'is lost or neglected by them that profess it, or disparaged among those that . . . have not entertained it. . . . These men, when they see so much religion placed by professors of Christianity in these things, which every intelligent man values but as forms, or inventions, or modes, or artifices, . . . are presently apt to censure and throw off all religion, and reckon all of the same make'. Hence there 'ariseth a most fruitful and most inevitable increase of atheism and contempt of religion'.[183] Hale began to compose 'a great design against atheism';[184] Wolseley wrote a book called *The Unreasonableness of Atheism*; Whitelocke registered his dismay at 'atheism, a wickedness increasing in these days'.[185] It is a mistake automatically to equate rationalism with religious indiffer-ence; and, as writers on religious freedom have often insisted, it may be another to attribute the emergence of arguments for toleration to indifference.[186] The devel-opment of claims for religious liberty, as it is reflected and articulated in the works of our three former Cromwellians, does not seem evidence of a decline of religious conviction. Rather it appears a stage in the process by which the Protestant God changes his character. He becomes a friendly monitor rather than an awesome dictator, a God in whom mercy is more conspicuous than justice; and Protestant-ism, the religion of faith, becomes a religion of works.

---

[182] Wolseley, *Liberty of Conscience*, ep. ded. (and see p. 304); *Judgement of the late Lord Chief Justice Sir Matthew Hale*, p. 25. Cf. Robert Ferguson, *A Sober Inquiry into . . . Moral Virtue* (1673), ep. ded. (to Wolseley).

[183] *Judgement of the late Lord Chief Justice Sir Matthew Hale*, pp. 16, 37, 39.

[184] *Works . . . of Matthew Hale*, i. 36–7.

[185] Whitelocke, *Quench not the Spirit* (1715 edn), pp. 52–3.

[186] The seventeenth-century pamphleteer Henry Stubbe planned to write a 'history of toleration' to prove the point: Stubbe, *Essay in Defence of the Good Old Cause*, 'Premonition'; Stubbe, *A Further Justification* (1673), pp. 70–1. Cf. Jordan, *Development of Religious Toleration*, i. 15–16, ii. 485–6.

4

Politics, Piety, and Learning: Cromwellian Oxford

In January 1651 the University of Oxford elected Oliver Cromwell its Chancellor. The Chancellorship, customarily held by a statesman or churchman or nobleman of high influence, was a powerful position, albeit one distant from the everyday affairs of the university. From 1629 to 1641 the Chancellor was Archbishop Laud. He used the post to achieve vigorous reforms, through which he hoped to make the university at once a source and an image of the religious and moral reformation of the wider nation.[1] For Oxford, with its sister university Cambridge, was the principal training-ground of the nation's guides and leaders. Most of the clergy were educated in one or other of the two universities. From the late fifteenth century an increasing proportion of the sons of substantial landowners, the dominant class of national and local government, had also been taught there, often at ages when in modern times they would have been at school.[2] Cromwell, like Laud, saw the universities as the nurseries of a godly society. Subjected to Laud's Anglican vision in the 1630s, Oxford was exposed to Cromwell's Puritan one in the 1650s. But where Laud succeeded to the Chancellorship in a time of domestic peace and institutional order, Cromwell acquired it in one of civil strife and institutional chaos.

In Laud's time the number of students at Oxford was higher than it had ever been, or than it would be again until the late nineteenth century.[3] Under Cromwell the university prospered on a different front. Its accomplishments in physics and chemistry and mathematics and astronomy and medicine won international recognition. Discussions and experiments in the lodgings of William Petty and Robert Boyle in the High Street, and of the Warden of Wadham College, John Wilkins, helped prepare the way for the achievements of the Royal Society after the Restoration. Those advances owed something to the placing of experimental thinkers in the university by friends or admirers among parliamentarians and

---

[1] Kevin Sharpe, 'Archbishop Laud and the University of Oxford', in Hugh Lloyd-Jones, Valerie Pearl, and Blair Worden, eds, *History and Imagination: Essays in Honour of H.R. Trevor-Roper* (1981), pp. 146–64.

[2] On Oxford in the sixteenth and seventeenth centuries see James McConica, ed., *History of the University of Oxford*, vol. 3: *The Collegiate University* (Oxford, 1986); and Nicholas Tyacke, ed., *The History of the University of Oxford*, vol. 4: *Seventeenth-Century Oxford* (1997).

[3] Stephen Porter, 'University and Society', in Tyacke, *History of the University of Oxford*, p. 33.

Cromwellians, though the motives for the appointments are not known.[4] In the main, however, the Puritan rule of Oxford had other preoccupations, which will be our subject: the securing of political obedience; the recovery of the university from the disruptions and disorder of the civil wars; and the building, upon those foundations, of a godly community. None of those goals could have been achieved quickly. The Puritans had to overcome resistance as fierce and powerful as they faced anywhere. They had to reconstruct an institution which, after the prosperity of the Laudian years, lay in ruins. As Anthony Wood, Oxford's antiquary, who lived there through the upheaval and became the university's historian, recorded bitterly but accurately, the civil war had left Oxford 'exhausted of its treasure', 'deprived of its number of sons'; 'lectures and exercises had for the most part ceased'; 'in a word there was scarce the face of an university left, all things being out of order and disturbed'.[5]

Since the Reformation, the Crown had kept an anxious watch on Oxford and Cambridge. It had extended its powers and patronage there and had monitored the conformity of the two universities to the religion of the state. University politics intertwined with national ones. In the Puritan Revolution they were inseparable from them. Oxford was the wartime capital of Charles I, a massively fortified garrison thickly crowded with soldiers and courtiers. Geographically, logistically, and emotionally it was the heart of the royal cause. Edward Hyde, the future Earl of Clarendon, who visited the university in 1642 and then lived in it as an adviser to Charles I and as the wartime Chancellor of the Exchequer, would recall that in the beginning of the fighting Oxford was 'the only city of England that' the king 'could say was entirely at his devotion'. Charles and his court resided in Oxford; the privy council and the royalist parliament met there; royal military strategy was formed there. It was to the university, rather than the town, that Hyde 'imputed' the 'integrity and fidelity' of the royal capital.[6] Cambridge, where Laudianism had also flown high, was captured for parliament at the start of the war. It was forcibly purged of the king's supporters during the fighting, under the direction of the Major-General of the Eastern Association, the Earl of Manchester.[7] At Oxford, by contrast, almost all those leading figures of the university who sympathized with the parliamentarian programme of 1641–2 soon left or were ejected.

With political and military affiliations went literary and religious ones. Oxford had a leading role in the writing of royalist political thought and polemic and poetry, and in the printing of royalist propaganda. Its royalism blended with a commitment to episcopacy and the Book of Common Prayer, so much so that political and religious allegiances can be indistinguishable. It was at Oxford that in

---

[4] Robert G. Frank, 'Medicine', in ibid., p. 544; Oxford University Archives (hereafter OUA), Reg[ister of] Conv[ocation] T, pp. 72, 73; Montagu Burrows, *The Register of the Visitors of the University of Oxford 1647–1658*, Camden Society, new series 29 (1881: hereafter Burrows), pp. cxx, 369n.; below, pp. 120, 156.

[5] Burrows, p. lviii.

[6] *CH*, ii. 375.

[7] J. D. Twigg, 'The Parliamentary Visitation of the University of Cambridge, 1644–5', *English Historical Review* 98 (1993), pp. 513–28.

1645 Henry Hammond, a Canon of Christ Church, the college at the centre of civil-war Anglicanism, published his *Practicall Catechism*, perhaps the work, more than any other, that characterized and shaped the Anglican counter-attack on the Calvinist theology of the victorious Puritans. Hammond's allies in the Anglican cause included the Dean—the head—of Christ Church, Samuel Fell; Samuel's formidable son John, another senior member of Christ Church, who in the Restoration would in turn become its Dean and a dominant figure of university politics; Robert Sanderson, Canon of Christ Church and Regius Professor of Divinity; and Gilbert Sheldon, Warden of All Souls College and future Archbishop of Canterbury, who with Hammond was personally close to Charles I.

When Oxford surrendered to the new model army in 1646, the royal military cause in effect fell with it. If anything, Oxford's royalism was intensified by defeat and by the university's treatment at its conquerors' hands. Parliamentarian control of the university was enforced by blunt military occupation and by brusque affronts to local law and custom. If devotion to the proscribed Anglican Church fortified royalism and blended with it, so did a sense of communal outrage. In September 1646 a group of Presbyterian divines was sent by parliament in the vain hope of preaching the university into religious conformity and political obedience. Next year came firmer and more systematic methods. In May 1647 parliament appointed a board of twenty-four Visitors to the university, who were to interrogate its members, and who were soon given powers to evict and replace parliament's opponents.[8] Among the Visitors was the parliamentarian grandee the Earl of Pembroke, who had succeeded Laud as Chancellor in 1641 when Laud, from his prison in the Tower, resigned. Pembroke had himself been replaced as Chancellor during the war by the royalist Marquis of Hertford. Now he resumed the office, and Samuel Fell, who had acted as Vice-Chancellor under Hertford, was deposed. The Visitors were instructed to identify teachers and office-holders who refused to take the Solemn League and Covenant (the test on which the purge at Cambridge had centred) or the Negative Oath (which committed its subscribers never to bear arms against the parliament), or who resisted the creation of the new Presbyterian Church. The arrival of the Visitation in Oxford was greeted by defiance, by contumely, and by a skilfully worded remonstrance, published in the university's name, which assailed both the Covenant and the legal basis of the Visitation. Clarendon, though he had himself left Oxford in 1645, would proudly recall that Convocation, the university's parliament,

> to their eternal renown (being at that time under a strict and a strong garrison put over them by the parliament, the king in prison, and all their hopes desperate), passed a public act and declaration against the Covenant, with such invincible arguments of the illegality, wickedness, and perjury contained in it, that no man of the contrary opinion

---

[8] There is a valuable study by Thomas Edward Reinhart, 'The Parliamentary Visitation of Oxford University, 1646–1652', Brown Univ. Ph.D. thesis, 1984. A number of Reinhart's conclusions are conveyed in condensed form in Ian Roy and Dietrich Reinhart, 'The Civil Wars', in Tyacke, *History of the University of Oxford*, pp. 720–31. The register-book of the Visitation is printed in Burrows, whose Introduction and editorial apparatus remain indispensable.

. . . ever ventured to make any answer to it; nor is it indeed to be answered, but must remain to the world's end as a monument of the learning, courage, and loyalty of that excellent place to eternity, against the highest malice and tyranny that was ever exercised in and over any nation.[9]

The rule of the Visitors would last until 1652. They kept long and hard hours,[10] as their Cromwellian successors in Oxford would do. At first they made little impact. The university's leaders, outwitting them by procedural devices and by what the Visitors called 'studdied delayes . . . to retard the great worke of reformation intended by the parliament',[11] isolated them from the running of the institution. Only in the spring of 1648, in response to the swelling, in the nation at large, of the anti-parliamentarian sentiment and hopes which produced the second civil war, was the great body of the members of the university interrogated. The Earl of Pembroke came to Oxford in April to launch the purge. Yet the royalist revival which provoked the Visitation into action also subverted it. So long as the outcome of the second civil war was uncertain, insolence and abuse were directed at the Visitation and at the soldiers of the city garrison on whom it depended to enforce its will. Anglican worship continued to be practised in the college chapels, where, as the Visitors lamented, there was 'great slacknesse in settinge up, and putting in execution' the Presbyterian Directory that was meant to replace it.[12] Royalist protest declared itself in ballads, in the lighting of bonfires, in the drinking of healths, in revelry, in ostentatious swearing and cursing. The university's officers dared not 'walk without soldiers'.[13] Proclamations by the Visitors were ripped from the gates of colleges or torn from their records. Keys, staves of office, and sole copies of legal or financial documents were stolen or concealed. 'Lybellouse, infamous, scurrilous, . . . abusive pamphletts' rained on the Puritan authorities.[14] Soldiers had to be called in to break down doors and gates and remove occupants of the colleges by force. The Visitor Francis Cheynell, whom parliament made President of St John's College, was only able to occupy his new lodgings after 'the doores' had been 'first violently broken down'.[15] Daniel Greenwood, parliament's choice as Principal of Brasenose College, took office after a 'guard of soldiers' had prevented the Fellows from electing a Principal acceptable to their own permanent or 'local' Visitor, a bishop, on whose authority they insisted even though parliament had abolished episcopacy.[16] John Fell's wife had to be carried from the Deanery of Christ Church on a chair into the quadrangle.[17] At the end of May and the beginning of June, following celebrations of the eighteenth birthday of the Prince

[9] *CH*, iv. 258.
[10] Burrows, p. 269.
[11] Ibid., p. 16.
[12] Ibid., p. 22.
[13] Bodl., Wood MS f. 35, fo. 305.
[14] Burrows, p. 34.
[15] Bodl., Wood MS f. 35, fo. 315ᵛ.
[16] F. J. Varley, 'The Restoration Visitation of the University of Oxford', *Camden Miscellany* 18 (1948), pp. 5–6.
[17] Roy and Reinhart, 'Civil Wars', p. 726.

of Wales,[18] to whom royalists looked for deliverance in the second civil war, the university was out of parliamentarian control. Sheldon was imprisoned and the arrest of Hammond was ordered, but the Puritans could not stop the gatherings of their followers. Defiance persisted into the winter, when at Christ Church, which the Visitors supposed themselves to have brought to compliance, Latin prayers and a Latin grace continued to be used. In the college hall 'high and profest Cavaliers' drank the king's health a few weeks before the regicide. Much the same happened in Balliol College.[19]

The universities were young communities, where many of the Fellows of colleges awaited the appointments to Church livings that would start their main careers. So a high proportion of the men brought before the Visitation were young. The demand to acknowledge the commission's authority confronted them, and their older colleagues, with problems of conscience of a kind recurrently posed by seventeenth-century demands for pledges of political obedience.[20] The university's members were required to state whether they accepted the authority of the Visitation. The small minority of them who readily submitted exposed themselves to 'malignity and opposition' from their colleagues.[21] Among the rest, many feared committing what the university, in an official declaration, called 'multiplied perjuries'.[22] Not only would submission acknowledge the legality of the parliamentary cause. It would recognize the Visitors' claim to override those local and collegiate authorities and oaths on which the ordering of the institution depended, and which informed its daily practices. Some members greeted the demand for submission with unflinching hostility. Yet there were less outright responses. Alongside the men who openly refused, there was as large a number who were resourcefully evasive. Some were conveniently absent when the Visitors summoned them. Others, having initially resisted, changed their minds. Others gave ingeniously ambiguous replies. Others still offered submissions which they would be glad to retract if the political wind were to alter. Amid the national turmoil and uncertainties of the late 1640s, the Visitors' efforts to separate friend from foe were baffled by the fluidity both of the university's population and of the political calculations of its members. The information and machinery of the Visitation were too restricted to permit the thorough execution of their decisions. About half of those listed for expulsion contrived to remain in their posts.[23] Men who slipped through the Visitors' net, remembering their friends among the less fortunate, sometimes succeeded in restoring them to their posts, or, when that

---

[18] Bodl., Wood MS f. 35, fo. 314; cf. Jesus College Archives (hereafter JCA), shelfmark 19, Bursars' Accounts 1621–53, p. 172.

[19] Bodl., Wood MS f. 35, fos 338, 339.

[20] John Spurr, 'Perjury, Profanity and Politics', *The Seventeenth Century* 8 (1993), pp. 29–50; Edward Vallance, *Revolutionary England and the National Covenant: State Oaths, Protestantism and the Political Nation, 1553–1682* (Woodbridge, 2005).

[21] Burrows, p. 78.

[22] Anthony Wood, *The History and Antiquities of the University of Oxford*, ed. J. Gutch, 2 vols in 3 (1792–6), ii. 524; cf. ii. 679.

[23] Roy and Reinhart, 'Civil Wars', p. 728.

endeavour failed, in enabling them to retain their chambers and free meals and even their teaching.

The Visitors had practical reasons for restraint in implementing the purge, even on occasion for winking at the avoidance of their commands.[24] The war had gravely depleted the ranks of Oxford's teachers and scholars. The evictions which the Visitors did carry out depleted them much further. The greater the number of Visitatorial evictions, the harder it became to find MAs and BAs statutably and intellectually qualified to fill the vacant posts—especially when the statutes of a college confined the positions to scholars who came from a region with which the college had connections, though the Visitors sometimes overrode that rule as the only way of supplying a quorum of Fellows, an irregularity that heightened the local sense of injury.

When the Visitors did order expulsions, or demanded changes in the colleges' conduct, their efforts were impeded by tensions between the Visitation and its masters at Westminster, which the university learned to exploit.[25] Until 1649 the Visitation was essentially a Presbyterian one, designed to impose on Oxford the Presbyterian rule which had already been enforced on Cambridge[26] (where appointments to replace the evicted members had been vetted by the predominantly Presbyterian Westminster Assembly of Divines[27]). When Cambridge was purged, however, the rival Independent alliance was only in its infancy. It came to unite Congregationalists, new model officers, and Erastian MPs, all groups suspicious of Presbyterian clericalism and intolerance. In the character of the Presbyterian inquisition into the consciences of the royalists at Oxford, the Independents recognized a threat to their own. The 'unwearied care and passionate endeavours' for the university's 'preservation' by its Erastian MP John Selden,[28] himself a giant of seventeenth-century scholarship, made him its most influential friend at Westminster.[29] Other MPs who proved valuable allies against the Visitors were Bulstrode Whitelocke, Nathaniel Fiennes (both of whom, with Selden, were on the standing parliamentary committee to which the Visitation was answerable[30]), and Sir John Trevor. Whitelocke was 'so universal a patron to all liberal studies';[31] Fiennes had many connections in Oxford and would be a powerful friend to it during the protectorate; Trevor was 'a great lover of learning', 'very obliging to several scholars' who were purged by the Puritans in Oxford and Cambridge, and possessing 'great interest'

---

[24] Reinhart, 'Parliamentary Visitation', p. 390; see too Burrows, pp. lxxvi, 133.

[25] Reinhart, 'Parliamentary Visitation', p. 334.

[26] David Laing, ed., *The Letters and Journals of Robert Baillie*, 3 vols (1841–2), ii. 386, 393; Henry Wilkinson Sr, *Miranda, Stupenda* (1646); Robert Johnson, *Lux et Lex* (1647), p. 43; Wood, *History*, ii. 543; Burrows, p. 22.

[27] Twigg, 'Parliamentary Visitation', p. 520.

[28] John Leland, *De Rebus Britannicis Collectanea*, ed. Thomas Hearne, 6 vols (1715), v. 282–3.

[29] For the depth of Oxford's gratitude to him, on that and other counts, see Bodl., Selden MS *supra* 109, fo. 452; cf. *CSPD 1654*, p. 405.

[30] Firth and Rait, i. 927. (W. C. Abbott's statement [Abbott, i. 444] that Cromwell was on the parliamentary committee rests on a misreading: *CJ* 14 May 1647.)

[31] John Davies, *Reflections upon Monsieur Des Cartes's Discourse* (1654), ep. ded.

in the appointment of their replacements.[32] All those men undermined the proscriptive activity of the Visitors. Their help enabled a number of heads and Fellows of colleges who resented the Visitation, but who were willing to curb or conceal their hostility to it, to survive it.[33]

Besides, as reformers the Visitors had their own inhibitions. The membership of the commission fell into two categories: laymen from outside Oxford, who had no immediate connection with the university, and most of whom played no active part in the Visitation; and clergymen, who were persistently involved in its proceedings.[34] Of the ten clergy, eight already held or had previously held posts in Oxford, and the other two soon did. The President of the board, Nathaniel Brent, had been made Warden of Merton College in 1622. An adversary of Laud's reforms in the 1630s, he was deposed by Charles I in the civil war, and was for a time replaced by the great William Harvey. He quietly resumed his office upon the fall of Oxford in 1646. Of the Visitors who were given new posts, most replaced royalists who had been evicted by the Visitation itself or by its parliamentary masters. Appointments to headships of colleges, which were made by parliament rather than by the Visitors, were bestowed on three of them. One of the three, Edward Reynolds, who became Dean of Christ Church, was also made Vice-Chancellor. Another, Francis Cheynell, was also appointed Lady Margaret Professor of Divinity. Another three Visitors were made Canons of Christ Church.

Two Visitors were regarded as the most zealous of them: Cheynell, that vigorous assertor of Calvinist doctrinal orthodoxy; and the elder of Oxford's two Henry Wilkinsons, 'Long Harry', who would be Cheynell's successor as Lady Margaret Professor.[35] In a sermon delivered two months after the surrender of Oxford, Wilkinson told the Commons that 'you have an university and a kingdome to purge, which lyes like the Augean stable, and it is a very vast businese to doe it'. He called for 'reformation in that place above others'. Yet his zeal was not uncompromising. His sermon advised parliament not to 'cast out' episcopalians, or others

---

[32] Walter Pope, The *Life of the Right Reverend Father in God, Seth Bishop of Salisbury* (1697), pp. 20–2; Seth Ward, *De Cometis* (Oxford, 1653), ep. ded.; cf. *CJ* 11 July 1659.

[33] Selden: Bodl., Tanner MS 456, fos 3, 5; Rawlinson MS d. 1070, fos 21–2; Selden MS *supra* 109, fo. 335; Wood MS f. 35, fo. 144; MS Lat. misc. c. 19, pp. 121–2; OUA, SP/E/5, fo. 48 (cf. fos 33–5); NEP/E/14(3); L. Twells, *The Life of Dr Edward Pocock*, in vol. i. (hereafter Twells, *Pocock*) of *The Lives of Dr Edward Pocock*, 2 vols (1816), pp. 131–2; Burrows, pp. lxvii–lxxii; Wood, *History*, ii. 537, 540; Reinhart, 'Parliamentary Visitation', pp. 294, 296, 405. Selden and Whitelocke: *SPC*, ii. 398–400; Wood, *History*, ii. 545–7; Whitelocke, *Memorials*, iv. 287; Bulstrode Whitelocke, *A Journal of the Swedish Embassy*, 2 vols (1855), ii. 492; Ruth Spalding, ed., *Contemporaries of Bulstrode Whitelocke* (Oxford, 1990), p. 206 (and see Spalding, *The Diary of Bulstrode Whitelocke* [Oxford, 1990], p. 595); Reinhart, 'Parliamentary Visitation', pp. 336–7; Roy and Reinhart, 'Civil Wars', p. 725; and compare BL Add. MS 37344, fo. 323, with Burrows, pp. 254, 257–8, 372. Selden and Fiennes: OUA, SP/E/5, fo. 34; Bodl., Wood MS f. 35, fos 144, 193ᵛ; Wood, *History*, ii. 544; cf. Peter Toon, ed., *Correspondence of John Owen* (Cambridge, 1970), pp. 94–5. For restraining influences among the parliamentary Independents see too H. Cary, ed., *Memorials of the Great Civil War in England from 1646 to 1652*, 2 vols (1842), ii. 415; *The Petition and Argument of Mr Hotham* (1651: the longer version of this tract), p. 8; cf. Bodl., Wood MS f. 35, fo. 358.

[34] Reinhart, 'Parliamentary Visitation', pp. 308, 368.

[35] Burrows, p. xxxi; Bodl., J. Walker MS c. 8, fo. 247&ᵛ; Wood MS f. 35, fo. 334; *Oxonii Lachrymae* (1649), pp. 3–5; Wood, *History*, ii. 612.

who might not 'close with every particular with you', 'if they will be quiet, and will not oppose or hinder you'. Since a 'tender usage and respect' might 'recover' them, and thus 'help you to build', 'it shall be your glory to recover and gaine such as these with love and the spirit of meeknesse'.[36] Perhaps his attitude sharpened when he experienced the intensity of Oxford's resistance to the Visitation, but his severity seems to have been directed only at outward defiance of parliament and Puritanism. Royalists understood his and Cheynell's basic allegiance to the university.[37] Even so, another Visitor, John Mills, had a 'great dislike, and detestation' of the two men's methods.[38] We shall find the Visitor Daniel Greenwood viewing with similar distaste an attack on the university's autonomy by a later Visitation.[39] The mild-mannered Edward Reynolds, happier as an uncontentious preacher than as a politician, remarked when accepting the Vice-Chancellorship 'how difficult it was for a man that had sequestered himself from secular imployments to be called to government, especially to sit at the sterne in these rough and troublesome times', when he 'did desire that good example and counsell might prevaile more in this reformation than severity'.[40] The Visitors found themselves facing two ways, as later Puritan rulers of Oxford, who came to power only during Cromwell's Chancellorship, would do. They knew that the success of their Puritan programme depended on external backing from parliament or the state. Yet they were themselves members of a university whose customs and communal sense were being violated by their own powers and deeds. If the Visitors needed support from outside, they were also reliant on acceptance and cooperation within. They found themselves delegating much of their business, particularly the choice of new appointments to replace the purged members, to other members of the university.

Pride's Purge and the execution of Charles I, by splitting the parliamentarian cause and the Visitation itself, weakened such support in Oxford as the Visitors had succeeded in building. There were further evictions from the colleges, where 'good affection' to the rule of the Rump was demanded of candidates not only for academic positions but for posts in the kitchens, butteries, and stables.[41] Desperate for a dependable base in Oxford, parliament and army condoned candid nepotism in the making of appointments and in the award of degrees, and unabashedly invoked allegiance to the state as a qualification for advancement.[42] The sons of the

---

[36] Wilkinson Sr, *Miranda, Stupenda*, pp. 27–9.
[37] Bodl., Tanner MS 456, fos 3, 5.
[38] Bodl., Wood MS f. 35, fo. 334; cf. Wood, *History*, ii. 612, 618.
[39] Below, p. 132.
[40] OUA, Reg. Conv. T, p. 11.
[41] In Exeter College the cook was dismissed 'for his misdemeanours and contempt of the authority of parliament' and replaced by one recommended 'for his great suffering and general affection to the authority of parliament'—with what culinary consequences we cannot say: Exeter College Archives (hereafter ECA), A. I. 6, fo. 42. The cook of Trinity College, who allegedly liked to help himself to drink from the cellar, 'often said' that 'the reformation intended by the Visitors was a deformation' (Burrows, p. 216). Problems of allegiance and conscience among servants are also visible in: New College Archives (hereafter NA), 9655, p. 50; Queen's College Archives (hereafter QCA), Register H, p. 131; Christ Church Archives (hereafter CA), D&C i. b. 3, p. 16; Burrows, pp. 60, 126, 130, 170, 226, 229, 236–7, 241–2; Varley, 'Restoration Visitation', pp. 19, 43, 53.
[42] OUA, Reg. Conv. T, pp. 6, 83, 92, 131; cf. Burrows, p. 206.

MPs Dennis Bond and Bulstrode Whitelocke were made Fellows of All Souls,[43] the first at the age of seventeen, the second aged fourteen.[44] There they joined the army's historian Joshua Sprigge and the Baptist army officer Hierome Sankey (or Zanchey), who was the tutor of Whitelocke's son James. Sankey rapidly became sub-Warden of the college and Proctor of the university. During what amounted to a state visit by the army after its suppression of the Levellers at Burford in Oxfordshire in May 1649, he presented Lord General Fairfax and his second-in-command, Cromwell, as Doctors of Civil Law. A succession of other army officers was also presented for degrees, the awards being 'called by some the Fairfaxian creation'.[45] When Puritan bosses of the neighbouring countryside were added to the Visitation[46] or became newly prominent on it, they and their relations were accordingly honoured or favoured by the university.[47]

In spite of the evictions and instrusions, Oxford remained permeated and surrounded by royalist conspiracy and hostility.[48] Lines of intelligence which in the first and second civil wars had connected Oxford to the wider royalist world remained open. In the neighbouring countryside there were landowners, among them the families of Cope, Stonehouse, Walter, and Falkland, who were tied both to the university and to the vanquished king's cause. After the regicide the city's castle was first expensively refortified and then, for fear that it would fall into enemy hands, slighted, alternative fortifications being built, to the university's dismay, in college grounds.[49] Oxford's geographical position, which had encouraged Charles I to establish his base there, made it the target or expected target of invading or rebel armies during the Interregnum: of Charles II during the invasion which culminated at Worcester in 1651; of John Penruddock when he led a royalist rising in Wiltshire in 1655; of George Monck and then John Lambert during the collapse of the Puritan cause in 1660.[50] After the final defeat of the royalists at Worcester, the event that stabilized Puritan rule in Oxford and in England, the royal arms were removed

---

[43] B. D. Henning (ed.), *The House of Commons 1660–1690*, 3 vols (1983), i. 676. Comparable favour was extended to a son of the rumper William Cawley and probably to a son of the army officer William Goffe: J. R. Bloxham, *A Register of…Magdalen College*, 7 vols (1853–81: hereafter Bloxam, *Reg. Magdalen*), v. 211, 213.

[44] Spalding, *Diary of Bulstrode Whitelocke*, p. 242.

[45] Anthony Wood, *Athenae Oxonienses*, ed. Philip Bliss, 4 vols (1813–20), iv. (*Fasti*) 127–55. The rumper William Stephens was made a Doctor of Civil Law in 1650: OUA, Reg. Conv. T, pp. 131, 137.

[46] *CJ* 23 May 1649. Cf. 13 September 1649; below, p. 101, n. 59.

[47] Burrows, pp. 171, 173, 204, 263, 277, 299, 476; OUA, Reg. Conv. T, pp. 16, 83, 168, 242; Bloxam, *Reg. Magdalen*, iv. 211.

[48] *CSPD 1649–50*, pp. 59, 60, 69, 175, 248, 337, 431, 461–2 (cf. pp. 303–4); *1650*, pp. 82, 254; A. Clark, ed., *The Life and Times of Anthony Wood*, 5 vols, Oxford History Society (1891–1900: hereafter Wood, *Life and Times*), i. 152, 161; cf. *Mercurius Politicus* 21 November 1650, pp. 391–2.

[49] Wood, *History*, ii. 646–7; *CSPD 1649–50*, p. 232; *1650*, pp. 127–8, 187, 578; *1651*, pp. 295, 383, 408, 416.

[50] Charles II: *CSPD 1651*, pp. 365, 403–4; Penruddock: below, p. 133; Monck: O. Ogle et al., eds, *Calendar of the Clarendon State Papers*, 5 vols (Oxford, 1869–1970), iv. 534; Lambert: *HMC Popham*, p. 176; Ludlow, *Voyce*, p. 111; Ronald Hutton, *The Restoration* (Oxford, 1985), p. 116.

from Oxford's walls and buildings.[51] Yet royalist plotting in and around Oxford would persist into the protectorate, if on a reduced scale.[52] There were government soldiers in Oxford, or close at hand, all through the Interregnum.

At moments of crisis for the Puritan cause, the military presence was supplemented by recruitment from within the university itself. A volunteer troop was formed in preparation against Charles II's forces in 1651.[53] When Penruddock and his fellow royalists rose in 1655, colleges sent men and weapons for a troop raised against them.[54] Yet the chief motive of the volunteers was not a taste for Puritanism or Puritan rule. What prompted the majority of them were a concern for the protection or 'defence' or 'security' of the city and university, and the fear of a return to the havoc of the 1640s.[55] As the leading figure of the university's government under Cromwell observed of Oxford during the crisis of 1655, 'self-preservation helps on the publike interest'.[56] In September 1649 the same priority had inspired the university's gratitude for the 'special service' of the local troops in 'quieting' the 'tumultuous soldiers in the garrison' during the Leveller mutiny in Oxford, which had appeared to threaten a breakdown of order.[57] There was a similar scare in 1658, when the 'insolence of the Anabaptists in Oxon rang very high' and an uprising was feared. Scholars kept watch, and procured weapons, 'for their own safety'. They were grateful for the 'vigilancy' of the government troop which calmed the threat, but for which, on the occasions when it enforced Puritan policies, they could have much less friendly feelings.[58]

In the period between the regicide and Worcester, the weakness of the Visitation was intensified and exposed by vituperative quarrels between it and its masters at Westminster. Tensions which had been contained before 1649 broke out. The parliament, having in that year become the government, was determined to be obeyed. Westminster and the Visitation had conflicting understandings of the status of the parliamentary standing committee. It was given additional members

---

[51] Wood, *History*, ii. 648.

[52] Abbott, iii. 746; *Mercurius Politicus* 21 June 1655, p. 5419, 27 May 1658, pp. 543–4; *Perfect Proceedings of State-Affaires* 23 August 1655, final page; *A Perfect Account* 29 August 1655, p. 1932; *Certain Passages of Every Dayes Intelligence* 29 August 1655, p. 58; Bodl., Rawlinson MS a. 27, p. 753; David Underdown, *Royalist Conspiracy in England 1649–1660* (New Haven, 1960), pp. 242, 246, 257, 260, 298.

[53] Wood, *History*, ii. 647; Wood, *Life and Times*, i. 167; Burrows, p. 354; *CSPD 1651*, pp. 336–7, 404, 416; NA, 9655, p. 5; 988: 15 September 1651.

[54] ECA, MS A. II. 10: 20 March 1655; JCA, shelfmark 19, Bursars' Accounts 1651–9: 1655, 'For a pistol . . .', and 'To the college trooper'; Pembroke College Archives (hereafter PCA), MS 4/1/1, fo. 23; OUA, NW/3/4, fo. 139; Reg. Conv. T, pp. 271–2; V. H. H. Green, *The Commonwealth of Lincoln College* (Oxford, 1979), p. 257; Barbara Shapiro, *John Wilkins 1614–1672: An Intellectual Biography* (Berkeley and Los Angeles, 1969), p. 257; and see *TSP*, iv. 595. It looks as if Joseph Williamson of Queen's, who would shortly be taking royalist private pupils to France, was enlisted in the troop: see the badinage in *CSPD 1655*, pp. 162, 246, 312.

[55] OUA, Reg. Conv. T, p. 72; Wood, *History*, ii. 646, 647, 668 (cf. ii. 696; Wood, *Life and Times*, i. 155, 194–5, 280, 303).

[56] Toon, *Correspondence of John Owen*, p. 83.

[57] OUA, Reg. Conv. T, p. 72; WP/β/21(4), pp. 267, 276; Wood, *Life and Times*, i. 155; *CSPD 1649–50*, pp. 303–5.

[58] Wood, *History*, ii. 683–4; Wood, *Life and Times*, i. 259, 368–9; Wood, *Athenae Oxonienses*, iv. (*Fasti*) 129.

and fresh energy in May 1649, after the army leaders had seen the condition of the university for themselves. At the same time parliament added the army officers Adrian Scrope and the Governor of Oxford, Thomas Kelsey, to the Visitation.[59] In the previous year Kelsey's responses to parliamentary orders had provoked furious ripostes from Westminster, which had seen its commands 'neglected and disputed' by him, 'whose duty it is to obey' them.[60] He and Scrope, and the Visitors they joined, were soon at odds with the standing committee. Was that committee, as the Visitors claimed, a mere body of appeal, to which aggrieved victims of the Visitation might resort? Or were the Visitors, as the committee itself maintained, merely the instruments of parliament, which might reverse their orders and overrule their recommendations as it wished? The university's residents were bemused by conflicting orders from the two bodies. During the ensuing procedural chaos the Visitors complained of the 'scorne and contempt' to which the committee's actions had reduced them.[61] They lamented, apparently with justice, that ignorance or misunderstanding of the facts of local power and personality had led the MPs into foolish decisions and appointments which infringed the committee's own stated policies. For 'wee that are here resident in the universitye cannot but know the state and condition of the colledges, and fitnesse of persons to be elected, rather than any that live remote from the place'. In turn the committee accused the Visitors of having brought parliament's authority into 'contempt' by contesting the decisions of the superior body.[62] The feud added to the complications which limited the eviction of Oxford's royalists.[63]

It also brought confusion and inconsistency to the implementation of a central policy of the Visitors: one with which the committee agreed in principle, but on which it gave instructions that often contradicted those of the Visitation and that were often not communicated to it. There was nothing the body of the university wanted more than the restoration of self-government, particularly in elections to college and university posts. Amid the political and religious divisions of the post-war years, no one expected the immediate fulfilment of that aim, which would have been fatal to the authority of the Visitation. Nonetheless the Visitors cooperated when they could with heads and Fellows of colleges in the re-creation of order and in making appointments to posts. Once the chief opponents of the Visitation in a college had been removed, and a party of the Visitors' own nominations to posts had been built up there, the college was given a large measure of autonomy and in the main was left to follow the electoral procedures required by its own statutes, though the Visitors continued to vet candidates for the posts. Colleges which achieved that position were described as 'settled' (or 'reduced'). Some

---

[59] *CJ* 23 May 1649; *HMC Popham*, p. 19. A further appointment at the same time, Thomas Appletree of Oxfordshire, joined another Puritan of the county, William Draper, an original member of the Visitation, who succeeded Kelsey as Governor of Oxford. Appletree was a tenant of Christ Church: CA, D&C i. b. 3, p. 32.

[60] *CSPD 1648–9*, pp. 270–2.

[61] Burrows, p. 318.

[62] Ibid., p. 323.

[63] It can largely be followed in ibid.; see too OUA, Reg. Conv. T, p. 72.

colleges, to achieve 'settlement', volunteered to elect candidates whom they knew the Visitors would favour. Some of the more recalcitrant colleges were not 'settled' until after the expiry of the Visitation in 1652, but the process was far advanced by then. Had it not been for the quarrel with the standing committee, the process might have been methodical. Instead it was bedevilled by inconsistencies and uncertainties.

In the autumn of 1649 there appeared a new cloud over Oxford, which would persist until 1651. This was the imposition of the Rump's 'Engagement' of loyalty to the Commonwealth. It required those to whom it was tendered to 'declare and promise, that I will be true and faithful to the Commonwealth of England, as it is now established, without a king, or House of Lords'. On 12 October, when parliament ordered the Engagement to be taken by men in all branches of public or official life, its standing committee was called on to ensure that the heads and Fellows of colleges, and all 'graduates and officers', take the Engagement, and that no one who had failed to take it could proceed to a degree or bear any office in the university.[64] The order also applied to Cambridge, to the supervision of whose affairs the committee's brief had recently been extended.[65] In November Oxford's Visitors commanded the heads of the colleges to impose the test and report the results to them.[66] The university's resident members, having previously been summoned to their college halls to declare whether they would submit to the Visitors' authority, were now to be assembled there to subscribe the Engagement.

We do not know whether all the heads obeyed the Visitors' command. Hostile colleges were capable of quietly ignoring their orders.[67] Where we do know the directive of November 1649 to have been observed, the only intelligible explanation of what happened next is that, at least for the most part, only residents who were willing to take the test turned up; and that the absence of the remainder was connived at both by the heads and by at least some of the Visitors. In December the university's leaders embarked on a subtle and protracted campaign against the Engagement, which involved them in a series of journeys to London. They were anxious to play down the opposition to the pledge within the university. Even the royalist survivors among Oxford's leaders did not want to provoke retribution by ostentatious defiance of the kind which the Visitation had encountered in 1647–8. The last thing they now felt the university needed, as it struggled to reconstruct itself after the chaos of the previous decade, was a further depletion of its members. Though hatred of the republic lived on in the university, its outward expression was by now confined to clusters of often intemperate scholars, whose protests had become an embarrassment to higher-placed survivors of the royal cause and to the foremost

---

[64] *CJ* 11, 12 October 1649.
[65] Ibid., 4 May 1649; cf. 8 June 1649.
[66] Burrows, p. 274; Bodl., Wood MS f. 35, fo. 355; Wadham College Archives (hereafter WCA), MS 4/82–3.
[67] QCA, MS 2Y/25.

defenders of the university's independence. Oxford's leaders hoped to impress on the government the readiness of the university's members to allow Convocation to issue a collective statement of submission in place of individual subscriptions; or, if that were unacceptable, to take the Engagement individually but in some modified form. For while 'very many' in the university did 'out of principles purely conscientious scruple' the Engagement, and baulked at committing themselves to the acceptance of kingless rule, they were ready to promise to 'live quietly and peaceably under the present government and . . . submit to them in all lawful things'.[68]

Though that initiative failed, it must have carried hopes of success. In the same winter there were moves outside Oxford for an accommodation that would exempt 'godly well-meaning men' who 'scrupled at the Engagement' from taking it. The Rump itself debated a proposal to spare people who could give other evidence of their 'good affection to the public peace'.[69] Thomas Fairfax, lord general of the army, was exempted in February 1650 on the ground that he had taken a less stringent pledge of fidelity as a councillor of state a year earlier.[70] The imposition of the Engagement divided the republican government, and thus made Oxford the object of a competition of impulses which gave it scope to obstruct the test. Some MPs saw the pledge as a means of converting the nation to kingless rule. To others it was merely an instrument for keeping the regime's opponents quiet, as Oxford offered to be. There were evidently those at Westminster, where Sir John Trevor and Bulstrode Whitelocke, valued friends of the university in the late 1640s, had survived parliament's own purge of December 1648, who supported the university's position.

Parliament's standing committee, divided within itself, at least seems to have been united in its attitude to the Visitation. The Visitors had been entrusted with the bulk of the decisions that produced the evictions and replacements of the late 1640s, but now the committee resolved to keep for itself the parallel decisions about the Engagement.[71] The Visitors were merely to report to the committee the names of the takers and refusers of the test.[72] A series of ad hoc orders from London for the enforcement or fuller enforcement of the Engagement reached Oxford's colleges in January, February, and April 1650.[73] Though some refusers were marked down for ejection, the orders had only a narrow effect. Not until June did parliament issue a general order for action to be taken against Oxford's non-subscribers, and even then the wording of its instructions left it an open question whether the standing committee was obliged, or merely empowered, to have them evicted and appoint replacements. A more forceful order, though still not a quite unambiguous one, followed in August.[74] In the following month, when the victory at Dunbar boosted

[68] OUA, Reg. Conv. T, pp. 84, 86; Twells, *Pocock*, p. 130.
[69] Blair Worden, *The Rump Parliament 1648–1653* (Cambridge, repr. 1977), pp. 229–31.
[70] *CJ* 28 December 1649, 20 February 1650.
[71] Burrows, p. 318.
[72] Ibid., p. 268; Bodl., Wood MS f. 35, fo. 355.
[73] QCA, Register H, p. 118; Bodl., Wood MS f. 35, fo. 356; Twells, *Pocock*, pp. 129–30.
[74] *CJ* 21 June, 16 August 1649.

the position of the more radical party in parliament, a new determination to enforce the test becomes discernible among its members.[75] Oxford's ensuing crisis persisted through the autumn and into the following spring. The last eviction of which we have notice, at University College, was in May 1651.[76] Thereafter the Engagement seems no longer to have been pressed on Oxford. It would be repealed at the outset of the protectorate in 1654.

Despite grave predictions,[77] the impact of the Engagement on Oxford was much smaller than that of the Presbyterian purge of 1648. It may be that most of those to whom it was offered at some point between 1649 and 1651 took it, but evasion of the test seems to have been widespread.[78] The most conspicuous departures wrought by the Engagement were from among the Visitors themselves. A principal effect of the pledge on Oxford, and perhaps one purpose of its imposition there, was to end the Presbyterian majority on the Visitation. The Presbyterian Visitors issued only vague orders for the taking of the test.[79] 'The truth is,' observed a royalist, 'they would not subscribe themselves, and so neither would they require us.'[80] By February 1650 the standing committee had restricted responsibility for the imposition of the test to those Visitors 'that have taken the Engagement'. Only the Independent members of the commission had done so. It was they who 'went from college to college' to press the test, and ordered the colleges to provide rolls of parchment with lists of their members, who were to sign alongside them.[81] There are two Presbyterian Visitors, Edward Reynolds, the university's Vice-Chancellor, and John Mills, who left Oxford and whose departure we can directly attribute to their refusal of the Engagement. Both were at Christ Church, the college where most of the other recorded evictions caused by the Engagement also occurred. Christ Church had been the house on which the Visitation had initially concentrated in 1647,[82] and was the one which most concerned the parliamentary authorities now. On both occasions it was those members of the college who were Canons of the Cathedral who bore the brunt. The demand for subscription at Christ Church lasted for seventeen months, from November 1649,[83] when other colleges were being mildly or circumspectly treated, until the college had been taken over by Independents in March 1651.[84]

There were good reasons for the government's concern to secure the submission of Christ Church. Contumacy, disorder, ostentatious swearing, and the drinking of

[75] QCA, MS 2Y/21 (cf. 2Y/32); Brasenose College Archives (hereafter BNCA), MS A. I. 12, fo. 74ᵛ.
[76] University College Archives (hereafter UCA), College Register 1509–1727, fo. 30.
[77] Twells, *Pocock*, pp. 130–2; Cary, *Memorials of the Great Civil War*, ii. 240.
[78] See the conflicting assessments of the extent of subscription in Whitelocke, *Memorials*, iii. 153; Wood, *History*, ii. 629–30 (see also Wood, *Life and Times*, i. 394); HMC *De Lisle and Dudley*, vi. 472.
[79] QCA, Register H, p. 117.
[80] Bodl., Wood MS f. 35, fo. 355.
[81] QCA, Register H, p. 118; Wood, *History*, ii. 629.
[82] Reinhart, 'Parliamentary Visitation', pp. 327, 339.
[83] Twells, *Pocock*, p. i. 128.
[84] Burrows, p. 329. Henry Stubbe, who as an undergraduate at Christ Church was not required to take the test, later claimed to have 'got' Reynolds 'to be turned out', but to have secured the survival of 'Cavaliers' in the college: unlikely boasts. James R. Jacob, *Henry Stubbe, Radical Protestantism and the Early Enlightenment* (Cambridge, 1983), p. 9.

healths persisted there.[85] Even after the evictions for refusing the Engagement, the college would remain a magnet for political defiance. In June 1651 there appeared a posthumous collection, published by the royalist bookseller Humphrey Moseley, of plays and poems by William Cartwright, a Christ Church man who had resided in royalist Oxford and been Proctor in 1643, the year of his death. By indirect wording the volume implies that the university had at that time been 'most learned' and 'most flourishing', but that its spirits and standards had drooped under 'the late Visitours'.[86] The volume has prefatory verses by royalist poets and polemicists which are full of covert but transparent royalist and Anglican shafts. A number of them were written by Christ Church men, and the volume has a Christ Church flavour. In the following year a sermon which Cartwright had preached at Christ Church was published, with a prefatory sigh for the time when England was 'governed by kings'.[87] Expressions of the college's royalism were not confined to literature. In September 1651 one of the college's senior members ('Students') was expelled after joining the king's army at Worcester.[88]

Reynolds, the Dean of Christ Church, and Mills, a Canon, seem to have withdrawn from the government of the college, or to have been removed from it, at some point during the summer of 1650.[89] Reynolds's unwillingness to subscribe was known from December 1649 and prompted the inception of the university's resistance to the test in that month.[90] There were strenuous and protracted efforts, inside and outside the university, to save him.[91] The prominent MP John Crewe (or Crew), who had been imprisoned by the army at Pride's Purge but who represented a strand of moderate Independent opinion that Cromwell was eager to reconcile, used 'earnest and solicitous endeavors' on Reynolds's behalf.[92] Another Canon of Christ Church who declined the Engagement, Edward Pocock (or Pococke), whom the Visitors had made Professor of Hebrew, was deprived of his canonry in April of the same year. Shy of controversy, he was nonetheless resolutely Anglican and royalist in his convictions. It looks as if he, like others, would have accepted a modified version of the Engagement, but he held out against the test itself, which would 'molest the peace of my conscience'.[93] In October the standing committee ordered that he be expelled from his other posts at Oxford. After two months of agitated discussion, a petition from the university succeeded in getting the order suspended, and Pocock was able to move to accommodation in Balliol.[94] Simon Ford, a Christ Church tutor whom Reynolds had recruited from Magdalen Hall, would remember having been 'cast out' after preaching in St Mary's, the

---

[85] CA, D&C i. b. 3, pp. 10, 16, 25; Burrows, pp. 304–5, 307, 319.
[86] *Comedies, Tragi-Comedies, with other Poems by Mr William Cartwright* (1651), title-page and preface. I have profited from discussions of this book with Nicola Whitehead.
[87] William Cartwright, *An Off-Spring of Mercy* (1652).
[88] Varley, 'Restoration Visitation', p. 36; cf. below, p. 176.
[89] Twells, *Pocock*, pp. 24–30; cf. OUA, Reg. Conv. T, p. 112. See too CA, D&C i. b. 3, pp. 61, 82.
[90] Wood, *History*, ii. 628–9; Twells, *Pocock*, pp. 128–9.
[91] *CJ* 14 March 1651; Ludlow, *Voyce*, p. 95; Bodl., J. Walker MS c. 8, fo. 217ᵛ; Burrows, p. xxxvii.
[92] Edward Reynolds, *Death's Advantage* (1657), ep. ded.
[93] Twells, *Pocock*, pp. 134–5.
[94] Ibid., pp. 128–41.

university church, 'against the republican Engagement'.[95] The Visitor Henry Wilkinson senior, another Canon of Christ Church, seems to have initially refused to subscribe, and to have been deprived accordingly, but to have been restored after changing his mind.[96] He did, however, long absent himself from meetings of the Visitation after the Engagement reached Oxford. He would never regain his earlier prominence on it. Wilkinson's ardent ally on the Visitation, Francis Cheynell, led a delegation from the university to carry its official response to the Engagement to Westminster.[97] He either signed the test or was allowed to evade it. He had strong supporters both on the parliamentary committee and in Oxford, where he had remained an active figure after the regicide. He did resign from St John's in September 1650, but only in order to relieve his penury by moving to a living in Sussex (a position which likewise either required him or should have required him to take the Engagement).[98] In January 1652 the parliamentary committee ordered that his tenure of the divinity professorship be prolonged for a few months, after which he resigned it.[99]

Aside from the deprived Visitors, we have evidence of only a handful of Oxford's residents being removed by the Engagement.[100] Though there were evidently voluntary resignations—we cannot say how many—by men who feared to be confronted by the test,[101] it scarcely reduced the Presbyterian majority among the Puritans who had come to occupy the leading positions in the university and the colleges. Even the removal of leading Presbyterians from the Visitation did not improve the body's relations with the parliamentary committee that supervised it. On the contrary the quarrel intensified after their departure. It turned less on issues of general policy, over which there were vacillations and divisions on both sides, than on assertions of power. In essence it became a contest, which had parallels in other spheres of the Rump's administration, between parliament on the one hand and, on the other, the soldiers and local officials on whose cooperation the regime was precariously dependent.

By the time of its termination in 1652, the Visitation, for all its difficulties, had finally worn down Oxford's royalism. It had replaced most of the heads of colleges, most of the Professors and Readers, and perhaps as many as two hundred Fellows. It had also appointed a small army of scholars to other posts, from whom would be drawn the majority of the Fellows elected over the remainder of

---

[95] Bodl., Wood MS f. 41, fo. 236ᵛ; Vallance, *Revolutionary England and the National Covenant*, p. 172.

[96] 'Illustrations of the State of the Church', *Theologian and Ecclesiastic*, vi. (1848), p. 221.

[97] OUA, WP/β/21(4), p. 267.

[98] OUA, Reg. Conv. T, p. 130.

[99] St John's College Muniments, Register III, pp. 426–31; Burrows, pp. 248–9; OUA, NEP/E/14 (5); Reg. Conv. T, pp. 97, 101, 165; Corpus Christi College Archives (hereafter CCCA), MS B/1/3/2, fo. 15ᵛ; Varley, 'Restoration Visitation', p. 2. If he did refuse the Engagement, he may have survived a narrow squeak in March 1651: OUA, Reg. Conv. T, p. 130 (cf. p. 138).

[100] Reinhart, 'Parliamentary Visitation', pp. 452–3; BNCA, MS A. I. 2, fo. 74ᵛ; QCA, MS 2Y/21; UCA, College Register 1509–1727, fo. 30; Vallance, *Revolutionary England and the National Covenant*, p. 172; see too Burrows, p. 475.

[101] Burrows, pp. lxxxvii, 130n.

the 1650s. The colleges of Cromwellian Oxford were essentially controlled by men whom the Visitors had intruded or vetted. The Visitation had laid the foundations on which the godly university of the Puritan imagination could be built. Never in the history of Oxford has more power been held by its would-be reformers.

Yet there were limits to that power, as events would show: limits imposed partly by the resilience of the institution; partly by the problems of translating Puritan ideas into practice; but partly too by the boundaries which had circumscribed the Visitors' achievement. The failures of Cromwellian rule in Oxford were to be as closely related as its successes to the legacy of a Visitation which had secured outward conformity to the Puritan occupation but had engendered small support for it. In general—though there were significant exceptions—those of the Visitors' appointments who had least experience of the university were those who lasted least long in it and made least impact on it. Despite the import of a number of many young men from Cambridge (a high proportion of them from Emmanuel and Queens' Colleges[102]), the majority of the Fellows introduced by the Visitors were Oxford men with Oxford loyalties. Their principal interests lay less in national politics or in Puritan reform than in their studies and careers—and in those endemic animosities of college life whose scope had been notably enlarged by the war and by the Visitation. Energy was absorbed by the 'many questions and differences about seniority' which were created by the Visitatorial intrusions, and which raised issues 'of profitt and precedencie'.[103] It was not only the rank and file of the newcomers whose appetite for reform was uncertain. Among Oxford's new leaders there arrived, alongside the eager initiators of reform, skilful politicians of more conservative outlook. The basic political divisions of the Oxford of Cromwell's Chancellorship would primarily arise not between the fresh appointments and those opponents of the Visitatorial purge who had survived it, but among the fresh appointments themselves.

Oliver Cromwell, a commoner, a regicide, and a Cambridge man, was an unconventional choice as Chancellor, made in unconventional times. His election in January 1651, when he was leading the parliamentary army in Scotland, occurred during a critical phase of the contest over the imposition of the Engagement at Oxford, and at a time of sharp dispute between the Visitation and the parliamentary committee. A year had passed since the Earl of Pembroke's death, which occurred at a low point in the fortunes and morale of the new republic.[104] The government, whose leaders knew the depth of anti-Puritan and anti-republican sentiment in Oxford, was troubled by the prospect of the university electing a

---

[102] Names and colleges of arrivals from Cambridge can be traced in J. and J. A. Venn, *Alumni Cantabrigienses*, 4 vols (Cambridge, 1922–7). For the incorporation of Cambridge men see OUA, Reg. Conv. T, p. 140. Cambridge had itself received an influx of students from Oxford during Laud's Chancellorship: J. B. Mullinger, *The University of Cambridge*, 3 vols (Cambridge 1873–1911), iii. 368.

[103] Burrows, p. 279; CA, D&C i. b. 3, p. 4; Varley, 'Restoration Visitation', p. 20. Such disputes were pervasive.

[104] Worden, *Rump Parliament*, pp. 224–5.

successor. On learning of the earl's death the standing committee, at a meeting at which it issued a demand for the enforcement of the Engagement in Oxford, also forbade the university to proceed to the choice of a successor, and appropriated the task to itself.[105] In August 1650 the committee likewise took over, for the length of the vacancy, the power of the Chancellor to make the appointment, an annual one, to Oxford's Vice-Chancellorship.[106] But the MPs knew how strongly the university's members wanted to be 'left to a free election of their own officers',[107] as its local statutes and customs required. On the principle which it also deployed in its dealings with the Visitors over collegiate elections, Oxford was ready to assure the government of its readiness to choose a Chancellor whose election would 'be to the abundant satisfaction of the state'.[108] After meeting a delegation from the university on 5 December, the standing committee resolved on the 26th that Oxford's members should be 'left to their free choice . . . as formerly'. Six days later, on 1 January, Cromwell was elected.[109] A delegation from the university travelled to Scotland to convey the instruments of office.[110]

He had acquired the Chancellorship only after a struggle on his behalf. In February 1650, less than a month after the order forbidding the university from making an election had been issued, there began moves, inside and outside Oxford, to circumvent it. A candidate was needed who would command the university's support and whom the regime would be ready to endorse. We know of the ensuing competition only from one of the unsuccessful candidates, the MP Bulstrode Whitelocke, and glimpse it only through his eyes.[111] His efforts to restrict the impact of the Visitation of the university would have been known and appreciated there.[112] A shameless networker, he had a joint social operator in Lambert Osbaldston, a former Headmaster of Westminster School who had suffered severe punishment for making criticisms of Archbishop Laud. Osbaldston had aided Whitelocke and Selden in their contests with the Visitors.[113] His own social contacts included the Countess of Nottingham, whose brother, a member of the university, told Whitelocke 'of good hopes of successe' in the election, '& that many of the schollars much desired it, & by the interest of him and & friends it was much furthered'. Unfortunately for Whitelocke, bigger beasts entered the field. 'After a little time',

---

[105] OUA, Reg. Conv. T, p. 120; QCA, Register H, p. 118.

[106] OUA, Reg. Conv. T, p. 118.

[107] Ibid., p. 105.

[108] OUA, WP/γ/2/1(i).

[109] OUA, Reg. Conv. T, pp. 118, 120; WP/γ/22/le.

[110] OUA, WP/β/21(4), p. 275.

[111] His account is in Spalding, *Diary of Bulstrode Whitelocke*, p. 254.

[112] Cf. OUA, Reg. Conv. T, pp. 252–3; below, p. 140. Much of his legal career had been based on the city of Oxford, where he had established a number of contacts and become Recorder and High Steward, though he found that the extent of his connections with the city, that permanent semi-adversary of the university, was counted an 'objection' to his candidacy. His son James, so young a Fellow of All Souls, was soon made colonel of the Oxford militia, though his service in it was interrupted when he was sent on Cromwell's expedition to Ireland, where he joined the general's lifeguard: *CSPD 1650*, pp. 36, 54, 105, 507; *1651*, p. 516; Whitelocke, *Memorials*, iii. 342; Spalding, *Diary of Bulstrode Whitelocke*, pp. 242–4.

[113] OUA, SP/E/5, fo. 48.

he records, he 'found that there were strong canvasses in the university, by one party for the lord president Bradshaw', who had presided over the trial of Charles I and become president of the republic's council of state, 'and by a stronger party for the lord generall [Cromwell] to be Chancellor'. Bradshaw can have won few friends in Oxford when in 1647 he had acted as counsel for parliament against the university's refutation of the legality of the Visitation. Whitelocke was assured that he himself might defeat not only Bradshaw but Cromwell too. Perhaps he would have done had Oxford's residents been free from external pressure. As it was, he had little chance. He decided 'not to stand in competition for it with either of these two great men'.

The government, anxious to present a united front to the nation, would have been loath to allow an open competition between Bradshaw and Cromwell. The contest was resolved, though we do not know how or where, behind the scenes— unless Bradshaw was the (unidentifiable) candidate for whom a single (unidentifiable) member of Convocation apparently cast a vote, in preference to Cromwell, at the election on 1 January.[114] It is likely that the rivalry for the post between Bradshaw and Cromwell had been hard-fought. In January 1649 the two men cooperated effectively, Cromwell mobilizing the trial of the king, Bradshaw steering it through. Since then, relations between them had been unhappy. In the winter of 1650–1, the time of his contest with Bradshaw over the Chancellorship, Cromwell wanted him removed from the presidency of the council of state, a goal the lord general eventually achieved nearly a year later.[115]

The conflict represented a divide at the heart of the regime, in which one party, with the lord president behind it, advocated confrontational politics, while the other, with the lord general behind it, sought conciliatory ones. The first group rejoiced in the memory of Pride's Purge and the regicide; clung to the principles which those deeds had represented; and demanded the conformity of the nation to them. The second wanted the government to put its revolutionary origins behind it. It sought the return to Westminster, and to local government, of men who had been alienated by the coup of 1648–9. The division between those viewpoints had been contained until the battle of Dunbar in September 1650, while the new government was struggling for its survival. Dunbar reduced the royalist threat sufficiently to allow the tensions within the government to emerge openly and to embolden the more radical spirits at Whitehall and Westminster. Bradshaw, himself a man with a taste for learning, attracted the friendship and devotion of two learned writers for the republic, John Milton and Marchamont Nedham. The prose of both men favoured his outlook.[116] Nedham's newsbook *Mercurius Politicus*, founded in June 1650, was its mouthpiece. In the aftermath of Dunbar, Bradshaw's allies won a series of victories in parliament. They got the statue of

---

[114] Ibid., SP/E/4, fo. 92; Reg. Conv. T, pp. 118, 120. The imputation that there was a dissenter was conceivably a slip of the pen, which produced the words 'but one' instead of 'not one'.

[115] Worden, *Rump Parliament*, p. 249.

[116] *LP*, chs 8–10; see too Edward Bagshaw, *A Practicall Discourse concerning God's Decrees* (1659), ep. ded. (to Bradshaw).

Charles I in the Old Exchange in London removed. In its place there were inscribed, in golden letters in the vacant niche, words proclaiming the demise of the tyrant and last of kings. 'These', observed Nedham's *Politicus*, 'are characters not to be blotted out by all the art under heaven.'[117] Bradshaw's party also persuaded the Commons to register its formal approval of the king's execution; to express its gratitude to the king's judges; and to give official commemoration to the second anniversary of the regicide on 30 January 1651. On that day bonfires, which had been a token of royalist sentiment in Oxford in 1648, were lit in colleges in Cambridge in 'thanksgiving' for the king's execution.[118] There had recently been serious royalist conspiracy in the region, which Bradshaw and his allies had been instrumental in uncovering. They secured the execution of some of the conspirators, in the face of moves for leniency by rival parties. It was *Politicus* that announced, at the start of January 1651, that some of 'the principal contrivers are obscured in some of the colledges'.[119]

Those political victories were bound to please what Nedham approvingly called the Commonwealth's 'party of its own throughout the nation'.[120] There must be no place, he urged, for 'lukewarm' or 'neutral' men in power, let alone for Presbyterians, whom he detested. The regicide, 'that heroick and most noble act of justice', was 'the basis whereupon the Commonwealth is founded. And if it ever be completed it must be by honouring and intrusting those noble instruments and hands, who laid the foundation, or now help with open hearts to carry on the building.'[121] Nedham knew how beleaguered the 'party of its own' was in the localities. There were active militia commissioners in Oxfordshire, with troops at their call, but support for them among the county's leaders and clergy was narrow, a deficiency which spurred Whitehall to have the Engagement enforced in the region.[122] In August 1650 *Politicus* printed a letter from Oxford 'touching the odd-affected university governors', and asking whether even the thorough imposition of the Engagement would be enough to secure the institution's compliance.[123] Three months later the newsbook published another letter, this one written from within 'the county of Oxon' to a Fellow of Oriel College, complaining that 'the whole work of carrying on the parliament's interest' in the local countryside lay on no more than four or five 'worthy instruments', who suffered 'base usage and contempt' as they contended with 'some malignant timorous justices, together with a sordid crue of priests (the like in no county for malignancy, disaffection, superstition, and ignorance . . .)'. The same spirit, reported the letter, was at work 'in the university'. The letter attacked a prominent figure among Oxford's

---

[117] *Mercurius Politicus* 22 October 1650, p. 162.

[118] John Twigg, *The University of Cambridge and the English Revolution, 1625–1688* (Woodbridge, 1990), p. 163.

[119] Nickolls, p. 39; *Mercurius Politicus* 2 January 1651, p. 491.

[120] Marchamont Nedham, *The Case of the Commonwealth of England, Stated*, ed. P. A. Knachel (Charlotesville, VA, 1969), p. 114.

[121] *Mercurius Politicus* 15 May 1651, p. 783.

[122] *CSPD 1649–50*, p. 431; *1650*, p. 430; *1651*, p. 126.

[123] *Mercurius Politicus* 8 August 1650, p. 144; cf. W. Jacobson, ed., *The Works of Robert Sanderson*, 6 vols (1854), v. 35.

Puritan leaders, the Presbyterian President of Corpus Christi College, Edmund Staunton. One of the Fellows of Staunton's college, Nedham's readers learned, had taken steps to prevent a sectary, a Captain Butler, from preaching in the neighbouring countryside.[124] Butler was one of the 'instruments' Nedham had in mind. The Rump looked to him to 'have a watchful eye' on the 'conflux of disaffected persons', and to help 'break them up'.[125]

In choosing Cromwell as Chancellor, Oxford's leaders were wise in their generation. Despite his absence in Scotland, and his earlier one in Ireland, he had had plenty of opportunity since the regicide to signal his attitude to the universities. He needed to, for there were misapprehensions which he was anxious to dispel. The brisk military methods by which he had thwarted the royalists in Cambridge in 1642 had not been forgotten. In the month following the regicide, the Anglican divine William Sancroft, Bursar of Emmanuel College Cambridge, and in later life Archbishop of Canterbury, wrote to his father from Cambridge: 'The universities we give up for lost; and the story you have in the country, of Cromwell's coming amongst us, will not long be a fable.'[126] That Cromwell in reality had no hostile intent was shown in May 1649, during the visit of the army leaders to Oxford after the Leveller defeat at Burford, when he and Fairfax stayed at All Souls, accepted their degrees in scarlet gowns, and were sumptuously feasted. The occasion indicates the prominence of the university in the army leaders' thinking. Fairfax had manifested his own esteem for scholarship on the fall of Oxford in 1646, when he ensured the protection of the Bodleian Library, of which he would himself be a munificent patron, from military depredation.[127] Now Cromwell in turn emphasized the commitment of the government to learning, without which 'no commonweal could flourish', and hinted that the regime would find new income for it.[128] He also indicated his political and ecclesiastical ecumenicalism by listening to sermons by two of Oxford's Presbyterian ministers.[129]

[124] *Mercurius Politicus* 21 November 1650, pp. 391–2. Staunton was himself one of the Oxford divines who preached in the county: Richard Mayo, *The Life and Death of Edmund Staunton* (1673), pp. 6–7, 38.

[125] *CSPD 1649*, p. 69. The same Captain Butler may have been one of the most determined and uncompromising members of the Commonwealth's 'party of its own' in the county; he may have had a particular interest in the reform of the university; and he may have had exalted contacts. It depends whether or how often the 'Butler' who appears in the evidence which prompts those suggestions is the man to whom *Politicus* refers: *CJ* 30 September 1648, 6, 15 April 1649, 28 June 1650, 9 August 1659; *TSP*, iv. 595; *CSPD 1651*, pp. 161, 180, 526; see too *1652–3*, p. 470. Nedham's 'Butler' could be the 'Captain Butler' who advanced a radical argument for liberty of conscience at the Whitehall debates in January 1649: cf. Firth, *Clarke Papers*, ii. 173, 272 with Christopher Durston, *Cromwell's Major-Generals* (Manchester, 2001), p. 46.

[126] Cary, *Memorials of the Great Civil War*, ii. 118; Twigg, *University of Cambridge*, pp. 153–6.

[127] John Aubrey, *Brief Lives*, ed. Andrew Clark, 2 vols (1898), i. 250–1. For Fairfax and the university see too Burrows, pp. lv, 210, 216, 220, 221, 224, 244, 264; OUA, Reg. Conv. Sb, pp. 128, 131; Reg. Conv. T, p. 55; *An Account given to the Parliament by the Ministers sent by them to Oxford* (1647), p. 52; CA, D&C i. b. 3, p. 55; Reinhart, 'Parliamentary Visitation', pp. 255–6, 296; Roy and Reinhart, 'Civil Wars', p. 723n.

[128] Abbott, ii. 73.

[129] Bodl., Wood MS f. 35, fos 341–2; Wood, *History*, ii. 620. One of them was the President of Magdalen Hall, Henry Wilkinson Jr. What was probably his sermon on that occasion can be found (if so, slightly mis-dated) in his *Three Decads of Sermons* (1660), pt. i, pp. 163–87.

After the visit the leading officers proposed the establishment of a new divinity lectureship in the university.[130]

In August, Cromwell crossed to Ireland. During his campaign there he gave concrete illustration of his readiness to aid learning's cause. In March 1650 the Rump passed legislation, which bears the mark of his influence, for the 'propagation of the Gospel' in Ireland. It created new funds for Trinity College Dublin, and appointed trustees of whom most were associates of Cromwell.[131] One of them was John Owen, his chaplain in Ireland and then Scotland, who while in Ireland took part in the survey of Trinity College that was prompted by the Rump's measure.[132] He would become Cromwell's lieutenant in the reformation of Oxford. Another was Jonathan Goddard, a member of Wilkins's scientific circle, who would also belong to the Cromwellian party there.[133] By now Cromwell's 'respects to piety and learning', and his 'generous designs of promoting them in other places', were understood in Oxford.[134] In April 1650 a panic hit the university when Edward Pocock, the distinguished Regius Professor of Hebrew, lost his canonry for refusing the Engagement and was threatened with the loss of his professorship. The university sent an 'express' over to Cromwell 'to desire him to intercede for the university'. Fairfax voiced his own concern on behalf of Pocock.[135]

Cromwell returned to England at the end of May 1650. A month later he left for Scotland at the head of the invading army. On the way he stopped at Cambridge, where he met a number of the university's leaders. We have only one account of his visit, from Sancroft, but Sancroft had no reason to invent an episode which was hard to square with his own demonological image of Cromwell. While Bradshaw's party demanded the vigorous imposition of the Engagement on the nation, Cromwell resisted that policy.[136] According to Sancroft, Cromwell assured the university's leaders 'that there should be no further proceedings against non-subscribers'. The pledge would have incensed Bradshaw. Cromwell, adds Sancroft, also told the leaders 'that he had desired' parliament's standing committee for the universities 'to petition the house, in his name' that the members of Cambridge University 'might be no further urged'. The story is bound to have reached Oxford, where at that time a 'Cambridg paper', 'communicated to the [Oxford] Delegates by a freind', was being discussed as a basis for reforms in both universities that might satisfy the government and keep it at bay.[137]

---

[130] *CJ* 23 May 1649.
[131] T. C. Barnard, *Cromwellian Ireland* (Oxford, 1975), pp. 198–9; Firth and Rait, ii. 356.
[132] Peter Toon, *God's Statesman: The Life and Work of John Owen* (Exeter, 1971), pp. 39–40. Another was Bulstrode Whitelocke's son James.
[133] For Goddard and Seth Ward see Ward's *Ismaelis Bulliandi* (1653), ep. ded.
[134] OUA, Reg. Conv. T, p. 135; Bodl., Wood MS f. 35, fo. 341; Wood, *History*, ii. 667.
[135] Twells, *Pocock*, p. 131; cf. pp. 102–3. For glimpses of Pocock's role in the university under the protectorate see OUA, NW/3/4, fos 100, 147.
[136] The Earl of Leicester, misunderstanding a report from his son, Viscount Lisle, who was on the Rump's council of state, supposed that Cromwell himself had refused the Engagement (*HMC De Lisle and Dudley*, vi. 472.) Lisle had in fact been writing about Fairfax, but the earl's misconception is revealing.
[137] OUA, Reg. Conv. T, pp. 109, 112.

Sancroft viewed Cromwell's remarks with scepticism. He expected that the general would change his tune once the Scots were beaten and the republic was strong enough to crush its opponents in England.[138] He was wrong. It is true that in the late summer and autumn of 1650 the purge of Cambridge proceeded. The removals wrought by the Engagement there were more numerous than the corresponding evictions at Oxford, though much fewer than the exclusions previously effected at Cambridge by the Presbyterians.[139] Because Cambridge had been purged of royalism in the mid-1640s, parliament had thereafter treated it gently (though there too the removals had been inadequate in local Puritan eyes[140]). In September 1649, the month before the imposition of the Engagement, the Rump did resolve on the establishment of a commission to conduct a new Visitation there, and instructed its standing committee to appoint its members.[141] Perhaps it did appoint them, and perhaps it was the men appointed who in March 1651 were discussing the reform of Cambridge's statutes.[142] If so, no action seems to have followed. Nonetheless the Presbyterian domination of Cambridge, which had suited the majority that prevailed in parliament until Pride's Purge, was a difficulty for the republic. The principal opposition to the Engagement in the nation was voiced and sustained by Presbyterians, not least because the test contradicted, or was taken to contradict, the Solemn League and Covenant. Less trouble was given by royalists, who found it harder to get objections into print, and some of whom in any case seem to have convinced themselves that a pledge to a diabolical regime carried no obligation to the conscience.[143]

Both before and after the defeat of the Scots, Cromwell wanted the holding of power in Oxford and Cambridge, as he wanted it in Whitehall and Westminster, to be based as broadly as was compatible with his programme of godly reformation. He sought the reconciliation of men who had opposed or been dismayed by the events that had brought the republic to power, and whose distaste he was ready to overlook if they would now collaborate with the regime. It seems to have been about a fortnight after accepting the Chancellorship that he wrote to an (unidentifiable) ally in London about recent developments in Oxford, where pressure from Whitehall and Westminster for the effective imposition of the Engagement was mounting.[144] His letter named three leading figures who had refused the test, and who had now lost their posts in consequence: Edward Reynolds, the

---

[138] Cary, *Memorials of the Great Civil War*, ii. 224–5.

[139] Twigg, *University of Cambridge*, pp. 155–61; Vallance, *Revolutionary England and the National Covenant*, pp. 171–2; Mullinger, *University of Cambridge*, iii. 375 ff.

[140] *HMC* vi. 202, 204, 207.

[141] *CJ* 13 September 1649; cf. 8 June 1649.

[142] Mullinger, *University of Cambridge*, iii. 408.

[143] Worden, *Rump Parliament*, pp. 231–2; see too *CSPD 1650*, pp. 47, 89. Perhaps the influence in Oxford of Robert Sanderson, whose discussion of the Engagement gave his readers scope for taking it (Jacobson, *Works of Robert Sanderson*, v. 17–36), helped some royalists to comply. The zealously royalist Fellow of Queen's Thomas Barlow, a friend of Sanderson, commended his casuistical writings: Barlow, *De Studio Theologiae* (1699), pp. 41–2.

[144] Burrows, p. 329; *CSPD 1651*, p. 126; Cary, *Memorials of the Great Civil War*, ii. 240; UCA, College Register 1509–1727, fo. 30.

Vice-Chancellor and Dean of Christ Church; John Conant, the Rector of Exeter College; and the Warden of Wadham, John Wilkins. Cromwell wrote that they, and others in the same predicament, were 'usefull & godly and willinge to give satisfaction if meanes could be used to keepe them in'.[145] Belatedly Reynolds did take the Engagement, but in a revised form of words (perhaps similar to ones which had been proposed by the university as a compromise) which diluted its meaning, and which the Rump declined to accept.[146] Conant, son-in-law to Reynolds, made a similar proposal on his own behalf, offering to subscribe with 'limitations and restrictions'.[147] Wilkins, who was prominent in the attempts to persuade parliament to modify or rescind the imposition of the Engagement on Oxford, did not take it himself.[148] He was no revolutionary. Whereas Owen exultantly proclaimed to the Commons, three months after the regicide, the current 'shaking and translating of heaven and earth',[149] Wilkins produced a treatise in the same year which he offered to the public as 'very seasonable to quiet and support the heart in these times of publick confusion'.[150] Yet he and Conant survived the imposition of the Engagement, and would become key supporters of Cromwell in Oxford. Though Reynolds had been one of the three ministers nominated by the army leaders in May 1649 for the delivery of divinity lectures in Oxford,[151] Cromwell did not succeed in saving him from the Engagement. He may in any case have doubted whether that emollient scholar possessed the political drive or acumen either to bring Christ Church to order or, as Vice-Chancellor, to effect the reforms in the university for which Cromwell hoped. He would certainly have questioned whether Reynolds, irenic though his temperament was, could be brought to accept Cromwell's programme of liberty of conscience.[152]

Or perhaps Cromwell simply wanted his own man in both posts: the man who acquired the Deanery in 1651 and the Vice-Chancellorship in 1652, the Independent divine John Owen. The standing committee offered the Deanery not to Owen but to another Independent minister, Joseph Caryl, who with Reynolds and Thomas Goodwin had been nominated by the army for the proposed divinity lectureship in 1649. Having pleaded in vain for Reynolds's reinstatement at Christ Church, Caryl accepted the post. There was then a delay, perhaps caused by Reynolds's offer of a modified subscription, or perhaps as a result of one more wrangle between the confronters and conciliators in the government. Caryl eventually decided to stay with his London congregation. In his place parliament appointed Owen, 'a person very powerful with the great ones'. His nomination divided the Commons, where it was opposed by Presbyterians but passed with the support of Cromwell's ally Sir Henry Vane. In the previous month, even though

---

[145] Abbott, iv. 947.
[146] *CJ* 14 March 1651; Ludlow, *Voyce*, p. 95.
[147] John Prince, *The Worthies of Devon* (1810), pp. 232–3.
[148] Twells, *Pocock*, pp. 136–7; *CJ* 17 August 1659.
[149] John Owen, *The Shaking and Translating of Heaven and Earth* (1649).
[150] John Wilkins, *A Discourse concerning the Beauty of Providence* (1649), title-page.
[151] *CJ* 23 May 1649; Burrows, p. 264.
[152] Cf. *CJ* 5 March 1660.

Owen had then held no post in Oxford, it was to him that Cromwell looked to work with Vane to preserve godly non-subscribers there.[153]

In his letter accepting the Chancellorship, Cromwell made two points. First, he had a lot else on his plate, and could not expect to give Oxford sustained attention. Secondly he voiced the hope 'that that seed and stock of piety and learning, so marvellously sprung up amongst you, may be useful to that great and glorious kingdom of the Lord Jesus Christ; of the approach of which so plentiful an effusion of the spirit upon those hopeful plants is one of the best presages'.[154] As Chancellor he never saw the university. After his return to Westminster in September 1651 that most sedentary of England's rulers, who had earlier marched across three kingdoms, never travelled as far from London as Oxford. His commitment to the reform of the university was consistent and determined. Yet he left the ordinary management of the institution to his agents there. He thus brought to his rule that air of slightly distant benevolence which Oxford welcomed in its Chancellors, and from which the Earl of Pembroke's role in the enforcement of the Visitation had been an offensive departure.

As lord protector, Cromwell presented some manuscripts to the Bodleian and made a financial contribution to the study of theology in Oxford. According to Anthony Wood, 'by these and other favours the university in general was devoted to' Cromwell, 'and ready upon all opportunities to express their affections'.[155] Wood's explanation is questionable, for Cromwell's financial generosity was of a kind conventionally expected of Chancellors. It was on a limited scale, and payment seems anyway to have been either discontinued or irregular.[156] If there was 'devotion to' him in Oxford, it is at least as likely to have had two other causes. One is his defence of it from figures bent on a more radical transformation of the university. The other is his readiness, which will have surprised and relieved anyone in Oxford who shared the view of his character held by Sancroft at Cambridge, to set limits to his interference in its affairs.

The limits were loose. His hand can be seen in critical appointments to leading positions in the university, as we shall find. He also took advantage of the opportunities customarily brought by the post to place men in lesser university or college posts. He procured the award of degrees and obtained dispensations from the full residence requirements for them. Degrees and dispensations were bestowed on friends or supporters or potential supporters; or on people whose course of education had been disrupted by the wars; or (a time-honoured category of dispensation) on men who were now on state service; or on Puritans who had undergone 'sufferings for . . . religion'.[157] His patronage was characteristically

---

[153] *CJ* 14 March 1651; Abbott, iv. 947; 'Illustrations of the State of the Church', vi. 221, 222. The divines Stephen Marshall and Philip Nye may also have been candidates: 'Illustrations', vi. 218.
[154] Ibid., ii. 392.
[155] Ibid., iii. 427; OUA, SP/E/4, fo. 100ᵛ; Bodl., Bodleian MS Add. d. 105, p. 8; Wood, *History*, ii. 667.
[156] *CSPD 1658–9*, p. 24; OUA, SP/E/4, fo. 100ᵛ; Bodl., Bodleian MS Add. 105, p. 8.
[157] Abbott, iv. 124–5.

eclectic.[158] Favours were extended to sectaries at one extreme and to members of royalist families at the other. In general, however, his resolve to be 'tender' and 'very sparing' in his requests, and to avoid the setting of 'precedents',[159] was upheld. He interposed no more than the parliament had done in the years before his election, or indeed than Fairfax had done while lord general of the army. The bulk of Cromwell's favours were bestowed in the year or so following his return to Westminster politics in September 1651, before, perhaps, he had grasped the complexities and delicacies of the job, to which a series of disputes arising from the memories and administrative disorder of wartime seems to have alerted him. In November 1651 he got the Visitation to appoint a Scotsman to a Fellowship at Queen's, only for the initiative to become entwined both with the quarrels between the Visitors and the standing committee and with political and financial problems within the college. It had to be cancelled.[160] In July 1652, when asked to sort out problems arising from the installation of parliamentarians in Fellowships of New College, he admitted to being 'altogether a strainger' to the college's rules, and breezily told the Commonwealth's supporters there to do what they judged 'fitt or convenient' to resolve the matter.[161] The Puritan rule of Oxford, which had arisen from civil havoc, retained more than its share of procedural abnormality.[162] Also in 1652, the Fellows of University College, being 'especially moved by a letter of recommendation' from Cromwell, elected to a Fellowship, in an 'irregularly pre-cipitated' vote, a young man who seems to have been an undergraduate in his first year, and who had convinced Cromwell of 'severall untruths'. That nomination, too, had to be unscrambled.[163] Thereafter Cromwell's interventions in appoint-ments, though they could be significant, were only occasional.[164] Neither Oxford nor Cambridge seems to have received anything like as many mandates for appointments from the protector as under the Tudor and Stuart monarchy.[165]

[158] It can be traced in ibid., ii. 394, 521, 532–3, 552, 554, 563, 565–6, 566, 582, 599, 601, iii. 110, 242, iv. 111, 124–5, 817; OUA, Reg. Conv. T, pp. 56, 159, 160, 161, 163, 176 (cf. Leland, *De Rebus Britannicis*, v. 288–9), 177–8, 224, 231, 241, 242–3, 304; CA, D&C i. b. 3, pp. 55, 59; D&C ii. c. 1, nos 50, 66; QCA, Register H, pp. 138, 140; NA, 9655, p. 51; MS 988: 2 January 1655; UCA, College Register 1509–1727: 1 September 1654 (cf. *CSPD 1654*, p. 294; OUA, Reg. Conv. T, p. 304); *CSPD 1654*, p. 259; W. D. Macray, *A Register of . . . Magdalen College*, new series, 8 vols (1894–1911: hereafter Macray, *Reg. Magdalen*), iv. 57, 58, 90; Wood, *Athenae Oxonienses*, iv. (*Fasti*) 185; Burrows, pp. 361 (cf. p. 365), 399; A. G. Matthews, *Calamy Revised* (Oxford, 1934), p. 397; below, pp. 117, 154, 175, 178–9, 187; Ludlow, *Voyce*, p. 86; and see Wood, *Life and Times*, i. 287. Cf. BNCA, MS A. VIII. 12: 23 July, 8 August 1653; MS B. I. d. 36: 16 July 1658.
[159] OUA, Reg. Conv. T, pp. 160, 176.
[160] QCA, Register H, pp. 136–41.
[161] NA, 9655, p. 5.
[162] Cf. Richard Ollard, *Clarendon and his Friends* (1987), p. 264.
[163] UCA, College Register 1509–1727: 3 November 1652.
[164] His appointment in October 1652 of delegates to carry out mundane functions of the Chancellorship (below, pp. 119–20) released him from the granting of dispensations proposed by the university.
[165] For Cambridge see Twigg, *University of Cambridge*, pp. 174–7. Richard Cromwell, Oliver's successor as Chancellor, may have been less reticent: Toon, *Correspondence of John Owen*, pp. 74–5; or Bodl., Tanner MS 69, fo. 182 (cf. below, pp. 185, 188 n. 668).

Until the end of 1653, when he was by far the most powerful person in England and yet, in terms of constitutional authority, was merely one among about two hundred members of the ruling parliament, Cromwell was ideally suited to the role, which Oxford had traditionally wanted from its Chancellors, of intermediary between government and university.[166] Once he became protector, that advantage was lost. If he was looked to as a mediator now, it was in the hope that he could be prevailed on to restrain his government's agents in Oxford. Yet the aims and tenor of his Chancellorship did not change. Oxford's 'seed and stock of piety and learning', and its potential contribution to the Puritanizing of England, were his abiding concern. Absent from Oxford himself, he needed a party there to do his work. As Chancellor he had been quick to create one.

The government of Oxford, as of England, was transformed by Cromwell's return to Westminster and Whitehall in September 1651. Previously he, like the parliament, had had to subordinate all other goals to the survival of the republic. Now his underlying aim emerged. He sought to combine reform with reconciliation. Ideally institutions were to be pressured, rather than coerced, into self-amendment. He wanted their essential structures to survive and be respected. His chief parliamentary ally in the pursuit of consensus,[167] his cousin Oliver St John, became Chancellor of Cambridge in November 1651, after the previous incumbent, the Earl of Manchester, who had conducted the purge of that university in the 1640s and been appointed to the office after the regicide, was removed from it upon his refusal to take the Engagement.[168] In the previous month Oxford's Visitors had indicated the Cromwellian stance. The goal of 'a full libertie of elections' in the colleges, they explained, was to be pursued 'in order to a more thorough reformation' of the university.[169] At the same time the military party on the Visitation withdrew from it, while John Conant, the Rector of Exeter College who had refused the Engagement, joined the commission.[170] In 1654 Conant would become Regius Professor of Divinity at the 'invitation' of Cromwell. It was but one of the favours bestowed by the protector on the man whom in 1657 he would make Vice-Chancellor.[171]

In the aftermath of the battle of Worcester men already close to Cromwell achieved prominence in Oxford alongside Conant. One was Jonathan Goddard, who had been his physician on the Scottish campaign, and who was installed as

---

[166] OUA, Reg. Conv. T, pp. 168, 169; *CJ* 11 June 1652; Bodl., Bodleian MS Add. d. 105, p. 10.
[167] Worden, *Rump Parliament*, ch. 13.
[168] *CJ* 4 November 1651; C. H. Cooper, *Annals of Cambridge*, 5 vols (1842–53), iii. 447–8.
[169] Burrows, p. 340.
[170] Ibid., p. 340. Thomas Kelsey, who had been the leading force in the military party, became Governor of Dover Castle in 1651.
[171] For Cromwell's assistance to Conant see Varley, 'Restoration Visitation', p. 2; John Conant Jr, *The Life of the Reverend and Venerable John Conant*, ed. W. Staunton (1823), p. 22; OUA, WP/3/4, fo. 198.

Warden of Merton College in succession to Nathaniel Brent, who died in 1652.[172] Another was Cromwell's Puritan brother-in-law Peter French, one of Oxford's recruits from Cambridge, who on the order of the parliamentary committee had replaced Edward Pocock in his canonry there.[173] French joined the Visitation in the autumn of 1651 with Conant and two other new appointments. Our first sight of him at Christ Church is on the same day as our first glimpse of Owen there. When Owen went to London for three months in 1652 to steer through his proposals for the reform of the national Church, he appointed French to deputize in his absence.[174] An 'excellent preacher', 'the best of all that party',[175] French would be one of the official preachers to the council of the protectorate, and would accordingly be given state lodgings in Whitehall.[176]

Although the authority to create new members of the Visitation formally lay with parliament's standing committee rather than with Cromwell,[177] his influence in the expansion of the body is unmistakable. Two further additions to the commission, the most striking ones, were the Independents John Owen and Thomas Goodwin. Despite his efforts on behalf of Presbyterians at Oxford, Cromwell's natural allies there were Independents: men who had supported the inauguration of the republic, and who supported his commitment to liberty of conscience. It was to Owen and Goodwin that he looked as the principal instruments for the reformation of Oxford, as of the religion of England. Owen had grown up near Oxford, been to school in the town, and attended the university until 1637, when his objections to Laudian ceremonialism had prompted him to withdraw from it.[178] Subsequently a minister in Essex, where, with many other Puritan divines, he enjoyed the patronage of the Earl of Warwick,[179] he acted as chaplain to parliamentarian troops at the siege of Colchester in 1648, where he came to know Cromwell's son-in-law Henry Ireton and other army officers. The Rump chose him to preach to it on the day after the execution of the king, and again following the defeat of the Levellers by Fairfax and Cromwell in May 1649. A few weeks before Cromwell's election to the Chancellorship, Owen publicly thanked him for 'daily spiritual refreshment and support—by inquiry into and discovery of the deep and hidden dispensations of God towards his secret ones— which my spirit is taught to value'.[180] In 1652 Cromwell politely eased the incumbent Daniel Greenwood, the Principal of Brasenose, who had been one of the initial Visitors, out of the Vice-Chancellorship.[181] He then appointed Owen, the

---

[172] Merton College Record (hereafter MCR), Registrum Collegii Mertonensis, pp. 385–7 (cf. pp. 396, 414).
[173] Twells, *Pocock*, p. 133.
[174] CA, D&C i. b. 3, pp. 39, 53.
[175] Pope, *Life of . . . Seth Bishop of Salisbury*, p. 44.
[176] *Perfect Proceedings* 22 March 1655, p. 4526; *Mercurius Politicus* 21 June 1655, p. 5419; *CSPD 1655–6*, p. 588.
[177] *CJ* 8 June 1649.
[178] Toon, *God's Statesman*, p. 9.
[179] Ibid., pp. 25–6.
[180] Ibid., p. 46; cf. p. 85.
[181] OUA, Reg. Conv. T, pp. 150–1, 170.

recent architect of the projected Cromwellian Church settlement, in his place. He would reappoint him for four successive years, so that Owen held the Vice-Chancellorship until 1657.

Both in Oxford and in England, Owen was one of 'the two Atlasses and patriarchs of Independency'.[182] Goodwin was the other. He had been a prominent figure in the rise of Congregationalism in the 1640s. After the overthrow of the Levellers at Burford the army leaders named him, with Reynolds and Caryl, for the proposed lectureship in divinity at Oxford. He preached with Owen to the Rump on a day of thanksgiving for the Levellers' defeat, when the House, 'with respect to' his 'great learning and worth', resolved to find a headship of a college for him. There may have been a simultaneous resolution to do the same for Owen.[183] In January 1650 parliament appointed Goodwin to the Presidency of Magdalen College.[184] Through their closeness to Cromwell, Goodwin and Owen gave Oxford an influence on the Cromwellian Church at least as great as that which it had exerted on the Laudian Church before it. It was they, and the party they built in the university, who designed or promoted the principal ecclesiastical initiatives of the Interregnum. What would become the system of Triers and Ejectors, which strove to Puritanize the nation's clergy, was designed by 'some heads and governors of some colledges in Oxford', Owen and Goodwin to their fore.[185] Cromwellian plans for a national Church settlement in 1654 were drawn up by Owen, Goodwin, 'and som [o]thers at Oxford'.[186] The 'rise' of the Congregationalist manifesto of 1658, the *Savoy Declaration*, which Goodwin submitted to the government, was a gathering of ministers at the Act (the university's annual parade of its lustre and learning) in Oxford that summer.[187]

In October 1652 Cromwell appointed a board of five men to carry out a number of the Chancellor's more routine duties. None of its members had been on the Visitation before Worcester, though three of them, Owen, Goodwin, and French, had now joined it. Goddard was the fourth. The fifth, the only one to hold an Oxford appointment before 1651, was the future bishop John Wilkins. He had been made Warden of Wadham in 1648. Though he too was an outsider, he had been accorded political prominence in the university from the time of his arrival.[188] It was he,

[182] Wood, *Athenae Oxonienses*, iv. 98.
[183] *CJ* 8 June 1649; Reinhart, 'Parliamentary Visitation', p. 472.
[184] *CJ* 8 January 1650. Cf. *CSPD 1651*, pp. 30, 214; Burrows, p. 264.
[185] *The Weekly Intelligencer* 6 April 1652, p. 409; *Severall Proceedings in Parliament* 1 April 1652, p. 2037.
[186] Johnston, *Diary*, ii. 246; above; Hunter Powell, 'The Last Confession: A Background Study of the Savoy Declaration of Faith and Order', Univ. of Cambridge M. Phil. thesis (2008), pp. 58–61; and see Geoffrey Nuttall, 'Presbyterians and Independents: Some Movements for Unity 300 Years Ago', *Journal of the Presbyterian Historical Society of England* 10 (1952), p. 12.
[187] *Mercurius Politicus* 21 October 1658, pp. 922–5; Powell, 'Last Confession', pp. 230–1. Cf. *CSPD 1657–8*, p. 30; *A True Catalogue, or, An Account of . . . by whom Richard Cromwell was Proclaimed* (1659), pp. 24, 61; Burrows, p. 384; Peter Gaunt, ed., *The Correspondence of Henry Cromwell 1655–1659*, Camden Society, fifth series 31 (2007), pp. 394–5; Toon, *God's Statesman*, pp. 1, 95, 103; Austin Woolrych, *Commonwealth to Protectorate* (Oxford, 1982), p. 341.
[188] Bodl., Tanner MS 62, fo. 189; cf. OUA, Reg. Conv. T, p. 12. On Wilkins see Shapiro, *John Wilkins*; C.S.L. Davies, 'The Family and Connections of John Wilkins, 1614–72', *Oxoniensia* 69 (2004), pp. 93–107.

Owen, and Goodwin who, in regular meetings over the remainder of Cromwell's Chancellorship, would do the main work of the board. For four years before his appointment at Wadham, Wilkins had been chaplain to the Elector Palatine, Charles Louis, who was staying in England with a subsidy from parliament, and who for a time was thought of as a possible parliamentarian candidate for Charles I's throne. Perhaps Wilkins's appointment at Oxford was indebted to the English contacts of the Elector, who had befriended Cromwell and the new model army in 1647.[189] Perhaps it was aided by Wilkins's patron the Independent grandee Lord Saye and Sele, who had a number of ties to Oxford, and whose regiment had briefly occupied it for parliament in 1642. At all events the new Warden had some elevated connections. So had his associates John Wallis and Seth Ward, who in 1649 were given favour at Oxford 'by order from above'.[190] The service of the Elector detained Wilkins from Oxford in the aftermath of his appointment there, but from 1649 he was a powerful figure in the university. After the death of Peter French in June 1655, Wilkins married his widow, Cromwell's sister Robina, a match which solidified his power in Oxford and made him 'the rising sun' there.[191] In the direction of university policy he was the chief rival to Owen, whom he eventually defeated.

For Wilkins and his scientific circle—especially Seth Ward, who had joined him at Wadham, and John Wallis—influenced the political as much as the intellectual history of Cromwellian Oxford. Thomas Sprat, in tracing the debt of the Royal Society to their meetings at Oxford in the 1650s, recorded that 'onely the satisfaction of breathing a freer air, and of conversing in quiet one with another, without being ingag'd in the passions, and madness of that dismal age', drew the circle together. For 'to have been eternally musing on civil business, and the distresses of their country, was too melancholy a reflexion: it was [the study of] nature alone, which could pleasantly entertain them.' Yet if Wilkins and his associates avoided politics in their scientific and philosophical discussions, elsewhere they immersed themselves in them. If Sprat's remarks give the impression of cerebral detachment on the circle's part, it is dispelled by his accompanying statement 'that it was in good measure by the influence, which these gentlemen had over the rest, that the university it self, or at least, any part of its discipline, and order, was sav'd from ruine'.[192] Walter Pope, the biographer of Seth Ward, made the point with

[189] Abbott, i. 433; S.R. Gardiner, *History of the Great Civil War*, 4 vols (1897–8 edn), iii. 344; cf. M. J. Braddick and Mark Greengrass, eds, 'The Letters of Sir Cheney Culpepper, 1641–1657', *Camden Miscellany* 33 (1996), p. 300. It may have helped that he had family connections (as did John Owen: Toon, *God's Statesman*, p. 2) with the Visitor Robert Harris: Davies, 'Family and Connections of John Wilkins', pp. 99–100 (cf. p. 106).

[190] OUA, Reg. Conv. T, p. 72.

[191] *CSPD 1656–7*, p. 51.

[192] Thomas Sprat, *The History of the Royal Society* (1667), pp. 53–6; cf. OUA, Reg. Conv. T, p. 97. Ward and Wallis are frequently seen together in Oxford politics. For their moderating instincts see NA, 1073; C. Nicastro, ed., *Lettere di Henry Stubbe a Thomas Hobbes* (Siena, 1973), p. 29. As a Presbyterian, admittedly, Wallis found it hard to agree with Wilkins and Ward in religion; and he was no friend to resurgent royalism in 1660 (Underdown, *Royalist Conspiracy*, pp. 295–6). For the cohesion of the Wilkins circle see also H. F. Kearney, *Scholars and Gentlemen* (1970), pp. 127–9.

characteristically extreme partisanship: 'Dr Wilkins, Dr Goddard, and perhaps two or three more . . . , us'd their constant endeavour to oppose the fury, and moderate the heats of the fiery, giddy party, and to advance the interest of learning'.[193] The diarist John Evelyn, a devotee of Crown and Church, approvingly noted the aim of Wilkins, 'my excellent and deare friend', 'to preserve the universities from the ignorant sacrilegious commander and souldiers'.[194] It was the policy of the Wilkins circle to sustain the forms and traditions of the university; to work for its independence from central power; to preserve figures unsympathetic to republican rule in their posts; to quieten the controversies which arose from Puritan reform; and to uphold Oxford's standing no less among royalists and neutrals than among parliamentarians.

Wilkins had avoided conspicuous commitment to either side in the civil wars. Unlike Evelyn he cannot properly be called a royalist in the period of Cromwell's Chancellorship. A better term for him would be monarchist. Until the fall of the protectorate, a Cromwellian monarchy seemed a far stronger possibility than a Stuart restoration. When in 1659–60 it began to seem that the pre-war dynasty might be restored after all, Wilkins readily transferred his allegiance to the Stuarts, and joined what the royalist Lord Colepeper called 'the monarchical party that before looked upon Cromwell as the fittest person to attain their ends by'.[195] It was only the exigencies of revolution that, for him and others, had lent attraction to the prospect of a Cromwellian monarchy, which, they hoped, would distance itself from its revolutionary origins and supporters. 'Royalist' is a better term for the eminent physician Ralph Bathurst, Vice-President of Trinity College under Cromwell and 'the principal and most constant of those who met in Dr Wilkins his lodgings in Wadham College'. In surviving the parliamentary Visitation, Bathurst would remember, 'I thought I had no more to do but to sit still and rest content with whatever befell under a prevailing party'. He had taken episcopal ordination during the civil war, and seems to have secretly arranged it for others under Cromwell. In 1651 he contributed to the covertly royalist collection of poetry that prefaced the posthumous publication of Thomas Cartwright's plays and poems. Yet, like all royalists—and neo-royalists—who took posts in Cromwellian Oxford, he made his compromises. After the Restoration he and others of his mind had motives to obscure or understate their past collaboration with Puritan rule. What had then seemed prudent adjustment to political reality could now, they were aware, be portrayed as 'a sordid, complying spirit'.[196] Bathurst chose to remember that he had had 'persons of unquestionably loyalty' to king and Church for his 'constant friends and intimate acquaintance', and that he had used the pretext of

[193] Pope, *Life of . . . Seth Bishop of Salisbury*, p. 46.
[194] E. S. de Beer, ed., *The Diary of John Evelyn*, 6 vols (Oxford, 1955), iii. 106, 165.
[195] *SPC*, iii. 493; cf. Matthew Wren, *Monarchy Asserted* (1659: published in Oxford), ep. ded. (to Wilkins).
[196] Robert South, *Sermons Preached upon Several Occasions* (1679), preface.

visiting patients to retain royalist contacts in the neighbouring countryside.[197] He chose to forget that he had served the state's navy as a physician during the Dutch war of 1652–4, 'with', as the Cromwellian authorities in Oxford recognized, 'much diligence and successe';[198] and that he had written, perhaps to compensate for his contribution to the Cartwright volume, paeans to Cromwell in the book of poems sent by the university to congratulate him on his assumption of the protectorate.[199]

Another contributor to the volume[200] was the distinguished Grecian and Oriental scholar Gerard Langbaine, Provost of Queen's College, where royalist sympathies were as potent as anywhere.[201] He had long made his commitment to the Stuart monarchy and to episcopacy, and his hatred of Puritanism and rebellion, abundantly clear.[202] He obstructed the progress of the Visitation,[203] and translated into Latin, for a continental audience, the defiant tract issued by the university against it.[204] Yet he contrived to remain in office. For to Langbaine, Keeper of the University Archives, friend to John Selden and James Ussher 'and the great Goliaths of literature', outward deference to the usurpers was a necessary price to pay for the preservation of his university and his college. When a royalist Fellow of Queen's urged him to rally the Fellowship in opposition to the Visitation, the Provost declined, explaining his disagreement with colleagues who 'fly so high upon the point of loyalty and privilege, as if they were ambitious of suffering'.[205] In that spirit he helped to sustain the reputation of a university which, under Cromwellian rule, was dependent for its distinction in secular learning on the presence of men who were out of sympathy with the partisan ambitions of Puritanism.[206] He seems to have played a part in the scientific meetings of the Wilkins circle.[207] Wilkins, who shared Langbaine's distaste for gestures of political defiance,[208] joined him in a skilful and unobtrusive policy of minimal tactical concession. There are five men whom we can name as the front rank of the university politicians of the 1650s: John Owen; Thomas Goodwin; John Conant;

---

[197] Thomas Warton, *The Life and Literary Remains of Ralph Bathurst* (1761), pp. 202–6; Clare Hopkins, *Trinity: 450 Years of an Oxford College Community* (Oxford, 2005), pp. 110, 123; and see Bodl., Rawlinson MS c. 421, fo. 70. For Wadham and Trinity see also Burrows, p. 337.

[198] Burrows, pp. 389–90. Another firm royalist, Richard Zouche, served on a court appointed by Cromwell to try the brother of the Portuguese ambassador in 1654. He may have prudently withdrawn from Oxford in 1650 to escape the Engagement: OUA, Reg. Conv. T, p. 112.

[199] See pp. 12–13 and p. 59 of Bodl., Wood Pamphlets 484 (12): Anthony Wood's copy of *Musarum Oxoniensium* (Oxford, 1654); cf. OUA, NW/3/4, fo. 66ᵛ.

[200] *Musarum Oxoniensium*, p. 51.

[201] Mordechai Feingold, 'Oriental Studies', in Tyacke, *History of the University of Oxford*, p. 484.

[202] See his many publications of the civil-war period.

[203] QCA, Register H, pp. 99–101.

[204] Reinhart and Roy, 'Civil Wars', p. 724.

[205] Wood, *Athenae Oxonienses*, iii. 446–7; Bodl., Wood MS f. 35, fo. 312; Leland, *De Rebus Britannicis*, v. 283–4; cf. Reinhart, 'Parliamentary Visitation', p. 351. For Langbaine's stoicism see also Bodl., MS Rawlinson Letters 89, fo. 108; QCA, MS 423, p. 150.

[206] That common characteristic of the intellectual fellow spirits of John Selden in Cromwellian Oxford can be glimpsed in Bodl., Selden MS *supra* 109, fo. 452.

[207] Margery Purver, *The Royal Society: Concept and Creation* (repr. 2009), pp. 112, 121–6.

[208] Bodl., MS. don. f. 39, pp. 206, 258.

Wilkins; and Langbaine.[209] Langbaine was the only survivor of Oxford's keen royalism in that select company, but behind him there stood less conspicuous figures of similar experience and outlook, a number of them at Queen's and its neighbour All Souls.

Such were the lines of battle in Cromwellian Oxford. We move now to the course of the conflict.

To posterity a tension is discernible in Cromwell's plans for Oxford and for England. Could his countrymen be both reformed and reconciled? Would not zealous reformation antagonize the interest groups and the moderate opinion he sought to reassure? And if he aimed to broaden the base of the revolution, must he not restore traditional forms and institutions—and thereby dull the sense of godly mission from which the energy of reforming Puritanism sprang? The course of Cromwellian politics, in Oxford as outside it, is largely explicable in terms of that dilemma. Yet Cromwell saw no contradiction. To him reform was the friend of stability. 'Reformation, if it be honest, and thorough, and just,' he assured parliament in 1656, 'will be your best security', and 'the liberty and prosperity of this nation depends upon reformation.'[210] In those convictions he was in the main current of parliamentarian Puritanism. It had run most powerfully in 1640–1, when Puritanism had seemed to speak for the nation, and when godliness had appeared the natural ally of political stability and health. The collapse of the Caroline regime had confirmed in Puritan minds the identification of instability with popery and wickedness. Those evils had allegedly flourished in pre-war Oxford and Cambridge, and in the continental seminaries to which some fathers had alternatively sent their sons. In the 1650s, Cromwellians hoped, the conquered universities of England—and of Ireland and Scotland—would become nurseries of orthodoxy and sobriety. To Oxford and Cambridge there would fall a duty fundamental to the creation of a godly commonwealth: the task of nurturing the pious ministry and magistracy which in turn would Puritanize, and so stabilize, the land.

The months after Worcester showed Cromwell that the task could not be left to the Rump, where the impetus for the reform of the universities, as of the nation, was paralysed by factional strife within the regime, much of it turning on his own largely unavailing conflicts with the civil power.[211] There were critical developments in the spring and summer of 1652, which alas are thinly documented. In April, when parliament was making alterations to its committee system, two readings were given to a bill of which we know only that it would have transferred the powers of the standing committee to 'several commissioners'.[212] The measure

---

[209] For the early stages of their collaboration see OUA, WP/*a*/10/11. His influence can be seen not only in his appointment to a number of leading positions and committees but in many politically important university documents of the 1650s that are in his hand. See too Roy and Reinhart, 'Civil Wars', pp. 719n., 723n. The readiness of Langbaine, Wilkins, and Owen to cooperate can also be glimpsed in Noel Malcolm and Jacqueline Stedall, *John Pell (1611–1685)* (Oxford, 2005), p. 149n.

[210] Abbott, iv. 270, 273.

[211] Worden, *Rump Parliament*, ch. 11.

[212] *CJ* 21 April 1652 (cf. Abbott, ii. 565).

vanished as a power struggle developed over the future government of the universities. In Oxford the Visitation, assuming that its own authority had lapsed with that of the standing committee,[213] promptly disbanded itself.[214] Was Cromwell behind its dissolution? A tract of February 1652, dedicated to him and intimating that he should be made king, appealed to his 'pity and power' to afford the university 'peculiar protection' against the 'prejudice' that Oxford's earlier 'malignant fever' had brought upon it. He was beseeched not to 'suffer her any longer to be committed to other hands than your own, and such as under you and nearer her, shall be thought fit to put her into'.[215] Just such a transition in the running of the university would occur in the summer.

The university's response to the end of the Visitation was the first episode in a new series of tussles over the relationship between Oxford and central government that would last until the twilight of the protectorate in 1659. In 1652 Oxford's leaders knew that the Puritan eagerness to reform the university had not abated. They also knew that a second Visitation was likely.[216] They expected it to consist of new, 'foreign Visitors', named by the republic. In June, to 'prevent' that threat, they produced their own proposal. They submitted it as a petition to parliament for a small body of Visitors 'residing upon the place', who would 'put an end to the work' left unfinished by the first Visitation. The document dutifully acknowledged that, despite the 'fair progress made' by the now extinct Visitation, 'there yet remain several things necessary to be done for the advancement of piety, the improvement of literature, and the good government of this place.' One of the tasks of the new body, as the petition uneasily recognized, would be the review of the statutes of the university and the colleges. In April 1651 parliament's standing committee had declared its resolve to have the statutes 'reduced to such a state as may render them most conducing to the advancement of true piety, and the interest of a Commonwealth', and had ordered the institutions themselves to propose alterations.[217] The pressure for change persisted.[218] The university's sense of vulnerability is indicated by the willingness of Gerard Langbaine, and of his ally and fellow royalist the distinguished civil lawyer Richard Zouche, Principal of St Alban Hall, to sign a petition which must have affronted their instincts, but behind which the competing parties within the university were ready to unite. The heads of the colleges signed almost to a man. The delegation to parliament included John Owen, Thomas Goodwin, and their political rival John Wilkins.

The breadth of backing for the petition is explicable only on the supposition which also makes Oxford's support for Cromwell's election as Chancellor the

---

[213] OUA, SP/E/4, fo. 70ᵛ; Wood, *History*, ii. 650.

[214] Cf. NA, 9655, p. 5. The committee may have felt that, the bulk of the colleges having been reduced to order, its main work had now been done (cf. QCA, Register H, pp. 142–3; MS 2Y/42).

[215] *Somers Tracts*, vi. 156.

[216] Bodl., Ballard MS 46, fo. 195.

[217] *Petition and Argument of Mr Hotham*, pp. 6–7, 103–5; cf NA, 9655, p. 11.

[218] Cf. the declaration of June 1652 by parliament's commissioners in Scotland announcing their intention of reforming the statutes of the universities there: F. D. Dow, *Cromwellian Scotland 1651–1660* (Edinburgh, 1979), p. 58 (see too p. 60).

previous year intelligible: that the university looked to him, as the tract of February 1652 did, to protect the university even as he strove to reform it. He was named at the head of the ad hoc committee to which parliament referred the petition. The university's friends Bulstrode Whitelocke and Sir John Trevor were appointed to it too.[219] Four days later, with an exceptional rapidity for which we must guess Cromwell to have been responsible, it made recommendations which endorsed the petition's proposals and which named prospective Visitors. The university's wish for an essentially internal rather than external Visitation was indulged by the recommendation that the Vice-Chancellor be a member ex officio.[220] In the event the stipulation was needless, for by the time the commission began work the Vice-Chancellor was John Owen, who was a member anyway. The clear majority of the new board were Independents: Owen and Thomas Goodwin, the Atlases of Independency; Samuel Basnett, the Independent sub-Warden of All Souls; and two of the firmest followers of Owen and Goodwin, both of them members of the congregation which Goodwin gathered in Magdalen and which met in his lodgings on Wednesdays: Francis Howell, Fellow of that college, and Thankful Owen, who had been appointed President of St John's in place of Francis Cheynell. In later life Thankful Owen would edit Goodwin's works and be buried beside him.[221] We shall encounter his closeness to John Owen. There were only two members of the new body who were opposed to Independency. During the first Visitation both of them had become heads of colleges of which they had been Fellows before the war. The first was John Conant of Exeter College. The second was the Presbyterian Edmund Staunton of Corpus Christi, whose hostility to sectarian preaching had been attacked by Marchamont Nedham in 1650.[222]

It would be a year before the second Visitation began its life. Within the university there was an expectation that its proceedings would start in September 1652.[223] In the event the Rump took 'no effectuall order' to implement the proposals submitted by the committee headed by Cromwell.[224] In June 1653, two months after expelling the parliament, and apparently acting on his authority as lord general,[225] he issued a commission empowering the Visitors who had been named in 1652 to act.[226] It does not survive, but we do know that, to the university's relief, it set a time limit, probably at a point late in 1654, to the

---

[219] *CJ* 11 June 1650.
[220] OUA, SP/E/4, fos 53–7; Wood, *History*, ii. 651–2; Burrows, p. 356n. It is perhaps a symptom of the partial assimilation of the first Visitation by the university that we find it meeting, in 1651, in the lodgings of the then Vice-Chancellor: QCA, Register H, p. 138 (though cf. below, pp. 131–2).
[221] For Goodwin's congregation see Wood, *History*, ii. 645; *Mercurius Politicus* 21 October 1658, p. 923; Bloxam, *Reg. Magdalen*, ii. 146–7.
[222] OUA, WP/β/21(4), p. 267.
[223] Bodl., J. Walker MS c. 9, fo. 195.
[224] *CJ* 2 March 1653; OUA, SP/E/4, fo. 62.
[225] Cf. Abbott, iii. 13, 34.
[226] Burrows, p. 357; OUA, SP/E/4, fo. 62. The suggestion by Wood (*History*, ii. 652) that Cromwell issued the commission in 1652 (rather than 1653) is unlikely. Wood attributes the delay between parliament's discussions in June 1652 and the first meeting of the Visitation to 'certain differences on foot in the university concerning them'. Such differences may have arisen, but if so we may guess them to have been extensions of developments in the capital.

Visitors' authority.[227] That provision conformed to Cromwell's own hope that England's institutions, once they had demonstrated their loyalty to the new order and their openness to Puritan reform, would be restored to their traditional forms.[228] The period of the second Visitation was the peak of the Independents' power in Oxford. Its opening meetings in June 1653 coincided with what the great Victorian historian S. R. Gardiner called the 'high water-mark of Puritanism'[229] and with the Independents' highest hopes of reformation, which infuse the slim records of the second Visitation. The hand-picked assembly of the pious that would become known as Barebone's Parliament had been summoned in place of the Rump. It had yet to meet, and no one knew that it would elude Independent control and, by its votes for radical reform, provoke a reaction in favour of Presbyterianism.

The first Visitation, though it had striven to promote Puritan worship and beliefs in Oxford, had had to give its main attention to the eviction and replacement of the refractory opponents of Puritan rule. That task having been virtually accomplished, the second Visitation could devote most of its labours to the achievement of godly reformation. A series of initiatives was taken to secure the appointment of pious tutors and for the provision of effectual preaching, of religious exercises, and of frequent prayer.[230] Alongside those measures the Visitors permitted or confirmed the return of all but the most recalcitrant colleges to a large measure of self-government. In elections to college posts they mainly contented themselves with vetting candidates whom the colleges had already chosen. Yet their criteria of eligibility were provocative. Candidates were required to produce testimonials vouching them to be not only studious and learned but 'truly godly', of 'approved godlinesse and integrity'.[231] 'Godly' credentials had been sought by the Visitors before, as they had by other Puritans in the university who maintained that electors to Fellowships should 'principally looke after holynesse'.[232] But only now was the requirement systematized. It applied to the university the procedures for the examination of candidates for Church livings which had been devised by John Owen, Thomas Goodwin, and their Oxford friends in 1652; which were debated by the Rump and Barebone's in 1652–3; and which were implemented by the board of Triers set up by the protectorate in 1654. The Triers, who like the second Visitation were an energetic and industrious body, were appointed to examine candidates for evidence of divine grace, holy conversation, knowledge of the Gospel, and capacity to preach it. John Owen, Thomas Goodwin, and Thankful Owen were the divines given pride of place on the board of Triers.[233]

---

[227] Wood, *History*, ii. 652, 661; OUA, SP/E/4, fo. 62.

[228] Cf. Worden, *Rump Parliament*, p. 267; Abbott, iii. 64, 67.

[229] S. R. Gardiner, *History of the Commonwealth and Protectorate*, 4 vols (New York, repr. 1965), ii. 340.

[230] The records of the second Visitation are in Burrows, pp. 356–99.

[231] Ibid., pp. 368–9.

[232] QCA, Register H, p. 140; CCCA, B1/3/2, fo. 15ᵛ; Henry Wilkinson Jr, *Three Decads of Sermons lately Preached to the University* (1660), pt. ii, p. 77.

[233] Firth and Rait, ii. 855–6; cf. Woolrych, *Commonwealth to Protectorate*, p. 341. Another energetic and industrious feature of ecclesiastical policy in the 1650s, the provision of financial

The imposition of the analogous test of godliness on Oxford provoked outrage from Gerard Langbaine, the Provost of Queen's, who had submitted to so much during the Puritan takeover of Oxford, but who now drew the line. Candidates at his college, he wrote to Selden, were being vetoed who 'were not known to these Visitors'—or 'those we call Visitors'—'to be regenerate'.[234] Langbaine, not one to make threats lightly, indicated that he would leave the university sooner than collaborate. In his eyes Puritan credentials were being preferred to scholarly ones. Henceforth the claims of the 'godly' to office in Oxford would be much resented and mocked. Yet Owen's party understood, as Cromwell did, the dependence of Puritan reform on the maintenance of the university's scholarly esteem. If the new Visitors ever overlooked that requisite, they were recalled to it by the explosive public campaign against the universities in 1653, when Oxford and Cambridge were assailed in the prints as strongholds of both Aristotelianism and Antichrist. In August, at the height of the scare, Owen, who in his youth had abbreviated his own studies at Oxford sooner than submit to Laudianism, was driven to seek out, for 'present use', a Laudian 'collection of such records as concerned the interests of the clergy'.[235]

The establishment of the protectorate under the Instrument of Government in December 1653 dashed the messianic hopes on which the attacks on the universities had thriven. The new regime, conscious that the extremism which had flourished under Barebone's had played into the hands of 'some malcontented gain-sayers' in Oxford,[236] anxiously publicized its commitment to preserve the institutions of learning. 'There is great joy in the universities for the present government under his highness the lord protector,' proclaimed a newsbook friendly to the regime two months after Cromwell's installation, 'for that learning will be cherished.'[237] Oxford was quick to congratulate Cromwell on his elevation, for 'we owe it to your favour that the university survives today', the protector having 'taken into your care the floundering world of letters'.[238] The congratulatory address was presented to the protector by John Wilkins.[239]

*

'augmentations' to godly ministers, was meant to apply to heads of colleges and other leading figures in the university, though there is conflicting evidence about the effectiveness of the arrangement: OUA, SP/E/3 (9–11); Reg. Conv. T, p. 168; Firth and Rait, ii. 373; ECA, A. II. 10: November 1650–November 1651; Burrows, pp. 246, 249, 251; *CSPD 1653–4*, p. 423; W. A. Shaw, *A History of the English Church during the Civil Wars and Commonwealth*, 2 vols (1900), ii. 575–7; G. B. Tatham, *The Puritans in Power* (Cambridge, 1913), pp. 131–2. See too (e.g.) TNA, SP 25/69: 4 April 1654; *CSPD 1654*, pp. 259, 268; *1656–7*, p. 375; *1658–9*, pp. 263–4; Bodl., Rawlinson MS d. 912, fos 3ʳ-4; Thomas Richards, 'The Puritan Visitation of Jesus College', *Transactions of the Honourable Society of Cymmrodorion* (1922–3), p. 49.

[234] Bodl., Tanner MS 52, fo. 60.

[235] OUA, Reg. Conv. T, p. 226; Leland, *De Rebus Britannicis*, v. 291–2.

[236] *Mercurius Politicus* 21 Sep. 1654, p. 3773.

[237] *Certain Passages* 17 February 1654, p. 38. Cf. *The Moderate Intelligencer* 22 March 1654, pp. 1342–3; *Severall Proceedings of State Affaires* 4 May 1654, p. 3807.

[238] Toon, *Correspondence of John Owen*, pp. 64–5.

[239] OUA, Reg. Conv. T, pp. 226–7 (and Burrows, p. 377n.); Wood, *History*, ii. 656; OUA, NW/ 3/4, fos 37, 66ᵛ; *Musarum Oxoniensum*.

If the inauguration of the protectorate released the university from its gravest fears, Cromwell's commitment to Puritanize it remained resolute. Any hope that systematic interference in Oxford's affairs would last only as long as the second Visitation was dashed. Among the ordinances passed by the protector and his council in 1654 was that of 2 September 'for the carrying on and perfecting of the reformation and regulation of the universities'.[240] It created a third—and last—Puritan Visitation, the second having held its final recorded meeting on the day before the passage of the ordinance. The decree introduced a new phase in the Cromwellian rule of Oxford, of which surviving documents give us some close and vivid glimpses.

The new body consisted, as the first Visitation had done, of both internal and external members. Alongside divines within Oxford a number of Puritan gentry, a high proportion of them from the neighbouring counties Buckinghamshire and Northamptonshire, were named. Again as on the first Visitation, however, it was not the outsiders who were expected to do the work or who did it. That was the task of resident members of Oxford. Most of the Visitors on the second Visitation were reappointed, and the party of Owen and Goodwin remained strong.[241] The ordinance set up parallel arrangements for Cambridge. Yet the protectorate, anxious to conciliate Presbyterianism, hesitated to challenge Cambridge's Presbyterian leadership. Like the decision to appoint a Visitation of Cambridge in 1649, the measure seems to have had little impact there.[242] It was with Oxford in mind that the ordinance was designed. As was 'sufficiently knowne' there, 'the first rise' of it 'did proceed from a petition presented as from the university'.[243] Though the petition does not survive, the impulse behind it is transparent. Owen and his party

[240] Firth and Rait, ii. 1026–9.
[241] The records of the third Visitation are in Burrows, pp. 400–39. Wood (*History*, ii. 661–3) has a story, which has been accepted by some modern authorities, that Owen was 'fool'd' into accepting the new Visitation by Thomas Goodwin, who got his own 'confidants' appointed on it. Thus finding himself a 'cypher', says Wood, Owen sided with the university against the Visitors, tried to have the ordinance which established them amended or annulled, and 'would not at all act among them'. In fact, as Wood's own narrative, and the documents on which it rests, amply show, and as we are about to find, Owen was an active member of the third Visitation and made every use of it. See too Burrows, pp. 402, 404–5, 435, 438; Wood, *History*, ii. 673–4. Wood was surely reading later differences between Owen and Goodwin back into the early stages of the Visitation. The conflict which he posits would make Owen's conduct in the episode we are about to view inexplicable. Besides, it is not conceivable that a disagreement between the protector and Owen, his right-hand man in Oxford, over the appointment of the Visitation would have left no evidence dating from the period of the episode, even in documents where Oxford's opposition to the ordinance receives detailed illustration. Burrows (pp. lxxix, ci), less at home in the 1650s than in the 1640s, compounds Wood's error. Even so, Owen and Goodwin may have cooperated as allies rather than friends, and it may be that some now irrecoverable quarrel between the two men lies behind Wood's supposition. John Wilkins referred in 1656 to occasions when Owen had indicated that his fellow Independents on the Visitation were not 'fit' to be 'intrusted' with the very powers which we shall see him urging them to assume in that year (OUA, SP/E/4, fo. 92ᵛ).
[242] Twigg, *University of Cambridge*, pp. 171–3; Mullinger, *University of Cambridge*, iii. 485. When the ordinance was debated in parliament in 1657 it seems to have been taken to have applied only to one 'university': *Burton*, ii. 64. A lukewarm assessment, from the government's perspective, of the condition of Cambridge can be found in the newsbook *The Publick Intelligencer* 14 July 1656, p. 688. The Independent divine Philip Nye told John Thurloe 'how fearfullie superstition increaseth at Cambridg' and at the Inns of Court: Bodl., Rawlinson MS a. 42, fo. 349.
[243] OUA, SP/E/4, fo. 78ᵛ.

were behind the ordinance. They had evidently chafed at the limits, and perhaps had baulked at the temporary remit, of the powers that the second Visitation had given them. On another occasion Goodwin revealed his readiness to exploit legal niceties in order to keep power at Oxford in the hands of Whitehall's nominees.[244] Owen, who stayed in London in the weeks before the ordinance reached the council,[245] now showed the same willingness. In 1647–8 the lay Independents in parliament had striven to defend the university's traditions against the Presbyterian Visitation of that time. The clerical Independents who held sway in Oxford in the 1650s, by contrast, were ready to confront the traditions. Unless the Visitors enjoyed sovereign power, they feared, the reform of Oxford might be stillborn. Above all the Independents sought the authority to alter the statutes of the university and colleges, without reference to protector or parliament. While Oxford was prepared to accept statutory reform, it insisted that local statutes could be legally altered only by parliamentary ones. Otherwise the university's charters and liberties would count for nothing.

The Instrument of Government empowered the protectoral council to pass ordinances which would be binding 'until order shall be taken in parliament concerning the same'.[246] Accordingly the government strove to complete a legislative programme for submission to the parliament that met on 4 September 1654. As that date approached, the drafting of ordinances became hectic: too hectic, as it turned out, for clarity and precision. Although the petition of Oxford's Independents for the new Visitation is likely to have been submitted months earlier, the ordinance reached the council only on 31 August, when it was rejected. Two days later, after discussions between councillors and the protector, a revised version passed the council, though only 'after diverse amendments at the table'.[247] Owen's critics in Oxford, perhaps aided by a leak from within the council, a normally secretive body, learned that the resistance had arisen at least in part from the extent of the powers given to the Visitors.[248] Even so the ordinance, as finally worded, gave the Visitation more power than at least some of the councillors intended. The measure startled the university by imposing no time limit on its tenure; by failing to provide, as the legislation for the Visitation of the later 1640s had done, a process of appeal from the Visitors to central government; and by stipulating that the new commission should have all the powers assumed by any previous Visitation of the university. On one reading, the reading favoured by Owen, the ordinance empowered the Visitors to act 'above and against statutes'; to alter them on their own authority; and also to assume the powers which the 'local' Visitors had held in the colleges.[249] In all those respects his interpretation awarded to the third Visitation powers which had not been allowed to the second.

---

[244] *TSP*, vii. 561.
[245] CA, D&C i. b. 3, p. 67.
[246] *GD*, p. 414.
[247] TNA, SP 25/76: 31 August, 2 September 1654.
[248] OUA, SP/E/4, fos 70ᵛ, 80.
[249] Ibid., fos 71, 83.

Though Owen's Vice-Chancellorship had its disasters, which derived largely from defects of his temperament, he was not a person to underestimate. 'The famous Independent John Owen', as John Evelyn called him after hearing his address at the Act of 1654, was a man of great physical and mental energy, an able and determined administrator, capable of 'a winning and insinuating deportment'[250]—and impatient of the political shortcomings of his closest allies. 'Some' Oxonians, he acknowledged, 'called' his tenure of office 'a lordly rule'.[251] Imposing as his qualities were, in Wilkins and his party he more than met his match. The university quickly mobilized itself against the ordinance of September 1654.[252] It submitted a series of objections and counter-proposals to a parliamentary committee to which, in October, the protectoral ordinances of 1654 were referred. The arguments used in those protests would often be repeated or developed in the years ahead, as the battle for Oxford's autonomy persisted. The ordinance prompted a proposal that instead of, or perhaps in addition to, the Visitors named by the ordinance, a substantial number be annually elected by the university itself. A petition was drafted for submission to Cromwell himself. It addressed the question, which again would figure prominently in the disputes ahead, of the local Visitors, whose role the Puritan occupation of Oxford had set in abeyance. As well as exercising powers in the colleges, they had had the function of assisting or protecting them in their dealings with the outside world. The university longed for their restoration. In some colleges, admittedly, the Visitor held his post ex officio as a bishop, and bishops had now been abolished. To meet the difficulty the university proposed that the episcopal Visitors be replaced, either by candidates chosen by the colleges themselves or by men to be named in a parliamentary statute. It also asked that, whatever rights the Visitation sought in the colleges, its powers there should not be allowed to exceed those which the colleges' own statutes gave to local Visitors.[253]

None of the ordinances submitted to the parliament of 1654, which was dissolved in January 1655, was confirmed by it. On one, contentious, reading of the Instrument, the protectorate was entitled to keep the ordinances in operation after the dissolution. It did so. Nonetheless, the refusal of the parliament of 1654 to give statutory sanction to the Instrument of Government threw the regime back on military rule. Cromwell's aspirations towards parliamentary legalism and political ecumenicalism, though never lost, were obscured or shelved for the next year and a half, the period that produced the rule of the Major-Generals.

Immediately after the dissolution of January 1655 the university was in revolt.[254] The rebellion was carefully managed. Although some members of the university

---

[250] de Beer, *Diary of John Evelyn*, iii. 105; Burrows, p. xl (from Anthony Wood).
[251] Peter Toon, ed., *Oxford Orations of Dr John Owen* (Callington, Cornwall, 1970), p. 44.
[252] The most illuminating source for the events of 1654–6 described here is OUA, SP/E/4, fos 90 ff. Wood's *History*, ii. 668–75, draws on that material, but the original is much more revealing.
[253] Cf. Wood, *History*, ii. 652.
[254] The situation was complicated in the winter of 1654–5 by contrasting developments at two colleges. At University College, of which the local Visitor was the university itself, Cromwell allowed the college to appoint a new Master, a move which appeared to suggest that he acknowledged the

were eager to 'blow the coals', and to 'aggravate' Owen's initiatives 'as such an unsufferable attempt as is not to be endured',[255] Wilkins and his friends were mostly successful in counselling restraint. They knew the insinuation which Owen's party was ready to make, 'privately', both in Oxford and in Whitehall: that the university was full of secret royalists who, the moment the state relaxed its control of Oxford, would challenge Puritan rule. Corresponding arguments were used to justify the rule of the Major-Generals in the nation at large. Though Oxford continued to think of Cromwell as its friend, the Vice-Chancellor, an intimate of the protector and the chief architect of his Church, had high influence at Whitehall. The dissolution of the parliament sparked a crisis in the university, which responded to it by resolving on a fresh petition against the Visitation. On 2 February 1655, in a bid to head off that initiative, John Owen's ally and fellow Visitor Thankful Owen arranged for a meeting to be held a week later, on the 9th, between the Visitors and their critics among the university's leaders.[256] On the 5th those leaders gathered at the lodgings of Gerard Langbaine, the Provost of Queen's, and 'prepared and agreed on' the views they would submit at the meeting.[257] The principal figures present were Langbaine himself; Wilkins; and the Warden of All Souls, the physician John Palmer, who had aided the survival of opponents of the Visitation in 1648. Though he had sat in the Rump, he was close to the royalist Langbaine. He had also been close to John Selden,[258] who had died in 1654 but whose spirit lived on in the leaders' deliberations.[259]

At 2 p.m. on 9 February, at the Dean's lodgings in Christ Church, the university's representatives were duly called in to a meeting of the Visitors. There Palmer rehearsed the arguments that had been agreed on in Langbaine's lodgings, and submitted a paper containing the representatives' pleas. The time for such 'extraordinary courses' as the third Visitation, he and his colleagues urged, was past. In the aftermath of civil war, they conceded, some such body as the first Visitation 'might' have been necessary, if only to secure for the victorious cause the political allegiance to which—as Wilkins's political circle was always careful to acknowledge—it had been and remained entitled. Yet that allegiance, after all, had now been achieved. Why therefore should not the traditional forms of self-government, and the traditional authority of local statutes, be restored? What need could there be of a continuing external authority, let alone one with the power of 'makeing and abrogating lawes'? Palmer, the ex-rumper, injected acidity into the proceedings by

---

traditional rights of the local Visitors, but which seems to have arisen from an embarrassing muddle: OUA, Reg. Conv. T. pp. 259–60; SP/E/4, fo. 81; Robin Darwall-Smith, *A History of University College Oxford* (Oxford, 2008), pp. 175–6; cf. UCA, College Register 1509–1727: 3 November 1652. At Jesus the Visitors are likely to have caused fresh alarm, just at the time—in early 1655—when the contest over their powers had reached a crisis, by crushing an attempt by the fifth Earl of Pembroke to reassert his right, as the local Visitor of the College, to judge a dispute there—a right which the Visitation unanimously claimed to belong to itself: Burrows, pp. 401–2; cf. *CSPD 1657–8*, p. 238.

[255] OUA, SP/E/5, fo. 92.
[256] Ibid., fo. 84ᵛ.
[257] Ibid., fos 77–8.
[258] Leland, *De Rebus Britannicis*, v. 282.
[259] Reinhart, 'Parliamentary Visitation', p. 404.

alluding to the arguments with which Cromwell had justified the forcible expulsion of the parliament in April 1653. Cromwell had castigated the Rump as a corrupt oligarchy, bent on the perpetuation of its arbitrary power. If 'rightly informed', Palmer suggested, the protector would now 'in probability' take the same exceptions to the new Visitation as 'in another and greater case'. For the 'unlimited and arbitrary power' which the ordinance gave to 'standinge Visitors', 'perpetuating power in the same hands', would surely constitute an insuperable temptation to corruption, 'yea even of godly men'.

The university's representatives, having submitted their proposals, were asked to withdraw to an adjoining room. A long wait was before them, for the Visitation was divided within itself. The Visitors eventually broke up, taking Palmer's paper with them, without informing the representatives that the meeting was over. It was after 9 p.m., 'the great bell haveing tolled', when Thankful Owen returned to tell them of the refusal of John Owen and the other Visitors to 'treate' with them further. They kept Palmer's paper and sealed it. The rebels, thwarted in Oxford yet confident of their support there, resolved to take the battle to London. Next day seven of the university's most prominent figures signed a letter relating the recent course of events to two colleagues in the capital, Jonathan Goddard (himself a member of the third Visitation) and Peter French, whose lives under the protectorate centred on Whitehall.[260] But for the absence of those mollifying figures from Oxford, Wilkins and his friends suggested to them, the breach in the university might have been avoided. Now the two men were asked to turn their Whitehall contacts to the university's advantage. Six of the seven signatories had been at the meeting in Queen's on the 5th: Langbaine, Palmer, Wilkins, Wilkins's allies Seth Ward and John Wallis, and the politically adept Professor of Natural Philosophy Joshua Crosse, who had helped the university to reclaim its right to elect its Chancellor in 1650–1.[261] The seventh, whose readiness to sign added weight to the challenge to Owen, was his predecessor as Vice-Chancellor, Daniel Greenwood.[262]

Goddard replied on his and French's behalf. He had sat in Barebone's, in effect representing the university's interests in it,[263] and had witnessed the threat which the assembly had posed to them. With others he looked to the protectorate for a new stability. He and French now offered Wilkins and his allies a counsel of caution. Was it necessary, they asked, to demand the rewriting of the ordinance? Whatever Owen and his allies might suppose, it was 'well knowne' in Whitehall that in the passage of the measure there had been 'no intent' to empower the Visitors to make or alter statutes, and that the Visitors were expected 'only to offer' recommendations for changes to the protector and parliament. So was it prudent, at a

---

[260] OUA, Reg. Conv. T, p. 308.

[261] OUA, WP/β/21(4), p. 275; for a glimpse of his character see William Stephen, ed., *Register of the Consultations of the Ministers of Edinburgh*, Scottish History Society, third series 16, p. 89.

[262] For Greenwood's opposition to Owen see too George Vernon, *A Letter to a Friend* (1670), p. 12.

[263] Woolrych, *Commonwealth to Protectorate*, p. 186.

time when the breakdown of the recent parliament and the mounting evidence of royalist conspiracy had deflected the government from its conciliatory path, to confront the protector's council with evidence of its legislative incompetence? Would not supporters of the Visitation be confident of persuading Cromwell that the resistance to the ordinance had sprung from 'a design to frustrate the reformation of the university', and that 'the leading persons are such as appear least zealous for the interest of religion and the power of godlinesse'? Wilkins and his friends took the hint. Owen, too, appeared to pull back; and the university 'upon confidence that the Visitors would use their power with due moderation and discretion . . . let the businesse fall asleep'.

For a time the confidence seemed justified. The Visitors held no meetings, or anyway no official ones, for the next three months.[264] The early spring of 1655 was a period of acute anxiety for the government. At the time of the attempted royalist rising in March, Owen mustered a troop of sixty horsed scholars and strove to mobilize the neighbouring countryside in the Commonwealth's defence. Reportedly he 'rode up and down like a spiritual Abeddon', 'rather like a Major-General than Vice-Chancellor'.[265] He was aided by the Principal of Hart Hall, Philemon Stephens, a member of the third Visitation, who commanded the troop under Owen.[266] At that crisis as in the infancy of the republic, the government's followers in the area had to contend with local hostility. The Commonwealth's 'party of its own' in Oxfordshire, headed by Thomas Appletree and William Draper, members of the first Visitation, served in the county militia which was raised in support of the regime of the Major-Generals, and on which Philemon Stephens served.[267] Yet the shortage of 'honest men' to advance the cause of Puritan rule in Oxfordshire persisted.[268] The county's JPs, as Owen complained to John Thurloe, Cromwell's Secretary of State, were 'cold and backward'. The Vice-Chancellor turned for help to neighbouring Berkshire, and asked Thurloe for blank commissions to raise a force there in association with 'sundry good ministers' of the county who had offered their assistance. Soon after Penruddock's rising the Vice-Chancellor discussed the condition of the region around Oxford, and no doubt of the university, with Cromwell and Thurloe in Whitehall.[269]

---

[264] Burrows, p. 402; Wood, *History*, ii. 667.
[265] Vernon, *Letter to a Friend*, p. 13. 'Abeddon' is presumably Abdon, the Judge of Israel, whose forty sons and thirty nephews were each mounted on an ass: Judges 12:13.
[266] Wood, *History*, ii. 668.
[267] *TSP*, iv. 595, 608.
[268] *Severall Proceedings of State Affaires* 2 March 1654, p. 3672.
[269] Toon, *Correspondence of John Owen*, pp. 82–5; Wood, *History*, ii. 668; ECA, MS A. II. 10: 20 March 1655; *Perfect Proceedings* 5 April 1655, p. 4569; Toon, *Oxford Orations*, p. 21. At Whitehall Owen put in a word for the family of his friend Unton Croke, a main figure both in the suppression of the rising and in the military defence of Oxford, who cooperated with him in the enforcement of Puritan rule there: Toon, *Correspondence of John Owen*, pp. 84–5, 121; cf. Spalding, *Diary of Bulstrode Whitelocke*, pp. 502, 503.

By late 1655 Owen was ready for a second trial of strength. The rule of the Major-Generals had now been regularized, and its programme of religious and social reformation announced. Owen introduced a comprehensive programme of reform for Oxford, which belonged to that wider policy or at least complemented it. For the present he was willing to pursue his programme, not through the Visitation, but through the normal constitutional procedures of the university, though he did not hesitate to bend them. Some of his proposals, for the tightening of educational discipline, were in large measure uncontroversial. There was agreement, too, on another subject. A dislike of compulsory oaths of allegiance had gained ground in England during the Puritan Revolution, when rival political and religious groups made so many competing demands for pledges of loyalty. Many at Oxford agreed with Owen's complaint that the university's regulations subjected its members to 'the needless multiplying of sundry oathes,...whereby the consciences of many have been wounded and entangled, and others layd under guilt of perjury, to the great dishonour of God'.[270] But the Vice-Chancellor had two other, much less acceptable, demands. One was for the abolition of the Act, which had become an occasion for frivolous pleasure. On one occasion Owen dragged the Terrae-Filius, the licensed satirist of the Act, from the stage with his own hands. The offender, who was supposed to restrict himself to the parody of philosophical disputations, had exceeded his brief and engaged in 'profaneness', 'obscenity', and 'personal reflections' on Owen himself.[271] Faced with the Vice-Chancellor's demand for the abolition of the Act, the university's Delegates, the guiding spirits of Convocation, offered a compromise which would 'new model' the occasion, purge its excessive hospitality, and reduce it to 'a serious philosophicall exercise'.[272]

In that modified form Owen's proposal would probably have passed if it had not become embroiled, alongside other plans for reform, with his second provocative demand, which was 'very displeasing to the university'[273] and which brought his Vice-Chancellorship to a crisis. This was for the abolition of 'habits'—gowns, hoods and caps. He allegedly judged habits 'totally superstitious'.[274] Perhaps he remembered Laud's insistence on them in the era when Owen had left Oxford in

---

[270] OUA, Reg. Conv. T, p. 281; SP/E/5, fo. 92. Cf. QCA, Register H, p. 116; Toon, *Oxford Orations*, p. 32.

[271] *A Complete Collection of the Sermons of John Owen* (1721), p. xi; Burrows, p. xli; Toon, *Oxford Orations*, p. 35. A recent trend had diminished the intellectual function of the Terrae-Filius: Mordecai Feingold, 'The Humanities', in Tyacke, *History of the University of Oxford*, p. 303. See too *CSPD 1655–6*, p. 289; Wood, *Life and Times*, i. 258, 300, 336; Wood, *History*, ii. 684–5.

[272] For an indication that the move to reform the Act may have had some effect see William Prynne, *The Lords Supper Briefly Vindicated* (1657), preface and p. 1.

[273] OUA, SP/E/4, fo. 91.

[274] Wood, *History*, ii. 668; cf. Toon, *Oxford Orations*, p. 10.

revulsion against the then Chancellor's rule.[275] Yet 'habits' were, as Wilkins observed, 'things common to us, with almost all the considerable corporations in England'. Wilkins thought Owen's war on them 'needless', 'when anyone that pleaseth doth take the liberty to neglect the use of them without control'. No one had been 'troubled' for that omission 'for many years, or like to be'. Having been repeatedly rebuffed by the Delegates, Owen resolved to outwit them. He sprang the proposal on the Delegacy on 25 December 1655, a day when, he perhaps reckoned, his opponents might be more convivially engaged.[276] He got it through, but his victory was short-lived. The decision was reversed when the Delegates met again in January. In March his proposal resurfaced, now as a demand not for the abolition of habits but for 'a general dispensation' from the local statutes that required them. The Delegates agreed, though only, it seems, after Owen had assured them that he did not intend to pursue the matter and after a number of those present had accordingly gone home.

On 10 April his reform programme came before Convocation.[277] Many of his proposals were voted through. Wilkins, anticipating charges of obstruction, was able to claim that 'more of a real publicke reformation' had been achieved at the meeting than by any of the Puritan Visitations. The achievement was not enough for Owen. He aroused antagonism by the number of 'great innovations being at one time proposed'; by his refusal from the chair to allow amendments in debate; and by his insistence on a contentious method of counting the votes. The meeting inflicted a substantial defeat on the Vice-Chancellor over 'the unhappy business of habits'. 'Extremely incensed', not only on that ground but because Convocation had not accepted his programme in its entirety, he berated the assembly as he ended its meeting. As the members dispersed, he summoned the Delegates and told them, no less angrily, that 'since he saw the Convocation would not, as hee desired, reforme itself, he would trouble them no more but meant to take another course'.

His meaning would become clear a few days later, on his return from a brief visit to the city of Coventry. His journey there gives us a glimpse of the national mission to which the Puritan rule of Oxford belonged. He went to Coventry to ordain the Independent pastor Samuel Basnett, the son of an alderman of that city. One of the Cambridge graduates whom the first Visitation had brought to Oxford, Samuel had been made a Fellow of All Souls and been a member of the second Visitation. In travelling to Coventry, as on many occasions in his life, the Vice-Chancellor was accompanied by his fellow Independent minister and fellow Visitor Thankful Owen, who preached with him before Coventry's godly. Thankful was President of St John's College, which had institutional links with the city. The reform

---

[275] Kenneth Fincham, 'Oxford and the Early Stuart Polity', in Tyacke, *History of the University of Oxford*, p. 202. The wearing of hoods on Sundays had been banned at Cambridge in May 1650: Bodl., Wood MS f. 35, fo. 359.

[276] Wilkins claimed that the meeting had been 'very thin', but it seems not to have been as thin as all that: OUA, Reg. Conv. T, p. 279; Bodl., MS Eng. hist. c. 310, fo. 81ᵛ.

[277] The resolutions of the Delegates between December 1655 and April 1656 are conveniently listed in Bodl., MS. Eng. hist. c. 310, fos 81–6ᵛ.

programme supervised by the Major-Generals was being eagerly pursued in Coventry, and Basnett, whose ministry received state support from 1656, would be a leading figure in its enactment there.[278] The Major-General for the region, the protector's cousin Edward Whalley, had recently visited the city and given 'encouragement' to its godly ministers.[279] In 1652 Whalley had headed the list, with John Owen immediately behind him, of the proposers to parliament of the scheme for ecclesiastical settlement that had been produced by 'some heads and governors of some colledges in Oxford',[280] and which was now the basis of the religious policies of the protectorate. Shortly before the arrival of the two Owens in Coventry, Whalley met the Puritan Mayor of the city, Robert Beake, in nearby Warwick.[281] Beake wanted a return to 'the ancient constitution', under Cromwell. He had despised the rule of the Rump, and had regarded its imposition of the Engagement as 'a sad and lamentable time'. He had been dismayed by the eviction from Oxford of Edward Reynolds, whom Owen had replaced.[282] Yet he was zealous for godly reformation, was a warm supporter of Basnett's ministry, and took pride in Owen's visit to Coventry.[283] Wilkins viewed the journey with mistrust, as he did Basnett and Thankful Owen.[284] Thankful Owen, who had been made a Fellow of Lincoln College in 1642 and had returned to the college after the civil war, was a man of spirited temper. In 1650, as sub-Rector of Lincoln, he poured 'contempts' on the parliamentary committee that supervised the Visitation, alleging, in splenetic language, that its appointments to Oxford posts had been governed by haste, ignorance, and favouritism.[285] It appears to have been Thankful Owen who declared, during the third Visitation, that he would sooner see the government of the university 'torn up by the foundation, rather then this gang', the opponents of the Vice-Chancellor's programme, 'should carry it'.[286]

Back from Coventry, the Vice-Chancellor summoned the Visitors. Having assured them that they had the authority to rescind and introduce statutes, he urged them to exercise it. The reforms which Convocation had refused would thus simply be announced as decrees at its next meeting. John Owen's plans did not stop there. He had resolved not merely to bypass Convocation but to overhaul it. 'The whole present frame' of the university's government was to be 'taken away'. During daily meetings of the Visitors, which lasted nearly a week, he addressed what he took to be the root of the problem: the voting rights of the body of MAs, many of

---

[278] Ann Hughes, *Politics, Society and Civil War in Warwickshire, 1620–1660* (Cambridge, 1987), pp. 283–4, 307, 311–12; Coventry City Archives, BA/H/Q/A79/246 (on Coventry and St John's).
[279] *TSP*, iv. 273.
[280] *CJ* 11 February 1653.
[281] Levi Fox, ed., 'Diary of Robert Beake, Mayor of Coventry, 1655–1656', Dugdale Society, *Miscellany* i. (1977), pp. 133–4.
[282] *Burton*, ii. 414–16, iii. 113.
[283] Hughes, *Politics, Society and Civil War*, p. 312; for Beake and Basnett see too Coventry City Archives, BA/H/Q/A79/230 (cf. /229, /231).
[284] OUA, SP/E/4, fo. 91ᵛ.
[285] Ibid., fos 41–5.
[286] Ibid., fo. 92ᵛ. There are notes on sermons by Thankful Owen in Oxford in Bodl., Rawlinson MS e. 199, fos 4ᵛ-6ᵛ.

whom were 'young men and averse to reformation', 'drones' unfit to be 'intrusted with government'. They were, indeed, 'such as would cut our throats'[287]—a phrase that was to be repeatedly echoed in Cromwell's opening speech to the parliament that met five months later, when the protector argued, in defence of the rule of the Major-Generals, that 'if nothing should be done but what is according to law, the throat of the nation may be cut'.[288] Owen's friends even claimed that Convocation, if left as it was, might vote to depose Cromwell from the Chancellorship, or, if the protector should choose to resign the office, elect a royalist to succeed him. Wilkins thought the threat unreal and the argument born of desperation. Even if such a challenge were to arise, he was sure, he and his friends would command the influence to check it. Nonetheless Owen and his allies determined that Convocation should be put under the control of 'godly and prudent men', who would choose which of the MAs to admit, and which not to admit, to its membership. If Convocation itself should rebel against the change, 'they talke of making use of the Major-Generall'.[289] There are three of the Major-Generals whom Owen might have had in mind. One is his ally at Whitehall Charles Fleetwood, whose area of command included Oxfordshire,[290] and who seems to have been present, in the following year, at the last of the Acts over which Owen presided.[291] The second is Fleetwood's Baptist deputy in the region, William Packer, who was in Oxford the month before Wilkins wrote, supervising the county militia, and who was there again three months after the letter was written.[292] Packer took a close interest in the city of Oxford, where he tried to win election to the parliament of 1656,[293] and where he would be the commanding officer in 1659.[294] It seems to have been Packer or his agents in Oxford who interrupted the connivance of the university authorities at gatherings of groups of royalists for worship.[295] The third possibility is that Owen had in mind his own close friend and ally Major-General John Desborough, whose own sphere of command was the West Country, but who took a close interest in Oxford's affairs.[296]

In April 1656 Wilkins told Goddard and French that the moves against the university's statutes in April 1656 were of 'huge concernment'. They 'strike at the subversion of all our charters. And I think we are the first corporation in England upon whom any such attempt hath been made'. Wilkins and his friends 'earnestly importuned' the Vice-Chancellor to withdraw from 'these high acts'.[297] They failed, but fortunately for them the divisions that had paralysed the Visitors at

---

[287] OUA, SP/E/4, fo. 92^v.

[288] Abbott, iv. 275.

[289] OUA, SP/E/4, fo. 92^v.

[290] Fleetwood was 'gallantly entertained' somewhere in the county during his return from Ireland to London in September 1655: *TSP*, iv. 32.

[291] PCA, MS 4/1/1, fo. 26.

[292] *TSP*, iv. 495, 608, v. 489.

[293] Durston, *Cromwell's Major-Generals*, pp. 90, 196.

[294] Godfrey Davies, *The Restoration of Charles II 1658–1660* (Oxford, 1955), p. 127.

[295] Below, p. 183.

[296] OUA, NW/3/4, fo. 70; *TSP*, iii. 345. (Owen is unlikely to have had Whalley in mind.)

[297] OUA, SP/E/4, fos 91–3.

their meeting in the Vice-Chancellor's lodgings in February 1655 had resurfaced. For the split among the Visitors of 1647–8, between harsh and gentle approaches to the reform of Oxford, had its parallel on the third Visitation. The counterweights to Owen's influence were a little stronger on the third Visitation than on the second, the body of 1653–4 which the new one replaced. John Conant had been reappointed. Although the Presbyterian Edmund Staunton had not been re-named, there were two Presbyterians on the third Visitation who, until the imposition of the Engagement, had been among the most active members of the first, but who had been omitted from the second. One of them, Robert Harris, was now in a sick and sleepy old age,[298] but he remained a substantial figure in Oxford politics. The other, Henry Wilkinson senior, had been the severe enforcer, with Francis Cheynell, of the first Visitation, though time and his Oxford career seem to have softened his approach. The Independent takeover of the first commission had diminished Wilkinson's role on it. His standing on the third Visitation, by contrast, must have been enhanced by Cromwell's desire to broaden the political base of the protectorate and by the return of Presbyterianism to parliamentary and public life.[299] Harris and Conant would have been beneficiaries of the same trend. The three men now questioned Owen's course. In doing so they had only limited room for manoeuvre. Even as he confronted the university's government, the Vice-Chancellor was able to exploit the authority of his own office within it, to which, after all, he had been appointed by the head of state. On the Visitation he was, strictly speaking, only one voting member among the rest, but other members hesitated to confront him and his Independent supporters on the body. They did not challenge the substance of his reforms, with which, to varying degrees, they are likely to have sympathized. With the encouragement of friends among Wilkins's party, however, they cast doubt on their own authority to enact them. They declined to proceed further until or unless their right to change statutes were confirmed in law, or at least until they had consulted with the non-resident Visitors, mostly men of moderate outlook who might be expected to exercise a restraining influence.

Thus checked, Owen returned to Whitehall in order to get his programme 'confirmed above'. He took all the relevant papers with him, leaving no copies even for his fellow Visitors.[300] Wilkins urged Goddard and French to counsel the Vice-Chancellor towards restraint. In the event Owen's mission was unavailing. In May, apparently through some bungle among the guards, he was arrested at Whitehall Gate, 'where he was coming to attend' upon some matter of 'public service'.[301] It was a symbolic mishap. His request for support over the Visitation evidently got lost amid the contests at Whitehall during the late spring and early summer of 1656 that led to the summoning of a new parliament, a development which in turn

[298] William Durham, *The Life and Death of . . . Robert Harris* (1660), p. 59.
[299] Below, p. 238.
[300] OUA, SP/E/4, fo. 93.
[301] TNA, SP25/127: 15 May 1656; *CSPD 1655–6*, p. 319; *1656–7*, p. 108; Toon, *God's Statesman*, p. 99.

heralded the demise of the rule of the Major-Generals and a return to Cromwell's conciliatory paths. Perhaps Wilkins's marriage to Cromwell's sister at some point in the same year was part of the story. It was in explaining the marriage that Evelyn wrote of Wilkins's aim 'to preserve the universities from the ignorant sacrilegious commander and souldiers'. Walter Pope stated that the match 'preserved the university from running into disorder and confusion'.[302]

In July the Act, which had been held annually since 1651, was cancelled, perhaps because of the feud over the character of the occasion; or perhaps because, with parliamentary elections in the offing, the government feared the gathering of ill-affected spirits in the university.[303] Or perhaps Owen, who in his discontent had absented himself from Oxford, vetoed the occasion.[304] In the same month the Puritan minister Ralph Josselin learned in his Essex parish that the Vice-Chancellor's war on 'habits' had made him 'a great scorne'.[305] The principal effect of his campaign, according to Pope, was a counter-productive one:

> It was very remarkable that all the antediluvian Cavaliers, I mean Fellows of colleges, who had the good fortune to survive the flood of the Visitation, and keep their places, and who had ever since lived retired in their cells, never medling with public affairs in the university, not appearing in the Convocation . . . came now as it were in troops, . . . habited in their formalities, to give their votes for their continuation, most of whose faces were unknown to the greatest part of the assembly.

For

> they who before car'd not before whether they wore caps or hoods, or not, now immediately procur'd them; never had the makers and sellers thereof a better vent for their ware, as it appeared the next Sunday; for there was then a greater number of scholars at St Marys in their formalities, than ever I saw before or since, and the use of them continued, tho' not to that heighth, till the happy Restoration of King Charles.[306]

Pope is a partisan and often unreliable witness. But other sources confirm that, in the summer, 'caps were never more in fashion than now', and that henceforth 'formalities' were 'on foot again'.[307] As in the later 1640s, so in the later 1650s,

---

[302] Shapiro, *John Wilkins*, pp. 111–13. Wilkins's wife was chief mourner, with her husband in attendance, at the funeral of Cromwell's beloved daughter Elizabeth in the month before the protector's own death: *Publick Intelligencer* 16 August 1658, p. 151.

[303] Puritan concern about the Act (like Puritan anxiety about horse-racing, which Major-Generals were suppressing at this time) arose from considerations of security as well as of morality. OUA, Reg. Conv. T, pp. 108–9; Wood, *History*, ii. 646, 670; Wood, *Life and Times*, i. 175; BNCA, MS A. II. 46, p. 26; OUA, SP/E/4, fo. 91ᵛ.

[304] OUA, Reg. Conv. T, p. 285; *CSPD 1656–7*, p. 51 (though cf. Bodl., MS Eng. hist. c. 310, fo. 86ᵛ). There had been doubts whether the Act would be held in 1655: *CSPD 1655*, pp. 207, 219.

[305] Alan Macfarlane, ed., *The Diary of Ralph Josselin 1616–1683* (Oxford, 1976), p. 374; cf. *CSPD 1655–6*, pp. 289, 294. Another 'formality' was personally embarrassing to Owen: his own title. The 'title of doctor', he explained when mocked on that account, 'was conferred on me by the university in my absence, and against my consent . . . nor did I use it till some were offended with me . . . for my neglect': Owen, *Works*, xiii. 302; cf. Richard Baxter, *Certain Disputations* (1657), pp. 484–5.

[306] Pope, *Life of . . . Seth Bishop of Salisbury*, pp. 42–3.

[307] *CSPD 1656–7*, p. 51; *1657–8*, p. 118; cf. Bodl., Tanner MS 52, fo. 98.

communal protest merged with royalist sentiment. Though royalism had mostly kept its head down in Cromwellian Oxford, it had never disappeared. The political leaders among Oxford's royalists and monarchists might warn against gestures of defiance, but they had to struggle to contain younger and hotter spirits. From 1656 a current of feeling in favour of old ways is increasingly perceptible in the university. The question, there as elsewhere, was whether the protectorate had the political capacity to absorb and accommodate that sentiment, and to transmute royalism into Cromwellianism.

   Owen had become an impediment to that aspiration. Though some of his less contentious reforms continued to be pursued by the Delegates after his defeat in Convocation in April 1656,[308] the days of his rule of Oxford were numbered. It fell victim to the conservative reaction which animated the parliament that met in September 1656, and to which Cromwell, even as he continued to press the cause of godly reformation (never more insistently than in his opening speech to the assembly), largely submitted. As usual when parliament met, the university took care to have its interests pressed at Westminster. Palmer and Wilkins and Langbaine all lobbied there. Wilkins's 'necessary stay' in London lasted nine weeks and involved a payment of ten shillings to 'the doorkeeper of the parliament house'.[309] The fate of the Visitation was not the university's only concern in the debates of the assembly,[310] and much of Wilkins's activity would have had Owen's support. Nonetheless, Owen's opponents pressed parliament to rid Oxford of the Visitation. They prepared a bill which would terminate its authority and restore the local Visitors. 'To continue for ever a Visitation, by persons unstatutable that are judges and parties, upon pretence of further reformation,' explained the proposers, 'may rather evidence the desire of rule and dominion in the pretenders, than any regard to the honour, liberties, or statutes of the university.' The present Visitors 'do rather nourish and foment, than appease differences'.[311] No doubt in support of that complaint, 'applications' were received by the university's old friend the MP Bulstrode Whitelocke, now a Commissioner for the Treasury, 'about Visitors of the University of Oxford'.[312] After 'a great deal of stir', the bill was dropped. Owen's party seems to have seen it off.[313] Yet if he won the battle he lost the war. In the spring of 1657 a parliamentary committee, charged with reviewing the ordinance that had created the Visitation, refused to recommend its endorsement, 'in regard the Visitors undertake to make laws against the fundamental laws'. In the Commons, Owen's close friend John Desborough, a Major-General and an advocate of military methods in politics, who had already defiantly but unsuccessfully resisted the parliament's attack on the Major-Generals, now struggled, again in vain, on Owen's behalf. 'Whatever reproach hath been cast upon' the Visitation, he told the House in late April 1657, 'it has been a great means to regulate the

[308] Bodl., MS Eng. hist. c. 310, fos 86, 87ᵛ, 92.
[309] OUA, NW/3/4, fo. 196; WP/β/21/4, pp. 293, 294 (cf. p. 305).
[310] Below, pp. 149, 155–6; *CJ* 27 January, 5 February 1657; NA, 4211.
[311] OUA, SP/E/4, fo. 96–8.
[312] Whitelocke, *Memorials*, iv. 287.
[313] Wood, *History*, ii. 680.

university, and to purge loose and profane persons'. Parliament nonetheless resolved that the Visitation be terminated in January 1658. Even that prolongation of its life was achieved only after pleas from Cromwell's councillors, and after a 'great debate' about the length of the extension. Cromwell uncomplainingly accepted the decision.[314]

In the same weeks Owen and Desborough were fighting a larger battle. In February 1657, to the consternation of their party, parliament offered Cromwell the Crown under a new constitution, the Humble Petition and Advice as it came to be known, which was designed to civilianize his rule and begin the restoration of the ancient constitution. Soon afterwards Richard Cromwell told his brother Henry that 'Dr Owen hath been very angry and went in great haste out of London'.[315] After Cromwell's elevation to the protectorate in 1653, Owen had hailed him, in verse, as England's Augustus.[316] At that stage, the restoration of single rule had had two attractions to such men as Owen and Desborough. It offered an escape from the anarchy of Barebone's; and it reduced the parliamentary obstacles that, since Worcester, had impeded the Cromwellian programme of godly reform and liberty of conscience. In 1657, by contrast, the proposal to make Cromwell king symbolized, in the same men's eyes, the betrayal and abandonment of the godly cause. Told that the protector was ready to accept the Crown, Desborough and Colonel Thomas Pride went to Owen and 'persuaded him to draw up a petition according to their desires'. The protector was furious.[317] Although he decided to refuse the offer, he was re-installed as protector in a ceremony that bestowed traditional features of regality on his rule under the Humble Petition. Owen's relations with him never recovered, even though Owen's final addresses as Vice-Chancellor two months later lauded the greatness of the political master who had appointed him.[318] He 'saw him not' for 'some long time before' the protector's death in September 1658.[319]

Owen's view of the kingship proposal was shared by Christopher Rogers, President of New Inn Hall, who had been a leading and energetic member of the first Visitation[320] and was active on the third. Of Oxford's ruling Puritans he was the most candidly radical in his politics. In 1648 he had prayed in the university church 'that God would open the king's eyes to lay to heart all that blood he had spilt'.[321] At the Restoration, when most Puritans accepted the legality of the king's return and kept quiet about their political pasts, he defiantly told the royal authorities that the parliament which enforced the Visitation in 1648 had been 'a

---

[314] *Burton*, ii. 63–4; *CJ* 28 April 1657. Cf. OUA, SP/E/4, fos 96–7, 100; Bodl., Bodleian MS Add. d. 105, p. 9. In the event the Visitors enjoyed a brief extension of their authority, apparently with Cromwell's blessing: TNA, SP 25/78, p. 840; Burrows, pp. 437, 439.

[315] Gaunt, *Correspondence of Henry Cromwell 1655–1659*, p. 221.

[316] *Musarum Oxoniensum*, p. 1; cf. p. 59.

[317] *Ludlow's Memoirs*, ii. 24–7.

[318] Toon, *Oxford Orations*, pp. 45, 47.

[319] Toon, *God's Statesman*, pp. 99–100; cf. Nicastro, *Lettere di Henry Stubbe*, p. 16.

[320] See esp. Reinhart, 'Parliamentary Visitation', pp. 321, 379.

[321] Bodl., Wood MS f. 35, fo. 309ᵛ.

lawful power'.[322] Like Thomas Goodwin at Magdalen College, Rogers combined his headship of his house with the role of pastor to a gathered church which met in it. With his congregation he saw in the proposal to crown Cromwell a symptom of a reactionary spirit in the nation. He and three pastors of similar congregations, one in Oxfordshire, one in Worcestershire, one in Gloucestershire, wrote to the protector on behalf of their flocks to urge him to refuse the offer. They observed 'to what a height the malignant and persecuting spirit is of late risen in the nation'; they noted the 'affronts and violence' which God's 'poore people . . . meete withal from that party, especially upon the rumor of the Major-Generalls being voted downe, under whom the Lord's people had comfortable protection'; they warned the protector against the 'temptations' with which the offer of the Crown 'encompassed' him; and they advised him that acceptance of it would lose him his saintly following, 'wherein wee humbly conceive (and as your highnesse hath often asserted) your preservation (under God) is absolutely wrapt upp'.[323]

Owen, ill and exhausted, gave up the Vice-Chancellorship in October 1657.[324] In addressing the university in his last months of office, he complained (in the Latin, always hard to turn into plausible English, of his official speeches) of 'wrongs and slanders' and of 'the many things I have suffered at the hands of men impelled by hate'.[325] He also insisted that he was resigning of his own volition, which he had had to press on 'certain very important men'.[326] Yet the protector can hardly have rued Owen's departure from office. In 1656 there had been a rumour that Owen would be replaced by John Wilkins.[327] In 1657 the place went instead to John Conant, whom the first Visitation had installed as Rector of Exeter College. Though a member of the second and third Visitations, Conant had repeatedly defended the university in its relations with central government. His election as Vice-Chancellor was greeted with 'a universal shout of a very full congregation'.[328] He would retain the post until the Restoration. In his way he was as earnest a Puritan reformer of Oxford as Owen, but his way was different. He was not minded to challenge the governing machinery of the university. In the 1640s he had refused to take the Solemn League and Covenant, apparently from a commitment to episcopacy, though episcopacy of a moderate kind. He joined in the addresses to Charles II at the Restoration, when a petition submitted on his behalf stated that he had been 'constantly loyal to the king's majesty'.[329] He was allowed to keep the headship of

[322] Varley, 'Restoration Visitation', p. 4; cf. Bodl., Wood MS f. 35, fo. 336.
[323] Nickolls, pp. 139–40. Rogers seems nonetheless to have cooperated with those members of the third Visitation who opposed Owen's stand against Convocation in 1656—a reminder, if so, of the customary complexities of university politics: OUA, SP/E/4, fo. 92ᵛ. For Rogers see too *CJ* 26 July 1659.
[324] Nicastro, *Lettere di Henry Stubbe*, p. 11; Bodl., J. Walker MS c. 9, fo. 188; cf. Toon, *Correspondence of John Owen*, p. 94.
[325] Toon, *Oxford Orations*, pp. 32–3, 41. I have used Toon's translations.
[326] Ibid., pp. 40, 44–5.
[327] *CSPD 1656–7*, p. 51.
[328] Conant Jr, *Life of . . . John Conant*, p. 24; cf. Wood, *Life and Times*, i. 359.
[329] BL, Harleian MS 7190, fo. 297.

his college 'in regard of his good behaviour'.[330] But he could not stomach the high Anglicanism of the Restoration. He left Oxford rather than submit to the Act of Uniformity of 1662.

Not only had Owen given way to Conant. Within the leadership of Independency he had been supplanted in Cromwell's favour by his fellow 'Atlas', Thomas Goodwin.[331] Goodwin had been intimate with the protector during the crisis over the Humble Petition and Advice, to which he had given useful backing. Cromwell and Thurloe, anxious to reward him for that service, arranged with Henry Cromwell for Goodwin to receive a secret source of income from an estate in Ireland[332] (where Owen himself had acquired lands[333]). Goodwin wanted the money because of his 'great desire . . . to separate himself to his studies, to perfect severall books, which he hath now under his hands, contayninge a body of divinity, and without doing of which he professeth he cannot dye in peace'.[334] Yet he was no recluse. In spite of his subsidy he remained at his post at Magdalen until 1660.[335] He was a sedulous politician who, in promoting the Puritan cause in Oxford, cultivated and mobilized high-placed contacts in Whitehall. In December 1657 it was reported that Owen had withdrawn from the course of sermons which he and Goodwin had for some years given on Sunday afternoons in the university church, 'and at the same university houre hath set up a lecture in the parish church, it is conceived in opposition, and to draine St Mary's'.[336] Perhaps it was there that Owen preached the sermon which he published in 1658 with the title *Of Temptation*, and which lamented that 'the prevailing party of these nations, many of those in rule', had succumbed to the enticements of Satan. Like other critics of the protectorate, among them John Milton,[337] Owen noted how the beguilements of self-advancement had been cloaked beneath 'pretences' to virtue.[338] It was Goodwin, not Owen, whom we find ministering to Cromwell at the protector's deathbed; praying at the ceremony in which Richard Cromwell accepted the succession;[339] welcoming Richard's rule on behalf of the Congregationalist churches;[340] and being imposed by the government on a resentful Commons as a preacher at the opening of Richard's parliament.[341] Owen, in preaching before the same assembly, boldly inveighed against 'old formes and ways taken up with greedinesse, which are a

[330] Varley, 'Restoration Visitation', p. 29.

[331] *TSP*, vii. 562; *Burton*, iii. 1–2.

[332] *TSP*, vi. 539, 55[4]; *CSPD 1657–8*, p. 318; Gaunt, *Correspondence of Henry Cromwell*, p. 368. The President's protégé and lieutenant at Magdalen James Barron, who had been favoured by Fairfax and Cromwell on their visit to Oxford in 1649, was subsidized in his university post by the protectoral council from 1654 (*CSPD 1654*, pp. 259, 268; Varley, 'Restoration Visitation', p. 18).

[333] *CJ* 15 September 1659.

[334] *TSP*, vi. 539.

[335] *CSPD 1659–60*, pp. 400–1.

[336] TNA, SP18/158, fo. 58. Cf. *CSPD 1657–8*, p. 118; Vernon, *Letter to a Friend*, p. 28.

[337] *LP*, pp. 258, 346.

[338] Owen, *Of Temptation* (1658), pp. 65–6 (cf. pp. 25, 28, 51, 72, 101, 104, 135); Toon, *God's Statesman*, p. 100.

[339] Davies, *Restoration of Charles II*, pp. 3, 6; cf. *Ludlow's Memoirs*, ii. 43.

[340] *Mercurius Politicus* 21 October 1658, pp. 921–5; cf. Davies, *Restoration of Charles II*, pp. 10, 49.

[341] BL Add. MS 5138, pp. 106–8.

badge of apostasy from all former ingagement and actings', and warned that England might 'return to its former station and condition'.[342] When the Rump was restored in May 1659, the parliament was swift to distinguish between its friends and the foes who had backed the monarchical tendencies of the late protectorate. It used uncharacteristically fulsome language to give 'very hearty thanks' to Owen for 'the seasonable word the Lord hath enabled him to deliver' to it at the opening of the session, but gave another cold reception to a sermon by Goodwin.[343]

If Owen was humiliated in 1657, neither his resignation nor parliament's decision to terminate the Visitation removed his appetite for the reform of Oxford, where, for all the intensity of the recent feuds, he was never shunned or isolated. In the last weeks of the commission's life he took part in its final battle, one in which the Visitors' appetite for institutional reform for once had the heads of the colleges,[344] and widespread opinion below them, on its side.[345] Like many reformers before and after them, the Visitors resolved to break the system by which Fellowships were sold at All Souls and New College. In no colleges had the successive Visitations made less headway. In both of them a reforming party found itself withstood by 'the major parte'. At All Souls, even after a wholesale appointment of new college officers[346] and the insertion of so many Fellows from outside—some of them of high intellectual attainment[347]—the Visitors complained in 1651 that the 'generall discipline' of the college was 'very much out of order', both in 'the publique worship of God in the chappell' and in 'scholastical exercises', a blight 'which is very much occasioned by the great necglect' of the college's officers.[348] In the 1650s we find the college's royalists meeting openly in a nearby coffee-house, or gathering for the playing of music by 'some ingeniose scholars'.[349] In 1657 the college contrived to appoint the Anglican divine Thomas Tomkins, a future chaplain to Gilbert Sheldon, to a probationary Fellowship.[350] If there were Puritan measures in the college during the Cromwellian years, the admittedly exiguous evidence does not record it. The Warden, John Palmer, was a more active occupant of the office

---

[342] Quoted by Paul Hardacre, *The Royalists during the Puritan Revolution* (The Hague, 1956), p. 134, and in Austin Woolrych's Introduction to *CPW*, vii., p. 61; cf. Davies, *Restoration of Charles II*, p. 95.

[343] *CJ* 8 May 1659; *CSPD 1658–9*, p. 352; Davies, *Restoration of Charles II*, p. 50; cf. *Burton*, iii. 1–2.

[344] Bodl., Tanner MS 340(i), fo. 123&ᵛ.

[345] For the battle see Burrows, pp. 418–34; *CSPD 1657–8*, pp. 181–2, 188, 236–7, 260, 277–9, and MSS there calendared; WCA, MS 4/116. Cf. OUA, WP/γ/22/1(i); QCA, MS 2Y/41; UCA, College Register 1509–1727, fo. 32; *CJ* 5 February 1657; *CSPD 1657–8*, pp. 188, 236–7, 277–8.

[346] Burrows, p. 287 and n.

[347] Ibid., p. cxx; S. J. D. Green and Peregrine Horden, *All Souls under the Ancien Regime* (Oxford, 2007), pp. 66–7.

[348] Bodl., Wood MS f. 35, fo. 365; Burrows, p. 315.

[349] Wood, *Life and Times*, i. 201; de Beer, *Diary of John Eveleyn*, iii. 106.

[350] Wood, *Athenae Oxonienses*, iii. 1046.

than has sometimes been supposed.[351] He may have been torn between reforming and conservative instincts.[352]

At New College the resistance to the Visitors in 1648, led by the Warden Henry Stringer, had been unanimous.[353] Parliament's standing committee replaced him, five days before the regicide, with George Marshall,[354] who had been chaplain to the parliamentarian troops in Oxford after the city's surrender in 1646.[355] By early 1650 Marshall had joined the Independent party on the Visitation.[356] He was close to Owen's friend John Desborough.[357] Unlike the other Visitors who were recruited between the regicide and Worcester, he remained an active member of the commission after that battle. Under the protectorate he received letters of intelligence from Hamburg, which he passed on to Cromwell, concerning the movements of exiled royalist clergy. His source was a minister whom Thomas Goodwin had sent 'at the request of the well affected' among the English merchant community there, which the civil wars had bitterly divided.[358] Marshall may have had his own use for the news, for he had to contend with royalist conspirators within the college's walls.[359] At New College as at All Souls, a number of committed supporters of the Puritan takeover had been intruded by the Visitation.[360] A series of initiatives for Puritan and disciplinary reform had ensued, but to little effect.[361] In 1650 there was 'great abuse of recreation through the excesse of it in the bowling green'.[362] In 1653, 'to the great scandal of the university', one of the chaplains, George How, a card-player of whom it was alleged that he never preached and that he spent half the morning in bed, raped a maid in the fields while returning from a drinking expedition to the nearby village of Iffley with a clerical colleague at the college.[363] (The companion, William Dennys, was sent on the disastrous expedition to Hispaniola the following year.[364]) Another resident of New College, Daniel Vivian, an expertly cantankerous Fellow who had outwardly cooperated with the parliamentarian takeover of Oxford but who may have been a secret royalist agent, was eventually expelled for a variety of misdemeanours, but only after giving endless difficulty both to his colleagues and to the Visitors. At one point the college had to pay for soldiers to guard his chamber.[365] At the Restoration he would win a handsome testimonial to

[351] All Souls College Archives (hereafter ASA), MS 401, fos 117–37.
[352] With the Principal of Hart Hall, Philemon Stephens, he served on the Oxfordshire militia commission in 1656 (*TSP*, iv. 595, 608).
[353] Bodl., Wood MS f. 35, fo. 310; Burrows, p. 127.
[354] Burrows, pp. 220–1.
[355] Anne Laurence, *Parliamentary Army Chaplains 1642–1651* (Woodbridge, 1990), p. 151.
[356] QCA, Register H, p. 118; Burrows, pp. 340, 350, 351 (cf. p. 239).
[357] *TSP*, iii. 345.
[358] Ibid., iii. 345–6.
[359] Ibid., iii. 329.
[360] For glimpses of their activity see NA, 9855, pp. 5, 11; 988: 15 September 1651; MS 4207: 1649, second term, 'to reform the college'; see too Burrows, p. 229.
[361] NA, 988. For the non-Puritan spirit at the college see also *CSPD 1655–6*, pp. 31, 124, 232.
[362] NA, 988: 31 May 1650.
[363] Ibid.: material at back of volume; Burrows, p. 361; Toon, *Correspondence of John Owen*, p. 121.
[364] Toon, *Correspondence of John Owen*, p. 121n.; cf. NA, 9655, p. 51.
[365] NA, 4207: 1649: fourth term (cf. the references to 'Lieutenant West' in the same term and in the third term); NA, 9655, reverse entries, fo. [1ᵛ]; TNA, SP 29/11, fo. 109; A. G.

the loyalty of his royalism, though the tribute it contained to his 'sober life and conversation' would have raised some Puritan eyebrows.[366] Under Richard Cromwell's protectorate, 'disorders, breaches of trust and violations of the statutes . . . and the scandalous lives and conversations, excesses of manners and other misdemeanours', drew the protector to announce a special Visitation of the college.[367]

Though the university's Visitors attempted to tackle the 'corruption' in the filling of Fellowships at New College, it was at All Souls that battle was joined.[368] The Visitors declared the 'corruption in the buying and selling of fellowships' there to be 'odiouse to God and all good men'.[369] 'The major parte of the Fellowes having an interest in keeping up this corruption', 'worthy, godly and deserving persons' were deterred from standing for election. In 1656 a 'testimony from heaven against that corrupt practice' gave the Visitors their chance. It 'pleased God to load and trouble the conscience' of one of the Fellows, who, 'the Lord pursuing his love towards him, with an effectuall worke of grace upon his heart', confessed to having paid £150 for his Fellowship. The 'godly and honest fellowes', and (at least outwardly) Warden Palmer, supported the Visitors.[370] Initially the Visitatorial assault received encouragement from Whitehall. Yet, as the weeks passed, the regime retreated into a cool neutrality. The reformers discovered how well connected their adversaries were. Although we cannot be certain, one ally is likely to have been particularly helpful to All Souls: the protector's elder son. Richard Cromwell, whom Oliver was tentatively grooming for the succession to the protectorate, was elected Chancellor, at the age of thirty, in July 1657, two months before Owen's replacement as Vice-Chancellor by Conant. It is possible, though the evidence is faint, that Oliver had wanted to give up the Chancellorship earlier; that, to test the water, he had floated the idea of securing Richard's succession to the office in the summer of 1655, when there were expectations that Oliver was about to take the Crown; and that in the event the protector had decided not to risk the stir of an election.[371] In the summer of 1657, Oliver's commitment to kingship in all but name having been demonstrated, and the end of the third Visitation being in sight, it evidently seemed safe to proceed.

Even so, the government moved cautiously. Richard's installation was held not in Oxford but in Whitehall. The new Chancellor's escort at the ceremony was John Wilkins, who from the outset established himself as his right-hand man at Oxford.[372] Those present included the royalists Gerald Langbaine and

---

Matthews, ed., *Walker Revised* (Oxford, 1948), p. 231; Burrows, pp. 53, 102n., 244–5, 363, 370–1, 377–85, 389, 404, 414.

[366] Bosher, *Making of the Restoration Settlement*, p. 159.
[367] NA, 9655, pp. 53–4.
[368] NA, 1085. Those were not the only colleges where corruption was suspected: QCA, MS 2Y/41.
[369] Burrows, p. 428; TNA, SP18/157, fo. 242.
[370] Burrows, pp. 428–9.
[371] *Weekly Intelligencer* 28 August 1655, pp. 6–7; OUA, SP/E/4, fo. 93.
[372] OUA, Reg. Conv. T, pp. 306, 308; *Mercurius Politicus* 30 July 1657, pp. 7955–6; *CSPD 1657–8*, pp. 215, 349; *1658–9*, p. 352; *Ludlow's Memoirs*, ii. 61.

Richard Zouche.[373] The government press reported that Richard's appointment was greeted in Oxford 'by the cheerful and unanimous suffrages of the whole Convocation'.[374] It was certainly unopposed. Owen's warning in the previous year that the nomination of a successor favoured by Richard's father might be challenged had proved empty. Five months later, in December 1657, in the midst of the battle between the Visitors and All Souls, Richard was added to his father's privy council. There he was one of two men given special responsibility for the handling of the dispute over the sale of Fellowships. The other was that conservative influence on the Cromwellian council[375] Nathaniel Fiennes, who had aided Oxford against the Visitors in the late 1640s. A son of Lord Saye and Sele, Fiennes belonged to a family which had long held rights as patrons of New College.[376] He represented the university in the parliament of 1656. It is likely to have been he who in 1654 had led resistance on the council to the award of sovereign powers to the third Visitation.[377] Now he and the new Chancellor worked closely together.

On Oliver Cromwell's death in September 1658 a maypole was set up in Oxford.[378] When Richard was proclaimed his successor as lord protector in front of the university church, the city's rulers 'were pelted with carret and turnip-tops by yong scholars and others who stood at a distance'.[379] It is the only recorded disturbance in England to have followed the proclamation.[380] Over the time ahead, defiance would take more serious and powerful forms. It was not directed at Richard himself. Although he was ready to intervene in the university's affairs,[381] he favoured traditional forms both as lord protector and as Chancellor. He befriended Presbyterians. He placed Edward Reynolds, whom the Engagement had removed from Oxford, on the Visitation to investigate the affairs of New College.[382] This was a different kind of commission from the three Visitations of the university in the previous twelve years. It was appointed not by the government but on the authority of the office of the local Visitor, the Bishop of Winchester, which Richard claimed to have devolved upon the state and thus upon him.[383] While the college's royalist and Anglican elements would hardly have welcomed the absorption of that authority by the protectorate, Richard's move did accord with

---

[373] OUA, NWA/3/4, fos 208–20. Wilkins's brother Timothy, a drinking friend of Anthony Wood (Davies, 'Family and Connections of John Wilkins', p. 105), was also there.

[374] *Mercurius Politicus* 30 July 1657, p. 7948.

[375] Below, p. 211.

[376] *CSPD 1657–8*, pp. 236–7, 278. See too *CJ* 30 December 1656, 23 January 1657; OUA, WP/β/21/4, p. 289; Bodl., MS Eng. hist. c. 310, fo. 88ᵛ; Firth and Rait, ii. 1077; *Burton*, i. 84, 353–4. In April 1660 William Lenthall, the Speaker of the Long Parliament, claimed to have been 'a great servant' to New College and the university 'in my public capacity', and implied that he had afforded them protection from outside powers. NA 9655, reverse entries, fo. [8]; below, p. 189.

[377] *CSPD 1654*, p. 346.

[378] Bodl., Wood MS d. 19(2), fo. 45.

[379] Wood, *Life and Times*, i. 259.

[380] Davies, *Restoration of Charles II*, p. 7.

[381] NA, 9655, p. 53; *CSPD 1657–8*, p. 236; Toon, *Correspondence of John Owen*, pp. 74–5.

[382] NA, 9655, p. 53.

[383] Ibid., p. 53.

the university's own readiness to accept new local Visitors as the price of the restoration of their offices.

Oxford's return towards institutional normality in the later 1650s was not untroubled. Under Richard it had to survive the continuing trials of strength at Whitehall over the direction of protectoral policy, between the monarchical party and the opposition to it led by Owen's allies Fleetwood and Desborough. The division had hardened and sharpened. As usual, conflict at the centre interacted with conflict in Oxford. John Wilkins had become a leading figure not merely in the university's affairs but in the nation's. Reportedly he, with John Thurloe and Lord Broghill, was one of the three innermost advisers of Richard's protectorate.[384] On Richard's succession Wilkins's party at Oxford immediately prepared a petition to the new protector, a copy of which survives among papers of Wilkins's ally John Wallis, and which repeated arguments that had been used against external Visitors since the appointment of the third Visitation. The petition addressed the new protector as the heir to England's 'princes', to his 'royall predecessors'. 'Some particular persons', it intimated, were striving for the appointment of yet another Visitation, which again would hold 'continuall and arbitrary power'. The advocates of the measure, it complained, were resorting, as usual by 'private insinuations', to the old argument that Oxford's entrenched royalism made it unfit for self-government. Emphasizing the university's loyalty to Richard, the petition rehearsed familiar arguments for the restoration of local Visitors to be appointed or confirmed by protector and parliament.[385]

The threat of a fourth Visitation must have been real and must have had backers in high places, for Wilkins's circle would not have drawn needless attention to it. Early in 1659, when Richard Cromwell's parliament met, 'the godly' of Oxford circulated a petition in favour of a new commission. Wilkins's associates moved again. A counter-petition, repeating the arguments of the address on Richard's accession, was prepared for presentation to parliament. We glimpse the involvement of Wilkins's ally Nathaniel Crewe of Lincoln College, who got young Anthony Wood to sign it. In the event, thanks apparently to conciliation by Vice-Chancellor Conant, neither petition was presented. Perhaps, like the university's leaders early in 1655, Conant decided that public remonstration would be counter-productive. Perhaps he sensed that the threat of a new Visitation could be trusted to evaporate.[386] At all events the time of 'extraordinary courses', to which

---

[384] *Ludlow's Memoirs*, ii. 61. Their ally Philip Jones was involved in Oxford's affairs: TNA, 25/158: 31 December 1657.

[385] Perhaps because protests against the prospective fourth Visitation tended to repeat those against the third, and perhaps because the account by Walter Pope revised the chronology to the advantage of his own importance in the story, contemporary recollections of the two series of episodes tended to get conflated and the events wrongly dated: OUA, SP/E/4, fos 91, 100; Pope, *Life of ... Seth Bishop of Salisbury*, pp. 34, 43; Thomas Wood, *An Appendix to the Life of ... Seth Bishop of Salisbury* (1697), pp. 27–9.

[386] For the struggle of 1658–9 see Bodl., Bodleian MS Add. d. 105, pp. 9–11; Conant Jr, *Life of ... John Conant*, pp. 28–30; Wood, *Life and Times*, i. 268; Wood, *History*, ii. 686; see too OUA, WP/β/21(4), p. 305.

Wilkins's party had called for an end during the crisis over the third Visitation, was over at last.

The conflicts between the Visitors and the visited of Cromwellian Oxford, and among the Visitors themselves, are a major portion of its history. Yet, acute as they could be, they are only a portion of it, and the rivalries that divided Owen and Wilkins are only a portion of its politics. Inevitably there were friendships across the parties, and enmities within them. Inevitably, too, a host of skirmishes arose, many of them parochial or personal, to complicate the principal divisions. But beside the story of conflict there is one of cooperation, over issues which brought Owen and Wilkins together in the university's defence. Even during the crisis over the wearing of habits in 1656, Wilkins was anxious to prevent Owen, or anyway to prevent the office of Vice-Chancellor, from being discredited.[387] Amid the earlier confrontation that was provoked by the ordinance for the third Visitation in 1654, the university 'with much unanimitie' chose Owen as its member of parliament, and remonstrated, unavailingly, when the Commons predictably disqualified him as a clergyman.[388] In the parliaments of the protectorate, no less than in previous parliaments, issues arose—the status of the civil law, for example—which touched on the university's common interests, and on which Owen's influence at Whitehall placed him in a strong position to fight its corner. He stayed in London for four weeks during the parliament of 1654 at the university's expense,[389] and acted again there on its behalf during the parliament of 1656.[390] If his presence in the capital sometimes counted against his rivals at Oxford, it could also further the aims they shared with him.

The Puritans came to reform Oxford, but also to preserve it. Mindful of the frequent association of Puritanism with unlettered philistinism, and conscious that the removal of distinguished scholars by the Visitors had hardened that sentiment,[391] they strove to get their religion identified in the public mind, as it was in their own thinking, with the pursuit of learning. In 1646 the elder Henry Wilkinson, even as he pressed the reform of Oxford on MPs, reminded them of the 'reproach' parliament suffered 'that you are no friend to the Muses'. His sermon proclaimed the 'neare affinity betwixt learning and religion', for 'the Lord himself hath had a great care of preserving learning and the arts, in regard he hath couched all kind of learning in the bowels of Scripture'.[392] William Prynne, who briefly

---

[387] OUA, SP/E/4, fo. 92^v.

[388] OUA, Reg. Conv. T, pp. 254–5; *pace* William Pittis, *Memoirs of the Life of the Late Reverend Dr South* (1721), p. 8. The distinction between clergy and laity, on which the disqualification was based, irked Cromwellians. A number of chaplains and preachers appointed by them at Oxford were not in holy orders: Varley, 'Restoration Visitation', pp. 25–6, 29–30, 43; cf. *CJ* 11 February 1653 ('Propagating the Gospel': clause 1). See too *CJ* 13 February 1660.

[389] OUA, NW/3/4, fo. 100; WP/β/21/4, p. 294.

[390] OUA, SP/E/4, p. 294 (cf. p. 305).

[391] See John Hall, *An Humble Motion to the Parliament for the Advancement of Learning, and Reformation of the Universities* (1649), p. 5.

[392] Wilkinson Sr, *Miranda, Stupenda*, pp. 36–7.

played an active part on the first Visitation, urged in support of it that 'true religion is a learned thing'.[393] Of course, Puritans knew that the training of the intellect, if separated from the exercise of faith, could be a sterile or dangerous pursuit. They knew how depraved was human reason and how empty its vanities.[394] Soon after Owen's appointment at Christ Church, the Commonwealth's rulers of Ireland reminded him that 'where learning is attained before the work of grace upon the heart, it serves only to make a sharper opposition against the power of godliness'.[395] He scarcely needed the lesson, convinced as he himself was that 'ability of learning and literature' was, without faith and election, 'of no use at all to the end and interest of true wisdom'.[396] Peter French echoed him: the 'search after true wisdom', he reminded 'the students' in a sermon at St Mary's, is 'not to be had in the books of philosophers, but Scriptures'.[397] Yet Oxford's Puritans held the intellect to have its indispensable uses—provided only that it was deployed with 'moderation', as a 'servant' to faith, 'keeping its due distance'.[398] Edward Reynolds warned that 'great learning' could 'coexist with monstrous wickedness', but he also knew that when 'seasoned with holiness' it advanced the understanding of the world of God's creation[399]—the goal to which the scientific exertions of the Wilkins circle were themselves directed. 'Piety and learning', 'religion and learning', 'godlinesse and learning', 'piety and literature': those phrases, which were in everyday use in society at large, were habitually employed by Oxford's ruling Puritans, as by Cromwell and their other political masters, to convey their understanding of the function of a university. Oxford's Puritans sought, in another form of words that became familiar, 'the right advancement of learning and the promotion of reformation'.[400]

Above all, Puritans valued the learning that was essential to theology. Owen, again conventionally, saw theology as 'the queen and mistress of the other branches of learning'.[401] 'Let orthodox religion remain' in the university, he declared in his valedictory address as Vice-Chancellor, 'and I am now pleased to die without hesitation'.[402] Theology apparently lost ground as an academic subject in Interregnum Oxford, where a reaction against the doctrinal warfare of the civil wars seems to have turned minds towards a study of the world and the universe as they are, not

---

[393] William Prynne, *The University of Oxford's Plea Refuted* (1647), p. 5.

[394] For Puritan attitudes to learning see John Morgan, *Godly Learning . . . 1560–1640* (Cambridge, 1986).

[395] Toon, *Correspondence of John Owen*, p. 51; cf. John Cook, *Monarchy, no Creature of Gods Making* (1652), ep. ded. and p. 134.

[396] Owen, *Works*, ii. 80.

[397] de Beer, *Diary of John Evelyn*, iii. 104–5. For French's preaching in Oxford see also Bodl., MS don. f. 41, fo. 69.

[398] Wilkinson Jr, *Three Decads*, pt. i, p. 74; pt. ii, pp. 7, 17, 76–7.

[399] Mordecai Feingold, 'Mathematical Sciences and New Philosophies', in Tyacke, *History of the University of Oxford*, p. 445; cf. William Dell, *A Plain and Necessary Confutation*, in Dell's *The Tryal of Sprits* (1653), pp. 1–2.

[400] QCA, Register H, pp. 124, 126.

[401] Toon, *Oxford Orations*, p. 15.

[402] Ibid., p. 40.

as divines said they ought to be.[403] The university's Puritans resisted that trend. They believed that the knowledge of the Bible in its original tongues was essential if the ministers trained at Oxford were 'to give the right sense of Scripture to the unlearned'.[404] The same expertise was requisite if the clergy were to answer those plausible objections to orthodox doctrine with which the sectaries and the sceptics of the Puritan Revolution were disconcertingly forward in confronting them. A Puritan plan of 1647 to fund pious students at Oxford stressed the need to 'make' the 'nation . . . more learned, for the saving of soules, because as those who 2 Pet. [3]. 16 were undiscipled and unprincipled did wrest things hard to be understood to their own destruction so doe many even now among us'.[405]

If theology had the first claim on learning, Owen did not suppose it to have an exclusive one. He gave encouragement to the secular subjects, and praised Oxford's 'outstanding mathematicians'.[406] No less than Wilkins was he concerned to strengthen the resources and morale of the university and to preserve a lay base for its support. The essential achievement of Owen's Vice-Chancellorship, in his own eyes, was to have saved the university from the havoc left by civil war.[407] Addressing it at the end of his period of office, he recalled that, at the outset of his tenure, Oxford and its Puritan rulers 'were a mere rabble and a subject of talk to the rabble'.[408] If his words had an element of self-justification, they scarcely exaggerated. Within the spectrum of Oxford politics Owen's readiness to alter the constitution of Convocation made him a radical figure, but he had no sympathy with those root-and-branch critics of the university who saw in its civil-war collapse an opportunity to re-design it on first principles. If Oxford were to be reformed, he recognized, it must first be restored. In the restoration, which occupied much of his labour, he and Wilkins discovered wide common ground.

During the earlier 1650s, the university gradually (if not always smoothly) succeeded in returning to its traditional procedures: the regular provision of lectures, the machineries of matriculation and examination, the rotatory appointment of Proctors, the functioning of the Chancellor's court. The annual Act was revived in July 1651, though in that first year it had to be held under military guard.[409] A general programme of physical repair was announced by the erection of scaffolding, the rhythm of hammers, the smell of fresh paint. Gradually, too, the

---

[403] de Beer, *Diary of John Evelyn*, iii. 105; the editor's Introduction to Tyacke, *History of the University of Oxford*, p. 17; Feingold, 'Mathematical Sciences', p. 441; cf. Toon, *Oxford Orations*, p. 16.

[404] *A Modest Reply, in Answer to The Modest Plea, for an Equal Common-wealth* (1659), p. 4.

[405] Robert Ibbitson, *Charitable Constructions* (1647), p. 1. Cf. Ann McGruer, *Educating the 'Unconstant Rabble'. Arguments for Educational Advancement and Reform during the English Civil War and Interregnum* (Newcastle upon Tyne, 2010), p. 108.

[406] Toon, *Oxford Orations*, pp. 15, 24–5, 34, 35; cf. Bodl., Selden MS *supra* 109, fo. 372.

[407] Toon, *Oxford Orations*, pp. 21, 40; cf. the tribute to Cromwell in *Mercurius Politicus* 9 December 1658, p. 59.

[408] Toon, *Oxford Orations*, pp. 40–1.

[409] Wood, *History*, i. 646; cf. Twigg, *University of Cambridge*, p. 154. It looks as if soldiers were present in later years too: BNCA, MS A. II. 46, p. 26 (1655); PCA, MS 4/1/1, fo. 26 (1657); NA, 4211 (1657).

military flavour of the civil war period, which had been sharpened in the late 1640s by an influx of disbanded soldiers who had come to study, disappeared, although the memories of war were sustained by the sight of troops in and around the city, as they were by the maimed ex-soldiers, and the refugees from the wars in Ireland and Scotland, who lingered at the college gates and in the quadrangles to beg relief.[410] With institutional restoration came administrative energy. The Puritans were determined to revive, even to improve, Oxford's academic standards. Vigorously they enjoined constant attendance at lectures and the regular performance of exercises; attacked such 'gross abuses' as the wining and dining of examiners and other 'great and scandalous abuses . . . of late crept in under pretence of entertainments and gratuities';[411] and insisted on the classical tongues as the languages of conversation.[412] Whether Puritan rule pursued those traditional goals of the university's governors more effectually than their predecessors it is not easy to say. But there was no want of trying, and at least some of the effort succeeded.[413] Anthony Wood, recalling the 1650s, remembered 'disputations and lectures, often; . . . we had then very good exercises in all matters performed in the Schooles; philosophy disputations in Lent time, frequent in the Greek tongue'.[414] John Owen himself counted among the achievements of his reign 'certain exercises newly established, and some restored anew, responsible scholarship to some extent regained'.[415]

The most pressing problems of reconstruction were the entwined ones of finance and student numbers.[416] In the colleges, financial problems had been created or exacerbated by the difficulties experienced during and after the war of collecting

---

[410] The evidence of such destitution, as of post-war rebuilding and redecoration, is widely distributed among the accounts of the university and of the colleges.

[411] OUA, NEP/*supra*/49, ii, fo. 157ᵛ; SP/E/4, fos 88, 102ᵇ; Reg. Conv. T, pp. 280, 283.

[412] Burrows, pp. 249, 266; Bodl., Wood MS f. 35, fo. 350; CCCA, B/5/1/1: 1653, second term; CA, D&C i. b. 3, p. 72; QCA, Register H, p. 115; MS 2Y/24, 26. The parliamentary authorities preferred English as the language of record-keeping. Their withdrawal from involvement in the colleges is sometimes marked by a return to Latin in the college records.

[413] The scientific enthusiasms of the 1650s were passed on to students with the university's support: OUA, NW/3/4, fo 26; WP/β/21(4), pp. 54, 56; [John Wilkins and Seth Ward], *Vindiciae Academiarum* (1654); Walter Charleton, *The Immortality of the Human Soul* (1657), p. 50. Music was probably the only subject of study to be slow to revive after the wars: [Wilkins and Ward], *Vindiciae Academiarum*, p. 29; OUA, WP/β/21/4, p. 296; NW/3/4, pp. 182, 226, 284; Reg. Conv. T, p. 292; Bodl., MS Eng. hist. c. 310, fos 84, 88ᵛ; but revive, at least to some extent, it apparently did: P. M. Gouk, 'Music', in Tyacke, *History of the University of Oxford*, p. 625. Pocock and Langbaine worked to establish proper founts for the printing and the study of Hebrew and Arabic: Bodl., Selden MS *supra* 109, fos 343, 349, 392, 403, 469; OUA, WP/β/21/4, pp. 287, 291; NW/3/4, p. 240 (cf. p. 148); NEP/*supra*/49, ii, fo. 168; and see Feingold, 'Oriental Studies'. Some light on the buying and reading of books in Puritan Oxford is cast by: UCA, MS Pyx J.J. fasc. 5; Oriel College Archives, MS II. G. 9, pp. 25, 123; Joseph Wells, *Wadham College* (1898), pp. 62–3; JCA, Benefactors' Book, pp. 51–8; see also CCCA, MS D/3/3 (library catalogue, with some entries probably of the 1650s).

[414] Wood, *Life and Times*, i. 300. Cf. Toon, *Oxford Orations*, pp. 16, 45.

[415] Toon, *Oxford Orations*, p. 16, 33, 45.

[416] On finance, see John Twigg, 'College Finances, 1640–1660', in Tyacke, *History of the University of Oxford*, pp. 773–802.

rents and tithes.[417] Only in the later 1650s were Fellowships, many of them previously kept vacant to save money, filled as a matter of course. At least until 1657, too, the university was apparently unable to resume the full payment of professorial salaries.[418] The threat of penury persisted,[419] despite Owen's rhetorical claim in 1657 that the university's treasury had increased ten-fold during his reign as Vice-Chancellor.[420] But at least emergency measures of retrenchment had become much less frequent. Undergraduate numbers were slow to climb in the 1650s. Although they gradually became respectable, they failed to reach the high levels of the 1630s, a period which, as Owen was uncomfortably aware, had in some eyes come to seem a golden age of the university.[421] The heaviest burden of numerical decline fell on the halls, those survivals of medieval halls of residence which had declined with the foundation and expansion of colleges in the Renaissance. Under Laud the halls, where allegiance to the Anglican Church was harder to enforce than in the colleges, had been refuges for Puritans. Now that Puritans were welcome in the colleges, some of the halls stood close to extinction—despite a fleeting period of revival in the late 1640s, which both in the halls and in the colleges brought in undergraduates whose studies had been postponed by the war.

Owen and his allies, anxious to revive Oxford's morale, and dependent on the traditional institutions of the university for its revival, did not embark lightly on their proposals for structural change. Their appetite for it was inhibited by the clamorous national movement for the overhaul of the universities: an impulse which reached its first peak amid the political turmoil of 1653 and its second in that of 1659, years when the very survival of the university seemed in doubt.[422] The movement, or aspects of it, had supporters within Oxford. Among them were two men who would argue vigorously for republican government in the

---

[417] CA, D&C i. b. 3, p. 10; OUA, Reg. Conv. T, p. 72 (cf. JCA, shelfmark 19, Bursars' Accounts 1631–53, p. 160); ASA, MS 401, fo. 117ᵛ (cf. JCA, MS 155: Ayleworth to Mansell, 16 December 1644); NA, 988: 31 May 1650; QCA, Register H, p. 132; Magdalen College Archives (hereafter MCA), MS C. II. 4. 13: 17 December 1649; September 1652; UCA, 'Duplicate Papers relating to the Visitation': 20 April 1648.

[418] OUA, Reg. Conv. T, pp. 168–9, 234; Burrows, p. 225; Bodl., MS Eng. hist. c. 310, fo. 91; Toon, *Oxford Orations*, p. 45; Toon, *Correspondence of John Owen*, p. 77; cf. *CSPD 1657–8*, p. 365.

[419] For the financial difficulties of the colleges in the Interregnum see, e.g., MCR, Registrum Collegii Mertonensis, p. 396; CA, D&C i. b. 3, p. 102; ii. c. 1, nos 43–4 (cf. no. 28); NA, 988: 2 February 1651, 4 January 1655; G. C. Richards and H. E. Salter, eds, *The Dean's Register of Oriel*, Oxford Historical Society, 84 (1926), pp. 331–2; UCA, Pyx J.J. fasc. 4: 20 August 1652; UCA, Smith transcripts, xi. pp. 140–9; Lincoln College Muniments (hereafter LCM), Md. Reg., fo. 101; H. W. C. Davis and R. Hunt, *A History of Balliol College* (revised edn, Oxford, 1973), p. 126; Burrows, pp. 302, 329–30, 374, 386–9.

[420] Toon, *God's Statesman*, p. 77.

[421] Toon, *Oxford Orations*, p. 8. Matriculation procedures were restored in 1650. The matriculations of the decade peaked in 1658. The numbers of high-born students are especially hard to calculate, but those of matriculands in the 1650s whose fathers were knights or of higher status were low, averaging around twelve a year. All calculations of matriculation levels in the 1650s are my own, but there is an essential discussion of the numbers of undergraduates, and of the difficulties of assessing the sources for them, in Porter, 'University and Society', pp. 31–5, 44.

[422] Toon, *Oxford Orations*, pp. 11, 21, 41; Toon, *Correspondence of John Owen*, pp. 64–5; *CSPD 1657–8*, p. 328. Falls in matriculation figures in 1654 and 1659–60 may be related to the extremist attacks on the universities.

national press in 1659: the Fellow of Lincoln College William Sprigge, who owed his appointment in Oxford in 1652 to the 'recommendation', supported by 'powerfull letters', of Oliver Cromwell;[423] and Henry Stubbe, that dextrous trouble-maker of Christ Church, who had joined the college in 1649, apparently as a protégé of Sir Henry Vane, at that time Cromwell's ally.[424] Yet the menace posed by the attacks on the universities was principally an external and hence, within Oxford, mostly a unifying one. The movement for the fundamental reform of learning was given voice during the revolution by John Milton and Samuel Hartlib and John Hall, by William Dell and John Webster, by Quakers and Fifth Monarchists. Cromwell kept his distance from it. Dell had officiated at the wedding of Henry Ireton with Cromwell's daughter in 1646. Yet in 1651 a report reached Cambridge that Cromwell had indicated his disapproval of Dell's tenets, which Dell was proclaiming as Master of Gonville and Caius College, the post to which the Rump had appointed him two years earlier.[425] Even so, the radical reform movement procured enough hints of support in high places to create profound anxiety in Oxford.[426] Some visionaries condemned all learning as an enemy to grace and truth. Some cast covetous eyes on the endowments of the monkish colleges. Others demanded a more utilitarian syllabus. Others still recommended the study of Paracelsian medicine or of the mystical teachings of Jacob Boehme.[427]

[423] LCM, Md. Reg., fo. 94; Varley, 'Restoration Visitation', p. 31. Cf. Burrows, p. 192; R. L. Greaves, 'William Sprigg and the Cromwellian Revolution', *Huntington Library Quarterly* 34 (1971), pp. 99–113; Green, *Commonwealth of Lincoln College*, p. 254.

[424] It is unfortunate that our knowledge of Stubbe's career in Oxford depends so heavily on his self-enlarging accounts of it: see Nicastro, *Lettere di Henry Stubbe*. For other glimpses of that career see *CSPD 1657–8*, p. 349; OUA, Reg. Conv. T, pp. 318, 321; Wood, *Athenae Oxonienses*, iii. 1075–6 (cf. UCA, MS D.D. 14); Wood, *History*, ii. 682–3; Varley, 'Restoration Visitation', p. 17. Stubbe's influence can be seen in the discontent at Christ Church expressed in CA, D&C ii. c. 1, no. 68 (cf. Longleat House, Thynne MS xii, fo. 166); *Sundry Things from Severall Heads concerning the University of Oxford* (1659).

[425] Cary, *Memorials of the Great Civil War*, ii. 372; *CJ* 4 May 1649; E. C. Walker, *William Dell: Master Puritan* (London, 1970), p. 105.

[426] John Lambert, the most powerful of Cromwell's councillors, took an interest in learning and in Oxford and may have been regarded as a favourer of educational experiment: John Webster, *Academiarum Examen* (1654), ep. ded.; OUA, Reg. Convoc. Sb, p. 126; Wood, *History*, ii. 687; *CSPD 1654*, p. 346; Barnard, *Cromwellian Ireland*, p. 218.

[427] General accounts of the agitation may be found in Mullinger, *University of Cambridge*, iii. 371–4, 447–71, 534–7; Richard L. Greaves, *The Puritan Revolution and Educational Thought* (Rutgers, 1970); Charles Webster, *The Great Instauration* (1975), esp. pt. iii; Twigg, *University of Cambridge*, ch. 8. See too Wood, *Life and Times*, i. 291–6; A. G. Debus (ed.), *Science and Education in the Seventeenth Century: The Webster—Ward Debate* (1970). For the demand for Behmenism see Nickolls, pp. 99–102. For Quakers, Fifth Monarchists, and other sectaries in Oxford: Wood, *Life and Times*, i. 190–1, 221, 293 (cf. David Underdown, *Pride's Purge* [Oxford, 1971], p. 350); *CSPD 1658–9*, p. 148; *TSP*, vi. 187; Hutton, *Restoration*, p. 87; Woolrych, *Commonwealth to Protectorate*, pp. 196–7; Nicholas Tyacke, 'Religious Controversy', in Tyacke, *History of the University of Oxford*, p. 596. Even during the earlier protectorate, a time of reaction against radical reform (although also of the peak of John Lambert's political influence), the university could not feel certain of the government's commitment to a learned and university-trained ministry: *Mercurius Politicus* 20 April 1654, p. 3429; cf. [Wilkins and Ward], *Vindiciae Academiarum*, p. 30.

In the vindication of Oxford and of learning, the party of Owen and the party of Wilkins joined forces.[428] The attacks of 1653 provoked a spirited vindication of the university's teaching methods by Wilkins's friend Seth Ward, the Savilian Professor of Astronomy. Owen would have concurred with the distinction drawn by Ward between 'the reall and solid wayes of knowledge' which were followed at Oxford and the 'windy impostures of magick and astrology' favoured by its opponents.[429] In 1654 the two parties joined on behalf of the famous Orientalist and theologian Edward Pocock, Regius Professor of Hebrew, who four years earlier, even though he had lost his canonry, had been kept in his professorship after a campaign by Wilkins, Langbaine and Selden. On that occasion a petition on Pocock's behalf, hailing him as 'a great ornament to this university', had won unanimous approval in Oxford, even the more strenuous Puritans within the university's leadership, Thankful Owen among them, pleading for him.[430] Now, in 1654, Pocock came under threat from another quarter. The Commissioners for the Ejection of Scandalous Ministers in Berkshire, where he held a living, proposed to evict him on account of his commitment to the Book of Common Prayer. John Owen, a leading designer of the system to which the Ejectors belonged, was shocked. Perhaps he learned of the episode from his allies among the Berkshire clergy, with whom he would collaborate the next year in organizing resistance to the royalist threat posed by Penruddock's rising.[431] 'Some few men of mean quality and condition, rash, heady, enemies of tithes', he wrote, were 'casting out' Pocock 'on light and trivial pretences'.[432] A delegation of four, consisting of Owen, Wilkins, Ward, and Wallis, journeyed to Berkshire to remonstrate with the commissioners: 'particularly Dr. Owen, who endeavoured, with some warmth, to make them sensible of the infinite contempt and reproach which would certainly fall upon them, when it should be said, that they had turned out a man for insufficiency, whom all the learned, not of England only, but of all Europe, so justly admired for his vast knowledge, and extraordinary accomplishments'. The shaken commissioners backed down.[433]

On other fronts, too, the university defended itself with unified determination. It lobbied resourcefully to protect the study of civil law from parliamentary criticism.[434] It lobbied no less resourcefully to forestall the creation of the college planned by Oliver Cromwell for Durham, a project in which the university saw a

[428] The university's self-defence: OUA, Reg. Conv. T, pp. 221–2 (cf. Wood, *History*, ii. 654); [Wilkins and Ward], *Vindiciae Academiarum*, p. 48), 226–7; Walker, *William Dell*, p. 132; Bodl., Selden MS *supra* 109, fo. 309; Leland, *De Rebus Britannicis*, v. 291–2; cf. Bodl., MS Lat. misc. c. 19, p. 57.
[429] [Wilkins and Ward], *Vindiciae Academiarum*, p. 36; cf. Toon, *Oxford Orations*, p. 35.
[430] Twells, *Pocock*, pp. 136–7; cf. Wood, *History*, ii. 555.
[431] Above, p. 133.
[432] Toon, *Correspondence of John Owen*, p. 83.
[433] Twells, *Pocock*, pp. 151–75.
[434] OUA, Reg. Conv. T, p. 252 (cf. Reg. Conv. Ta, p. 50); SP/E/4, fos 63, 100; WP/γ/22/1(h); WP/γ/23/1(16); Bodl., MS Eng. hist. c. 310, fos. 88, 92; *CSPD 1657–8*, p. 272; Wood, *Life and Times*, i. 187; Wood, *History*, ii. 667; *CJ* 21–2 November 1656; Toon, *Correspondence of John Owen*, pp. 76–9; Brian P. Levack, 'Law', in Tyacke, *History of the University of Oxford*, pp. 561, 567–8. Cf. Bodl., Bodleian MS Add. d. 105, p. 9; *CSPD 1654*, p. 354.

prospective rival, and which Richard Cromwell, when he succeeded his father as lord protector, allowed to sleep, to Oxford's gratification.[435] The steersmen of the Durham scheme favoured Baconian principles of educational reform which had their supporters in Oxford, among them William Petty at Brasenose and two Fellows of Lincoln who were allocated posts at the prospective new college: Robert Wood, an advocate of decimalized currency, whom the Visitors had brought to Oxford, and Cromwell's protégé William Sprigge. Petty owed his presence at Oxford to military favour. His career there was launched in 1649, with the university's grudging acceptance, through the influence of the local military governor, the Visitor Thomas Kelsey.[436] Petty enjoyed a privileged position in the university thereafter.[437] His ideas had common ground with those of Samuel Hartlib, who had added an apocalyptic dimension to Bacon's programme.[438] Yet Petty was too often away from Oxford to make a durable impression on the development of studies there. The reaction both of Owen's friends and of the Wilkins circle to Hartlib's proposals was unwelcoming. Hartlib's wish for a post at Oxford was blocked, and his schemes for reform were ignored.[439]

Less unified, admittedly, was Oxford's reaction to proposals for a fundamental revision of the university and college statutes, to replace or anyway overhaul the Laudian reforms. The aspiration was extensively canvassed in 1649–52.[440] Owen would have liked to rewrite the university statutes from scratch. A month before his resignation from the Chancellorship he replied to a request from Henry Cromwell in Ireland for a copy of them, for use in the development of Trinity College Dublin. Owen urged a different course on Henry, whom he wanted to sponsor the drafting, in England, of 'a body of orders and statutes' which might be applied in the universities both of England and of Ireland. For the existing statutes of Oxford and Cambridge, 'beinge framed to the spirit and road of studys in former days, will scarsly upon consideration be found to be the best expedient for the good ends of godlinesse and solid literature'. The new ones envisaged by Owen would be 'suited to the present light, interest of state and advantagious discourse of

---

[435] Bodl., Bodleian MS Add. d. 105, p. 9; OUA, WP/β/21/4, p. 305; Reg. Conv. T, pp. 339–42; Conant Jr, *Life of...John Conant*, pp. 26–7; Wood, *History*, ii. 687–94.

[436] OUA, Reg. Conv. T, pp. 73, 75.

[437] BNCA, MS B. I. D. 36: 7 March 1651, 16 July 1658; MS A. I. 2, fo. 74ᵛ; MS A. II. 44, pp. 32, 35; *CSPD 1653–4*, p. 208. Cf. Frank, 'Medicine', p. 544; Webster, *Great Instauration*, pp. 81–2.

[438] Cf. Barnard, *Cromwellian Ireland*, pp. 217–18. For Hartlib's ideas see Charles Webster, *The Great Instauration* (1975); Mark Greengrass, Michael Leslie, and Timothy Raylor, eds, *Samuel Hartlib and Universal Reformation* (Cambridge, 1994); Timothy Raylor, 'Milton, the Hartlib Circle, and the Education of the Aristocracy', in Nicholas McDowell and Nigel Smith, eds, *The Oxford Handbook of Milton* (Oxford, 2009), pp. 382–406.

[439] Leland, *De Rebus Britannicis*, v. 288–9. Hartlib did have friends at Oxford, among them Henry Langley, Master of Pembroke College (*CSPD 1653–4*, pp. 53, 143, 206, 454; G. H. Turnbull. 'Notes on John Durie's *Reformed Libarie-Keeper*', *The Library*, 5th series 1 (1946), p. 65; Webster, *Great Instauration*, pp. 193–4); but such radical sympathies as Langley may have possessed are unlikely to have been gone deep: Bodl., MS don. f. 39, fos 166 ff.

[440] Above, p. 124; OUA, NEP/*supra*/49, ii, fos 139–68; WP/6/21/4, pp. 276–7; WP/7/6/2; SP/E/5, fo. 55; QCA, Register H, p. 116; WCA, MS 4/90; Wood, *History*, ii. 651–2; Reg. Conv. T, p. 148; Burrows, pp. 259, 261, 264; C. E. Mallet, *A History of the University of Oxford*, 3 vols (1924–7), ii. 388n.; Webster, *Great Instauration*, pp. 194–6, 523–8; and see *HMC Leyborne–Popham*, p. 80.

literature'.[441] The main objections to the existing statutes seem to have centred on the political and ecclesiastical loyalties which the Laudian code enjoined. But to less radical spirits that feature seemed merely an embarrassing anachronism, one which, it was claimed, had been satisfactorily met in 1650–1, when the university—perhaps as part of its efforts to persuade the government that the imposition of the Engagement there was needless—declared that no statute 'contrary to the word of God or the law of the land' was binding.[442] An overhaul of the statutes would have been a major undertaking, beyond the already overstretched resources of Puritan time and energy. Gerard Langbaine skilfully contained the movement for it. The Puritans had no antiquarian expertise to match his, or that of his friend and fellow royalist the Regius Professor of Civil Law Richard Zouche, who had himself been involved in the drawing up of the Laudian code,[443] and who had joined Langbaine in publicly defending the university against the Visitors in 1647.[444] In any case the revision of the statutes, much as Owen would have liked it, was low on his agenda. In pursuing his policy of reconstruction he found that the existing statutes, however deficient, were indispensable landmarks. It is characteristic of the Puritans' experience in Oxford that they much more often found themselves demanding the observance of old statutes than proposing new ones.[445] The Laudian code survived their rule.

The Puritan government of Oxford, then, was characterized by institutional caution. But it did not lack zest or ambition. Cromwellians tended to see institutional forms as means to be either used or discarded in the pursuit of godly ends. They looked more to good men than to good laws as the instruments of reform. In Oxford they sought to make men good through three principal means: the definition and inculcation of orthodox doctrine; the preaching and teaching of God's saving word; and the purification of morality.

Since the Reformation it had been the duty of the universities, in John Owen's words, 'to defend, improve, give and add new light unto old truths'.[446] The war against popery had been on one front a war of theology and scholarship. It remained one. Prominent advisers of the protector were persuaded to support a scheme, which he apparently favoured,[447] to turn St Mary Hall (in what is now the northern quadrangle of Oriel College), 'not at present made use of, or endowed', into a research institute where 'tenne godly able men' would compose 'a generall

[441] Toon, *Correspondence of John Owen*, pp. 100–1. Cf. pp. 50–1; Bodl., MS Eng. hist. c. 310, fo. 91ᵛ; Barnard, *Cromwellian Ireland*, p. 200.
[442] OUA, Reg. Conv. T, p. 122 (cf. p. 141); NEP/*supra*/49, fos 139 ff.; Bodl., Wood MS f. 35, fo. 349; Wood, *Life and Times*, i. 173–4; Wood, *History*, ii. 636–7; NA, 9655, p. 11.
[443] Fincham, 'Oxford and the Early Stuart Polity', p. 201.
[444] Roy and Reinhart, 'Civil Wars', p. 724.
[445] See e.g. Burrows, pp. 82, 223, 228, 259, 294, 313, 426; QCA, MS 2Y/30; WCA, MS 4/116; Mayo, *Life and Death of Edmund Staunton*, pp. 16–17. Cf. Bodl., Wood MS f. 35, fo. 359; Shapiro, *John Wilkins*, p. 92.
[446] Owen, *Works*, xi. 11.
[447] BL Add. MS 32093, fo. 400ᵛ.

synopsis of the true reformed Protestant religion', and so at last make the rectitude of Calvinist teaching unanswerably plain to England and to Europe.[448] Had the project been executed, St Mary Hall would have offered a shelter to refugee Protestant scholars from the Continent, a class to which Puritan Oxford was always generous.[449]

Upon the leading Puritans of Cromwellian Oxford there fell, as they believed, the responsibilities which had been sustained by the foremost figures of English reformed theology, among them John Jewel, Thomas Morton, James Ussher, Joseph Hall, John Davenant, and John Prideaux.[450] All those men had been bishops. Before the reign of Charles I there had been a predominant tradition of militant Calvinism in Oxford theology, which had been comfortably combined with loyalty to the episcopal Church. Under Cromwell the tradition was restored, albeit now in a post-episcopalian world.[451] Owen was among the Puritan heads who, in their youths, had witnessed the subversion of Calvinist doctrine in Laudian Oxford. In recalling that shameful period they found one consoling memory: the resistance which had been led from Exeter College by Prideaux, the college's Rector for thirty years before the civil war and the university's Regius Professor of Divinity for twenty-six. He had been Vice-Chancellor five times. The younger Henry Wilkinson ('Dean Harry', a former pupil of 'Long Harry'), Principal of Magdalen Hall, proudly recalled that Prideaux 'gave Arminius a dreadful blow' at Oxford.[452] The university's Puritans paid Prideaux public tributes during the first Visitation, and his hold on their hearts and minds survived his death in 1650.[453] Their admiration was sharpened by a sense of common experience. For even though the political convulsion of the 1640s had delivered the guardians of Calvinist orthodoxy from Laudianism and brought their movement to power, there were times when they felt as intellectually beleaguered in the 1650s as Prideaux had done in the 1630s. Throughout England, and across Europe, the leaders of Puritan

---

[448] Ibid., fos 399–400ᵛ; R. A. Beddard, 'A Projected Cromwellian Foundation at Oxford and the "True Reformed Protestant Interest"', *History of Universities* 15 (1997–9), pp. 155–191. The amending hand in the document was that of Bulstrode Whitelocke. Also involved was the Cromwellian divine Hugh Peter, on whose interest in Oxford see also R. A. Beddard, 'A Traitor's Gift: Hugh Peter's Donation to the Bodleian Library', *Bodleian Library Record* 16 (1999), pp. 374–390. For proposals comparable to that for St Mary Hall, see *Perfect Proceedings* 14 July 1656, p. 688; John Dury, *An Earnest Plea for Gospel-Communion* (1654); Stephen Geree, *The Golden Mean* (1657), p. 4. Cf. BL Add. MS 4364, fo. 15; Mullinger, *University of Cambridge*, iii. 349.

[449] Toon, *Oxford Orations*, p. 36; cf. Robert Vaughan, *The Protectorate of Oliver Cromwell*, 2 vols (1839), i. 19. References to grants of money to distressed Protestants are scattered though the accounts of colleges. The Puritan preoccupation with the conversion of Jews and Indians was also well represented in Oxford.

[450] Owen, *Works*, xi. 497; Toon, *Oxford Orations*, p. 16; Wilkinson Jr, *Three Decads*, pt. i, preface, pt. iii, p. 23; Joshua Hoyle, *A Rejoinder to Master Malone's Reply* (1641), ep. ded.; *Genuine Remains of that Learned Prelate Dr Thomas Barlow* (1693), pp. 51, 191–2; *The Works of Robert Harris* (1654 edn), preface; Barlow, *De Studio Theologiae*, p. 46.

[451] Tyacke, 'Religious Controversy', pp. 569 ff.

[452] Wilkinson Jr, *Three Decads*, preface.

[453] Burrows, pp. xxvii–xxxiii; BNCA, MS A.VIII.13: 12 November 1659; Bodl., Wood MS f. 45, fo. 130; Michael Ogilvy, *Fratres in Malo* (1660), p. 29; Wilkinson Jr, *Three Decads*, preface; Henry Wilkinson Jr, *Two Treatises* (1681), p. 47; *Genuine Remains of . . . Thomas Barlow*, p. 181; cf. CA, D&C i. b. 3, p. 5.

Oxford observed the corrosive advances of Pelagianism and scepticism. Those tendencies did not merely challenge the Puritans' theological convictions. By emphasizing ethics above doctrine, they questioned the very primacy of faith.

Their most alarming doctrinal manifestations were Arminian and Socinian teachings. Puritan and Cromwellian Oxford went to war on those soul-destroying heresies,[454] which reasserted, in the face of the Calvinist emphasis on the helpless depravity of fallen man, the dignity of human reason and the rightful capacities of the human will.[455] Puritan heads of house observed the perilous attraction exerted by those positions among the young of Cromwellian Oxford, and recalled their comparable, and catastrophic, youthful appeal in pre-war Oxford.[456] In the 1640s Owen had written vigorous defences of the doctrine of predestination. Now, as Vice-Chancellor, in hours snatched between committees and on his journeys to London, he composed hundreds of thousands of words to expose the subtle hypocrisy and logical fallacies of Arminian and Socinian claims.[457] He fought the battle on two fronts: the first against what he considered to be the Socinian writings of Hugo Grotius and of Grotius's disciple Henry Hammond, whom the parliamentary Visitors had expelled from the college which Owen now ruled; the second against the Oxford graduate John Biddle, whose anti-Trinitarian treatises the protector's council instructed Owen to answer.[458] To Owen's literary efforts the Puritan leaders lent eager support: Conant, Staunton, Harris, Henry Wilkinson junior; Henry Langley, Master of Pembroke College; Joshua Hoyle, formerly Professor of Divinity at Trinity College Dublin and now Master of University College and Oxford's Regius Professor of Divinity; and Lewis du Moulin, Camden Professor of History.[459] In 1650 the university commissioned Francis Cheynell 'to set forth a book in vindication of the Trinity'.[460] Owen, his ally in that cause, was said to be under

---

[454] The campaign can be followed in Robert Crosse, *Exercitatio Theologica* (1651); Edward Bagshaw, *Dissertationes Duae anti-Socinianae* (1657); John Wallis, *Mens Sobria* (1657); Henry Hickman, *Concio de Haeresium Origine* (1659); Henry Hickman, *A Review of the Certamen Epistolare* (1659); Edward Bagshaw, *A Practicall Discourse concerning God's Decrees* (1660); Henry Hickman, *Laudensum Apostosia* (1660); Burrows, pp. l, lxv. Cf. *An Account given to the Parliament by the Ministers sent to Oxford* (1647); Macray, *Reg. Magdalen*, iv. 91–2; Durham, *Life and Death of... Robert Harris*, pp. 94–5.

[455] Above, p. 66.

[456] Wilkinson Jr, *Three Decads*, preface.

[457] Owen, *Works*, xi. 16, xiii. 209, 213, 299. See also Bodl., MS Lat misc. c.19, pp. 63–4; Toon, *God's Statesman*, pp. 40, 83; Toon, *Oxford Orations*, p. 16.

[458] H. R. Trevor-Roper, *Catholics, Anglicans and Puritans* (London, 1987), pp. 224–5; Sarah Mortimer, *Reason and Religion in the English Revolution: The Socinian Challenge* (Cambridge, 2010).

[459] Bodl., Rawlinson MS e. 199, fos 4, 30, 56–8, 114, 151; Wood MS f. 45, fo. 128 (cf. fo. 46&ᵛ); MS Lat. misc. c. 19, pp. 63–4, 70, 74; OUA, Reg. Conv. T, pp. 39–42, 97, 342 (cf. pp. 349–52); BL, Harleian MS 3998, fos 114–41 (cf. Bodl., Rawlinson MS c. 945, pp. 26, 361–411, 425–9, 520; MS don. f. 40); Conant Jr, *Life of... John Conant*, pp. 13, 18, 20; Wood, *Life and Times*, i. 300, 444–5; Robert Harris, *A Brief Discussion of Man's Estate* (1653), p. 65; Wilkinson Sr, *Miranda, Stupenda*, p. 36; Wilkinson Jr, *Three Decads*, preface; pt. i, pp. 75, 116, 175; pt. ii, pp. 18, 97–8, 162; pt. iii, pp. 3, 23, 28; the preface by Wilkinson Jr to Nicholas Clagett, *The Abuse of God's Grace* (1659); Lewis du Moulin, *Paraenesis ad Aedificatores* (1656); William Fulman, *A Short Appendix to the Life of Edmund Stanton* (1673); Bloxam, *Reg. Magdalen*, i. 57 n.

[460] OUA, Reg. Conv. T, p. 97.

his influence.[461] Perhaps it was parliament's own concern for doctrinal orthodoxy that led the Rump's standing committee to stipulate that Cheynell be continued in his divinity professorship despite his role in the university's resistance to the Engagement.

True doctrine needed to be defined and defended in print. Yet it was in sermons that it could best be made vivid and be stamped on the university's young imaginations. The promotion of preaching in the university and colleges had been a goal of the first Visitation from its outset, and remained a priority of all Oxford's Puritan rulers. As Henry Wilkinson junior explained, 'a sermon preacht now, if the Lord work by it, may doe good many a yeare after', not only among its hearers but among the audiences or associates to which they in turn would in due course bring its fruits.[462] He rejoiced in the profusion of preaching in Oxford. 'The spirituall manna of the word', he told the university in 1658, 'is plentifully rained down amongst you. You never had more frequent, never more profitable preaching.'[463] He returned to the theme in 1660: 'for these thirteen years past there hath been sermons more constant, and more practical edifying preaching amongst us, then the oldest alive can remember ever before in this university'.[464] George Trosse, a tense and devout undergraduate at Puritan Pembroke from 1658, would be grateful to have been at Oxford at a time 'when there were so many sermons preached, and so many excellent, orthodox, and practical divines to preach them'. The college, he remembered, was 'kept in very good order' on the Sabbath by the 'repetition' of sermons, by the frequent administration of the sacrament, and by communal prayer; 'besides which, after supper, all collegiate duties having been dispatch'd, three or four hopeful religious lads came to my chamber, and with them I was wont to repeat and pray'. In that era, he recalled, 'was religion in its glory in the university'—and, he added, 'a qualification for respect and advancement'.[465] Philip Henry, later a celebrated Nonconformist, had supported the king's cause, and at Christ Church had been indebted to the guidance of the Anglican divines Hammond and John Fell. He declined to submit to the Visitation, and was spared eviction from the college only by the protection of his kinsman the Earl of Pembroke, the then Chancellor.[466] Under the Puritan rule of Oxford he came round, and in 1652 he became a Student of his college. In Interregnum Oxford, he would remember, 'serious godliness was in reputation'. He

> would often mention it with thankfulness to God, what great helps and advantages he had then in the university, not only for learning, but for religion and piety... and besides the publick opportunities they had, there were many of the scholars that us'd to meet together for prayer, and Christian conference, to the great comforting of one

---

[461] Frederick J. Powicke, *A Life of the Reverend Richard Baxter* (1924), i. 123. Cf. Matthew Sylvester, ed., *Reliquiae Baxterianae* (1696), pt. ii, p. 197; above, p. 79.
[462] Wilkinson Jr, *Three Decads*, pt. i, p. 182.
[463] Ibid., pt. iii, p. 33; cf. pt. i, p. 235.
[464] Ibid., preface.
[465] *The Life of the Rev. Mr George Trosse* (1714), pp. 81–2; Douglas MacLane, *Pembroke College* (1900), p. 134.
[466] Burrows, p. 72.

anothers hearts in the fear and love of God, and the preparing of them for the service of the Church in their generation.[467]

No doubt the memories of Oxford's Puritans (no less than of its royalists) were distorted by the anti-Puritan reaction of the Restoration, when the university became, in at least some Dissenting eyes, a 'nursery of Baal's priests'.[468] Distance then lent enchantment to the Cromwellian era. George Trosse, who remained at Pembroke for five years after the Restoration, bleakly recorded the change in 1660 when the Puritan community in the college was broken up.[469] Even so, the recollections of Restoration Nonconformists are in keeping with evidence from the institutional records bequeathed by the 1650s. They are supported too by the testimony of Anthony Wood, not a man enamoured of Puritan rule but an admirer, however reluctantly, of its achievements in both learning and religion: 'discipline, strict and severe . . . catechising, frequent; prayers, in most tutors' chambers every night . . . sale of books, especially practicall divinity, very much'. There was, he thought, 'too much' praying and preaching, for 'some would carry on those exercises a whole week together'.[470] So frequent were the sermons and devotional and catechistic exercises and biblical discussion groups that the timetable grew overcrowded. A special time was Thursday afternoon, when the godly would hurry from the exercise at Edmund Staunton's lodgings in Corpus to catch a similar meeting in Christ Church.[471]

Such gatherings represented the voluntary element of Puritan worship. There was a strenuous element of compulsion too. The university and many of the colleges issued strict orders for courses of preaching and praying; for the 'repetition', before their heads or tutors, of the sermons which pupils had heard; and for the catechizing and nightly devotional guidance with which tutors were likewise entrusted.[472] Here the initiatives of the Visitations complemented those generated from within the university. The concern to secure 'the election of Fellowes that are godly' persisted.[473] For it was the tutors of England's future ministers and magistrates who held the key to the nation's spiritual health. As the younger Henry Wilkinson, for whom this was a recurrent concern, put it, 'in doing good to one scholar, you may do good to a whole parish or city'.[474] Working parties of Puritan Fellows and tutors were set up to devise means of enhancing pious worship in the colleges,

---

[467] *An Account of the Life and Death of Mr Philip Henry* (1699), p. 17 (though cf. Toon, *Correspondence of John Owen*, pp. 79–81). For Henry see too *Musarum Oxoniensium*, p. 22.

[468] Ludlow, *Voyce*, p. 9.

[469] *Life of . . . George Trosse*, p. 82.

[470] Wood, *Life and Times*, i. 300–1.

[471] Wilkinson Jr, *Three Decads*, preface; *Life of . . . George Trosse*, p. 81; Burrows, pp. 335–6; Wood, *History*, ii. 645; Mayo, *Life of Edmund Staunton*, p. 17.

[472] Burrows, pp. 27, 248, 302, 358, 359–60, 372, 374, 382, 390, 411–12, 415–16, 430, 434, 454; Bodl., MS Eng. hist. c. 310, fos 86, 90; OUA, SP/E/4, fo. 99; Wood, *Life and Times*, i. 166; Wood, *History*, ii. 644–6, 656; CA, D&C i. b. 3, pp. 24–5, 62; CCCA, MS B/5/1/1: 1649, 1653; LCM, Md. Reg., fo. 94; NA, 988: 3 July, 2 August 1650, 8 December 1651, 15 February 1653; WCA, MS 2/2, pp. 7–8, 10.

[473] WCA, MS 4/116.

[474] Wilkinson Jr, *Three Decads*, pt. ii, p. 78.

and to ensure the punishment of 'such who scoffe at sermons, public ordinances, and ministers'.[475] There was emphasis on the obligation of young MAs to preach in the university and the neighbouring countryside, a practice which was encouraged by the Rump in October 1651, the time of Cromwell's highest influence in the assembly.[476] The experience they would thus gain, and the practical advice they would be given by the seniors who heard them, would prepare them for their cures of souls, it being 'one maine end of the university', as the second Visitation explained on behalf of the initiative, 'to traine up men . . . that they may be able (when the providence of God shall call them) to publish the Gospel of Christ to the conversion and building up of soules to eternal life'.[477]

If the university were to be made fit for God's eyes, the establishment of sound doctrine and worship and preaching would not be enough. The monuments of superstition must be suppressed. Images of Christ, of the Virgin, and of saints, on gates and in churches and college chapels and the Cathedral at Christ Church, were removed or painted over.[478] Organs were taken from most of the colleges, Christ Church among them, and from the church of St Mary's, where the erection of a 'large' pulpit confirmed the new priorities.[479] There were even attempts to end the use of holy names for churches and feast days, although, as most Puritans seem to have grasped, the Christian nomenclature of Oxford ran too deep to be extinguished, at least in the short term.[480]

With the suppression of popery went the drive for moral reformation. The licentiousness and debauchery against which Puritans had so long remonstrated had to be extinguished. War was waged on alehouses and brothels, on neglect of the Sabbath, on hunting, and on the 'mirth and jollity' of the tennis court and the bowling green.[481] Stern injunctions were issued against the 'excess and vanitie' of personal appearance that blossomed, no doubt in anti-Puritan protest, in the aftermath of the regicide. The taste for 'exotick garbes', 'worse then [in] former

---

[475] WCA, MS 4/118.
[476] *CJ* 28 October 1651.
[477] Burrows, pp. 372, 374, 416; Toon, *God's Statesman*, pp. 56–7; Wood, *History*, ii. 647, 671; *Account of the Life and Death of Mr Philip Henry*, p. 17.
[478] The changes in the physical appearance of the chapel at Magdalen under Thomas Goodwin may, however, have been limited: de Beer, *Diary of John Evelyn*, iii. 109; Wood, *Life and Times*, ii. 161 (though cf. Bloxam, *Reg. Magdalen*, ii. cviii).
[479] On the policy of demolition and suppression see Wood, *History*, ii. 648–9; Nicolas K. Kiessling, ed., *The Life of Anthony Wood in his Own Words* (Oxford, 2010), p. 70; Burrows, p. 114 n.; C. G. Robertson, *All Souls College* (1889), p. 127; de Beer, *Diary of John Evelyn*, iii. 109. College organs and chapels: CA, MS i. b. 3, pp. 2, 40; *Sundry Things from Severall Hands concerning the University of Oxford* (1659), p. 10; Wood, *Life and Times*, i. 309 (Merton); Bloxam, *Reg. Magdalen*, ii. cxv and n.; St Mary's: OUA, NW/3/4, pp. 182, 204, 226, 231, 244; WP/β/21(4), p. 277 (cf. p. 326); *CSPD 1655–6*, p. 289; Gouk, 'Music', p. 629.
[480] OUA, NEP/*supra*/49, ii, fos 140–1; Wood, *Life and Times*, i. 174, 197; CCCA, B/5/1/1: 'Festu . . .'. Cf. e.g. MCR, Registrum Collegii Mertonensis, p. 385; LCM, Md. Reg., fo. 91ᵛ; Bodl., Rawlinson MS d. 912, fos 1–2; H. E. D. Blakiston, *Trinity College* (1898), p. 142.
[481] OUA, Reg. Conv. T, pp. 30, 109; Wood, *History*, ii. 645–6; Burrows, p. 284; Bodl., MS Eng. hist. c. 310, fo. 89ᵛ; CCCA, MS B/5/1/1; NA, 988: 31 May 1650 (bowls); Wilkinson Jr, *Three Decads*, pt. i, pp. 29, 161, 230–1. For the iniquities of tennis: Bodl. MS Wood f. 35, fo. 359; OUA, SP/E/4, fo. 42; and for both sports see Firth and Rait, ii. 1250.

ages', produced a craze for 'boots and spures and bote-hose-tops' and for the 'phantasticall' wearing of ribbons, of 'even all the colours of the rainbow', on hats, round waists, on breeches. Other fads were the dyeing and powdering and 'crisp[ing]' of hair and the wearing of love-locks. By May 1650 the Puritan rulers of Oxford were faced with a sartorial revolt, which the parliamentary committee, the Visitors, and the heads of colleges combined to confront.[482] This was the month when the Rump, tracing its own political problems to divine anger, passed its Adultery Act to combat 'the abominations and crying sins ... wherewith the land is defiled and Almighty God highly displeased'.[483] It was also a time of national economic hardship, when, as Henry Wilkinson junior lamented, luxurious self-display offered an insensitive contrast to what, as 'any tradesman ... will tell you', was the grievous condition of the poor. There were, Wilkinson reminded the university, 'many poore householders' who 'have much adoe to keep themselves alive', and whose families could be maintained 'a great while' by the money that was mis-spent on gaudy costumes. 'I cannot hold my peace', expostulated Wilkinson, 'to see such vanities and prodigious sights.'[484] If the complaints that reached parliament's standing committee from Oxford in 1650 were correct, sartorial extravagance was but one aspect of the 'licentious' and 'disorderly' and 'unseemely' carriage not only of Commoners but of Scholars, whose 'new-fashions, long haire, hounds and horses' were judged a novel iniquity.[485] Sartorial extravagance and comparable forms of self-display seem to have survived the measures and declamations against them.[486] At the end of John Owen's Vice-Chancellorship, when 'habits' and 'formalities' had again become familiar in the university church, Wilkinson felt impelled in a sermon there to assail those who

> cry up irreverent gestures in the worship of God. For any in time of divine worship to be laughing one upon another, it argueth a slight and vain spirit. To have ones hat on one side according to the swaggerers fashion; or partly off, according to a careless, slovenly fashion, hanging in their eyes, is a scandalous, irreverent, offensive gesture, while the preacher is praying.[487]

So Cromwellian Oxford did not conform to the ideal of Geneva. If some of the young devoured compulsory sermons, others skipped them or, if they attended, let

---

[482] Burrows, pp. 294, 313; PCA, MS 4/1/1, fo. 4; CA, D&C i. b. 3, pp. 24–5; QCA, Register H, p. 124; MS 2Y/30; OUA, Reg. Conv. T, pp. 108, 109; Bodl., Wood MS f. 35, fo. 359; Wood, *Life and Times*, i. 300; Wood, *History*, ii. 635. The fashion for boots and spurs revived an 'old humor': Mark Curtis, *Oxford and Cambridge in Transition* (Oxford, 1959), p. 144. I suspect that the story that Vice-Chancellor Owen powdered his hair was a *canard*, perhaps concocted over a pot of ale by George Vernon, who studied at Brasenose in the 1650s, and Anthony Wood: Wood, *Life and Times*, i. 221, 405; Vernon, *Letter to a Friend*, p. 13. Wood's account of Owen's dress, in which the Vice-Chancellor's informality is equated with vanity, likewise seems fanciful.

[483] Keith Thomas, 'The Puritans and Adultery', in Donald Pennington and Keith Thomas (eds), *Puritans and Revolutionaries* (Oxford, 1978), p. 263.

[484] Wilkinson Jr, *Three Decads*, pt. ii, pp. 18–19.

[485] QCA, Register H, pp. 124, 126, 127; Burrows, p. 313.

[486] Wood, *Life and Times*, i. 299–300.

[487] Wilkinson Jr, *Three Decads*, pt. ii, pp. 18, 168; cf. Clagett, *Abuse of God's Grace*, p. 15, and Wilkinson's preface to that work.

their attention wander.[488] Owen was torn between satisfaction at the advances of Puritanism in Oxford and despair at their limits. The breakdown of order and discipline in the civil wars, he lamented at the outset of his Vice-Chancellorship, had produced in Oxford an abatement of the 'reverence due to superiors' and 'a licentiousness almost Epicurean', so that 'a very large section of the students are now—alas—wandering beyond all bounds of modesty and piety'. In the years ahead he fought the 'stubbornness and deplorable contempt of religion', and the 'blindness and ignorance . . . concerning the things of God', that he observed in 'very many'. Yet, as often in Puritan accounts of the communities where they lived or worked, there was light amid darkness. Already in 1651 Wilkinson rejoiced in the presence, amid the general debauchery, of 'a sprinkling of young men, who are grave, serious, studious and breath[e] after God'.[489] With time Owen could remark on 'a great number of men, distinguished in every kind of virtuous pursuit', whose piety and merits were Oxford's answer to the 'calumniators' of its moral standards. Even as he castigated the negligence and indolence of so many members of the university and their habits of absence from doctrinal instruction, he rejoiced in 'the revival of theological disputations' and in the flourishing of 'well-attended discourses breathing piety . . . and sensibilities schooled in sacred pursuit . . . and piety brought back from its exile and defeat'.[490]

Those goals were Cromwell's too. The protector, who in accepting the Chancellorship had looked to Oxford for a 'seed and stock of piety', told parliament in September 1654 that

> God hath for the ministry a very great seed in the youth of the universities; who instead of studying books, study their own hearts. I do believe, as God hath made a very great and flourishing seed to that purpose, so I believe [of] this ministry of England, that, I think in my very conscience, . . . God will bless and favour, and hath blessed it to the gaining of very many souls. It was never so upon the thriving hand since England was, as it is this day.[491]

Not for the only time in addressing his parliaments, the protector was echoing thoughts recently voiced by Owen in Oxford. At the Act two months earlier, the Vice-Chancellor had looked forward to 'an eventual harvest . . . such as to load the very furrows. We have . . . a harvest in the blade, young men of great promise of rich fruition.' By 1655 Owen felt sufficiently pleased with the advances of Puritanism to assure the university that it had never 'nourished a greater number of innocent and saintly souls than it does now'.[492] Three years later an adviser of Henry Cromwell in Ireland, the minister Thomas Harrison, seeking grounds for consolation on the death of Henry's father, included among them 'the observation of our brethren in England' that there were 'so many hopeful young men coming on to the ministry' there: 'their parts more raised, their lives more reformed, the council of God more

---

[488] Wilkinson Jr, *Three Decads*, pt. ii, pp. 173, 180–1.
[489] Ibid., pt. ii, p. 76.
[490] Toon, *Oxford Orations*, pp. 15–16, 43; cf. Wilkinson Jr, *Three Decads*, pt. ii, p. 76.
[491] Abbott, iv. 273.
[492] Toon, *Oxford Orations*, pp. 16, 24.

clearly revealed then formerly'.[493] Such claims would be vindicated after 1660 by the contribution which ministers who had been trained at Puritan Oxford made to Restoration Nonconformity.[494]

The failures of Puritanism as a movement of reform are often conspicuous enough.[495] In Oxford they are perhaps most tellingly demonstrated by the huge popularity of Francis Osborne's worldly, cynical book *Advice to a Son*, which allegedly 'did instil principles of atheism into young gentlemen'. It was printed in Oxford in 1655 and was in its sixth edition by 1658. The attempts of Vice-Chancellor Conant to suppress it only increased its sales.[496] At the height of its popularity Jeremy Taylor urged 'the necessity of stopping the progression of blasphemy and atheism...at Oxford'.[497] Yet the shortcomings of godly reform, in Oxford and the nation, can easily be misunderstood or exaggerated. The very frequency of Puritan injunctions against wickedness is sometimes interpreted as testimony to the ineffectiveness of the Puritan movement. It might equally well be viewed as evidence that Puritans were setting themselves impossible standards, against which their efforts of evangelism could only be judged ineffective. In one sense Puritanism throve on the evils it sought to suppress. However distressing the wickedness of the reprobate, its persistence offered Oxford's Puritans the reassurance, even as they mingled with the great body of the university in its everyday activities, of a distinctive and collective identity. It was as a 'select number' that the godly formed gathered churches, met for prayer in college rooms, or were chosen by devout heads for supplementary religious instruction.[498] Their distinctiveness was demonstrated when, amid the variety of services and exercises, voluntary gatherings of Puritans drawn from across the university clashed with compulsory services enjoined by the regulations of one or more of their colleges. Though the first Visitation tried to reduce the problem in 1651 by the adjustment of timetables, there was sympathy on the commission, and on the third Visitation too, with the preference of the godly for worshipping together and for separating themselves from contemporaries who resented or were indifferent to the new forms of worship.[499]

[493] Thomas Harrison, *Threni Hybernici* (1659), p. 20.

[494] Matthews, *Calamy Revised*, p. lxi, notes that among the Nonconformist ministers whose biographies appear in his volume, Cambridge men outnumber Oxford men by nearly three to two. If we confine our calculations to those of Matthews's ministers who were educated at the universities in the 1650s, we find that Oxford, although still behind Cambridge, is markedly less so.

[495] They have been emphasized and well illustrated in recent scholarship. See especially Derek Hirst, 'The Failure of Godly Rule in the English Republic', *Past and Present* 132 (1991), pp. 33–66; Christopher Durston, 'Puritan Rule and the Failure of Cultural Revolution, 1645–1660', in Durston and Jacqueline Eales, eds, *The Culture of English Puritanism 1560–1700* (Houndmills, 1996), pp. 210–33; and Durston, *Cromwell's Major-Generals*.

[496] Wood, *Life and Times*, i. 257; Wood, *History*, ii. 684. The university also lamented the influence of Thomas Hobbes on students: George Lawson, *An Examination of the Political Part of Mr Hobbes's Leviathan* (1656), preface; John Wallis, *Due Correction of Mr Hobbes* (1656).

[497] Bodl., Tanner MS 52, fo. 199.

[498] *Life of... George Trosse*, p. 81; Conant Jr, *Life of...John Conant*, p. 14.

[499] Burrows, pp. 335–6; Wood, *History*, ii. 644–6, 670–1; cf. QCA, Register H, p. 122.

To a degree, then, Puritans were a community within a community. Their associations not only extended across the colleges but stretched into the town, where, in the cause of common worship, the godly party among the citizens submerged their jurisdictional resentments against the university.[500] Edmund Staunton, President of Corpus, preached in the city, 'in which he...sow[ed] many harvests of precious seed'.[501] Robert Harris, President of Trinity, an accomplished preacher,[502] accepted an invitation from 'well-affected citizens' to catechize and instruct them at gatherings which were also attended by 'scholars'.[503] Perhaps it was those meetings that George Trosse had in mind when he remembered how Harris, 'that excellent and grave divine', would weekly practise 'the catechising of young lads', for Trosse 'had...a great deal of religious acquaintance both in the university and the city, among the students and townsmen; by praying and conversing with whom now and then, I doubt not but I gain'd much spiritual advantage to my soul'.[504]

If the Puritans of town and gown acquired a feeling of solidarity, an unsavoury episode of November 1651 suggests that the despisers of Puritanism in the two communities may likewise have developed a sense of common cause. Possibly the story got exaggerated,[505] but the event was serious enough to require the intervention of the council of state and of Cromwell. A gathered congregation in which town and gown were represented was set upon by a gang of scholars and townsmen, who reportedly invaded the service, hummed and hissed, pushed and shoved, stamped their feet, and lewdly molested the women. The congregation blamed the episode on the recent withdrawal of the garrison, 'who were (almost) the onely visible support' of Oxford's godly against 'the malignant party'. The elect could no longer 'adventure out of our houses after day light is downe, without danger of our lives'.[506] The following year the godly of one college (perhaps All Souls), preparing to pluck down an image of Christ from the front gate, found themselves so 'exclam'd against' by 'the neighbours and passers-by' that their exploit had to be delayed until dead of night.[507] It is a measure of the strengthening of Puritan rule in Oxford that the godly would scarcely have felt so exposed by the time of the protectorate.

[500] A key figure in the collaboration was the city father John Nixon, whose contacts with Thomas Goodwin's Magdalen were close: MCA, MS C. II. 4. 9: September 1652, 25 November 1652, 23 January 1653; C. II. 4. 13: 10 December 1652; Bodl., Rawlinson MS d. 715, fo. 218. For Nixon's relations with the university see also *TSP*, iv. 595; Spalding, *Diary of Bulstrode Whitelocke*, pp. 502, 503; Firth and Rait, ii. 974; OUA, SP/E/4, fo. 59; Longleat House, Thynne MS xii, fo. 162; Wood, *History*, ii. 560.
[501] Mayo, *Life of Edmund Staunton*, pp. 16–17.
[502] Pope, *Life of...Seth Bishop of Salisbury*, pp. 47–8; Wilkinson Jr, *Three Decads*, pt. iii, p. 74.
[503] Durham, *Life and Death of...Robert Harris*, p. 44; cf. Wilkinson Jr, *Three Decads*, pt. i, p. 161.
[504] *Life of...George Trosse*, pp. 81–2. For the godly party in the city see also Burrows, p. 354; *Mercurius Veridicus* 21 April 1648, p. 3; UCA, 'Duplicate Papers': petition of Oxford citizens.
[505] Wood, *History*, ii. 646.
[506] OUA, SP/E/4, fos 45, 47, 100–105ᵛ; *CSPD 1651–2*, pp. 81–2; Wood, *History*, ii. 647–8.
[507] Bodl., J. Walker MS c. 9, fo. 195. Cf. Robertson, *All Souls College*, pp. 126–7; Bloxam, *Reg. Magdalen*, ii. cxviii.

Naturally there were disagreements within the Puritan community and among its leaders. Above all there was the division between Presbyterians and Independents. Members of both groups were prominent in the national organizations of their movements.[508] Occasionally the debate flared during the Interregnum. Owen's contribution to it in 1656–7 may have hastened his downfall.[509] Yet for most of the 1650s a truce was observed. The challenge presented by the sects to the very principle of national Church government, and to the status of the ministry and of ministerial ordinances, persuaded Oxford's Presbyterians and Independents to emphasize the ecclesiastical principles which they held in common. Even during the contest over the Engagement in 1650, the zealous Presbyterian Francis Cheynell pleaded, in a work sponsored by the university, for a 'union' between 'godly Presbyterians and Independents'.[510] The shared commitment of the two denominations to Puritan doctrinal orthodoxy and Puritan reform is one reason why, even when Independents had taken control of the first Visitation, the removal of Presbyterians by the Engagement was so limited in scale. Among the Cromwellian heads of colleges there were more men whom we can either tightly or loosely call Presbyterian than there were Independents. Alongside the common purposes of the two parties there were tactical considerations which brought them together. Under Cromwell, Presbyterians knew they could hope to win influence at Whitehall only in collaboration with Independents, who in turn saw, in such collaboration, a means of refuting the allegation that Independency was 'the sink of all heresies and schisms'.[511] Independents also hoped, by befriending moderate Presbyterians, to isolate the more 'severe' or intolerant ones,[512] as Cromwell himself sought to do. Though hard-line Presbyterians bitterly attacked Owen's Independency in national debate in 1656–7, their campaign made little headway within Oxford.

---

[508] For Oxford's place in the national Presbyterian network (where a main contact was the London attorney and bookseller Samuel Gellibrand), see OUA, Reg. Conv. T, pp. 51, 78, 128, 140; Bodl., MS don. f. 39, fo. 212 (visit of the leading Presbyterian minister Simeon Ashe to Oxford); Wilkinson Jr, *Three Decads*, pt. iii, p. 24; Wood, *History*, ii. 697; Barnard, *Cromwellian Ireland*, p. 127. Under the protectorate, as earlier, Presbyterians were eager to provide financial support for godly students who would become ministers—a preoccupation strengthened by their conviction that the status and the attractions of a clerical career had been weakened by the economic damage, the political uncertainties, and the ecclesiastical vacillations of the Puritan Revolution and by the anticlericalism which it had fostered. Edmund Calamy, *The City Remembrancer* (1657), ep. ded.; Thomas Case, *Sensuality Dissected* (1657), pp. 78 ff.; Christopher Fowler and Simon Ford, *A Sober Answer to an Angry Epistle* (1657), p. 19; [Matthew Poole?], *A Model for the Maintaining of Students* (1658); Richard Baxter, *The Crucifying of the World* (1658), sig. f4; Nathaniel Hardy, *The Olive-Branch* (1658), p. 37; Thomas Watson, *A Plea for Alms* (1658), pp. 38–9; N. H. Keeble and Geoffrey F. Nuttall, eds, *Calendar of the Correspondence of Richard Baxter*, 2 vols (Oxford, 1991) i. 99, 264–5, 290, 292–3, 326–7, 334, 380, 382, 386; *Mercurius Politicus* 6 November 1656, p. 7355; 20 November 1656, p. 7388; 27 November 1656, p. 7397; *CJ* 22 November 1656; cf. Ibbitson, *Charitable Constructions*.

[509] Nicastro, *Lettere di Henry Stubbe, passim*; Owen, *Works* xiii. 217–18, 299–300.

[510] Francis Cheynell, *The Divine Trinity* (1650), sigs b4–5ᵛ; OUA, Reg. Conv. T, p. 97. Cf. Durham, *Life and Death of… Robert Harris*, pp. 97–8; *CSPD 1653–4*, p. 416.

[511] *Mercurius Politicus* 21 October 1658, pp. 922–5.

[512] Cf. *Paraenesis ad Aedificatores*, by Owen's ally Louis du Moulin, ep. ded., with *Mercurius Politicus* 11 September 1656, p. 7231; 2 October 1656, p. 7275; 2 April 1657, p. 7701. See too Owen, *Works*, xiii. 298.

In 1646 the elder Henry Wilkinson had told parliament that the conciliation of its political opponents in Oxford might 'help you to build' a following there.[513] If that had then seemed a motive for cooperation with flexible royalists and Anglicans, how could Puritans now refuse the same argument for cooperation among themselves? Oxford's Presbyterians and Independents were agreed on the need to meet the shortfall of godly ministers in the parishes, a deficiency which even the combined resources of the two parties would have been hard pressed to rectify.[514] The Pelagian threat brought home their shared subscription to doctrinal Calvinism. They were again at one in their determination to secure godly preaching and worship in Oxford, and to purge the university of vice and superstition. The appreciation of their common priorities produced warm friendships. John Owen thought of Henry Wilkinson junior, a theologically rigid Presbyterian committed to the Solemn League and Covenant, as an 'old and faithful friend', and the sentiment was evidently returned.[515] Wilkinson had eagerly supported the first Visitation during its earlier, Presbyterian phase. In a university sermon of November 1648 he exhorted the Visitors, as a hostile source reported, 'to goe on, and make a thorough reformation, not to [leave] any thinge of Baal, not the stampe of Dagon', 'to leave neither roote nor branch of the old stock', for 'there could be noe quiet while they stay'.[516] Then came Pride's Purge, the regicide, republican rule. Wilkinson was a Presbyterian in politics as in religion. Whereas Owen accepted an invitation to preach to the Rump on the day after the king's execution, we find Wilkinson warning in a sermon of March 1649 that, where there is rule without law, 'might will prevaile above right'. Two months earlier a tract by John Goodwin, *Right and Might Well Met*, had provoked Presbyterian hostility by its defence of Pride's Purge. Wilkinson's sermon pleaded for the 'just rights and priviledges' of the university, to which the republic, the Visitation's new master, posed a new threat.[517]

Yet if Wilkinson were to aid the 'thorough reformation' to which, like Owen, he was committed, he had to accommodate himself to what to him and other Presbyterians was lawless rule. Like royalists, Presbyterians preserved their values under the republic by outward conformity. Wilkinson preached complaisantly before Cromwell at Oxford in May 1649, and survived the imposition of the Engagement. Over the 1650s the differences between Oxford's Presbyterians and Independents about issues of national politics, keenly felt as they could be,[518] were largely suspended in the service of the common Puritan cause—at least until the cause began to collapse in 1659. Confident that piety would produce loyalty to pious government, the Puritan rulers of Oxford preferred, almost as much as the Wilkins circle did, to avoid discussion of politics. It is a striking feature of Cromwell's Chancellorship that, as far as we can tell, the Puritans who did his

[513] Above, p. 98.
[514] For cooperation on that front see *CJ* 3 August 1659.
[515] Bodl., MS Lat. misc. c. 19, pp. 63–4, 68, 70–1.
[516] Bodl., Wood MS f. 35, fo. 333ᵛ.
[517] Wilkinson Jr, *Three Decads*, pt. i., pp. 100, 152, 160.
[518] e.g. Bodl., MS Lat. misc. c. 19, pp. 140–1.

work in Oxford subjected the university only to religious, never to political, indoctrination.

There was much in the Puritans' programme that was not exclusively Puritan. It was widely sensed that the wealth which had been brought to Oxford by sons of gentry since the Reformation had corrupted frugal medieval habits.[519] Fathers of all persuasions would have been pleased by the measures taken in Cromwellian Oxford to correct the 'idleness and debauchery' of undergraduates who 'misspend their time and money'; to suppress the street-brawling that had allegedly become fashionable; to ensure that the sons of noblemen and gentlemen worked diligently and, if they were studying for degrees, adhered to the regulations for them; to compile a register of approved tutors—those 'pro-parents', as Henry Wilkinson junior called them;[520] and to monitor the tutorial supervision of undergraduates.[521] Puritanism may have been the creed of a party, but it can also be viewed in a broader light, as a tendency that characterized (even if it never monopolized) a historical period, an era which preceded and then transcended the divisions of civil war. The disciplinary, educational, and sartorial injunctions imposed by Oxford's Puritan rulers often echoed those announced two decades earlier by its Laudian ones.[522] While their enemies might quarrel with many aspects of the Puritans' understanding of the duties of a godly ministry, there were pastoral needs and responsibilities which all sides acknowledged. When the royalist Chancellor of Cambridge, the Earl of Holland, expressed on the scaffold in 1649 the hope that God would make his university 'a nursery to plant' pious ministers there, so 'that the souls of the people may receive a great benefit',[523] he voiced sentiments that crossed the civil-war divide.

So did Edward Hyde, Earl of Clarendon, when his *History of the Rebellion*, even as it reviled the wickedness and 'stupidity and negligence' of Puritan rule and the 'wild and barbarous depopulation' wrought by the first Visitation, paid an unexpected and signal tribute to Cromwellian Oxford—even if he gave the credit to divine providence rather than to the Cromwellians. Clarendon, who became Chancellor at the Restoration, would recall that the university of the Interregnum had 'yielded a harvest'—that metaphor again—'of extraordinary good and sound knowledge in all parts of learning; and many who were wickedly introduced [by the Puritans] applied themselves to the study of good learning and the practice of virtue, and had inclination to that duty and obedience they had never been taught', 'little inferior to what ... was before its desolation', so that at the Restoration the returning king found the institution 'abounding in excellent learning'.[524]

---

[519] Burrows, pp. xiii–xiv.

[520] Wilkinson Jr, *Three Decads*, ii. 17.

[521] Burrows, p. 313; Bodl., Wood MS f. 35, fo. 359; MS Eng. hist. c. 310, fo. 82; QCA, Register H, p. 124; CA, D&C i. b. 3, p. 61; OUA, Reg. Conv. T, pp. 279–80; Wood, *Life and Times*, i. 300; Wood, *History*, ii. 254; WCA, MS 4/116. For the likelihood of parental approval see BL Add. MS 37344, fo. 323; *CSPD 1659–60*, p. 258; Burrows, pp. xxxiii, 366.

[522] Burrows, p. xvi; Sharpe, 'Archbishop Laud and the University of Oxford'; cf. Mullinger, *University of Cambridge*, iii. 269 n.

[523] Mullinger, *University of Cambridge*, iii. 359.

[524] *CH*, iv. 259 (though cf. *TSP*, vii. 817, 819).

Clarendon was at one with Puritan sentiment in his pleas, as Chancellor, for a further reformation of the university. His demand for the removal from Oxford of 'all dissolute and debauched persons' who failed to conform to 'the sobriety and manner of a collegiate life' echoes an attempt of the parliamentary standing committee a decade earlier to impose 'the sobriety and decency that is requisite among persons that make profession of civility and learning'.[525] Clarendon lamented, as Cromwell and other Puritans did, the tendency of Englishmen to educate their children in popish countries abroad.[526] The sternly Calvinist tutor at Magdalen, Henry Hickman, though a firm opponent of episcopacy,[527] knew that not all Cavaliers were frivolous or debauched. He extended financial relief and the hand of friendship to 'sober, serious, peaceable royallists', whom he distinguished from their less virtuous political sympathizers.[528]

Even the Calvinist understanding of the doctrine of predestination, an interpretation which could be so divisive, had its Cavalier as well as its Roundhead adherents—just as it had had its devotees among the most devoted clerical supporters of the Laudian ascendancy. Oxford's civil-war royalists, distressed as they were by the Puritan destruction of the Church of England, nonetheless contained a party whose Anglicanism was firmly Calvinist in doctrine: the party of James Ussher, of John Prideaux (in whose house Ussher lived), and of Prideaux's colleague at Exeter College Henry Tozer.[529] All three men were revered by the Puritans of Cromwellian Oxford.[530] At the high point of the university's disobedience during the second civil war, Tozer was seized by soldiers in Carfax Church, and banned from preaching, because he 'seduced the people'. He was then arrested, again by soldiers, in Exeter College, where he was sub-Rector and where, with 'high contempt', he had denied the Visitation access to keys and papers. Yet the Visitors, having formally expelled him from the college, enabled him to keep his chambers and his allowance.[531] John Conant, Exeter's Rector under Cromwell, 'could not mention Tozer's name without respect'.[532] In 1658, on the second anniversary of the death of James Ussher, 'a great confluence of scholars and strangers' gathered in the hall of Christ Church to hear a sermon in Ussher's honour.[533]

---

[525] Burrows, p. 313.

[526] Abbott, iv. 494; OUA, Reg. Conv. Ta, p. 80; *CT*, pp. 313–48.

[527] Bosher, *Making of the Restoration Settlement*, p. 120.

[528] Hickman, *Review of the Certamen Epistolare*, ep. ded. Cf. de Beer, *Diary of John Evelyn*, iii. 105. Admittedly the hand was extended the more urgently as the Puritan cause crumbled and the Restoration approached.

[529] Bosher, *Making of the Restoration Settlement*, p. 60.

[530] Prideaux: see p. 158 above. Tozer: Bodl., Wood MS f. 35, fos 171ᵛ, 200ᵛ, 316, 320ᵛ; Wood MS f. 45, fo. 136; MS Rawlinson Letters 89, fos 108, 137; Burrows, p. 211; Conant Jr, *Life of... John Conant*, pp. 8–9. He nonetheless left to minister to a congregation in Holland. Ussher: Bodl., MS Eng. hist. c. 310, fos 87ᵛ, 88ᵛ; du Moulin, *Paraenesis ad Aedificatores*, preface; Peter Heylyn, *Certamen Epistolare* (1651), pp. 118, 124–5; *CSPD 1656–7*, p. 271 (see too Hoyle, *Rejoinder to Master Malone's Reply*; Bodl., MS Rawlinson Letters 52, no. 4).

[531] Burrows, pp. cx–cxi, 114n., 139n., 211, 217; ECA, MS A. I. 6, fo. 42; Roy and Reinhart, 'Civil Wars', p. 728.

[532] Burrows, p. lxxv (quoting Anthony Wood).

[533] *Publick Intelligencer* 4 April 1658, pp. 129–30.

Then there was John Owen's former tutor at Queen's, Thomas Barlow, a lifelong friend of Owen[534] but also an intimate associate of the leading Anglican clerics George Morley, Henry Hammond, and Robert Sanderson.[535] There was no more bitter an opponent of the Roundhead cause, or of the post-war Visitation, than Barlow. In a sermon of 1643 he had urged royalists to 'fight the good fight of faith' against the parliamentarians, who 'vow and covenant to maintain the religion and true worship of God, and yet prophane his house, imprison his ministers, and with sacrilegious hands rob God of his portion; this is such a phrency as Christendome till now never heard of'.[536] In 1647 Barlow exhorted 'this brave, but now bleeding university' not to let 'any base, or degenerous fear' soften its readiness to suffer a 'glorious martyrdom' and to shed blood in 'soe great, and good a cause'.[537] Yet he survived the purge, and in 1658, on Langbaine's death, became Provost of Queen's. Barlow's doctrinal Calvinism, and his hatred of Arminianism and Socinianism, were unyielding.[538] He shuddered to recall the moment in Laudian Oxford when, at a disputation chaired by Prideaux, the young Gilbert Sheldon had introduced the heretical principle that the pope was not the Antichrist.[539] A follower of Barlow among the Fellows of Queen's was the 'strict Calvinist' Thomas Tully, like Barlow an Anglican and royalist.[540] He became Principal of St Edmund Hall in 1658, and rapidly revived that hitherto expiring house by his efficient rule and energetic fundraising.[541] In the Interregnum, believed John Owen's friend Lewis du Moulin, Barlow and Tully 'did keep this university of Oxon from being poyson'd with Pelagianism, Socinianism, popery etc.'.[542]

Not all Oxford's rulers, admittedly, welcomed the Puritans' insistence on Calvinist orthodoxy. Gerard Langbaine shared the distaste of his friend John Selden for the appetite for heresy-hunting with which adversaries of that orthodoxy, especially in its Presbyterian form, associated it.[543] Members of the Wilkins circle, who believed that the theological rigidity and contentiousness of Puritanism were

[534] Toon, *God's Statesman*, p. 6.

[535] Beddard, 'Restoration Oxford', pp. 808–9; OUA, Reg. Conv. T, p. 7; Bodl., Wood MS f. 35, fo. 121ᵛ; *Genuine Remains of . . . Thomas Barlow*, p. 244.

[536] QCA, MS 424, pp. 54–5, 59.

[537] Bodl., Wood MS f. 35, fos 112ᵛ, 121, 144.

[538] *Genuine Remains of . . . Thomas Barlow*, pp. 72–83, 122–40, 181; Bodl., Tanner MS 52, fos 212–13; Rawlinson MS c. 945, pp. 443–58, 503–16; Wood MS f. 35, fos 46–46ᵛ; Thomas Barlow, *De Studio Theologiae* (1699), pp. 48, 55–63; John Prideaux, *Manuductio ad Theologiam Polemicam* (1657), preface; Wilkinson Jr, *Three Decads*, preface; William Sheppard, *Sincerity and Hypocrisy* (1658); cf. Nancy L. Matthews, *William Sheppard: Cromwell's Law Reformer* (Cambridge, 1984), pp. 33, 64.

[539] *Genuine Remains of . . . Thomas Barlow*, pp. 191–2.

[540] Wood, *Athenae Oxonienses*, iii. 1055–9; cf. QCA, MS 521: 'T.T.'.

[541] Bodl., Wood MS f. 28, fo. 306; OUA, SP/37 (Matriculations 1648–62), p. 553; A. B. Emden, 'The Old Library', *St Edmund Hall Magazine* 5 (1943–8), pp. 39–40; Dorothy Gardiner, ed., *The Oxinden and Peyton Letters 1642–70* (1937), pp. 229–30. Cf. Bodl., MS Top. Oxon f. 31, pp. 16–18; MS Lat. misc. c. 19, pp. 132–45.

[542] Wood, *Athenae Oxonienses*, iii. 1058. Oxford's Calvinist tradition survived into the Restoration: Beddard, 'Restoration Oxford', pp. 833–7.

[543] Bodl., Selden MS *supra* 109, fos 380, 452.

weakening the hold of Christianity itself, were sniped at by doctrinaire Calvinists who described them as 'meer moral men, without the power of godliness', and who accused them of elevating the ethical above the doctrinal content of religion.[544] Wilkins, in language characteristic of Protestant opposition to Calvinist fundamentalism, warned from a university pulpit against 'wresting hard places of Scripture', and against the practice of men who 'vehemently engage themselves in . . . opinions that are grounded upon places hard to be understood'.[545] Whereas Oxford's Presbyterians and Independents contended over their rival formulae of church government, Wilkins 'maintained in his colledge', late in 1656, 'that no form of church government is *iure divino*'.[546] In the following year he is said to have advised Cromwell to restore episcopacy.[547] If so he probably recommended it in a pragmatic spirit, perhaps as the partner of monarchy, which he and his friends wanted Cromwell to assume in the same year.

Yet the 'moral men' were at one with Calvinists in their diagnosis of the spiritual malaise of the time, however different some of their recommendations for its cure might be. Like other opponents of theological dogmatism,[548] Wilkins and Ward lamented the proliferation of 'sceptics', 'epicures', and 'atheists' in terms which might have been Owen's.[549] The moral earnestness of the Wilkins circle had its Puritan dimension. Wilkins devoted strenuous labours to the composition of conventional works on providence and prayer and preaching, subjects in the staple diet of seventeenth-century Protestant instruction. He attended John Conant's sermons at St Mary's Church together with Ward, who himself often preached there without obligation or reward.[550] Wilkins recommended preachers to Cromwell's council from the ranks of Oxford's young men, among them the son of Edward Reynolds.[551] The Wadham of Wilkins and Ward was both a jolly and a cultivated college, where guests of the 'that most obliging and universally curious Dr Wilkins', the 'ever curious Dr Wilkins', 'the greatest curioso of his time', could find 'magnificent entertainment' in the hall, and where, in the gardens laid out by him, visitors heard beehives humming, watched 'water-works of pleasure' producing 'an exquisite rainbow', and were startled by a speaking statue.[552] Queen's under Langbaine was jolly and cultivated too. There was free, high-spirited jocularity

---

[544] Pope, *Life of Seth . . . Bishop of Salisbury*, pp. 43–4. Cf. Bodl., MS don. f. 39, pp. 256–8; MS don. f. 41, pp. 76–8; Shapiro, *John Wilkins*, p. 67.

[545] Bodl., MS. don. f. 39, p. 258.

[546] Nicastro, *Lettere di Henry Stubbe*, p. 21.

[547] Shapiro, *John Wilkins*, p. 68.

[548] Above, p. 90.

[549] John Wilkins, *Ecclesiastes* (1656), p. 12; John Wilkins, *Of the Principles and Duties of Natural Religion* (1675), p. 1; Seth Ward, *A Philosophicall Essay* (1655), pp. 1–2, 80; Bodl., MS don. f. 42: Ward's sermon of 8 December 1661 (and see Seth Ward, *A Sermon preached before the Peers* [1666], p. 1); cf. Owen, *Works*, xvi. 289, 348.

[550] Conant Jr, *Life of . . . John Conant*, p. 19; Pope, *Life of . . . Seth Bishop of Salisbury*, p. 24. Cf. Bodl., Rawlinson MS e. 199, fos 82ᵛ–4; Shapiro, *John Wilkins*, ch. 3; Toon, *Oxford Orations*, pp. 14, 19 (n. 14).

[551] *CSPD 1654*, p. 427.

[552] de Beer, *Diary of John Evelyn*, iii. 105–6, 110; Wood, *Life and Times*, i. 257; Shapiro, *John Wilkins*, pp. 120–1, 135–6.

about wine and women. Yet in the two colleges, amid the cheer, the practical jokes, the music, and the hunting, we catch glimpses of sombre introspection, regular devotion, frequent preaching, the repetition of sermons, troubled prayer: features of religious life to which even the more convivial members of that afflicted generation could be susceptible.[553]

Yet generations pass. When Puritan rule collapsed in 1659–60, it was among young men that royalist enthusiasm was most widely noticed. In the eyes of many of them, Puritanism, the religion under whose sway they had grown up, had been a destructive force, a source of bloodshed and chaos and misery. The youthfulness of Oxford's community at times seems to have been in itself a cause for undisguised regret among its Puritan educators, who despaired of youth's light-headedness, its 'frothy wit', its perilous indifference to eternal verities. At times Owen almost equated youth itself with folly and ignorance and arrogance.[554] Puritans sensed the passing of their own generation and the contraction of their social following. Behind the Independents' demand for sovereign power for the third Visitation there lay the fear that time was not on their side: that reform must be achieved soon or not at all. Robert Harris, the President of Trinity, a survivor from late Elizabethan Puritanism, thought 'the power of godliness' to be now 'much abated', and 'did much bewail the vast difference (in garb and practice) twixt new and old professors'.[555] His close friend Henry Wilkinson junior,[556] who had the virtues and examples of late Elizabethan Puritans ever in his eyes,[557] judged that 'the good old Puritans' had become 'very few'.[558] John Owen's 'complaint that the Masters are too young', which had animated his demand for the overhaul of Convocation in 1656, reflected his anxiety lest the battle for the political, ecclesiastical, and ethical dispositions of the coming generation was being lost.[559] At the first Anglican services to be held openly in Oxford in 1660, the church 'was always full of young people purposely to hear and see the novelty'.[560] The anti-Puritan outlooks acquired by numerous youths of the 1650s would become clear later in the century. Alongside the ranks of future Dissenters in Cromwellian Oxford who submitted to its Calvinist teaching, there were large numbers of young men who in the later Stuart age would become leading high churchmen, or who would crow

---

[553] For Wadham see WCA, MS 2/2, pp. 7, 8, 10; 4/118; Shapiro, *John Wilkins*, pp. 120–2. For Queen's see *CSPD* for the period of the protectorate, s.v. Williamson, Joseph; Williamson's prayer in TNA, SP18/205, fos 168–70; Wood, *Life and Times*, i. 290. There was much factional fighting in both colleges: Burrows, pp. 362, 396–7 (Wadham); *CSPD 1656–7*, p. 51 (Queen's).

[554] Wilkinson Jr, *Three Decads*, pt. ii, pp. 4–16; Toon, *Oxford Orations*, pp. 16, 32, 43; OUA, Reg. Conv. T, p. 72.

[555] Durham, *Life and Death of... Robert Harris*, p. 95.

[556] For the friendship see Wilkinson Jr's preface to Clagett, *Abuse of God's Grace*; Wilkinson Jr, *Conciones Tres* (1654), pp. 175, 184–90; Wilkinson Jr, *Three Decads*, preface, and pt. iii, p. 74.

[557] Wilkinson Jr, *Three Decads*, pt. i, pp. 57, 161; pt. ii, pp. 13, 87, 168; Bodl., MS Lat. misc. c. 19, p. 60.

[558] Wilkinson Jr, *Three Decads*, pt. i, p. 75.

[559] OUA, SP/E/4, fo. 92.

[560] Wood, *History*, ii. 704; cf. Bosher, *Making of the Restoration Settlement*, pp. 40, 140–1, 170, 173, 211–12.

over the executions of the Rye House plotters in 1683 and of the Duke of Monmouth in 1685, or who would be non-jurors after 1688.[561]

George Trosse believed that godliness had flourished in his time at Oxford because 'most' of the houses had had 'religious governors'.[562] For the greater part of the era of Cromwellian rule, ten of the eighteen colleges had as their heads men whom we can call zealous Puritans,[563] as did most of the halls. Four more colleges (All Souls, Jesus, Merton, and Wadham) had heads to whom Puritan reform could look for varying degrees of support.[564] The heads of the other four (Balliol, Lincoln, Oriel, Queen's) can be called royalist or neo-royalist. Ultimately it was in the colleges that the battles for the Puritan reformation of Oxford were won and lost. It is time to make a tour.

The college which came closest to meeting the Puritan ideal was Magdalen under Thomas Goodwin. Puritans had been repelled by the condition of Magdalen in the time of Laudianism, which had captured it for its programme.[565] Some colleges which had shown strong Anglican or royalist sympathies before the Cromwellian era managed to preserve at least something of that characteristic during it, but in Magdalen the purge effected by the first Visitation enabled Puritanism to build afresh. In consequence the college's personnel would occupy a high proportion of the time of the royalist Visitation that came to Oxford at the Restoration[566]— rather as royalist Christ Church had been the college to give the first Puritan Visitation the most concern. In his youth, under the inspiration of that prominent divine Richard Sibbes, Goodwin had been a model Puritan tutor at Cambridge, inculcating godly principles, winning souls, helping to extend the nation's Puritan network. At Magdalen he sought 'to bring in young men that were godly, both

[561] See e.g. Bloxam, *Reg. Magdalen*, v. 223–9 (cf. v. 236; Burrows, pp. cvi–cvii); John Fitzwilliam, *A Sermon preached at Cottenham near Cambridge* (1683); Joseph Foster, *Alumni Oxonienses*, 4 vols (1891–2), i. 129 (Nathaniel Bisby). Wadham, Christ Church, and Queen's were especially productive of future high churchmen, for reasons that will emerge. There were Tory politicians in the making, too. Thanks to the History of Parliament Trust (see Henning, *House of Commons*) we can trace the careers of the Oxford men who sat in the House of Commons in the later seventeenth century. Though calculations of this kind are too fraught with difficulties, and demand too heavy simplification, for much weight to be placed on them, there does seem to be a difference—not sharp, but perceptible nonetheless—between the members who had been at Oxford in the Interregnum and those who were there before or after it. The products of the Laudian and of the Restoration university were a little more likely to be Whig than Tory, or to possess outlooks that would soon attract the labels Whig and Tory. The products of Cromwellian Oxford were a little more likely to be Tory than Whig, or, as we might say of the years before the two parties emerged in the exclusion crisis of 1679–81, proto-Tory than proto-Whig. Henning, *House of Commons*, i. 4, gives the numbers and the allegiances of Oxford's graduates in Restoration parliaments (but does not divide them into generations: here the—inevitably tentative and imprecise—calculations, based on Henning's biographies, have been my own). On the limits of Whiggism in the Oxford of Charles II see Beddard, 'Restoration Oxford', pp. 867–9.

[562] *Life of . . . George Trosse*, p. 81.

[563] Brasenose, Christ Church, Corpus, Exeter, Magdalen, New, Pembroke, St John's, Trinity, University.

[564] On Jesus College see however Richards, 'Puritan Visitation of Jesus College', esp. p. 29.

[565] Burrows, p. cxiii; and see Bosher, *Making of the Restoration Settlement*, p. 89.

[566] Varley, 'Restoration Visitation'; *CSPD 1660–1*, p. 187.

Fellows and scholars, that should serve God in the ministry in after-times'.[567] He was highly successful. His gathered congregation drew Puritans—Presbyterians and Independents alike—from across Oxford into the college, and supplied energetic preachers to the neighbouring parishes. The Puritans teaching at Magdalen in the 1650s included the future prominent Dissenters John Howe and Theophilus Gale; the university politicians James Barron, who would be the editor, with Thankful Owen, of Goodwin's posthumous works, and Francis Howell; the influential tutor Thomas Cracraft, who became Goodwin's Vice-President; and the controversialist Presbyterian Henry Hickman, who had been one of those 'sent for' from Cambridge' by the first Visitation,[568] and who was the 'stated preacher' of the congregation which met next to Pembroke and which George Trosse attended.[569] Goodwin's Magdalen was the college where Puritan divines sent their sons: the fathers included Edward Reynolds, John Conant, Philip Nye, Sidrach Simpson, John Tombes, and Thomas Fairfax's chaplain Isaac Knight. Of all the colleges, Magdalen supplied the largest number among the ministers who would be ejected from their livings in the 1660s.

Not far behind were Exeter and Christ Church.[570] At Exeter, John Conant, active in 'new peopling of his college', was an able governor, whose high standards would be lauded but scarcely exaggerated by Dissenting posterity. He revived the academic and spiritual reputation, and the 'ancient and wholesome discipline', which had characterized the college under Prideaux, whose pupil he had been, and whose post as Regius Professor of Divinity he acquired. Puritan exercises and godly conduct were strictly enjoined by Conant, who as Vice-Chancellor, according to his son, 'used frequently to take his rounds at late hours to ferret the young students from public and suspected houses'.[571] At Christ Church, not an easy college to govern, John Owen waged a vigorous campaign of moral and spiritual reform, as Reynolds had done before him.[572] As he was apparently aware,[573] his absences in London did not help him. Yet there was plenty of reforming energy in his absence, for Christ Church boasted a number of Oxford's most influential Puritan politicians, among them Henry Wilkinson senior, Henry Cornish (a beneficiary of Cromwell's favour in 1652[574]), and Ambrose Upton. Like Magdalen's, the Puritan contacts of Christ Church stretched across the university. Most

---

[567] *The Works of Thomas Goodwin*, 12 vols (1861–6), ii. xxxi.

[568] Varley, 'Restoration Visitation', p. 10.

[569] *Life of . . . George Trosse*, p. 81; Hickman, *Concio de Haeresium Origine*, ep. ded.

[570] My calculations, which are based on the biographical entries in Matthews, *Calamy Revised*, are admittedly an imperfect test of the Puritanism of the colleges, especially since not all Puritans became Nonconformists and not every Nonconformist was a Puritan; but the calculations do reveal patterns. For the contribution of Cromwellian Exeter to Restoration Nonconformity see also Patrick Collinson, *The Elizabethan Puritan Movement* (1967), p. 129.

[571] Conant Jr, *Life of . . . John Conant*, pp. 11–12, 25; cf. John Conant, *Sermons Preach'd on Several Occasions* (1694), pp. 207–8. For the spiritual life of Exeter see too E. S. de Beer, ed., *The Correspondence of John Locke*, 8 vols (Oxford, 1976–89), i. 631.

[572] For his rule at Christ Church see Toon, *God's Statesman*, pp. 53–63.

[573] OUA, SP/E/4, fo. 92ᵛ.

[574] CA, MS i. b. 3, p. 59; for Cornish see too his statement in QCA, MS 521.

immediately they reached neighbouring Pembroke, the college of George Trosse, where the Presbyterian Henry Langley was an energetic head.[575]

Nonetheless a querulous spirit persisted in Christ Chruch. Surviving royalists and Anglicans voiced protests, both within its precincts and in tippling-houses where adversaries of Puritanism gathered, against Owen's regime. One Student who had refused to submit to the Visitation, but had hung on to his post, persistently 'traduced' the new rulers of the college. In 1653 he 'publiquely affront[ed]' the Dean and Chapter in the dining hall when, in accordance with the directives of the second Visitation, they announced 'their intentions of repetition of the sermons every Lords Day in the evening in the chapel'.[576] Two months later another Student, who had likewise contrived to return to the college after his ejection by the first Visitation, to which he had subsequently given a lot of trouble, preached a funeral sermon in an Oxford church where royalists worshipped. His address contained, as the second Visitation recorded, 'matter of profanation and abuse of Scripture, tending much to the palliation and extenuation of grosse miscarriages, to the strengthening of the wicked and sadning of the hearts of the godly, whereby God hath beene much dishonoured and the university scandalized and prejudiced'.[577] In 1659 a group of Christ Church scholars stole away with the purpose of joining Sir George Booth's rising against the restored Rump, the regime at that time supported by Owen. One of them allegedly had a commission from the king.[578] Shortly before the rising the theologian and Student Robert South preached a fiercely anti-Puritan sermon in St Mary's which assailed the Dean's principle of liberty of conscience.[579] Perhaps South sharpened the wording in the version which he rushed into print in the month of the Restoration, when, presenting himself as an uncompromising Anglican, he had his participation in Cromwellian rule to explain.[580] Yet he seems to have been secretly ordained in 1658 'according to the rites and ceremonies of the Church of England',[581] and his Anglican commitment was recognized at the Restoration, when he promptly became chaplain to Clarendon and the university's Public Orator.[582] In the 1650s he had evidently been a thorn in Owen's side.[583] South was a product of Westminster School, whose headmaster, Richard Busby, was a staunch royalist. A number of the Westminster Scholars at the college in the 1650s had Tory or episcopal futures.[584]

---

[575] PCA, MS 4/1/1. See also Job Roys, *The Spirit's Touchstone* (1657), ep. ded. (to Langley); *Mercurius Politicus* 27 January 1659, p. 192. Notes on sermons by Langley are in Bodl., Rawlinson MS e. 199, fos 56ᵛ-58ᵛ.
[576] CA, D&C i. b. 3, p. 62. Cf. p. 31; ii. c. 1, no. 66.
[577] Burrows, pp. 304–5, 370.
[578] Ogle, *Calendar of Clarendon State Papers*, iv. 399.
[579] South, *Sermons Preached upon Several Occasions*, pp. 43–4.
[580] Ibid., preface; Pittis, *Memoirs of... Dr South*, p. 5; and see Bodl., Rawlinson MS c. 421, fo. 70.
[581] Pittis, *Memoirs of... Dr South*, p. 10.
[582] *ODNB*: Robert South.
[583] Pittis, *Memoirs of... Dr South*, pp. 6–10.
[584] CA, D&C i. b. 7, fos 8ᵛ–9; cf. Toon, *God's Statesman*, pp. 61–2. For divisions in the college see too QCA, MS 521: 'The Humble Addresses of Christ Church'.

If the leading Puritan college was Magdalen, the house most closely linked to it was Magdalen Hall under the Presbyterian Henry Wilkinson junior. He believed that the Fellows of Magdalen College had been ready to elect him unanimously to their Presidency when parliament imposed Goodwin upon them in 1650, though the Rump's preference for the Independent Goodwin is not surprising. Wilkinson harboured similar hopes later in the decade, when Goodwin professed a yearning to retire.[585] Despite his disappointments he was apparently content at Magdalen Hall, to which, as to the university at large, he was devoted.[586] As Principal he modelled his rule on the godly and expansionist regime of his predecessor John Wilkinson, under whom he had long served, and after whose example he 'took all the ways necessary to make his house flourish with young students'.[587] While he stood no chance of matching the very high numbers of the 1630s, he did enable Magdalen Hall, alone of the halls, to maintain an intake with which an average-sized college would have been pleased.[588] For the most part the halls of the mid-century are virtually without records, but if Wilkinson practised at Magdalen Hall what he so often preached at St Mary's Church he must have been a vigilant disciplinarian. At New Inn Hall the politically radical Christopher Rogers had been Principal since 1626, except during his enforced absence in the first civil war. So far as we know, his reign was untroubled during the Cromwellian years, as were those of Philemon Stephens and Tobias Garbrand in two barely surviving bodies, Hart Hall and Gloucester Hall;[589] but none of those three institutions was in a condition to contribute much to the Puritan advance.

In the colleges things were easier for the Puritan heads, though all of them had to contend with the residue of the royalist and Anglican outrage at their appointments. Sometimes the evidence allows only tentative assessments of their performance. As far as we can tell, St John's under Thankful Owen did not experience the successful impetus for reform that was injected elsewhere by his friends Goodwin and John Owen, even though the eviction of royalists by the first Visitation had been more thorough there than in many houses, and even though a remarkably high number of ministers sent their sons to the college during his reign. At Brasenose, Daniel Greenwood, the stop-gap Vice-Chancellor of 1650–2, whose appointment at the college had been so resented by the Fellows, was reputed 'a severe and good

---

[585] Bodl., MS Rawlinson Letters 52, no. 90; *TSP*, vi. 539, vii. 561; *CSPD 1657–8*, p. 338; *1659–60*, pp. 400–1; cf. the remarks on his character by James Barron and Thankful Owen in *Works of Thomas Goodwin*, ii. xxx–xxxi.

[586] Bodl., Wood MS f. 45, fos 128–40; Ballard MS 46, fos 93–8; Clagett, *Abuse of God's Grace*, preface.

[587] Wood, *Athenae Oxonienses*, iv. 285. For the character of Wilkinson's regime see also TNA, SP29/11, fo. 43; SP29/14, fo. 146; BL Add. MS 11610, pp. 204–7; Wood, *Life and Times*, i. 413–16; cf. OUA, Reg. Conv. T, reverse entries, p. 1.

[588] Matriculation figures from Magdalen Hall in the 1650s averaged about twenty a year: in the 1630s they had averaged around fifty a year.

[589] Garbrand became a Student of Christ Church in 1659, and was later a Nonconformist divine. Matthews, *Calamy Revised*, p. 217.

governor',[590] but there is little sign of reforming vigour in the college, where he may have had enough to do to keep the college in order. At Corpus, enduring bitterness may likewise have curtailed the achievement of Edmund Staunton, a man bent on the extinction from England of idolatrous worship, of the pleasures of the maypole, of the abuse of the Sabbath.[591] His rule was later praised by his devotee Richard Mayo, whose ministry in Surrey, where he deputized for Staunton after the latter's move to Oxford in 1648, had been subsidized by the Cromwellian regime.[592] Staunton 'took great care', recalled Mayo, 'to introduce and elect into the colledge such as he either saw or heard to have some appearances of grace'.[593] It is a persuasive claim.[594] Yet the President's mastery of his house was apparently uncertain.[595] Puritanism never captured Trinity College. There, too, there had been overwhelming resistance to the first Visitation. Yet the commission had brought relatively few expulsions.[596] The college's President Robert Harris, though an industrious Visitor and eager Puritan, seems not to have been a confrontational figure. During his rule of Trinity 'there was ever a fair correspondency' between the parties.[597]

Thus the support of an intruded head, while a necessary condition of Puritan reform, was not a sufficient one. There were other colleges with new governors which again were too divided or unsettled for reform to be practicable. Their number probably included Merton, whose Warden, Jonathan Goddard, in any case no zealot, was so much away. The previous Warden, Nathaniel Brent, though President of the first Visitation, had broken with it after it had been taken over by the Independents. Merton was one of the colleges to have given the first Visitation least trouble in the late 1640s. Yet 'excessive and immoderate drinking, and frequent swearing and cursing', and 'a malignant spirit against the honest partie in the colledege and universitye', survived the purge there. The 'divers miscarriages and misdeameanors' of Anthony Wood's brother Edward, a Fellow, contributed to the fractious spirit.[598] At University College, whose affairs were dominated by its debts, neither Joshua Hoyle, who was much incapacitated by illness and who died in 1654, nor Francis Johnson, whose succession to him was encouraged or anyway

[590] Burrows, p. xxxiv (from Anthony Wood); above, p. 94; cf. the Puritan tribute to his Vice-Chancellorship in Bodl., J. Walker MS c. 9, fo. 195. The new chapel built in Brasenose during his reign, the fulfilment of an old aspiration, was not a distinctively Puritan building.
[591] Edmund Staunton, *Rupes Israelis* (1644), ep. ded.; Reinhart, 'Parliamentary Visitation', p. 409; see too Staunton's *Phinehas's Zeal* (1645).
[592] *CSPD 1657–8*, p. 377.
[593] Mayo, *Life of Edmund Staunton*, pp. 17–18.
[594] CCCA, B1/3/2, fo. 15[v].
[595] Cf. Reinhart, 'Parliamentary Visitation', pp. 436–7. Staunton may have had an unfairly bad press in the later Stuart period (see Fulman, *Short Appendix to the Life of Edmund Stanton*; Bodl., J. Walker MS c. 8, fo. 247), but the Visitation Register for the 1650s does not show his rule in a flattering light. His disciplinary endeavours are evident in CCCA, MS B5/1/1.
[596] Bodl., Wood MS f. 35, fo. 309; Roy and Reinhart, 'Civil Wars', p. 729.
[597] Quoted by Blakiston, *Trinity College*, p. 139; cf. Bloxam, *Reg. Magdalen*, ii. 162, 164.
[598] Burrows, pp. cix, 322.

endorsed by Cromwell, seems to have impressed his Puritan values on the college.[599]

Two colleges in the Turl were in disarray. The dark feuds of Jesus College reduced that house to administrative chaos and exposed the intruded Principal Jonathan Roberts to charges of embezzlement and eventually to dismissal.[600] In 1638, as a young Fellow, Roberts had been expelled by the previous Principal, Francis Mansell, partly for his 'covetous and worldly inclinations' and failure to repay money he owed the college.[601] Mansell, who had striven to build up the college and to heal its internecine strife, was an intimate friend of Gilbert Sheldon, whom he joined in the resistance to the first Visitation. In 1648 the standing committee at Westminster found Mansell 'guilty of high contempt and denyall of authority of parliament', and appointed Roberts in his place. Ten months later Mansell had to be ordered to hand over the keys and seals of the college to his successor, which he refused to do.[602] Even after losing that battle he contrived to return to Jesus in 1651. He resided there, and commanded the college's deference, throughout the Interregnum.[603] His relations with Principal Roberts we are left to imagine. The royalism of civil-war Wales, the college's main recruiting-ground, ran deep among its members. Leoline Jenkins, alumnus of Jesus and its future Principal, had served in the royalist army in Wales and had thereafter stayed with Mansell there before returning to Oxford in 1651, the year of Mansell's own return to Jesus. Having denounced the Engagement as criminal and sinful, and having recently been cited for sedition by parliamentary authorities, he reached Oxford from Wallingford Castle with a message for John Wilkins from David Jenkins, the royalist judge imprisoned in the castle, who thanked Wilkins for the 'civilities' he had already bestowed on Leoline and begged his 'further favour and protection' for him. It was indeed Wilkins's protection that enabled Leoline to live in the town until 1659, infusing Anglican principles into his pupils and teaching royalist sons who in happier times would doubtless have been sent to the colleges. Jenkins would remember taking his own pupils abroad with him when Wilkins departed for Cambridge in 1659.[604] If so, the action is a striking testimony to Wilkins's role as a shelterer of the king's followers. Perhaps at the instigation of Francis Mansell, and perhaps too at that of James Vaughan, another of the college's royalists, the bishop James Ussher retained rights of hospitality in Jesus, which he had acquired before the civil war, until his death in 1656, though he may not have used them.[605]

---

[599] Darwall-Smith, *History of University College*, pp. 173–9.

[600] For that dispute, which surfaces frequently in Burrows, see also OUA, WP/*a*/38(1); and Richards, 'Puritan Visitation of Jesus College', which presents Roberts in a highly unsympathetic light.

[601] JCA, MS 156: 'Dr Mansell's apologie'.

[602] Burrows, pp. 105–6, 222, 228.

[603] JCA, MS BB a. 6–9; Burrows, pp. lxxvi–vii, cxvii.

[604] W. Wynne, *The Life of Sir Leoline Jenkins*, 2 vols (1724), i. i, ii. 643, 645–50; JCA, MS 153: letter of 12 July 1651; MS 156.

[605] JCA, MS BB a. 2–3, 6–7; Ernest G. Hardy, *Jesus College* (repr. 1998), pp. 100–1. For Vaughan: Bodl. Selden MS *supra* 109, fo. 450; Nicastro, *Lettere di Henry Stubbe*, pp. 18–19; Pope, *Life of . . . Seth Bishop of Salisbury*, p. 45; Richards, 'Puritan Visitation of Jesus College', p. 18.

God's Instruments

Across the street at Lincoln College, the Rector, Paul Hood, was not a Puritan appointment. A royalist and Anglican, he was the only head of a college to survive in that office from pre-war days into the Cromwellian years. He had collaborated with the parliamentarian cause in 1641–2 but had managed to stay on after the royalist takeover. Through a mixture of compliance and evasiveness he had likewise kept his place during the first Visitation.[606] But he commanded none of the authority that enabled Gerard Langbaine, another royalist who swallowed Puritan rule, to be so effective a governor of Queen's. In 1650–1 Hood, the butt of unconcealed contempt from his juniors, was 'articled against by some of the Fellows' and was 'upbraided' with 'timerousnesse' by the sub-Rector, Thankful Owen (who had yet to move to St John's). It was Hood's and Lincoln's misfortune to have become embroiled in the quarrel between the first Visitation and the Rump's standing committee. Hood had given offence within the college by his acquiescence in the admission, at the committee's behest, of a small group of Fellows who had been imported from Cambridge in the cause of reformation, but whose characters proved to have been gravely misjudged by the committee, which appointed them over the Visitors' heads. The newcomers brought with them the strange customs of academic dress, and the peculiar Latin pronunciation, that Oxford men associated with Cambridge.[607] Worse were their drunken and chaotic conduct, their bizarre affectations of manner, their 'dangerous influence to youth', and the 'rude and unbeseeming noises' that emanated from their chambers. Their behaviour gave 'grief' to 'the honest partie of that house' and provoked a series of quarrels which brought the Fellows to blows in the dining hall and the street. The party of William Sprigge and Robert Wood, the educational reformers, was not a force for emollience.[608] While neighbouring Jesus College, despite its internal feuds, achieved a measure of reconstruction in the 1650s, Lincoln withered. In the 1650s it attracted scarcely more than a quarter of the number of undergraduates it had admitted in the 1630s, a fall far greater than that suffered by any other college.[609] During the later years of the Interregnum a group of Fellows was led by Nathaniel Crewe, a 'rotten Cavalier' as John Owen was alleged to have called him,[610] who was elected to his Fellowship in May 1656.[611] The group became increasingly open in their royalist preferences and in their repudiation of the revolution with which the Rector had complied. Crewe, a future royal chaplain

[606] Bodl., Wood MS f. 35, fo. 312; Burrows, pp. 19n., 343.
[607] OA, SP/E/5, fo. 42; Wood, *Life and Times*, i. 148–9, 300; Wood, *History*, ii. 634–6.
[608] The principal sources for the quarrels are Burrows; LCM, Md. Reg.; OUA, SP/E/4, fos 41–5; 'Illustrations of the State of the Church', vi. 167–8. See too Varley, 'Restoration Visitation', pp. 30–1, 40–42; *CSPD 1660–1*, p. 273. Lincoln's account books are also useful. For Sprigge, see also Bodl., MS e. mus. 77, p. 380. V. H. H. Green, 'New Light on Rector Hood', *Lincoln College Record* (1979–80), pp. 11–13, adjusts the assessment of Hood given in Green's *The Commonwealth of Lincoln College* (1979).
[609] The college had only about seven matriculands a year in the 1650s.
[610] Andrew Clark, ed., 'Memoirs of Nathaniel Lord Crewe', *Camden Miscellany* 9 (1895), p. 5.
[611] LCM, Md. Reg., fo. 101.

and Bishop of Durham, was probably a protégé of John Wilkins. By 1660 the Rector seems to have been under Crewe's control.[612]

If, as Puritans hoped, the colleges were to produce a godly ruling class, it would not be enough for them to recruit students from Puritan backgrounds. They must attract members of other families. Sons of royalists and Anglicans must be drawn to Puritan colleges and make Puritan friends. Here Cromwellian rule failed. To apply a simple but revealing measurement, there were only two colleges, the Christ Church of Owen and the Wadham of Wilkins, where we find a significant number both of sons of royalists and of future Dissenters. Even there the two categories rarely overlapped. Philip Henry, the Anglican turned Puritan at Christ Church, was an exception to a rule. Wilkins's ability to attract families from across the political spectrum gave his college an undergraduate population half as high again as that of the 1630s, an achievement without rival in Cromwellian Oxford,[613] and one the more striking when we observe the college's condition in 1650, when its debts had required the suspension of three Fellowships and three Scholarships.[614] The first Visitation had brought a high rate of expulsions from Wadham.[615] Yet it was 'especially those then stiled Cavaliers and malignants' who sent their sons there in the 1650s. The royalist rebel John Penruddock, who was executed in 1655, and the royalist judge David Jenkins were among them.[616] Jenkins had been repeatedly in danger of execution for treason at parliament's behest between 1648 and 1650. He had remained in prison in 1651, when he thanked Wilkins for the loan of 'the book and papers' and for 'your courtesie and civility to me', which, since Jenkins was in no condition to reciprocate, was 'a favour of the ancient stamp'.[617] There were six future bishops at the Wadham of the Interregnum to guide the young: Wilkins, Ward, Thomas Sprat, William Lloyd, Gilbert Ironside, and Walter Blandford. The wits Sedley and (a very young) Rochester were there, as was Christopher Wren, who retained his rooms in Wadham after his election to a Fellowship of All Souls in November 1653.[618]

Wadham and Christ Church were among the four colleges with the largest undergraduate populations in the 1650s. The others were Exeter and Queen's.

[612] The main source for the conflicts surrounding the rise of Crewe is LCM, Md. Reg. (esp. fo. 105); see also Wood, *Life and Times*, i. 268, 274, 290, 332–3, 362; BL Add. MS 34769, fo. 63. Crewe's election to the Fellowship followed soon after that of Richard Knightley, to whose family both he and Wilkins were connected. All three families had links with that of Lord Saye and Sele, who was a patron of the Sprigge family, and who had influence at the college (Md. Reg., fo. 99ᵛ). He regarded Cromwell's rule as a lawless usurpation (Bodl., Carte MS 80, fo. 749). His grandson, the son of Nathaniel Fiennes, matriculated from Lincoln in 1655.

[613] Matriculations from Wadham were about seventeen a year in the 1630s, twenty-five a year in the 1650s. My principal means of identifying sons of royalists in Cromwellian Oxford has been to compare entries in the university matriculation register and in Foster, *Alumni* with M. A. E. Green, *Calendar of the Committee for Compounding*, 5 vols (1899–1902) and other standard printed sources for the civil wars.

[614] Burrows, p. 288; Twigg, 'College Finances', p. 796.

[615] Roy and Reinhart, 'Civil Wars', p. 729.

[616] Pope, *Life of . . . Seth Bishop of Salisbury*, p. 28; and see Henning, *House of Commons*, iii. 223–4. The Penruddock family evidently had connections with royalists in Jesus: JCA, MS 156.

[617] Wynne, *Life of Sir Leoline Jenkins*, ii. 643.

[618] Shapiro, *John Wilkins*, p. 118.

Those four were also the most public-minded of the colleges. Among them they produced around three-fifths of the MPs of the later seventeenth century who had been at Cromwellian Oxford.[619] Unlike the other three colleges, Puritan Exeter had few sons of royalists among its pupils.[620] Queen's under Langbaine provides a striking contrast. An unusually high proportion of its Fellows had contrived to survive the first Visitation. Known as the house 'resorted to by all that were Cavaliers or of the king's party',[621] its character can be arithmetically illustrated. In the Interregnum it was the college with the largest number of sons of royalists among its pupils; it was the college, ahead even of Christ Church, with the largest number of matriculated undergraduates whose fathers were knights or of higher rank; and there was scarcely a future Dissenting minister on its books.[622] Only one other house preserved so distinctly royalist a character: Oriel, a smaller college, where the proportion of sons of royalists was even higher than at Queen's. The royalist Provosts Richard Sanders (or Saunders) and his successor Robert Say (or Saye), both of whom declined to submit to the first Visitation but survived it, resisted all efforts to impose Puritanism on their house with obstinacy, even insolence.[623] In 1659 conspirators from the county met in the Provost's lodgings and planned a rising in the Stuart cause to which the college would contribute.[624] At the Restoration, when the Puritan alterations to forms of worship were reversed, Oriel spent a 'great' sum 'in adorning the chancel' of the university church.[625] A royalist flavour also seems to have survived in Cromwellian Balliol, whose Master, Henry Savage,[626] parliament's surprising choice as successor to the intruded Puritan George Bradshaw in 1651, had no more love for Puritanism or rebellion than had the heads of Queen's and Oriel.[627]

So the Puritans and the royalists of Cromwellian Oxford often kept themselves apart.[628] Even more perhaps than the Puritan network, the royalist community stretched beyond the colleges into the town, where it included men who had been

---

[619] My calculation is based on the biographical entries in Henning, *House of Commons*.

[620] On the rough assessment which is all that is possible, Exeter was likewise alone of the four in producing more future Whig (or proto-Whig) MPs than Tory (or proto-Tory) ones. There was a comparable dearth of royalist sons at Puritan Magdalen.

[621] Henning, *House of Commons*, iii. 458–9.

[622] It was also, by the same crude calculation, the college which produced most future Tory or proto-Tory MPs.

[623] Saye's royalism: TNA, SP29/4, fo. 216; Bodl., Rawlinson MS c. 421, fo. 70; Underdown, *Royalist Conspiracy in England*, p. 265. Oriel's royalism and defiance: Burrows, pp. 383, 386, 395; Wood, *History*, ii. 654 n.

[624] Beddard, 'Restoration Oxford', p. 810.

[625] OUA, WP/β/21/4, p. 326.

[626] Davis and Hunt, *History of Balliol College*, pp. 122–30; cf. Balliol College Archives (hereafter BCA), Computi 1615–62: Baptist term 1652, gift to 'poore gent. formerly in the k[ing]'s service'.

[627] BCA, College Register 1514–1682, esp. pp. 263–4; Bodl., Rawlinson MS c. 421, fo. 70; Henry Savage, *Balliofergus* (1668), ep. ded. and pp. 105, 118, 122, 125 (cf. Tyacke, 'Religious Controversy', p. 596). Perhaps the appointment of a Master with royalist sympathies helps to explain why Balliol's undergraduate numbers rose promisingly in the earlier 1650s; but they then fell again.

[628] de Beer, *Diary of John Evelyn*, iii. 106; Wood, *Life and Times*, i. 201.

expelled by the first Visitation. At Magdalen parish church their protests took provocative forms.[629] Other devotees were more discreet, but no less committed. Some worshippers attended services held on Sundays and holy days in the house of the city alderman Samson White, 'the little Welsh-Hall' as it was known on account of the connections of the congregation with Jesus College, whose ex-Principal Francis Mansell officiated there. In 1655, fearing to be forcibly suppressed during the crackdown on royalism by the Major-Generals, White's assembly disbanded itself. Some leading members of the flock slipped away into exile. Mansell also worshipped at a larger congregation, which was apparently three hundred strong in term-time, at the house of Thomas Willis, the experimental scientist, in Merton Street. In his youth Willis had been a servant in the family of Sir George Stonehouse, a royalist with connections in Oxford. Willis enlisted for the king in the civil war. Like other leading Anglicans of Cromwellian Oxford he was a friend of Gilbert Sheldon. He took episcopal orders amid the collapse of episcopacy. So did three of those who would worship in his home in the 1650s, Robert South, John Dolben, and the royalist agent Richard Allestree. Dolben and Allestree, victims of the first Visitation, had been Students of Christ Church, as South now was. Willis's house was the heart of the Anglican community in Oxford. At the Sunday services that were held there, the sacrament was administered by John Fell, another of the evicted Students of Christ Church, whose sister Willis married in 1657. Anglican forms were observed 'with such circumstances of primitive devotion and solemnity as was hardly to be paralleled elsewhere during the storm of that persecution'. The ejected scholar and zealous episcopalian Leoline Jenkins, who worshipped there as well as at White's congregation, would remember that 'the Church itself might be said to have retir'd to that ... upper chamber' in Willis's house.[630]

Like White's, Willis's services came under threat from the rule of the Major-Generals in 1655. Unlike White's they were allowed to outlast it. Perhaps the authorities judged that Anglicans could more easily be watched if they stayed in Oxford than if they were dispersed from it. It was said that Willis's fellow worshippers, with other royalists and Anglicans, owed their survival in Oxford to the interposition of John Wilkins, who protected them from John Owen's desire to evict them.[631] Wilkins is bound to have befriended their cause, discreetly but firmly. An early biographer of Owen, however, tells us that the Vice-Chancellor himself 'suffered' the congregation 'to meet',[632] a claim which, though not disinterested, is plausible. Owen had, after all, come to the rescue, in conjunction with Wilkins, of the royalist and Anglican Edward Pocock in 1654. Anthony Wood tells us that John Fell, Owen's evicted predecessor as Dean, resided not only in Willis's

[629] Burrows, p. 370; Wood, *Life and Times*, i. 146, 161; Wood, *History*, ii. 704; and see Kiessling, *Life of Anthony Wood*, p. 192.
[630] Wynne, *Life of Sir Leoline Jenkins*, i. v; Jenkins, *Life of Fancis Mansell*, pp. 22–3; Wood, *History*, ii. 613; Wood, *Athenae Oxonienses*, iv. 194; Beddard, 'Restoration Oxford', pp. 804–6 (cf. p. 877).
[631] *Genuine Remains of ... Thomas Barlow*, preface; cf. Pittis, *Memoirs of ... Dr South*, pp. 6–10.
[632] *A Complete Collection of the Sermons of John Owen* (1721), p. xi.

house in Merton Street, which was close to Christ Church, but for part of the time in rooms of Willis 'in Canterbury Quadrangle pertaining to Ch[rist] Church'. If so, the habitation was within shouting distance of the Dean's own lodgings, and close enough to the back gate for Fell to slip in and out of the college.[633] If he did reside there, a situation prevailed at Christ Church that paralleled the survival of the royalist ex-Principal Francis Mansell in Jesus. Whatever the Vice-Chancellor's stance towards Willis's congregation, there is a contrast between its survival and the fate of the Quakers whom he got whipped from Oxford.[634] There must have been Cromwellian connivance at other Anglican activity at Oxford. Oxford men travelled to the Oxfordshire village of Launton, reportedly in their hundreds, to be ordained or confirmed by the former Bishop of Oxford, Robert Skinner, whose activity cannot have been unknown to the authorities.[635]

There survives, fittingly in Jesus College, a striking documentary witness to the depth of Anglican sentiment in Cromwellian Oxford. It reveals a secret collection organized in Oxford in 1654 for distressed bishops in exile. Among the contributors we find, alongside the names of royalists who had been expelled from the university, those of Gerard Langbaine, Thomas Barlow, Thomas Tully, and the future bishop Thomas Lamplugh at Queen's; of Rector Hood of Lincoln; and of two veterans of civil-war royalism who had survived at All Souls, Martin Aylworth and John Prestwich.[636] The collection is likely to have been organized by the deposed Principal of Jesus, Francis Mansell, and by his protégé Leoline Jenkins, another devotee of Gilbert Sheldon.[637]

Since it was the restoration and preservation of order, not any appeal of Puritanism, that made Puritan rule acceptable to Oxford, the habit of submission to it was rapidly eroded when, after the fall of the protectorate in 1659, order began to collapse. On the king's restoration in the following year a new Visitation was appointed to undo the purge of 1648. Among its members was Thomas Lamplugh, who under Puritan rule had escorted candidates for Anglican confirmation or ordination to Skinner's parish at Launton.[638] With his friend Joseph Williamson of the same college he found favour at court in 1660. In Lamplugh's papers there survives a testimonial drafted on Ward's behalf by, or perhaps for, the royalist Visitation of that year. During the civil war, Ward had been imprisoned at

---

Wood, *Athenae Oxonienses*, iv. 184.

Toon, *God's Statesman*, pp. 76–7. Cf. Burrows, p. xlii; Toon, *Correspondence of John Owen*, pp. 61–2.

Bodl., Tanner MS 48, fo. 25; Kenneth Fincham and Stephen Taylor, 'Episcopalian Conformity and Nonconformity, 1640–1660', in Jason McElligott and David L. Smith, eds. *Royalists and Royalism during the Interregnum* (Manchester, 2010), pp. 18–43; Fincham and Taylor, 'Vital Statistics: Episcopal Ordination and Ordinands in England, 1646–1660', *English Historical Review* 126 (2011), pp. 319–44.

JCA, MS 154; cf. S. L. Jenkins *The Life of Francis Mansell* (1854), pp. 23, 26. Cf. Bosher, *Making of the Restoration Settlement*, pp. 36–7.

Bodl., Wood MS f. 31, fo. 158.

Bodl., Tanner MS 48, fo. 25.

Cambridge after refusing the Solemn League and Covenant. At Oxford he apparently avoided taking the Engagement, with Wilkins's protection.[639] In 1654 he accompanied Wilkins to London to congratulate Cromwell on his accession to the protectorate.[640] Yet during the same decade he was appointed Precentor of Exeter Cathedral by its deposed bishop, Ralph Brownrigg (who also ordained William Lloyd, one of the future bishops, alongside Ward, at Wadham). During Cromwellian rule, as the testimonial on Ward's behalf remembered, he had 'zealously... asserted the liberties' of the university 'from those amongst our selves, who have endeavoured to invade them'.[641] Ward had been willing to cooperate with Puritan rule and to seek to influence and modify it, but he can have shed no tears for its passing. Soon after the Restoration he was denouncing before his king 'the late days of darkness' and the rebellious principles which had produced them.[642] Soon, too, he reaped his episcopal reward.

Ralph Bathurst, Ward's friend at Trinity, believed that by the eve of the Restoration 'the generality of the university was, for the most part, come about to wish well to the [ancient] government both of Church and state, as by law established'.[643] In February 1657 the university's Puritan authorities felt the need to attempt action against the 'bad influence' of those of its members who had been 'cast out' by the first Visitation, but who were now 'returning' as if 'by right'.[644] The initiative succumbed to the mounting confidence of royalist sentiment, which in the late 1650s secured the election or re-election to Fellowships, in some cases with the assistance of Richard Cromwell,[645] of men who had been purged by the first Visitation. The appointment of a younger figure, Gilbert Sheldon's future chaplain Thomas Tomkins, a fierce denouncer of Puritan politics and religion in the Restoration, at All Souls in 1657 belonged to the same trend. Plainer still was the tendency in elections to headships. On that front the Puritans won their last victory in 1657, in a battle fought largely in London. At Jesus College, Seth Ward was proposed 'by the direction of Dr Mansell' as successor to the deposed Jonathan Roberts, and was elected in October. His candidacy was 'much backed by Wilkins, but not by Owen'. The Wilkins circle had for once overreached itself. Ward and 'the Fellows who chose him' were—reportedly—summoned to Whitehall and 'severely reprimanded', prominent among them the royalist James Vaughan. Thomas Goodwin's friend the Independent Francis Howell was installed in Ward's place.[646] Next year, however, Goodwin's bid to

---

[639] Pope, *Life of... Seth Bishop of Salisbury*, pp. 2–3, 20–1, 44–5.

[640] OUA, WP/β/21(4), p. 284.

[641] QCA, MS 521: companion document to paper dated 19 June 1660.

[642] Seth Ward, *Against Resistance of Lawful Powers* (1661), ep. ded. and pp. 5, 26–7, 33.

[643] Warton, *Life and Literary Remains of Ralph Bathurst*, p. 206.

[644] Toon, *Correspondence of John Owen*, p. 95; WCA, MS 4/118.

[645] Bloxam, *Reg. Magdalen*, ii. cvii; Toon, *Correspondence of John Owen*, pp. 74–5 (an undated letter of which I infer the date from its last sentence: cf. CA, D&C ii. c. 1, no. 66); Wood, *Athenae Oxonienses*, iii. 881; WCA, MS 4/118.

[646] JCA, MS BB a. 8: 24 October 1657; Bodl., Nicastro, *Lettere di Henry Stubbe*, p. 21; Pope, *Life of... Seth Bishop of Salisbury*, pp. 42, 45–6; Richards, 'Puritan Visitation of Jesus College', p. 74; cf. Bloxam, *Reg. Magdalen*, ii. 149. Howell seems to have restored order to the college's finances: JCA,

have Thomas Cracraft, his Vice-President at Magdalen, imposed as President of Trinity from Whitehall was thwarted by the Fellows there. They elected William Hawes, who had declined to submit to the first Visitation. In September 1659, after Hawes had died, they chose Seth Ward in his place. Trinity had learned the advisability of proceeding to a swift election before the Puritans could interfere.[647] The same method was used at Queen's, where on Langbaine's death in February 1658 the vacancy was instantly filled by Thomas Barlow,[648] a choice wherein 'everyone' in the college 'without reluctancy cheerfully concurred'.[649] It was in the same year that Barlow's royalist friend at Queen's, Thomas Tully, was made Principal of St Edmund Hall. The tactic of instant replacement was used again at Wadham, where, on the appointment of Wilkins as Master of Trinity College Cambridge by Richard Cromwell in 1659, the Fellows rapidly named the future bishop Walter Blandford to succeed him.[650] Also under Richard's protectorate the royalist Michael Woodward was made Warden of New College, 'after a great controversie and difference'.[651] On his own authority he then restored the royalist servants in the college who had been removed by the first Visitation, 'well knowing of the unjust sufferings of the said evicted persons'.[652]

As the chaos of the late Interregnum grew, John Fell remarked with pardonable exaggeration that England was witnessing 'more governments on foot than all Europe has had for centuries of years'.[653] In October 1659, five months after the overthrow of the protectorate, Richard offered to resign the Chancellorship in view of 'the signall changes of the hand of God towards mee',[654] though in the event he retained the office, powerlessly, until the Restoration. The rule of England was in the hands of a divided clique, whose tenure of power was unacceptable to most Puritan opinion in Oxford. Its cause cannot have been helped by the attempts of the restored Rump, unavailing as they were, to reimpose the Engagement on Oxford and Cambridge.[655] The Rump announced that the universities would be both 'countenanced and reformed'.[656] That dual aim had been Cromwell's too, but by now the polarization of the Puritan cause had made the combination of the two goals barely possible. The swelling conservative opinion of the late Interregnum echoed the Rump's concern to 'countenance' the universities but kept quiet about their 'reform'.[657] By January 1660 the Rump itself was content to profess its

shelfmark 19, Bursars' Accounts 1651–9: annual signatures; Bodl., Jesus College MS DD a. 8–9 (see esp. October–November 1657). Cf. *CSPD 1657–8*, p. 238.

[647] *TSP*, vii. 561; QCA, MS 521: 'June 19. 1660'; Trinity College Archives, Register A, fos 86ᵛ, 88–90; Ward; Pope, *Life of . . . Seth Bishop of Salisbury*, pp. 47–8; Varley, 'Restoration Visitation', p. 8.

[648] QCA, Register H, pp. 155, 157.

[649] *ODNB*: Thomas Barlow.

[650] WCA, MS 2/1, pp. 115–16.

[651] NA, 9655, p. 53.

[652] Varley, 'Restoration Visitation', p. 43; cf. Burrows, p. 229.

[653] Longleat House, Thynne MS xii, fo. 144.

[654] OUA, Reg. Conv. Ta, p. 1.

[655] *CJ* 17 August 1659; cf. 9 August 1659, 14, 15 February 1660.

[656] *Mercurius Politicus* 26 May 1659, p. 454.

[657] See e.g. the Oxfordshire petition of February 1660 in *CSPD 1659–60*, p. 361 (cf. p. 336); *OPH*, xxii. 89.

concern to 'settle', 'encourage', and 'uphold' the universities.[658] Pleas for their traditional standing and purposes figure repeatedly in the political polemic of the late Interregnum, a sentiment on which the propaganda of the exiled court was careful to play.[659] In 1654 the protectorate had exploited the reaction against the sectarian movement of the previous year, whose targets had included the universities. At the time when the sectarian programme was revived in 1659, the protectorate declined and fell, so that there remained no effective Puritan authority to which opponents of the radical reformers might look for shelter.

In the summer of that year, as the revolution started to implode, Oxford became once more a city under military occupation.[660] Royalist conspiracy, now widespread in the nation, flourished in the town and the colleges and neighbourhood and won encouragement from the pulpits.[661] In July, when soldiers were searching the houses and college stables for arms, the Act had once more to be cancelled.[662] In August, New College issued a tart rebuff to Charles Fleetwood, now commander-in-chief of the new model army, who had urged the college to restore the Independent minister Stephen Charnock to the Fellowship which the parliamentary authorities had procured for him in 1650. Charnock, who was eager to see the universities reformed,[663] had been a useful assistant to the Visitation of 1653–4. It had named him to a committee to investigate the malpractices of the recalcitrant royalist Fellow Daniel Vivian; had then made Charnock a Dean of Divinity; and had then appointed him sub-Warden.[664] In the university he became a Proctor. But in 1655 he went to Ireland, where Fleetwood gave him a lectureship, and where, after Fleetwood's departure from Ireland later in the same year, he became a chaplain to Henry Cromwell, a post for which, the next year, Oliver Cromwell procured him leave from his college. By 1659 he had prolonged his absence beyond the statutory limits. The college reminded Fleetwood that at some earlier point it had been 'menaced' with legal proceedings on Charnock's behalf by 'other persons... that were concerned in the supply of our vacancies'. Fleetwood's request for his readmission was refused.[665]

In August 1659 John Owen attempted, at the behest of the Rump's council of state, to repeat his exertions of 1655 and raise a troop of horse in Oxford and the adjacent countryside. In that earlier year his call had been answered. Now it was 'stiffly denied', despite, or perhaps because of, the arrival of his ally John Desborough, who with Fleetwood had joined a Congregationalist church recently

[658] *CJ* 21 January 1660.
[659] *SPC*, iii. 521.
[660] *CSPD 1659–60*, pp. 52–3, 76, 110, 195; Wood, *Life and Times*, i. 288.
[661] Ogle, *Calendar of Clarendon State Papers*, iv. 186, 295, 386–7, 399, 648–9; *CSPD 1658–9*, p. 353; *1659–60*, pp. 61, 69, 76, 157, 195, 242, 250; Wood, *Life and Times*, i. 279–80, 368–9; Underdown, *Royalist Conspiracy in England*, p. 275; Henning, *House of Commons*, iii. 493.
[662] OUA, Reg. Conv. T, pp. 348–9; Reg. Conv. Ta, p. 7; Wood, *Life and Times*, i. 268.
[663] Aidan Clarke, *Prelude to Restoration in Ireland* (Cambridge, 1999), p. 252; cf. pp. 247, 280.
[664] Burrows, pp. 170, 370, 380–1, 392.
[665] NA, 1067; cf. 9655, p. 51 and reverse entries, fo. [1]; *ODNB*: Charnock, Stephen.

'gathered' by Owen,[666] to help him.[667] Desborough and Owen, who in the spring of 1657 had agitated against the prospective enthronement of Oliver Cromwell, had again acted together in the cabals of the spring of 1659 that produced the fall of Richard Cromwell. Owen's political interventions kept him in London for much of that year, when they seem to have commanded more of his attention than the affairs of his college.[668] He kept company in the capital with Thankful Owen,[669] whom shortly after the Restoration the Oxfordshire militia would discover, together with Francis Johnson, the intruded Master of University College, on John Owen's family estate in the village of Stadhampton, where reportedly the soldiers also found six or seven cases of pistols.[670]

The former Vice-Chancellor's resistance to the monarchical trend of the late Interregnum was doomed. In January 1660 Henry Wilkinson junior complained of the 'lascivious scurrilous ballad[s]' being sung in Oxford's 'alehouses and taverns', the drinking of healths, 'carrowsing', and 'other sinfull jollities'. He warned 'God's owne people' that 'now is the time of their triall', when they 'may be brought unto straights and miseries'.[671] Next month 'the news of a free parliament' was greeted in Oxford by bonfires and bellringing. Rumps were roasted in Queen's College and tossed at the windows of John Palmer, the dying Warden of All Souls, who had been given leave of absence from Oxford to take his seat in the restored Rump Parliament the previous year.[672] On Palmer's death, Gilbert Sheldon, having spent the Interregnum in retreat with Cavalier families, was quietly reinstated.[673] In March the Long Parliament, now afforced by the Presbyterian members who had been purged in 1648, dismissed Owen from Christ Church and restored Edward Reynolds and John Mills, those victims of the Engagement, to their places there. It then cancelled all the expulsions, in Oxford and elsewhere, that the Engagement had caused, and resolved that the Engagement itself be expunged from the parliamentary record.[674] The university had already shown its liking for Mills by electing him, albeit after a contest, as one of its two members in Richard Cromwell's parliament, the other being the lawyer Matthew Hale, John Selden's friend, who had acted as counsel for the university in its struggle with the first Visitation and had occasionally been employed by it since.[675]

---

[666] Gaunt, *Correspondence of Henry Cromwell*, p. 475.

[667] *CSPD 1659–60*, p. 110; Wood, *History*, ii. 696.

[668] Toon, *God's Statesman*, pp. 107–119. Owen stood up to Richard Cromwell in Oxford: Toon, *Correspondence of John Owen*, pp. 74–5.

[669] *CSPD 1659–60*, p. 221; *CJ* 26 July 1659.

[670] Toon, *God's Statesman*, p. 123 n.; *ODNB*: Thankful Owen; cf. *CJ* 13 March 1660. Congregationalist churches had mobilized themselves into regiments in 1659: e.g. Spalding, *Diary of Bulstrode Whitelocke*, p. 526; Christopher Feake, *A Beam of Light* (1659), p. 38.

[671] Wilkinson Jr, *Three Decads*, pt. iii, pp. 160, 170.

[672] ASA, MS 401, fo. 135; cf. Whitelocke, *Memorials*, iv. 397.

[673] Wood, *Life and Times* i. 303–4; Longleat House, Thynne MS xii, fos 150, 152, 156; Green and Horden, *All Souls*, p. 68. See too Beddard, 'Restoration Oxford', pp. 810–15.

[674] *CJ* 3, 12, 13 March 1660. For Reynolds's and Mills's restoration see also Longleat House, Thynne MS xii, fo. 156; Wood, *Life and Times*, i. 307; CA, D&C i. b. 3, pp. 93–4.

[675] OUA, Reg. Conv. T, pp. 332–3; WP/β/21(4), pp. 267, 305. Hale seems to have been first choice, and John Palmer and William Petty to have been Mills' rivals for the second seat (which the

Owen's departure, and that of other Independents in 1659–60, was in the first instance a victory not for royalists but for Presbyterians, who hoped for the dominance in Oxford that they had only temporarily achieved in the late 1640s.[676] On 14 March 1660, the day after it had rescinded the expulsions wrought by the Engagement in Oxford, the restored Long Parliament enjoined the leaders of the two universities to consider 'how the colleges and halls may be put in classical presbyteries'.[677] Yet the current of royalist feeling, in Oxford as outside it, bore Presbyterianism before it.[678] By March the Oxfordshire militia was in hands satisfactory to royalists.[679] In the contest of March and April 1660 over the university's representation in the Convention, the assembly which would restore Charles II, John Fell canvassed openly and tirelessly in the king's cause.[680] Oxford did not merely spurn George Monck's candidate, the Speaker William Lenthall, who claimed to 'have stood between' the university and 'many threatening dangers in times past'.[681] It turned on university politicians who had proposed Monck himself in preference to an unambiguously royalist candidate.[682] The erection of maypoles added to the Puritans' discomfort.[683] When the king returned in May, Oxford was 'perfectly mad', its rejoicing being greater than that of 'any place of its bigness'.[684] Surplices and the Book of Common Prayer came into common use in advance of the official commands for their restoration.[685] The university's printing press, which had produced a book of poems to congratulate Cromwell on becoming protector in 1654, now published verses to the returning king.[686]

Yet, for all the enthusiasm for the Restoration, the royalists who took over the university found it in disarray. The political turmoil of the previous year had generated a corresponding disorder in Oxford's academic and administrative life.[687] The problems were compounded by the absence in London of many leading figures eager to attract royal favour or forestall royal retribution. In July the Act, which Oxford's Puritan rulers had so often been unable to hold, was cancelled by its royalist ones on account of 'the present discomposure' of the university.[688] Another purge, and another feat of reconstruction, would be needed to restore order. This

Instrument of Government had removed, but which had now been restored): *Mercurius Politicus* 6 January 1659, p. 235; see too Spalding, *Diary of Bulstrode Whitelocke*, pp. 502, 503.

[676] Cf. Bosher, *Making of the Restoration Settlement*, p. 127; Wood, *History*, ii. 697. Departure of other Independents: *CJ* 13 March 1660; Bloxam, *Reg. Magdalen*, ii. cxvii; NA, 1067; Bodl., Rawlinson MS d. 912, fo. 361&ᵛ.
[677] *CJ* 14 March 1660.
[678] For doomed hopes of Oxford Presbyterians in 1660 see too Bosher, *Making of the Restoration Settlement*, p. 127.
[679] *SPC*, iii. 697; cf. *CJ* 15 March 1660.
[680] Longleat House, Thynne MS xii, fos 152–64.
[681] NA 9655, reverse entries, fo. [8]; and see Davies, *Restoration of Charles II*, pp. 329–30.
[682] OUA, Reg. Conv. Ta, pp. 10–12; Longleat House, Thynne MS xii, fos 152–64; Wood, *Life and Times*, i. 311–13.
[683] Wood, *Life and Times*, i. 314.
[684] Ibid., i. 317; Wood, *History*, ii. 697–8.
[685] Wood, *History*, ii. 698. Cf. Bodl., Rawlinson MS d. 912, fos 1–2; NA, 4214.
[686] OUA, WP/β/21(4), p. 312.
[687] CA, D&C i. b. 1, fo. 8ᵛ; MCA, Liber Computi 1660; cf. OUA, SP/E/2(16).
[688] OUA Reg. Conv. Ta, p. 17; Wood, *Life and Times*, i. 320.

time, however, the eviction of the university's rulers had the support of the community. There was no need, now, for the military occupation and enforcement on which the first Visitation had been dependent. In September 1660 the university reminded the government of 'that misery and slavery under which they have long groaned'.[689] Restoration Oxford would be as potent and reliable a source of religious and political conservatism as any in the nation.[690]

Nonetheless, the mood of rejoicing in 1660, and the hardening of anti-Puritan and anti-Roundhead sentiment in the years thereafter, conceal subtleties of feeling. On the Visitation which followed the Restoration, as on the Puritan ones before it, most of the work was done by active members of the university. Of their number, most had held high posts in Cromwellian Oxford. Their appointment to the commission dismayed less pliant supporters of the Stuarts who, in Oxford as elsewhere, found their hopes of a monopoly of reward and compensation frustrated.[691] Six of the new Visitors had been Cromwellian heads of house: Paul Hood of Lincoln (now Vice-Chancellor), Thomas Barlow of Queen's, Robert Say of Oriel, Walter Blandford of Wadham, Michael Woodward of New College, and Richard Zouche of St Alban Hall. Only two members of the new commission, Martin Llewellyn, now Principal of St Mary Hall, and John Oliver, now President of Magdalen College, had been expelled in 1648, and Oliver was anyway one of the less active members of the commission. The Visitation restored other victims of 'the iniquitye of those times' to their posts,[692] removed their replacements, and deprived members who had made their political or religious opposition to the Restoration clear.[693] Some of them proved hard to evict.[694] Arguments that had challenged the legal authority of the Puritan Visitations were now levelled against those of the royalist one, though this time more from desperation than from conviction.[695]

In spite of such provocations a number of Puritan appointments were allowed to stay,[696] among them the heads of Exeter College and Magdalen Hall, John Conant and Henry Wilkinson junior, even though they dragged their feet over the reimposition of Anglican worship in their houses.[697] Perhaps the Visitors shared Clarendon's pleasure—perhaps they sent him reports which prompted it—in the learning of so many of the intruded Puritans.[698] A tone of civility and restraint, even of reluctance, runs through the commission's records,[699] a sentiment that is likely to have been encouraged from Whitehall.[700] Anthony

[689] OUA, Reg. Conv. Ta, p. 50.
[690] Beddard, 'Restoration Oxford', pp. 803–4, 852–3.
[691] Wood, *History*, ii. 700.
[692] Varley, 'Restoration Visitation', p. 20.
[693] Ibid., pp. 4, 22, 29–30. Cf. *HMC Popham*, pp. 182–8; Bosher, *Making of the Restoration Settlement*, p. 161.
[694] Ibid., pp. 7, 40–3 (cf. p. 34).
[695] QCA, MS 521: statement by Henry Cornish.
[696] Cf. Wood, *History*, ii. 701–2.
[697] TNA, SP29/11, fo. 43; 29/14, fo. 146; cf. Ludlow, *Voyce*, p. 182, on Wilkinson Sr.
[698] Above, p. 169; cf. *CT*, pp. 324–5; but see Beddard, 'Restoration Oxford', pp. 850–1.
[699] See esp. Varley, 'Restoration Visitation', pp. 25–7, 29, 32, 42, 59, 62.
[700] Cf. *CSPD 1660–1*, pp. 174, 209. The Restoration Visitors, like their Puritan predecessors, had to bend some rules: Coventry City Archives, BA/H/Q/A79/246a.

Wood had a point when he drew a contrast between the 'great cruelty' of the Visitation in 1648 and the 'moderation, and a requital of good for evil' that prevailed at the Restoration.[701] In turn, the majority of the Puritans who had to surrender their positions to royalist claimants seem to have distanced themselves from the refractory minority and to have accepted their own departure without a sense of injustice. At Jesus College the Independent Francis Howell disowned his occupancy of the Principalship and acknowledged the evicted Francis Mansell to be 'most worthy of the same'.[702] Mansell's own conduct at the Restoration was dextrously conciliatory. Alongside the Fellows and Scholars who were restored with him at Jesus there were a number of Puritan appointments whom, as he explained to the Visitation, they were 'well content' to see remain in post. In Cromwellian Oxford the emotional wounds of civil war, though they had never healed, had been assuaged.

For it is a mark, perhaps a definition, of a community that it can bind, and intermittently unite, even members of it who on most matters will disagree or who will generally avoid each other's company. Cromwellian Oxford is the Oxford of the young Anthony Wood, who studied at Merton from 1647 to 1652 and remained in the university, without a post, through the remainder of the Puritan period. In May 1648, according to his own account, he had faced eviction for declining to acknowledge the authority of the Visitation, only to incur the fury of his mother and brother, who 'told him that he had ruined himself, and must therefore go a begging'. After his mother's intercession with the Warden, the President of the Visitation Nathaniel Brent, 'he was conniv'd at and kept in his place, otherwise he had infallibly gon to the pot'.[703] Were it not for Wood's antiquarian zest and his preservation of documents, the history of the Puritan rule of the university could scarcely be written. Even so he can be a misleading guide. That is partly because his grasp of party alignments, and occasionally of chronology, is uncertain. More fundamentally it is because of his taste for caricature. He misrepresented not only Puritans but many of the royalist survivors, whom he despised as time-servers. Sometimes the retrospective accounts of Cromwellian Oxford which he based on the university's records are less revealing than the diary notes he had kept in the 1650s and the personal recollections in which he drew on them. In them we see a university less sharply polarized, and more alive to its common humanity, than that portrayed by Wood elsewhere.

The high point of his week was the musical session where the 'natural and insatiable genie he had to musick' found its outlet. The Puritan rulers of Oxford, Wood acknowledges, 'encouraged instrumentall musick, and some there were that had musick meetings every week in their chambers'.[704] Musical activity crossed the political and religious divides. The 'usual company' with whom Wood played

---

[701] Wood, *History*, ii. 701; cf. Hardacre, *Royalists during the Puritan Revolution*, p. 140.
[702] Varley, 'Restoration Visitation', p. 3.
[703] Wood, *Life and Times*, i. 144.
[704] Ibid., i. 298.

included royalists, intruded Puritans, and a Roman Catholic.[705] In their spirited gatherings a wrong political or ecclesiastical opinion was a less serious offence than a wrong note. Even in a time of revolution, national events may not be the most pressing preoccupation of students and scholars. The partisan loyalties of Puritans and royalists, deep and divisive as they could be, were time and again softened or sublimated by common enthusiasms, by scholarly collaboration, or by private kindness. Gerard Langbaine's allegiances of Church and state did not stop him from inviting a Presbyterian colleague to baptize his son 'after the new cut, without godfathers'.[706] They did not stop Langbaine's royalist lieutenant at Queen's, Thomas Barlow, who had so boldly resisted the first of the Visitations, from fearing anxiously for the life of his friend and former pupil John Owen when Owen was gravely ill during the crisis over the third one,[707] or from interceding with the Earl of Clarendon on Owen's behalf at the Restoration.[708] They did not stop Ralph Bathurst, the Vice-President of Trinity, despite his claim that he 'scarce knew, or was knowne to, any of' the Puritan 'party',[709] from calling in his close friend the royalist physician Thomas Willis to help him tend Robert Harris, the octogenarian Puritan President, as the emphysema that would kill Harris advanced.[710]

Wood's restrospective characterizations distort not only Oxford's past but his own.[711] For all the reactionary sentiments of his later years, he had not been untouched by the Puritan influences around him. The friends of his youth included the intruded Fellows of Lincoln William Sprigge and John Curteyne, in whose company he mocked the return of Anglican ceremonies at the Restoration.[712] Sprigge and Curteyne, it is true, were among the less solemn of the Cromwellian newcomers. Yet it is not the frivolous Wood who notes appreciatively the funeral sermon that was given for his brother Edward, whose own sermons Anthony edited. The preacher was Edward's Puritan tutor Ralph Button, a Fellow of Merton whom the first Visitation installed at Christ Church and who sat on the second. Button's ministrations, Anthony gratefully observed, had helped Edward 'to make a most religious end', an end which Anthony piously described not as death but as 'falling asleep'.[713] It is not the frivolous Wood who is moved by the death of a friend to compose reflections on the 'fraile estate of man' which are conventionally Puritan, even predestinarian.[714] Even in later life Wood could find virtues to remember in the earnestness and energy of Cromwellian rule, which he contrasted

[705] Ibid., i. 173, 204–6, 273–5, 316.
[706] *CSPD 1656–7*, p. 51.
[707] Bodl., J. Walker MS 9, fo. 188.
[708] *Dictional of National Biography*: Thomas Barlow.
[709] Warton, *Life and Literary Remains of Ralph Bathurst*, p. 205.
[710] Blakiston, *Trinity College*, p. 146 (cf. pp. 151–2); Hopkins, *Trinity*, p. 123; cf. Bloxam, *Reg. Magdalen*, ii. 162, 164.
[711] Cf. Burrows, pp. lii–liii.
[712] Wood, *Life and Times*, i. 281, 378; Bodl., Wood MS f. 44, fos 329–37; Wood MS f. 45, fos 155, 158.
[713] Wood, *Life and Times*, i. 197–8, 200; Edward Wood, *That Which May be Known to God by the Book of Nature* (1656), sig. A2ᵛ; cf. Toon, *Oxford Orations*, p. 28.
[714] Bodl., Wood MS f. 45, fo. 150.

with the sloth and debauchery of the present. Like many royalists of the Puritan Revolution, he reserved his hatred for rigid Presbyterians. Though he found much to condemn and mock in the Independents, he reveals, intermittently and some-times inadvertently, a certain respect for them.[715] He favourably compared the educational and disciplinary standards of Cromwellian rule to those of the Restor-ation era, 'when scholars were more given to liberty and frivolous studies', to 'playes' and 'drollery'.[716] That is the serious, even sombre side to Wood. Yet even in the 1650s another side is more commonly visible: that of the cheerful young man who was often in the alehouse; whose 'silly frolicks' included an expedition to Kingston Bagpuize, west of Oxford, where he and his friends dressed as poor fiddlers to beg for money; and who was led, blushing, to play his violin before an appreciative and convivial audience at John Wilkins's dinner-table.[717] The glimpses of daily existence disclosed by Wood's descriptions of his youth confirm what our larger story has suggested: that the Puritans made a profound impact on Oxford; and that the more they changed it, the more it remained the same.

---

[715] Cf. Burrows, p. xxv.

[716] Wood, *Athenae Oxonienses*, iii. 1068; Wood, *Life and Times*, i. 360, 422–3, 465, ii. 212; Kiessling, *Life of Anthony Wood*, pp. 192–3; above, pp. 152, 161.

[717] Wood, *Life and Times*, i. 189–90, 257; cf. de Beer, *Diary of John Evelyn*, iii. 105–6, 110.

5

Cromwell and his Councillors

How are monarchs or other single rulers to be counselled? The fate of realms depends on the qualities and influence of the ruler's advisers. Under the Tudors the Crown (if the monarch was of adult age) chose whether and when to take and follow advice. There was a council—from the time of the early Tudors the privy council—which customarily advised the monarch, and whose members conventionally included high officers of state and great magnates. It was often said or supposed that actions of the king which were stated to have the approval of his council had, or ought to have, more authority than ones without it. Sometimes the principle had been asserted or implied in medieval statutes and manifestoes and treatises, and it can be found again in the sixteenth century. Yet there was no constitutional machinery to enforce it, and none to impede the sway of royal favourites beyond the council-chamber. In seeking the provision of good counsel and the Crown's acceptance of it, sixteenth-century commentators looked less often to legal provision than to humanist principles of ethics and education. Kings and their advisers, it was urged, should be trained in virtue and wisdom and public spirit, and be taught to shun their opposites.[1]

In the early Stuart period a constitutionalist approach, one with medieval antecedents, came to the fore. Less was now said about the education of counsellors, more about the functioning of the royal council, a body which seemed sometimes ineffective (especially during the sway of James I's favourites),[2] sometimes an instrument of arbitrary government (especially under Charles I). The change reflected a partial shift of political culture, from ethical or psychological prescriptions for good government towards institutional or regulatory ones.[3] Pressure for reform of the council achieved nothing before 1640, but the Long Parliament resolved to achieve it. In the proposals for settlement that it pressed on the king before and during the civil war, it made two demands. The members of the privy council must be named, or at least approved, by parliament, the nation's and the ruler's 'great council'; and the privy council must be answerable to parliament, perhaps in some measure representative of it. Those ideas were adapted

---

[1] For humanist thinking on counsel see John Guy, 'The Henrician Age', in J. G. A. Pocock, ed., *The Varieties of English Political Thought, 1500–1800* (Cambridge, 1993), pp. 13–46. I have discussed the subject in my *The Sound of Virtue: Philip Sidney's 'Arcadia' and Elizabethan Politics* (1996), q.v. 'counsel'.

[2] Clayton Roberts, *The Growth of Political Responsibility in Stuart England* (Cambridge, 1966).

[3] Cf. Alan Cromartie, *The Constitutionalist Revolution . . . 1450–1642* (Cambridge, 2006), p. 204.

or developed in the constitutional proposals of the army in 1647–9 and of the Rump in 1653.[4] Under the republic of 1649–53, however, the parliament, having replaced the king, insisted on the subordination of the council of state, whose membership it appointed annually, to itself. Parliament, as the nation's 'great council', was itself taken to need no conciliar restraint. Though the Rump's council was to a large degree the initiator of policy, it exercised no formal check on the parliament's powers. It answered to a sovereign parliament as the pre-war council had answered to a sovereign king.

Only under the protectorate would the council become a formal component of the constitution, with an official and guaranteed relationship both with the ruler and with parliament.[5] In many, perhaps most, practical respects the alteration barely affected the everyday functions and practices of the body. Except when the protectoral constitutions required departures from them, the council followed the procedural forms of its pre-war predecessor. Like Charles I's council, and like the Rump's too, it was an executive as well as an advisory body. It made and implemented decisions about the preservation of law and order, supervised the administration of the revenue and local government, and involved itself in the workings of justice and trade and poor relief. It issued warrants and directions, investigated and resolved disputes, and interrogated political malcontents and suspects. Yet the constitutional background to those practices had changed. In its executive capacity the council had often seemed, not a limit on arbitrary tendencies in the Crown, but a weapon of them. Memories of the 'council table' of Charles I, which had 'bit' like a 'serpent',[6] persisted through the civil wars. The Instrument of Government, which brought Cromwell to power, responded to that sentiment by injecting an element of parliamentary accountability into the council's proceedings. In practice that provision did not much impinge on the body's daily dealings. It supplied a warning against conciliar misconduct, but in the event Cromwell's parliaments did not subject any councillor to formal oversight or rebuke, even though MPs were ready to criticize the conduct of the council in general terms.

The Instrument had more to say on another subject: the council's relationship with the protector. Here, at least on paper, there was a change in the basis of government. Royal will, it seemed, was replaced by conciliar rule. Whereas kings had selected their own councillors, Cromwell's were appointed by the Instrument. His inauguration in December 1653 was arranged on the council's authority. At the ceremony of his installation he declared that he had become protector 'seeing that it was the will of God and the pleasure of the council', whose inception can

---

[4] Peter Gaunt, 'The Councils of the Protectorate, from December 1653 to September 1658', Univ. of Exeter D.Phil. thesis, 1983; for the Rump see Blair Worden, *The Rump Parliament 1648–1653* (Cambridge, repr. 1977), pp. 372–3.

[5] The significance of the subject of the Cromwellian council was established by Gaunt's 'The Councils of the Protectorate' and his '"The Single Person's Confidants and Dependants"? Oliver Cromwell and his Protectoral Councillors', *Historical Journal* 33 (1991), pp. 537–60. Like any worthwhile historical topic, the Cromwellian council will sustain more than one interpretation, and I have gone my own way within it; but readers of Gaunt's meticulous work will recognize my debt to it, the extent of which could not be economically particularized in the notes that follow.

[6] *Burton*, iii. 89.

thus be said to have somehow preceded his own.[7] It might be answered that on that occasion the councillors were merely exercising, albeit in so untraditional a way, the traditional function of the council as the depository of authority—at least if no parliament were in session—during a breakdown of government or a succession crisis (or in the rule of a minor).[8] If so, the Instrument nonetheless gave a new formal embodiment to that notion. It stipulated that the council should elect succeeding protectors (unless parliament were sitting, in which case parliament would make the choice; but the Instrument provided for future parliaments to be, like pre-war ones, occasional and short-lived bodies). Though the council lost that power under the Humble Petition and Advice in 1657, it was the council that, reverting perhaps to its traditional emergency role, proclaimed the succession of Richard Cromwell in September 1658 and vouched for its legitimacy.[9]

The other powers given to the council by the Instrument of Government affected the regular course of government. Two months after Cromwell's inauguration the leading propagandist of the new regime, Marchamont Nedham, hailed the new interaction of protectoral, conciliar, and parliamentary power as an enactment of the classical principle of mixed government. Under the Instrument, he asserted, the council embodied the 'admirable counsel of aristocracie'. It blended with and supported the monarchical element that was vested in the protector and the democratic one vested in parliament.[10] Nedham was adapting the argument of Charles I's *Answer to the XIX Propositions* in 1642, which, in a temporary concessionary spirit, had portrayed the English constitution as a mixture of monarchy, aristocracy, and democracy. Nedham ascribed to the wisdom of the council the aristocratic role which the *Answer* had attributed to the House of Lords.[11] He used his classical categories to highlight the conciliar restraints on the protector laid down by the Instrument. The constitution required the protector to administer the government with the council's 'assistance', and to rule 'in all things by the advice of the council'. Only with its 'consent' could he 'dispose and order' the armed forces, make peace or war, or call parliaments supplementary to the triennial ones stipulated by the Instrument. Only thus, too, could he raise non-parliamentary revenue. Only thus could he impose the interim legislation permitted by the Instrument until the meeting of the parliament of 1654, or make additions to the membership of the council.

The council was not merely to be a curb on the protector. It would to a degree be a representative body of the nation. In some matters—as in the arrangements for the election of succeeding protectors—the council was to act as a substitute for parliament when none was sitting. The Instrument provided for parliament to acquire, over time, a large say in the council's composition. Once the first

[7] Abbott, iii. 137–8.
[8] Possibly the same memory influenced the plans of the army and parliament in 1647–53 for a council to hold power during 'intervals' of parliamentary rule.
[9] *CSPD 1658–9*, p. 129; *Mercurius Politicus* 9 September 1658, pp. 803, 804; cf. *GD*, p. 415.
[10] Marchamont Nedham, *A True State of the Case of the Commonwealth* (1654), p. 51.
[11] J. G. A. Pocock, *The Machiavellian Moment* (Princeton, 1975), pp. 354, 361. Nedham's description had been anticipated by John Whitgift: Cromartie, *Constitutionalist Revolution*, p. 136.

parliament of the protectorate had met in September 1654, the constitution declared, a new councillor could be appointed only from a list of six candidates drawn up by parliament, and then reduced by the existing councillors to two, from whom the protector would choose one—though, as no councillors were appointed between that month and the termination of the Instrument, the provision was never invoked. If the protector was restricted in the hiring of councillors, he had no official say in the firing of them. Parliaments of the early seventeenth century had wondered how to guarantee protection for councillors who gave unwelcome advice from the ruler's disfavour. Under the Instrument, councillors could not be removed for their opinions. They could be dismissed only for corruption or comparable wrongdoing, and only after an investigative process which would be shared between parliament and council and from which the protector would be excluded[12]— though that arrangement, too, was never called into use.

The Humble Petition and Advice, which replaced the Instrument in 1657, supplied looser constitutional prescriptions than its predecessor and left more to the ruler's discretion. A number of the powers and responsibilities vested in the council by the Instrument were removed, and the choice of the 'new' protectorate was silently left to Cromwell himself. Nonetheless the principle of conciliar government remained. The protector was still obliged to 'exercise' his 'government over these nations by the advice of [his] council'. He would still need its approval in nominating additional councillors, whose appointments would also require the subsequent endorsement of parliament. He still needed its consent in managing the armed forces during the intervals between parliaments; and his successors would be allowed to appoint leading military and naval officers only by the same authority, though that limitation was not imposed on Cromwell himself. As under the Instrument, only the council and parliament together could remove individual councillors.[13] By provisions added to the Humble Petition at Cromwell's own prompting,[14] the protector could pay out money only on the council's advice, and could appoint leading officers of state only with its consent, which in turn would require subsequent ratification by parliament.

Such were the terms on which the councillors of the protectorate held office. By the standards of the age they were a small body. The size of councils is an essential determinant or conditioner of their character and authority. Over the sixteenth and early seventeenth centuries the size had varied greatly.[15] Under James I and Charles I it fluctuated between around twenty and around forty members. The Long Parliament, perhaps remembering that the membership had been smaller under Queen Elizabeth, favoured a reduction. No one wanted the council to be too small, for then it might become a 'cabinet council', the instrument of a clique. But large councils were agreed to be weak councils, deficient in both focus and secrecy, and

---

[12] They could, however, be suspended by protector and council until parliament met.
[13] *GD*, pp. 447–64.
[14] Abbott, iv. 492–3.
[15] G. R. Elton, 'Tudor Government: The Points of Contact. II: The Court', *Transactions of the Royal Historical Society*, fifth series 25 (1975), pp. 195–211.

too easily bypassed not only by monarchs but by their favourites. In 1642 parliament proposed a minimum of fifteen councillors and a maximum of twenty-five.[16] It kept within those limits in establishing its own semi-conciliar bodies: the committee of safety set up in the same year, and the committee of both kingdoms appointed in 1644. In 1648, however, parliament, like the Crown before it, yielded to inflationary pressure. The committee of both houses which was set up in that year had thirty-nine members. The council of state established by the Rump in 1649 had forty-one. Perhaps there were too many interests in parliament to be accommodated within a smaller body; or perhaps, amid the breakdown of the monarchy and of its departments of state, the burden on councillors was expected to be greater.

The protectorate returned to the earlier thinking of the Long Parliament. The process of reduction had begun under Barebone's Parliament, whose council had only thirty-one members. In the Instrument of Government and the Humble Petition a maximum of twenty-one was declared. The Instrument required a minimum of thirteen, which was always sustained. But the maximum allowed by the two protectoral constitutions was never reached. The members exceeded sixteen only for a brief period in 1654, when they rose to eighteen. Despite frequent predictions of purges and new appointments, there was a striking continuity in the council's composition. Here, too, Cromwellian rule broke with the pattern of the governments of the previous four years, which had established the practice of replacing half the councillors each year. Seventy-eight men were appointed to the council of state under the Rump, and forty-six under Barebone's. There were only twenty councillors over the five and a half years of the protectorate. Fourteen of them were in post from 16 December 1653.[17] Four more had been added by the summer of 1654, and a further two by the end of 1657. Three members withdrew, two in 1654–5, one in 1657. In 1658 the composition of the council survived the succession of Richard Cromwell unchanged.[18]

Constitutional arrangements may determine the formal powers of a council and establish a framework for its relationship with the ruler. The relationship itself, however, will depend not on machinery but on the men who exercise it: on the characters, and the interaction, of the ruler and his advisers. Who then were Oliver Cromwell's councillors? To look over their names is to be reminded how far the revolution had come since its inception. Only one councillor who had had significant stature in 1640–2—Nathaniel Fiennes—is among them.

Between the fall of Barebone's on 12 December 1653 and the proclamation of the protectorate four days later, protracted discussions among the army officers and their civilian collaborators preceded the choice of the initial members. Nedham,

---

[16] *GD*, p. 251.

[17] I hope to discuss the circumstances of their appointment elsewhere.

[18] One councillor (the Earl of Mulgrave) died shortly before Oliver, one (Francis Rous) shortly after him.

who emphasized the role that the constitution had given to the people's representatives in the selection of future councillors, defensively explained that it would
have been impracticable to implement that principle at the outset of the protectorate, when 'we were, in the beginning of a new government, necessitated to create a
little world out of chaos, and bring form out of confusion; so that there was an
absolute necessity, that some who are known to be persons of integrity, and firm for
the present settlement, should at the same instant be taken in, to carry on the
work'.[19] Cromwell accepted the initial composition of the council as part of the
contract by which he assumed power. Yet his was manifestly the decisive voice in
the choice of names. After the dissolution of the Rump in April 1653, he had
chosen an interim council on his own authority as captain-general of the forces. He
might as well have been formally allowed to name the councillors in December, for
they fell into one or in most cases both of two categories which centred on him.

The first, in which we can place eight of them, can be called Cromwell's affinity.
There were the army officers Charles Fleetwood, his son-in-law, and John Desborough, Oliver's brother-in-law and his comrade-in-arms from the start of the civil
war. There was Henry Lawrence, the council's president, who had been Cromwell's
landlord, and fellow dissenting Puritan, in St Ives. There was Lawrence's cousin Sir
Gilbert Pickering, of a family of Puritan gentry in Northamptonshire, who had
long been Cromwell's closest ally among the civilian MPs of the Long Parliament.
There was Pickering's own close ally, the Yorkshireman Walter Strickland, another
invaluable supporter of Cromwell in that assembly. There was Philip Jones, a
further old friend and parliamentary supporter of Cromwell and the tenant and
supervisor of his estates in South Wales. There was Pickering's brother-in-law
Edward Montagu, yet another old friend of the protector, who had a radical teenage
past in the new model army, when he had formed a close bond with Pickering's
own close brother Colonel John Pickering.[20] Finally there was Richard Major of
Hampshire, who can only have owed his place on the council to the fact that he was
Richard Cromwell's father-in-law.

The other category, which contains all but one of the thirteen, is the moderate or
Cromwellian party in Barebone's. (The exception is Fleetwood, who was serving in
Ireland in 1653 and would take his seat on the council only on his return to England in
1655.) As well as those already named, there were the former soldier William Syden-
ham of Dorset; Francis Rous, who had been John Pym's stepbrother and the Speaker of
Barebone's; Anthony Ashley Cooper, the future Earl of Shaftesbury; Viscount Lisle,
son and heir of the Earl of Leicester; and Sir Charles Wolseley, a son-in-law of Lord
Saye and Sele. The leaders of the party had drawn ever closer in the later stages of
Barebone's, when they took control of foreign policy and intelligence[21] and united
against the radical threat in domestic policy. It was they who, with army officers,

---

[19] Nedham, *True State*, pp. 45–6.
[20] *The Harleian Miscellany*, 8 vols (1744–6), iii. 457; TNA, SP28/22, fos 158, 165, 168, 268, 273,
289–90; 28/25, fos 206, 267–8, 289. Montagu and Sir Gilbert Pickering, although often on opposite
political sides during the protectorate, were on good personal terms, as Montagu's correspondence in
the Carte papers in the Bodleian shows.
[21] *CSPD 1653–4*, pp. 90, 223, 286; Bodl., Rawlinson MS a. 8, p. 175.

cleverly organized the abdication of the assembly on 12 December. Four days later they took their places at the centre of power.

Because Cromwell's supporters in Barebone's resisted the radicals' assaults on Chancery and lay impropriations, they are sometimes thought of as a conservative force. But the radicals' triumphs in Barebone's were not the victory of reform over reaction. They were rather the appropriation and extension of a more limited, but no less earnest, programme for the reform of Church and law, which Cromwell and his allies had urged since the victory at Worcester, and which they would continue to press under the protectorate. Most of the councillors, as we might expect, were strenuous Puritans. Most of them were friends—some of them eloquent and thoughtful friends[22]—to liberty of conscience. Seriousness of religious purpose took bookish forms among Cromwell's councillors. Four of them wrote, and another of them commissioned, prose published in God's cause.[23]

When the army leaders selected the members of Barebone's in the summer of 1653, the choice of radical nominees was balanced by the appointment of moderates. Some of the latter group were surprising nominations which again suggest Cromwell's hand. During the Rump period he had urged Henry Lawrence and Edward Montagu, who had withdrawn from the Long Parliament at Pride's Purge, to return to the cause.[24] Now, invited to join Barebone's, they acceded. Cromwell's earlier approaches to them had belonged to his attempts to reconstruct, at least in large measure, the parliamentary party which Pride's Purge had shattered. He had been more successful in his contentious policy of attracting former royalists to the service of the new regime, such as George Monck and Matthew Hale. Now two ex-royalists were appointed to Barebone's: Cooper, who had been raised from political obscurity by his membership of the Hale commission on law reform, the body set up by the Rump in the winter of 1651–2 in response to Cromwell's pressure;[25] and Wolseley, a hitherto unknown figure who was in his early twenties. Wolseley's father, a baronet, had been killed fighting for the king, and the family's estates had been sequestered. In 1653 Sir Charles himself, according to a hostile but knowledgeable source, was 'converted from a Cavalier in a good hour'.[26] Cromwell, who welcomed such pliancy, was less fond of ideological rigidity, even in God's cause. There was not a single signatory of the king's death warrant on the protectoral council.

The fourteenth initial councillor, the only one not to fall into either of the two categories, was the most powerful of them. This was John Lambert, the designer of the Instrument of Government, who had seized political control in December 1653 and imposed the new constitution on the army, but who left the council when the Instrument lapsed in 1657. His relations with Cromwell, despite the shared military exploits of the two men, had long been uncomfortable, and he had steered

---

[22] *Burton*, i. 56–7, 68–9, 88, 173; above, pp. 70, 87–90.
[23] Authors: Lawrence, Rous, Skippon, Wolseley; commissioner: Mulgrave (*ODNB*).
[24] Abbott, ii. 328.
[25] For other indications of proximity between Cromwell and Cooper see Abbott, iii. 86, 105.
[26] *Harleian Miscellany*, iii. 456.

clear of the experiment of Barebones, which he judged misconceived. He and his fellow leading officers, Fleetwood and Desborough, formed the military component of the initial council. They were joined, four days after the proclamation of the protectorate, by another eminent military figure, that veteran of the new model army Philip Skippon, the fifteenth appointment, who had appeared to have retired from public life.

The Instrument permitted the protector and the council between them to add a further six councillors before September 1654, when the first parliament of the protectorate was to meet. In the event only three were appointed. Perhaps the industrious Humphrey Mackworth, a little-known lawyer who joined in February 1654 and would die in December, was added in order to aid the programme of law reform, which the protector was pressing around that time.[27] Lord Saye and Sele's son Nathaniel Fiennes, who according to a royalist report was 'brought in by Lawrence',[28] joined in April, and the Earl of Mulgrave, long a friend[29] and parliamentary ally of Cromwell, in June. None of the four men—Skippon and those three—who were added to the initial council in 1653–4 had been members of Barebone's.

The appointment of the two new councillors of 1657 followed the introduction of the Humble Petition and Advice. The first was John Thurloe, hitherto the secretary to the council, who since December 1653 had had a 'place at the board'.[30] It was an important place, but it did not carry formal membership or allow him a vote. He too belonged to Cromwell's affinity, having for some time worked privately for him and, for still longer, for Cromwell's cousin and intimate friend Oliver St John. Though Thurloe had not been a member of Barebone's, he had had, behind the scenes, an influential role in the Cromwellian party in the assembly. He was soon joined on the council by the final appointment, Richard Cromwell, in one of a series of moves designed to prepare the protector's elder son, who had had no substantial political experience, for the succession.

Kings had faced a recurrent dilemma in the selection of their councillors. Should they choose them for their judgement or competence or industry, or should they appoint men of high social or political standing whose commitment to the regime would carry weight, or satisfy interest groups, in the wider nation?[31] It seems likely that Mulgrave, the only peer on the council, owed his appointment at least partly to that status. He appears to have accepted nomination on condition of the settlement of a financial grievance.[32] The choice of two other councillors may have offered

[27] *CSPD 1654*, pp. 31, 54, 252, 281; TNA, SP25/75: 15 August 1654, item 17; above, p. 86. Mackworth's name was proposed to Cromwell by the council in the protector's presence (*CSPD 1653–4*, pp. xxxix, 382), but the government newsbook *Mercurius Politicus* simply reported (16 February 1654, p. 3273) that Mackworth had been 'added' to the council 'by his highness'.

[28] *CSPD 1655–6*, p. 80.

[29] Abbott, i. 646.

[30] *CSPD 1654*, p. 309.

[31] Elton, 'Tudor Government . . . II'.

[32] *CSPD 1651*, p. 497; *1653–4*, pp. 165–6, 384; *1654*, pp. 197, 230, 322; *1655*, pp. 62, 100; TNA, SP25/75: 20 March 1655; *Severall Proceedings of State Affaires* 31 August 1654, p. 4065; cf. Abbott, iii. 321 (Mackworth).

some reassurance to that middle ground of Puritan opinion which, while it disliked ecclesiological or doctrinal rigidity, viewed the spread of the sects with anxiety. One was Rous, who had been born in 1579 and was a veteran of the age's political and religious conflicts.[33] The other was Skippon, who was troubled by the sectarian excesses of religious liberty.[34] There may have been a second motive for the appointment of Skippon, whose presence could be expected, by virtue of his long-standing relationship with the London militia, to offer satisfaction among Cromwell's supporters in the City.

Mulgrave, Rous, and Skippon were, together with Richard Major, the councillors who worked least hard and made least impact at the board. Of the more influential councillors, seven—Lisle, Montagu, Wolseley, Strickland, Pickering, Cooper, and Sydenham—were from substantial landed families, though they were scarcely magnates.[35] Perhaps it is the social standing of Mulgrave and Lisle, the first an earl, the second heir to an earldom, that explains why one or other of them tended to take the chair in Lawrence's absence;[36] or perhaps it was their air of semi-detachment from the regime, which distanced them from the factional rivalries of others, though Lisle played a significant part in the council's activities. He showed no trace of Puritan enthusiasm. Though his capacities were not always highly regarded,[37] he inherited, together with the wide and cultivated interests of the Sidney family,[38] their expertise in diplomacy. He shared it with the hard-working Strickland, who had had a demanding training as the Long Parliament's ambassador to the Netherlands. Strickland had extensive Dutch connections and sympathies, as perhaps did Lawrence, a Baptist who had emigrated to Holland under Laud. Some councillors acquired major posts outside the council. Sydenham and Montagu were made treasury commissioners, Fiennes a Commissioner of the Great Seal. Two councillors left Whitehall for extensive periods, Montagu as an admiral, Desborough as Major-General in the West Country.[39] Three members, Pickering, Strickland, and Jones, were as much courtiers as councillors. They handled most matters relating to the protector's household. Strickland and Pickering were, amid

---

[33] For his position on liberty of conscience see J. Sears McGee, 'Francis Rous and "scabby or itchy children": The Problem of Toleration in 1645', *Huntington Library Quarterly* 67 (2004), pp. 401–22.

[34] *Burton*, i. 48–50.

[35] For their social backgrounds see Austin Woolrych, *Commonwealth to Protectorate* (Oxford, 1982), esp. p. 199.

[36] The only other councillor to do so was Nathaniel Fiennes.

[37] M. J. Braddick and Mark Greengrass, eds, 'The Letters of Sir Cheney Culpepper, 1641–1657', *Camden Miscellany* 33 (1996), p. 291. Woolrych, *Commonwealth to Protectorate*, pp. 313–14, thinks of Lisle as 'lazy', but see Bulstrode Whitelocke, *A Journal of the Swedish Embassy*, 2 vols (1855), i. 41, ii. 456.

[38] Hilary Maddicott, 'A Collection of the Interregnum Period: Philip, Lord Viscount Lisle, and his Purchases from the "Late King's Goods", 1649–1660', *Journal of the History of Collections* 11 (1999), pp. 1–24; Blair Worden, 'Classical Republicanism and the Puritan Revolution', in Hugh Lloyd-Jones, Valerie Pearl, and Blair Worden, eds, *History and Imagination: Essays in Honour of H. R. Trevor-Roper* (1981), pp. 185–90. In the Restoration, Lisle would acquire distinguished contacts in the world of poetry and drama, as would Wolseley, who was himself a poet.

[39] With Jones, Desborough also had responsibilities in naval administration.

their other duties, fetchers and carriers, escorting ambassadors to and from audiences and sometimes acting as translators during them.

Cromwell's councillors can be hard to know. The protectorate, alive to the dangers of leaks and informers and internal disloyalty, was a secretive regime, which foreign ambassadors found unusually hard to penetrate. Few of the councillors had public profiles. In the government press, reports of the members' activities normally referred to them collectively and not by name. Other observers who described the workings of the council tended to get the names of its members wrong. As far as the civilian administration was concerned—for the army was another matter—this was not a government of grandees. The language of the over-mighty subject, and of corrupt and parasitic favourites, which had flourished under the monarchy is rarely heard in the reign of Oliver. That was partly because of his own over-might. But it may also have been because of the carefully even distribution, in his dealings with the more active of the civilian advisers, of his marks of attention and esteem.

Cromwell, who was fifty-four when he became protector, was surrounded by younger men. Rous, admittedly, was twenty years his senior, while Strickland, Lawrence, Skippon, Mackworth, and Major were of his generation. But of the other fourteen of the twenty councillors, none in 1653 was older than around forty-five; eleven (all but Fiennes, Desborough, and Pickering) were below forty; and three (Montagu, Wolseley, and Richard Cromwell) were appointed in their twenties. Only four members of the council had belonged to the Long Parliament from its outset, and few of the councillors had held high office before Barebone's. Cooper, it is true, had sat in the Short Parliament of 1640, and seven councillors had come into the Long Parliament in by-elections. Even so, the council's combined political experience was limited. Lawrence, the hard-working president, had been a scarcely-known figure before 1653. For him as for others, Barebone's was a steep learning curve. Even Fiennes, a veteran of the Long Parliament, had ceased to sit at Pride's Purge, and so had not shared in the experience of government under the Rump. His appointment was nonetheless a catch for the protectorate. He soon became a leading figure in the formation and articulation of its policies, both foreign and domestic.

The councillors were entitled to salaries of £1,000 a year (though, like other government stipends, theirs got into arrears). That stipulation caused public resentment.[40] Yet it seems to have been meant as a substitute for the haphazard and no less unpopular assortment of perquisites and gratuities which had hitherto been substitutes for salaries, and which allegedly had corrupted the public service.[41] At all events the protectoral councillors earned their pay. Attendance records, when measured against those of royal councils, were on the whole high.[42] They tell only part of the story, for to the hours spent at the council board we must add the labours of preparing the council's business, implementing its decisions,

---

[40] *Burton*, i. civ, iv. 48; *Ludlow's Memoirs*, i. 371–2; cf. *OPH*, xxii. 370.
[41] G. E. Aylmer, *The State's Servants* (1973), pp. 110–11.
[42] E. R. Turner, *The Privy Council of England*, 2 vols (Baltimore, 1972), i. 319–20.

attending council committees, and contributing to endless informal consultations. There was a limit to what could be left to the council's thinly staffed secretariat. Numerous witnesses testified to the hectic activity of the councillors and to their long and late hours. Even before the civil war, when the privy council had acted within an established constitutional framework, its members had needed great energy.[43] The task before Cromwell's councillors was more daunting, for together with the ordinary business of government they confronted all the obstacles arising from the illegitimacy or alleged illegitimacy of their tenure of power; from the remaining divisions of civil war; from the challenges of conspiracy by both Cavalier and Roundhead malcontents; from the heap of unresolved grievances and disputes bequeathed by wartime administration; and from the task of sustaining a great army and navy. Though much of the burden was carried by standing committees outside the council, its members bore a huge load. Like the Rump, and like Barebone's, the protectorate came into existence as a hastily improvised regime, which had to make up its procedures as it went along. Like those earlier regimes it inherited a great backlog of business. It grew ever more behind, and its delays became notorious.

A fashion has arisen of describing the relations among the inner circles of early-modern English politics as 'collegial'. The phrase is apt, provided we do not romanticize it. For there are colleges and colleges. The protectoral council was a claustrophobic body, consisting of a small and rarely changing group of men who met day upon day behind a long series of closed doors;[44] who forever passed each other in the passageways of Whitehall; and who slept in state lodgings close to their work unless they could get back to town houses of their own or escape for a while to the country air. They habitually prayed or attended sermons or fasted together. They endured periods of great strain, when the direction or even survival of the regime stood in doubt. As happens in small colleges, external challenges could sometimes unite, sometimes divide. The councillors came firmly together on one issue which, if they had debated it, say, as backbench MPs, would surely have divided them. In indignant response to the royalist conspiracy of 1655 they introduced and rallied behind the hated decimation tax, the levy on royalist estates which appeared to breach the indemnity granted by the Rump to royalists three years earlier.[45] On other matters they faced parliament—as privy councils had often done—with a divided front. But whatever their disagreements, the daily demands of business required the maintenance of working relationships. Sometimes, as in all regimes of the era, friendships or family ties crossed lines of division, or habitual allies found themselves at odds. Only rarely and momentarily do we glimpse the undercurrents

[43] Kevin Sharpe, *The Personal Rule of Charles I* (1992), pp. 265 ff. The abolition of the Court of Requests by the Long Parliament added to the duties that would fall on the councils of the Interregnum.
[44] *The English Civil War: A Contemporary Account* [taken from the *Calendar of State Papers Venetian*], 5 vols (1996), iv. 168; *Calendar of State Papers Venetian*, xxx. 142–3. I suspect that the gatherings to which the Venetian ambassador was referring were not formal council meetings but informal ones in Cromwell's own chamber. Cf. Abbott, iv. 727.
[45] Gaunt, 'Councils of the Protectorate', pp. 204–5.

of affection or exasperation, or the release of laughter or the explosions of temper, that will visit any body of men who encounter each other's voices and mannerisms day after day.

Contemporary comment on the stature of the councillors was unflattering. They were said to want 'heads' and 'hearts', to lack 'resolution', and to suffer from excessive 'caution'.[46] Ambassadors, accustomed to aristocratic courtesies, bemoaned the 'ignorance', and the consequent diplomatic solecisms, of the councillors.[47] They remarked on their propensity to haggle like 'merchants' at the expense of the larger diplomatic picture.[48] Some of that comment is perhaps attributable to monarchist animus, or to the need of agents of foreign powers to explain to their masters their own failure to make diplomatic headway with a stubborn regime. There was plenty of logistical competence among the councillors. There was plenty of toughness too, not only in the military leaders but among the civilians also. Jones, Pickering, and Major were, or were said to be, ruthless in the management of their lands; Sydenham had had a reputation as a ruthless soldier; Strickland had been an exacting diplomatic negotiator. The protector's council might well have been equal to a normal political setting. The rule of the Long Parliament had shown how much political and administrative ability was to be found outside the customary circles of Whitehall, and how quickly it could develop under the pressure of events. Cromwell, who was renowned for 'knowing men better than any other man' and for 'suiting instruments for work',[49] was an able recruiter of flexible administrators who would do his will, and of men able to give practical cast to his aspirations. Yet breadth of political vision, and independence of mind, fared less happily under his shadow. The two councillors of obvious political stature, Lambert and Cooper, were the ones who broke openly with him.

Lambert—'his lordship' as he contrived to be called in the council's minutes, apparently on the strength of his appointment as Lord Deputy of Ireland in 1652, which Cromwell had aborted—arrived with Oliver for the protector's first formal appearance at the council.[50] From 1653 to 1657 he enjoyed a standing far above the rest of the councillors, even though he was obliged to observe the same forms of deference to the protector as they. His stature was given public recognition when he rode in the protector's coach to the openings of Oliver's two parliaments. He had dominated the discussions that followed the termination of Barebone's, when the

[46] Gaunt, 'Single Person's Confidants', p. 540; *TSP*, iii. 498; Peter Gaunt, ed., *The Correspondence of Henry Cromwell*, Camden Society, fifth series 31 (2007), p. 143; Clyve Jones, ed., 'The Correspondence of Henry Cromwell, 1655–1659, and Other Papers, from . . . Lansdowne MSS 821–823', Univ. of Lancaster M.Litt. thesis (1969), pp. 579–80, 781; Michael Roberts, ed., *Swedish Diplomats at Cromwell's Court*, Camden Society, fourth series 36 (1988), pp. 32, 140, 273, 284 (cf. p. 32); Ruth Spalding, ed., *The Diary of Bulstrode Whitelocke* (Oxford, 1990), p. 464. I am most grateful to Mr Jones for making his thesis available to me.

[47] Roberts, *Swedish Diplomats*, pp. 208–9, 289–90; Spalding, *Diary of Bulstrode Whitelocke*, p. 431. Cf. Bodl., Carte MS 114, fo. 265ᵛ; Clarendon MS 59, fo. 354; Abbott, iv. 251.

[48] Bodl., Carte MS 114, fo. 215 (cf. Robert Vaughan, ed., *The Protectorate of Oliver Cromwell*, 2 vols [1839], i. 43); Roberts, *Swedish Diplomats*, p. 286.

[49] *TSP*, iv. 54, vi. 609; cf. *CH*, vi. 91.

[50] TNA, SP25/47, p. 9.

abyss of anarchy yawned, and had given Cromwell and his cause a lifeline. Perhaps—for we have mainly to guess at his dealings with Oliver in those hectic days—some understanding or half-understanding was reached at that time that Lambert would be a kind of second-in-command of the government, perhaps too that Cromwell would favour him as his successor. At all events Lambert's superiority over the other members of the council has many indices. In the available evidence he appears as the only councillor to host a meeting of the council in his own Whitehall lodgings;[51] to be 'spared' attention on minor matters in order to concentrate on major ones;[52] to be visited at his home (at Wimbledon) by the protector;[53] and to dine with his wife at Cromwell's table.[54] During his time on the council he was apparently the only member to have his own intelligence service,[55] and the only one to draft letters in Cromwell's name.[56] When, in July 1656, after a period of torrid conflict within the government, Lawrence's presidency suffered a crisis of authority, it was Lambert who resolved it.[57]

Ambassadors, politicians, and favour-seekers all recognized his exceptional standing and courted his attention. In main areas of policy, especially the army, Scotland, and (at least until Fleetwood's return from it in 1655) Ireland, his was the pre-eminent voice on the council, as chairman or leader of committees and as the introducer of reports and discussions.[58] He is the only councillor we ever see challenging Cromwell's views head-on. It happened, as we learn from a document in the hand of Edward Montagu, at a meeting of councillors in July 1654, when Lambert incisively criticized the protector's project to invade the Spanish empire in the new world and indeed the government's general priorities. Montagu recorded speeches only by Cromwell and Lambert: it looks as if the others sat mute, like hushed spectators at tennis.[59] The removal of 'the great man'[60] from the council in 1657, though a relief to his opponents within the regime, was also a blow to its competence, for without him the momentum of decision-making ran down. Together with his ability the government missed his equability and civility, which could paper over disagreements.[61] Commentators agreed that his outward complaisance masked private ambition. They asserted that, while it was in his own interest for the regime of which he was the designer to run effectively, he harboured

[51] *CSPD 1654*, p. 367.
[52] TNA, SP25/75: 3 February 1654, item 27.
[53] *TSP*, iv. 587.
[54] Ibid., ii. 257.
[55] *CSPD 1655–6*, p. 244; *TSP*, iii. 329.
[56] TNA, SP25/75: 23 March 1655; SP25/76: 20 July 1655, 31 July 1655.
[57] Ibid., SP25/77: 29 July 1656.
[58] Like many aspects of Cromwellian politics, Lambert's role emerges more forcefully from the council's records than from the printed calendars of them. (I cite the calendars, rather than the original MSS, when those MSS add nothing significant to them.)
[59] Firth, *Clarke Papers*, iii. 207–9. The meeting is likely to have been an informal gathering of Cromwell and the councillors, not a formal session: *CSPD 1654*, p. xl; *Severall Proceedings of State Affaires* 27 July 1654, p. 3985; below, pp. 219–20.
[60] *TSP*, vi. 74.
[61] Spalding, *Diary of Bulstrode Whitelocke*, p. 390; Gaunt, *Correspondence of Henry Cromwell*, pp. 138, 154 (cf. p. 137); Abbott, iv. 415; cf. Bodl., Carte MS 213, fo. 301.

a secret disloyalty to the protector, even perhaps a readiness, if it proved the only route to the succession, to depose him. If, as was alleged, Cromwell called him 'bottomless Lambert', the epithet seems warranted, for Lambert had a way of outwardly encouraging the prospect of the hereditary succession of Richard Cromwell, but by methods that alerted his listeners to the problems it would pose.[62]

Bulstrode Whitelocke, a dependable weathercock, took pains to cultivate Lambert, 'he being a person in great favour with the army, and not without some close emulation from Cromwell'.[63] In 1656 the protector was reportedly 'in an extraordinary rage' and 'passion' at Lambert's conduct towards him.[64] Some claimed that Lambert was taking over control of the army by courting popularity among his juniors and fixing the promotion of his supporters. That was an exaggeration. He indeed had a significant, and to the protector a potentially dangerous, role in military politics and administration. Yet Cromwell kept a close watch on promotions,[65] especially when his own power base might be in question.[66] The protector entrusted much military business to a committee or committees of officers appointed by him and dominated by his faithful followers Edward Whalley and William Goffe. When the trial of strength between Cromwell and Lambert came in 1657, Lambert drew back and fell from power.

According to a royalist newsletter of March 1656, Lambert 'is daily in council and carries all before him as he thinks best'.[67] Next month another royalist newsletter stated that Lambert 'hath the protector in a string'. It added that 'the council do for the most part affect him, though at present they seem to stick close to the protector'; and that Lambert's fellow Yorkshireman Mulgrave, and 'one or two more' of the council, were his 'creatures'.[68] Again we may be sceptical. The Cromwellians would hardly have deserted the protector for Lambert, who lacked (though he could intermittently assume) their godly demeanour and language. Mulgrave, whom Cromwell had been eager to add to the council, would continue to serve after Lambert's withdrawal.[69] Despite Lambert's opposition, 'most' of the council supported Cromwell over the expedition to the new world.[70] Even so, Lambert—so long as he worked within the boundaries of political compliance—was an obvious rallying point for the significant element of the council's

---

[62] *TSP*, ii. 681, 684, 685; François Guizot, ed., *History of Oliver Cromwell*, transl. A. R. Scoble, 2 vols (1854), ii. 475; Worcester College Oxford, Clarke MS xxix, fo. 109. Cf. *English Civil War*, iv. 342; Roberts, *Swedish Diplomats*, p. 326.

[63] Whitelocke, *Journal of the Swedish Embassy*, ii. 458–9; Longleat House, Whitelocke MS xv, fo. 71.

[64] Thomas Carte, ed., *A Collection of Original Letters . . . 1641 to 1660*, 2 vols (1739), ii. 89–90; cf. Abbott, iii. 764–5.

[65] Henry Reece, 'The Military Presence in England', Univ. of Oxford D.Phil. thesis (1981), ch. 3.

[66] e.g. Bodl., Rawlinson MS a. 27, p. 499 (cf. *TSP*, iii. 568); Gaunt, *Correspondence of Henry Cromwell*, p. 133; *TSP*, iii. 193–4, 217.

[67] Carte, *Original Letters*, ii. 89.

[68] *TSP*, iv. 676.

[69] He would, it is true, decline to sit in the 'Other House', but that was perhaps because of a refusal to betray the peerage (the apparent reason for his decision not to sit on the Rump's council of state in 1649).

[70] *TSP*, i. 761.

membership that was troubled by the drift back towards monarchy. If he did aspire to the succession, the Humble Petition and Advice, which left the succession to the will not of the council or parliament but of Cromwell himself, removed his chances.

The Swedish ambassador thought that 'the two leading men in England' (after Cromwell) were Lambert and Fleetwood.[71] Fleetwood had little of Lambert's sharpness of mental or political focus, but he did possess a following among the 'saints' that Lambert could not match. At his London home, Wallingford House, formerly a royal palace, the saints egged him on.[72] He was a potential rival to Lambert for control of the army and perhaps for the succession. After the introduction of the Humble Petition in 1657, some of Lambert's power, on and off the council, was taken over by Fleetwood.[73] But the two men had made common cause earlier in that year, when they and their fellow general Desborough, the 'three great men' as Thurloe called them,[74] stood out against the crowning of Cromwell.

In the early stages of the protectorate it was common knowledge that the government wanted to increase the council's number to its maximum of twenty-one. Within days of the proclamation of the regime 'the persons already settled in the council' were expected to be 'suddenly' increased to that number.[75] The addition of Philip Skippon on 20 December 1653 was apparently achieved through the intermediacy of his friend the Congregationalist minister Philip Nye, that pillar of Cromwell's ecclesiastical establishment.[76] On the previous day Nye, after talking to Henry Lawrence, had put out a feeler to Lord Wharton,[77] who had been a grandee of the Independent party in the 1640s. Of all the Roundheads who had withdrawn from the cause at Pride's Purge, Wharton was perhaps the one whom, in the Rump period, Cromwell had been most eager to woo back to it.[78] Lawrence himself had been brought into the Long Parliament through Wharton's patronage.[79] On 1 January 1654 the French ambassador reported that Cromwell had sent invitations to three powerful figures to join the board.[80] They are likely to have included another Independent grandee, William Pierrepoint, 'the prime man', as another observer wrote, whom 'the protector aims to get in'.[81] Pierrepoint's political companion Oliver St John is

[71] Roberts, *Swedish Diplomats*, p. 238.
[72] *TSP*, iv. 405–6.
[73] *CSPD 1657–8*, pp. 33, 47, 92.
[74] *TSP*, vi. 281.
[75] Bodl., Carte MS 103, fo. 198. Cf. Carte MS 131, fo. 253ᵛ; *TSP*, i. 632, 755; TNA, PRO 31/92/ 3, fos 103, 116; *Mercurius Politicus* 22 December 1653, pp. 3052–3.
[76] *Harleian Miscellany*, iii. 456.
[77] Bodl., Carte MS 103, fo. 198.
[78] Abbott, i. 646, ii. 189–90, 328–9, 453.
[79] David Underdown, 'Party Management in the Recruiter Elections', *English Historical Review* 80 (1968), p. 242, and the sources at Underdown's n. 4.
[80] TNA, PRO 31/92/3, fo. 117.
[81] *TSP*, i. 755. There were a number of men, such as Robert Tichborne (a member of the council of state under Barebone's) and Sir William Roberts, to whom the regime habitually turned to fill administrative or advisory roles, and whom we might expect to have been candidates for membership of the council in the early stages of the protectorate. If they were, Cromwell evidently preferred to hold out for more substantial figures.

also likely to have been among them. Those and perhaps other initiatives on the same front may be one reason why the publication of the Instrument (which named the councillors) was held back until early January 1654. When that constitution was replaced by the Humble Petition in 1657, there were expectations within the regime of 'alterations' to the council's composition.[82] Again it was taken for granted that the government wanted to fill the vacant places.[83] Prediction looked particularly to the recruitment of Pierrepoint and St John,[84] to whose names were soon added those of Lord Broghill and Cromwell's new son-in-law Lord Fauconberg.[85] Yet all but two of the empty places—the ones taken by Thurloe and Richard Cromwell—remained unfilled.

There were arguments against making fresh appointments. Prospective candidates could usefully be kept waiting and hoping.[86] The smaller the council, the greater the chance of cohesion and the less risk to confidentiality. In 1657 MPs may have suspected that the limited size of the existing council had enabled the protector to control it too easily.[87] Yet the gains in authority that would have accrued to the government from the addition of men of substance would have been considerable. The two whose absence from the council's membership was most widely remarked, Pierrepoint and St John, often advised Cromwell secretly, with the aim of steering his regime in a civilian and parliamentary direction. But Pierrepoint's 'conscience' forbade him to hold office under him.[88] What of the consciences of the councillors themselves? Their various perspectives had afforded them ways of justifying the coup of December 1653 to themselves. They could reason that the return to single rule, to which they had no objection in principle, had been the only means to preserve the nation from the chaos threatened by Barebone's; or that, through a necessary exertion of arbitrary power, it had opened the way to an end to it; or that Cromwell's pre-eminence, which divine providence had sanctioned, entitled him to the supreme authority which the emergency of 1653 required him to exercise; or that his supremacy was warranted by his determination to promote godly rule and ensure liberty of conscience for its friends. Those arguments might seem readily persuasive until the parliament of 1654 met, when the Instrument was to be submitted for parliamentary sanction. But what happened if that sanction was refused? What if force had to be used—as indeed happened after eight days—against a parliament that in any case had been

---

[82] Vaughan, *Protectorate of Oliver Cromwell*, ii. 216. Cf. *TSP*, vi. 428–9; Abbott, iv. 574–5; *English Civil War*, v. 53.

[83] *English Civil War*, v. 53, 56, 61.

[84] *TSP*, vi. 404; cf. *The Case of Oliver St. John* (1660), p. 3.

[85] William Stephen, ed., *Register of the Consultations of the Ministers of Edinburgh*, 2 vols (Scottish History Society, 1921–30), ii. 47; Abbott, iv. 665; *Harleian Miscellany*, iii. 459; cf. *TSP*, vii. 388.

[86] Whitelocke, *Journal of the Swedish Embassy*, i. 322.

[87] Compare *Burton*, i. 408 with Gaunt, *Correspondence of Henry Cromwell*, pp. 297–8. Although the Humble Petition and Advice stipulated only a maximum, and no minimum, number of councillors, it may be that parliament intended (what the Venetian ambassador seems to have supposed the document to require: *English Civil War*, v. 53) that the full number be appointed.

[88] *TSP*, iv. 469; cf. below, p. 242.

chosen on the government's own restrictive terms? The military leaders on the council, it is true, seem to have stood firm when the purged parliament attacked the Instrument.[89] But some of their civilian colleagues felt differently. Two of them unofficially withdrew during the parliament, reportedly to Cromwell's grave displeasure.[90] Richard Major left Whitehall for his native Hampshire, where he remained on civil but distant terms with the central government.[91] The other departure was more significant. Anthony Ashley Cooper withdrew after a vain attempt to civilianize Cromwell's rule by getting parliament to offer him the Crown.[92] His subsequent opposition was so strong that the council excluded him from the parliament of 1656. In the parliament of 1659, where he joined forces with the anti-protectoral rumpers, he compared Cromwellian rule to the tyranny of Caesar Borgia.[93] Major and Cooper are unlikely to have been the only councillors troubled by the constitutional breakdown of the winter of 1654–5. Some members of the council had worked with MPs in the hope of finding common ground and of getting the new constitution through the Commons.[94] Cromwell's sudden dissolution of the assembly in January 1655 dashed that hope. The termination of the parliament was reportedly 'against the opinion of the council'.[95]

The narrow base of support for the protectorate was not the only obstacle to the expansion of the council. Existing councillors, whose consent would be needed for new appointments, might be troubled by them. So might the government's followers beyond Whitehall. Cromwell's instinct for political balance produced poises so delicate that the slightest shift would endanger them.[96] He strove to preserve not only balance but the appearance of it, for men whom he needed to keep happy watched the composition of the council as a key to the intentions and sympathies of the regime. The appointment, by and under the Instrument, of councillors who had arranged the end of Barebone's, or who had steered clear of the regicide and the Rump, induced suspicion and dismay among radicals.[97] In January 1654, when the coup of the previous month was causing heart-searching in Ireland among the English commissioners who had ruled it for the Rump and Barebone's, one of them wrote to the councillor Philip Jones that they 'listened very narrowly' to see 'what kind of persons you call to your council', and whether 'sober zealous Christians' would control it or 'whether you alloy them with a

---

[89] Firth, *Clarke Papers*, iii. 10–11.

[90] *English Civil War*, iv. 236.

[91] *CSPD 1654*, pp. xlii–iii; *TSP*, iv. 238, 239, 363, 764, v. 397. Illness may have confirmed him in his absence.

[92] Firth, *Clarke Papers*, iii. 16.

[93] Gaunt, *Correspondence of Henry Cromwell*, p. 466; Gaunt, 'Single Person's Confidants', p. 539.

[94] This is shown by the names of the tellers in the debates of the parliament, and by a comparison of *A Representation concerning the late Parliament, in the Yeer 1654* (1655), p. 21, with Bodl., Carte MS 74, fos 110–15.

[95] Bodl., Clarendon MS 49, fo. 343; cf. *TSP*, iii. 58; but see too Spalding, *Diary of Bulstrode Whitelocke*, p. 400.

[96] Below, p. 236.

[97] *Ludlow's Memoirs*, i. 371–2; *The Protector (so called) in Part Unvailed* (1655), p. 55.

mixture of persons carnal'.[98] Comparable vigilance awaited Oliver's decisions about the composition of the council in 1657, and Richard Cromwell's decisions on the same subject upon his accession.[99] Most of the suggestions for the expansion of the membership would have brought in 'persons' whom saints would have judged 'carnal'. Early in 1655 the protector seems to have contemplated the addition of the lawyers Bulstrode Whitelocke and John Glyn,[100] and soon afterwards there was 'much speaking' of the political Presbyterian Sir John Hobart's 'being of the council'.[101] Whitelocke, at least, would have jumped at the chance.[102] Yet the appointment of those figures would not merely have impeded the protector's programme of law reform. It would have given ammunition to critics who portrayed the protectorate as a return towards the old forms of government, which the three men favoured.

The balance struck on the council was between those who hoped, and those who feared, that those forms would be restored. The first view was that of Sir Charles Wolseley, whose departure from his family's royalism was never profound, and who had half-returned to it by the time of the Restoration; of Nathaniel Fiennes; of Edward Montagu, whose radicalism of the 1640s had been long overlaid, and who, alone of Cromwell's councillors, would work his way across to royal favour in the Restoration (when his membership of the Cromwellian council would be discreetly removed from the record[103]); of John Thurloe, who had intrigued for the crowning of Cromwell before his own appointment to the council and remained eager for it thereafter (provided it could be achieved without a fatal split within the government); and of Thurloe's close ally Philip Jones, who hammered the amended Humble Petition and Advice through parliament after other backers had pulled out.[104]

The rival view was that of the three generals—Lambert, Desborough, and Fleetwood—and of their civilian allies in the resistance to the Humble Petition: Sydenham, Strickland, and Pickering. Those men had welcomed or accepted Cromwell's elevation in 1653, but had no liking for the thought of a hereditary succession. Fleetwood and Desborough encouraged men who had broken with Cromwell in 1653 to air views critical of the regime, and sought to shield them

---

[98] J. Mayer, 'Inedited Letters of Cromwell, Colonel Jones, Bradshaw and Other Regicides', *Transactions of the Historical Society of Lancashire and Cheshire*, new series 1 (1860–2), p. 220.

[99] *TSP*, vii. 388, 436; *Mercurius Politicus* 23 September 1658, p. 846; 7 October 1658, p. 891.

[100] Firth, *Clarke Papers*, iii. 20–1 (cf. Godfrey Davies, *The Restoration* [Oxford, 1955], p. 31; *CPW*, vii. 66). Since, from September 1654, new conciliar appointments were, by the terms of the Instrument, to be drawn from short-lists chosen by parliament, the appointments would have broken the government's own rules; but the rules of the Instrument were in any case of uncertain status from January 1655.

[101] *TSP*, iii. 328.

[102] Whitelocke, *Journal of the Swedish Embassy*, i. 5, 322; Spalding, *Diary of Bulstrode Whitelocke*, pp. 401–2, 438.

[103] TNA, SP18/42, no. 49 (though see too E222[29], last page; E223[3], p. 3058).

[104] His achievement can be traced in *Burton*, vol. ii. Like Lambert's, Jones's stature on the protectoral council is more evident in the council's records than in the calendars of them. Thurloe would die after collapsing into Jones's arms.

from the consequences[105]—not unusual behaviour amid the rivalries of seventeenth-century court politics. Only the support of the two men can have given any weight to a proposal of June 1658—which the protector would have accepted only *in extremis* if at all—that the rumpers Sir Henry Vane, Edmund Ludlow, and Nathaniel Rich be brought on to the council.[106] Fleetwood's and Desborough's friend Sydenham,[107] who as far as we know was never personally close to Cromwell, was the civilian councillor most offended by the Humble Petition and most resistant to it.[108] Alone of Oliver's councillors, he joined the generals in deposing Richard in 1659 and was immediately welcomed aboard the restored Commonwealth.[109] For a time in the summer of 1657 he and Pickering refused the councillors' new oath of loyalty, and were at risk of losing their places.

There may have been something faintly patronizing in Cromwell's treatment of 'honest Pickering',[110] whom Whitelocke saw as a toady of the protector.[111] He was described as 'so finical, spruce and like an old courtier'.[112] We see why when we glimpse him tickling the vanity, or soothing the hurt pride, of colleagues.[113] Yet he was prone to doubts about Cromwell's political elevation and about his military methods. He tended to remove himself from Whitehall when unhappy with Cromwell's decisions. He absented himself for a period following the inauguration of the protectorate,[114] and was not present at the urgent meetings that followed the dissolution of parliament in January 1655.[115] He slipped away again in early 1657, when the kingship proposal was brought forward; again in the summer when the Humble Petition was introduced; and, for a long period, in December, at the moment when the council proposed the addition of Richard Cromwell to its numbers.[116] Though appointed, with the bulk of the councillors, to Cromwell's 'Other House', he did not attend it.[117] Yet he never broke with the protector. It looks as if he was brought to accept the Humble Petition by his personal ties to Cromwell; or by the emotional pressure which Oliver exerted on his followers at moments of crisis; or by the pomp and perquisites of power.[118] The advocates of kingship had their sensitivities too. Wolseley and Montagu were deflated and

[105] Fleetwood: *Ludlow's Memoirs*, i. 416, 431, 432, ii. 16; *TSP*, iii. 246, iv. 100, 107–8; Desborough: John Streater, *Secret Reasons of State* (1659), pp. 18–19.

[106] *TSP*, vii. 154–5.

[107] Ibid., vii. 490; *CSPD 1658–9*, p. 354; cf. Gaunt, *Correspondence of Henry Cromwell*, p. 475.

[108] *TSP*, vi. 311, vii. 490; Bodl., Carte MS 228, fo. 84; cf. *Burton*, i. 257–8, 274–5, ii. 291–2, 299.

[109] *CSPD 1658–9*, p. 354; Gaunt, *Correspondence of Henry Cromwell*, pp. 509, 512, 513; cf. *CJ* 3 August 1659.

[110] Abbott, i. 645; Whitelocke, *Journal of the Swedish Embassy*, i. 7–8, 14.

[111] Whitelocke, *Journal of the Swedish Embassy*, i. 10.

[112] Woolrych, *Commonwealth to Protectorate*, p. 200.

[113] *Burton*, i. 193, 361–2.

[114] *CSPD 1653–4*, pp. xxxvii–viii.

[115] *CSPD 1655*, p. xxv.

[116] *CSPD 1657–8*, pp. liii, 206; Firth, *Clarke Papers*, iii. 114; Bodl., Carte MS 73, fo. 175. Note too his unhappiness about the regicide: *TSP*, v. 674; TNA, SP25/62: 19 February 1649.

[117] Gaunt, 'Councils of the Protectorate', p. 233.

[118] Firth, *Clarke Papers*, iii. 69, 129, 141; Bodl., Carte MS 73, fo. 187[v].

disenchanted by Cromwell's refusal of the Crown in 1657, and Montagu was away from Whitehall for long periods after his return from naval service.[119]

The protector's answer to the division among his followers was to be, in political language and machinery as in iconography, half a king.[120] Even so, royal associations more often than not prevailed, increasingly so with time. In the spring of 1654, while the new court was taking form, the council moved from the large chamber which the Commonwealth's councils of state had occupied into the old royal council-chamber (though it sometimes met elsewhere, usually in Cromwell's own lodgings or, late in his life, at his palace at Hampton Court); and its members went to chapel in Whitehall 'full of state'.[121] In 1657, when the council was re-named 'the privy council', its members officially became what they had often been unofficially called, 'lords of the council'. There were now other regal or neo-regal titles. The council's minutes, which previously had recognized Thurloe only as its secretary, acknowledged him as Principal Secretary of State, and soon afterwards Sir Gilbert Pickering and Philip Jones were decked out with the accoutrements of the offices, which hitherto they had held only informally, of Lord Chamberlain and Controller of the Household.[122]

Cromwell liked to emphasize the constitutional restraints which the powers given to the protectoral council imposed on him. He had accepted the office of protector, he told parliament in 1654, only because the Instrument 'limited me and bound my hands to act nothing to the prejudice of the nations without consent' of the council. In the intervals between parliaments, he added, the council took parliament's place, exercising an 'absolute . . . negative' over him.[123] In 1657 he reminded a parliamentary audience that he could 'do nothing but in [co-]ordination with the council'.[124] The powers given to the council at his bidding in 1657, he remarked, would be 'a safety' to the chief magistrate and a security to the nation.[125]

His statements, which echoed and were echoed by those of apologists for the regime,[126] were made with a purpose. They were meant to help reconcile opponents of his usurped authority, both across that wide body of conventional opinion which objected to arbitrary and military rule and among people who saw his elevation as a betrayal of the 'good old cause'.[127] MPs, it is true, varied in the

[119] Gaunt, *Correspondence of Henry Cromwell*, pp. 247–8; Abbott, iv. 536; *CSPD 1657–8*, pp. lii, 79; Bodl., Carte MS 73, fo. 145. Cf. *TSP*, vi. 662; Firth, *Clarke Papers*, iii. 114.
[120] For the iconography see Laura Knoppers, *Constructing Cromwell: Ceremony, Portrait, and Print 1645–1661* (Cambridge, 2000).
[121] BL Add. MS 37345: 3 March 1654.
[122] Below, pp. 234–5; Bodl., Rawlison MS a. 55, fo. 327.
[123] Abbott, iii. 455, 460.
[124] Ibid., iv. 488.
[125] Ibid., iv. 492–3.
[126] Nedham, *True State*, pp. 39, 45, 51; Nedham, *The Observator, with a Summary of Intelligence* 7 November 1654; *A Letter from a Person in the Country to his Friend in the City* (1656), p. 9.
[127] Gaunt, 'Single Person's Confidants', p. 553, assesses Cromwell's statements differently.

degrees of their interest in the constitutional position of the council. Though there were sharp attacks on the body in both of Cromwell's parliaments,[128] neither its powers nor its composition were at the forefront of the constitutional arguments. In the embittered Commons' debates of 1654–5 there was far less discussion of the council's position in the constitution than of parliament's.[129] The assembly approved in principle of the powers held by the council in relation to the protector, and proposed to extend them.[130] MPs who favoured conciliar limitations on his power cited his statements in support of them, in some cases as a warrant for demanding further restrictions.[131] There were moves in the same parliament to extend the powers which the Instrument gave to parliament over the council.[132] Even as they stood, the arrangements made by the Cromwellian constitutions for parliament's relationship with the council may have helped to win acceptance for those documents. The formidable Presbyterian MP John Birch, who had been a leading opponent of the Instrument in the parliament of 1654, explained in 1659 that he had fought in the civil war largely to win for parliament the right to approve the members of the council; and that the fidelity to that principle of the Humble Petition (which unlike the Instrument had the parliamentary sanction that Birch thought essential) was a reason for supporting the new constitution.[133] Yet alongside the concern for constitutional restriction a different and perhaps alternative conception of the council lived on, in which it was seen as a body of the ruler's friends, whom he liked and could trust. There was a 'necessity', it was urged in the parliament of 1654, 'that there should be some personal knowledge, opinion and affection between the protector and his council'.[134] Here as elsewhere in the Puritan Revolution, the constitutional aggressiveness of Roundhead MPs, and their interest in constitutional formulae, vied with an alternative attitude: a reluctance to affront the awe or impair the dignity of majesty or to tell rulers how to govern.

The Humble Petition silently passed over the previous history of the protectorate, which it implicitly dismissed as an illegality. It made no mention of the Instrument of Government, or of the council it had appointed. It assumed rather than stipulated that the protector would have a 'privy council'. It did, on that assumption, lay down conciliar restraints on his will, but there was no visible repetition now of the attempt which had been made in the Instrument to give the council the appearance of one of three balanced components (protector,

---

[128] S. R. Gardiner, *History of the Commonwealth and Protectorate*, 4 vols (New York, 1965 edn), iii. 182 n.; *Burton*, i. 281, ii. 289–90. Cf. *Burton*, iii. 197, 259, 275, 455 ff., iv. 67, 72; *TSP*, vii. 626.

[129] The council does not figure in Andrew Marvell's poem on the 'First Anniversary' of the protectorate, which lauds the Instrument of Government and the constitutional relations of protector and parliament.

[130] *GD*, pp. 427–47.

[131] *Burton*, i. cv, cvi; ii. 288.

[132] *TSP*, iii. 57; *Burton*, i. xli, xliv–vi, liii–lv, civ–cvii.

[133] Ibid., iv. 61–2.

[134] *Burton*, i. cv; cf. the wariness of the Grand Remonstrance on this point: *GD*, p. 205. In the Restoration the former Lord Broghill, who had been a prominent figure under Cromwell but not a member of the council at Whitehall, wrote a play which has the place of royal friendship as a theme: Blair Worden, 'Favourites on the English Stage', in J. H. Elliott and L. W. B. Brockliss, eds, *The World of the Favourite* (1999), p. 164.

council, and parliament) of the constitution. The names of the two members who were added after his investiture under the new constitution, John Thurloe and Richard Cromwell, ought to have been submitted for parliamentary approval, but there is no sign that they were, though perhaps they would have been if the session of early 1658, when the submissions could have been expected, had lasted longer.[135] The notion, which had been commended by Nedham in 1654 as a basic principle of the Instrument of Government, that parliaments should select the protectoral councillors had evidently not struck roots. Cromwell's ambassador in France, Sir William Lockhart, thought that Richard's 'birthright' should have 'spared' him even the 'formalities' by which the council was required to agree to his appointment.[136] In the debates on the Humble Petition in 1657 there was some gingerliness in discussing not only the composition of the council but its powers. Perhaps some MPs feared lest divisions on the issue might obstruct the passage of the new constitution.[137]

Hardline advocates of the sovereignty of parliament, the principle that had prevailed from 1649 to 1653, had no such inhibitions. To them it was not enough that the council could veto resolutions by the protector. If there had to be a protector at all, they wanted him to be denied a veto over the council.[138] Even so, Cromwell could hope that the guarantee of powers to the council might win over discontented rumpers and saints and soldiers. His request for additions to the council's powers in the Humble Petition can be at least partly attributed to his eagerness to make the new constitutional arrangements acceptable to friends as well as foes.[139] No one was more in need of reassurance than the councillor John Desborough, whose support for the protectorate seemed, during the kingship crisis, to have ended. Yet he was reconciled, and helped to steer the amended document through the Commons. Echoing words that Cromwell had used of the Instrument, the constitution to which Desborough had been firmly committed, he emphasized the council's role under the Humble Petition, a document which, if he read it, he cannot have understood, for he evidently supposed it to have preserved the earlier conciliar restrictions on the protector intact.[140]

Cromwell had further motives for emphasizing the council's powers. Foreign ambassadors and agents, maddened by the circular proceedings and delaying tactics of the regime, and exasperated by its failure to supply consistent and coherent answers to their questions, grew weary of the line taken by Cromwell and his advisers: that the protector, in negotiating with foreign powers, could not, or anyway preferred not, to act against the will, or anticipate the deliberations, of

[135] Cf. *CJ* 24 October 1654. If the parliament of 1654 had accepted the legitimacy of the Instrument, it would have had the duty of vetting the members who had been added to the council in 1654.
[136] *CSPD 1657–8*, p. 266.
[137] *Burton*, ii. 288–90.
[138] *CSPD 1653–4*, p. 303; cf. *The Case of Matthew Alured* (1659), p. 11.
[139] Abbott, iv. 471–2, 493–4.
[140] *Burton*, ii. 55.

the council,[141] the regime's 'oracle' as the French ambassador sarcastically put it.[142] Cromwell used similar tactics when questioned by critics of his domestic policies. He 'could not' abolish tithes, as to his lasting regret he had rashly promised to do in his exaltation after the victory at Dunbar, because 'he was but one, and his council allege it is not fit to take them away'.[143] He did not grant more liberty to Anglican clergymen because he had been 'advised by his council' against it.[144] In the protectoral parliaments, attacks on the council centred on two government policies which attracted wide hostility. The first was the government's exclusion of large numbers of MPs from both assemblies. It would be naïve to suppose that Cromwell played no part in that process.[145] Formally, however, the Instrument of Government left the vetting of the elected members wholly to the council,[146] which consequently bore the odium of it. The second issue was the decimation tax. The only mention of the council in Cromwell's long speech at the opening of parliament in 1656 referred to its role in the imposition of the tax (a policy to whose introduction he had himself been fully committed).[147] The Commons, following the ancient practice of attacking advisers rather than rulers, duly blamed it on the council.[148] The council knew its traditional duty to shoulder responsibility for the ruler's deeds. In 1657 it shielded him from the fury of Sir Thomas Fairfax by accepting responsibility for the continued imprisonment of Fairfax's son-in-law, the royalist Duke of Buckingham.[149] When Cromwell's sons Richard and Henry rose to prominence, in line with his transparent wishes,[150] the council took on the role of overcoming his professed resistance to their elevation.[151]

Most of the time, protector and council worked in harmony and spoke with a single voice. The routine business of government passed uncontentiously (if generally slowly) between the two. Protector and council often left items of business to each other's discretion, and did not usually mind whether a matter that would go before

---

[141] e.g. *TSP*, iii. 381, iv. 178, 683, v. 266; Gardiner, *History of the Commonwealth and Protectorate*, iii. 114 n.; Abbott, iv. 625 (cf. iv. 24).

[142] *TSP*, ii. 669.

[143] Firth, *Clarke Papers*, ii. xxxvi; cf. Abbott, iii. 103.

[144] Abbott, iv. 70; see too *Ludlow's Memoirs*, ii. 12.

[145] See e.g. *Severall Proceedings of State Affaires* 17 August 1654 (under 10 August).

[146] *GD*, p. 412.

[147] Abbott, iv. 269.

[148] *Burton*, i. 273, 281. The council risked provoking parallels to the tyrannical proceedings of Charles I's 'council table' by taking on the burden of summoning Sir Henry Vane (TNA, SP25/77: 5 September 1656, item 30; *The Proceeds of the Protector against Sir Henry Vane* [1656]), and Edmund Ludlow (*CSPD 1655–6*, p. 139) before it. Cf. O. Ogle et al., eds, *Calendar of the Clarendon State Papers*, 5 vols (Oxford, 1869–1970), ii. 325; but also below, n. 186.

[149] TNA, SP 25/78: 1 December 1657; *TSP*, vi. 617, 648.

[150] As well as the familiar sources for the public roles given to Richard and Henry Cromwell, see the eminence accorded to Henry by the secretariat of the council of state in minutes of council meetings in the month before Oliver's assumption of the protectorate: TNA, SP25/4-6; 25/72: from 17 November 1653.

[151] Abbott, iii. 756; *CSPD 1654*, pp. 321, 328; *1655*, pp. 42, 57 (cf. TNA, SP25/75: 12 March 1655), 146; *1657–8*, p. 206 (cf. p. 26); TNA, PRO 31/3/92, p. 103.

both of them reached protector or council first.[152] But what happened if differences arose? Did the council, or any of its members, have the appetite or capacity for a trial of strength? Observers remarked not on the powers of the council but on its weakness. It was 'like a nose of wax, which will wind and turn which way the single person pleases';[153] its members were Cromwell's 'creatures'[154] or 'dependants' and had 'no other share in the government than the name of councillors';[155] England was governed not by 'a council and protector' but by 'protector and council';[156] the Instrument of Government gave the council only the 'semblance' of power in relation to Cromwell.[157] Henry Cromwell was told by his father-in-law, Francis Russell, who was in a good position to know, that 'all' the protector's council 'rides upon one horse; I meane, he counsels himselfe'; which Russell, who had a low view of the councillors' ability, thought was as well.[158] Whatever their relations with Cromwell on paper, it was believed, the councillors were too feeble or unintelligent or sycophantic to be an effective counterweight to his will.[159] Some, but not all, of those charges came from hostile sources. It nonetheless seems telling that the regime's critics, who might have blamed its failings—as critics had customarily blamed those of pre-war regimes—on the excessive influence of the ruler's advisers, instead commented on their impotence.

Were the charges accurate? We know of the council's proceedings mainly through its minutes. As far as we can judge—for they are imperfect records—they indicate that in areas of policy where the council's consent was specifically required, Cromwell invariably observed—occasionally, perhaps, even exceeded[160]—his obligations;[161] and that the run of the government's other decisions came to him as

---

[152] e.g. Abbott, iii. 618; *TSP*, ii. 113, iii. 335.

[153] Gaunt, 'Single Person's Confidants', p. 540.

[154] *A Copy of a Letter from an Officer of the Army in Ireland* (n.d.: 1656?), p. 17.

[155] Bodl., Clarendon MS 59, fo. 355; cf. *English Civil War*, iv. 166.

[156] Gaunt, 'Single Person's Confidants', p. 540. See also *A Brief Relation containing an Abbreviation of the Arguments urged by the Late Protector* (1659); *OPH*, xxi. 301.

[157] TNA, PRO 31/3/92, fo. 104; cf. BL Add. MS 5138, p. 153.

[158] Gaunt, *Correspondence of Henry Cromwell*, pp. 297–8. The equine metaphor was conventional in discussions of councils: *Burton*, i. 408; Cromartie, *Constitutionalist Revolution*, p. 224.

[159] Spalding, *Diary of Bulstrode Whitelocke*, pp. 400, 417, 464; *TSP*, vi. 617; Gaunt, 'Single Person's Confidants', p. 540; cf. BL Add. MS 5138, fo. 153.

[160] E.g. TNA, SP25/75: 20 February 1655, item 15; SP25/76: 20 July 1655, item 5; cf. *Burton*, iii. 334.

[161] The main difficulty is the uncertainty in contemporaries' minds of the distinction between 'advice' and 'consent'. One would expect the difference to have been that the protector—though he liked to inform the nation that his actions accorded with the council's advice—was bound only to listen to that advice, not to accept it. But when, for example, clause 23 of the Instrument entitles the protector to call emergency parliaments 'with the advice of the major part of the council', 'advice' must, at least in practice, mean the same as 'consent'. (The rulers of the protectorate were not alone in their uncertainty: *GD*, pp. 251, 432, 445, 453 [bottom paragraph]; see too the uneasy discussion in *Burton*, ii. 288–9.) Clause 30 of the Instrument allowed the protector to pass interim legislation until September 1654 'with the consent of the major part of the council', but the ensuing ordinances, though they often mention that 'consent', at other times invoke instead—or, at still other times, as well—the council's 'advice'. Interpretation is plagued by the infelicities of Cromwellian drafting. One ordinance invoked a non-existent 'authority abovesaid': Firth and Rait, ii. 1000. One proclamation by the protector, a sensitive one of February 1655 (Abbott, iii. 626–7), failed to mention, as his others did, the council's approval, but the best guess is that that was merely an error of wording. More

recommendations 'offered to his highness as the advice of his council'. The recommendations were formally enshrined. The councillors passed resolutions containing the advice they wished to submit to him, occasionally after putting them to the question, a formal procedure that the royal privy council had sometimes followed. There was a special emphasis on procedural formalities in the passage of the interim ordinances of the first months of the protectorate, when the council adopted parliamentary procedures for the enactment of legislation.[162] The reduction in the council's powers under the Humble Petition did not visibly lessen Cromwell's readiness to seek its approval. Only occasionally during the protectorate—and rarely if ever on a point of fundamental principle—did he veto a recommendation or refer one back for modification.[163] Otherwise he accepted the council's proposals without demur.

Yet, as the Roman historian Tacitus famously taught, observance of the forms of power may conceal rather than reflect the substance. What was the relationship between form and substance in Cromwell's relations with the council? The question might be easier to answer were it not that the council's records, bulky as they are, are substantially incomplete. We learn from other sources of numerous council meetings of which the minutes supply no record. When those sources mention meetings of which we do have a minuted record, they often—more often than not—refer to items of discussion which the minutes themselves do not record. There are two main reasons for that deficiency of the evidence. The first is the existence of a 'private book'—or 'secret book'—in which the clerks recorded sensitive information, and which has not survived[164] (though occasional extracts from it have done[165]). It is likely to have been substantial, and to have recorded, among other things, many decisions on foreign policy, the army and navy, and the dangers of conspiracy.[166]

The second reason is that the formal meetings of council were supplemented by informal, unminuted ones, which seem, at least normally, to have been held elsewhere than in the council-chamber, sometimes in advance of formal ones held later in the day.[167] The only visual glimpse of a council meeting that we have shows Cromwell sitting in his 'great chair at the upper end of the table', his head covered

---

complications are raised by the flawed wording of the hastily composed Instrument of Government. Article 5, in referring to the 'aforesaid' advice of the council, evidently refers back not to article 4 (which I think likely to have been a late addition to the Instrument) but to article 3. The formal statements of kings had often acknowledged the 'advice' of their councils.

[162] Gaunt, '"To Create a Little World . . . "', in Little, *Cromwellian Protectorate*, ch. 6.

[163] TNA, SP25/47, p. 41; 25/48, p. 49; 25/77: 13 November 1656, item 8; *CSPD 1656–7*, p. 208.

[164] TNA, SP25/48, pp. 24–5; 25/77: 17 December 1656, item 1; *CSPD 1655*, pp. 150, 202 n.; TNA, PRO 31/17/33, p. 183.

[165] *TSP*, iii. 16–17; Bodl., Rawlinson MS a.15, pp. 105–6; *CSPD 1655*, p. 202 n.

[166] Sometimes the surviving minutes of a meeting record only a small item or small items, which cannot have been the main business of the day.

[167] *Severall Proceedings of State Affaires* 10–31 August 1654 (under 3, 7, 10, 24 August); cf. 23 March 1654 (under 18 March); 11 May 1654 (under 9 May). Compare too ibid., 23 March 1654, p. 3710, with *CSPD 1654*, p. xxxvi. Those two explanations are not complete, for some formal decisions which are not mentioned in the surviving minutes were not sensitive ones and are unlikely to have been confined to the 'private book': e.g. Ann McGruer, *Educating 'The Unconstant Rabble':*

while the councillors' were bare.[168] That was on a ceremonial occasion, when non-councillors were being honoured by an audience. What formalities were observed at official meetings when no outsiders were present we cannot say, but we might guess unofficial gatherings of councillors to have been marked by the blunt informality that is characteristic of many of Cromwell's recorded conversations, a tone that would have suited his temperament.[169] There was a second likely attraction of unofficial gatherings of the council. Official ones, then as in earlier times, were tied to agenda on which large items mingled with small ones. Unofficial ones gave scope to freer and broader discussion of general issues of policy. Cromwell is recorded as having attended about 40 per cent of the official meetings.[170] The proportion will increase (we can only guess how much) if we assume that, as seems more than probable, he was present more often at discussions of the kind that were recorded only in the 'private book' than at others. The council was used to holding official meetings without him, but the unofficial meetings, when we know anything of them, seem at least normally to have centred on his presence.[171]

It is when we move from the formal to the informal gatherings that the substance of power begins to peep through the forms. Outside its official meetings, the council lost its collective identity. Often the protector would discuss matters with 'some' or a 'few' of the councillors, chosen by him.[172] He frequently saw ambassadors or other visitors with a selection of councillors beside him. On occasion—in line with royal precedent[173]—he took 'some' of the councillors with him to Hampton Court.[174] Often he consulted a small number of councillors together with men who were not on the council, and whose views seem to have carried as much weight as theirs. During the kingship crisis of 1657—to take only the most striking of the many examples—he spent hours at a time 'shut up' with a group of five advisers which consisted of the councillor Wolseley and the council's secretary Thurloe but also Pierrepoint and two other non-councillors of large and persistent influence at Whitehall, Broghill and Whitelocke. The five men's 'counsel', recorded

Arguments for Educational Advancement and Reform during the English Civil War and Interregnum (Newcastle upon Tyne, 2010), pp. 163–4, 170–1.

[168] Whitelocke, *Journal of the Swedish Embassy*, ii. 447. The audience was not recorded in the minutes of the council's formal meeting on that day (*CSPD 1654*, pp. 244-5), but perhaps occurred during it.

[169] As in Firth, *Clarke Papers*, iii. 207–9. Cf. *Ludlow's Memoirs*, ii. 12

[170] Gaunt, 'Single Person's Confidants', p. 552.

[171] Our sources for informal meetings, and for unminuted items at formal ones, are mainly the newsbooks, but they are supplemented by reports of ambassadors and other outsiders (who could not always tell or know the difference between formal and informal meetings, and whose accounts must be read in that light). On one occasion the distinction between formal and informal meetings appears to have collapsed, when a resolution (for the release of the poet Edmund Waller from prison), taken at an informal meeting in Cromwell's lodgings, was communicated to a formal council meeting later in the day as a fait accompli: TNA, SP25/76: 6 March 1656, item 37. Perhaps there were other such cases which have left no record.

[172] e.g. Roberts, *Swedish Diplomats*, pp. 256, 278; Abbott, iv. 24, 400; *TSP*, iii. 101; *Ludlow's Memoirs*, i. 432–6; cf. Whitelocke, *Memorials*, iv. 153–4.

[173] Turner, *Privy Council*, i. 92–3.

[174] *Perfect Proceedings of State Affaires* 28 June 1655 (under 22 June); *English Civil War*, iv. 183, 294; cf. e.g. *Severall Proceedings of State Affaires* 23 March 1654, p. 3715.

Whitelocke, 'was accepted and followed by him in most of his greatest affairs',[175] a statement in which we can allow for self-congratulatory exaggeration, as well as for the frailties of Whitelocke's memory, but not for invention. Cromwell also liked to take advice from bodies outside the council, some of them standing committees, others ad hoc ones which were named by him and to which a councillor or councillors might but might not be appointed. Often he consulted such bodies before submitting a matter to the council or after receiving a recommendation from it.

Even in the management of formal meetings of the council, Cromwell showed that he meant to rule. Though his interest in the details of the council's recommendations was intermittent and selective, it was sufficiently vigilant to keep the councillors on their toes (and to add to the backlog of business). Cardinal Mazarin's belief that Cromwell 'had a perfect knowledge of all things' in his administration[176] was as true as the constraints of time and health allowed the protector. Though the council made many of the arrangements for the conduct of its business, Cromwell decided on them when he chose to. It was he who resolved that the councillors should be paid, and how much[177]—whereas the council 'humbly' left his own pay as lord general to his discretion.[178] In the early protectorate he took a series of steps which announced his authority. It was he who appointed the politically lightweight Henry Lawrence as the council's president.[179] He 'ordered and declared', 'being now present in council', the names of the council's commissioners to negotiate with the French and Spanish ambassadors.[180] When it suited him he named other commissioners of the council—'his' commissioners, as they were commonly called—for diplomatic tasks.[181] He named the members of the council's committees for diplomacy, security, religion and the treasuries and its commissioners for law reform.[182] When, early in its life, the council decided on its working procedures, he revised them so as to enable him to summon formal meetings even if not all the members had been notified of them.[183] The council's subsequent attempts to keep to a timetable of formal meetings were at the mercy of the protector's practice of calling them—and of summoning only those members who happened to be available—as he wished.[184]

When Cromwell told parliament that he could do 'nothing' without the council, he was alluding to the stipulation in the Instrument that he be advised by it 'in all things'. The phrase was of uncertain meaning. If it had been taken to mean 'in

[175] Spalding, *Diary of Bulstrode Whitelocke*, p. 464 (cf. p. 477).
[176] P. A. Chéruel, ed., *Lettres du Cardinal Mazarin*, 9 vols (Paris, 1872–1906), vi. 464.
[177] *CSPD 1657–8*, p. 113.
[178] *CSPD 1655*, p. 251.
[179] *CSPD 1653–4*, p. 360.
[180] TNA, SP25/75: 4 April 1654, items 15, 16.
[181] Ibid.: 30 May 1654, items 1–2; Guizot, *History of Oliver Cromwell*, ii. 457; *TSP*, iii. 528.
[182] TNA, SP25/76: 20 June 1654; *CSPD 1654*, p. 31.
[183] TNA, SP25/47, p. 25.
[184] Abbott, iv. 429; *TSP*, iii. 101, 381, iv. 266, vi. 360; Spalding, *Diary of Bulstrode Whitelocke*, p. 389; TNA, SP 25/78: 31 December 1657, item 25; 25 March 1658, item 1; cf. *Severall Proceedings of State Affaires* 23 March 1654, p. 3721.

every detail', it would have imposed a degree of restriction that no one seems to have envisaged. Even the parliament of 1654, which looked to the council as a means of restricting the protector's powers, proposed that the phrase be dropped.[185] Cromwell issued many orders and warrants, gave many promises, wrote many official letters, of which the council learned only afterwards[186] if at all—and which, as far as we can see, provoked not a squeak of protest from it. The council uncomplainingly recognized that many decisions were beyond its reach. Frequently it sent representatives to 'know' or 'receive' Cromwell's 'pleasure', in matters great and small.[187] It made little difference when that 'pleasure', once ascertained by the council, came back to him as a recommendation. In January 1654 the council's draft minutes recorded the protector's 'special command' that the hardship of John Lilburne, then a prisoner in the Tower, be alleviated. The minute was erased, no doubt in a spirit of constitutional propriety, and the decision was returned to Cromwell as a proposal by the council, which he duly accepted.[188] But there were many more 'special commands' or 'special directions' (a number of them early in the protectorate, when the ground rules were being laid),[189] and there was more rubber-stamping.[190] Communications to the council of his 'desire' or 'pleasure', or 'will and pleasure', or his recommendations 'in an especial manner', met with instant compliance.[191]

As far as his knowledge and energy allowed, he kept control of appointments to posts: not only to military positions (which the Instrument implicitly reserved to him) but to civilian ones. The council learned after the event whom Cromwell had 'pitched upon' as an agent to be sent to France in 1655; or the names of those he had chosen the previous year to try Dom Pantaleon de Sa, the brother of the Portuguese ambassador, for murder; or the identity of commissioners for victualling the navy who had been appointed by his 'special order' in February 1658.[192] In 1656, when new commissioners for the customs were about to be appointed, it was 'in his highnesse' breast, who the persons shall bee'.[193] In 1657, though he

---

[185] *GD*, pp. 406, 430–1. It did not reappear in the Humble Petition and Advice.

[186] e.g. TNA, SP25/76: 18 January 1656 (Lawrence to Major-General of Northampton etc.); *CSPD 1655–6*, p. 176. In the parliament of 1659 much was made of the fact (if fact it was) that Robert Overton had been arrested in January 1655 on a warrant of Cromwell, not of the council: *Burton*, iv. 152 ff. For other arrests on Cromwell's orders see TNA, SP25/75: 20 February 1655, item 7; *CSPD 1655–6*, p. 239.

[187] e.g. TNA, SP 25/75: 19 June 1654, item 19; 5 December 1654, item 6; 1 March 1655, item 4; SP25/78: 23 July 1657, item 25; 27 October 1657, item 5; 31 December 1657, item 25; 4 May 1658, item 27.

[188] TNA, SP25/47, pp. 40, 64.

[189] e.g. TNA, SP25/47: 29 December 1653, items 11, 13; SP18/68, no. 25; SP25/112 p. 185; cf. Bernard Capp, *Cromwell's Navy* (Oxford, 1989), p. 188.

[190] e.g. TNA, SP25/75: 8 May, items 1, 2; 27 June 1654, item 5; 9 March 1655, item 2.

[191] That is most evident in the council's handling of petitions which reached it accompanied by expressions of Cromwell's wishes for action.

[192] *CSPD 1654*, p. 156; *1655*, p. 235; *1657–8*, p. 291.

[193] Gaunt, *Correspondence of Henry Cromwell*, p. 94. One of those appointed was Pickering's cousin the protectoral placeman Edward Horseman, who named his sons Oliver and Gilbert (Woolrych, *Commonwealth to Protectorate*, p. 385). For Pickering's patronage see also James A. Winn, *John Dryden and his World* (1987), pp. 79–80.

consulted others—councillors apparently among them—over the composition of the Other House, he made up his own mind.[194]

There was, it is true, a shift over time. Though Cromwell, except when severely ill, never lost his capacity for decisive intervention or for the scrutiny of matters that preoccupied him, he was made a less animating force by age and ill health and by his increasingly frequent absences at Hampton Court. Despite the reduction in the council's powers under the Humble Petition, much that he would earlier have controlled passed into its hands over the last year or so of his life,[195] so that the body inadvertently acquired a measure of training for the altogether larger role that it would acquire under Richard Cromwell.[196] It was not a happy experience, for during Oliver's illnesses councillors discovered how badly they missed 'the main wheele to carry on our publique affaires',[197] and how little of substance they could achieve or agree on without him.[198] In the last year of his rule there were areas in which the government virtually ground to a halt.[199]

Foreign ambassadors who were invited to think of the council as the centre of decision-making were not fooled for long. Sometimes they were told a different story: that, for example, the council's representatives could not move forward with negotiations because 'his highness hath not yet declared unto them his intentions'.[200] Such explanations played their own part in the game of delay, but foreign ambassadors understood—as did England's ambassadors when they sent home their reports—that Cromwell was the initiator and arbiter of policy. The protector's correspondents within England assumed it too, not least those at or near the centre of power—including the Major-Generals, the councillor Desborough among them. Foreigners and natives alike perceived that the way of reaching Cromwell was not through the council but through John Thurloe.[201] Everyone agreed that it was through Thurloe's hands that all business passed; that it was he who sifted the protector's correspondence and screened him from unwelcome representations; that he was the person to 'move' Cromwell or to 'get' or 'procure' or 'hasten' things from him; that he was the figure most likely to be present, and was commonly the only one present, when Cromwell received visitors. Even he was excluded from key

---

[194] Bodl., Carte MS 73, fo. 150; *TSP*, vi. 648; Turner, *Privy Council*, i. 327.

[195] That transition cannot be exactly charted. Gaunt ('Single Person's Confidants', p. 559) dates it a little later than I do, from February 1658. It can, I think, be sampled at: TNA, SP25/78: 6 August 1657, item 7; *TSP*, vi. 680–1; *CSPD 1657–8*, pp. 150–1 (with which cf. e.g. BL Add. MS 48500, fo. 102), 155 (item 2); cf. *Burton*, iv. 367. In Richard Cromwell's parliament the council, much more a parliamentary target under Richard than under Oliver, took the rap for the handling of the diplomatic crisis in the Baltic near the end of Oliver's life: *Burton*, iv. 478; Gaunt, *Correspondence of Henry Cromwell*, p. 465; *TSP*, vii. 626.

[196] For that role see e.g. *TSP*, vii. 516–18; *Mercurius Politicus* 11 November 1658, p. 164; Bodl., Clarendon MS 59, fo. 355.

[197] Gaunt, *Correspondence of Henry Cromwell*, p. 97.

[198] *TSP*, iv. 18, 493, vi. 493, 817, vii. 294–5, 320, 354. Gaunt, 'Single Person's Confidants', p. 551, takes an alternative view.

[199] *TSP*, vi. 568–9, vii. 38, 320; Bodl., Carte MS 73, fo. 143.

[200] *TSP*, iii. 7. Cf. ii. 744; Roberts, *Swedish Diplomats*, p. 248.

[201] Cf. below, pp. 228, 230.

decisions.[202] Thurloe was too shrewd to jeopardize his position by seeking to manipulate the protector, whose skill in detecting motives he knew. Self-effacement was Thurloe's style. Through it he sustained an anomalous position which encapsulates the relations of power within the regime. For his official function until 1657 was to service, not the protector, but the council. He indeed exercised that role—even if his work at the board seems often to have consisted of bringing before it, for its endorsement, decisions which Cromwell had already made. Thurloe liked to indicate in his letters that the forms of conciliar rule were being observed. Yet in the mass of his surviving correspondence the council's activities are only occasionally a central presence.[203] The heart of power lay elsewhere. It was glimpsed, during a political crisis of 1656, by a visitor to Whitehall who looked from a window and saw Cromwell, Thurloe, and Lambert 'deepley engaged in the garden'.[204]

Cromwell, who always watched his back, was said to rule the councillors by deceiving them.[205] He certainly kept a close eye on them. If they, who broadly shared his view of the world and his hopes for changing it, did not back him, who would? Within and around the council there was plenty of argument, of jostling for position, of 'tugging',[206] which is intelligible only on the assumption that Cromwell would take account of the advice he received. The protector, who customarily indulged plain speaking, is unlikely to have encouraged, or seen much to gain from, the sycophancy of which councillors were accused. He had learned the merits (though also the snags) of frank debate and collective decision-making in the military and political councils of the new model army. Most of his time as protector he spent talking to people, sounding them, debating with them, urging them, reassuring them, flattering them. What leader of men has spent more time discussing and arguing? In such conversations the councillors played their part—though theirs was far from the only part—in the formation of his opinions and plans. Yet he seems to have done most of the talking, and at least normally to have got his way.[207]

There was, however, a solitary side to him too, the side that tended to take over his personality as his most difficult (and eruptive) decisions approached. Even Thurloe could not read his mind. 'Whatever resolutions his highness takes', he

---

[202] e.g. C. H. Firth, *The Last Years of the Protectorate*, 2 vols (1909), i. 35–6.

[203] We must be wary here, for most of the documents with which Thurloe can be assumed to have serviced the council (and which would reveal more about how the triangular relationship between protector, Thurloe, and council functioned) are lost. The fluke preservation of Thurloe's surviving papers (*TSP*, i., preface) has also to be set against the disappearance of most of the letters sent to president Lawrence; but the chance survivals from Lawrence's in-tray, and the occasional references to them in other documents, do not modify the picture I have proposed: TNA, SP25/76: 11 January 1656, item 16; *TSP*, iv. 271–2, 320; cf. *Proceeds of the Protector against Sir Henry Vane*, p. 1. The loss of the papers of Cromwell's personal secretary William Malyn, who had occasional dealings with the council, may also distort the picture in favour of Thurloe's influence, but perhaps only marginally, for Thurloe's rise put Malyn in the shade.

[204] Gaunt, *Correspondence of Henry Cromwell*, p. 152.

[205] Roberts, *Swedish Diplomats*, p. 249.

[206] Spalding, *Contemporaries of Bulstrode Whitelocke*, p. 52; *TSP*, vii. 56.

[207] Whitelocke, *Journal of the Swedish Embassy*, ii. 453–5; Spalding, *Diary of Bulstrode Whitelocke*, pp. 389–90, 391, 408–9; *Ludlow's Memoirs*, i. 431–2, ii. 10–13 (cf. i. 432–6); *CSPD 1655*, pp. 281–2; Firth, *Clarke Papers*, iii. 207–9.

remarked during the kingship crisis of 1657, 'will be his own.'[208] When Cromwell overruled the opposition to his decision to dissolve the first protectorate parliament, one of the opponents reflected that the protector was 'positive in his own judgements and resolutions'.[209] He brushed aside objections to the dissolution of the second protectorate parliament—again a lone decision—in the same spirit.[210]

In some matters the council did take its own, limited initiatives. It 'desired' Cromwell to adopt a particular procedure, or gave him reasons for one, or pointed out practical or legal obstacles to his wishes, or reminded him of unfinished business.[211] He depended on councillors to coach him in matters which visitors might raise with him—and to rescue him, in conversations with outsiders, from his senior moments.[212] But practical assistance was one thing, the assertion of power another. As far as its records or other sources tell us (and in the stream of reports and gossip by newswriters there would surely be at least some evidence to hint to us) the council never offered him collective advice that contradicted his own known wishes. It lacked not only the unity of purpose to do so but the motive or the will. When it had uncomfortable points to raise, it did not stand on the constitutional ground that was theoretically available to it. Instead it dispatched one or more of its members to explain the situation tactfully to him. The nearest it came to collective criticism was in August 1654, when it sent his friends and courtiers Pickering, Strickland, and Jones to him, armed with a delicate euphemism. The repair of Whitehall for the protector's occupancy, they were to explain, was not being 'managed in so regular way as were to be wished, nor the charge thereof ordered as may be best for his highness's service'.[213]

Cromwell could not expect (perhaps he would not even have welcomed) the agreement of the councillors with his every policy. A majority of them seem to have dissented from his wish for a land base in Flanders, though if so they came round.[214] Foreign policy was a divisive area, with respect both to the Franco-Spanish conflict and to the rivalry of Sweden and the United Provinces.[215] Yet his control of diplomacy was generally taken for granted.[216] Useful as the diplomatic expertise of some councillors must have been to him, he would, as Thurloe once

---

[208] *TSP*, vi. 219.

[209] Spalding, *Diary of Bulstrode Whitelocke*, p. 400.

[210] *TSP*, vi. 788–9. Cf. Abbott, iv. 727–8; Spalding, *Diary of Bulstrode Whitelocke*, p. 485.

[211] *CSPD 1654*, pp. 186, 346, 397; *1655*, p. 48; *1655–6*, pp. 192, 394; *1656–7*, pp. 97, 113–14, 281, 300; *1657–8*, pp. 226, 233; TNA, SP25/75: 7 February, item 1; 19 May 1654, item 9; 25/77: 3 March 57, item 29; 25/78: 31 December 1656, item 25; 6 August 1657, item 21.

[212] Roberts, *Swedish Diplomats*, pp. 14–15, 195–6, 266–7.

[213] TNA, SP25/75: 17 August 1654.

[214] Guizot, *History of Oliver Cromwell*, ii. 583; Abbott, iv. 654, 658.

[215] The pro-Dutch Strickland was balanced by the pro-Swedish Lisle (Roberts, *Swedish Diplomats*, p. 13 and *passim*). It is possible, though the evidence is faint and inconclusive, that councillors talked Cromwell out of his desire for an ambitious offensive and defensive league with France: *TSP*, i. 761 (cf. iv. 470); Guizot, *History of Oliver Cromwell*, ii. 529–30; Bodl., Carte MS 114, fo. 253&ᵛ; Chéruel, *Lettres du Cardinal Mazarin*, vi. 175. But if so there is no sign of any stand against him.

[216] e.g. TNA, SP25/75: 20 February 1655, item 7; *CSPD 1655–6*, pp. 6, 20; Vaughan, *Protectorate of Oliver Cromwell*, i. 268, 334–5; *TSP*, ii. 137, 153; Roberts, *Swedish Diplomats*, pp. 248–9.

put it, 'cast within himself' to decide on his course.[217] There were divisive issues at home too. Yet in neither foreign nor domestic matters did the protector ever find himself in the position of Elizabeth I, who had had to engage in power struggles with her council and to reject its recommendations of policy.[218] In the great bulk of the protectoral council's records, or in Thurloe's voluminous correspondence, there is never a hint that Oliver has been overruled by his councillors.[219]

Perhaps the conciliar restraints on him which the wording of the Instrument of Government stipulated were always unlikely to be realized in the volatile conditions of the protectorate, whose formidable ruler had come to power by such forceful and unconventional means. Perhaps the constitution, had it lasted and had the regime won national consent, would have worked differently under Cromwell's successors, whose councils would in time have been composed of parliament's nominees,[220] and who would themselves be unlikely to command the automatic stature that Oliver had earned. If there was a long-term vision in the drafting of the Instrument, which extended beyond the peculiar circumstances of Cromwell's rule, perhaps it is glimpsed here. In the meantime the forms of conciliar

---

[217] *TSP*, i. 762.

[218] Worden, *Sound of Virtue, q.v.* 'council'.

[219] There are two recorded occasions in the protectorate, both of them arising from the conservative shift in Cromwellian politics that was announced and furthered by the introduction of the Humble Petition and Advice in 1657, when the evidence suggests the possibility, though it is a thin one, that a proposal put by the protector to the council was challenged. If so the resistance was defeated. Both episodes concerned major appointments by Cromwell. In October John Thurloe reported to Henry Cromwell that 'after some debate, the counsell here have, upon his highness's nomination, consented, that your lordship be the Deputy' of Ireland. He added that the body had 'alsoe advised' that all but one of the members of the late Irish council be reappointed; and 'that all the other votes about Ireland were very unanimous, noe man dissenting' (*TSP*, vi. 599). Henry's appointment was a humiliating affront to the councillor Charles Fleetwood, whose direct role in the government of Ireland it ended. Our problem is to know (a) whether, by the nouns 'consent' and 'vote', Thurloe meant a formal process, and (b) whether he had in his mind a clear distinction between 'consent' and 'advice', words that were used so interchangeably in accounts of the council's procedures. The answer to both questions is perhaps likely to be no, since by the terms of the Humble Petition Henry Cromwell's appointment did not need the council's 'consent' (though it did require the subsequent approval of parliament: *GD*, p. 454). The episode is not recorded in the council minute-book, which does however record the other of the two episodes. It occurred three months earlier, on 13 July, at the first meeting of the council under the new constitution. This time there was a formal vote, which in this case the Humble Petition did require (ibid., p. 453). The protector 'this day nominated John Thurloe, Secretary of State, to be a member of council, which was, by vote of the council, upon the question, consented unto' (TNA, SP 25/78: 13 July 1657). The appointment occurred at a sensitive time, for it was also on the 13th that Cromwell ordered Lambert, whom Thurloe in effect replaced on the council, to give up his commissions (Abbott, iv. 577; and see Gaunt, *Correspondence of Henry Cromwell*, p. 300). The word 'vote' is a rare appearance in the council records, and there may have been some uneasiness about its use (TNA, SP 25/47: 23 December 1653, item 5). But seventeenth-century 'votes' were more often than not unanimous, and putting the question was more often than not a purely formal procedure. Probably the council was placing on record, in case of any subsequent parliamentary investigation into its doings at a delicate moment, its observance of a process required by the Humble Petition. It would have been hard to mount a case against Thurloe's appointment, and if a case had been made we would surely hear of it. Fleetwood and Desborough were present, but Pickering and Sydenham, who sympathized with them and with Lambert over the Humble Petition, and whose votes would have been essential to a serious challenge to the nomination, were not.

[220] There is an analogy of a kind with the summoning of Barebone's. Its members were chosen by the army, but their successors, in ensuing parliaments, were to be chosen by the electorate.

restraint were more impressive than the substance. Under the Humble Petition the forms themselves were reduced.

There is admittedly one episode, a significant one in the protectorate's annals, which at first glance brings Cromwell's command of the council into question. The appearance is nonetheless deceptive. It hides a truer image of the relations of power within Cromwell's entourage—and strengthens a Tacitean understanding of them. In the early summer of 1656 the Major-Generals were summoned to Whitehall to discuss the government's mounting problems, and especially the question whether to summon a parliament to raise urgently needed money. A decision to do so was reportedly taken at the end of May, but if so renewed uncertainty followed, and it was only on 1 July that the issuing of the writs was publicly announced.[221] May and June were a time of frantic and confused discussion in Whitehall[222] when the normal courtesies of debate broke down.[223] Cromwell opposed the summoning of a parliament, but eventually gave way. Two newsletters, which could have had a common source, report the protector as recalling that episode in February 1658, at a meeting with discontented army officers. In one of them, written by the royalist scholar William Dugdale, the protector is said to have remembered that, 'being advised by his council, he yielded, though he professed it, in his own judgement, no way seasonable'.[224] In the other, anonymous, letter, Cromwell 'told the officers . . . that he was against the calling of the late parliament. But the councell urged it soe'.[225] Yet a year earlier, in an address to army officers in February 1657 of which we have fuller and more dependable records, he had said something different. He then stated that, when he had argued against the calling of parliament, the alternative view was carried, not by the council, but by the army officers themselves, who were 'impatient . . . till a parliament was called'.[226]

Perhaps the newswriters of 1658, in reporting that Cromwell had referred to the advice of the council, got their facts wrong. But if they got them right, how do we explain the discrepancy between the words of February 1657 and those of February 1658? Was he, on the second occasion, once more passing the buck? It is true that the council would have been involved in the decision to call the parliament. By the terms of the Instrument, Cromwell could summon a parliament in 1656 only with its approval. No doubt—albeit in one of those decisions of which we have no

[221] Abbott, iv. 169, 198.
[222] Roberts, *Swedish Dipomats*, pp. 295, 303; *English Civil War*, iv. 289–90, 298.
[223] Roberts, *Swedish Diplomats*, p. 284; Gaunt, *Correspondence of Henry Cromwell*, p. 146.
[224] *HMC* v. 177 (Sutherland MSS).
[225] David Underdown, ed., 'Cromwell and the Officers, February 1658', *English Historical Review* 83 (1968), p. 107.
[226] Abbott, iv. 414, 417–18. Cromwell said that he 'gave my vote against it', but in that context 'vote' may simply have meant 'voice'—or he may have been seeking, as elsewhere in the speech, to highlight the political influence the officers had exerted.

record—it gave it.[227] Yet he seems to have consulted the Major- Generals and army officers before he turned to the council. It was the daily discussions of the Major-Generals, among themselves and with Cromwell, that were at the centre of events around the time the decision to call the parliament was reportedly taken.[228] If the views of individual councillors carried weight during the episode, it was not at the formal meetings of the council, from which Lambert, Desborough, and Fleetwood for a while absented themselves,[229] and which indeed were suspended during the critical debates.[230] In his speech of February 1657 Cromwell accused the officers of having 'garbled' the members who were elected to the parliament: of having 'kept out and put in whom you pleased'. Constitutionally the examination of members was the responsibility of the council, which indeed exercised it. The forms were observed. Yet Cromwell's words make sense only on the assumption that the council had had, at the least, guidance from the military. The 'garbling' of MPs took place in early September,[231] when a meeting of officers had just gathered at Whitehall.[232]

Army men, like the councillors, daily trod the passageways of Whitehall. Cromwell had long made a habit of arranging meetings of civilian and military politicians, which were essential if his cause were to be held together. The practice continued through the protectorate, a regime which after all had been brought into being by the cooperation of officers and MPs in arranging the dissolution of Barebone's. In the summer of 1655, when there were moves afoot to make Cromwell king, army officers had a 'large conference' with the protector and the council.[233] The 'junto' of nine men which he set up to resolve the impasse over the constitutional future among his advisers in 1658 was a mixture of officers and councillors.[234] The distinction between civilians and soldiers should not be overdrawn, for a number of civilian councillors had had military experience, and had formed bonds with soldiers, in or since the civil wars.[235] Among the opponents of kingship there were friendships that tied the ex-soldier Sydenham to Fleetwood and Desborough; the civilian Sir Gilbert Pickering—who had been close to the new model army in the 1640s through his military brother—to Fleetwood[236] and to Major-General Boteler;[237] and Pickering's own intimate civilian ally Strickland to Boteler and

---

[227] *TSP*, v. 176. Three years earlier, explaining to parliament the purge of September 1654, he indicated that it would have been unnecessary had the government followed his own preference, which was to impose a test of allegiance on MPs before their 'first entrance into the House, but this was declined, and hath not been done'. He does not say who 'declined' it. Fleetwood, in Ireland at the time, wished that Cromwell's proposal had been followed: *TSP*, ii. 620.

[228] Abbott, iv. 169–70; *TSP*, v. 63; Roberts, *Swedish Diplomats*, p. 303; *Civil War in England*, iv. 295.

[229] Gaunt, 'Councils of the Protectorate', p. 179.

[230] Gaunt, *Correspondence of Henry Cromwell*, p. 149 (cf. p. 125); *CSPD 1655–6*, p. 303.

[231] Gaunt, 'Single Person's Confidants', p. 555.

[232] Firth, *Clarke Papers*, iii. 71.

[233] *A Perfect Account* 6 June 1655 (under 5 June).

[234] *TSP*, vii. 192, 269; cf. Firth, *Clarke Papers*, iii. 145.

[235] Philip Jones continued to supervise his regiment in South Wales well into the protectorate.

[236] *TSP*, vi. 37; cf. TNA, SP28/258, fo. 613. On the Pickering brothers see Glenn Foard, *Colonel John Pickering's Regiment of Foot 1644-1645* (Whitstable, 1994), ch. 7

[237] *TSP*, iii. 172, 192, 328, iv. 190, 550; *CSPD 1655–6*, p. 65; Bodl., Rawlinson MS a. 32, p. 77 (inaccurately reproduced in *TSP*, iv. 234).

Major-General James Berry[238] and perhaps to Lambert too.[239] It is likely that in the crisis of 1656 the civilians followed the generals, as Pickering and Sydenham would do in opposing the Humble Petition.[240] At all events, the conflict around Cromwell in 1656 turned not on the council but on Thurloe and his military opponents, Lambert, Fleetwood, and Desborough.[241]

The council itself included four Major-Generals: Lambert, Desborough, Fleetwood, and Skippon. If Cromwell, in one of those senior moments, did muddle the parts that had been played by the Major-Generals and the council in the crisis of 1656, the error becomes intelligible once we recognize the dominance the army leaders could exert over their civilian colleagues. As in Tacitus, the power of the legions lay behind the civilian forms. That is why some observers of the regime, when describing its politics, either attributed decisions in which the council was involved solely to the army,[242] or spoke of 'the council and army men' or 'the court party and soldiery'.[243] During the weak rule of Richard Cromwell there would often be heard the old charge of 'evil counsel', which was directed mainly at Thurloe and his civilian ally, Jones.[244] Yet on the only occasion on which the same phrase is reported under Oliver, it was directed, not at the civilian councillors, but by a civilian at the generals who were opposed to kingship.[245] Oliver's civilian councillors might appeal to his judgement or conscience or friendship. But the man who had conquered three kingdoms, and who had destroyed both sides—the king and the Long Parliament—of the civil war, was unlikely to be diverted from his goals by a Sir Gilbert Pickering or a Walter Strickland. Thurloe noted that Cromwell said things to Pickering so that they would get back to Fleetwood, to whom Pickering 'tells all'.[246] The protector would hardly have troubled to say things to Fleetwood so that they would get back to Pickering.

In the later stages of Oliver's protectorate the supporters of kingship, infuriated by the army's continuing political pretensions, wished to see the composition of the council 'turned' in their own favour.[247] Yet they were at least as much concerned to

[238] *TSP*, iii. 328, iv. 546.

[239] The evidence is shadowy, but—especially when set beside the collaboration of the two men with their fellow Yorkshireman the rumper Luke Robinson—suggestive: *CJ* 25 May 1652, 24 February, 15 May, 18 June 1657; *Burton*, i. 320; *CSPD 1655–6*, p. 107; *1656–7*, p. 41; *TSP*, iii. 385, vi. 292–3; Bodl., Carte MS 228, fo. 86; Patrick Little, *Lord Broghill and the Cromwellian Union with Ireland and Scotland* (Woodbridge, 2004), pp. 132, 133, 136. Strickland's position as captain of the guard at Whitehall, and Lambert's large role in the reorganization of the protector's lifeguard, involved cooperation between them: TNA, SP18/181, no. 13. (Sometimes, as allies did, Lambert and Strickland disagreed.)

[240] For Sydenham and Lambert, see also Stephen, *Register of Consultations*, ii. 47.

[241] Roberts, *Swedish Diplomats*, p. 284; Gaunt, *Correspondence of Henry Cromwell*, pp. 146, 152.

[242] e.g. cf. *TSP*, iii. 512 with *Perfect Account* 6 June 1655 (under 5 June).

[243] *Burton*, i. lxxxvii–viii; Bodl., Carte MS 228, fo. 81.

[244] *TSP*, vii. 507 (cf. vii. 490, 659); *Burton*, iii. 268 (cf. iii. 259, iv. 197). Cf. Gaunt, *Correspondence of Henry Cromwell*, pp. 465, 482–3; G. F. Warner, ed., *The Nicholas Papers*, Camden Society, 4 vols (1886–1920), iv. 84; Abbott, iv. 678.

[245] Gaunt, *Correspondence of Henry Cromwell*, p. 519; cf. *Burton*, iii. 308.

[246] *TSP*, vi. 37.

[247] Ibid., vi. 810, 810–11, 858; Gaunt, *Correspondence of Henry Cromwell*, p. 245; Jones, 'Correspondence of Henry Cromwell', p. 461.

procure regiments for those advocates of a Cromwellian monarchy, Fauconberg and the councillor Montagu, an aspiration which assumed a symbolic status amid the political divisions of the late protectorate.[248] It was the 'well regulateing' or 'well constituting the councell and army' that Henry Cromwell sought in the spring of 1658. The 'well-framing of the army', he thought, would keep the next parliament 'steady', which in turn would resolve the problem of the council's membership; but there was no point in calling a parliament 'untill the army be sufficiently modelled'.[249] John Hobart of Norfolk (admittedly a tart opponent of the regime, though one with an ear near the centre of power) opined that the council was 'perfectly awed' by Cromwell and his '30,000 myrmidons'.[250] The Venetian ambassador—admittedly an erratic source, though one not without a feel for the broad picture—described the protectorate as 'military rule', in which the council was given a role merely to keep up the 'appearance of a republic'.[251] Perhaps those statements were exaggerations. Yet they contain an essential truth, which times of crisis brought to the surface: that the destiny of Cromwellian England lay not at the council table, but in the decisions of the generals and of the captains and soldiers behind them; and that the council, however valuable to Cromwell as a source of assistance, mattered as a locus of power only because the generals sat on it.

[248] Bodl., Rawlinson MS a. 61, fo. 394; *TSP*, vi. 699, 858; Gaunt, *Correspondence of Henry Cromwell*, p. 407; TNA, PRO 31/17/33, pp. 52–3, 128–9, 143; Bodl., Clarendon MS 59, fo. 222; Ogle, *Calendar of Clarendon State Papers*, iv. 19; Bodl., Carte MS 73, fo. 220.
[249] *TSP*, vi. 810, 811, 858.
[250] Bodl., Tanner MS 52, fo. 159ᵛ.
[251] *English Civil War*, v. 8–9 (cf. iv. 166).

6

Cromwell and the Protectorate

On 24 February 1657 John Thurloe, whom observers agreed to be the '*intimus*' and '*fac totum*' and 'right-hand man' of the lord protector,[1] wrote to George Monck, commander-in-chief of the occupying English forces in Scotland, to report the presentation to parliament, on the previous day, of the Remonstrance that offered to make Oliver Cromwell king. This was the document that, after modification by the Commons, would become the Humble Petition and Advice. Thurloe, an inveterate shaper of news, remembered the disaffection among the forces in Scotland that had followed Cromwell's elevation to the protectorate in December 1653, and he feared the renewal of discontent now. So he gave Monck information about the Remonstrance that would enable the general, on whose cooperation Thurloe could rely, to 'satisfie any . . . who may have scruples about this bussines'. One point Thurloe particularly wished to put across: that the move to crown Cromwell owed nothing to the personal ambition of which the protector was widely suspected. Thurloe 'assured' Monck that the Remonstrance 'arises from the parliament only; his highness knew nothinge of the particulars untill they were brought into the House'.[2] The claim is supported by a report of the Dutch ambassador in London, who was well informed about the Remonstrance: 'the whole business is so managed, that the protector is left out of it'.[3] The management must have been adroit. Four days before the presentation of the Remonstrance, a copy of it had been seen in the hands of Oliver's son and prospective successor Richard.[4] Those who also saw the document in advance included that 'discontented and dangerous person', as Monck called him,[5] William Packer, the commander of the protector's own regiment of horse, whose hostility to the Humble Petition would result in his own dismissal from the army a year later.[6]

Cromwell was practised at not knowing. He had achieved a larger feat of ignorance in December 1648. Having stayed in the north of England, in ruminative mood, while the revolution of which he had become the leading spirit neared its climax of Pride's Purge and the regicide, he travelled south so slowly as to reach the capital only on the evening of the day that Colonel Pride had had the army's

---

[1] Michael Roberts, ed., *Swedish Diplomats at Cromwell's Court, 1655–1656*, Camden Society, fourth series 36 (1988), pp. 114, 127, 146, 159, 162, 280, 289.
[2] Firth, *Clarke Papers*, iii. 89–90.
[3] *TSP*, vi. 85.
[4] C. H. Firth, *The Last Years of the Protectorate*, 2 vols (1909), i. 129n.
[5] *TSP*, vi. 807.
[6] Firth, *Last Years of the Protectorate*, i. 129n.

leading opponents in the Commons arrested.[7] On his arrival he was able to declare—according to the admittedly garbled but, on such a point, essentially reliable source in which the statement has come down to us—'that he had not been acquainted with this design'.[8] Five years after the purge there was a feat of ignorance more impressive still. On 12 December 1653 he succeeded, even as lord general of the army, in being unaware of the military coup that terminated the rule of Barebone's Parliament, the body which he had summoned, on his authority as lord general, five months earlier. The decision was managed by his own advisers, who persuaded the assembly to return its power to him. Yet in September 1654 he assured another parliament, 'in the presence of divers persons here, who do know whether I lie in that, that I did not know one tittle of' the resignation of Barebone's.[9] Four days after its expiry he was installed as lord protector under the new constitution, the Instrument of Government. In the same speech of 1654 he told parliament that he had not been 'privy' to the 'counsels' that led to the drawing up of the Instrument, and appealed to 'the gentlemen that undertook to frame' the constitution as witnesses.[10]

There is no more dextrous a political art than knowing how not to know. Equally there is none likelier to arouse mistrust. Cromwell was universally mistrusted. His elevation in 1653 had long been predicted, not only by royalists but by critics on his own side. Among MPs, Levellers, and sectaries, there were men whom he had courted or sounded and who were left to reflect on what, in bitter retrospect, they took to have been the duplicitous purposes of his advances of friendship. The supposition that his avowals of godliness, and his commitment to liberty of conscience, were masks for his own advancement, or were means to it, was not only made by observers in whose minds we might suppose Puritan religious experience to have been a blind spot: Clarendon, Hobbes, foreign rulers and ambassadors. It was held by men who had been bound to him in spiritual exertion, among them Sir Henry Vane[11] and Cromwell's brother-in-law Valentine Walton,[12] whose son's death by a cannon-shot at Marston Moor had prompted that memorable letter of consolation from Oliver.[13] Observers of his conduct, sometimes intimate ones, remarked on the 'temptations' to which he was vulnerable[14] (a weakness, admittedly, that Puritans commonly detected in each other). His sympathizers were outnumbered by his haters, and the hatred was most intense not among royalists but among his former allies.

---

[7] David Underdown, *Pride's Purge* (Oxford, 1971), pp. 148–50.
[8] *Ludlow's Memoirs*, i. 211.
[9] Abbott, iii. 454–5.
[10] Ibid., iii. 455.
[11] Above, pp. 26–7.
[12] *TSP*, vii. 795.
[13] Abbott, i. 287.
[14] *TSP*, ii. 620, iii. 294; *Burton*, iii. 165, 211; Bodl., Rawlinson MS a. 39, fo. 528; *A Copy of a Letter from an Officer of the Army in Ireland* (n.d.: 1656?), p. 20; Abbott, iv. 879 (cf. iii. 89); *Somers Tracts*, vi. 314; *The Humble Representation . . . of . . . Churches . . . in South-Wales* (1656), p. 19; Peter Toon, *God's Statesman: The Life and Work of John Owen* (Exeter, 1971), p. 100 (cf. pp. 55–6; above, p. 143); cf. *LP*, p. 328.

At some point between the parliament of 1654 and that of 1656, an anonymous polemicist alleged that the protector had told the Scottish politician John Hay, second Earl of Tweeddale, 'that there was something amiss in the Church and state, ... and as for those things that were amiss in the Church, [he] hoped to rectify by degrees, as opportunity presented itself; but before [he] could do this work, the Anabaptists must be taken out of the army, and this [he] could not do with sharp corrosive measures, but it must be done by degrees'.[15] We cannot tell whether Cromwell said such a thing. Yet in Tweeddale's country, as Thurloe appreciatively observed, Monck successfully undertook the 'weeding out of the army troublesome and discontented spirits'.[16] Henry Cromwell confronted the Anabaptists in Ireland and strove to 'keep them from power' there.[17] He and his followers were urged to be 'patient', 'for a while', until the protector's approval of Henry's policies could be made open.[18] Henry himself hoped that his father would 'at length' 'distinguish ... true freinds from others', and that 'by degrees' he would 'wind out power and armes out of the hands of' Henry's own enemies in England, to whom Anabaptists looked for protection.

Over the course of the protectorate, people who had rejoiced in the regicide or in the abolition of monarchy, or who wanted far-reaching change in the Church or the law or the universities, saw their cause in retreat. Leading figures—Fleetwood in Ireland, Robert Lilburne in Scotland, John Lawson in the fleet, John Owen at Oxford University—who, even though they had come on board the protectorate, retained sympathy for colleagues who had not, lost their places or their influence. William Sheppard, to whom, until the parliamentary session of 1656–7, Cromwell looked to draw up extensive reforms of the legal system, was then eased from the picture.[19] Presbyterian divines were increasingly welcomed to court, among them John Howe, a scourge of heresy who became chaplain to the protector;[20] and Thomas Manton, who had sided with the Presbyterian majority in parliament against the new model army in 1647, but who conducted the prayers at Cromwell's installation under the Humble Petition,[21] and who prayed with him on the last day of the protector's life.[22] On the council the alliance of Thurloe and Philip Jones,[23] men eager for Cromwell to be king, gradually outreached the influence of civilian colleagues dismayed by that prospect. Among the regime's administrators and diplomats, such pragmatic figures as George Downing and Sir William Lockhart, too young to have been shaped by those experiences of the

---

[15] *TSP*, iii. 150.
[16] Ibid., vi. 873.
[17] Ibid., ii. 149–50, 162–4; T. C. Barnard, *Cromwellian Ireland* (Oxford, 1975), p. 107.
[18] Peter Gaunt, ed., *The Correspondence of Henry Cromwell 1655–1659*, Camden Society, fifth series 31 (2007), pp. 168, 178.
[19] Nancy L. Matthews, *William Sheppard, Cromwell's Law Reformer* (Cambridge, 1984), pp. 62, 132, 223.
[20] *ODNB*: 'Howe, John'; and see Lee Prosser, 'Writings and Sources XXII: The Palace of the Republic', *Cromwelliana* 2009, p. 82.
[21] *ODNB*: 'Manton, Thomas'.
[22] Frances Henderson, ed., *The Clarke Papers V*, Camden Society, fifth series 27 (2005), p. 272.
[23] Above, p. 211.

1620s which had forged the political Puritanism that destroyed Charles I, replaced superannuated ideologues.

And yet how slow was the shift, and how incomplete. Always Cromwell had one eye on the resistance it encountered. The opposition, like so much else in protectoral politics, turned on perceptions of his character. Had he not, it was demanded, succumbed to allurements of the will or the self, or to the slipperiness of high places? Had he not, like King Jehu in the Second Book of Kings,[24] used a programme of godly reformation as the engine of his own advancement, and abandoned or fatally compromised it once the advancement had been achieved? Was it true, it was suspiciously asked early in the protectorate, that he was 'serv'd upon the knee' at table?[25] And if, as he sometimes indicated, he wanted to preserve the spirit of a commonwealth even as he parted from its constitutional forms—or if, as he liked to insist, he did not intend the government to pass to members of his own family[26]—then why did he not, as proof of his 'sincerity', make provision for the exclusion of his sons from the succession,[27] a proposal which seems to have been advanced during the discussions of the content of the Instrument of Government in the days before its introduction?[28] Not only was there hostility to his rule from outside the regime, from politicians and 'saints' whom he would have carried with him if he could. There was unease, and often more than unease, within it. Army officers who had been bound to Cromwell from dark and humble days— John Desborough, Edward Whalley, William Goffe, James Berry—were accustomed to a frank egalitarianism in their dealings with him that the deferences of the new court seem to have done nothing to soften.[29] Those officers had allies among the civilians on the council in William Sydenham (himself a former soldier), Walter Strickland, and Sir Gilbert Pickering,[30] who monitored no less closely the protector's contentions with temptation.

Historians may never agree whether it was from choice or necessity—whether from conscience and conviction, or from a recognition of facts of power—that the protector restrained the counter-revolutionary trend which he simultaneously encouraged, and positioned himself midway between the two pressures. Either way, a persistent ambiguity was worn on the face of power. Was the protector, or was he not, a kind of king? Earlier protectors had been, not kings, but temporary substitutes for them. The title was familiar to the nation only as an interim expedient, suited to the reign, and a substitute for the rule, of a minor or a

---

[24] Worcester College Oxford, Clarke MS xxvii, fo. 6; *Somers Tracts*, vi. 474; and see below, p. 300.
[25] *TSP*, ii. 163.
[26] Gaunt, *Correspondence of Henry Cromwell*, p. 76; Abbott, iii. 756; cf. above, p. 216.
[27] 'Johannes Cornubiensis', *The Grand Catastrophe* (1654), p. 13.
[28] TNA, PRO 31/3/92, fo. 103; cf. *Ludlow's Memoirs*, i. 370.
[29] Desborough: *LP*, p. 328; Whalley: Clyve Jones, ed., 'The Correspondence of Henry Cromwell, 1655–1659', Univ. of Lancaster M.Litt. thesis (1969), p. 213; Goffe: Abbott, i. 541; *Conscience-Oppression: or, a Complaint of Wrong Done to the People's Rights* (1657), p. 52; Berry: *TSP*, iv. 274, 498 (cf. vii. 365). For the egalitarian spirit among the officers see too Gaunt, *Correspondence of Henry Cromwell*, p. 277.
[30] Above, p. 211.

disqualified monarch.[31] He himself told parliament in 1657 that he had expected his tenure of the office to be 'temporary, to supply the present emergency'.[32] He had undertaken it, after Barebone's had attacked property rights and threatened to overhaul the legal system, 'not so much out of hope of doing any good, as out of a desire to prevent mischief and evil, which I did see was imminent upon the nation'.[33] Government propaganda tirelessly justified the coup of December 1653 as the nation's escape from the anarchy to which Barebone's had almost reduced it. Yet, whereas a time-limit had been set on the rule of Barebone's,[34] the new constitution was apparently designed for posterity. The regime's conduct in its early stages did nothing to discourage that perception. The Instrument entitled the government, during the first nine months of its existence, to pass ordinances 'for the peace and welfare of these nations where it shall be necessary', which would carry authority until or unless parliament subsequently rescinded them.[35] One might suppose that they, too, would have been emergency measures. Yet some of the ordinances went well beyond the immediate claims of 'necessity' and aimed to secure lasting changes in the Church, the law, the universities.[36] There was nothing temporary, either, about the repair and refurbishment, on a regal scale, of the protector's palaces from early in 1654.[37]

During Oliver's rule there ran frequent rumours that the great offices of state that had accompanied the rule of kings would be revived, and that a Lord Chancellor or Lord Treasurer or Lord High Admiral or Lord Privy Seal was about to be appointed.[38] Instead his councillors preserved a collective anonymity. It is true that visiting ambassadors, and sometimes Englishmen, were invited to know Thurloe as 'Secretary of State', the title by which posterity also recognizes him, or even as 'Principal Secretary of State'.[39] He was accorded those titles in formal minutes of the council after his admission to its membership in 1657.[40] Yet there was no official announcement of his appointment and there is no official record of it.

[31] See e.g. Nathaniel Bacon, *An Historical and Political Discourse* (1760 edn), [part] ii. 79–82.
[32] Abbott, iv. 481; cf. iii. 138.
[33] Ibid., iv. 470.
[34] Ibid., iii. 67.
[35] *GD*, p. 414.
[36] On them see Peter Gaunt, '"To Create a Little World out of Chaos": The Protectoral Ordinances of 1653–1654 Reconsidered', in Patrick Little, ed., *The Cromwellian Protectorate* (Woodbridge, 2007), pp. 105–26.
[37] On it see Paul Hunneyball, 'Cromwellian Style: The Architectural Trappings of the Protectorate Regime', in Little, *Cromwellian Protectorate*, pp. 53–81.
[38] *TSP*, i. 645, iii. 538; Roberts, *Swedish Diplomats at Cromwell's Court*, p. 80; Firth, *Clarke Papers*, iii. 42–3; Ruth Spalding, *Contemporaries of Bulstrode Whitelocke* (Oxford, 1990), p. 52; the newsbooks for the first half of June 1655; *Certain Passages of Every Dayes Intelligence* 24 August 1655, p. 52; 28 September 1655, p. 25; O. Ogle et al., eds, *Calendar of the Clarendon State Papers*, 5 vols (Oxford 1869–1970), ii. 359. See too *GD*, pp. 413, 416.
[39] TNA, SP 18/67, no. 56; 25/75: 6 August 1657, item 6; Abbott, iii. 774, 784; *CSPD 1655*, p. 128; *1656–7*, p. 82; *Severall Proceedings of State Affaires*, 29 December 1653, p. 3509; 23 March 1654, p. 3715; 6 April 1654, p. 3749; Roberts, *Swedish Diplomats*, p. 74; *TSP*, ii. 106, 245, vi. 428, vii. 64; F. P. G. Guizot, *History of Oliver Cromwell and the English Commonwealth*, trans. A. R. Scoble, 2 vols (1854), ii. 436 (though cf. ii. 446–9). In the minutes of the protectoral council he was often called 'Mr Secretary', the courtesy title that had customarily been given to Secretaries of State.
[40] TNA, SP25/78: 6 August 1657, item 7; cf. *CSPD 1657–8*, p. 26.

He was Secretary of State and he wasn't. In the status of Cromwell's '*intimus*', indeed, ambiguity approached an art form. Until 1657, when he was made a member of the council, the only post Thurloe officially held was as its 'secretary'. Yet in December 1653 an ambiguously worded order of that body implied that he was a councillor in all but name.[41] Ambiguity extended, too, to Sir Gilbert Pickering and Philip Jones. From 1655, when they were informally reported to have been given the posts of Lord Chamberlain and Controller of the Household respectively, until the winter of 1657–8, when they seem, through some protracted and to us invisible process, to have formally assumed them, the two men held the offices and they didn't.[42] Semantic ambiguity was also preserved on other fronts. Sometimes Cromwell employed the royal 'we'; sometimes he eschewed it; sometimes he got muddled between the two practices. In official communications he referred to the government's executive body sometimes as 'his' or 'our' council, in the way that a monarch might do; sometimes as 'the council', a term more appropriate to the largely independent body of state envisaged by the Instrument; and sometimes as 'the council of state', which had been the official term for the executive bodies of the Rump and Barebone's, but which, while it was often used colloquially to describe the council of the protectorate, had no formal meaning under it.[43] Here too the introduction of the Humble Petition in 1657 brought some formalization of nomenclature. Yet ambiguity had not lost its scope. It seems safe to infer, from Cromwell's complaisant silence on the subject during the negotiations over the new constitution, that its designers anticipated his acceptance of its original and ingenious solution to the dilemma over the succession: his successor was to be neither hereditary nor elected, but nominated by him. The arrangement enabled him to sustain ambiguity unto his deathbed: he nominated Richard to succeed him, and he didn't.[44]

[41] TNA, SP25/75, p. 10 (*CSPD 1653–4*, p. 309).

[42] Firth, *Clarke Papers*, iii. 47, 141; Bodl., Carte MS 73, fo. 187ᵛ; *CSPD 1657–8*, p. 344. It is possible that Nathaniel Fiennes was given some kind of informal recognition as Lord Privy Seal in the summer of 1655: Firth, *Clarke Papers*, iii. 42; *CSPD 1655*, p. 278; and the sources cited at n. 38 above. Perhaps the elevations signalled in the summer of 1655 were intended to be formally announced but were abandoned once the proposal, current at that time, to enthrone Cromwell had been dropped.

[43] The solecism assumed comical forms when it mingled with his uneasy forays into the royal 'we': TNA, SP18/69, no. 71; 18/76, no. 7; 18/99, no. 58. (The term 'council of state' did, it is true, also live on outside the heart of power.) Other confusions or moments of inconsistency can be glimpsed in *TSP*, ii. 285; Abbott, iii. 296–7, 507, 809. The suggestion in Peter Gaunt's admirable article, '"The Single Person's Confidants and Dependants"? Oliver Cromwell and his Protectoral Councillors', *Historical Journal*, 32 (1991), p. 553, that Cromwell used the word 'we' to refer to decisions taken by him together with the council could explain only some of the cases.

[44] Historians consequently cannot agree whether he did: *CPW* vii. 4–5; Jonathan Fitzgibbons, '"Not in Any Doubtfull Dispute"? Reassessing the Nomination of Richard Cromwell', *Historical Research* 83 (2010), pp. 280–300. The Humble Petition said nothing about the succession on the deaths of future rulers. In that and other respects the concentration by the framers of the constitution on its provisions for Oliver's own government reflects the provisional and temporary spirit of the document, a feature that would cause problems when the Humble Petition was debated in the parliament of his son Richard.

Ambiguity was the instrument of balance. In Ireland, even when, in 1657, two years of ambiguous, not to say contradictory, command were ended by Henry Cromwell's appointment as Lord Deputy, his rival and counterweight Fleetwood retained his capacity to undermine him at Whitehall, while the membership of the Irish council, as Henry complained, was 'looked upon as a mere balance of three against three'.[45] In June 1658 the protector appointed a body of nine to decide on the next political move. On it the rival parties were so carefully poised—four against four, with a neutral in between—that agreement was unattainable.[46] There was, urged Henry Cromwell and his allies, an answer to the paralysis that afflicted the regime in its later stages: an end to the 'bare balance or aequilibrium', which 'will not serve',[47] and a reconfiguration of the personnel both of the English council and of the military high command.[48] Thus could the protector subdue the 'depraved appetites' of the 'sick minds'[49]—Fleetwood, Desborough, and their associates—who obstructed the desire for a monarchical settlement, and by whom, as Henry's new brother-in-law Lord Fauconberg told him, Henry himself was 'so very much feared and hated'.[50] Instead the shift towards monarchy halted; as Oliver's end approached, there were expectations within the regime of 'civill warres after his death';[51] and in that 'miserable posture' of affairs Fauconberg prepared to confront his and Henry Cromwell's enemies over control of the army.[52] Nine months after Richard's succession a regime that had awed Europe was destroyed from within when Oliver's son-in-law Fleetwood and his brother-in-law Desborough toppled his elder son.

Royalists, who had looked to Cromwell's death for a revival of their fortunes, were disappointed. Clarendon, perceiving only the external power of the government and unaware of its internal contentions, remembered that, 'contrary to all expectation at home and abroad', Richard succeeded with a smoothness that an established dynasty might have envied.[53] Sir Charles Firth, the master-historian of the protectorate, was likewise impressed by its standing in the last phase of Oliver's life. He noted the protector's continuing decisiveness, and stressed the humbling of royalist conspiracy. In February 1658, alarmed by the power of the agitation against his rule in the Commons, in the army, and in the city of London, Cromwell had to hail a hackney-carriage to get him from Whitehall to Westminster in time to dissolve the parliament before it could receive a mass petition demanding the restoration of the 'supreme power' of the Commons. A newswriter portrayed him as a fallen Samson: 'the poor man seems to speake and act much like one that have lost his locke of strength, and wisedome that once he had'.[54] Yet to Firth the dissolution, dramatic as it was, was a response to a merely temporary problem posed by the creation of the

[45] *TSP*, vi. 506.   [46] Ibid., vii. 193, 269.   [47] Ibid., vi. 858.
[48] Cf. above, pp. 228–9.   [49] *TSP*, vi. 93.   [50] Ibid., vii. 451.
[51] Ibid., vii. 348; cf. vii. 269.   [52] Ibid., vii. 365, 366.   [53] *CH*, vi. 98.
[54] David Underdown, 'Cromwell and the Officers', *English Historical Review* 83 (1968), p. 107. 'Surely he hath not wanted Dalilahs to deprive him of it', the newswriter added cryptically.

'Other House', the second parliamentary chamber established by the Humble Petition. Firth regarded the feats of Robert Blake's navy, and the acquisition of Mardyke and Dunkirk, in the later part of Oliver's rule as vindications of his diplomatic ambitions—even if the means had not been found to pay for them or sustain the army at home.[55]

Firth's is a salutary perspective. The government of England after the civil wars would never have been easy. Profound hostility to any regime that emerged from them, and serious threats to its survival, were inevitable. To Cromwell, 'difficulties' were an expectation and a norm.[56] In April 1658, when to the divisions within the government and army there were added the prospects of royalist insurrection and foreign invasion, a visitor at court reported that 'the protectors party were full of unquiettnes & alarums, & yet it pleased God to keep up their spirits from being daunted'.[57] The army and navy behind the regime were formidable. The opposition of royalists and former rumpers and discontented soldiers was overcome, and the defeat of opponents tends to boost the morale and authority of governments. Any seventeenth-century administration which established itself in power, as the protectorate did, could count on instincts of submission, which derived partly from concern for the preservation of public order, partly from a readiness to accept the providentialist credentials of de facto rulers.[58] There is nonetheless an alternative perspective on the protectorate: one that emphasizes, not its success in securing obedience, but the narrowness and shallowness of its political base.

Because the protectorate brought a return to government by a single ruler, and because it crushed the alien plant of non-monarchical rule, it has become customary to think of it as, in David Underdown's words, 'a half-way house on the road to 1660'.[59] The return to single rule indeed brought Cromwell advantages. Had he gone further and become king, the replacement of one dynasty by another would have provided a familiar kind of resolution of civil strife, which de facto thinking would have endorsed. Every Roundhead would have had at least something to dread from a return of the Stuarts, a prospect against which a Cromwellian monarchy might seem the most effective bulwark. Outside the Roundhead fold there were many, particularly among younger men who had grown up amid the havoc of the civil wars and yearned for an end to it, who would have supported a Cromwellian monarchy as the likeliest means to the return of civil peace. Only when that prospect faded after Oliver's death did 'the monarchical party that before looked upon Cromwell as the fittest person to attain their ends by'[60] begin to look instead to the return of the Stuarts. Until that time the protectorate, wrote Underdown,

[55] C. H. Firth, *Oliver Cromwell and the Rule of the Puritans in England* (1900), pp. 425–6, 428; Firth, *Last Years of the Protectorate*, ii. ch. 12. A similar picture is painted by Austin Woolrych, 'The Cromwellian Protectorate: A Military Dictatorship?', *History* 75 (1990), pp. 226–8.

[56] Above, p. 8.

[57] Ruth Spalding, ed., *The Diary of Bulstrode Whitelocke* (Oxford, 1990), p. 489.

[58] Above, pp. 49–50.

[59] David Underdown, *Somerset in the Civil War and Interregnum* (Newton Abbot, 1973), p. 175.

[60] Above, p. 121.

was 'a government closer to the hearts of the gentry than any since the civil war',[61] though he emphasized that it was not as close as all that, and he anyway made a large exception for the period of the rule of the Major-Generals. Certainly the government strove from the outset to widen its support. It immediately withdrew the Engagement of loyalty to kingless rule that the Rump had divisively imposed.[62] It distanced itself from the memory of the regicide.[63] From an early stage it made known its willingness to offer favour or amnesty to MPs who had been leading opponents of the army in the late 1640s.[64] Parliamentary elections brought political Presbyterians—men who, or whose allies or members of whose families, had been driven from parliament in 1648—back to Westminster, first in 1654, then in 1656, then, under Richard Cromwell, in 1659. A great many constituencies which had been denied representation in the Rump regained it—though the purges of Oliver's parliaments left a sizeable number still deprived. There were intermittent initiatives to conciliate royalists and Anglicans, and there was a frequent readiness to wink at their dissent, provided it was peaceable—though those concessions were unlikely to impress victims of the Major-Generals and the decimation tax, the non-parliamentary levy on royalists which financed the Major-Generals' rule. In some counties established families returned to the agencies of local government—though, if a single pattern emerges from the diversity of regional experience that modern studies of the shires in the 1650s have uncovered, it is that the more the leading families involved themselves in the running of the localities, the more the counties were able to put local priorities ahead of Whitehall's.

Up to a point the ambiguity on the face of Cromwell's power worked. He offered a middle way. The government's leading polemicist, Marchamont Nedham, commended the Instrument because 'the frame of government appears so well bounded on both sides against anarchie and tyrannie'.[65] Nedham had made the same claim on behalf of the Commonwealth of 1649–53: it was 'the only bank which preserves us from the inundations of tyranny on the one side and confusion on the other'.[66] But the middle way he had then saluted was one between Levellers and royalist or Presbyterian forces of reaction. In 1654 he could intimate that the Commonwealth, which he now portrayed as a period of both arbitrary and disordered rule, had itself been one of the two extremes. Now, too, the middle way accommodated rather than excluded Presbyterians. An MP of 1659 spoke approvingly of the 'mediocrity' between a republic and monarchy which the protectorate had created.[67]

---

[61] David Underdown, 'Settlement in the Counties', in G. E. Aylmer, ed., *The Interregnum: The Quest for Settlement* (1972), p. 174.

[62] Firth and Rait, ii. 830–1.

[63] *LP*, p. 142.

[64] *SPC*, iii. 223–4; *Certain Passages of Every Dayes Intelligence* 24 February 1654, p. 47 (cf. *TSP*, iv. 347); *The Faithfull Scout* 24 February 1654, p. 1314. Cf. *CSPD 1653–4*, pp. 401–2; *1654*, p. 54, item 25; Worcester College Oxford, Clarke MS xxvi, fo. 83.

[65] Marchamont Nedham, *A True State of the Case of the Commonwealth* (1654), p. 52.

[66] Marchamont Nedham, *The Case of the Commonwealth of England, Stated*, ed. Philip Knachel (Charlottesville, VA, 1969), p. 111.

[67] *Burton*, iii. 360.

The regime had another advantage. By ending the long and unbroken period of parliamentary rule, it lowered the political temperature. The temperature was always high when seventeenth-century parliaments were sitting, and the Long Parliament had sat almost continuously. Now parliaments were to meet at regular but distant intervals. The end of republican rule altered the political mood. When, in Richard Cromwell's parliament, former rumpers glorified the memory of their own rule, other MPs were moved to protest. The years of the Rump, recalled one, were 'not such halcyon days, but they brought tears to the eyes of the best men. . . . All errors, opinions and blasphemies, got root in that time; levelling principles, agreement of the people, nothing monstrous but that time produced. When we make the comparison, we may bless God we are on this side the waves and surges that those times produced.'[68] That was hardly fair on the Rump, which had broken the Levellers and moderated or resisted demands for liberty of conscience, but at least in the protectorate there were no *Agreements of the People*. Those whom, under the Commonwealth, Nedham had saluted as the Commonwealth's 'party of its own throughout the nation', the often confrontational functionaries who condemned existing institutional practices in Church and state, and who hoped to see 'lukewarm' and 'moderate' parliamentarians removed from central and local government,[69] were themselves largely displaced after 1653. In the parishes, though there was not yet order, there was in general more calm. The protectorate had replaced the Commonwealth, recalled one MP of 1659, 'to heal the disorder and confusion: as well to keep out the mischiefs of arbitrariness, on one hand, and confusions on the other hand'.[70] Even at a low ebb of the protectorate's fortunes, in March 1655, an MP who had been a victim of Pride's Purge could tell Thurloe: 'I am fully perswaded, if you keepe quiet above, and grow towards a settlement, the coun[t]ies will quietly setle.'[71]

Cromwell had not devoted his life to the Puritan cause merely in order to 'keepe quiet'. The chances of a nationally acceptable 'settlement' under the Instrument of Government were impaired by his unceasing commitment to godly reformation and liberty of conscience. Yet the protectorate had a larger flaw than the divisiveness of his goals. Its basic problem, which derived from its military basis, was its illegitimacy, which undermined and countered all the benefits of single rule. The most fundamental aberration from Roundhead ideals in the 1650s was not the parliamentary rule on either side of the protectorate. It was the protectorate itself. Recent advances in the study of seventeenth-century parliaments are indebted to the challenge levelled by Conrad Russell and other historians at 'Whig' interpretations. Yet something has been lost by Russell's insistence that parliament was 'an event' rather than 'an institution'. It was both. The event mattered because the institution mattered. The politically inspired exploration of medieval parliamentary history by seventeenth-century lawyers and antiquaries involved the recovery not

---

[68] Ibid., iii. 113–14.
[69] *LP*, pp. 188–9; above, p. 110.
[70] *Burton*, iii. 267.
[71] *TSP*, iii. 227; cf. Underdown, 'Settlement in the Counties', p. 181.

merely of tactically useful precedents but of a vision of parliament as the great council of the realm, where ultimate authority, and with it emergency powers, lay: a council, that is, entitled in the last resort not merely to give advice to kings but to make decisions without them. How else can we explain the confidence of the Long Parliament in 1642, when it claimed to control the militia; bypassed the royal veto; asserted that, as the repository of the community's will, it was entitled to place necessity above the law; and took over the executive? Then, as was believed to have happened so often in medieval times, an emergency or hiatus of government had returned power to its proper source. The Puritan Revolution being a protracted emergency or hiatus, the principle would be repeatedly reasserted by the truncated parliaments which it produced: in 1649, when kingship was abolished; in the parliaments of 1654 and 1657, when parliament took the settlement of the nation on itself; in 1659, when the Rump was restored; and in the assumption of power by the 'free parliament', or Convention, which resolved to bring the king back in 1660. The creation of the protectorate, which flouted the decisions reached and laws passed by parliament in 1649, was a flagrant violation of a widely accepted principle.

Edward Hyde, Earl of Clarendon, would time and again remember the king's difficulty, even after the Long Parliament had appropriated executive powers, in constructing a royalist case that would overcome the 'reverence' and 'veneration' and 'superstition' that were 'generally... entertained for parliament', that 'fatal disease' by which 'the whole kingdom was misled', and which, Hyde judged, gave Westminster an unassailable advantage in the recruitment and maintenance of armies.[72] Other royalists shared his assessment: parliament had become an 'idol'; it was 'a word that... carried armies in it'.[73] There may have been sour grapes in such judgements, but there was also a rueful recognition of a fundamental obstacle to the royalist cause. At least Hyde managed to persuade the king, in royal declarations of 1642, implicitly to renounce his earlier non-parliamentary rule, and to explain that his own actions were directed not against 'the dignity, privilege and freedom of parliaments', 'whose freedom distinguishes the condition of his majesty's subjects from those of any monarchy in Europe',[74] but only against the 'seditious' ringleaders who had perverted the institution.[75] The king declared it obvious 'that it is impossible for him to subsist without the affections of his people, and that those affections cannot possibly be preserved or made use of but by parliaments'.[76] At his trial and on the scaffold he remembered to insist on his respect for the 'privileges' of parliament.[77]

---

[72] *CH*, i. 476–7 (cf. i. 532), ii. 82, 461, 479 (cf. ii. 25), iii. 117, 181, 259, v. 281.

[73] John Bramhall, *The Serpent Salve* (1643), sig. A3; G. F. Warner, ed., *The Nicholas Papers*, 4 vols, Camden Society, 1886–1920, iv. 105, 152. Cf. *The Copy of a Letter from a Lincolnshire Gentleman* (1660), p. 3; *SPC*, iii. 289.

[74] *CH*, ii. 202, 279.

[75] Ibid., ii. 66, 149.

[76] Ibid., ii. 202.

[77] David Iagomarsino and Charles J. Wood, eds, *The Trial of Charles I* (Hanover, NH, 1989), pp. 81, 140.

Of course, no one among Charles's opponents in the Long Parliament aimed at what they inadvertently achieved: a parliament in permanent session, allegedly exercising a tyranny of its own. Parliaments were regarded as supreme in the sense that they were the source and sanction of legitimate rule. They were not expected, in normal circumstances, to administer it. The one basic constitutional point about which the parliament of 1654–5 found it easy to agree with the protector was that parliaments should not be 'perpetual'.[78] Equally, MPs did not want new parliaments to be too frequent. When medieval precedents suggested to them that parliaments ought to be summoned once if not twice a year, most of them shrank from the logic of their own antiquarianism. The supremacy attained by the Long Parliament was full of contradictions. The more the assembly claimed to be acting as the representative of the people, the less representative it became. The trial of the king was carried out on the authority of a House of Commons which invoked its own supremacy in vindication, but which had had to be forcibly purged of its majority for that purpose.

MPs on the parliamentarian side in the civil wars responded in varying ways to the dilemmas about constitutional authority with which the revolution unexpectedly presented them from Pride's Purge onwards. Some pronounced all the regimes of 1648 to 1659 illegal. Others aimed to steer Puritan rule back to constitutional legality. Some became committed to kingless rule. Others converted to royalism. Some held to their positions obdurately: others altered or compromised them in the light of events. What in most cases cut across those positions was an assumption that without parliamentary consent there was no legitimate basis of government— even if disagreement often flared about how consent could or should be identified and achieved. If the record and memory of the rule of the Rump worked to the protector's advantage, at least the Rump had been a remnant of a constitutionally elected parliament, whose rights it had proclaimed as the basis of its power.[79] It had, as one of its less zealous members would recall in 1659, a 'root' in 'law' which the constitutions of the protectorate had never acquired.[80]

More than two hundred MPs were willing to sit in the Rump.[81] They had earlier pledged themselves, with the rest of the Long Parliament, to the ancient constitution of king, Lords, and Commons. A majority of them were opposed to Pride's Purge and the execution of the king, the events that brought the Commonwealth to power. Yet in the circumstances of 1649 they accepted, as the only alternative to military rule, the unicameral rule of the House of Commons and its annexation of the powers of the other two estates—a decision to which the next chapter will return. The Rump made clear its view of Pride's Purge by voting to omit Henry Ireton and Thomas Harrison, the MPs who as army officers bore most responsibility for it, from the council of state set up after the regicide.[82] In

---

[78] Abbott, iii. 459; *Burton*, i. xxxii, xl; *CJ* 14, 15 November 1654.
[79] Below, ch. 7.
[80] *Burton*, iv. 58.
[81] The conduct and motives of its members, and the composition of the membership, are described in my *The Rump Parliament*.
[82] Ibid., p. 180.

December 1648 Ireton had wanted to go further and dissolve the Long Parliament.[83] MPs hoped that by prolonging it, even in a purged form, even under the shadow of military intervention, and even after the overthrow of the ancient constitution, they could preserve the principle of parliamentary supremacy. The prominent rumper Bulstrode Whitelocke thus explained his readiness, even as he repudiated the regicide, to turn for salvation after it to the supremacy of the Commons: 'Unavoidable necessity hath put us upon those courses, which otherwise perhaps we should not have taken'.[84]

If the rule of the Rump in 1649 was a parliamentary alternative to military rule, the protectorate replaced parliamentary rule by a military usurpation. In that sense the termination of Barebone's was a more profound alteration of the revolution's course than the expulsion of the Rump eight months earlier. Even if Barebone's was chosen not by the electorate but by the army, at least Cromwell, in what he tried to make a formal act of transference, 'devolve[d] and intrust[ed] the supreme authority and government' into its hands.[85] In 1654 his stance was different. Having submitted the Instrument of Government to parliament for approval, he would not take its refusal for an answer.

During the Rump's rule Cromwell strove, in the face of opposition within the regime, to secure the return to active politics of MPs who had been excluded in December 1648 or had absented themselves thereafter.[86] We might think that as protector, eager as he remained to reconstruct the parliamentarian party of the 1640s, he had his chance. Yet scarcely any members of the Long Parliament who had ceased to sit in the Long Parliament in 1648 can be found anywhere near the centre of his regime. The permanently vacant seats, about a third of the whole, on the protectoral council, to which he hoped to appoint parliamentarian grandees, signal his failure.[87] The refusal of William Pierrepoint's 'conscience' to allow him to serve on it was a telling blow. Pierrepoint had been prominent on the moderate wing of the Independent party.[88] Under the protectorate only one of Pierrepoint's colleagues in the party's leadership, Nathaniel Fiennes, joined Cromwell's government. Presbyterian survivors of the Long Parliament were on still more distant terms with the regime. Though they are to be found in significant numbers at Westminster under the protectorate, they are rarely glimpsed in Whitehall.

If Presbyterian MPs purged by Colonel Pride were absent from the heart of protectoral power, few former rumpers were to be found there either. It might be answered that a high number of rumpers, perhaps even a majority of them, had played little part in the executive machinery of the republic, and were the kind of country gentlemen whom we would sooner expect to find running their estates than occupying posts in Whitehall. Yet nearly eighty of the Rump's members had

---

[83] Underdown, *Pride's Purge*, pp. 140–1.
[84] Whitelocke, *Memorials*, ii. 526. The points made in this paragraph are developed in Chapter 7.
[85] Abbott, iii. 67.
[86] Blair Worden, *The Rump Parliament* (Cambridge, repr. 1977), p. 277.
[87] It is derided in *Copy of a Letter*, pp. 17–18.
[88] Above, p. 209; Valerie Pearl, 'The "Royal Independents" in the English Civil War', *Transactions of the Royal Historical Society*, fifth series 18 (1968).

sat on one or more of its annual councils of state, its executive arm.[89] In 1653 most of them vanished from the political scene. That year was one of those occasions in politics when a generation leaves the stage (though in this case the generation would in large measure return, in 1659–60). It was not the Long Parliament but Barebone's, whose rule can be seen in retrospect as the auditions for the protectorate, that supplied a large proportion of the officials—members of the army committee; admiralty commissioners; excise commissioners; and so on—who ran Cromwell's government.[90]

There were exceptions to the rule. Seven former rumpers served, with varying perspectives and varying degrees of commitment, on the council of the protectorate, both under the Instrument of Government and under the Humble Petition and Advice: Philip Jones, Francis Rous, Philip Skippon, Walter Strickland, Sir Gilbert Pickering, William Sydenham, and Charles Fleetwood.[91] Yet even among those names there was unease. Outside the council there were eleven professional lawyers who seem to have made the transition from parliamentary to protectoral service easily enough, and to whose identity and behaviour we shall come. But only three other rumpers appear to have held office in the central administration of the protectorate: Luke Hodges of Gloucestershire, who became an excise commissioner; William Masham of Essex, who was made a treasury commissioner;[92] and John Lowry, formerly Cromwell's fellow MP for Cambridge, who was given a post in the customs.[93] For all we know there may have been a number of other rumpers who, like Robert Bennett of Cornwall,[94] would have been glad to be invited to serve in similar ways—just as there may have been Presbyterians who would have accepted office but whose views, especially on liberty of conscience, would have made them unacceptable. Yet there was a limit to the number of experienced politicians whose service Cromwell could afford to refuse. Some rumpers outside his regime made gestures of amity towards it. Thomas Pury signed 'a declaration gratulatory' submitted to the protector by the city of Gloucester in February 1654.[95] There was a handful of other rumpers in the provinces whom the protectorate may have thought of as among its friends. One was John Bingham, the governor of the Isle of Wight, a neighbour, relation, and old ally of the protectoral councillor William Sydenham;[96] another was Sir William Strickland of Yorkshire, brother of the councillor Walter Strickland;[97] others were Dennis Bond and John Trenchard of Dorset.[98] Yet the friendships, if such they were, may

---

[89] Worden, *Rump Parliament*, p. 26.

[90] Woolrych, *Commonwealth to Protectorate*, pp. 384–5. Woolrych is the essential guide to the politics of 1653.

[91] The ageing army officer Sir William Constable also supported the protectorate: E999[12], p. 4.

[92] *CSPD 1653–4*, p. 309; *1654*, p. 284; *Ludlow's Memoirs*, i. 372.

[93] Andrew Barclay, 'The Lord Protector and his Court', in Little, *Oliver Cromwell in Perspective*, p. 205. Cromwell also conferred a barony on his cousin the rumper Edmund Dunch.

[94] Woolrych, *Commonwealth to Protectorate*, pp. 389–90.

[95] *Severall Proceedings of State Affaires* 23 February–2 March 1654, p. 3673.

[96] TNA, SP25/77, pp. 311–12; Worden, *Rump Parliament*, p. 29.

[97] *TSP*, iv. 593.

[98] *CSPD 1655–6*, p. 354.

not have gone deep.[99] Occasionally former members of the Rump can be seen addressing the regime with prudent politeness when they had petitions or private concerns to press in Whitehall.[100] Yet outward civility to rulers has never, on its own, been evidence of support for their rule.

Other rumpers were drawn into public service but without looking like enthusiasts for the protectorate. Two of them served the regime abroad: Robert Blake, the great admiral of the fleet, and Richard Salwey, who was appointed ambassador to Constantinople. It is probable that both men thought of themselves as acting for their country rather than for its present government. Blake showed no commitment to the regime, and Salwey's loyalty to it was doubtful.[101] The slippery John Jones became brother-in-law to the protector and gave practical support to the government in his native Wales,[102] but the favour bestowed on him was keenly opposed by Henry Cromwell, who remembered Jones's republican past and thought him still 'dissatisfied'.[103] Some rumpers, though not many, were appointed as commissioners for the public faith, and a larger quantity, alongside a great number of other parliamentarians or Puritans, as commissioners for the ejection of ungodly ministers. At least six were named to the council of trade.[104] Yet it seems unlikely, at least in most cases, that the rumpers appointed to those bodies were consulted before their appointments or that they ever took them up. A number of rumpers did retain their customary involvement in local government. In the absence of other evidence, however, their willingness cannot be interpreted as betokening more than a determination to preserve the workings of their communities or their own places in them. Some, among them five MPs from Buckinghamshire who acted as militia commissioners in the county under the Major-Generals,[105] were willing to assist the government against the Cavaliers, the 'common enemy' as parliamentarians of various hues liked to call them.[106] Yet that attitude, too, is no indication of a liking for Cromwell's rule. It was shared by Matthew Alured, one of the 'three colonels' who mounted a conspiracy against the protectorate during the first of its parliaments,[107] and for whose life Charles Fleetwood had to plead after Alured's conviction by a court-martial.[108] Thomas Scot, a prominent rumper and a zealous

---

[99] Sir John Trevor of Surrey is another candidate (*CSPD 1655–6*, p. 354; see too TNA, SP25/153: 1 January 1657, item 1), but the evidence does not always allow us to distinguish him from his son John.

[100] *TSP*, iv. 644 (William Masham's father and fellow rumper Sir William Masham), v. 711 (Thomas Scot), vi. 624 (Dennis Bond); Bodl., Rawlinson MS a. 24, p. 74 (James Ashe).

[101] *TSP*, iv. 589.

[102] Ibid., iv. 413.

[103] Ibid., iv. 606; cf. Ludlow, *Voyce*, p. 248.

[104] Abbott, iv. 64 (Godfrey Bosvile and William Purefoy), 97 (John Jones); *CSPD 1655*, p. 240 (Oliver St John, Dennis Bond, and Thomas Chaloner).

[105] *TSP*, iv. 583: George Fleetwood, Richard Ingoldsby, Edmund West, Cornelius Holland, and Simon Maine.

[106] The rumper John Dove, the sheriff of Wiltshire who was captured by the royalist rebels of March 1655, subsequently assisted the government in their suppression: *TSP*, iii. 318–19.

[107] Ibid., iv. 359. An opponent of the protectorate in Cheshire, Robert Duckenfield (who like Alured was not an MP, but who like him had been happy to serve the Rump), offered to receive from Cromwell a 'handsome military command' to fight on the Continent, but was unwilling to accept a commission 'within this nation': ibid., iii. 294.

[108] Ibid., ii. 733.

opponent of the protectorate, who had run the Commonwealth's intelligence system, was prepared to pass information about royalist conspiracy to Thurloe, his successor in that post.[109] In Sussex another MP who had exerted great influence in the Rump, Herbert Morley, agreed to assist the Major-General in the county 'to the utmost' as a JP, but not otherwise.[110] He was ready—readier than he wanted his neighbours to know—to aid the government in the raising of seamen and in combatting royalist conspiracy or piracy on the county's coast.[111] Nonetheless the council, which knew his underlying antipathy to the government, excluded him, as it did Scot, from the parliament of 1656.[112]

It is no surprise to find men who by 1659 would be known as 'commonwealths-men'—Scot, Sir Arthur Hesilrige, Sir Henry Vane, Ludlow, John Weaver—in conflict with the protectorate. But the hostility among former rumpers was more widespread. At its heart was not republican but parliamentarian sentiment, of which commitment to kingless rule was an extreme or eccentric form. The protectorate knew of the dislike of its own existence among prominent rumpers who, as far as we can see, never developed a principled opposition to single rule: Valentine Walton,[113] Sir William Brereton of Cheshire,[114] Thomas Fell of Lanca-shire,[115] Robert Wallop, Nicholas Love, and Robert Reynolds of Hampshire.[116] Opposition broadened from the time of the dissolution of the first protectorate parliament in January 1655. Clarendon thought that there had been no greater origin of the civil wars than the 'precipitate dissolution of parliaments' in the 1620s;[117] and that the sudden dissolution of the Short Parliament in 1640 was 'the most immediate cause (that is, the contrary had been the most complete cure) of all that hath since gone amiss'.[118] Both parliaments of the protectorate were dissolved precipitately and acrimoniously, as the Rump and Barebone's and Richard Cromwell's parliament were. The dissolutions of 1655 and 1658, carried out against the advice of at least some of Cromwell's councillors and confidants, were heavy blows to the regime.

Until January 1655 there was a chance that, albeit in a revised form, the Instrument of Government could acquire parliamentary sanction. After it the government was cast back on the military authority that had brought it into being. One rumper who took his stand was the judge Francis Thorpe. He had opposed the regicide, but in March 1649 had delighted the Rump by declaring on its behalf that the people

---

[109] Ibid., iii. 350, v. 711.

[110] Ibid., iii. 161; cf. below, p. 259 (on the rumper Richard Norton).

[111] Ibid., iii. 369, iv. 549, 573–4. On Morley, and the conduct of Sussex MPs associated with him, see Anthony Fletcher, *A County Community in Peace and War: Sussex 1600–1660* (1975).

[112] *TSP*, v. 490.

[113] Peter Gaunt, 'The Councils of the Protectorate', Univ. of Exeter Ph.D. thesis (1983), p. 129; cf. *TSP*, vii. 587.

[114] *TSP*, v. 313.

[115] Ibid., iv. 423.

[116] Andrew Coleby, *Central Government and the Localities: Hampshire 1649–1689* (Cambridge, 1987), pp. 72, 78.

[117] *CH*, i. 5.

[118] Ibid., i. 103, 182–3.

were 'the original of all just power'.[119] Now he refused to implement Cromwell's treason ordinance, was dismissed, and became a sturdy opponent of the regime.[120] Another protesting rumper was Cromwell's former friend Sir Peter Wentworth,[121] who had collectors of non-parliamentary taxation arrested in his native Warwickshire, and who was summoned to Whitehall for his pains. There—according to our garbled but here again essentially reliable source, Edmund Ludlow's *Memoirs*—he told Cromwell to his face that 'by the law of England no money ought to be levied upon the people without their consent in parliament'.[122] How could John Hampden, had he still been alive, not have concurred? The rumper Lord Grey of Groby, who had stood at Colonel Pride's side during the purge of 1648, was now arrested for conspiring against the protectorate. There was a more substantial figure—not a rumper—among the politicians disaffected under the protectorate.[123] Sir Thomas Fairfax, who had accepted the rule of the Rump in 1649, would collude with former rumpers in Richard Cromwell's parliament, where, conspicuously, he 'allways' sat at the side of Sir Arthur Hesilrige.[124] In that assembly he took his stand, as MPs had done in 1642, against the ceding of the control of the militia to the ruler.[125] In December 1657 Fairfax was reported to have declared that 'since the dissolving' of the Long Parliament in 1653, 'which was broke up wrongfully, there was nothing but shifting and a kind of confusion'.[126]

The military origins of the protectorate plagued its quest for settlement. On the ninth day of its first parliament, 12 September 1654, the protector, dismayed by the assembly's opposition to the Instrument of Government, forcibly purged the Commons. Members who wished to resume their seats were required to subscribe to a loosely worded 'Recognition' that engaged them to fidelity to the protector and to acceptance of the government 'as it is settled in a single person and a parliament'. In one sense the purge was successful. In the opening days of the parliament, Cromwell had been opposed by two formidable sets of politicians. There were the leading Presbyterians, at their head John Birch, John Bulkeley, and Sir Richard Onslow, men who had been imprisoned at Pride's Purge. And there were the rumpers, headed by Hesilrige and Scot, who had been forcibly expelled in 1653. In the initial sessions of the parliament the two groups attacked the Instrument. The purge of 12 September removed most of the hardline rumpers.[127] The event was in

---

[119]   *ODNB*: Francis Thorpe; see too below, p. 284.

[120]   S. R. Gardiner, *History of the Commonwealth and Protectorate*, 4 vols (repr., New York, 1965), iii. 298–9. (The breach came only in 1655. Thorpe had been 'suspended' from the judicial circuit in February 1654, but only because the government had other work for him: *CSPD 1653–44*, pp. 373, 407, 412. He was reappointed to the circuit in November 1654.)

[121]   Abbott, i. 346.

[122]   *Ludlow's Memoirs*, i. 414.

[123]   Ibid., i. 414; Gardiner, *History of the Commonwealth and Protectorate*, iii. 226–7, 229, 269.

[124]   BL Add. MS 5138, pp. 118, 128; *Burton*, iii. 48; *TSP*, vii. 615–16.

[125]   *Burton*, iii. 273.

[126]   *TSP*, vi. 706, vii. 84. When parliamentary rule was restored in May 1659 Fairfax was appointed to the council of state, though he did not take his seat (*CSPD 1658–9*, pp. xxiv, 349; *1659–60*, pp. xxiii–xxv) and we cannot tell whether he agreed to the appointment.

[127]   This can be deduced from the names of members which appear, or do not appear, in the *Journal of the House of Commons* thereafter. The only significant exception was Herbert Morley.

a sense the opposite of Pride's Purge, for this time it was the Presbyterians who survived. They were ready to negotiate with Cromwell, as in 1648 they had been willing to negotiate with Charles I.

Yet no more than the rumpers who had decided to return to parliament after the regicide were they enthusiasts for their course. After the purge of September 1654 a number of them withdrew for a time and hesitated before resuming their seats. It was the Presbyterians' turn to face the argument from necessity. Some of them, including John Birch and probably John Bulkeley, returned only after several weeks and after extensive debate among themselves, after which they resolved to 'give way to the present necessity'. The 'sin' of the pledge that was now required of them, decided one of the Presbyterian MPs, lay with its 'imposers', not its 'subscribers'.[128] There was much in the Instrument of Government that the Presbyterians would have wanted to revise even if it had been introduced through some constitutional and civilian mechanism. They contended strongly against the provisions of the document for liberty of conscience and concerning the control and pay of the armed forces. Yet their basic objection was not to the content of the Instrument. It was to its genesis in armed force. The MPs were willing to sanction the general outline of the Instrument, but on one condition: that the authority of the constitution, and of the protector himself, be acknowledged to derive from parliament itself, not from the soldiers who had introduced it. On that premise his rule from December 1653 to September 1654 had been a usurpation, which must be wiped from the record. Only now, through the consent of parliament, would his regime acquire legitimacy. No one in the assembly other than the court party seems to have been impressed by Cromwell's claim that since December 1653 the readiness of judges or justices to sit, or electors to vote, or political organizers in towns or counties to send him addresses, indicated that the nation had consented to his rule.[129]

To make its point the parliament of 1654–5 adopted a fiction. Even as it went through the Instrument, revising its clauses, it affected to be drafting a bill of its own devising. Only a month before the dissolution did the assembly give itself leave 'to consider of the printed document, intituled The Government of the Commonwealth' (the name under which the Instrument had been published).[130] Five years later John Bulkeley told the Commons that, 'in the bowels of it', the Instrument 'took away your rights'. That he had in mind the genesis rather than the content of the Instrument is indicated by his acknowledgement that the constitution itself 'had much good in it'. If only Cromwell and parliament could have agreed on its revision, he intimated, England would have acquired 'a happy government and foundation for posterity'.[131]

---

[128] Henry Ellis, ed., 'Three Letters Illustrative of English History', *Archaeologia* 25 (1832), 139–40; and see *Burton*, i. xxxv–xxxvi.

[129] Abbott, iii. 456–7; *Burton*, i. xxix, xxx.

[130] *CJ* 19 December 1654 (though cf. 14 September 1654).

[131] *Burton*, iii. 107.

Uncompromising assertions of the sovereign rights of parliament were made in the debates of 1654–5. We might expect them to have been voiced solely by Hesilrige's party. It may indeed have been they who, on the day before the purge of September 1654, described 'the former government, by king and parliament', as 'but an usurpation upon the common right'.[132] Perhaps it was they who, in the same debate, insisted that 'the supreme power was originally in the people'; but they were not alone in thinking it.[133] When 'the more moderate men on both sides' turned the debate towards a search for common ground, 'the sense and opinion of the House ran generally' in favour of the principle of parliamentary supremacy. 'The government', it was agreed, 'should be in the parliament and a single person, limited and restrained as the parliament should think fit'.[134] That view prevailed in the Commons after the withdrawal of the rumpers, when the right of parliament to 'limit and restrict' the protector's powers continued to be asserted.[135] Thus when the question arose whether Cromwell's successor should be chosen by parliament or by the executive council of the protectorate, it was 'agreed on all sides, that it was an original fundamental right, inherent in the parliament, to choose their supreme officers'.[136] 'There is no Englishman', it was proclaimed, 'but will rather part with his life, his liberty, his estate... than with the just rights and freedoms of the people'; and 'the legislature was ever in the people'.[137] The Commons decided that any power which the protector might hold to veto legislation would be bestowed as the 'gift' of parliament, though under pressure from the court 'the more moderate' members persuaded the Commons to 'change the word "give" into "declare"'.[138]

Between the parliament of 1654–5 and that of 1656–8 there are significant contrasts.[139] In 1654–5 court and council were mainly united in defence of the Instrument. In 1656–7, the time of the first session of the second protectorate parliament, court and council were split, and the rival parties took the battle to parliament. A number of courtiers and councillors joined the MPs who brought the Remonstrance into the House, and who commanded a strong majority for it. They commanded it because Presbyterians who had opposed the Instrument in 1654 supported the new constitution of 1657, as they would support it again in 1659. Why that contrast? There were differences of content between the Humble Petition and the Instrument of Government, the constitution which the Humble Petition was meant to replace. Yet, like the differences in 1654 between the Instrument and the bill into which the parliament converted it, they were not the nub of the matter. In 1654 and 1657 alike, parliament adopted its own constitution. The contrast lay in the attitude not of MPs but of Cromwell, who was hostile to the first

---

[132] Ibid., i. xxx.
[133] Ibid., i. xxix; below, pp. 284–5.
[134] Ibid., i. xxxii; cf. iii. 142.
[135] Ibid., i. lvi.
[136] Ibid., i. liii.
[137] Ibid., i. lxv; cf. i. xxx–xxxi.
[138] Ibid., i. lxvi–vii; *CJ* 10, 11 November 1654.
[139] The two assemblies are penetratingly analysed in Patrick Little and David L. Smith, *Parliaments and Politics during the Cromwellian Protectorate* (Cambridge, 2007).

parliamentary constitution but welcomed the second. In 1657 the negotiations between parliament and protector were, outwardly at least, as amicable and courtly as in 1654 they had been antagonistic. Yet the principle on which the Presbyterians had taken their stand three years earlier was preserved. The Humble Petition, having reminded the protector that 'the ancient and undoubted liberties and privileges of parliament...are the birthright and inheritance of the people,... wherein every man is interested', pointedly requested 'that you will not break or interrupt the same'.[140] The phrase is testimony to the affinity of feeling which, across such deep differences of political standpoint, bound the successive victims of the army's treatment of parliaments, for 'interruption' was the standard accusatory term for Cromwell's expulsion of the Rump in April 1653.[141]

If, in 1654, MPs denied Cromwell's right to impose his rule on them, in 1657 they questioned, in their discussions with him over parliament's offer of kingship, his right to refuse a constitution which the people's representatives were pressing on him: pressing, moreover, not as a basis for negotiation but to be accepted or rejected in its entirety—though he characteristically contrived to wriggle out of that stipulation. During the talks between Cromwell and the parliamentary delegates, Nathaniel Fiennes, in his capacity as an MP, told Cromwell that the new constitution, while it was modestly called a 'petition', was 'in some sort a petition of right', which Cromwell had an 'obligation' to accept.[142] Sir Charles Wolseley concurred: the protector should 'give the people leave to choose their own servant; that is a due you cannot, you will not certainly deny them'.[143] Perhaps the conduct of Fiennes and Wolseley had its tactical aspect. Councillors of Cromwell, they needed to assure their colleagues in the Commons of their own esteem for parliament's constitutional role. Their master Cromwell, who in 1657 was as concerned not to alienate parliament as in 1654 he had been ready to confront it, was careful to declare himself 'obliged to acquiesce' in parliament's 'determination'[144]—though when it came to it he wriggled again. Yet it was the Commons' perception of its supreme function in the resolution of the nation's constitutional crisis that enjoined his and his councillors' professions of subordination. The MP Sir Richard Onslow, the veteran Presbyterian MP who had been prominent in the opposition to the Instrument of Government in the parliament of 1654, but who in 1657 urged Cromwell to accept kingship, told the protector during the negotiations that, whatever the differences which the civil wars had created about forms of government, 'all ought to submit to the judgement of a parliament'.[145]

Wide as the parliamentary backing for the Humble Petition was, it cannot properly be interpreted as support for the government. It was support for the party within the government which wanted not to entrench the protectorate but to change it: to turn it into a parliamentary, and civilian, monarchy. The Presbyterians

[140] *GD*, p. 449.
[141] *LP*, pp. 41, 341, 343.
[142] *Somers Tracts*, vi. 380.
[143] Ibid., vi. 360, 514.
[144] Abbott, iii. 445. Cf. iii. 453, 468–9; and Sir Henry Vane's recollection in *Burton*, iii. 178.
[145] *Somers Tracts*, vi. 377.

who had opposed the Instrument in 1654, and who backed the Humble Petition in 1657–9, had not, or mostly had not, become courtiers. Sir Richard Onslow was fairly described by Henry Cromwell's agent Anthony Morgan as 'head of the country party for' the Humble Petition.[146] With Presbyterian or country party support—for the two had become hard to distinguish—the Humble Petition secured parliament's consent, even after Cromwell had procured amendments to it. Yet his refusal of the Crown, at the army's behest, showed how little security for civilian and parliamentary rule the new constitution gave. Supporters of the Humble Petition lost heart and hope and their party was broken.[147] In the months before his refusal, the opposing faction, led by Fleetwood and Desborough, had seemed in decline. Cromwell's rejection of the Crown revived its fortunes and thus erected what proved to be a permanent block to the civilianization of the regime.

Two years later Fleetwood and Desborough would bring down Richard Cromwell. To MPs, Richard, being 'without guile or gall',[148] and being unlikely to lead military coups against parliament as his father had done, had much to be said for him as a potential parliamentary monarch, if only—but it proved too big an 'if'—he could control the generals. The rumper and lawyer John Stephens, who had no love for the protectorate,[149] had found the 'little fingers of the Major-Generals . . . heavier than the loins of the greatest tyrant kings that went before'. Now he was 'glad to find one in possession'—Richard—whose instinct was to 'rule according to the law, and not the sword'. Stephens feared, however, that the 'many . . . military persons' in the Other House, who did not share Richard's civilian 'principle', would thwart that aspiration. For that reason Stephens saw no hope from the Humble Petition, and looked instead to a full return to the 'ancient fabrick' of the constitution. But he was outnumbered. The Humble Petition, having been advanced as an anti-military constitution by parliament in 1657, won majority support in the parliament of 1659 on the same ground. It was because of that majority that the army destroyed the assembly.[150]

There had, however, always been an underlying frailty in the movement for the Humble Petition. The parliament that presented it had been summoned by a government which owed its power to a military coup, and which had failed to secure statutory sanction even from the forcibly purged parliament of 1654. A large number of MPs, probably at least a hundred,[151] were excluded from the parliamentary session of 1656–7. It was, as Sir Arthur Hesilrige would remark in 1659, 'a forced parliament, because some of us were forced out; an imperfect parliament, a

---

[146] Gaunt, *Correspondence of Henry Cromwell*, p. 205. Cf. *TSP*, iii. 161, and John Bulkeley's speech in *Burton*, iv. 347.

[147] Firth, *Last Years of the Protectorate*, i. 193–8; Patrick Little, *Lord Broghill and the Cromwellian Union with Ireland and Scotland* (Woodbridge, 2004), pp. 157–63; Fletcher, *County Community in Peace and War*, p. 315; cf. Little and Smith, *Parliaments and Politics*, pp. 107–8.

[148] *Burton*, iii. 132; Little and Smith, *Parliaments and Politics*, p. 160.

[149] Andrew Warmington, *Civil War, Interregnum and Restoration in Gloucestershire 1640–1672* (Woodbridge, 1997), pp. 118, 120.

[150] The point is astutely conveyed by Little and Smith, *Parliaments and Politics*, esp. ch. 7.

[151] Little and Smith, *Parliaments and Politics*, pp. 89–90.

lame parliament, so much dismembered'.[152] That may be one reason why Richard Cromwell's government decided to seek the ratification of the Humble Petition in1659 by what Hesilrige and others allowed to be a 'free parliament'. It was the first parliament of the Interregnum whose membership had not been determined or truncated by the army or its civilian instruments. Hesilrige had been ejected from power in 1653, but his attitude to military intervention was not peculiar to rumpers, as the protest in the Humble Petition against the 'interruption' of 1653 reminds us.[153] A price Cromwell had to pay for securing the new constitution was the readmission in January 1658 of MPs who had been excluded from the first session of the parliament. It was Hesilrige and his ally Scot who exploited that concession, but again the feeling against the exclusion of MPs was much broader.[154] The Humble Petition, observed one member who had not been in the Rump, had 'but a sandy foundation', which the parliament 'should not build upon.... I pray, observe the manner of obtaining that law', when so many members 'were kept out by force'. Besides, he added, the passage of the Humble Petition had depended on the members, largely government nominees, who sat, without statutory warrant, for Ireland and Scotland.[155]

The majority, in their eagerness for a settlement, were ready to wink at those transgressions. MPs liked the Humble Petition in proportion to the extent that they judged it to advance, or to be capable of advancing, the freedoms of parliament and of the subject. They took those liberties to be indispensable to the return of political health and stability. The Presbyterian Griffith Bodurda, who favoured the crowning of Cromwell in 1657,[156] looked to the Humble Petition as 'a foundation.... More is done thereby, than has been done these sixty years for the liberty and privileges of the people.'[157] John Birch, a leader of the opposition to the government in the parliament of 1654, now remembered that 'our parliaments could not be free by the Instrument.... Were it no more, but for this freedom of parliament, I should be in love with the Petition and Advice.'[158] Few were so enthusiastic, or supported the constitution without qualification, but most thought it better than nothing. At least the Humble Petition was a parliamentary document, which took the place of a constitution that originated with the army. It was a start. And it restored some sense of constitutional order. The regime's claim that the protectorate had terminated a period of anarchy was aided by memories, which the government assiduously kept alive, of the social and institutional panic caused by Barebone's Parliament. But as an MP of 1659 said, the rule of the Major-Generals,

[152] *Burton*, iii. 101. Cf. iii. 204–5, iv. 58; BL Add. MS. 5138, p. 133.
[153] Above, p. 249.
[154] Cf. *Burton*, ii. 443; and note the call for 'liberty of admission into the House', as well as for 'free elections', in the preface to a legal treatise, dated in the month before the second session met, which proclaimed the rights and powers of parliament: John Doddridge, *The Several Opinions of Sundry Learned Antiquaries* (1658).
[155] *Burton*, iii. 118–19.
[156] Little and Smith, *Parliaments and Politics*, p. 117.
[157] So says the source, but did the speaker say, or mean, 'sixteen years'? BL Add. MS 15861, fo. 98; *Burton*, ii. 433.
[158] *Burton*, iv. 61.

which 'had no foundation in parliament', had itself brought 'confusion and anarchy'.[159] 'I look upon the Humble Petition', said another member, 'as the ark that has preserved us in the deluge of anarchy and confusion.' So the House should 'allow it, at least, as a ladder for your building. Afford it a standing, until your fabric be finished.'[160] Cromwell claimed to have rescued the nation from the 'arbitrary' government of the Rump,[161] but what, again, could have been more 'arbitrary' than the rule of the Major-Generals? If the Humble Petition were not confirmed, observed an MP in 1659, 'we leave the nation to an arbitary government. Any government is better than no government, and any civil better than a military government.'[162]

Yet when the protectorate fell, and the Humble Petition with it, who lamented their passing? The spirit of the document had always been pragmatic, and with its overthrow by the generals it lost its pragmatic point. In 1659–60, as the revolution disintegrated, there were stray, despairing thoughts of restoring Richard, but there is no sign that those who made the suggestion supposed that the Humble Petition, let alone the Instrument of Government, was recoverable. Thus the only two written constitutions to have been implemented in English history, the first imposed by the new model, the second aborted by it, fell to dust. On Richard's fall and the restoration of the Rump, large numbers of rumpers who had boycotted the protectorate returned, bringing their portion of the displaced generation back with them. William Purefoy of Warwickshire, apparently aged nearly eighty, who had disliked the protectorate and had retreated into semi-retirement under it, returned 'rejuvenated' to Westminster.[163] The lawyer Oliver St John, Oliver Cromwell's cousin and close friend, who had been Hampden's counsel and then a parliamentary grandee both before Pride's Purge and in the Rump, had subsequently given backstairs advice to both protectors. Yet, while he had hesitantly continued to sit as Chief Justice of the Common Pleas, he had evaded the exercise of political office. Cromwell had him appointed as a treasury commissioner,[164] but there is no indication that he took up the post. After the restoration of the Rump in May 1659, by contrast, he served on its council of state.[165]

Other rumpers in the legal profession had responded differently to Cromwell's elevation. The MPs who had served as the Rump's attorney-general and solicitor-general, Edmund Prideaux and William Ellis (or Ellys), remained in their posts. The rewards of office made Prideaux a rich man in the 1650s. He and Ellis were made baronets by Cromwell three weeks before the protector's death.[166] The Rump's three Commissioners of the Great Seal, John Lisle, Sir Thomas Widdrington, and

[159] Ibid., iii. 567.
[160] Ibid., iii. 510.
[161] Abbott, iii. 455; cf. iii. 435, 453; C. C. Weston and J. R. Greenberg, *Subjects and Sovereigns: The Grand Controversy over Legal Sovereignty in Stuart England* (Cambridge, 1981), p. 51.
[162] *Burton*, iv. 56.
[163] Ann Hughes, *Politics and Civil War in Warwickshire, 1620–1660* (Cambridge, 1987) p. 292.
[164] *CSPD 1654*, pp. 284, 411; *1655*, p. 173; *CJ* 24 October 1654.
[165] *CSPD 1658–9*, pp. xxiv, 349; *1659–60*, pp. xxiii–xxv; Warner, *Nicholas Papers*, iv. 150; and see above, pp. 208–9.
[166] Abbott, iv. 866.

Prideaux's friend Bulstrode Whitelocke, held to their posts in December 1653.[167] Nicholas Lechmere of Worcestershire acquired a new legal office; William Lenthall, the former Speaker of the Long Parliament, remained Master of the Rolls and would accept membership of Cromwell's Other House; his son John retained his post as one of the Six Clerks of Chancery and would be knighted by the protector. Lislibone Long, whom Cromwell also knighted,[168] and the brothers Nathaniel and Francis Bacon became the protectorate's Masters of Requests. Roger Hill served the protectorate as a sergeant-at-law.[169] The compliance of all those lawyers with a system of rule whose illegality deterred others might prompt us to cynical reflections on the careerist priorities of their profession in illegal times. Their adaptability was doubtless enhanced by the panic in the legal profession when Barebone's voted to abolish the Court of Chancery, and by the relief when Cromwell's elevation removed that threat. William Lenthall, who in 1654 helped to secure regional support for the new government,[170] reflected after the protector's installation that on the eve of it the nation had stood 'upon the brincke . . . of confusuon and desolation'. In the Rump, the close cooperation of establishment lawyers in the House had been decisive in defeating radical proposals for law reform.[171] The same lawyers had been excluded from Barebone's, almost with disastrous consequences for their profession. In the light of that experience, they did not find voluntary abstinence from protectoral politics an attractive option.

Yet it was not only the vested interests of lawyers that were at stake, at least in their own perception. To lawyers, at least, the law and its survival were deeper considerations than forms of government. Without law there could be neither liberty nor order, and without liberty and order there could be no society or civility.[172] In revolutionary times those priorities might require some flexibility about the occupancy or forms of political power. With other lawyers, William Lenthall saw Cromwell's elevation in December 1653 as a prerequisite, which in the circumstances could only be attained through military means, of the demilitarization of politics. He told himself that the new government, under which 'our laws have ther freedom and countenance and property challenges her own without interruption', would 'produce much happinesse and safety to all . . . and as much settlement to our lawes and liberties'.[173] Thurloe, himself a lawyer, hoped the same. Anticipating words of Cromwell to parliament, he proclaimed at the outset of the protectorate that the regime would bring an end to 'arbitrariness' in government.[174] Perhaps his assertion would have been vindicated had the protector reached agreement with the parliament of 1654 or taken the Crown in 1657. There proved, however,

---

[167] For the friendship see Spalding, *Diary of Bulstrode Whitelocke*, p. 528.

[168] Abbott, iv. 360.

[169] Worcester College Oxford, Clarke MS xxvi, fo. 12ᵛ; Thomas Walkeley, *A New Catalogue of the Dukes . . .* (1658), p. 175; cf. Abbott, iii. 671. Another lawyer-rumper, the regicide William Say, may have been passed over: Bodl., Rawlinson MS a. 10, p. 320.

[170] *Severall Proceedings of State Affaires* 2 March 1654, p. 3673.

[171] Worden, *Rump Parliament*, ch. 6.

[172] Cf. below, p. 384.

[173] Spalding, *Contemporaries of Bulstrode Whitelocke*, p. 166.

[174] Ibid., p. 374.

to be narrow limits to the constitutionalism of the regime introduced by the Instrument of Government. Even before the parliament of 1654–5 had met, William Ellis, the solicitor-general, had to remonstrate against the council's readiness to bypass the legislative claims of parliament.[175]

While it lasted, the Humble Petition offered, to the lawyers as to others, the hope of escape from arbitrariness. Ellis had sat in the Rump, but had had no respect for its military foundation. In January 1649 he moved for a writ of Habeas Corpus on behalf of William Prynne, that fiercely protesting victim of Pride's Purge.[176] Ellis was not involved in 'making the Petition and Advice', but in Richard Cromwell's parliament he urged the Commons to adhere to the new constitution, for 'if we lose this foundation we must go to Major-Generals, and the Instrument of Government, that had no foundation in parliament'.[177] In the same assembly Lislibone Long was ready to overlook scruples about the constitutional basis of the Humble Petition because, as he recalled in 1659, 'there has been peace and tranquillity under' it.[178] His old and close ally Nicholas Lechmere,[179] who with so many lawyers wanted Cromwell to take the Crown in 1657,[180] was similarly indulgent. He looked to the Humble Petition as a basis not only for law but for liberty. In proposing the Humble Petition, he remembered in 1659, MPs

> looked upon their rights as in a bleeding condition. They, in a fair way, did redeem the people's rights. It was a petition of right, and brought the heads of our liberties above the water; so that though that parliament did not fully recover all the rights, they went a great way.

Lechmere's speech 'ran over the Petition and Advice, wherein our rights and liberties were restored as by that Petition of Right'. So the shortcomings of the constitution could be borne with. It 'pretends not to perfection. It says only, it will provide some remedy. It does not totally, but in degrees, restore our liberties. In some places it may be amended.'[181] In the event, like the Rump and Barebone's and the proposed parliamentary constitution of 1654–5, it succumbed to the army. Once it had done so, the lawyers shed no tears for it.

Then there is the Suffolk lawyer Nathaniel Bacon, who in the 1640s had been a prominent administrator in the Eastern Association. Bacon's *An Historicall Discourse of the Uniformity of the Government of England ... with a Vindication of the Antient Way of Parliaments in England*, published in 1647 and followed by a *Continuation* in 1651, has been called 'the English *Franco-Gallia*'.[182] With resourceful scholarship he claimed that Saxon and medieval history showed the

---

[175] Gaunt, '"To Create a Little World"', pp. 121–2.
[176] Underdown, *Pride's Purge*, p. 194.
[177] *Burton*, iii. 566–7.
[178] Ibid., iii. 191.
[179] Worden, *Rump Parliament*, p. 30.
[180] Cf. the annotation on p. 5 of *Twelve Queries Humbly Proposed* (1659), E983[3].
[181] *Burton*, iii. 586–7.
[182] Glenn Burgess, *The Politics of the Ancient Constitution: An Introduction to English Political Thought 1603–1642* (1992), p. 96.

English monarchy to be properly elective and contractual and to be subject to parliamentary supervision, though, he lamented, arbitrary rule had over time eroded those principles. His book would be frequently reprinted, and be invoked by politicians, in the later seventeenth century and the eighteenth.[183] Bacon, like Ellis, had joined the Rump only in early June 1649. He did not become a regular member of it, and would later speak scathingly about its rule.[184] But he also hesitated to endorse the protectorate. After the purge of the parliament of 1654 he waited for a month before resuming his seat.[185] So it seems a surprise to find him acting, by July 1655, as a Master of Requests (though characteristically it is not clear whether he had been formally appointed). He became the only rumper, other than those on the council, to play a bigger part in the government of the protectorate than of the Commonwealth before it. But we can sense what he was up to: he was trying to help change the government from within. Through the crowning of Cromwell, he evidently thought, politics could be freed of military intervention, and a return to medieval, civilian, constitutional principles of rule could be achieved. From early 1656 we can watch him seeking to nudge the regime towards kingship. When Cromwell referred petitions to the council which the Masters of Requests had brought before him, Bacon and his brother Francis, with surreptitious impropriety, directed the documents to 'the', or 'his', 'privy council',[186] the term that would be re-introduced to the constitution only in 1657, when the Humble Petition adopted it in order to give the institution a regal flavour. Nathaniel gave his backing to the Humble Petition 'for peace and unities sake'. Yet in doing so he was seeking, not an enhancement of the protector's powers, but on the contrary the definition and limitation of them by parliament, on what he took to be medieval principles. He wanted to leave the protector no room for negotiation over the new constitution, which Cromwell must either take or leave.[187]

Or there is Bulstrode Whitelocke. Never have a politician's autobiographical self-vindications more calamitously backfired. His readers might have more sympathy

---

[183] *ODNB*: Bacon, Nathaniel; and see *The Works of Lord Bolingbroke*, 4 vols (1841), ii. 140-1.

[184] Underdown, *Pride's Purge*, pp. 367, 373; Worden, *Rump Parliament*, pp. 73, 127; below, p. 277.

[185] Ellis, 'Three Letters Illustrative of English History', p. 140; *CJ* 10 October 1654.

[186] TNA, SP18/126, no. 123, 125; 18/127, no. 19; 18/128, nos 5–6, 56, 78–9, 82; 18/129, nos 25, 57, 69–70, 110; 18/130, nos 77–8. His readiness to adopt that tactic must have caused him unease. For Bacon, who had studied the history of royal councils, believed the 'privy council' to have often been an instrument of prerogative powers, which had been illegitimately exercised at the expense of the 'public council' or parliament. Properly, he maintained, regal councils had been and should be subordinate to parliaments: 'the privy council is never more like itself, than when it is an epitome of the common-council of the kingdom'. The council should perform some of parliament's functions when no parliament was sitting, and its membership should be selected or controlled by parliament, though he recognized that under a public-spirited monarch such as Queen Elizabeth, whose government he thought of as parliamentary, a council might rule well without such formal constraints (Bacon, *Historical and Policical Discourse*, i. 112, 119, 201, ii. viii, 16–21, 80, 83–5, 117–18, 157, and [second pagination] 168–9). The provisions of the Instrument of Government and, to a lesser extent, of the Humble Petition and Advice broadly corresponded to his views on the council (above, p. 197). See too below, n. 212.

[187] BL Add. MS 5138, pp. 254-5; *Burton*, ii. 21. The rumper-lawyer John Stephens, though taking issue with Bacon over the practicality of the Humble Petition, shared his medievalist perspective on it.

with his criticisms of the protectorate had he not disclosed to posterity how tickled he was by the attention and favour Cromwell bestowed on him, and how resentful that he did not bestow more of them.[188] After the dissolution of parliament in 1655, Whitelocke was among the defectors. He resigned, with Sir Thomas Widdrington, as a Commissioner of the Great Seal sooner than implement Cromwell's extra-parliamentary ordinance for the reform of the court of Chancery. For 'to execute that as a law upon mens estates & rights which [I] knew to be no law, but an exorbitant power', 'when I knew that those who made it had no legal power to make a law, . . . would be a betraying of the rights of the people of England, and too much countenancing of an illegal authority'.[189] A month later he accepted a lucrative post as a treasury commissioner instead. There is an unmistakable dimension of self-serving retrospect in his accounts of his pleas to Cromwell to revert to parliamentary and legal courses, as in much else in his recollections of his conduct in the Interregnum. Even so, his dismay at the 'wholly illegall' rule of the Major-Generals, and at other breaches of constitutional methods by the protector, is plain enough.[190]

Like Nathaniel Bacon, Whitelocke explored medieval history in a book that would be put to Whiggish use in the eighteenth century.[191] He also visited the subject in a manuscript 'Historie of the Parlement of England', of 'our great, publique, supreame generall counsell of the nation'.[192] He believed 'the ancient constitution of the polity of our nation' to be 'government . . . by parliament'. That constitution had 'continued to our times, wherein the king was the supreme officer', and had survived the removal of the kingly office. 'Every government which the people chooseth', he maintained, 'is certainly lawful, whether kingly or other.' Bacon would have entirely concurred. With Bacon, too, Whitelocke believed the English monarchy to have been elective, even though both men accepted that the nation, in electing its kings, had come to endorse the practice of hereditary succession.[193] Again with Bacon, Whitelocke favoured mixed forms of government and regarded England's ancient constitution as one. With Bacon he wanted Cromwell to take the Crown and supported the Humble Petition, though he had 'several' objections to its content (which he does not specify).[194] Yet in other circumstances his commitment to parliamentary supremacy, and to the principle of political consent, could assume non-monarchical forms. It could also lead him into different company from that of the other lawyer MPs: most strikingly that of the Leveller John Wildman, with whom he formed a devoted friendship. In 1655, after Cromwell's failure to win parliamentary sanction for the Instrument, Whitelocke received a copy of the vituperative declaration in which Wildman

[188] Bulstrode Whitelocke, *A Journal of the Swedish Embassy*, 2 vols (1855), i. 5, 322, ii. 457; Whitelocke, *Memorials*, iv. 188; Spalding, *Diary of Bulstrode Whitelocke*, pp. 401–2, 414, 438, 464, 476, 477, 478.
[189] Spalding, *Diary of Bulstrode Whitelocke*, p. 407; Whitelocke, *Memorials*, iv. 204.
[190] Spalding, *Diary of Bulstrode Whitelocke*, pp. 400, 415, 417, 477, 485, 488, 489.
[191] Charles Morton, ed., *Whitelockes Notes upon the Kings Writt*, 2 vols (1766), i. xxii.
[192] BL Stowe MS 333.
[193] Whitelocke, *Journal of the Swedish Embassy*, i. 309–11, 330.
[194] Whitelocke, *Memorials*, iv. 289.

sought to incite an armed rising against 'the tyrant Oliver Cromwell' in defence of 'native rights and freedoms': a document, remarked Whitelocke, wherein 'there was too much of truth'.[195] In late 1659 he and Wildman came together to draft 'the form of a free state', a document which proscribed the rule of a single person and adopted the Leveller principle that the people may impose restraints on their delegates in parliament.[196]

Whitelocke was outraged by Cromwell's expulsion of the Rump in 1653, when 'this great parliament' was 'routed' by its 'servants'. He remembered that 'all honest and prudent indifferent men were highly distasted at' the coup,[197] and that in 1659 'many others' had, with him, welcomed the return of the Rump 'for setling the peace and liberty of the nation, and the more because they were upon the first right and foundation of that Long Parliament, which had done so great things'.[198] Yet the army, the creator and destroyer of every regime of the Interregnum, soon expelled the Rump for the second time. If ever in the Puritan Revolution two bodies ought to have been able to find common ground of policy, it was the restored Rump and the army which restored it. Yet they quarrelled vehemently and irreparably over the issue of civilian command of the forces. For the principle of parliamentary supremacy, which in the civil war had been defended against the king, had since 1647 faced an alternative enemy in the new model, ironically a body that in its programme of political reform had done so much to champion it. In 1659–60 the conflict destroyed the revolution. A mortal blow was the second dismissal of the Rump in October 1659. Herbert Morley, the Sussex grandee and prominent rumper who had kept his distance from the protectorate, was moved to an indignation that no opponent of Charles I's treatment of parliaments had surpassed. The army, he and others who challenged its authority alleged, had revived an 'old court design, to affright Englishmen out of their . . . love to a parliament', and out of 'their hereditary and birthright privilege of making their own laws, by which they shall be governed'. In the present crisis there were 'many thousands of our mind who know no help, under God, like that of a parliament', for which 'the spirit of the free-born Englishmen' was yearning.[199]

In 1659–60 accusations of 'sword-government', of rule by 'muskets' and 'red-coats', were hurled at the army by victims of its various purges of parliaments.[200] Now as in 1640, opponents of arbitrary rule looked to parliament as the nation's only salvation and as the instrument of the nation's will, a will which was closer to unity in 1660 than at any point in the intervening twenty years. They turned first to the restoration of the MPs who had been excluded by Colonel Pride, and then to

---

[195] Ibid., iv. 187; Spalding, *Diary of Bulstrode Whitelocke*, p. 401.
[196] Longleat House, Whitelocke MS xxiv, fos 399–400; Spalding, *Contemporaries of Bulstrode Whitelocke*, pp. 459–60. In the Restoration, when he allowed significantly more powers to the Crown than Bacon had done, Whitelocke's writings tended to overlay his earlier views, which are accordingly hard to recover.
[197] Whitelocke, *Memorials*, iv. 6.
[198] Spalding, *Diary of Bulstrode Whitelocke*, p. 514.
[199] *TSP*, vii. 772; cf. vii. 794.
[200] See e.g. ibid., vii. 772–3, 797.

the holding of the free elections that would produce the Convention. In 1642 the cry thrown in Charles I's face in the streets of London, 'Privileges of parliament!', had announced the collapse of his authority in the capital: in 1659–60 the cry for 'a free parliament', or 'a full and free' or 'free and full parliament', set the avalanche of the Restoration in motion. From the time when the Presbyterian MP Sir George Booth appealed during his rising of 1659 for 'a free parliament', the demand for one was widespread. By early 1660 it was 'the desires and hopes and expectation of all';[201] 'the nation in general' was 'lifting up its vows to heaven for a free and full parliament'; now as 'in all times', a free parliament was 'the darling of the nation'.[202] 'A full, and free parliament . . . by the . . . experience of all ages hath been found the best and only expedient for providing remedies to be applied to so great and general mischiefs.'[203]

The demand had its tactical dimension. It suited royalists and Presbyterians, in a skilfully coordinated petitioning campaign, to suspend the differences between the two parties by calling for a parliament whose 'freedom' would allow it to settle the nation as it chose. The term was often used as code for the return, in some form, of the monarchy, a goal which no one dared openly proclaim until shortly before the event, but to which royalists expected a free parliament to lead. Yet when, in February 1660, the prospect of a free parliament prompted the lighting of bonfires of celebration, it was far from clear that the return of kingship would follow. General Monck, whose arrival in London had caused the celebration, was still declaring an unambiguous commitment to the preservation of kingless rule. The Restoration was the restoration of parliament before it was the restoration of the monarchy, which was restored through parliament's choice. During the approach to the Restoration, the exiled court and its English contacts recognized that any propaganda which affronted the public esteem for parliaments would be self-defeating. In that time there were very few arguments for the *iure divino* rights of kings. Equally there were very few pleas for the House of Lords, or demands that the Commons become a lower House again.

Instead there was a great deal of the language of liberty, of Magna Carta, of the Petition of Right, of the privileges of parliament. The freedom of parliaments was 'the great charter of the people of England', and 'whoso toucheth them, toucheth the apple of their eye'. They were 'the bulwarks and defence of our liberties', 'the great patron and guardian of our persons, liberties, and properties'. After the havoc of the civil wars they were 'the only probable means, under God, left us for the rights, freedom, peace and safety', 'the only probable means of our recovery and settlement'.[204] 'Our glory and comfort consist in our privileges and liberties, the inheritance of all the free people of England, the grand privilege of being represented in parliament, without which we are no better than vassals'. 'Only consent of

---

[201] Robert Latham and William Matthews, eds, *The Diary of Samuel Pepys*, 11 vols (1970–83), i. 1.
[202] Thomas Fuller, *A Happy Handfull, or Green Hopes in the Blade* (1660), pp. 15, 32; William Prynne, *A Brief Narrative* (1659), pp. 1–2.
[203] *The Declaration of Sir Charls Coot . . . at Dublin* (1660), p. 5.
[204] Fuller, *Happy Handfull*, pp. 10, 15, 31–2; *The Publick Intelligencer* 9 January 1660, p. 999; Prynne, *Brief Narrative*, pp. 1–2.

the people in a free parliament' could end the troubles.[205] The success of Monck, during the early months of 1660, in moving from apparent support for the Rump to insistence on the Restoration becomes explicable when we remember the common commitment to parliamentary authority that underlay those otherwise opposing positions, and when we recall his own timely demands that 'noe forme of government bee established over these nations butt by parliament', whose 'resolutions' he would ever 'reverence . . . as infallible and sacred'.[206]

In March 1660 Lord Broghill, the Anglo-Irish peer who had been behind the Humble Petition and Advice, looked to a parliamentary solution again, even though he feared that the return of the king would be disastrous to his own interests. For men should 'obey . . . whatever a free parliament will enact'.[207] When, in the previous month, Monck temporarily resisted pressure to restore the members who had been purged in 1648, on the ground that if they were readmitted they would restore the king, one of those who protested was the rumper Richard Norton of Hampshire, once a close friend of Oliver Cromwell. Under the protectorate he had been willing to 'keepe Portsmouth', where he was made governor of the garrison in 1655, 'safe' against a royalist invasion or insurrection,[208] but that was all. To Cromwell's dismay he refused to cooperate with the rule of the Major-Generals,[209] which permanently alienated him from Puritan rule. Now, in 1660, he told Monck that 'freedome of parliament was the just right and interest of the nation, and if they [parliament] thought it fitt to bring in the Turke they ought not to be imposed on to the contrary'.[210] Herbert Morley for his part decided that a parliamentary monarchy, under the Stuart house, would be better than a military republic, as did another rumper who had opposed the single rule of the protectorate, Alexander Popham. Even the most entrenched republicans conceded that in 1660 the nation, however foolishly or wickedly, had consented to the king's return.[211] It had never consented to the military rule of Oliver Cromwell.[212]

[205] *CSPD 1659–60*, pp. 344–5.

[206] Firth, *Clarke Papers*, iv. 22, 98.

[207] *TSP*, vii. 859.

[208] Gaunt, *Correspondence of Henry Cromwell*, p. 202.

[209] *TSP*, iv. 238.

[210] Coleby, *Central Government and the Localities*, p. 81; cf. pp. 21, 33, 71 (though also p. 79); *TSP*, iv. 452; Jason Peacey, 'The Upbringing of Richard Cromwell', in Patrick Little, ed., *Oliver Cromwell: New Perspectives* (Basingstoke, 2009), pp. 250–1.

[211] *LP*, p. 362.

[212] As this book goes to press, I learn that a surreptitiously published tract of 1655, *A Representation of the Late Parliament, in the Year, 1654* (cited above, p. 210 n. 94; below, p.270 n. 89), which indignantly attacked Cromwell's behaviour in that assembly, is attributed in a copy of the Cambridge University Library, in a contemporary hand, to 'Nathaniel Bacon, Master of Requests'. Bacon's views and character are discussed on pp. 255–6 above and in the next chapter. The tract was evidently written by a member of the parliament who sat after the purge of September, as Bacon did; and it conforms to views he expressed elsewhere. If the pamphlet is his, it not only illustrates his own hostility to the regime in 1654–5. It also sharpens the point that the willingness of lawyers to serve the regime, and their endeavours to civilianize it, are far from indicating approval of it. I hope that the arguments of this and the next chapter are afforced by an article which appeared too late for me to make use of it: James S. Hart Jr, 'Rhetoric and Reality: Images of Parliament as Great Council', in Michael J. Braddick and David L. Smith, eds, *The Experience of Revolution in Stuart Britain and Ireland* (Cambridge, 2011), pp. 74–95.

7

Kingship, the Commonwealth, and Single Rule

On 17 March 1649 the Rump, the remnant of the House of Commons left by Pride's Purge four months earlier, abolished the office of king. Two days later it abolished the House of Lords. Two months later it declared England a Commonwealth and Free State.[1] The period of kingless rule that followed is unique in English history. How had it come about?

There had been nothing in the political thought of the age to foretell it. The English had long been used to discussion of the nature of their monarchy. Was it absolute or limited, 'pure' or 'mixed'? Was it answerable to its subjects, or only to God? Could it be legitimately resisted if it degenerated into tyranny? Was the succession hereditary or elective? Over the century and more before the civil wars we find, alongside countless commendations of monarchy as a system of rule, frequent acknowledgements of its problems and disadvantages. Yet its flaws were normally depicted in abstract or general terms, not with particular reference to English traditions or circumstances. There was no visible disposition to question the sanctions of law, time, and custom which rooted and solemnized the kingly office, or the dependence of the nation's order and unity on its existence. No one who went to war in 1642, and few if any at the war's end in 1646, wanted or expected kingship to be abolished. Even the boldest polemicist on parliament's behalf assured his readers that it 'intended' no 'change of government', and that it meant only to restore the 'balance' of the 'mixed' constitution.[2] During the war it would not have been difficult to envisage the deposition of Charles I, a course which some MPs may indeed have favoured,[3] or his death at his enemies' hands. Kings had been deposed and killed before. But their removal had never brought the kingly office into question. Always one king had replaced another.

Early Stuart parliaments saw themselves, not as critics of the 'ancient constitution', but as its defenders and preservers. The constitution was held to guarantee both the rights of the Crown and the liberties of the subject. Under the early Stuarts, who had more to say about the entitlements of the Crown than of the subject, the constitution seemed under threat. Alarmed by statements of councillors

---

[1] *GD*, pp. 384–8.

[2] Blair Worden, '"Wit in a Roundhead": The Dilemma of Marchamont Nedham', in Susan D. Amussen and Mark Kishlansky, eds, *Political Culture and Cultural Politics in Early Modern England: Essays presented to David Underdown* (Manchester, 1995), p. 314.

[3] S. R. Gardiner, *History of the Great Civil War*, 4 vols (1897–8 edn), i. 367–8; M. J. Braddick and Mark Greengrass, eds, 'The Letters of Sir Cheney Culpepper, 1641–1657', *Camden Miscellany* 33 (1996), pp. 142, 192, 304.

and courtiers and divines, MPs feared 'the utter dissolution and destruction' of the 'politic frame and constitution of the commonwealth',[4] or detected a design, as the future Cromwellian councillor Francis Rous put it, 'to alter and subvert the frame and fabric of this estate and commonwealth'.[5] The Grand Remonstrance of 1641 declared parliament's 'most dutiful and faithful intentions and endeavours of restoring and establishing the ancient honour, greatness and security of this Crown and nation'.[6] In 1642 parliament empowered its captain-general, the Earl of Essex, to lead forces to prevent 'the whole frame of the ancient and well-tempered government of this realm' from 'being dissolved and destroyed'.[7] MPs aimed to rescue the monarchy from the discredit which, they alleged, had been wrought by its bid to extend its powers. That goal survived the king's defeat. In 1646 parliament confirmed its devotion to government by the three estates of king, Lords, and Commons and its purpose of 'making' Charles 'a great and happy prince'.[8] In 1648 it would repeatedly restate its commitment to the preservation of the three estates.[9]

The revolution of 1649 looked, as its leaders acknowledged, like an abrupt betrayal of that commitment. They had an answer. As they told the nation, the change of constitution was a 'consequence' of the king's execution on 30 January;[10] and his execution had been made unavoidable by his own actions. Though parliament had been 'confident' in 1646, they explained, that he would accept defeat and submit to the will of his victors, he had proved 'obstinate' in the 'maintenance of his usurped tyranny'.[11] 'Nothing was wanting' in the Commons 'that if possible he might have saved the government and himself with it'. Yet he had 'defied' all 'applications . . . made to him, still imploring him to be reconciled'.[12] His duplicity in negotiation, his treacherous alliance with the Scots, and the insurrections of the second civil war had shown peace and security to be incompatible with his survival. MPs who rejected the treaty that was worked out in the Isle of Wight in the autumn of 1648 maintained that it would have surrendered the cause, political and religious, for which the country had bled.[13] In any case it would not have worked, for the king would have striven to extract himself from it and would have continued to exploit the national sentiment that had swelled in his favour since 1646. The second civil war had proved that 'it was impossible to continue him alive', for 'so long as he was above-ground, in view, there were . . . risings in all places, creating us

[4] Quoted by Glenn Burgess, *Absolute Monarchy and the Stuart Constitution* (New Haven, 1996), p. 48.
[5] Quoted by Glenn Burgess, *The Politics of the Ancient Constitution* (Houndmills, 1992), p. 176.
[6] *GD*, p. 206.
[7] Firth and Rait, i. 14.
[8] *OPH*, xix. 75.
[9] C. C. Weston and J. R. Greenberg, *Subjects and Sovereigns: The Grand Controversy over Legal Sovereignty in Stuart England* (Cambridge, 1981), p. 74.
[10] *OPH*, xix. 360.
[11] Ibid., xix. 76–7.
[12] *Burton*, iii. 173.
[13] Cf. Abbott, iii. 54.

all mischief'.[14] The MPs who had survived Pride's Purge found themselves 'constrained', as 'the last refuge', to 'change their former resolutions' and bring him
to execution.[15] Their predicament, they might have added, was parallel to that
of Elizabeth I in confronting the threat of his grandmother, Mary Queen of Scots,
in 1587.

The prudential considerations that brought Charles to execution merged with
sentiments of higher pitch and intensity. Behind the requirements of 'necessity',
explained regicides, there lay the commands of 'providence',[16] which insisted on
the enactment of divine justice. The punishment of 'delinquents' around the king
had been a principal and consistent parliamentarian war aim. Now the chief
offender himself would be dispatched. Cromwell, though normally reticent, during
the protectorate, about the events of 1648–9, at one point of his rule rejoiced to
remember those divinely appointed developments, which had brought 'offenders to
punishment'—and which had 'also', he added, produced 'the change of government'.[17] Charles had to die because, as he was told at his trial, 'to acquit the guilty is
of equal abomination as to condemn the innocent'.[18] The king's judges and their
accomplices recalled from the Old Testament how God visits vengeance on lands
whose magistrates bear the sword of justice in vain. They were conscious 'how
much we have already provoked and tempted God by the neglect of impartial
justice, in relation to the innocent blood spilt and mischief done in the late wars'.[19]
The king's execution was 'the most comprehensive, impartial, and glorious piece of
justice that ever was acted'.[20] Some went further. They cited Psalm 149 to claim the
honour that awaits God's servants who punish wicked kings.[21] They drew a
'resemblance' between the regicide court and God's 'judging of the world at the
last day by his saints'.[22] 'To have made an agreement' with the king, explained John
Cook, who had been prosecuting counsel at the trial, would have been 'to put a
crown of gold upon him and a crown of thorns upon Jesus Christ', while 'the saving
of him had been the beheading of all holiness and righteousness'.[23] If those
perceptions mocked the earlier readiness of the 'saints', while there had seemed a
prospect of the king's submission, to save and restore him, then that was how
providence worked. God had shown up the man-made calculations of his servants.
From the political fragmentation of 1648, when no one party could control or

[14] *Burton*, iii. 109.
[15] *OPH*, xix. 77; *Burton*, iii. 109.
[16] Bodl., MS Eng. hist. c. 487 (Edmund Ludlow, 'A Voyce from the Watch Tower'), pp. 1083–5;
Ludlow, *Voyce*, pp. 131, 143; *Burton*, iii. 97, 173.
[17] Abbott, iii. 54.
[18] David Iagomarsino and Charles Wood, eds, *The Trial of Charles I: A Documentary History*
(Hanover, NH, 1989), p. 117; Proverbs 17:15.
[19] *OPH*, xix. 35. Cf. *LP*, pp. 179–82; above, pp. 57–8.
[20] John Cook, *King Charls his Case* (1649), p. 39.
[21] Ludlow, *Voyce*, pp. 138, 234; Bodl., MS Eng. hist. c. 487, p. 1084.
[22] Ludlow, *Voyce*, p. 234; Cook, *King Charls his Case*, p. 40; Michael Fixler, *Milton and the Kingdoms of God* (1964), p. 157.
[23] John Cook, *Monarchy, no Creature of God's Making* (1652), ep. ded.

predict events, he had taken his followers into unforeseen circumstances, where his implacable will must be enacted by dauntless means.

In 1649 as in 1642, Charles I's reign was portrayed as an attack on the ancient constitution. He died for deserting and perverting the kingly office. He was convicted as a tyrant who had been a traitor to his people and shed their innocent blood in war.[24] The *Remonstrance* of November 1648 which announced the army's intention of bringing him to justice, and the pronouncements of the purged parliament and of the court it appointed to try him, built their case on an interpretation of the character of the English monarchy which, by itself, would have carried extensive support among the MPs who opposed the trial. In 1625 Charles had been 'admitted', in what the army's *Remonstrance* called a 'mixed state',[25] to rule as a 'limited monarch' with 'limited power'. By his 'trust', his 'office', and his coronation oath, he had been obliged to rule 'according to the law of the land', 'for the good and benefit of his people, and for the preservation of their rights and liberties'.[26] Instead 'the regal power, which was intended for the weal and defence of the people', was 'turned against them'.[27] He had sought 'an unlimited and tyrannical power to rule according to his will'.[28] If he had been allowed to regain his power, 'his monarchy and our slavery' would have been 'absolute, and probably for ever'.[29] His accusers did not think that the perversion of the monarchy had necessarily begun with him. The royal prerogative, they alleged, had made 'encroachments' under his predecessors, though Charles I had 'exceeded' them all 'in the destruction of those whom he was bound to preserve'.[30] But the proceedings against him, though they rested on a firm repudiation of the principle of unaccountable monarchy, implied neither the necessity nor the desirability of abolishing kingship itself.

Not until a week after Charles's execution did the Commons debate the constitutional future. 'The king being dead', as the new rulers accurately told the nation, 'the next consideration fell upon his children'.[31] The steersmen of the revolution of 1649 were committed to the view that the English monarchy was properly elective. They nonetheless hesitated to repudiate the hereditary principle, even though pragmatic considerations might have pointed them to a forthright renunciation of it. The king's two elder sons, Charles Prince of Wales

---

[24] Cf. Martin Dzelzainis, 'Milton and the Regicide', in Paul Hammond and Blair Worden, eds, *John Milton: Life, Writing, Reputation* (Oxford, 2010), pp. 91–105.

[25] *OPH*, xviii. 176.

[26] *GD*, p. 377; *OPH*, xviii. 182.

[27] *OPH*, xviii. 504.

[28] *GD*, p. 377.

[29] *OPH*, xviii. 210.

[30] *GD*, p. 357; *OPH*, xix. 64, 75–6; cf. Bulstrode Whitelocke, *A Journal of the Swedish Embassy*, 2 vols (1855), i. 234–5.

[31] *OPH*, xix. 71. Cf. Whitelocke, *Memorials*, ii. 521–2; Lucy Hutchinson, *Memoirs of the Life of Colonel Hutchinson*, ed. James Sutherland (Oxford, 1973), p. 191. I know of no evidence for the statement of John Morrill and Philip Baker ('Oliver Cromwell, the Regicide and the Sons of Zeruiah', in Jason Peacey, ed., *The Regicides and the Execution of Charles I* [Houndmills, 2001], p. 30) that Cromwell wanted the trial of the king to be deferred until after 'the introduction of the new constitution and the holding of fresh elections'.

and James Duke of York, remained in arms against the parliament and were bent on the recovery of the throne. Their ambitions helped broaden the hatred of Charles I into a hostility to the Stuart 'line' or 'race',[32] 'that cursed family',[33] whose admission to the throne in 1603 had broken biblical advice by the bestowal of the Crown on a foreigner or 'stranger'.[34] That sentiment would be nurtured by government propaganda from 1650, when Charles II's campaign to reclaim the throne by invasion from his native Scotland imperilled the survival of England's new government. Yet the *Remonstrance* of November 1648, in outlining the options that would be available once Charles I had been removed, included among them the enthronement of James Duke of York, the future James II, if he could be brought to submit to terms acceptable to the army. The 'estate and revenue of the Crown' would be 'sequestered, and all the matter of costly pomp or state suspended for a good number of years', while redress was sought for the 'desolations and spoils of the poor people' wrought by the Stuart family; but that punishment would be only temporary.[35] In the previous year the army leaders had offered generous terms to Charles I himself. Their mood was not generous now, but their instinct still pointed them towards the preservation of kingship. Their openness to a Stuart succession was not logically inconsistent with the principle of elective monarchy which the *Remonstrance* proclaimed.[36] Opponents of theories of absolute or divine-right monarchy argued that, insofar as the hereditary principle had prevailed in England, it was a gift of the nation, which for reasons of courtesy and convenience had elected the linear heir, but which might at any time choose not to. If James could be brought to behave as a limited monarch, his election might be a means to heal the nation's wounds. Yet in explaining the change of government in 1649 parliament acknowledged the 'obvious' 'objection . . . of injustice to disinherit those who have a right and title to the Crown'.[37]

Facts, not principles, doomed the Stuart succession. Forty winters later, in 1688–9, when James II lost his throne, an acceptable alternative king was available in his son-in-law, William of Orange. Had there been a comparable candidate in 1649 there would have been no republic. The succession of a Stuart could conceivably have provided a basis for national accommodation in 1649 if Charles I had been merely deposed rather than brought to the block. The hardening of royalist hearts by his execution ruled the possibility out. It would anyway have divided the regicides themselves. At least some of the civilians among them had viewed the army's plan to restore Charles I in 1647 with suspicion. The same men would have been dismayed by the succession of either of his elder sons. An informal meeting of a group of MPs at the end of December 1648, when the king's fate was not yet certain, agreed both that he should not remain on the throne and that neither of his elder sons should succeed him. Some of those present did favour a proposal, of

---

[32] *Burton*, iii. 97; *Somers Tracts*, vi. 100, 103.
[33] *Burton*, iii. 108.
[34] *OPH*, xix. 66; *Somers Tracts*, vi. 175; Ludlow, *Voyce*, p. 225.
[35] *OPH*, xviii. 228–9.
[36] Ibid., xviii. 234.
[37] Ibid., xix. 72.

which we hear other reports around the same time,[38] to enthrone their nine-year-old brother, Henry Duke of Gloucester, who was in parliament's hands and who 'might be educated as [it] should appoint'.[39] Charles himself, just before his death, forbade the duke from compliance. Once Charles was dead, royalists would have viewed an enthroned Henry, as they would have seen an enthroned Prince of Wales or Duke of York, as a prisoner to be freed. The scheme was abandoned. It was floated again three years later, when the royalist cause had been crushed and the new rulers could determine future constitutional arrangements from a position of relative strength. Only then, too, would suggestions for the crowning of Oliver Cromwell be audible. In 1649 the national revulsion against the king's execution, and the fractures and weaknesses and divisions of the parliamentarian cause, would have precluded the crowning of anyone outside the Stuart house.

Even in the absence of an alternative king, the Rump resolved to abolish kingship only after a 'long and quick debate' on 6 and 7 February.[40] The parliament took another six weeks to pass the act of abolition, in a notably thin House from which most of its opponents had absented themselves. If 1649 is the most revolutionary moment in English constitutional history, no revolution has proclaimed itself more cautiously. The act was accompanied by an official *Declaration*, drawn up by the rumper Bulstrode Whitelocke. Even after amendments in the Commons had made it 'much sharper' than he 'had drawn it',[41] it was predominantly defensive in tone. It explained the change of government, as other statements on the Rump's behalf would do, as the sole means to end the civil wars. 'In human probability, as affairs then stood', there was no other 'safe way for a sure peace and prevention of future troubles, and to avoid a succession of misery'.[42] The *Declaration* did not exult in the arrival of kingless rule. Instead it stated that the question 'may justly be admitted' whether parliament should continue kingship or 'change that government'.[43] The Rump, as its apologists explained, had 'not' been 'obliged' to preserve the old forms.[44] The abolition of kingship was 'lawful' and 'not unlawful'.[45] So it was up to opponents of the change to explain why it should 'not' have been carried out.[46] As in vindications of the regicide, 'necessity' was invoked. The Rump, stated the March *Declaration*, had judged the alteration of government 'necessary' and had been 'necessitated' to it.[47] The prominent rumper Sir Henry Vane would recall that he and his colleagues had been 'brought', 'step by

---

[38] David Underdown, *Pride's Purge* (Oxford, 1971), pp. 170, 183.

[39] Whitelocke, *Memorials*, ii. 481. Whitelocke, who compiled his account in retrospect, is a source as problematical as he is essential: Blair Worden, 'The Diary of Bulstrode Whitelocke', *English Historical Review* 108 (1993), pp. 123–34. In this book I have tried to use his evidence discriminatingly, but we must allow for distortions of his memory.

[40] Whitelocke, *Memorials*, ii. 521–2.

[41] Ibid., ii. 555.

[42] *OPH*, xix. 72; cf. xix. 360.

[43] Ibid., xix. 72.

[44] *Mercurius Politicus* 3 October 1650, p. 277.

[45] 'Eleutherius Philodemus', *The Armies Vindication . . . in reply to Mr William Sedgwick* (1649), table of contents and p. 5.

[46] e.g. Whitelocke, *Memorials*, iii. 373.

[47] *OPH*, xix. 64, 75.

step', to that 'necessity'.[48] It was indeed 'the confession on all hands' that 'necessity' had impelled the change of government.[49] Again 'providence' enforced 'necessity'. MPs would remember how 'the providence of God' had 'ordered' the change or had 'conducted' them to it, or how 'it pleased God, by well-known steps, to put a period, and bring that government to a dissolution'.[50] Again providence had confounded human calculation and taken its agents into unknown paths.

Did no one think the abolition of kingship desirable in itself? Rhetorical complaints against the failings of 'princes' had long been heard from writers and politicians who had never thought to propose a change of constitution. Statements made in 1646–8 echoed the rhetoric, but there was now a chance that it would lead to action. In 1648 the MP Sir Thomas Wroth sighed for 'any government rather than that of kings. . . . From devils and kings good Lord deliver me!'[51] Abolition may have been discussed, perhaps around the same time or a little earlier, at a meeting at Cromwell's house in London, where there were probably Levellers present.[52] Two years earlier the Leveller Richard Overton had warned parliament against 'the intolerable inconvenience of having a kingly government', and urged it 'never to have any more' kings.[53] Yet the Levellers soon retreated from that thought. Instead they envisaged the rule of a king who would have no share in the legislative authority. He would be a 'chief officer' or 'public officer' or 'officer of trust',[54] given revocable executive powers by the people's representatives in parliament, who would be his superiors. At Putney in 1647, it is true, there were statements which can be taken as demands for the abolition of king and Lords. Yet their wording was ambiguous. What aroused the Levellers' ire at Putney was not the prospect of the survival of kingship but the misplaced generosity of the peace terms which the army leaders had offered Charles.[55]

The question of kingship was not the Levellers' priority. Their basic concerns were the transformation of the relationship between parliament and electorate and the achievement of social reforms. Once they had got their fellow parliamentarians to pledge themselves to that programme, it would be time enough to think about the future of the monarchy.[56] In the weeks before the regicide they wanted to keep Charles on the throne, at least until their own programme were accepted (though they came round to the abolition of kingship after his death[57]). In those weeks there seems to have been only one tract which argued for a change of government, and

---

[48] *Burton*, iii. 173, 176; BL Add. MS 5138, p. 157; above, p. 242.
[49] *Somers Tracts*, vi. 382, 384. Cf. Marchamont Nedham, *A True State of the Case of the Commonwealth* (1654), pp. 6–8; *Burton*, iii. 173, 222; Whitelocke, *Journal of the Swedish Embassy*, i. 377.
[50] *Burton*, ii. 389, iii. 109, 176 (and see iii. 361). Cf. *OPH*, xix. 35; above, pp. 58–9.
[51] David Underdown, ed., 'The Parliamentary Diary of John Boys', *Bulletin of the Institute of Historical Research* 33 (1966), p. 156; cf. *Burton*, iii. 534.
[52] *Ludlow's Memoirs*, i. 384–5. The passage, which is likely to owe much to adjustments by its posthumous editor, is hard to assess; cf. above, p. 59, and below, n. 328.
[53] D. M. Wolfe, ed., *Leveller Manifestoes of the Puritan Revolution* (repr. 1967), p. 116.
[54] Wolfe, *Leveller Manifestoes*, pp. 113–14, 283, 285.
[55] Firth, *Clarke Papers*, i. 376, 377, 386.
[56] Wolfe, *Leveller Manifestoes*, pp. 203–4.
[57] Whitelocke, *Memorials*, ii. 541.

then in ambivalent terms. It criticized the Levellers for their failure to explain what they would place 'in the room' of what they would 'pull down'.[58]

The phrases 'chief officer' and 'public officer' and 'officer in trust' were taken up by the army leaders and by MPs to signify the kind of king which they, in turn, might allow or have allowed.[59] Since such an 'officer' would be the servant of parliament and would hold power only under its aegis, the question whether or not to appoint one could seem a matter of convenience—of the suitable arrangement of constitutional machinery—rather than of constitutional principle. Proposals would surface during the Interregnum for some English equivalent to the toothless dukes or doges of Venice. They were, however, tentatively and uneasily voiced, and were rarely particularized. Attitudes towards the restriction of regal power had an old ambivalence that would not go away even now that the monarchy had broken down.[60] Often the same people who wanted to curtail bad kings were eager to empower good ones. It had been the job of kings to protect their subjects and maintain public order; to defend and unify the realm and purge its abuses; to dispel faction and check oligarchy; to control or reform the Church; to impress foreigners by their might and by their freedom of political manoeuvre. How could a ruler subordinated to every whim of parliamentary masters meet those obligations? Political thinkers faced a recurrent dilemma: how to deny kings the capacity to do 'hurt' or 'mischief' to their subjects, but at the same time to enable them to do good.[61] Other mental inhibitions held back demands for the emasculation of royal power: the imaginative hold of majesty; the Aristotelian vision of royal excellence; the identification of king or prince with country; above all perhaps the sense, in a society that had known only kingly rule, of peering hazardously into the unknown. Parliamentarians of the Puritan Revolution were equipped with arguments which would have justified, and which logically perhaps demanded, severe restrictions on kingly (or, under Cromwell, protectoral) power, but from which many of them drew back. Even the Levellers seem to have hesitated before the implications of their constitutional principles for the future of the monarchy.

Between Pride's Purge and the regicide, as Whitelocke would remember, 'all men were at a gaze what would be the issue'. 'There were everywhere too many talkers, and few with much judgement.'[62] The parliament did not merely need to find legal foundations for the trial and punishment of the king. It had to anticipate the legal void that would be created by the vacancy of the throne—whether temporary or

---

[58] Philodemus, *Armies Vindication*, p. 50.

[59] *GD*, p. 357; *OPH*, xix. 72; Iagomarsino and Wood, *Trial of Charles I*, p. 120. The portrayal of the king as an 'officer', whose function was to implement the people's will, was not confined to militants and regicides. See e.g. Nathaniel Bacon, *An Historical and Political Discourse* (1760 edn), [part] i. 29; above, pp. 248, 256; Weston and Greenberg, *Subjects and Sovereigns*, p. 64.

[60] Blair Worden, *The Sound of Virtue: Politics in Philip Sidney's 'Arcadia'* (1996), pp. 246–52; *LP*, pp. 231–2.

[61] e.g. Cook, *Monarchy, no Creature*, pp. 129–30; *Burton*, iii. 267, 320 (cf. 334); cf. George Savile, Marquis of Halifax, 'The Character of a Trimmer', in Halifax's *Miscellanies* (1717 ed.), p. 87.

[62] Whitelocke, *Memorials*, ii. 486; cf. Hutchinson, *Life of Colonel Hutchinson*, p. 191.

permanent—after his death.[63] Some thought was given to the question what 'settlement' might follow the proceedings against him,[64] though the issue was overshadowed and repeatedly postponed by the preparations for his trial. There were vague intimations that there might be a 'change of government', though there were also hints that there might not be.[65] At the meeting of MPs in late December where the installation of the Duke of Gloucester was proposed, 'some' of those present 'were wholly against any king at all'.[66]

Among them would surely have been the close allies Henry Marten and Thomas Chaloner, the leading members in the Commons' discussion of its own constitutional position in the weeks on either side of the regicide.[67] They were unconventional figures in that Puritan assembly, for neither of them had a Puritan bone in his body. Neither would have used providentialist arguments. Marten was an old antagonist both of the powers and of the trappings of kingship, a stance that had earned him expulsion from the Commons in 1643, which was lifted only after three years. There is no sign that he or Chaloner had ever argued for the abolition rather than the curtailment of monarchy, but in the crisis that preceded the regicide they would have been the first to say that monarchy was disposable. Chaloner, an intellectually cosmopolitan figure,[68] guided through a thin House on 15 January a declaration explaining the Commons' unwillingness to negotiate further with the king.[69] Its last sentence, which nothing earlier in the document leads its readers to expect, rhetorically announces the House's intention to settle the kingdom 'in a more happy way, by the authority of parliament, than can be expected from the best of kings'. Whether the words were meant to exclude all kingly rule, or merely the rule of any king save on parliament's own terms, was unclear, perhaps deliberately so.[70] At all events, the declaration brought no change in parliament's position. When judgement was passed on Charles twelve days later the Commons forbade, not the appointment of a future king, only the proclamation of one 'without the free consent of the people in parliament'.[71]

Any solution to the constitutional uncertainty would have to satisfy the army. Cromwell and his son-in-law and political partner Henry Ireton, the author of the army's *Remonstrance*, belonged with Marten and Chaloner to a small group of MPs to whom leading constitutional issues were being principally entrusted. The attitude of the army leaders to forms of government was bluntly flexible. Cromwell thought the issue 'but a moral thing. It is but as Paul says "dross and dung in

[63] *CJ* 2, 9, 10, 23, 27 January 1649.
[64] Ibid., 2, 8, 9 January 1649.
[65] Iagomarsino and Wood, *Trial of Charles* I, p. 122; *CPW*, iii. 207; Philodemus, *Armies Vindication*, pp. 3, 20, 61.
[66] Whitelocke, *Memorials*, ii. 481.
[67] *CJ* 19 December 1648, 4, 8, 9, 15, 27, 30 January, 6, 15, 16 February, 7 March 1649.
[68] Blair Worden, 'Classical Republicanism and the Puritan Revolution', in Hugh Lloyd-Jones, Valerie Pearl, and Blair Worden, eds., *History and Imagination. Essays in Honour of H. R. Trevor-Roper* (1981), pp. 184–97; *LP*, pp. 73–5.
[69] *CJ* 15 January 1649; cf. 19 December 1648.
[70] *OPH*, xviii. 513.
[71] *CJ* 27, 30 January 1649.

comparison of Christ".[72] Kingship, in Cromwell's mind, was to be retained or removed as providence should direct and in accordance with his own programme of godly reformation and liberty of conscience. It was always his inclination, so long as practicality allowed, to preserve as broad a power base as possible, and to shun action that would split the Roundhead cause. Perhaps by mid-January, certainly by early February, he had concluded that practicality did not permit the survival of kingship. It was on Cromwell's motion, proposed with Ireton's support, that the House voted for abolition on 7 February.[73] As so often, he had adjusted his will to 'providence and necessity'.[74] There was, he would recall four years later, 'a remarkable imprint of providence' on the change of government.[75] A further four years later he would maintain that 'providence' had 'laid' the title of king 'in the dust'.[76] It was a subject on which he had vacillated, but in February 1649 he was certain of God's will.

Having resolved to abolish kingship, the Rump found arguments for its abolition. The old, and until recently abstract, criticisms of monarchical rule were pressed into service. The act of abolition stated that 'for the most part, use hath been made of the regal power and prerogative to oppress and impoverish and enslave the subject; and that usually and naturally any one person in such power makes it his interest to encroach upon the just freedom and liberty of the people'.[77] The *Declaration* accompanying the act enlarged upon those claims, in passages which can be attributed to Marten and Chaloner, and which are at odds with the mainly defensive tone of the document. They, or some of them, must be the parts of the text which made it 'much sharper'. 'Very few' of England's kings, alleged the *Declaration*, had 'performed that office with righteousness, and due care of their subjects' good'.[78] A government without kings would be 'a better one'.[79] It would free the nation from the expense of royal courts and households, those drains on national prosperity. With an eye to the social and economic discontent which, amid the hardship of the late 1640s, was animating the Leveller cause, the *Declaration* asserted that trade is likelier to flourish under a republic and the poor to be relieved.[80] It also linked kingship to 'the Norman slavery' and to the 'oppression' of the poor by 'great lords'.[81] Those passages, too, are likely to have been composed with the Levellers and their readers in mind. Marten, Edmund Ludlow, and a small number of other MPs were friends of the Levellers.[82]

---

[72] Firth, *Clarke Papers*, i. 370; Philippians 3:8. Cf. *Ludlow's Memoirs*, i. 184–5; above, p. 59.
[73] *Burton*, iii. 97, 123; below, p. 282.
[74] Clement Walker, *Anarchia Anglicana* (1649), p. 54; *LP*, p. 87.
[75] Abbott, iii. 54.
[76] Ibid., iv. 473.
[77] *GD*, p. 385.
[78] *OPH*, xix. 64.
[79] Ibid., xix. 72.
[80] Cf. ibid., xviii. 236.
[81] Ibid., xix. 73, 79.
[82] *CJ* 12 May, 25 October 1649; Jack R. McMichael and Barbara Taft, eds, *The Writings of William Walwyn* (Athens, GA, 1989), pp. 151, 375, 436, 437; William Haller and Godfrey Davies, eds, *The Leveller Tracts 1647–1653* (repr. 1964), pp. 204, 211, 373, 421, 422; Wolfe, *Leveller Manifestoes*, pp. 164, 322; *The Weekly Intelligencer* 26 May 1659, pp. 89–90; John Lilburne, *The Upright Mans*

In principle they broadly supported their programme, even if they differed from them over the realities of power. Outside that circle there can have been little enthusiasm in the Commons for the more socially challenging premises of the manifesto, or even for its more familiar criticisms of monarchy. The *Declaration* would not have passed in a fuller House. Later manifestoes in the parliament's name would rarely if ever repeat its arguments. Polemicists for the regime would sometimes do so, as we shall see, but a wider range of writers on its behalf would turn to the neo-Hobbesian thesis which demanded obedience to any government, whatever its constitutional form, that commands the sword or protects its subjects.[83]

The change of government had been improvised, confused, and at moments perhaps panic-stricken. The new rulers scratched around to discover what forms of diplomatic address were or had been used by other kingless states.[84] They were 'necessitated' to discover how the United Provinces had met the legal and procedural challenges posed by its recent renunciation of Habsburg rule.[85] The Commons also faced what its March *Declaration* acknowledged to be a 'weighty' objection to the change: the nation's regard for its ancient laws and customs as the guarantees and badges of its freedom. Anxiously the regime explained that the alteration would bring amendments only to the forms of the law, not to the substance.[86] Yet the law ran in the king's name. Could it run without him? From 1642 parliament had passed legislation without the king's consent, though it had called its measures 'ordinances' rather than 'acts'. In 1643 it had authorized the use of a new Great Seal. But those had been holding measures, required, as parliament explained, by Charles's desertion of his office. Now that kingship had been abolished, and its powers taken over by the Commons, a new basis both of legislative and of executive authority must be found.[87]

Faced with those challenges the new rulers, as a knowledgeable observer would remember, 'knew not what to do', 'were at a loss what to do'.[88] Their answer was to invent a fiction or 'shadows':[89] 'Keepers of the Liberty of England', or *Custodes Libertatis Angliae*. The term supplied an incorporeal substitute, in the absence of a king, for a *Custos Regni*.[90] The expedient could not prevent the resignation of half the senior judges. And it would leave an awkward question unresolved: just what

---

Vindication (1653), pp. 6–8; Nigel Smith, 'Popular Republicanism in the 1650s: John Streater's "Heroick Mechanics"', in David Armitage, Armand Himy, and Quentin Skinner, eds, *Milton and Republicanism* (Cambridge, 1995), p. 46; below, p. 328 n.

[83] Quentin Skinner, 'Conquest and Consent: Thomas Hobbes and the Engagement Controversy', in G. E. Aylmer, ed., *The Interregnum: The Quest for Settlement* (Houndmills, 1972), pp. 99–120.

[84] *CSPD 1649–50*, pp. 113–17.

[85] *Somers Tracts*, vi. 383.

[86] *OPH*, xix. 78–9.

[87] Whitelocke, *Memorials*, ii. 491.

[88] *Somers Tracts*, vi. 383, 384.

[89] *Burton*, iii. 179; cf. *A Representation concerning the Late Parliament* (1655), p. 2.

[90] Cromwell seems to have been told that the office of protector would be a substitute for the 'Keepers': *Somers Tracts*, vi. 380, 382–3; cf. *GD*, p. 400. Even in March 1660 the 'Keepers' proved indispensable: Firth and Rait, ii. 1463, 1470.

did the act for the abolition of kingship abolish?[91] In its passage through the Commons the measure was described as an act for 'the taking away kingship', and as one for 'the abolishing the kingly office',[92] the title which was given to it on its promulgation. Four months later the Rump would state that the act had 'utterly abolished the said kingly office'.[93] But had it?

The text of the act is perplexingly worded and smacks of confusion in committee. It proscribes, not kingship *tout court*, but the tenure of the office of king by 'any single person'. The nation has 'found by experience, that the office of a king in this nation and Ireland, and to have the power thereof in any single person, is unnecessary, burdensome, and dangerous to the liberty, safety, and public interest of the people'. 'Any one person in such power'—which might be taken to mean undivided or unlimited power?—tends to encroach on the people's liberty 'to promote the setting up of their own will and power above the laws, that so they might enslave these kingdoms to their own lust'. So 'the office of a king in this nation shall not henceforth reside in or be exercised by any single person', and 'no one person whatsoever' is to 'hold the office, style, dignity, power or authority of a king'. It is therefore to be treason to promote 'any one person whatsoever' to that end.[94] It may be that those pronouncements reflect not only a desire to retain the possibility of a return to limited monarchy, but a vain hope of squaring two conflicting sets of legal advice: one arguing that the office of king could be detached both from its title and from the form of government which the king had headed, and could be transferred to the collective magistracy of parliament; the other that it could not, and that the government's power, legislative and executive, must be placed on a new legal foundation.[95] Still, a way forward had been found. Parliament's measures became 'acts' again, and a new Great Seal was made by the sole authority of the Commons. On the day after the decision to abolish kingship a workman was brought into the Commons with his tools, 'who in the face of the House, upon the floor, broke the old Seal in pieces'.[96]

After the passage of the act abolishing kingship on 17 March it took the Commons two more months to produce a further act to establish a government in kingship's place. It was briefly, not to say cursorily, worded. It had no preamble, always a sign of division or irresolution among the Rump's members. Its single sentence summarily announced that 'the people of England' and of its dominions and territories 'are hereby constituted, made, established and confirmed to be a Commonwealth and Free State by the supreme authority of this nation, the representatives of the

[91] The question has been opened up by Alan Cromartie, *Sir Matthew Hale 1609–1676* (Cambridge, 1995), pp. 59–60; idem, *The Constitutionalist Revolution ... 1450–1642* (Cambridge, 2006), pp. 268–9, 273. I am grateful to Professor Cromartie for discussion of the subject.

[92] *CJ* 20 February, 5, 7, 17, 23 March, 2, 7 April 1649.

[93] Firth and Rait, ii. 169.

[94] *GD*, pp. 384–7.

[95] Cf. the statement of Francis Thorpe quoted by Cromartie, *Constitutionalist Revolution*, p. 268 with *Somers Tracts*, vi. 356–7, 372 (where the 'Master of the Rolls' is William Lenthall, who had been Speaker in 1649), 380, 382–3.

[96] Whitelocke, *Memorials*, ii. 523.

people in parliament...and that without king or House of Lords'.[97] Again the phrasing suggests trouble in committee. Why both 'Commonwealth' and 'Free State'? On the face of it the combination was tautological. Political commentary of the sixteenth and seventeenth centuries habitually recognized the existence, past and present, of two kinds of government. The first were kingdoms or monarchies or principalities. The second were variously called commonwealths, free states, free commonwealths, popular governments, popular states, or republics.[98] Occasionally members or supporters of the new government would call it a 'popular government' or 'popular state' or 'popular model',[99] as they would occasionally call it a 'democracy',[100] but the regime's official language shunned those terms.

Initially the Rump did think of calling its government a republic. The pledge of allegiance drawn up for members of the new council of state in February 1649 enjoined their commitment to 'the government of the nation for the future, in way of a republic'.[101] The March *Declaration* vindicated the government of a 'free state' and of a 'republic' (though it did not couple the terms).[102] In the four years ahead, members and supporters of the regime would occasionally refer to it, informally, as a republic.[103] Yet over the same period formal documents rarely if ever used the word (though in its diplomatic proceedings the Rump did translate 'Commonwealth' into *Respublica*, the Latin noun from which it had taken or largely taken its rise). The Rump became wary of 'free state' too.[104] Though the *Declaration* had announced the government's intention to settle the nation 'in the way of a free state',[105] official uses of the term were scarce after the legislation

---

[97] *GD*, p. 388.

[98] The descriptive term 'commonwealths and free states' could occasionally be found: e.g. Pedro Mexia, *The Imperiall History* (1623), p. 865. It is conceivably relevant that Bulstrode Whitelocke, a key figure in the passage of the act of May 1649 (Whitelocke, *Memorials*, iii. 31), knew Mexia's book, which he used in his own writing on politics (BL Stowe MS 333, fos 109–10). The vocabulary that distinguished between monarchies and non-monarchies coexisted with the Aristotelian classification of governments as monarchies, aristocracies, democracies, and their variants.

[99] e.g. *Somers Tracts*, vi. 79; *Burton*, iii. 586.

[100] e.g. *Somers Tracts*, vi. 78. There were also writers who commended the Rump as an aristocracy or compared it to one: *A Discourse between Monarchical and Aristocratical Government* (1649); Cook, *Monarchy, no Creature*, ep. ded.; Fixler, *Milton and the Kingdoms of God*, p. 153.

[101] *GD*, p. 384; *CJ* 20 February 1650.

[102] *OPH*, xix. 63, 72, 75, 76, 79, 80.

[103] e.g. John Hall, *The Grounds and Reasons of Monarchy* (1650), pp. 12, 51; *Somers Tracts*, vi. 168, 175; Whitelocke, *Memorials*, iii. 373.

[104] Conventionally 'free state' had two meanings, both of them derived from the Latin *civitas libera*. In the first, the Rump's meaning, 'free' referred to the freedom of citizens from princely or state control. In the second it meant (as 'free city' did) a political community, whatever its form of rule, that was free from external control (so that, for example, John Donne [*Pseudo-Martyr*, 1610, table of chapters] could assert that the pope had 'no more right over the kingdom of England, than over any other free state whatsoever'). The two meanings tended to overlap, because kingless states, in Switzerland and Italy and the Netherlands, were often threatened by powerful monarchies. The common phrases 'little republic' and 'petty republic' reflect the tendency of overlap too (as perhaps does Milton's hope that every county could become 'a little commonwealth': *CPW*, vii. 383). The conflation of the two kinds of liberty was mocked in chapter 21 of Hobbes's Leviathan, in words that can be compared with: Thomas Bayly, *The Royal Charter Granted unto Kings* (1649), p. 87; *Burton*, iv. 10; Thomas Hobbes, *Behemoth*, ed. Paul Seaward (Oxford, 2010), p. 118.

[105] *OPH*, xix. 63.

of May.[106] Outside parliament the term was favoured by radical spirits, who welcomed the revolution of 1649 as a springboard for more fundamental changes in politics and society, which would produce a 'state . . . really free'.[107] Those men liked, in referring to the present government, either to use 'free state' on its own[108] or to reverse the order of the words to 'Free State and Commonwealth'.[109]

The Rump's own everyday term for the new regime was 'Commonwealth'.[110] Whereas 'free state' and 'republic' intimated that an alien form of rule had been imported, 'commonwealth' had comforting native associations. The English knew they already lived in a commonwealth. For although 'commonwealth' was often used to denote kingless rule, its most frequent meaning—like that of its Latin equivalent *respublica*—was simply a state or country, whatever its form of government. (So, for example, an MP of 1640 could declare that 'we exceed all other commonwealths'.[111]) Until 1649 the Long Parliament normally used 'commonwealth' interchangeably with 'kingdom' (or 'nation' or 'realm'). The Rump had to avoid 'kingdom' (and 'realm'), but 'commonwealth' meaning state, and commonwealth meaning a form of government, cohabited in its official language, so closely that it can be impossible to tell which meaning was intended. Thus the two ideas of nationhood and kingless rule were brought together. On the coinage issued by the new regime, the words 'The Commonwealth of England' were accompanied by the arms of the nation, not by any indication of its form of government.[112]

'Commonwealth' had a second helpful connotation. It—or 'commonweal'— meant the general good or a communal identity. Though 'republic' could mean that too, it rarely did so, whereas the benign resonances of 'commonwealth' were written into English political consciousness. Long-established language voiced men's responsibility to 'serve' the 'commonwealth', to seek its 'benefit' or 'advantage', to

---

[106] Firth and Rait, ii. 566; and see the rumper Francis Rous's *The Bounds & Bonds of Publique Obedience* ([August] 1649), pp. 56–7. The Rump did impose the term on Scotland after its conquest of it: C.S. Terry, *The Cromwellian Union* (Edinburgh, 2002), pp. xxii, 20 ff.; cf. *CJ* 4 October 1653.

[107] *Mercurius Politicus* 25 March 1652, p. 1475.

[108] James Freize, *A Second Why Not* (1649), p. 1; Marchamont Nedham, *The Case of the Commonwealth of England, Stated*, ed. Philip A. Knachel (Charlottesville, Va., 1969), p. 123; *Somers Tracts*, vi. 169, 174; Cook, *Monarchy, no Creature*, ep. ded.; *A Copy of a Letter from an Officer of the Army in Ireland* (n.d.: 1656?), pp. 2, 4, 5, 12; cf. Philodemus, *Armies Vindication*, p. 62.

[109] *MSP*, p. 31; Nedham, *Case of the Commonwealth*, pp. 115, 116; Nedham, *True State*, p. 12; *Copy of a Letter*, p. 6; Thomas N. Corns, Ann Hughes, and David Loewenstein, eds, *The Complete Works of Gerrard Winstanley*, 2 vols (Oxford, 2009), ii. 8; *CJ* 4 October 1653.

[110] Here I bring my trowel to an expanding archaeological site: Phil Withington, *Society in Early Modern England* (2010), pp. 134–68; Mark Knights, 'Towards a Social and Cultural History of Keywords and Concepts by the Early Modern Research Group', *History of Political Thought* 31 (2010), pp. 427–48; Early Modern Research Group, '*Commonwealth*: The Social, Cultural and Conceptual Contexts of an Early Modern Keyword', *Historical Journal* 54 (2011), pp. 659–87. I am grateful to Professor Knights for commenting on a draft of this chapter.

[111] Judith Maltby, ed., *The Short Parliament (1640) Diary of Sir Thomas Aston*, Camden Society, fourth series 35 (1988), p. 121; cf. above, p. 261.

[112] *CJ* 25 April 1649; Sean Kelsey, *Inventing A Republic. The Political Culture of the English Commonwealth, 1649–1653* (Manchester, 1997), pp. 89–92, interestingly notes the 'proliferation' in corporations, under the Rump, of maces bearing the arms of the Commonwealth. I am not convinced that he is right to think of them as 'republican'.

'defend' or 'preserve' it and its 'safety' from 'danger' to it. In 1643 John Milton lamented that men trapped in loveless marriages become 'unserviceable and spiritless to the commonwealth', 'unactive to all public service, dead to the commonwealth'.[113] The Levellers, who liked to draw on the communal associations of 'commonwealth', protested when their enemies sought to make them 'useless and unserviceable to the commonwealth'.[114] The same associations were carried by 'commonwealthsman' or 'commonwealthman'. A commonwealthsman sought and acted for the common or public good: through neighbourliness, or the discharge of a magistrate's or minister's duties, or the design of schemes for social justice or economic improvement, or other manifestations of a consciousness that we live not for ourselves but for our country or fellows.[115] Another meaning of 'commonwealth' denoted the civil as distinct from the spiritual or ecclesiastical sphere of life. So people habitually spoke of 'Church and commonwealth' or 'Church or commonwealth'. Correspondingly the virtues of a commonwealthsman were expected to partner, in the same person, those of a 'Christian' or a 'Church man'.[116]

Until 1649 the king was often described as integral to the commonwealth. 'No commonwealth can be rightly a commonwealth without a king', explained a political commentator of 1600.[117] Yet an alternative descriptive practice presented king and commonwealth as separate beings.[118] There was nothing necessarily confrontational about that perspective. Normally the relationship between the two was mentioned or assessed in either commendatory or neutral terms. Even so, 'commonwealth' was a word that princes needed to watch—rather like 'patriot', which shared some of its resonances. 'A king', it was agreed, 'ought to be called (and so in truth to be) the father and nourisher of the commonwealth.'[119] But what happened if he was not? It was a commonplace, one which James I was 'wont to' endorse,[120] that kings exist for the sake of their subjects, not subjects for the sake of

---

[113] *CPW*, ii. 347, 632.

[114] Haller and Davies, *Leveller Tracts*, p. 278.

[115] e.g. John Ponet, *A Shorte Treatise of Politike Power* (1556; facsimile reprint, 1970), sig. Dvii; [George] *Herbert's Remains* (1652), p. 39; George Whetstone, *The English Myrror* (1586), 'Induction' to 'The Third Booke'; Markku Peltonen, 'Rhetoric and Citizenship in the Monarchical Republic of Queen Elizabeth I', in John F. McDiarmid, ed., *The Monarchical Republic of Early Modern England: Essays in response to Patrick Collinson* (2007), p. 109; Richard Cust, 'Reading for Magistracy: The Mental World of Sir John Newdigate', in ibid., pp. 191–2, 194. The same outlook had informed the thinking of the men known to historians as the 'commonwealth men' or 'commonwealth party' of mid-Tudor England (Whitney R. D. Jones, *The Tudor Commonwealth 1529–1559* [1970], p. 217), but I have not encountered evidence that they used those terms of themselves.

[116] e.g. Lloyd Berry, ed., *John Stubbs's Gaping Gulph* (Charlottesville, Va, 1968), p. 53; *Herbert's Remains*, p. 39; Samuel Fawcet, *A Seasonable Sermon for these Troublesome Times* (1641), p. 4; Richard Baxter, *A Holy Commonwealth*, ed. William Lamont (Cambridge, 1994), p. 158; George Sykes, *The Life and Death of Sir Henry Vane Kt.* (1662), p. 113.

[117] John Floyd, *The Picture of a Perfit Common Wealth* (1600), p. 2; cf. John Doddridge, *The Several Opinions of Sundry Learned Antiquaries* (1658), p. 96: 'king, and ... country ... whose weals cannot be separated'.

[118] e.g. Dale Hoak, 'Sir William Cecil, Sir Thomas Smith, and the Monarchical Republic of Tudor England', in McDiarmid, *Monarchical Republic*, p. 39; Cromartie, *Constitutionalist Revolution*, p. 38.

[119] Ralph Holinshed, *The Second Volume of Chronicles* (1587), p. 267.

[120] *Burton*, iv. 119.

kings. On that premise John Ponet had written under Queen Mary that 'men ought to have more respects to their country than to the prince: to the common wealth than to any single person. For the country and common wealth is a degree above the king'.[121] The parliaments of Charles I called his 'evil counsellors' and other instruments of his power 'enemies'—or 'Achans'[122]—of 'the commonwealth'.[123] 'Great liberty', complained a royal declaration penned by Clarendon, 'was used in voting men enemies of the commonwealth (a phrase his majesty scarce understood)'; it was 'a brand newly found out (and of no legal signification) to incense the people by, and with which the simplicity of former times was not acquainted'.[124] Although the tactic was occasionally returned on the parliamentarians, royalists of the civil war seem in the main to have been wary of the word 'commonwealth'.[125] The king was called an 'enemy to the commonwealth' at his trial. The derisive laughter with which he greeted the accusations against him may have been provoked at least partly by that phrase.[126]

In the civil war, parliament gave encouragement to its supporters by acknowledging their 'good service' to 'the commonwealth'.[127] The new rulers of 1649 annexed such sentiments to the change of government.[128] A conventional view of kingship, which went back to Aristotle, held that true kings serve the common good, tyrants their own interests. England's monarchs, asserted the Rump, had failed that test. They, Charles most of all, had preferred their own 'particular' or 'selfish' interests to 'the public interest'. The new government promised to reverse that priority, so that 'the people's welfare' would be 'preferred before the particular interests of them that govern'. Now the nation would find rulers committed to 'the good of the commonwealth', 'the good of the people', 'the good of the nation', 'the public good', 'the good of the whole', 'the common good, which is the true and ultimate end of government'.[129] The termination of kingship 'being for the good of the commonwealth, no commoner of England can justly repine at' it.[130]

Such pledges aroused unrealistic expectations. The regicide was a deracinating experience, which, if it induced desolation in some quarters, raised heady hopes in others. Here the Rump's propaganda proved all too effective. Reformers who unavailingly claimed that the common good required extensive law reform, or an

---

[121] Ponet, *Short Treatise*, sig. Dvii.

[122] *CH*, i. 511.

[123] *GD*, pp. 3, 83; *CH*, i. 503, 508, 551, iii. 29, 145.

[124] Ibid., iii. 68, 201.

[125] Withington, *Society in Early Modern England*, p. 154.

[126] Iagomarsino and Wood, *Trial of Charles I*, pp. 63–4, 108. Tyranny had long been represented as the adversary of the 'commonwealth' or 'commonweal' (e.g. Thomas Starkey, *A Dialogue between Reginald Pole and Thomas Lupset* [1948], pp. 102, 110–11). From 1649 it would be said that where there was tyranny there was no commonwealth: Jonathan Scott, *Commonwealth Principles: Republican Writing of the English Revolution* (Cambridge, 2004), p. 117; William Walker, *'Paradise Lost' and Republican Tradition* (Turnhout, 2009), pp. 68–9.

[127] *CH*, iii. 179; Firth and Rait, i. 263, 1218; cf. i. 431.

[128] e.g. *CJ* 24 February 1649, 4 October 1650, 18 March 1651; Firth and Rait, ii. 555.

[129] *OPH*, xviii. 505, 539 (cf. 173, 174), xix. 7, 54, 64, 152, 188; *GD*, p. 382. Cf. *Burton*, iii. 109–10.

[130] *OPH*, xix. 77.

end to tithes or monopolies or other forms of social oppression, or a fresh approach to poor relief, would protest that the change of government had proved to be merely 'notional'; that it had achieved not 'a full commonwealth's freedom' but only the 'name' of a 'commonwealth'.[131] 'Hitherto in the change of our government nothing material has yet been done', complained one reformer to Cromwell in 1650, 'but a taking the head of[f] monarchy and placing upon the body or trunk of it the name or title of a commonwealth, a name applicable to all forms of government, and contained under the former'.[132] In the same year Cromwell himself, who was always alert to the argumentative possibilities of the term commonwealth, delighted his more radical followers by reminding the Rump that 'if there be any one that makes many poor to make a few rich, that suits not a commonwealth'.[133] In writing to the Commons the following year he urged 'that the common weal may more and more be sought, and justice done impartially'.[134] In 1656 he suggested to parliament that 'commonwealths men', whose opposition to his own government he represented as disdain for the common good, had 'little enough' justification for claiming the label.[135] In the same year the political thinker James Harrington questioned whether the 'commonwealthsmen' who wanted to restore the Rump 'really intended the public', for otherwise they 'are not truly such' but rather 'hypocrite[s], and the worst of men'.[136]

The Rump's deficiencies as an instrument of public good were likewise assailed by royalists and Presbyterians, who maintained that 'a commonwealth', as a form of government, 'was never for the common weal',[137] or that 'the commonwealth . . . is now become the private wealth of every particular saint'.[138] If the Rump's assertion of parliamentary sovereignty in January 1649 was in itself in tune with widespread parliamentarian sentiment, the uses to which that sovereignty was applied provoked an antagonism no less broad. First there were the military origins of the Rump's rule. Then there were the features of that rule. The regicide; the cost, intrusiveness, and military basis of the regime; the allegations against rumpers and office-holders of peculation and other forms of financial self-seeking; ecclesiastical anarchy; the cries for radical reforms in the press; the same demands from low-born and strident officials and commissioners to whom the removal of a large proportion of the parliamentary party from central and local government had given a new prominence; the prolongation and intensification of the divisions of civil war, which the

[131] Haller and Davies, *Leveller Tracts*, p. 277; Corns et al., *Complete Works of Gerrard Winstanley*, ii. 287; *Mercurius Politicus* 2 June 1659, p. 471. Cf. Abbott, iii. 53–4; Ruth E. Mayers, *1659: The Crisis of the Commonwealth* (Woodbridge, 2004), pp. 151–2. The complaints about the 'name' of a commonwealth echoed Sir Thomas More, *Utopia*, trans. Ralph Robinson (repr. 1859), pp. 157, 159. Classical authors may lie behind it too: cf. Walker, *'Paradise Lost' and Republican Tradition*, pp. 163, 209.
[132] *MSP*, p. 31; cf. William Sprigge, *A Modest Plea, for an Equal Commonwealth* (1659), preface.
[133] Cf. Abbott, ii. 325; cf. e.g. *Ludlow's Memoirs*, i. 254.
[134] Abbott, ii. 433; cf. ii. 73, iii. 53–4.
[135] Ibid., iv. 267.
[136] James Harrington, *'The Commonwealth of Oceana' and 'A System of Politics'*, ed. J. G. A. Pocock (Cambridge, 1992), p. 62.
[137] *Burton*, iii. 262.
[138] Walker, *Anarchia Anglicana*, p. 212.

peace negotiations terminated by Pride's Purge had been meant to end: those aspects of the Rump's rule made 'commonwealth', as a term for a form of government, unpalatable to those who resented them. In Richard Cromwell's parliament in 1659 the thought of the rule of 'a commonwealth' was 'odious' to MPs.[139] Nathaniel Bacon, who had sat in the Rump, now reminded the House 'of the tyranny of a commonwealth. Look into Carthage; Athens.'[140] Yet whereas friends of kingship derided the Rump's adoption, in the 'unfree state' which it had created, of the phrase 'free state',[141] it was for the regime's perversion of the word 'commonwealth', not for its use of the term itself, that they attacked it. However distasteful the Rump's rule made the word, it would not necessarily have sounded alarming at the outset of its government in 1649. It was the most unrevolutionary term available. Although, when used of a form of government, 'commonwealth' normally indicated the absence of kingship, and although the Rump itself created 'a Commonwealth . . . without king or House of Lords', another usage of the noun allowed a 'commonwealth', as a form of government, to be presided over by a king.[142] Nathaniel Bacon, in a treatise of 1647–51, stated that since the time of the Saxon constitution, that 'beautiful composure', England had been a healthy kind of 'commonwealth', a 'mixed commonwealth' with a king. He thought of the English 'commonwealth' in classical terms, as a mixture of the three components of government, monarchy, aristocracy and democracy, whose English counterparts were the king, Lords, and Commons. 'Democracy' was properly its predominant form,[143] though to his regret it had often been overborne by aristocracy or monarchy.[144]

[139] *Burton*, iii. 283; cf. iii. 157, 344, 362, iv. 10, 185.
[140] Ibid., iii. 123; BL Add. MS 5138, p. 136.
[141] Blair Worden, 'The Politics of Marvell's Horatian Ode', *Historical Journal* 27 (1984), pp. 543–4; cf. *OPH*, xix. 223. There was similar mockery of the term 'Keepers of the Liberty of England', which royalists judged appropriate to a country that had become a prison.
[142] The same, admittedly, was (or became) true of 'free state'. A writer of 1652, seeking the introduction of a monarchical element into the constitution, told of 'the good use may be made of kings in a free state' (*Somers Tracts*, vi. 174). After the civil wars the view would emerge that England was a free state under its kings: *Whitelockes Notes upon the Kings Writt*, 2 vols (1766), ii. 343; Scott, *Commonwealth Principles*, p. 352. The view would become commonplace in the eighteenth century.
[143] Bacon, *Historical and Political Discourse*, i. 138.
[144] Because of disagreements between, or uncertainty on the parts of, the two diarists from whose accounts the third volume of *Burton* is compiled (BL Add. MS 5138; Add. MSS 15861–3), we cannot always be sure whether it was Nathaniel or his brother Francis who delivered speeches recorded under their surname in Richard Cromwell's parliament of 1659. Nathaniel is usually the likely answer; and if or when it is the wrong one, then we can say that Francis's views and perspectives were in close accord with those set out in Nathaniel's treatise on English history. One or other of the brothers described the Humble Petition as 'not so much a new constitution, as a reviving of the old with taking off exorbitances'; maintained that 'the people of England have a right to the single person and two houses of parliament, and it cannot be taken away without their consent'; and asserted that 'it is our undoubted constitution to be governed by a single person and a parliament. There was never any other government . . . in England' (*Burton*, iii. 122, 357. Cf. iv. 34; BL Add MS 5138, p. 136). Nathaniel's support for the Humble Petition, and for the principle of mixed monarchy, shows the compatibility of those positions with a conviction that 'the supreme power' lies in 'the people' and its representatives (Bacon, *Historical and Political Discourse*, e.g. i. 8, ii. 75). His book not only provided a series of historical illustrations—on such subjects as the royal veto, the control of the militia, and the right of parliament to legislate in the king's absence—which justified, by a series of (mostly unstated) analogies, the resistance by parliament, 'the representative body of the kingdom' (i. 76, 131), to Charles I in the

The protectorate, which Bacon served as a Master of Requests, replaced the rule of the unicameral Rump by the principle of a single person and parliament. Yet, like the Rump, it termed its rule a 'commonwealth' (though it eschewed the Rump's 'free state'). The Rump had called itself 'the Parliament of the Commonwealth': Cromwell's title was 'Lord Protector of the Commonwealth'.[145] The choice of phrase, as MPs acknowledged, offered a counterweight to the charges of absolute and arbitrary rule that were heaped on him.[146] The parliament of 1654, though it had many objections to the constitutional foundation of the protectorate, endorsed that title. So did the parliament of 1657 after he had refused its offer of the Crown.[147]

No more than the Commons before 1649 did the Rump seek constitutional innovation. Few of its supporters did either. If for the time being we leave aside James Harrington and his many imitators, the politics and political thought of the Interregnum were virtually barren of novel constitutional design. From time to time we hear that individuals are drawing up innovative proposals that will soon be completed or published or be in the mail, but they came to nothing.[148] Constitutional novelty was commonly associated with Platonic or utopian fantasy.[149] The Rump's aim in establishing the 'Commonwealth and Free State' was not to create a new form of government. It was to preserve what was left of the old, the remnant of the Commons which had survived Pride's Purge.

The premises on which the Rump would base its claim to rule were first articulated as a constitutional basis for the trial and execution of the king. To proceed against him it had to bypass not only the royal veto but the House of Lords, where Pride's Purge and the prospective trial had provoked deep antagonism, and where few members continued to sit. The Commons met that challenge

---

civil war (e.g. i. 95–6, 127–9, 174, 187–8, ii. 9, 60, 86, 102–6, 168–72). It also made claims which corresponded to ones made by the king's judges in defence of the regicide. Bacon insists, for example, on the right of subjects to bring to account kings who break the conditions on which they have been elected (i. 200–1), and on the definition of treason as an offence against the people rather than against kings (i. 61, 121, ii. 45, 149–50).

[145] *GD*, p. 405. The full title was 'Lord Protector of the Commonwealth of England, Scotland and Ireland, and the dominions thereunto belonging'. That was a sleight of hand, for the legislation for the union of the three nations after Cromwell's conquest of Ireland and Scotland had not been completed. The act abolishing kingship in March 1649 had spoken (amid characteristically confused wording on the subject) of 'the Commonwealth of England and Ireland', and the arms of the new regime had carried an Irish harp alongside the cross of St George. Yet subsequent legislation and pronouncements by the Rump assumed or implied that Ireland was not part of the Commonwealth. *GD*, p. 387; *OPH*, xix. 62, 108; Firth and Rait, ii. 20, 559, 598 (cf. ii. 933, 935); *CJ* 4 October 1650 (cf. 25 April 1649, 8, 19 November 1656).

[146] *Burton*, iii. 267, 321, iv. 143; *LP*, pp. 143–4.

[147] *GD*, pp. 427, 448, 459; cf. e.g. *CJ* 10 November 1656.

[148] *MSP*, pp. 32–3; Blair Worden, 'Harrington's "Oceana": Origins and Aftermath, 1651–1660', in David Wootton, ed., *Republicanism, Liberty, and Commercial Society* (Stanford, 1994), p. 118. Cf. Philodemus, *Armies Vindication*, p. 64; Henry Stubbe, *The Commonwealth of Oceana put in the Ballance* (1660), preface.

[149] *Burton*, iii. 144; CJ 25 January 1658; Walker, *Anarchia Anglicana*, p. 14; Haller and Davies, *Leveller Tracts*, p. 120; Baxter, *Holy Commonwealth*, p. 126; Mayers, *1659*, p. 16.

with a clarity and candour that stand in contrast to its confused and gingerly moves against the office of king. On 4 January the House declared, without a contested vote, that 'the people are, under God, the original of all just power'; that the Commons, 'being chosen by, and representing the people, have the supreme power in this nation'; and that whatever the Commons 'enacted, or declared for law . . . hath the force of law', even if 'the consent of king, or House of Peers, be not had thereunto'.[150] Those assertions enshrined the view of Henry Marten, to whom the power of legislation derived solely from the people and was 'the supreme badge of supreme power'.[151] They were an ironic triumph for the Levellers, to whom the supreme power of the Commons was likewise an article of faith: ironic because the Leveller leaders were bitterly opposed to Pride's Purge and the establishment of the new government. When, earlier, petitions of the Levellers had addressed the Commons as the supreme power of the nation, the House had voted the phrase seditious.[152] The Levellers wanted a new contract between parliament and electorate. By contrast the Rump's resolutions of 4 January, which declared that 'all the people of England are concluded by' the Commons' votes of that day, imposed the proceedings against the king on the electorate whether it liked them or not[153]— even though most of the constituencies were not represented between Pride's Purge and the regicide, when the House struggled to maintain its quorum of forty members.

The Moderate, a Leveller newsbook, viewed the resolutions of 4 January with understandable scepticism. 'How many were of this mind a month ago', it asked, 'beside Henry Marten and seven more?'[154] Seven likely names indeed come to mind: Chaloner, Edmund Ludlow, Thomas Scot,[155] Lord Grey of Groby (who had helped to carry out Pride's Purge),[156] Alexander Rigby,[157] Cornelius Holland,[158] and Sir Thomas Wroth.[159] Their viewpoint now found its moment. 'The power and supreme authority of the Commons of England', the president of the regicide court, John Bradshaw, told the king, was the 'root' of the proceedings against him, 'which this court will

---

[150] *CJ* 4 January 1649.
[151] C. M. Williams, 'The Anatomy of a Radical Gentleman: Henry Marten', in Donald Pennington and Keith Thomas, eds., *Puritans and Revolutionaries: Essays in Seventeenth-Century History presented to Christopher Hill* (Oxford, 1978), p. 130.
[152] *OPH*, xix. 44–5.
[153] Even so, the notion that MPs were 'delegates' of the people was widely accepted by members: *OPH*, xix. 35; Williams, 'Anatomy of a Radical Gentleman', p. 131; Sykes, *Life and Death of Sir Henry Vane*, p. 98; *CJ* 8 October 1659; Ruth Spalding, *Contemporaries of Bulstrode Whitelocke* (Oxford, 1990), p. 460; cf. *Burton*, iii. 101–2. Note too the Rump's acknowledgement in March 1649 that governments properly derive from 'Agreement[s] of the People': *OPH*, xix. 64.
[154] *The Moderate* 9 January 1649, p. 245.
[155] *CJ* 19 December 1648, 4 January, 16 February, 7 March 1649; *Burton*, ii. 387–90, iii. 108–9, 219.
[156] *CJ* 6 February 1649; Maurice Ashley, *John Wildman* (1947), p. 88.
[157] Haller and Davies, *Leveller Tracts*, pp. 211, 421, 448; Blair Worden, *The Rump Parliament 1648–1653* (Cambridge, repr. 1977), p. 39.
[158] Haller and Davies, *Leveller Tracts*, pp. 206, 210, 414, 420, 421, 448.
[159] Above, p. 266; *Burton*, iii. 413–14.

not admit a debate of'.[160] The doctrine broke sharply with the Long Parliament's previous commitment to restore the ancient constitution of king, Lords, and Commons. A majority of its members refused to accept it. They declined to sit in the Rump or were excluded from it. Yet there were well over a hundred other members who, having withdrawn or been excluded, and having kept clear of the regicide, returned to the Commons after it and accepted the premises of the votes of 4 January as the basis of the Rump's rule for the next four years. A number of them served not merely as MPs, a position which required only a limited sense of collective responsibility, but as members of the executive council of state. How did they persuade themselves to comply with the revolution of 1649?

Stark as it was, the parliament's change of constitutional stance in 1649 obscures a degree of continuity. From one perspective the real revolution had been accomplished in 1642, by the parliament's novel assertion that the Crown had no 'negative voice' or veto,[161] and by its complementary insistence, in vindicating its struggle with the king, on its own representative character.[162] The parliament for which sovereignty was claimed (in a range of theoretical formulations) in 1642 and in the civil war consisted of king and Lords as well as Commons. Yet the king had removed himself, and there was an awkward question for the upper House too. If the king had no veto because he did not represent the people, why did the Lords have one? 'How a double negative' should rest in king and Lords, wrote Nathaniel Bacon, 'is to me a mystery. . . . For it is beyond reach, why that which is once by the representative of the people determined . . . should be dis-determined by one or a few, whose counsels are for the most part . . . grounded upon private inconvenience.' Though he was apparently in favour of a second chamber of some kind, he always regarded the lower House as the constitutionally superior body. He did not lament the passing of the Lords in 1649.[163] The parliamentarian Sir Cheney Culpepper of Kent, who detested the upper House and saw the Commons as the 'natural mother' or 'first parent of all government',[164] thought that the debates of the civil war had made 'the true authority of parliaments better and more generally understood'.[165] The new power of the principle of representative government is shown by the eagerness of the army leadership in the later 1640s, and the readiness of the Rump in the early 1650s, to sweep away rotten boroughs and transform the

---

[160] Iagomarsino and Wood, *Trial of Charles I*, p. 111. (Bradshaw was not himself a member of the Rump.)

[161] On the novelty of that position see *Burton*, iii. 182, iv. 74.

[162] Derek Hirst, *The Representative of the People? Voters and Voting Rights in England under the Early Stuarts* (Cambridge, 1975), pp. 178–93.

[163] Bacon, *Historical and Political Discourse*, ii. iii–xii, 176. The second part of Bacon's treatise, published in 1651, included a separately paginated preface which was perhaps inserted after the rest of the book had been prepared. It indignantly replies to a tract of August 1649 in which William Prynne maintained the constitutional superiority of the upper over the lower chamber. The concluding sentence of the preface, while not necessarily to be taken as a vindication of the abolition of the Lords, casts an indulgent eye on it. Though Bacon was no Leveller, his treatise is pervaded by a congenital mistrust of the tendency of peers or 'great men' to pursue 'private' interests in opposition to the 'public' concern of the Commons; cf. BL Add. MS 5138, pp. 254–5.

[164] Braddick and Greengrass, 'Letters of Sir Cheney Culpepper', pp. 201, 206; cf. pp. 146, 153, 197–8, 217, 302.

[165] Ibid., pp. 232–3.

electoral map, a goal that would be achieved by the Instrument of Government.[166] Henry Ireton, a principal if not the principal initiator of that movement, also favoured proposals to rename 'parliaments' as 'representatives',[167] a suggestion followed by the Rump in its bill for a 'new' or 'equal representative'. Before 1649 the Commons had not the power or motive to overthrow the upper House. Yet there was plenty of resentment at its 'negative voice'[168] and its other powers, a sentiment intensified by the lukewarm attitude of the majority of the peers towards the war effort of 1642–6 and by the apparent sympathy of many of them for the royalist resurgence in 1648.

In 1642 Lords and Commons had claimed sovereign power in order to get round the dereliction of the king. In 1649 the Commons claimed the same power to get round the dereliction of the Lords. The votes of 4 January 1649 left the upper House a subsidiary role at most. Its abolition on 6 February, which immediately preceded the debate on the future of kingship, was not preordained. By that time the Commons had begun to re-fill. The vote that paved the way for abolition was passed, by forty-four votes to twenty-nine, only after 'a long and smart debate'. Marten and Ludlow were the tellers in favour.[169] There is some slender evidence to suggest that the abolition may have been unpopular in the nation at large.[170] Nonetheless it attracted much less attention, and proved much less contentious, than the removal of kingship. The Rump was not the only unicameral parliament of the 1650s. Only in 1657 would parliamentary proposals for a second chamber arise. Presbyterians in the parliament of 1654, disgruntled as they were on other grounds, accepted without protest the provision for unicameral parliaments in the Instrument of Government, and incorporated it into their own proposed constitution. In 1657 it was as 'the great council and representative of the three nations' that the unicameral Commons 'tendered' the Humble Petition and Advice 'by a general and universal consent of the three nations'.[171] The history of Oliver Cromwell's two parliaments shows the easy compatibility of a belief in parliamentary sovereignty with a commitment to kingship. The second of the parliaments wanted to make him king, and there was powerful support in the first for doing so.[172]

The majority of the MPs of the Interregnum who accepted the transition to a single chamber did so without enthusiasm. Even among those who voted for it in January 1649, or sat at other times between the purge and the regicide, there were men who viewed the proceedings of those weeks with dismay. They kept their seats only in order 'to preserve the face of the civil authority'[173] and

---

[166] Worden, *Rump Parliament*, ch. 8.

[167] *Somers Tracts*, vi. 357, 366. Cf. Braddick and Greengrass, 'Letters of Sir Cheney Culpepper', pp. 185–6.

[168] See e.g. *Burton*, ii. 388, 390.

[169] *CJ* 6 February 1649; Whitelocke, *Memorials*, ii. 521.

[170] *Burton*, iii. 124, 363.

[171] *CJ* 7 April 1657; *Somers Tracts*, vi. 339. Cf. *GD*, p. 449; *OPH*, xxi. 266–7.

[172] Firth, *Clarke Papers*, iii. 16. In the debates on the parliament's constitutional bill, the title by which Cromwell would rule was for a time left undecided, perhaps in order to keep the option of kingship open: *CJ* 10 November 1654; cf. *GD*, p. 427.

[173] Ludlow, *Voyce*, p. 143.

'not to leave all to the sword'.[174] The conflict between soldiers and civilians, which had transformed the parliamentarian cause in 1647, persisted even when the army had purged its Presbyterian opponents. Army and parliament sought to shift the responsibility for the king's trial on to each other.[175] The army, having wanted to dissolve the parliament by force, had only resolved on the lesser step of a purge at the entreaty of MPs who shared its desire to bring the king to justice or would be ardent supporters of the sovereign rule of the Commons. The purge caused unease in some of them, hostility in others. The widow of the regicide John Hutchinson would remember his hatred of the army and of 'the shackles' it had placed on the Commons.[176]

The prominent rumper Sir Arthur Hesilrige, who was in the north of England in December and January, was more specific. It was, he recalled with mordant irony in 1659, 'by advice of the army' that 'we turned our selves into a Commonwealth'— or, as another version of his speech has it, 'We turned ourselves into a Commonwealth by advice of the soldiers among us.'[177] For 'what else [should] we do?' 'Two of the three estates were thus gone. Then, for the third estate, that, God knows! had been much shattered and broken.'[178] In Hesilrige's mind it had been the Rump's achievement to establish the principle of parliamentary sovereignty, and to have built national power and prosperity, out of the havoc which the army had created. Hesilrige had apparently favoured the restoration of Charles I on the terms worked out in the Isle of Wight before Pride's Purge, a coup with which he had had 'nought to do'.[179] Yet it was he who steered the act that made England a Commonwealth and Free State through the Rump.[180] Of the four leading civilian MPs of the Rump period, only one, Thomas Scot, was present between the purge and the execution. The others were Hesilrige, Vane, and St John. St John made it clear to the army officers in 1651 that he wanted a return to monarchy. Vane disapproved of the regicide court and attributed the trial to Cromwell and 'the soldiers'. Yet from February 1649, like Hesilrige, he worked assiduously for the new government. Vane and Hesilrige were at one with Cromwell in attributing the revolution of 1649 both to 'providence' and to its instrument, 'necessity'. Hesilrige remembered how God's 'wonderful hand', uprooting human expectation, had wrought blessings from destruction. 'A nation, that had been blasted and torn, began . . . exceedingly to flourish.'[181] Hesilrige made a parallel point about Cromwell's expulsion of the Rump in 1653, an evil whose disastrous consequences, by the same 'wonderful' providence, had brought home the sanctity of the very principles of parliamentary sovereignty

---

[174] Whitelocke, *Memorials*, ii. 481.
[175] Ibid., ii. 480.
[176] Hutchinson, *Life of Colonel Hutchinson*, p. 214.
[177] BL Add MS 5138, p. 130; BL Add. MS. 15862, fo. 29. The transcription in *Burton*, iii. 97 is misleading (though the labours of the editor, J. T. Rutt, who transcribed Burton's diary were heroic).
[178] *Burton*, iii. 97; cf. iii. 101.
[179] Ibid., iii. 96, iv. 76.
[180] *CJ* 30 April, 1 May 1649.
[181] *Burton*, iii. 97.

and political consent which the coup had desecrated.[182] Vane for his part remembered how God, 'who knows best what that work is, which he hath to bring forth', had destroyed the peace negotiations in the Isle of Wight; and how, through 'unavoidable necessity', the events of 1649 had restored the 'natural right' of parliament and nation. They had laid a 'foundation' of 'the supreme judicature' of 'the representative of the nation', and so had freed the people from 'bondage'.[183]

We must allow for embittered distortions in the memories of rumpers whom the army had driven from power in 1653. Many of those members were again forcibly excluded in 1654, and were prevented from taking their seats in 1656. Yet retrospect explains only so much. In 1651, during the Rump's tenure of power, we find a printed attack on the memory of Charles I, so bold that it has been mistaken for Milton's, reminding readers that the rumpers, whatever their shortcomings, 'are of the old legal election, and the relicts of the old form'. The blame for 'the maiming or lessening the number and quality of the old form', maintained the tract, lay with the army, not with 'those that remain faithful to their trust, for some kind of government the people must have'.[184] The regicide lawyer John Lisle explained in a private paper that 'the violation of the privilege of parliament' by the purge had not destroyed the parliament's 'authority'. What was left of the Commons was 'the higher power ordained by God', to which 'providence' and biblical injunction had enjoined his obedience.[185]

If any deposit of lawful government remained after the purge, it lay in the Commons. MPs who, at least since 1642, had believed in the sovereignty of parliament had now to adapt to a world where only a remnant of that sovereignty survived. It was the very principle of parliamentary sovereignty that enabled them to do so. In February 1649 an 'engagement' or pledge was required of prospective members of the new council of state. A number of them refused to take a test that committed them to endorse the purge or the regicide. They made no difficulty when a new test, devised by Cromwell and Sir Henry Vane in consultation with them, required only acceptance of the sovereignty of the Commons. The Earl of Denbigh pledged himself to 'acknowledge' the Commons as 'the supreme authority of this nation' and promised to 'live and die with them', both because 'the liberty and freedom of the people is so involved' in their rule and because 'now there is no other power in England but that of the House of Commons'. Three other peers, Pembroke, Salisbury, and Mulgrave, replied, at least 'for the general matter', in the same terms. So, probably, did a number of rumpers.[186] The peers who thus deserted the upper House were derided at the time, and have been mocked by

---

[182] BL Add. MS 5138, p. 127.

[183] *Burton*, iii. 173-6.

[184] *The Life and Reigne of King Charls* (1651), p. 225; cf. the attitude of the rumper William Heveningham related in Worden, *Rump Parliament*, p. 45.

[185] Bodl., MS. Eng. hist. c. 487, pp. 1083–5. Cf. Ludlow, *Voyce*, pp. 143, 268; *OPH*, xix. 22, 77–8; *Burton*, iii. 356–7. One of the MPs who had opposed the regicide but who accepted membership of the council of state, Bulstrode Whitelocke, remembered explaining that the 'protection' afforded him by the new government required his 'obedience' (Whitelocke, *Memorials*, ii. 526).

[186] *CJ* 19 February 1649; TNA, SP 25/62, p. 3; Burton, iii. 174 n.; Whitelocke, *Memorials*, ii. 537, 538; Ann Hughes, *Politics and Civil War in Warwickshire, 1620–1660* (Cambridge, 1987), p. 223.

historians, for craven cowardice or opportunism. Yet how else might they, and the commoners who joined them, have helped to keep a parliamentary and civilian authority in being? Thomas Fairfax, the lord general, who was committed to civilian rule and had been unhappy about the regicide, undertook, as a member of the new council, to 'adhere to this present parliament, in the maintenance and defence of the publick liberty and freedom of this nation'.[187] His compliance could not have been taken for granted. In the following year he would embarrass the regime by resigning sooner than lead an army into Scotland against the Presbyterians there. The acceptance of the new Commonwealth by the rumper and lawyer Francis Thorpe could not have been taken for granted either. He would break with Cromwell in the protectorate. In 1658 he would 'acknowledge the old constitution, by Lords and Commons, to be the best constitution'.[188] He is likely to have held the same view in 1649. Yet in the circumstances of that year he stoutly defended the sovereignty of the Commons and was involved in the passage of the act declaring England a Commonwealth and Free State.[189]

The Rump and its apologists did not think of the resolutions of 4 January 1649 as committing the parliament to kingless rule. The votes created or demonstrated the Commons' entitlement to change the government if it chose. They did not indicate what change, if any, it should make. It was on the inherent right of the people's representatives to alter governments, not on the choice itself, that polemic on behalf of the purge and regicide or of popular sovereignty centred in the weeks around the king's death.[190] In vindicating the termination of kingship, MPs enunciated their right 'to alter or change any government' 'when they shall judge it to be no longer for the good and safety of the people'.[191] The House asserted a 'natural right and inherent power to take up or lay down what form of government we think fit, and judge most convenient to our own preservation, safety and welfare'.[192] The MPs 'may…erect such a form as themselves conceive most convenient'.[193] In 1649 they debated 'what government the people of England shall choose'.[194] Denbigh promised to serve 'what government' the Commons 'shall set up'.[195]

The Rump's assertion of its 'natural right', though discredited in the nation at large by the violence that facilitated it, in itself accorded with a widespread sentiment. Across the parliamentarian spectrum there was broad agreement that, as Nathaniel Fiennes, who had boycotted the Rump, put it in 1657, 'God hath so declared his will concerning all forms of government, that they are wholly at the pleasure and disposition of men to be continued and altered and changed according

---

[187] *CJ* 20 February 1650.
[188] *Burton*, ii. 447.
[189] Whitelocke, *Memorials*, iii. 31; Cromartie, *Constitutionalist Revolution*, p. 268.
[190] e.g. John Warr, *The Priviledges of the People* (1649); *The Moderate* 9 January 1649, p. 237; *The Moderate Intelligencer* 11 January 1649, pp. 1825–6; *CPW*, iii. 207.
[191] *Burton*, iii. 109; *OPH*, xix. 31.
[192] *OPH*, xix. 147; cf. *Mercurius Politicus* 22 April 1652, p. 1539.
[193] *Mercurius Politicus* 3 October 1650, p. 277.
[194] *OPH*, xix. 31.
[195] *CJ* 19 February 1649; cf. Philodemus, *Armies Vindication*, p. 61.

to the exigency of affairs'.[196] The choice, it would have been no less widely agreed, lay in parliament. In the most conservative of the parliaments of the protectorate, that of Richard Cromwell in 1659, the opposition of Hesilrige, Scot, and their allies to a 'single person' was doomed, whereas their 'doctrine' that 'all power is in the people', and that it had 'reverted into' the Commons on Cromwell's death, proved an effective weapon.[197] The constitutional proposals of the parliaments of 1654 and 1657 rested on parallel premises. In 1654 even 'the moderate sort' among the critics of the Instrument of Government 'were for the parliament alone' to have 'the legislative power' and to determine and restrict the protector's executive power.[198]

The priorities of the parliamentarian party of the civil wars are reflected in the negotiations between Cromwell and the Commons' delegates over the proposal to crown him in 1657. Fiennes, urging the offer of the title on him, explained that in 1649 'one parliament thought the [present] state of affairs required the taking away of the name and office of king', and that now 'this parliament judgeth the present state of affairs requireth the restoring of it'.[199] Lord Broghill, who headed the party behind the Humble Petition, agreed: 'what one supreme authority may suppress, another may erect'.[200] Broghill, like Fiennes, had opposed the change of 1649. Yet in 1657, finding themselves in a comparable predicament to that of the creators of the Commonwealth eight years earlier, the two men looked back on its establishment with some indulgence, as the best or only course available to MPs hemmed in by 'necessity'. In that necessity, the Commonwealth had at least supplied a government. Amid the disintegration of the Puritan cause in February 1660 a petition from aldermen of the city of London told parliament 'that they found some persons for a monarchical, some for a commonwealth, some for no government at all. The last they did dislike. For the other, they would not presume to direct, but should acquiesce, and submit to the determination of parliament.'[201]

The new regime of 1649 did not argue that kingless rule was appropriate to all societies at all times. It claimed no right to export its constitutional revolution to the Continent, and denied any wish to 'intermeddle with the ... government of any other kingdom or state'. Its respect for the traditional forms of diplomatic address to monarchs obliged Milton, as the Commonwealth's Latin Secretary, to address a letter on the government's behalf to 'The Most Serene and Potent Prince, Philip IV, King of Spain'. The Rump justified the change of government as the right

---

[196] *Somers Tracts*, vi. 381 (cf. vi. 384). The breadth of opinion behind the position can be sampled at: *OPH*, xx. 272; *The Second Speech of the Honourable Nathanael Fiennes* (1641), pp. 3–4; John Goodwin, *Anti-Cavalierisme* (1642), pp. 7–8; Thomas Case, *A Sermon preached before the Honourable House of Commons . . . 22 August 1645* (1645), p. 26; *OPH*, xx. 272; *Burton*, iii. 186, 521; Firth, *Clarke Papers*, iv. 12; Nedham, *True State*, pp. 5, 8; Baxter, *Holy Commonwealth*, p. 214; BL Add. MS 37343 (MS of Bulstrode Whitelocke), fos 117–18; Algernon Sidney, *Court Maxims*, ed. Hans Blom and E. Haitsma Mulier (Cambridge, 1996), p. 38; Algernon Sidney, *Discourses concerning Government* (Indianapolis, Ind., 1990), pp. 490–1, 549–50; Sykes, *Life and Death of Sir Henry Vane*, p. 101; below, pp. 366, 395.

[197] H. M. Margoliouth, ed., *The Poems and Letters of Andrew Marvell*, 2 vols (Oxford, 1971 edn), ii. 307.

[198] *Burton*, i. xxxii; cf. above, p. 248.

[199] *Somers Tracts*, vi. 381.

[200] Ibid., vi. 384.

[201] *CJ* 23 February 1660.

decision to take in the exceptional context of 1649, when no other means of preserving the nation and its liberties were visible. It was a pragmatic choice, in which the advantages of the alteration were weighed against the disadvantages. Arguments for kingless rule advanced on the Rump's behalf tended to be relative rather than absolute. So forthright a polemical spirit as the pamphleteer John Hall was content to assert that men could be 'more happy' under kingless than kingly rule, or that 'republicks may be as just and authoritative as king-ships'.[202] Even in providentialist vindications of the change, biblical or apocalyptic zeal is less frequent than in the more exclamatory endorsements of the regicide.

There is no decisive evidence that any rumpers believed, during their tenure of power in 1649–53, that republics were inherently superior to other forms of government. The widow of the regicide MP Colonel Hutchinson would state, in distant retrospect, that in 1659 her husband had judged the people's freedoms to be best preserved 'in a free republic'—free, she meant, from military force—rather than in 'a single person', but her words suggest that it was only in that year, when (as we shall find) the climate of constitutional discussions had changed, that he came to think in that way.[203] She does not imply that even in 1659 his preference, which she too presents as relative rather than absolute, was an animating ideal. In Richard Cromwell's parliament of that year another rumper, Robert Bennett, who had 'no principle engaging me to any particular form of government', declared that he had 'liked a commonwealth well' in 1649–53, and that he would favour it now 'if you were *tabula rasa*'. But he would not recommend it 'at this time, when we are so full of distraction'.[204] It is hard to think that during their tenure of power many rumpers would have resisted a return to some form of single rule if altered circumstances had made the change propitious. At a meeting arranged by Cromwell at the Speaker's house in December 1651, leading lawyers among the MPs present, Oliver St John, Bulstrode Whitelocke, and Sir Thomas Widdrington, demonstrated that they regarded the change of 1649 as temporary and that they wanted the parliament to set up some kind of mixed monarchy. Cromwell agreed.[205] Nathaniel Bacon would have concurred too.

The Rump saw itself as a parliament first, a commonwealth second. The *Declaration* of March 1649 did passingly relate that MPs, in deciding to end kingship, had 'received encouragement, by their observation of the blessing of God upon other states', past and present, which were not monarchies: republican Rome, modern Venice, Switzerland, and the Netherlands. But they did not claim to have been inspired by those examples or profess a wish to emulate them.[206] The iconography

---

[202] Hall, *Grounds and Reasons*, pp. 12–13.
[203] Hutchinson, *Life of Colonel Hutchinson*, p. 214.
[204] *Burton*, iii. 266, 360. Cf. iii. 520–1; BL Add. MS 5138, p. 192; above, p. 243.
[205] Whitelocke, *Memorials*, iii. 372–4.
[206] *OPH*, xix. 72–3. The civil war had, however, generated an interest in the balloting boxes used in Venetian politics: Braddick and Greengrass, 'Letters of Sir Cheney Culpepper', pp. 198, 260, 265, 271, 275; cf. *CJ* 10 October 1646. During the civil war Marchamont Nedham had glanced admiringly at the 'free states' of the United Provinces: Worden, '"Wit in a Roundhead"', p. 317.

of the regime did not allude to them.[207] In March 1649, around the time of the abolition of kingship and of the *Declaration* supporting it, we do find Milton, the newly created Latin Secretary, who may have been dissatisfied with the constitutional settlement of 1649 and have wished for further changes,[208] adding a classical flourish to the draft, penned by Henry Marten, of a letter from the parliament to the senate of Hamburg. Milton headed it *Senatus Populusque Anglicanus*. The wording did not survive parliament's scrutiny.[209] Perhaps Marten had encouraged or connived at the phrase. Yet he seems to have had little interest in foreign republics.[210] The sovereignty of the lower House was the preoccupation both of Marten,[211] who in his own words 'always adored' the Commons,[212] and of his friend Chaloner.[213] Before long Milton had aligned his position with the parliament's. In February 1650, admittedly at a low point of the Rump's fortunes,[214] he explained to the King of Portugal on the Rump's behalf that 'we were finally driven to the point where, if we wished to save the nation, we had to alter the form of government'. In addressing the King of Spain on the same day he described the change of government as a 'plan' which the new rulers had 'at last . . . conceived . . . for recovering our liberty'.[215] It was not, as he publicly conceded a year later, an ideal one: 'our constitution is what the dissensions of the time will permit, not such as were to be desired'.[216]

The regime referred to itself usually as 'the Parliament of the Commonwealth', sometimes as 'the Parliament and Commonwealth', but often simply as 'the Parliament'. It was primarily as a parliament that it required foreign states to address it;[217] it was parliament's supremacy that it required them—and its repentant enemies in England—to acknowledge;[218] and it was the 'honour' of the parliament that its ambassadors were instructed to defend. It was as members of the parliament, not as rulers of a republic, that MPs wanted their deeds to be memorialized in pictures or on medals.[219] The new Great Seal of 1649 carried a picture of the Commons in

---

[207] The Rump's 'attitude' to 'the whole issue of what to do with the legacy' of the Stuart monarchy in such matters has justly been called 'fundamentally preservationist': Kelsey, *Inventing A Republic*, p. 38.

[208] Blair Worden, 'Milton's Republicanism and the Tyranny of Heaven', in Gisela Bock, Quentin Skinner, and Maurizio Viroli, eds, *Machiavelli and Republicanism* (Cambridge, 1990), p. 235.

[209] *CPW*, v. 478.

[210] Williams, 'Anatomy of a Radical Gentleman', p. 136.

[211] Ibid., p. 134.

[212] Ludlow, *Voyce*, p. 295.

[213] David Scott, 'Motives for King-Killing', in Peacey, *Regicides and the Execution of Charles I*, pp. 140–1.

[214] Worden, *Rump Parliament*, pp. 222–32.

[215] *CPW*, v. 505, 507.

[216] *WJM*, vii. 29. What might Milton have meant? Having a classical disposition in favour of mixed constitutions, perhaps he was troubled by the Rump's failure to create one.

[217] *CJ* 30 January 1650; *OPH*, xix. 492.

[218] *CSPD 1649–50*, p. 117.

[219] Kelsey, *Inventing a Republic*, pp. 57, 95–6, 216. Three decades later, it is true, Algernon Sidney would eloquently compare the accomplishments of the Rump, in which he had sat, with those of other republics. 'In a few years', he remembered, 'good discipline, and a just encouragement to those who did well, produced more examples of pure, complete, incorruptible, and invincible virtue than Rome or Greece could ever boast; or if more be wanting, they [=than?] may easily be found among the Switzers, Hollanders and others: but 'tis not necessary to light a candle to the sun.' (Sidney, *Discourses concerning*

session, with the words, penned by Marten,[220] 'In the First Year of Freedom, by God's Blessing Restored'. That 'freedom' was not republican rule, which the parliament did not pretend to be 'restoring'. It was the nation's right, which Nathaniel Bacon's treatise celebrated, to hold sovereign parliaments or 'national meetings in council'. 'A most happy way', declared the act abolishing kingship, 'is made for this nation . . . to return to its just and ancient right, of being governed by its representatives or national meetings in council, from time to time chosen and entrusted to that purpose by the people.'[221] Parliament explained in May 1649 that it was for the very 'purpose' of ensuring 'that the people shall for the future be governed by its own representatives or national meetings in council' that the 'Commonwealth' had been set up.[222] The point was confirmed by Sir Henry Vane. When the MPs of 1649 declared the abolition of kingship to be 'the only happy way of returning to their own freedom', he would recall, 'their meaning was that thereby the originall of all just power was in the representatives of the people and was reserved wholly to them'.[223]

In April 1653 it was Cromwell's abolition of the parliament, not the consequences for the republic, that enraged MPs. Rule without a single person, after all, survived the Rump. Barebone's, the assembly that succeeded it in July, claimed the sovereign power, again as 'the Parliament of the Commonwealth', that the Rump had held—the difference being that Barebone's was set up, and its membership chosen, by a military power which had destroyed what remained of a duly elected parliament and had usurped its authority. When opponents of the protectorate called for the return of the Rump, or for the election of parliaments that would be free from the government's control, it was at Cromwell's abolition of parliamentary supremacy, and at its consequences for the rights and liberties of the subject, that their resentment was directed. On the return of the Rump in 1659 it was the restoration of the parliament, not of the Commonwealth, that was publicly celebrated. It was in the chance to renew their 'service' to the parliament, not to the Commonwealth, that restored rumpers expressed delight.[224] They informed the nation that the parliament had been restored and, 'with it', the form of government set up in 1649.[225]

Government, p. 216; cf. pp. 276, 278). Whether he had thought like that at the time is another matter. Long years of exile after the Restoration had evidently played tricks on his memory. During them he seems to have convinced himself of a fantasy about the establishment of the new government in 1649, which he portrayed as an attempt to select the best features of ancient republican constitutions 'and make a perfect composition' (Jonathan Scott, *Algernon Sidney and the English Republic 1623–1677* [Cambridge, 1998], p. 15). Those constitutions, as he acknowledged in the book in which he hailed the classical 'virtue' of the rumpers, were 'mixed' as distinct from 'pure' forms of government, a difference from the unicameral Rump which his recollections overlooked.

[220] *CJ* 9 January 1649; Whitelocke, *Memorials*, ii. 492.
[221] *GD*, p. 386. Cf. Iagomarsino and Wood, *Trial of Charles I*, p. 61; *OPH*, xix. 379.
[222] Firth and Rait, ii. 120; cf. *GD*, p. 359.
[223] BL Add. MS 5138, p. 157; cf. *Burton*, iii. 176.
[224] Mayers, *1659*, p. 32.
[225] Firth and Rait, ii. 1299; cf. *Burton*, i. xxx.

Admittedly there were incentives of expediency for the Rump to place public emphasis on the parliamentary basis of its rule, which was continuous with the Roundhead cause, rather than the republican one, which was a departure from it. Yet expediency only confirmed the injunctions of instinct and conviction. Since 1640 the cause of the Long Parliament had taken over its members' lives. The change of government in 1649 did not alter the rumpers' perceptions of the causes and purpose of the civil war. In their minds it remained what it had been for their colleagues in parliament before the purge: a struggle for liberty and for the rule of law. Ideas of liberty had been adapted and extended since 1640. Yet the old language of 'rights and liberties', of 'the true English liberty', remained pervasive, inside and outside parliament. It was here, not in any pursuit of 'republican' goals, that the political passions of MPs lay. Marten was driven by the conviction that 'the English nation is a free people undeniably possessed of liberty in their persons, and property in their goods'. In the civil war he promoted a bill 'for the confirmation of the subjects' liberties in their persons'.[226] From 1653 men who were determined to restore the freedom and 'supreme trust' of parliament would bemoan, in language that had been conventional in the opposition to Charles I, the protector's affronts to 'our fundamental rights and liberties', 'the just rights and liberties of our country', 'our native rights and freedoms', 'the ancient liberties of England, settled by Magna Charta, the Petition of Right and other laws'.[227] Liberty was guarded by the power of law-making. In 1658 Thomas Scot, who had been a leading and zealous regicide and one of the architects of the Commonwealth, asked parliament 'what was fought for' in the 1640s 'but to arrive at that capacity to make your own laws?'[228] He was courting, admittedly to unorthodox political ends, an orthodox parliamentary sentiment to which he himself subscribed. The same can be said of the conduct the following year of his close parliamentary ally Hesilrige when he portrayed his own quarrel with the protectorate as one between the principle of 'the laws' and that of 'arbitrary power'.[229] Before 1649 parliament had attempted the preservation or recovery of liberty and law, and the thwarting of tyranny, through the machinery of the ancient constitution, which it had not questioned. It was the Rump's argument in 1649 that in present circumstances the same goals could be best attained, or only attained, through a change of government.

If the termination of kingship in 1649 derived from contingency and necessity rather than from conviction, an obvious question arises. How was it that the issue of single rule came, over the next eleven years, to polarize and ruin the Puritan cause? The neo-monarchical rule of the protectorate, and the non-monarchical rule on either side of it, both occupied about half the Interregnum of 1649–60, the

---

[226] Williams, 'Anatomy of a Radical Gentleman', pp. 129–30.
[227] *The Humble Petition of Several Colonels of the Army* (1654); Whitelocke, *Memorials*, iv. 183, 184, 187.
[228] *Burton*, ii. 390.
[229] Ibid., iv. 152. Cf. *The Armies Dutie* (1659), p. 6; Bacon, *Historical and Political Discourse*, i. 9.

protectorate being a little the longer of the two. Oliver Cromwell never became king, but the differences between kingship and the protectorate he accepted in December 1653 would be increasingly hard to tell. The act abolishing kingship in 1649 forbade the rule of 'any one single person': the Instrument of Government brought Cromwell to power as 'one person . . . the style of which person shall be the lord protector'.[230] In May 1659, on the fall of the protectorate, rule by a 'single person' was again outlawed. It remained so until the Restoration a year later. During the non-monarchical phases of the Interregnum it was treasonable to deny the 'supreme authority' of the Commons: during the protectorate it was treasonable to deny the protector's role in the 'supreme authority'.[231] By 1659 the central power struggle of the Roundhead cause was being commonly described as one between 'the single person men' and their opponents.

If republican arguments did not cause the abolition of kingship, they arose from it. The abolition created its own emotions and expectations and polemical needs. It unleashed impulses which would work their way into the calculations and professions of politicians. Their absorption into practical politics was a slow process. It took nearly ten years. Along the way it acquired a second stimulus: the coups of 1653 which first removed the Long Parliament and then made Cromwell protector.

Once in power, the Rump had to entrench itself. Its diverse membership needed a distinctive identity, which would help it to hold the regime together and to combat the threats to its survival. The wars in Ireland and Scotland might easily spread to England. Unless the new government could establish a base in public opinion it might easily unravel. As an MP put it in 1659, England's rulers would be wise to settle on a form of government 'as far from' the old monarchical one 'as we can, lest it bring in the old line'.[232] Any initiative within the government towards a return to single rule would have seemed evidence of weakness and of concession to the regime's parliamentarian as well as royalist enemies. So rumpers who had expounded the ideal of limited monarchy in January 1649 dropped it. Government publications contained almost no discussion of mixed constitutions, and acknowledged no middle ground between 'tyranny' and its own rule. The *Declaration* of March 1649 described the abolition of kingship as a change 'from tyranny to a free state', thanks to which the people would not have 'any more a king to tyrannize over them'.[233] Subsequent polemic equated 'monarchy and tyranny'. It targeted 'the haughty tyranny of royal power'.[234] Such assertions must have caused unease among the rumpers, especially on the backbenches, but propaganda was largely in the hands of regicides, Thomas Scot and John Bradshaw at their head, who had been decisive figures in the events that terminated the monarchy. After the huge

---

[230] *GD*, pp. 384–7.

[231] Firth and Rait, ii. 120–1, 832.

[232] *Burton*, iii. 268; cf. iii. 414.

[233] *OPH*, xix. 76, 80; cf. xix. 187.

[234] *CPW*, v. 479–80; Nedham, *Case of the Commonwealth*, p. 127; Marchamont Nedham, *The Excellencie of a Free-State* (1656: a work mostly taken from editorials of Nedham's *Mercurius Politicus* in 1651–2), *passim*; John Hall, *The Grounds and Reasons of Monarchy*, 'The First Part', *passim*.

risks they and their allies had taken in 1649, there could be no going back. They had crossed a Rubicon.

By 1650 Bradshaw was promoting arguments which were still more distant from the thinking of most MPs, who were in no position to resist them. To help counter the threat from Charles II—'Tarquin', as newsbooks for the Rump called him— John Hall and, on a larger scale, his and Bradshaw's friend Marchamont Nedham described not merely the evils of tyranny but the inherent superiority of republics.[235] In his book *The Case of the Commonwealth* in 1650, and then in the editorials of his newsbook *Mercurius Politicus* in 1651–2, Nedham rejoiced in the virtues and achievements of the Roman republic and of other states that had broken free of monarchy. He implied, as the Rump itself would not have done, that the 'freedom' restored in 1649 was that of kingless rule, for 'England consisted of free-states until the Romans yoked it'.[236] Even in his writings, however, attacks on kingship were always tied to, and never overtook, the arguments about consent, representation, and parliamentary sovereignty that were the heart of parliament's constitutional claims after Pride's Purge as before it. Nedham summoned 'Roman stories' in doubtful support of the propositions that 'the supreme authority' properly lies 'in the hands of the people's representatives, in . . . their supreme assemblies'.[237] His celebration of the civic vitality of classical antiquity was partnered by a more conventional concept of liberty, one to which the parliament of the 1640s would have subscribed. Liberty, 'the most precious jewel under the sun',[238] would protect the people from the state. England, he promised in proposing the restoration of rule without a single person in 1656, could become a 'quiet habitation' where 'none might make the people afraid'.[239]

In 1651, the victory at Worcester brought the regime security. Immediately the Rump turned its attention to 'the further settlement of this commonwealth'.[240] Immediately, too, Nedham embarked on the second, bolder stage of his republican arguments. Among MPs, resistance to the return of kingship persisted, but it remained pragmatic rather than ideological. In the winter of 1651–2 there was private discussion, promoted by Cromwell, of a return to monarchy. There was renewed thought of enthroning the Duke of Gloucester, even perhaps of negotiations to restore the now powerless Charles II or his brother James on parliament's terms.[241] There were also moves, though their source is unknown, towards the enthronement of Cromwell himself.[242] The prospect would have appalled large numbers of MPs, who resented the military basis of his power and suspected him of

---

[235] See my forthcoming edition of Nedham's *The Excellencie of a Free-State*, to be published by Liberty Fund.

[236] *Mercurius Politicus* 22 April 1652, p. 1540.

[237] Ibid., 30 October 1651, p. 1157.

[238] Ibid., 30 October 1651, p. 1157.

[239] Nedham, *Excellencie*, preface.

[240] *CJ* 9 September 1651.

[241] Whitelocke, *Memorials*, iv. 372–4; Abbott, ii. 584; Cook, *Monarchy, no Creature*, p. 129; Kelsey, *Inventing A Republic*, p. 169; cf. *Mercurius Politicus* 20 February 1651, pp. 591–2.

[242] The idea was floated in the press and provoked warnings against it: *Somers Tracts*, vi. 153, 174; Cook, *Monarchy, no Creature*, p. 53; *LP*, pp. 92–9 (cf. Scott, *Commonwealth Principles*, p. 269).

pursuing personal ambition. In debates they opposed his programme of religious and social reform. There were suspicions of Cromwell in the army too, but it was the army that stood most to gain from the political elevation of its own lord general. Before Worcester the Rump had had to survive the threat from royalism. Now it had to survive threats from its own soldiery. That conflict, in turn, militated against any initiative within parliament for a return to kingship in the foreseeable future.

It was on the holding of parliamentary elections, not on arguments about kingship, that the conflict centred. As in the army debates of 1647, forms of government were a less central issue than the relationship between parliament and the nation it represented. In the act abolishing kingship the Rump had promised to hold elections 'so soon as may possibly stand with the safety of the people'.[243] The nation's hostility to its new rulers, and the campaigns in Ireland and Scotland, enjoined repeated delays. Government manifestoes explained or indicated that only once the Commonwealth was past its 'infancy', only when the electorate had 'tasted the sweets of peace and liberty', only when the country had found 'rest' from the 'pressures' of the massive taxation and military occupation on which the Rump's survival depended, would elections be practicable.[244] Meanwhile the nation deserved a respite from political alterations. 'England is not as France', as Thomas Scot, employing a conventional simile, had told Cromwell in November 1650, 'a meadow to be mowed as often as the governors please; our interest is to do our work with as little grievance to our new people, scarce yet proselytised, as is possible.'[245]

Until Worcester the postponement of elections did not divide the regime. After the victory it set parliament against army. Worcester had ended the royalist threat, but not the Rump's unpopularity, which was the obstacle to speedy elections. MPs had an answer. They would win over the electorate by ambitious foreign and commercial policies which would raise the nation's prosperity and self-esteem. They would build up shipping and trade. They would break the maritime and economic power of the Dutch, with whom the Rump went to war in 1652.[246] At the same time the parliament would reduce the size, and with it the political aspirations, of its army, which in any case the government's naval and commercial ambitions would sideline. Those policies would take time. The desperate difficulties of the earlier part of the Rump's rule, and the contumely it had earned, would have to be forgotten. At the time that Cromwell expelled the parliament, rumpers believed, the nation had discovered only the burdens of their rule, not yet its benefits.[247] It seems likely that, while it remained in power, the Rump looked to the next parliament to provide, as the supreme council of the nation, a long-term settlement of the constitution. Meanwhile a country that had undergone so many 'changes' would be spared further ones.[248]

[243] *GD*, p. 386; cf. *OPH*, xix. 187.
[244] *OPH*, xix. 189, 194; Nedham, *Case of the Commonwealth*, pp. 125, 127.
[245] *MSP*, p. 28.
[246] *Burton*, iii. 111–12.
[247] Cf. ibid., iii. 557.
[248] Ibid., iii. 112.

After the Rump had been expelled, its members recalled the triumphant achievements, not of the Commonwealth, but of 'that glorious parliament',[249] 'the Great
Parliament', 'this great parliament which hath done so great things', 'the most
memorable parliament that ever was since Magna Charta', 'this assembly famous
through the world for its undertakings, actions, and successes'.[250] Normally those
tributes were salutes to the assembly's exploits before as well as after Pride's Purge,
an event which rumpers thought of as a truncation of, not as a breach with, the
fuller body. Parliamentarian enemies of the Rump had a different view of its rule.
As one of them recalled in 1659, 'The Long Parliament did great and glorious
things for the first eight years. Then, I confess, it is best to sigh them out in
sorrowful silence.'[251] He was reacting against the praise by rumpers of their own
exertions in power. They remembered how their own prudence, energy, and
administrative skills had laid the foundation for the conquests of Ireland and
Scotland, exploits for which the army had been prone to claim the sole credit.
The regime had got the upper hand in the Dutch war, which Cromwell had
subsequently ended on needlessly lenient terms.[252] A crack navy had been built
up. So did not the achievements of the Rump prove kingship to have been, as the
Rump had declared, 'unnecessary', indeed an obstacle to the national well-being?
Did they not show republics to be a superior form of government? Maybe some
MPs drew and relished such conclusions. Yet there is nothing, in the admittedly
exiguous records of the Rump's politics, to say so, and nothing to indicate that its
members had been converted by the republican propaganda it had sponsored.

Men who did commend republican forms of rule in the 1650s did so, as a rule, as
critics, not friends, of the Rump. The rule is not straightforward, for some of them
had been involved in its government: Harrington's friend and literary partner
Henry Neville as an MP, and Milton and Nedham as polemicists. But members
of the Rump, that heterogeneous assembly, were not all admirers of their own
regime. To Neville and his close associates the Rump was 'tyrannical', 'an oligarchy,
detested by all men that love a commonwealth'.[253] Its 'notorious unskilfulness'
showed that it 'would never have made a government'.[254] Harrington thought the
Rump an oligarchy too. The 'single council of the people, pretending to be a
parliament', he wrote, was 'so new a thing that neither ancient nor modern
prudence can show . . . the like'.[255] Harrington wanted a true 'commonwealth'
that would show up the failings of the Rump's rule. Milton and Nedham, for

[249] Hutchinson, *Life of Colonel Hutchinson*, p. 214.
[250] Whitelocke, *Memorials*, iv. 6; *Burton*, iv. 131, 586; Ludlow, *Voyce*, pp. 217, 248. Cf. *The
Faithfull Scout*, 13 May 1659, p. 19; Slingsby Bethel, *The World's Mistake in Oliver Cromwell* (1668),
pp. 2–3; Mayers, *1659*, p. 192. By contrast, the author or authors of a pamphlet which complained
that the Rump had achieved 'the name only of a free state' had wanted it to achieve 'a glorious
commonwealth': *Copy of a Letter*, pp. 2, 5.
[251] *Burton*, iii. 120.
[252] Ibid., iii. 97, 111–12, 388–91, 394 (though cf. iii. 178).
[253] Ibid., iii. 134; BL Add. MS 5138, p. 141; Add. MS 15862, fo. 45; Caroline Robbins, ed., *Two
Republican Tracts* (Cambridge, 1969), p. 180.
[254] Worden, 'Harrington's "Oceana"', p. 118.
[255] Harrington, *'Commonwealth of Oceana'*, ed. Pocock, pp. 64–5.

their parts, had at best mixed feelings about the Rump. Milton privately despaired of the insularity of the rumpers, at their ignorance of the political prudence of classical antiquity and Renaissance Italy.[256] Nedham's writing for the government in 1650–2 attempted to give its rule a classical and republican aura. Its members, he proclaimed in 1650, were 'every way qualified like those Roman spirits of old'. In 1651, when the Rump was hoping for an alliance with the Dutch rather than the war that ensued the next year, he urged a 'union of those great republics', which would be 'formidable to kings'. When the war came he likened it to Rome's mighty struggle against its rival republic Carthage, and described England as 'the most famous and potent republic in this day in the world', indeed, with the exception of Rome itself, 'the greatest and most glorious republic that the world ever saw'.[257] Such language may have struck a popular chord among his readers.[258] So may the persistent echoes in his polemic of the Rump's momentary appeal, in March 1649, to the socially oppressed, and his complaints about the 'lordly interest' of 'an hereditary titular nobility'.[259] Kingship, he explained, is not merely a form of government but a 'lordly interest of dominion'. 'The name king' might have been abolished in 1649, but only an assault on oppressive social privilege would remove 'the thing king', which could lie 'in the hands of one, or of many'.[260]

Yet Nedham, as so often in his career, was playing a dextrous double-game. He was ever capable of half-distancing himself from political masters who, anxious to see his nimble pen deployed on their behalf rather than against them, had to swallow his departures from their thinking.[261] In his mind as in Neville's the Rump was an oligarchy. Its rule, he intimated, embodied the survival of 'the thing king'. Wanting not the 'grandee...government' of the Rump but 'the form of a real republic',[262] he proposed the introduction of some equivalent to Rome's tribunes as a counterweight to the landed interest which dominated the Commons. Perhaps Henry Marten and a handful of other rumpers looked benevolently on some of Nedham's more socially adventurous assertions. Yet it looks as if Marten, who, despite his eloquence, was generally on the losing side in the Rump, had no more illusions about the assembly than his and Chaloner's friend Neville had. After the expulsion of the Rump either Marten or one of his associates complained that it had 'understood nothing of a commonwealth but the name'.[263]

*

[256] *CPW*, v. 451; Worden, 'Classical Republicanism', pp.190–1; *LP*, pp. 192, 200–1.
[257] *LP*, pp. 127, 182, 219; John Selden, *Of the Dominion of the Seas*, trans. and ed. Nedham (1652), ep. ded. and p. 483; cf. Milton's tribute in *CPW*, vii. 420–1.
[258] Other newsbooks, popular in form, would imitate his illustrations from classical history. And see Nigel Smith's essay on John Streater, 'Popular Republicanism in the 1650s' (above, n. 82). There are close parallels between Nedham's and Streater's writings.
[259] *Mercurius Politicus* 19 February 1652, pp. 1410, 1412.
[260] Ibid., 23 October 1651, p. 1143; 19 May 1659, p. 443.
[261] *LP*; and my forthcoming edition of his *Excellencie of a Free-State*.
[262] *Mercurius Politicus* 15 January 1652, p. 1338, 19 February 1652, p. 1412; cf. Mayers, *1659*, p. 182.
[263] Williams, 'Anatomy of a Radical Gentleman', p. 135.

Oliver Cromwell removed the king in 1649, the parliament in 1653. The second coup generated hatreds less widely held than the first, but no less intense. Much of what is often described as the republican thought of the 1650s is better thought of as anti-Cromwellianism. Hostility to Cromwellian rule nonetheless became, with time, hostility to all single rule.

Cromwell had no interest in the principle of parliamentary supremacy, save when he could make political use of it. By December 1653 he had had enough of it. The absence of any 'check' on the Rump's power, he maintained, had produced 'arbitrary' government.[264] He wanted power for himself with which to implement the programme the Rump had refused to accept. He would not have been interested in ruling as a Venetian doge, a role, in any case, which his temperament would have precluded. From December 1653, when he became protector, the legislative power, which the Rump had claimed to lie solely in itself, was shared between 'one person' and parliament. The subordination of the executive to the sovereign legislature had been a cardinal premise of the Rump's rule. Sir Henry Vane remembered in 1659 that it was 'because they would not put the executive power out of their hands' that the Rump's members had invented the fiction of the 'Keepers of the Liberty of England'.[265] The Rump's executive power had been placed in a council of state which was subordinate and accountable to the Commons—just as a king whom MPs might in other circumstances have entrusted as a 'chief officer' or 'supreme officer' would have been. That arrangement, together with the mistrust of the council of state by backbenchers, kept the parliament in permanent session, as it had been before Pride's Purge. From December 1653 Cromwell and his executive council were largely independent of parliament, which was now to be confined to occasional meetings. Early propaganda of the protectorate reproached the Rump for having failed to separate executive from legislative power. In 'the keeping of these two apart, flowing in distinct channels', it was explained, 'there lies a grand secret of liberty and good government'.[266] Men who were outraged by that attitude regarded the title by which Cromwell ruled as a secondary issue. They played little if any discernible part in the resistance to the offer of the Crown in 1657. The underlying parliamentarian objection to the protectorate would have stood whether he had taken the title of king or not. Just as Charles I had been arraigned as a tyrant rather than a king, so it was on Cromwell's 'tyranny', together with the military usurpation that was alleged to make him if anything a worse tyrant than Charles, that manifestoes hostile to his rule dwelled. The chief opposition to the offer of the Crown in 1657 came from within the army, whose leaders had themselves offered it to him in December 1653. They would have accepted, even welcomed, a return to kingship provided it served their purposes. In 1653 they wanted Cromwell to use the kingly office to carry out their programme. In 1657 he would have become the parliament's king, appointed to civilianize the regime, ease the army out of politics, and tame movements of religious and social radicalism.

---

[264] Abbott, ii. 589, iii. 459–60.
[265] *Burton*, iii. 179.
[266] Nedham, *True State*, p. 10.

During the kingship crisis of 1657 the movement against the rule not merely of Cromwell but of any 'single person' had yet to gather strength. Foundations had nonetheless been laid. The foreign exploits of the kingless regime of 1649–53, trumpeted by Nedham's eloquence, had entered public consciousness. The thinking of James Harrington, which had percolated before the appearance of his *Oceana* in 1656,[267] may also have played its part, though it would be only in 1659 that his constitutional programme made a wide impact. Yet there were other, more powerful, sources from which hostility to single rule would arise.

Even before 1649 the breakdown of the institutions of Church and state, and the convulsion of civil war, had generated radical expectations. The regicide and the abolition of king and Lords gave them a new and striking impetus, which the Rump could not contain and of which it became the target. 'Lordly' conduct and character, attacked by Nedham, were denounced too by Gerrard Winstanley, who maintained that the 'tyranny of one over another, as of lords of manor over the common people . . . ought to be taken away with the kingly office, because they are the strength of the ancient prerogative custom'. Nedham and Winstanley both professed to speak for 'the people', by which they tended to mean right-thinking people. 'The people', according to Winstanley, 'are much rejoiced' in the end of the monarchy and in the proclamation of a 'free commonwealth', 'as being words forerunning their freedom, and they wait for their accomplishment'. Like Nedham, Winstanley claimed that 'the kingly power' could lie not only in 'one' but in 'many' hands. But where Nedham had argued in secular terms, to Winstanley the Rump's 'kingly power' was 'the power of unrighteousness, which indeed is the devil'. Earthly kingship, explained Winstanley, usurped 'the power of Almighty God', whose 'kingly power of righteousness' would 'tread all covetousness, pride, envy and self-love . . . under his feet, and take the kingdom and government of the creation out of the hand of self-seeking and self-honouring flesh'—the 'tyrant-flesh', as Winstanley also called it—'and rule the alone king of righteousness in the earth; and this indeed is Christ himself'.[268]

Winstanley's beliefs lay outside the political and theological mainstream of the Interregnum. So did the call of Fifth Monarchists, another movement generated by the revolution of 1649, and of other sectaries for 'No King but Jesus'.[269] Yet those aspirations were only extreme signals of a broader movement of the spirit, whose adherents knew the use God makes of his servants to obliterate principalities and powers that obstruct his will. Biblical denunciations of 'the kings of the earth' (or 'the great potentates of the earth') were voiced by men close to the centre of power. The prominent regicide Edmund Ludlow, who thought that even though Charles I 'was not the Antichrist spoken of by the Apostle, yet was he one of the kings that gave his power to the Beast', commended the king's execution 'as it related to

[267] Worden, 'Harrington's "Oceana"', pp. 113–22.
[268] Corns et al., *Complete Works of Gerrard Winstanley*, ii. 33, 87, 108–9.
[269] Henry Haggar, *No King but Jesus* (1652); Myers, *1659*, pp. 216–17.

the advancement of the Gospel of Christ, and the setting up of his rule and sceptre'.[270] The king's death, he hoped, would be 'such an example' to 'the beasts of prey' that 'the kings of the earth might be kept more in awe'. Here Ludlow may have been following, as he did elsewhere, the footsteps of John Cook, his ally in Ireland in the early 1650s, who wanted the regicide to be 'an example to other kingdoms . . . that the kings of the earth may hear, and fear, and do no more so wickedly'.[271] Cook indicated how the intensity of that and similar yearnings had worn down his own instinctive hope for reform by a virtuous single ruler.[272] 'Majesty', he had decided, was 'a term not fit for any mortal man', and to bestow it on one was 'high treason against the majesty' of the Lord.[273] The regicide had created or heightened an alertness to the intermixture of 'religious' and 'civil' idolatry and superstition, and to the parallels between popery and the adoration or 'idolizing of kings'.[274] Such sentiments did not in themselves preclude the rule of godly or virtuous single persons, a possibility which Cook contemplated with an ambivalent mind in 1652,[275] and to which Ludlow seems to have remained open during Cromwell's rule.[276] They were in essence directed against a spirit, not a form, of power. Their spiritual cast tended to direct attention away from questions of form. Where forms of government were attacked on spiritual grounds, the republican one of the 1650s could be as vulnerable to criticism as the protectoral one. Nonetheless, the criticism helped create the mental climate within which debates over single rule would be conducted towards the end of the decade.

That climate is unintelligible if we confine ourselves to the secular strands of opinion to which the attention of historians of political thought is often restricted. Even in the writings of the 1650s which pleaded for the emulation of classical political example, pagan precepts merged with Christian ones. A tract printed twice between Pride's Purge and the regicide, arguing that a 'free state' encourages men 'to the study of wisdom, truth, justice, &c.', drew on the writings of Aristotle, Virgil, Machiavelli, Bodin, and Lipsius—and asserted that 'the Lord is now risen up and doing his great work, throwing down and breaking to pieces the proud powers of the earth both civil and ecclesiastical. . . . All powers and places in opposition to Christ are but dry stubble'.[277] James Harrington detected, in the wisdom of classical republics, principles of constitutional design of which the pristine Hebrew commonwealth was the original pattern. He had no time for the perspective of such writers as John Cook, who in seeking 'civil prudence for governing a state and commonwealth' looked to 'the sacred fountain of Scripture rather than the puddles of history',[278] and John Rogers, that advocate of a 'theocratic' commonwealth who

[270] Ludlow, *Voyce*, pp. 144, 208; cf. J.P. Kenyon, *The Stuart Constitution* (Cambridge, 1966), p. 327; Sidney, *Court Maxims*, p. 89.
[271] Cook, *King Charls his Case*, p. 40.
[272] Cook, *Monarchy, no Creature*, p. 50.
[273] Ibid., p. 42.
[274] e.g. Hall, *Grounds and Reasons*, p. 22; *Somers Tracts*, vi. 87; *LP*, pp. 175–6, 186, 206, 234. Cf. Nedham, *Case of the Commonwealth*, p. 114; *CSPD 1653–4*, p. 307; below, p. 336.
[275] Cook, *Monarchy, no Creature*, p. 53.
[276] *Ludlow's Memoirs*, i. 420; cf. *Armies Dutie*, p. 27.
[277] Philodemus, *Armies Vindication*, preface and pp. 41, 63, 64.
[278] Cook, *Monarchy, no Creature*, p. 5.

scorned the 'pagan' and 'popish' models that he accused Harrington of having 'fetched from Athens and Venice'.[279] Harrington was angered when writers denounced his hero Machiavelli as 'irreverent or atheistical' for comparing Lycurgus and Solon with their fellow lawgiver Moses.[280] It was the spread of literacy and learning by the Romans, Harrington reminded his readers, that had laid the social foundations of the spread of Christianity.[281] To Harrington, as to Milton,[282] pagan and Christian instruction reinforced each other. Harrington's classicism coexisted easily with apocalyptic thinking. The system of rule that he proposed would reclaim 'freedom of soul' from 'earthly trash' and from 'the bondage of sin'.[283] If God the Father had ruled the Hebrew polity, God the Son would rule the immortal commonwealth of Harrington's devising.[284]

Harrington looked forward to the transformation not only of England but of the world. One point on which he agreed with his critic the minister Richard Baxter was that, as Baxter had it, 'the same principles that prove it sordid and impious to value our personal prosperity before that of the common-wealth do prove it as bad to value the good of one common-wealth before the universal kingdom of God on earth'.[285] 'The late appearances of God unto you', Harrington told the English, had not been 'altogether for yourselves'. Ciceronian ideas blended with messianic ones in his assertion that a truly constituted commonwealth would have a 'duty', as a 'minister of God upon earth', to 'aspire unto the empire of the world', and so liberate the oppressed subjects of the tyrannies of the Continent, whose cries God had heard.[286] The regicide, together with the epidemic of continental revolutions in the middle decades of the century, gave a new headiness, in the writings of Harrington and others, to an old dream of a military campaign that would sweep from northern to southern Europe and clear the Continent of popery and tyranny: the vision that is either proclaimed or derided (or both) in Andrew Marvell's 'Horatian Ode' of 1650, where Cromwell 'to all states not free | Shall climacteric be'.[287] The aspiration was enhanced, too, by the war with the Dutch of 1652–4, whose most zealous advocates saw it as a means towards the purification of international Protestantism and its unification against popery and Antichrist.[288]

Did God favour republican rule? Harrington was only one of many who believed the early Hebrew polity to have had no king. John Cook was sure that the Rump

---

[279] John Rogers, *Diapoliteia: A Christian Concertation with Mr Prin* (1659), pp. 76, 82; Myers, *1659*, p. 221. The charge about Athens was untrue.

[280] J. G. A. Pocock, ed., *The Political Works of James Harrington* (Cambridge, 1977), p. 629.

[281] Harrington, *'Commonwealth of Oceana'*, ed. Pocock, p. 48.

[282] *LP*, pp. 161–3.

[283] Harrington, *'Commonwealth of Oceana'*, p. 19.

[284] Ibid., p. 232.

[285] Baxter, *Holy Commonwealth*, p. 79.

[286] Harrington, *'Commonwealth of Oceana'*, pp. 229–33.

[287] Worden, 'Politics of Marvell's Horatian Ode', p. 535. Cf. *The Protector (so called) in part Unvailed* (1655), p. 57; Christopher Hill, 'The English Revolution and the Brotherhood of Man', in Hill, *Puritanism and Revolution* (1958), ch. 4.

[288] Steven Pincus, *Protestantism and Patriotism. Ideologies and the Making of English Foreign Policy, 1650–1668* (Cambridge, 1996).

had 'settled that form of government which was appointed for God's peculiar people'.[289] There were many alternative interpretations. Bulstrode Whitelocke and Nathaniel Bacon found parallels between the early Hebrew polity and the ancient English constitution of king and parliament.[290] In any case, was the form of rule in the Hebrew state, which was agreed to have been directly ruled by God, necessarily to be emulated in lands where he had left the design of governments to human agency and choice?[291] Even the Israelites, after all, had been allowed to cast off the divinely appointed form, when God permitted them, against his advice, to choose a king to reign over them. Ludlow remarked on the error of their choice but approvingly observed that at least their kings had been 'chosen by the free vote of the people'.[292] Nonetheless the supposition that the Hebrew government supplied a 'first pattern' of kingless rule[293] acquired a following in the Interregnum. If God intended England to be a second Israel, the chosen people of the new dispensation, then the pattern might have a special authority.[294]

New Testament texts were invoked too. The classical streak in Milton's suspicion of kings converged with his conviction, first announced in 1651, that Christ's rebuke to the sons of Zebedee, who sought exaltation above their brethren, revealed heaven's dislike of kingly domination.[295] For no form of government, he explained in 1660, 'comes nearer' to Christ's teaching 'than a free commonwealth', where the

---

[289] Cook, *Monarchy, no Creature*, ep. ded.

[290] BL Add MS 37343, fo. 14ᵛ; *Whitelockes Notes upon the Kings Writt*, ii. 57, 257; Bacon, *Historical and Political Discourse*, i. 70; cf. Baxter, *Holy Commonwealth*, p. 214.

[291] Nedham denied that the 'theocracy' of 'the government of the Israelites under Moses, then Joshua and the judges', all rulers whom he thought of as kingly, was applicable to other nations: *Mercurius Politicus* 22 April 1652, pp. 1538–9.

[292] Ludlow, *Voyce*, pp. 138, 220.

[293] Mayers, *1659*, p. 221.

[294] In the first chapter of his powerful recent study of the influence on political thought of the revival of rabbinic studies after the Reformation (*The Hebrew Republic: Jewish Sources and the Transformation of European Political Thought* [Cambridge, Mass., 2010]), Eric Nelson detects a change in attitudes towards forms of government in the England of the 1650s. A pluralist approach, which accepted that God allowed for variety and human choice in political constitutions, gave way, in 'many' writers, to a prescriptive one, which insisted that God had enjoined a uniform principle. Some took the divine model to be a monarchy, others a republic. Thus 'monarchy was now either required or forbidden; there was increasingly little middle ground'. To 'a startling degree', 'this debate' was 'shaped and radicalized by the Christian encounter with "Talmudists"' (pp. 51–2). Nelson seems to me to overstate his case, both in his accounts of the two writers, Harrington and Milton, on whom he concentrates, and in his brief assessment of the controversies to which their writings belonged. I am not persuaded that the equation of monarchy with idolatry which Nelson traces to rabbinic writing need have had that source (or that Harrington's own views can be equated with those of the 'Talmudists' whom he cites). The hardening of positions discerned by Nelson seems to me best explained by the changes of political atmosphere described by this chapter. Nonetheless, he directs us to a dimension of Puritan political thought which, however much or little it may have owed to rabbinic studies, has been under-explored. Writers who wanted a republic in England, and who thought that the Hebrew government which God had ordained had been a republic, saw biblically enjoined principles of rule at work in that polity. They urged it as an inspiration and example, sometimes even as a model of divine wisdom which no human prudence could hope to match; and many of them thought that divine providence demanded kingless rule in present-day England.

[295] *WJM*, vii. 155; *LP*, pp. 43–4. Cf. *CPW*, iii. 486, vii. 155; Williams, 'Anatomy of a Radical Gentleman', pp. 123–4.

greatest men 'are not elevated above their brethren'.[296] Though Milton had by that
time turned wholly against single rule, his biblical positions need not have been
incompatible with it, if some means could have been devised of utilizing the merits
of kings while limiting their powers. Nathaniel Bacon, alluding to Matthew 11:30,
argued that the Saxon kingdom had been 'above all others likest unto that of
Christ's kingdom, whose yoke is easy, and burden light'.[297]

What such sentiments were not compatible with, in the minds of an increasing
number of people during the protectorate, was the rule of Cromwell (even if Bacon
himself came to accept it). Not merely was that rule flagrantly unconstitutional. It
was sinful. In the obloquy that was heaped on Cromwell, the misgovernment of
the country was blamed on the misgovernment of his soul. Within Cromwell's
circle as without it, his apparent proclivity towards worldly political calculation or
manipulation was closely watched. In complaints about his rule as protector, the
old point that single rulers tend to pursue their own rather than the public interest
was given a Puritan cast, as it had been in attacks by the godly on Charles I. The
'self-seeking, slavish and enslaving spirit' of Cromwell's government was attributed
by Sir Henry Vane and his friends to 'that great idol . . . self-interest . . . a frame of
spirit directly contrary to Christ's, serving to promote and advance the great . . .
interests of the devil in the world' and to plant 'the throne and seat of the Beast'.[298]
Thirsters after righteousness, it was alleged, were 'trodden under foot', 'and such
only promoted to ride in the chariot with Jehu'—another deliverer of his people
who had turned tyrant—'who had their hearts right with his heart'.[299] At the
ceremony at which Cromwell took his oath of office under the Humble Petition
and Advice, the Speaker of the parliament—perhaps as a peace-offering to the
soldiers and Congregationalists and sectaries who had opposed the offer of the
Crown, but perhaps as a warning on parliament's own behalf—invoked a text that
was commonly used against Cromwell as against Charles I before him, Deuteronomy 17:20, to remind the protector that his 'heart' should not be 'lifted up above
his brethren'.[300]

Opponents of the protectorate of varying outlooks and experiences—former
rumpers; disaffected army officers; sectaries—came together under the slogan
'the good old cause'. It was artfully deployed.[301] Sometimes its users competed
over the meaning of the phrase, but as a rule its value lay in its very looseness and
uncertainty. Some adherents of the good old cause had opposed Cromwell since
April 1653 if not earlier, some since December 1653. Others had broken with him

---

[296] *CPW*, vii. 359–60.

[297] Bacon, *Historical and Political Discourse*, i. 70.

[298] Quoted by Scott, *Commonwealth Principles*, p. 251; cf. pp. 217–18.

[299] Blair Worden, *Roundhead Reputations: The English Civil Wars and the Passions of Posterity*
(2001), p. 58. For Cromwell as Jehu see too Haller and Davies, *Leveller Tracts*, p. 443; William
Sheppard, *Sincerity and Hypocrisy* (1658), pp. 23–4; *A Brief Relation containing an Abbreviation of
the Arguments* (1659), sig. A2; above, p. 233; cf. *CPW*, vi. 698.

[300] *OPH*, xx. 156; cf. *Burton*, iii. 282.

[301] Barbara Taft, 'That Lusty Puss, The Good Old Cause', *History of Political Thought* 5 (1984),
p. 459.

during the protectorate. Some had put the principle of parliamentary sovereignty first. Others cared more for liberty of conscience or godly reformation. In 1656 one of the Major-Generals, Thomas Kelsey, yearning for 'that blessed haven of reformation endeavoured by us', and distressed by the fillip given to the contrary spirit by the outcome of the parliamentary elections of that year, advised the protector that 'the interests of the people of God' were 'to be preserved before a thousand parliaments'.[302] Rumpers outraged by their own expulsion from power were thrown together with men who had welcomed the parliament's overthrow or who anyway shed no tears for its memory, and who looked for salvation to the fresh elections which the Rump had long resisted. Yet only with a united front could Cromwell's opponents hope to destroy him. A widely circulated tract, *XXV Queries*, published early in Richard Cromwell's parliament, urged the 'necessity for those of the old parliament, the officers and soldiers of the army, and all others that pretend to be friends to the good old cause, to lay aside all personal animosities . . . and to unite . . . and . . . to promote principles of public interest and common right and freedom'.[303] Where the groups to which the pamphlet appealed could not agree on policies, at least they learned to cite common memories and experiences, real or imagined, of a cause they could agree to be both good and old.[304] Its prosperity or adversity was measured by its emotional temperature, as its adherents observed the alternate withdrawals and returns of God's 'presence and blessing' among them, the advances of 'the work of the Lord' and the times when it 'seemed to stand still'.[305] Men yearned for the 'primitive lustre' of the cause, for the return of its 'virgin days'.[306] Before Pride's Purge, the cause had been 'a very pitiful, dull, dry, lean, barren, ill-favoured thing', but with the death of the king 'it became, and appeared on a sudden in the eyes of thousands, the most lovely, lively, growing, sparkling, prosperous cause of all the earth. . . . The power and spirit of our cause was great and high after the king's death more than at any time before.'[307] Not all leaders or followers of the cause spoke of it in so exalted a strain, but a language of forsaken godliness or virtue was of wide help in hiding the cracks within the movement

Cromwell's betrayal of the cause gradually persuaded its adherents of the wickedness, not merely of the abuses of single rule, but of single rule itself. The evils of Charles I's reign could be blamed on one man or one family. Now that they were replicated by Cromwell, it seemed that they might be inherent in the occupancy of single power. 'How many thousands beside the army', asked the republican John Streater on the fall of the protectorate, 'were of opinion, if any man under heaven might be trusted, Gen. Cromwell might be trusted with absolute

---

[302] Quoted by Christopher Durston, *Cromwell's Major-Generals* (2001), p. 199.

[303] Quoted by Austin Woolrych, 'The Good Old Cause and the Fall of the Protectorate', *Cambridge Historical Journal* 13 (1957), pp. 138–9.

[304] Cf. Firth, *Clarke Papers*, iii. 140.

[305] *The Moderate Publisher* 4 February 1653, p. 710. Cf. *OPH*, xxi. 368; *Mercurius Politicus* 26 May 1659, p. 462; Woolrych, 'Good Old Cause', p. 161.

[306] Woolrych, 'Good Old Cause', p. 139.

[307] Christopher Feake, *A Beam of Light* (1659), p. 35.

power?'[308] Milton had given the protectorate half a chance. In its early stages he had kept to his long-held view that forms of government should vary according to prevailing political and ethical conditions. Single rule might be suitable to some states, unsuitable to others. In 1654 he found arguments for the single rule of Cromwell, if Cromwell could only show himself to be supremely virtuous.[309] By the time of the protector's death Milton had lost that hope and had come to view the protectorate as a tyranny. In 1659–60 he declared his opposition to the rule of any 'single person', even to 'the fond conceit of something like a Duke of Venice'.[310] He wanted a government 'where no single person, but reason only swaies'. In 1656 Milton's hero Sir Henry Vane had thought that the executive power, which should be 'distinct from' the 'legislative power' but 'subordinate to' it, might be 'intrusted into the hands of one single person, if need require, or in a greater number, as the legislative should think fit'.[311] By 1659 the experience of Cromwellian rule had convinced him that 'too great is the burthen for a single person, because liable to temptation'.[312] The thought of the pamphleteer William Sprigge moved in the same direction. Pleading for 'an equal commonwealth' in 1659, he explained that he had previously been 'strongly possessed with a fond opinion of the indifferency of all forms of government', but had come to grasp that even the 'name' of a single person must be proscribed.[313]

In early 1649 the Rump forbade the exercise of kingly 'power' by 'any single person', but its anxious wording did not rule out a constitutional role for one. When, in the following winter, it demanded national subscription to an 'Engagement' of loyalty, it required obedience to 'the government as it is now established, without a king or House of Lords', but did not stipulate the exclusion of a 'single person' from government.[314] After the Rump's restoration in 1659, by contrast, the parliament, seeking to beat off the Cromwellian interest, demanded the renunciation of government by a king, House of Lords, or 'any' or 'every single person'.[315] In the same year the term 'free state' acquired a wider currency. Even the Rump and its members, who had been wary of it in the early 1650s, became readier to use it.[316] The Rump's Engagement of 1649–50 had demanded submission to the 'Commonwealth': now it was rephrased to require obedience to the 'Commonwealth and Free State'.[317]

Hostility to single rule was one thing. Agreement how to replace it was another. Advocates of parliamentary sovereignty had to make common cause with thinkers

---

[308] John Streater, *The Continuation of this Present Session of Parliament Justified* (1659), p. 13; cf. *Faithfull Scout* 13 May 1659, pp. 19–20.

[309] *LP*, chs 11–14.

[310] *CPW*, vii. 374, 427.

[311] *Somers Tracts*, vi. 311–12.

[312] *SPC*, iii. 506. Cf. Sykes, *Life of Sir Henry Vane*, p. 100; *Armies Dutie*, p. 15.

[313] Sprigge, *Modest Plea*, pp. 1, 7.

[314] *GD*, p. 391.

[315] Firth and Rait, ii. 1273, 1304; *CJ* 3, 7 May, 3 September 1659, 6 January, 14 February 1660; *OPH*, xxii. 60 (cf. xxi. 401); cf. *Mercurius Politicus* 14 July 1659, p. 589.

[316] e.g. Firth and Rait, ii. 1299–1300; *Burton*, iii. 176; above, p. 257; cf. e.g. *OPH*, xxii. 171.

[317] *CJ* 14 February 1660.

who were indifferent or hostile to that ideal, or who continued to lament the Rump's failure to lay the foundations of a true 'commonwealth'. Those tensions persisted through the protectorate and survived it. Nonetheless, the pressures of opposition gradually narrowed the gaps of perspective. Unfortunately, problems of evidence make that development exceptionally hard to pinpoint, for we are dependent for glimpses of it on slanted accusations by Cromwell and the head of his intelligence service, John Thurloe, who had reasons to exaggerate the extent of anti-monarchical sentiment in the opposition to Cromwellian rule. Even so, a probable pattern can be detected.

The first parliament of the protectorate, which sat from September 1654 to January 1655, supplied a focus for conspiracy by disaffected officers and soldiers.[318] According to notes later made by Thurloe, the conspirator John Wildman told his ally Colonel Robert Overton in late 1654 (or perhaps at the start of 1655) that 'there was a party which would stand right for a commonwealth'. Yet the manifestoes compiled by Wildman and his close associates during the parliament say next to nothing about a 'commonwealth'. They are pleas for the freedom of parliament.[319] Thurloe's assertion was amplified, but not particularized, by Cromwell. In dissolving the parliament he referred to conspiracies that had flourished during its session. There were plotters who 'pretend commonwealth's interest', and there was a 'party of men, called Levellers, and who call themselves commonwealthsmen'.[320] 'Levellers' was here a smear to cover the coalition of plotters. In his opening speech to his next parliament, in 1656, the protector claimed that the 'Levelling party hath some access lately [to a party that?] goes under a finer name or notion. I think they would be called commonwealths men'.[321]

Thurloe and Cromwell knew that the esteem of the word 'commonwealth' had suffered by its annexation by the Rump. The protector played on that association in April 1657, in a retrospective justification of his expulsion of the Rump. If the parliament had had its way, he remembered, its successor would have been 'a commonwealth's government, why, we should have had fine things then! We should have had a council of state and a parliament of four hundred men executing arbitrary power without intermission.'[322] The word 'commonwealth' gave him

---

[318] Barbara Taft, '*The Humble Petition of Several Colonels of the Army*: Causes, Character, and Results of Military Opposition to Cromwell's Protectorate', *Huntington Library Quarterly* 42 (1978), pp. 15–41.

[319] *Humble Petition of Several Colonels* (cf. Taft, '*Humble Petition*', p. 23); Whitelocke, *Memorials*, iv. 187; cf. *SPC*, iii. 289.

[320] Abbott, iii. 574, 585; cf. Whitelocke, *Memorials*, iv. 183–4. The diarist of the parliament of 1654, Guibon Goddard, tells us that in its opening days there were MPs hostile to the Instrument of Government (among whom we may guess those zealots for the Commons' supremacy Bradshaw, Hesilrige, and Scot to have been at the fore) who 'disputed as if they had been in the schools, where each man had liberty to propose his own Utopia, and to frame commonwealths according to his own fancy, as if we had been in *republica constituenda*, and not in *republica constituta*' (*Burton*, i. xxxi–xxxii). It seems likely that the diarist meant to describe, not a frenzy of fresh constitutional design, but merely an impractical insistence on a return to first political principles. The diarist habitually presents the concern of the opposition as parliamentary sovereignty, not 'framing commonwealths'.

[321] Abbott, iv. 267.

[322] Ibid., iv. 487; cf. iv. 501.

further opportunities for denigration. From Tudor times there remained memories, though they were much diminished, of its association with designs of social turbulence and subversion on behalf of the common or 'base and poorer sort'.[323] That connotation, which underlay his association of 'commonwealthsmen' with 'levelling', would be exploited more fully by him in February 1658, when, in dissolving parliament, he complained of moves to establish 'a commonwealth', where 'some tribune of the people might be the man that might rule all'. Behind that initiative he detected 'endeavours . . . to stir up the people of this town into tumultuating', which were attracting 'the meanest people that go about the streets'.[324]

Polemical attacks on the protectorate in Cromwell's lifetime did not in fact use the word 'commonwealthsman' (or 'commonwealthsmen'). The noun had yet to stand for a political position. When in the 1640s the Leveller William Walwyn had commended 'common-wealths men', he had used the word only in its conventional sense, to mean servants of the common good.[325] A writer who lauded the regicide in 1651 acknowledged that there had been 'most noted common-wealths men' among the civil-war royalists.[326] In 1652 Marchamont Nedham tried to give the word an anti-monarchical cast by indicating that the common good could prevail only in a republic. The English, he urged, should learn to 'be true commonwealth's men, and zealous against monarchic interest, in all its appearances and encroachments whatsoever'.[327] But no one at the time seems to have followed his lead.[328] Nedham's statement was republished in June 1656, in a tract published to influence the elections to the parliament that would meet in September. Yet when, in November 1656, Harrington's *Oceana* referred to rumpers and their

---

[323] Withington, *Society in Early Modern England*, pp. 142–4. The influential denigration of 'commonweal' by Sir Thomas Elyot, quoted by Withington, was absorbed by the *Remains of Sir Walter Raleigh*, which was often reprinted in the seventeenth century (e.g. 1657 edition, pp. 3, 8).

[324] Abbott, iv. 731, 732; cf. C. H. Firth, ed., 'Letters concerning the Dissolution of Cromwell's Last Parliament, 1658', *English Historical Review* 7 (1892), p. 106. In Richard Cromwell's parliament Sir Arthur Hesilrige felt it necessary, in defining his stance of opposition to the protectorate, to explain that 'I am no Leveller' (*Burton*, iv. 77). Cromwell's phrase 'some tribune of the people' was perhaps suggested by Marchamont Nedham: cf. *LP*, p. 351.

[325] McMichael and Taft, *Writings of William Walwyn*, pp. 99, 397.

[326] *Life and Reigne of King Charls*, pp. 221–2.

[327] *Mercurius Politicus* 11 March 1652, p. 1458.

[328] John Toland, the posthumous editor of Edmund Ludlow's autobiography, who was fighting his own battles over the terms 'commonwealth' and 'commonwealthsman', has Ludlow writing of the role of 'the commonwealth party' and 'the commonwealthsmen' in events from 1646: *Ludlow's Memoirs*, i. 146, 177, 184–5, 186, 212–13, 391, ii. 28, 46. Even if Toland reproduced Ludlow's (lost) manuscript accurately, those passages would be no evidence that the terms were used at that time, since Ludlow himself wrote in retrospect, after the Restoration. In fact Toland, whom we sometimes find inserting 'commonwealth' language into the part of Ludlow's text that does survive, is likely to have invented them. Ludlow himself does refer to 'the commonwealth party' in Richard Cromwell's parliament in 1659 (*Voyce*, p. 121), but by that year the phrase had come into use. He also looks back at discussions with 'my commonwealth friends' before the trial of Charles I (*Voyce*, p. 166). He must have meant the Levellers and those MPs, Ludlow among them, who had held discussions with them. John Lilburne refers to those MPs as 'the honest men of the parliament as they were called': Toland at one point changes Ludlow's phrase 'the honest party' to 'the common-wealth party' (*Voyce*, p. 97; *Ludlow's Memoirs*, ii. 284).

supporters, loosely and unsympathetically, as 'commonwealthsmen',[329] he did not indicate that they used the word of themselves. A tract published during the kingship crisis of 1657, *A Copy of a Letter written to an Officer of the Army by a true Commonwealths-man, and no Courtier*, was a plea for the return of hereditary monarchy in the cause of the common good.

If the word 'commonwealthsmen' had acquired some derogatory associations, opponents of the protectorate may have felt as much incentive to avoid it as Cromwell did to deploy it. It is always possible that in 1654–7, the period of the Instrument of Government, hopes of a 'commonwealth', as a form of government, figured more widely in the discussions of Cromwell's opponents than in their public statements. It seems, nonetheless, that there was a turning-point in the vocabulary of opposition at some point after the protector's investiture under the Humble Petition and Advice, and the prorogation of parliament, in June 1657. The passage of the Humble Petition, and the offer of the Crown to Cromwell, induced new thinking among opponents of those moves. If the Humble Petition was the kind of thing parliamentary sovereignty would produce, then appeals to that principle would, on their own, be an inadequate and hazardous strategy. The passage of the new constitution implicated parliament not merely in the drift back towards monarchy but in the movement, which we can loosely call Presbyterian, of social and religious reaction. In the face of it a new position was needed that would distinguish adherents of the good old cause not merely from Cromwellians but from Presbyterians too. The drive by the Commons in 1657 to convert the protectorate into a civilian and conservative monarchy was a sobering development for friends of the good old cause. There had been a similar Presbyterian impulse in the purged parliament of 1654, but that parliament had stood up to the protector, and in any case its failure had given new heart to disaffected rumpers and their allies. The new parliament had befriended him and given his rule parliamentary sanction.

Yet if the introduction of the Humble Petition had in that respect strengthened his rule, it had in other ways made it more vulnerable. In early 1658 his government faced the severest test with which opposition within the Roundhead cause ever presented it. The party that had constructed the Humble Petition and Advice had been demoralized and dispersed by his refusal of the Crown, a decision which correspondingly gave fresh heart to opponents of the conservative direction of the regime. In the second session of the parliament, which met in January, he lost control of the Commons. It had sat for just over a fortnight when he moved frantically to dissolve it. The MPs who had been forcibly excluded from the first session had been allowed back to the second. They found an easy target. The Humble Petition had created, with vulnerable imprecision, a second chamber, the 'Other House', as a substitute for the Lords. A conventional explanation of the constitutional function of the Lords had lain in the independence of its members, or of enough of them, from the Crown. By contrast the new

---

[329] Harrington, *'Commonwealth of Oceana'*, pp. 61–2; cf. Pocock, *Political Works of James Harrington*, pp. 574, 600.

chamber was to be nominated by Cromwell. Though the names were to be submitted to the Commons for approval, the protector had acquired a new and potentially formidable machine of patronage. That was not the purpose of the designers of the Humble Petition, who had seen the power of nomination which it gave him merely as a price worth paying for a move back towards the ancient constitution. In time, they hoped, the old peers, or at least the parliamentarian ones, would be restored and the Other House be converted into the House of Lords. Cromwell saw more immediate benefits in the new chamber. It would be a means of rewarding friends and supporters with office, of binding potential trouble-makers into the regime, and of blocking unwelcome initiatives from the Commons.

The newly restored MPs, headed by Hesilrige and Scot, those champions of the unicameral Commons, vigorously attacked the newly created body. This time we have evidence from outside the court. The diarist of the parliament, Thomas Burton, recorded a long speech by Scot which warned Oliver Cromwell's courtiers that 'the administrations of God's government are against you. Is not God staining the glory and pride of the world? Is there anything but a commonwealth that flourishes? Venice against the pride of the Ottoman family. All their mountains are pulled down. God governs the world, as he governs his church, by plain things and low things.' Scot's speech, protested another member, 'wholly tends to a common-wealth, so I hope it will need no answer. . . . We have had sad experience of . . . a commonwealth.'[330] What Scot said in the chamber seems to have reflected a development of opinion outside it. Encouraged by the debates in the Commons, public protest against the regime had acquired a new breadth and boldness. A petition with a huge list of signatures was drawn up in the City for submission to the Commons, whom it urged to reclaim 'the supreme power and trust which the people (the original of all just power) commit unto them'. Cromwell, in alluding to the agitation at the dissolution of the parliament, did not refer to that demand, which he had as much reason to bypass as the petitioners had to highlight it. Instead he mentioned 'inventions', which had been formed since the passage of the Humble Petition, 'of (really) designing a commonwealth', and of current attempts 'to draw the army to the state of a question, a commonwealth, a commonwealth'. It was now that he alluded to plans for a 'commonwealth' where 'some tribune of the people might be the man that might rule all'.[331] Thurloe likewise emphasized the demand for 'a commonwealth' at this time. Discontent in the army, headed by William Packer, the commander of Cromwell's own cavalry regiment, survived the dissolution and led to the dismissal of Packer and five other officers. Thurloe, reliant as ever on George Monck to steer opinion in Scotland, reported to him that the officers, in explaining their dissatisfaction to Cromwell, 'seemed to speak much of the goodness of a commonwealth'.[332] Samuel Hartlib, writing from Thurloe's office to an English envoy abroad whose support the government was anxious to retain, described the City petition as 'for a commonwealth'. He called it a

---

[330] *Burton*, ii. 389, 395; cf. ii. 330.
[331] Abbott, iv. 731–2.
[332] Firth, *Clarke Papers*, iii. 140.

'dangerous design' which 'would have gathered like a snowball' but for 'the resolute and sudden dissolving of the parliament'.[333]

The petition did not call for a commonwealth. Yet this time the government was probably right to discern such an ambition at work. Loaded as the regime's allegations are, they are a little less airy and slender than its earlier ones. When set beside Scot's speech they are also more persuasive. At all events, the tendency of which Cromwell and Thurloe had complained had become unmistakable by the end of 1658. In December, as the election campaign for Richard Cromwell's parliament got under way, Thurloe alleged that 'the commonwealthsmen have their daily meetings, disputing what kind of commonwealth they shall have, taking it for granted that they shall pick and choose'.[334] Firm evidence supports his claim. Unfortunately part of it survives only in a hostile account, which was drawn up for him, but the report includes a transcription of a manifesto which has every mark of authenticity. Drawn up after Richard Cromwell's accession, with the aim of winning over the army, it brought together the claims of parliamentary sovereignty and republican rule. It stated 'that liberty consists in the people's being master of the supreme authority . . . as also that the disposition of the people of England at this time is wholly inclined and adapted to the government of a republic'. In developing that second claim the remonstrance offered 'a model of a common-wealth'. The account submitted to Thurloe gives details which there is no reason to doubt. The 'model' was based on Harrington's *Oceana*.[335] That evidence is complemented by a source independent of the government, a tract of 1659, *The Armies Dutie*. It printed 'faithful advice to the soldiers', from 'several honest men', which had been contained in two letters sent in the same month, December 1658, to Charles Fleetwood, the new commander-in-chief of the army. It too was based on Harrington's teaching. If the subscribers who put their initials to the tract are the people they seem likely to be, then Henry Marten, Henry Neville, and John Wildman were making common cause with discontented soldiers.[336]

In Richard Cromwell's parliament in the spring of 1659, the goal of a 'common-wealth', without a single ruler, had become the basis, half-proclaimed, half-concealed, of the political programme not only of Neville but of Scot and Hesilrige. The concealment was tactical.[337] Those men, wanting to build a broad party of support in the Commons, professed or intimated a willingness to keep Richard Cromwell in power, provided the protector's authority were acknowledged to derive from parliament and to be limited by it. 'I am not against a single person', declared Hesilrige, 'but against that monster prerogative'.[338] A number of former rumpers and their sympathizers said much the same. The government was not fooled.

---

[333] Robert Vaughan, ed., *The Protectorate of Oliver Cromwell*, 2 vols (1839), ii. 442; cf. Firth, 'Letters concerning the Dissolution', p. 107.

[334] *TSP*, vii. 541.

[335] Bodl., Rawlinson MS a. 61, p. 401.

[336] *Armies Dutie*; cf. *CPW*, vii. 103 n.

[337] For Neville see Worden, 'Harrington's "Oceana"', pp. 126–32.

[338] *Burton*, iv. 77. Cf. iii. 112–13 (Scot), 132 (Neville), iv. 152 (Heselrige); BL Add. MS 5138, pp. 172–3, 177–8 (Vane); Cook, *Monarchy, no Creature*, p. 53; *Armies Dutie*, p. 27.

'They pretend they are for a single person', wrote one of Thurloe's employees, the MP Andrew Marvell, to another, 'but we know well enough what they mean.'[339] The parliamentary diarists Guibon Goddard and Thomas Burton were sceptical too. So was the MP who accused Hesilrige and Scot of aiming at 'a commonwealth', 'opposite to a single person'.[340] Their and their allies' goal became transparent when the parliament had been dissolved and the protectorate had fallen. They had no time for 'single persons' now. It was during the parliament of Richard Cromwell that the political meaning of 'commonwealthsmen', and with it 'the commonwealth party', acquired widespread use. The words were employed to describe Hesilrige, Neville, and their allies.[341] Whether those MPs used them themselves during the parliament we cannot be sure, but by the summer, at least, 'commonwealthsman' had ceased to become a mere political stigma. It had become a political badge, worn by men to whom the fall of the protectorate had been a deliverance.[342] Whereas in 1657 the term 'commonwealths-man' had been adopted for the title of a pamphlet in favour of hereditary monarchy, in titles of 1659 it meant an opponent of single rule.[343] That was not the only shift of political vocabulary wrought by the events of 1659. Used as we are to thinking of the last phase of the civil wars as a twilight, we can forget how open the future then seemed. No party and no programme could be confident of success. From the chaos and uncertainty there arose fresh thought and fresh alliances. Language responded to them. The adoption of 'commonwealths-men' by friends of the good old cause was one instance. Another, which we shall follow in the next chapter, was the spread of the phrase 'civil and religious liberty', which likewise gave the good old cause some common ground.[344]

A further word, which hitherto had been barely familiar, circulated too, if less widely. Until 1659 'republican', as a noun or adjective, had been scarce. As an adjective it (or 'republical') had had a neutral meaning, to signify the world of politics or public life.[345] The word had a friendly usage too, to mean—like 'commonwealthsman'—a servant of the community or the common good. It was in that sense that a pamphleteer of 1657 wrote that 'in every village there is some excellent republican'.[346] It also had a hostile signification. It had been used

---

[339] Margoliouth, *Poems and Letters of Andrew Marvell*, ii. 307.

[340] *Burton*, iii. 113.

[341] Ibid., iii. 502; BL Add. MS 5138, p. 114; *SPC*, iii. 425, 440, 444, 453; G. F. Warner, ed., *The Nicholas Papers*, 4 vols (Camden Society, 1886–1920), iv. 80, 83, 84, 104, 155; William Stephen, *The Consultations of the Ministers of Edinburgh*, 3 vols (Edinburgh, 1921–30), ii. 156; Baxter, *Holy Commonwealth*, p. 214.

[342] Cf. Baxter, *Holy Commonwealth*, p. 214.

[343] *The Honest-Design: or, The True Commonwealths-man* (1659); *A Common-wealth, and Commonwealths-men, Asserted* (1659).

[344] Around the same time another term, 'interest', which had long offered political interpreters an instrument for the assessment or prediction of the conduct of competing individuals or parties, acquired a keener, more analytical, more sceptical edge. J. A. W. Gunn, *Politics and the Public Interest in the Seventeenth Century* (1969), pp. 48–52. After a decade without the monarchy, parliamentary debate about the constitution had lost its hallowed tones. In 1659 it was characterized by plain speaking and candid homespun metaphors.

[345] Cook, *Monarchy, no Creature*, p. 27; cf. *Miltons Republican-Letters* (1682).

[346] John Beale, *The Herefordshire Orchards* (1657), pp. 38–9. Could the word, as an adjective, have a bolder signification? In 1651 a disciple and collaborator of Nedham, Charles Hotham (*Corporations*

scornfully to describe opponents of tyranny in a manuscript treatise of the 1620s,[347] and may have been occasionally deployed to brand parliamentary critics of the early Stuarts as enemies of monarchy.[348] In 1653–6 we sometimes find England's present rulers being attacked or mocked as 'republicans'.[349] It was only in 1659, however, that the political meaning of 'republican' came into anything like general use. People who then got called 'commonwealthsmen' or 'the commonwealth party' were also termed 'the republicans' or 'the republican party'.[350] They did not use the second pair of terms of themselves, but the coupling was another response to the spread of the anti-kingly sentiment.

There were tight limits both to the practical impact and—James Harrington's writings aside—to the conceptual originality of the republican thought of 1659. The army leaders could agree on no other alternative to the protectorate they had toppled than the restoration of the Rump. The newly proliferating language of republics and free states did not replace the old one of parliamentary virtues, which more often absorbed than yielded to it. In 1659–60 Milton retrospectively praised the Rump both as 'the famous parliament' and—in *The Readie and Easie Way to Establish a Free Commonwealth*—as 'a glorious rising commonwealth'.[351] The old language of liberty and the law persisted too. 'The most frequent distinguishing terms between monarch and commonwealth', observed a tract of 1659, 'are *servitus* and *libertas*.'[352] In the same year John Streater, an eager advocate of classical republican models, was content to define the 'good old cause' in the conventional parliamentarian terms of 'security of life, liberty and estate. The laws of this country speak no other language'.[353] 'A free state', he explained 'is the ruling of a people ... by laws that are superior to private interest.'[354] A majority of the rumpers still eschewed fresh constitutional design and remained pledged to unicameral parliaments. Other political actors broke free of that commitment. In the army and the

Vindicated, pp. 26–8), attacked the 'oligarchy' of the Rump. The country, he protested, should have 'not the shadows of a free commonwealth' but 'the substance of a right republican government of the nation by its own representatives, or national meetings in council'. 'I am', he explained, 'a servant of the *respublica*, not *curia*, *Romana*, a votary to a true commonwealth, not a decemvirate' (a noun repeatedly used against the Rump in Nedham's own explorations of Roman history). Yet Hotham simultaneously recalled his regret at the abolition of 'our limited monarchy'. 'Republic' as the common good, and 'republic' as a form of rule, stand in an uncertain relationship in his mind.

[347] J. P. Sommerville, *Royalists and Patriots: Politics and Ideology 1603–1640* (1999 edn), p. xiii.
[348] We have only the word of foreign ambassadors, writing in their own tongues, for that development: L. J. Reeve, *Charles I and the Road to Personal Rule* (Cambridge, 1989), p. 132; David Norbrook, *Poetry and Politics in the English Renaissance* (revised edn, Oxford, 2002), p. 159.
[349] Théophile Brachet, sieur de la Milletière, *The Victory of Truth* (1653), p. 8; William Prynne, *The First and Second Part of a Seasonable...Vindication* (1655), preface (penultimate page); Harrington, '*Commonwealth of Oceana*', p. 184; *SPC*, iii. 316.
[350] *Burton*, iv. 342, 344, 378; BL Add. MS 5138, p. 173; Warner, *Nicholas Papers*, iv. 84; William Prynne, *The Re-Publicans and Others Spurious Good Old Cause* (1659), *passim*; Prynne, *A True and Perfect Narrative* (1659), *passim*.
[351] *CPW*, vii. 420–1.
[352] *Common-wealth, and Commonwealths-men, Asserted*, p. 6.
[353] Streater, *Continuation*, p. 1.
[354] John Streater, *A Shield against the Parthian Dart* (1659), p. 16.

churches, many who had been dissatisfied with the earlier rule of the Rump had turned to the protectorate. Now that Cromwellian rule had failed them, they needed new constitutional ideas. Yet they struggled to devise them. The only innovative proposal in 1659 to come to the political forefront was the call (which took various forms) for a second, unelected parliamentary chamber, a select senate, which like the Cromwellian 'Other House' would shield the godly and their cause from the electorate.

That scheme adopted but, in its oligarchical tendency, perverted the constitutional proposals of Harrington, who eschewed the partisanship of Interregnum politics but whose ideas were now appropriated by partisans. His determinist argument, which explained that monarchical rule was superannuated and that Cromwell's attempt to revive it had been doomed, supplied an assurance to champions of the good old cause that they had history on their side. Other writers had suggested, metaphorically, that the old constitution had succumbed, after so many centuries, to old age.[355] Now Harrington gave the idea an analytical base. He likewise gave a scientific dimension, or at least the appearance of one, to a perception that had flourished since the early seventeenth century: that the peerage was in decline and the House of Lords with it.[356] His international perspective found an audience too. Scot's speech in January 1658—'Is there anything but a commonwealth that flourishes?'—may bear its influence. Harrington's insistence on agrarian laws to restrict aristocratic wealth also found its champions. It was taken up in 1659 by opponents of single rule who were also critical of noble oppression, of 'covetousness', of 'greed', of the 'vast unsatiable desire ... after riches'.[357]

In the winter of 1659–60, when the Puritan cause imploded but when the might of the army seemed to preclude the return of the monarchy, Harrington's arguments attracted interest on a wider front. Adaptations and truncations of the old constitution having all broken down, his promise that a new, soundly designed one, which would end the destructive passions of the last two decades and restore harmony and stability, caught a mood even among readers with no bias against monarchy. They had learned the truth of his assertion that 'for a nation to be still upon the cast of a die, to be ever upon trepidation as to the main chance of government, is a dreadful state of things'.[358] His friend John Aubrey observed that the new doctrine became 'very taking, and the more so because, as to human foresight, there was no possibility of the king's return'.[359] But when, as winter

[355] e.g. Nedham, *Case of the Commonwealth*, p. 13. Cf. *Mercurius Politicus* 22 April 1652, p. 1538; *Somers Tracts*, vi. 87; Braddick and Greengrass, 'Letters of Sir Cheney Culpepper', p. 356; *Burton*, iii. 89; Andrew Marvell, 'An Horatian Ode', line 35.
[356] Pocock, *Political Works of James Harrington*, p. 45; Bacon, *Historical and Political Discourse*, ii. 178; Theodore Rabb, 'The Role of the Commons', *Past and Present* 92 (1981), p. 77.
[357] Sprigge, *Modest Plea*, preface and pp. 112 ff.; cf. Petrus Cunaeus, *De Republica Hebraeorum*, ed. Lea Campos Boralevi (Florence, 1996), p. 61.
[358] Pocock, *Political Works of James Harrington*, p. 692.
[359] John Aubrey, *Brief Lives*, ed. Andrew Clark, 2 vols (1898), i. 290–1.

turned to spring, that 'possibility' grew, Harrington's thinking was discarded. Now the language of a 'free state' yielded to that of a 'free parliament'.

During the monarchical reaction of the Restoration, memories of the 'Commonwealth' of the Interregnum attracted wider and deeper revulsion. In the early years of the Restoration the government seems to have sought to adapt the word to its own uses. During the trials of the regicides the prosecutor Heneage Finch declared 'the king to be head of the commonwealth', which 'was an inanimate lump without him'.[360] The titles of early statutes of the Cavalier Parliament promised benefits to 'the commonwealth'.[361] But as a benign noun the word would fade. 'Commonwealthsman' suffered discredit too. Early in the Restoration, in the clamour for revenge on Puritan rule, a royalist argued 'that the commonwealth is not safe, while common-wealths-men remain alive'.[362] In a narrative of Richard Cromwell's parliament published after its dissolution in 1659, the MP Slingsby Bethel described the part played in it by 'the commonwealthsmen' or 'the party that was for the commonwealth', of which he was one. When the tract was republished in the Whig cause in 1680, the terms were prudently changed to 'the country party'.[363]

The odium would persist. 'Commonwealthsman' was still used to denote servants of the public good, but sparingly and as a secondary meaning. A dictionary first published in 1735 defined 'a commonwealthsman' as 'a stickler for a commonwealth government; also one who acts for the good of the commonwealth'.[364] Fourteen years earlier the 'true Whig' Robert Molesworth complained of the 'great discouragement' that was visited on friends of 'public liberty' by 'the heavy calumny thrown upon us, that we are all commonwealthsmen; which (in the ordinary meaning of the word) amounts to haters of kingly government'. For though the 'true construction' of the term, and of 'commonwealth', denoted care for 'the good of the whole', 'foolish people' had been 'frighten[ed]' out of that usage by 'the anarchy and confusion which these nations fell into sixty years ago, and which was falsely called a Commonwealth'.[365] 'Republican' was an alternative term of abuse, which had likewise lost its benign meaning. By now no one would have commended as 'republicans' the people 'in every village' who served the common good. From the early 1680s, the time of the exclusion crisis and the Rye House

---

[360] Ludlow, *Voyce*, p. 202.

[361] *Statutes of the Realm*, v. (1819): 'An Act for Prevention of Vexations' (1661); 'An Act for the Punishment of Unlawfull Cutting' (1663); 'An Act for Drayning of the Fenn' (1664–5).

[362] Sykes, *Life and Death of Sir Henry Vane*, p. 93; cf. p. 107.

[363] Slingsby Bethel, *A True and Impartial Narrative* (1659), pp. 5, 7, 12–14; Bethel, 'A Brief Narrative', in Bethel's *The Interest of Princes* (1681), pp. 333 ff.

[364] Benjamin Defoe, *A New Dictionary* (1735).

[365] Robert Molesworth, *The Principles of a Real Whig* (1775 edn), pp. 5, 6–7. Cf. *The Commonwealths-man Unmasqu'd* (1694: a reply to Molesworth); James Harrington, *The Oceana of James Harrington and his Other Works*, ed. John Toland (1700), p. vii; *Miscellaneous Works of Mr John Toland*, 2 vols (1747), ii. 227; *Cato's Letters*, 4 vols (1723–4), iii. 17; *The Works of Lord Bolingbroke*, 4 vols (Philadelphia, 1841; repr. Farnborough, Hants, 1969), i. 408. See too Rachel Hammersley, *The English Republican Tradition and Eighteenth-Century France* (Manchester, 2010), pp. 14–15; Blair Worden, 'Republicanism and the Restoration', in Wootton, *Republicanism, Liberty and Commercial Society*, pp. 190, 444; Worden, *Roundhead Reputations*, pp. 150–3.

Plot, 'republican' acquired a new breadth of usage, which associated Whigs with the past convulsions and fanaticism of Puritan rule. The same tactic was used in William III's reign against a new generation of Whig writers, who looked back admiringly on the regicide but who found themselves having to deny any 'republican' intentions.

The perception that 'republican' aims had animated the revolution of 1649 has travelled uncontested down the centuries. They had not. Even though MPs who had fought to preserve the constitution in the 1640s became complicit in its wreckage, they had not changed their spots. The principle that had provided justification for some of the rulers whom the regicide brought to power, and inspiration for others, was the sovereignty of parliament.

Here too the Restoration would bring a reaction. A principle which had been brought to the fore by the parliamentarian cause would survive its collapse, but would be confined to a restricted and vulnerable political base until 1688. Then the Revolution gave it enduring new life. That chronological trajectory supplies one of a series of parallels between the ideas discussed in this chapter and those to be explored in the next.

8

Civil and Religious Liberty

In 1845 the Whig interpretation of seventeenth-century English history, which had attracted widening support in recent decades, was assailed in two books that would become famous: Benjamin Disraeli's novel *Sybil*; and Thomas Carlyle's edition of the *Letters and Speeches of Oliver Cromwell*. Both authors struck at what to them was a blindly complacent catchphrase: 'civil and religious liberty'. *Sybil* presents an archetypal 'great Whig family', the Greymounts, who rose on the ruins of the monasteries, and who in the seventeenth century opposed what Disraeli represents as the benevolent social policies of the Stuarts. At the time of the Revolution of 1688 the then Earl of Greymount became 'a warm supporter of "civil and religious liberty"'. It was 'the cause', adds the narrator in a swipe at a second Whig slogan, 'for which Hampden died in the field and Russell on the scaffold'.[1] Where Disraeli's target was Whig social oppression, Carlyle's was the modern identification of the Cromwellian cause with the materialist Whig conception of progress. The spiritual aspirations of the Puritans, Carlyle maintained, had become unintelligible to a society obsessed by the mundane 'babblements' of parliamentary reform, free trade, and 'the cause of civil and religious liberty all over the world'.[2]

Neither author could stem the tide. In 1847 Cromwell's biographer Merle d'Aubigné proclaimed that the lord protector had 'carried into the practice of the seventeenth century that famous motto which is the glory of the greatest Englishmen of the nineteenth, "civil and religious liberty all over the world"'.[3] In 1848, the year of European revolutions, the reformer Joshua Toulmin Smith, recalling England's own upheaval of the mid-seventeenth century, told his kindred spirit Robert Owen that 'two centuries ago, when the friends of reform had to show their earnestness by going forth with harness on their backs, my fathers fought for reform, and for civil and religious liberty', 'on the security of which every reform and every advance of truth and knowledge depend'.[4] In the same year the *York Herald*, taking up the debate about Cromwell that had recently permeated the national and local presses, declared that the England of the present day possessed ever more of

---

[1] *Sybil*, Book I, Chapter 3.

[2] *The Works of Thomas Carlyle*, 30 vols (1896–9), xxviii. 164, xxix. 296 (cf. xxvii. 79); Charles R. Sanders and Kenneth J. Fielding, eds, *The Collected Letters of Thomas and Jane Welsh Carlyle* (Durham, NC, 1970–), xx. 124; Thomas Carlyle, *Historical Sketches of Notable Persons and Events in the Reigns of James I and Charles I*, ed. Alexander Carlyle (1898), p. 271.

[3] Merle d'Aubigné, *The Protector* (Edinburgh, 1847), p. 305.

[4] Quoted by Ben Weinstein, '"Local Self-Government is True Socialism": Joshua Toulmin Smith, the State, and Character Formation', *English Historical Review* 123 (2008), p. 1224.

the 'blessings' of 'civil and religious liberty' for which he had contended.[5] In 1859 another biographer of Cromwell, Alessandro Gavazi, explained that Oliver 'took up arms to preserve the civil and religious liberties of England'.[6] In 1876 the militant agricultural labourers of Naseby, at their annual gathering at the obelisk that marked the Puritan victory there, heard a lecture on 'Civil and Religious Liberty'.[7] In 1899 Sir Richard Tangye, that ardent collector of Cromwelliana, hailed the protector as 'the man who made civil and religious policy possible'.[8] A host of other nineteenth-century writers on Cromwell or the Puritan cause, among them the master-historian of the Interregnum C. H. Firth, invoked the phrase.[9]

It had a long ancestry. From 1688 until the Great War it served a basic component of Whig or Liberal power: the alliance of a political programme with Dissent or Nonconformity and with the principle of religious toleration. While the term 'civil and religious liberty' was, as we shall find, far from new in 1688–9, it is from then that it is a continuously pervasive presence, though its persistence and spread have not been studied, if indeed they have been noticed. The term had its variations, which were usually, though not always, synonymous with it. In place of 'religious' we find 'spiritual' or 'Christian' or 'ecclesiastical'. Instead of 'liberty' we find 'freedom' or 'right'. Or the noun is plural: 'liberties', 'rights', 'freedoms'. Or the adjectives are reversed: 'religious and civil liberty', and so on. Or we find such formulations as 'liberty, civil and religious'. Sometimes another phrase, 'liberties as men and Christians', or variations on it, did the same work. Of the family of phrases, 'civil and religious liberty' and 'civil and religious liberties' are the commonest.

For a century from 1689 the terms were ceaselessly deployed to salute, and to inspire commitment to, the legacy of the Glorious Revolution. In 1688 James II's attack on 'the civil and religious liberties of his country',[10] an assault that had placed 'our civil and spiritual liberties in so much danger',[11] had been thwarted; and then William of Orange had secured 'the preservation of our civil and religious liberties', 'the supreme earthly blessings of civil and religious liberty'.[12] The terms were summoned—especially around the time of the rising of 1745—to signify the values and interests that were under threat from the combination of Jacobitism and popery. A commitment to civil and religious liberty, it was insisted, held or should hold England together. The entrenchment of the Hanoverian dynasty was 'what every Englishman ought to have greatly at heart', because 'it secures to us the

---

[5] *York Herald*, 9 December 1848.

[6] Alessandro Gavazi, *Justice to Oliver Cromwell* (1869), pp. 6, 12.

[7] Pamela Horn, 'Nineteenth Century Farm Workers', *Northamptonshire Past and Present* 4 (1972), p. 168.

[8] Stuart Reid, *Sir Richard Tangye* (1908), p. 201.

[9] Blair Worden, 'Thomas Carlyle and Oliver Cromwell', *Proceedings of the British Academy* 105 (2000), pp. 166–7 and n. 226.

[10] Joseph Priestley, *An Essay on the First Principles of Government, and on the Nature of Political, Civil and Religious Liberty* (1771), p. 34.

[11] Thomas Sprat, *The Bishop of Rochester's Second Letter* (1689), p. 54.

[12] John Withers, *The Whigs Vindicated* (1715), p. 7; Peter Peckard, *The Nature and Extent of Civil and Religious Liberty* (1783), p. 34.

enjoyment' of 'those great blessings', 'civil and religious liberty'.[13] Like all enduring slogans, the phrase meant different things to different people and at different times. The most fervent of its eighteenth-century users tended to be Dissenters or anti-establishment Whigs,[14] who pointed to gaps between the ideal of civil and religious liberty and present practice. But the phrase also had countless employers high in respectability. The Test and Corporation Acts, those grievances of the Dissenters, were held by Sir William Blackstone to 'secure both our civil and religious liberties'.[15] Admittedly the annexation of the phrase by the social radicalism of the 1790s caused a 'great ferment' and 'great clutter and clamour',[16] and prompted Edmund Burke to deride 'the cause of compulsory freedom, civil and religious'.[17] In the main, however, friends of established power, rather than repudiating the phrase, deployed it to their own ends and indicated that radicals had misunderstood or perverted its correct meaning.

Until around the time of the Reform Act of 1832, when the parliamentarian cause of the civil wars began to command a breadth of admiration that first rivalled, and then surpassed, the veneration of the Revolution of 1688–9,[18] it was more usual to associate the cause of civil and religious liberty with the later upheaval, which had preserved the ancient constitution, than with the earlier one, which had destroyed it. Blackstone took 'the great rebellion' to have produced, not liberty, but 'slavery, both civil and religious'.[19] Mainstream Whigs were eager to bury its memory. Yet there were bolder Whig spirits who did apply the phraseology to the Puritan struggle. Even before 1688, during the Tory reaction earlier in that decade, the understandably anonymous editor of state letters which had been written by John Milton for the Puritan regimes had already found proof in them of the zeal of 'our predecessors' for 'civill, and religious rights'.[20] In the late 1690s John Toland, that devotee of Milton's memory, promoted the perception that the civil wars had been fought in the cause of 'civil and religious liberty'. So, in the mid-eighteenth century, did two men who frequently advertised their own commitment to 'civil and religious liberty', Richard Baron and Thomas Hollis. Their lead was followed by two writers on seventeenth-century history who were indebted to Hollis's assistance: Cromwell's biographer William Harris, who saw the parliamentarian cause as a struggle for 'civil and religious rights' against 'king and priest'; and Catharine Macaulay, who lamented that Archbishop Laud had been 'entirely

---

[13] Hugh Hume, Earl of Marchmont, *A Serious Address to the Electors of Great Britain* (1740), p. 31; cf. Thomas Mortimer, *The National Debt No National Grievance* (1768), p. 38.

[14] Rachel Hammersley, *The English Republican Tradition and Eighteenth-Century France* (Manchester, 2010), pp. 7, 16–18, 33, 42, 55–6, 68, 124, 191, 200, gives examples of their preoccupation and shows that it was exported to pre-Revolutionary France.

[15] Sir William Blackstone, *Commentaries on the Laws of England*, 4 vols (1800), iv. 438.

[16] Thomas Davis, *King and Government: a Discourse on Occasion of the Great Ferment about Civil and Religious Liberty* (1791), p. 11.

[17] Edmund Burke, *Reflections on the Revolution in France* (Dublin, 1790), p. 16.

[18] Blair Worden, *Roundhead Reputations: The English Civil Wars and the Passions of Posterity* (2001), pp. 227–8.

[19] John Seed, *Dissenting Histories: Religious Division and the Politics of Memory in Eighteenth-Century England* (Edinburgh, 2008), p. 124.

[20] *Miltons Republican-Letters* (1682), preface.

ignorant of the utility, equity, and beauty of civil and religious liberty', and who described Charles I's followers as 'enemies to the civil and religious liberties of their country'. Harris and Macaulay, echoing an assertion of Hollis, agreed that what Harris called the 'best pens' of the Puritan cause had written 'in behalf of civil and religious liberty'.[21]

At first sight the application of the term to the Puritan Revolution may seem emblematic of the anachronistic distortion with which the modern world charges Whig history. The term did not exist in the civil war of 1642–6, and the participants, or most of them, would not have understood it. Yet Whig historians spoke more truly than they knew. The phrase 'civil and religious liberty' was the creation of the Puritan Revolution. Nowhere to be found in the England of 1640, it is everywhere in the England of 1660. In its development, Oliver Cromwell played a decisive part. That may surprise us. Whig theories of religious toleration rested on different premises from his own conception of liberty of conscience.[22] His use of force on parliaments was remembered by Whig historians as an assault on civil liberty. He nonetheless proves to have been, inadvertently, a founder of a Whig way of thinking.

The parliamentarians who went to war in 1642 confronted Charles I on grounds of both politics and religion. But what was the connection between the two issues? Were they innately tied by some common principle? Or had they merely been brought together by the government's attacks on parliaments and Puritans at once? The king's opponents agreed that during the personal rule of Charles I, when 'the Puritan and patriot were equally persecuted',[23] there had been 'oppression' both of 'estates' and of 'consciences',[24] especially when victims of Laudian persecution were punished by the civil power. It was commonly alleged that prelates and papists had conspired to introduce, as a means to destroy the defenders of godliness, a 'tyranny . . . in the state'[25] that had inflicted both 'temporall and spirituall tyrannies'.[26] Puritans and parliamentarians spoke often of the conjunction of 'popery and tyranny' or 'popery and slavery'. So they rejoiced in the early work of the Long Parliament, when 'the yokes which lay upon our estates, liberties, religion, and conscience; the intolerable yokes of Star-Chamber, and terrible High-Commission', were 'broken'.[27] Such language was not new. Sixteenth- and early

---

[21] William Harris, *An Historical and Critical Account of the Life of Oliver Cromwell* (1762), table of contents and pp. 43, 202; Catharine Macaulay, *The History of England from the Accession of James I*, 5 vols (1769–72), iv. 59, 134, v. 195; cf. Helen Darbishire, ed., *The Early Lives of Milton* (1932), p. 215. For Hollis and Baron see the Introduction to my forthcoming edition of Marchamont Nedham, *The Excellencie of a Free-State* (Indianapolis, Ind., 2012).

[22] Above, Chapter 3.

[23] John Bryan, *A Discovery of the Probable Sin* (1647), p. 10.

[24] See e.g. *GD*, p. 137; Jack R. McMichael and Barbara Taft, eds, *The Writings of William Walwyn* (Athens, GA, 1989), p. 123; Woodhouse, pp. 395, 444.

[25] *CH*, ii. 328.

[26] *CPW*, i. 725; cf. Joseph Caryl, *The Workes of Ephesus Explained* (1642), p. 47.

[27] Stephen Marshall, *A Peace-Offering to God* (1641), p. 45.

seventeenth-century Protestants had used similar phraseology in warning or complaining of tyrannical rule by Catholic monarchs.[28] Now the language was directed at the combined threat of popery and absolutism from within the Stuart state and Church.

What opponents of Charles I did not say before the civil wars, and what earlier antagonists of popery and tyranny had not said, was that a principle of liberty connected their political concerns and their religious ones. The difference between protesting against joint oppressions and calling for joint liberties may sound to be one merely of words. It was not. The political and religious movements were brought together by what they were against, but not by what they were for. Since the Reformation, Europe's beleaguered Protestants, especially Calvinist ones, had frequently made common cause with opponents of absolutist or tyrannical tendencies in the state. They had supported arguments for the limitation or accountability of monarchs; or for the principle of political consent; or for the powers of representative institutions; or for freedom of political speech; or for tyrannicide.[29] Yet the alliance of religious with political dissidence was based on common interest or needs rather than on a shared principle.[30] Often a joint sense of oppression made the alliance heartfelt, but even then it did not create any conceptual link between the two causes. In England, in any case, mainstream Puritans more readily looked to the strength of the state than to limitations on it to curb the power of the Church.[31]

In the prelude to the civil war, as in the earlier political contests on the Continent, 'liberty' meant liberty in secular affairs. Parliament claimed to be acting for 'public liberty' or 'native liberty' or, more commonly, for the 'liberty' or 'liberties' of 'parliament' or 'the subject' or 'the people': liberty which, together with the rule of law and the rights of property and the 'privileges' of institutions and individuals, had been attacked by the illegal taxation and arbitrary imprisonments of Charles's regime. In 1640–2 parliament did not speak of 'religious liberty'. What it complained of were threats to, or 'innovations' in, 'religion'. It defended 'the true religion' or the 'Protestant' or 'reformed' religion. Parliamentarians did insist that orthodox doctrine, which the Laudian regime had suppressed, should have 'free passage' or be 'freely taught'. But the impulse behind that demand was not tied or analogous to their demands for the liberty of the subject. It was a yearning for reformation, to which the necessary means would be discipline and enforcement. Parliamentarians demanded the 'extirpation' of popery and superstition and idolatry, which assaulted or obstructed

---

[28] See e.g. George Garnett, ed., *Vindiciae, Contra Tyrannos* (Cambridge, 1994), pp. 173, 178; John Gouws, ed., *The Prose Works of Fulke Greville Lord Brooke* (Oxford, 1986), p. 14.

[29] Two recent articles have reminded us of the force of those alliances in England and added to our knowledge of them: M. P. Winship, 'Freeborn (Puritan) Englishmen and Slavish Subjection: Popish Tyranny and Puritan Constitutionalism, c. 1570–1606', *English Historical Review* 124 (2009), pp. 1050–74; Nicholas Tyacke, 'The Puritan Paradigm of English Politics 1558–1642', *Historical Journal* 53 (2010), pp. 517–50.

[30] There are some astute observations on this point in John Coffey's valuable forthcoming essay, 'Civil Liberty and Liberty of Conscience in Calvinist Resistance Theory'.

[31] Cf. Winship, 'Freeborn (Puritan) Englishmen', p. 1069.

Gospel truths, and the restoration or advancement of religion in its 'power' or 'purity', to which the Gospel's 'free' passage was essential. The calls for it were accompanied by despairing complaints about the government's or the Church's allowance of 'freedom' to the publication of popish tenets.

The parliamentarian language before the civil war persisted during it. It explained that parliament was contending both for 'religion' and, in the civil sphere, for 'liberty' or 'liberties'. Parliament's was the 'cause' of 'religion and liberties',[32] of 'religion and liberties both together',[33] which had become 'in-twisted'.[34] The parliamentary Protestation of 1641 committed its subscribers to the defence of 'the true reformed Protestant religion' and 'the lawful rights and liberties of the subject'.[35] In the years thereafter, that definition of the parliamen-tarian programme would be echoed time and again in vindications and polemic. Those great pledges of parliamentarian loyalty in 1643, the Solemn League and Covenant and the Vow and Covenant, respectively pledged their adherents to 'the preservation and defence of the true religion and liberties of the kingdoms',[36] and to the recovery of 'the true Protestant reformed religion, and the liberty of the subject'.[37] When the Commonwealth came to power it reminded the nation that 'religion in its purity, and public liberty, were the ends which, from the begin-ning, we had before our eyes'.[38] Royalists naturally scorned parliament's preten-sions. As the king's commissioners wearily reminded their parliamentarian counterparts at the treaty at Uxbridge in 1645, 'the defence of the Protestant religion, the liberty and property of the subject, and the priviledges of parliament' had been 'made the cause and grounds' of 'a war of near four years'.[39] Yet royalists spoke the language too. In the war of words between king and parliament that preceded the war, and in the polemical exchanges during it, both parties claimed to stand for 'religion' and 'liberty' against the depredations of the enemy.[40] 'Both sides', a preacher to the Commons observed in 1643, 'pretended religions defence, and kingdoms liberties'.[41] It is on the parliamentarian side, however, that the linguistic story to be told in this chapter lies.

The pairing of 'religion' and 'liberty' would persist long after the phrase 'civil and religious liberty' had become widespread. We find it in the Bill of Rights of 1689, which spoke for 'the Protestant religion and the lawes and liberties of this kingdome',[42] and in numerous apologias for the Revolution of that year. By that

---

[32] Francis Woodcock, *Ioseph Paralled by the Present Parliament* (1646), p. 24.
[33] Herbert Palmer, *The Necessity and Encouragement, of Utmost Venturing for the Churches Help* (1643), p. 62.
[34] Thomas Coleman, *Gods Unusuall Answer to a Solemne Fast* (1644), p. 16.
[35] *GD*, p. 156 (*pace* John Vicars, *Jehovah-Jireh*, [1644] p. 200).
[36] *GD*, p. 269.
[37] Michael Braddick, *God's Fury, England's Fire* (2008), p. 293.
[38] *OPH*, xix. 179. Cf. Firth and Rait, ii. 456; Abbott, ii. 283–5.
[39] T. H. Lister, *Life and Administration of Edward, First Earl of Clarendon*, 3 vols (1837–8), i. 250.
[40] A reading of the succession of declarations and remonstrances conveniently reprinted in Clarendon's *History of the Rebellion* will confirm the point.
[41] Thomas Coleman, *The Christians Course and Complaint* (1643), ep. ded.
[42] W. C. Costin and J. S. Watson, *The Law and Working of the Constitution*, 2 vols (1952), i. 68.

time, writers who would speak of 'religion and liberty' in one breath would talk of 'civil and religious liberty' in another. To an increasing number of people the two terms now often meant the same thing, or much the same thing.

To see how and why that change came about, we must first look more closely at some linguistic practices. Sometimes the practices are complex, for there were standard phrases that could have more than one meaning. There are consistent usages nonetheless.[43] In the 1640s 'civil liberty' was not a frequent term, while 'religious liberty' was a still less common one. The adjective 'civil' betokened a sphere of life, to be distinguished from, or contrasted with, other spheres. So there were 'civil' as distinct from 'military' or 'martial' rules or activities. Or there was the 'civil' as distinct from the 'common' branch of the law. There was also 'civil' as distinct from 'natural' life. That last distinction created a use for the term 'civil liberty', which could distinguish, from 'natural liberty', the freedom for which a particular framework of law or society provides or to which subjects have consented.[44] 'Civil liberty' had, however, a further meaning, which was, or became, more common, and in which its relationship with the phrase 'religious liberty' would, in time, be forged. For there was another area of life distinct from the 'civil' sphere: the 'religious' one. 'Civil liberty' could thus mean liberty in the secular sphere. When used in that way it meant the same as those more common phrases, 'public' or 'native liberty' or 'the liberty of the subject'.[45] People who spoke of 'civil liberty' in the year or so before the civil war did so to indicate which of the two areas of parliamentarian grievance, the secular and the religious, they were talking about. But (with the occasional exception, to which we shall come) they did not link the term to any conception of religious 'liberty', or give any intimation that they took 'liberty' to be under threat outside the 'civil' sphere. Thus in 1641 the MP Nathaniel Fiennes blamed the prelates not only for 'the introducing of . . . superstition and idolatrie' but for 'the evils which wee have suffered in our civill liberty, and the right of our proprieties'.[46] In 1642 Milton, who wrote of 'civil liberty' more than

---

[43] The history of vocabulary is no easy subject. Rich new opportunities—together with some hazardous temptations—have been brought to it by the digitalization of historical documents, which allows us to seek out patterns of phrasing by pressing buttons on a keyboard. Yet a student of the seventeenth century who applies that method to a broad topic confronts a great obstacle. The volume of material that can be digitally searched is (unless in a scholarly undertaking of mammoth ambition) too large, and yet (at least at the time I write) constitutes too small a proportion of the entire range of seventeenth-century publications, for any analysis to be systematic. Perhaps, when the infancy of historical digitalization is past, scientific tests will become practicable, though there would have to be a mental revolution beyond present imagination before searching could be a substitute for reading, or before it could recapture the shades and subtleties of linguistic habit. Meanwhile a survey such as the present one, which makes extensive use of search mechanisms but is also largely independent of them, must rest on some vulnerable impressions. At some points of my argument, scholars who have read (or remembered) different sources might reach different conclusions, though I hope that the outline of the story I tell is firm.

[44] See e.g. Stephen Marshall, *An Expedient to Preserve Peace and Amity* (1647), pp. 12–13.

[45] The distinction that would grow in the eighteenth century between 'civil' and 'political' liberty does not affect the argument of this chapter.

[46] *A Speech of the Right Honourable Nathanael Fiennes* (1641), p. 9; cf. e.g. *CH*, i. 494.

most, remarked of the bishops that 'they who seek to corrupt our religion are the same that would inthrall our civill liberty', with the result that the causes of 'religion, and . . . native liberty' had become 'inseparably knit together'.[47]

The term 'civil liberty' would become widespread, and would overtake 'native' or 'public liberty', only when changes in religious thinking had brought the term 'religious liberty' into common use. It was as a result of the same changes that the joint pursuit of freedom in secular affairs and freedom in religious ones became an intelligible and then a common aspiration. When that happened, the familiarity of the distinction between civil and religious life made 'civil liberty' (rather than 'natural' or 'public liberty') the obvious term to speak for the first of the two goals, and to partner 'religious liberty'.

'Religious liberty' achieved its currency by processes of linguistic conflation, which brought together concepts that had been distinct. On the rare occasions when we find 'religious liberty' used in England before the end of the first civil war, it has connotations very different from the ones that would align it with 'civil liberty'. It bore the same meaning as phrases which had far wider currency, and which were likewise remote from 'civil liberty'. They were 'Christian liberty' and 'spiritual liberty' (or sometimes we find 'Gospel liberty'). Those phrases would undergo the same shifts of meaning as 'religious liberty', so that their association with 'civil liberty' likewise became first comprehensible and with time instinctive. Until then, the two spheres of liberty could not meet, for they belonged to different orders of experience and value. 'Civill liberty' was understood to be about the relationship of the outward man, which 'is man's prerogative', to the state or the magistrate. Christian liberty was understood to be about the relationship of the inward man, 'which is God's prerogative', to Christ, whose blood has purchased it.[48] By Christ's blood, it was agreed, 'we are made free, . . . but this oure liberte is spirituall and not temporal'.[49] Christian liberty emancipates the soul from 'the bondage of sinne',[50] from 'the power of sin, Satan, death, hell, and condemnation'.[51] It liberates us from fear, from our lusts and passions and wills, from the 'flesh'. It frees us from the 'self'. 'We must learn', enjoined that doyen of Puritan theology William Perkins in expounding the principles of Christian liberty, 'to detest whatsoever is of our selves, because it wholly tends to bondage.'[52] The central text of Christian liberty was Galatians 5:1: 'Stand fast therefore in the liberty wherewith Christ hath made us free, and be not entangled again with the yoke of bondage.' By common interpretation of that passage, the word 'yoke' referred to the Jewish Law. It could mean the Jewish rites and observances—circumcision, or rules governing the eating of

[47] *CPW*, i. 923–4.

[48] William Perkins, *A Commentarie or Exposition, vpon the Fiue First Chapters of the Epistle to the Galatians* (1604), p. 366; George Downame, *The Doctrine of Christian Libertie* (1634), pp. 2, 9; below, p. 334.

[49] Thomas Becon, *A Pleasaunt Newe Nosegaye* (1553), unpag.

[50] Marshall, *Expedient*, p. 29.

[51] William Perkins, *A Godlie and Learned Exposition upon the Whole Epistle of Jude* (1606), p. 77.

[52] Perkins, *Commentarie or Exposition*, p. 366; cf. Raymond P. Stearns, *The Strenuous Puritan: Hugh Peter 1598–1660* (Urbana, Ill., 1954), p. 213.

meats—which were abrogated by the Gospel. But it could mean much more than that. It could cover the whole burden of sin and death from which Christ set us free. Puritans incorporated Galatians 5:1 into their vision of the process of conversion and salvation. They applied II Corinthians 3:17, 'Where the spirit of the Lord is there is liberty', to the same theme.

Not merely did civil liberty and spiritual liberty belong to different spheres. In one respect they had opposite rules. As Romans 6:18–22 explained, 'freedom from sin' makes men 'servants to God'. In Puritan eyes—though not in theirs alone— Christ's servants undergo an experience which, to those who have not shared it, seems a paradox. They exchange the 'yoke of bondage' for a glorious subjugation, the 'yoke', or 'absolute subjection', of Christ's 'law of liberty'. To be 'bound' by that subordination is the source of 'the truest liberty', of 'perfect liberty'.[53] The 'liberty of the subject' frees or protects us from the restraints of civil power, but Christian liberty releases 'power' in the believer's spirit,[54] bringing 'confidence'[55] and 'purity' to the soul.[56] It is a condition independent of the political or social arrangements of mankind. Following Luther,[57] Calvin emphasized that 'spiritual liberty may very well agree with civil bondage'.[58] Luther and Calvin stressed the point because they were alarmed by what they believed to be a widespread misunderstanding or misapplication of the doctrine of Christian liberty by Anabaptists and antinomians.[59] Their anxiety was shared by an army of sixteenth- and seventeenth-century writers (among them many whom we think of as radical in their theology or political thought), who alleged that sectaries were interpreting freedom from sin as freedom to sin, or were making 'Christian liberty' a pretext for 'licence' or 'licentiousness' or 'wantonness' or indulgence of 'the flesh', or were deploying the doctrine to challenge political or social authority. The Westminster Confession

---

[53] John Brinsley, *The Sacred and Soveraigne Church-Remedie* (1645), p. 28; Francis Cheynell, *A Plot for the Good of Posterity* (1646), p. 38; Marshall, *Expedient*, p. 29; Mary Cary, *The Resurrection of the Witnesses* (1648), pp. 21–2; David Como, *Blown by the Spirit: Puritanism and the Emergence of an Antinomian Underground in Pre-Civil-War England* (Stanford, Calif., 2004), pp. 297, 298. Writing outside Puritanism, but arguing against the claims of papal infallibility that likewise affronted Puritans, William Chillingworth urged the removal of that 'tyranny' and looked to the restoration of Christians 'to their just and full liberty of *captivating* [my italic] their understanding to Scripture only' (quoted by B.H.G. Wormald, *Clarendon: Politics, History, Religion* [Cambridge, 1951], p. 259).

[54] John Lilburne, *A Light for the Ignorant* (1638), p. 14.

[55] Nicholas Byfield, *A Commentary: or, Sermons* (1623), p. 674; William Struther, *A Looking Glasse for Princes and People* (1632), p. 5.

[56] Walter Balcanquhall, *A Large Declaration concerning the Late Tumults in Scotland* (1638), p. 64.

[57] Woodhouse, pp. 224–5.

[58] Ibid., p. 192. Cf. Desiderius Erasmus, *An Exhortation to the Diligent Study of Scripture* (repr. Amsterdam, 1973), sig. G5v; Anthony Burgess, *A Treatise of Original Sin* (1658), p. 306. Professor Tyacke, to whom I am grateful for constructive discussion of the subject, maintains ('Puritan Paradigm', p. 528) that a 'key concept' in a 'novel fighting creed' forged by Marian exiles in the 1550s 'was what they called "Christian liberty", defined' 'as a half-way house between the tyranny of the Roman Catholics and the "licencious libertie" of' the Anabaptists. I have not encountered that definition. The exiles seem to me to have used the term in the senses I describe here. I have a similar difficulty with the phrases 'Christian and . . . civic liberties', and 'intertwined civic and ecclesiastical alarm', used by Winship, 'Freeborn (Puritan) Englishmen', pp. 1050, 1051.

[59] Harro Höpfl, *The Christian Polity of John Calvin* (Cambridge, 1982), pp. 35–8.

of Faith, following in that monitory tradition, explained that people 'who, under pretence of Christian liberty, . . . oppose any lawful power . . . resist the ordinance of God'.[60]

The accusations were of doubtful validity, at least in England.[61] The more extreme the sectaries, the likelier they generally were to distinguish between the world and the spirit, between fleshly and spiritual freedom.[62] Nonetheless, the charges were understandable, for there were pressures of both theology and politics that made the separation of Christian liberty from earthly preoccupations difficult to sustain. Here we encounter the complexity of linguistic practice. For while the meaning of 'Christian liberty' I have been describing was the primary one, the term had another meaning, which confronted the believer with challenges of this world as well as of the next. Though less widespread, the second meaning was still a frequent one. It signified the immunity or exemption of churches from the secular power. An alternative term for that immunity, with which this second sense of 'Christian liberty' was synonymous, was 'ecclesiastical liberty'. The second meaning of 'Christian liberty' was agreed to be far inferior to the first. As John Colet, a friend to 'the Churches liberte' or exemption, had observed, it was of an incommensurately lower order than 'the trewe libertye', 'the spirituall lybertie of Christe'.[63]

Conceptually the difference between the two kinds of Christian or religious liberty was clear. In practice it could be difficult to keep them apart. English Protestants often gave a hostile meaning to 'ecclesiastical liberty', to refer to the privileges claimed and abused by the Catholic Church in its relations with the lay power.[64] But they also spoke in defence of ecclesiastical or 'Christian' liberty against the threat which popery posed to Protestantism.[65] Paul had enjoined that Christ's followers, whose bond with him had made them his 'freem[e]n', must not be 'the servants of men' (I Corinthians 7:23). The injunction was normally taken, un-contentiously, to signify that Christ's followers can serve him only if they guard their souls against the enslavement of worldly pursuits. But what happened if man, who cannot serve two masters, was ordered by rulers of Church or state to observe religious practices that disobeyed Christ's precepts? Most Protestants agreed that in that sense Catholicism, which denied 'the true light and liberty of the Gospel'[66] and withheld from those who were subjected to it ordinances that were among the

[60] Woodhouse, Introduction, p. 66.
[61] See Como, *Blown by the Spirit*, pp. 281–307, 352.
[62] The point is brought out in the Introduction to Woodhouse.
[63] *The Sermone of Doctor Colete, made to the Conuocation at Pauls* (1530), sigs C4ᵛ–5.
[64] *CH*, ii. 72, iii. 483.
[65] e.g. Thomas Bilson, *The True Difference between Christian Subiection and Unchristian Rebellion* (1585), p. 382. Civil-war royalism protested against the invasion by parliamentary legislation of the rights of the Church of England, which had been guaranteed by the king's coronation oath (*CH*, ii. 72, iii. 483). Magna Carta had enjoined the preservation of the 'rights and liberties' of the Church (John Witte, *The Reformation of Rights. . . . Early Modern Calvinism* [Cambridge, 2007], p. 27). Cf. below, n. 105.
[66] Ian Breward, ed., *The Work of William Perkins* (Abingdon, 1970), p. 520.

means to salvation, strove to 'oppresse Christian libertie'.[67] On the same premise it was argued, across the spectrum of Protestant opinion, that 'our liberty in the Gospel' entitled or obliged Protestants in Catholic lands to refuse the imposition of false worship.[68] Establishment Protestants were less comfortable when the devotional practices of the Church of England were themselves identified as impediments to salvation or as revivals of Jewish ceremonialism, and were thus likewise portrayed as affronts to Christian liberty. Under Archbishop Laud, when the base of establishment Protestantism narrowed, the conviction that official ecclesiastical policy was contrary to Christian liberty broadened accordingly.

The term 'Christian liberty' took on other practical dimensions. It was common theological ground that the abrogation of Jewish ceremonies had made many matters of worship 'things indifferent'. Establishment Protestantism maintained that, precisely because they were indifferent, the state or the Church was entitled to enforce its own choices. In opposition there came the claim that unfettered worship in things indifferent was a privilege of 'Christian liberty'. Were the vestments which the ministers of the Elizabethan Church were required to wear, it was asked, 'consistent with ecclesiastical and Christian liberty'?[69] Baptists and separatists maintained that any participation in false worship, even perhaps in any worship imposed by the state, was a sin against 'Christian libertie', or against 'the liberties and priviledge of all the subjects of Christ', an offence which Christ's servants should 'dare' not commit.[70] The requirement to 'worshipp inventions & traditions of men', explained the separatist Henry Barrow, is 'contrary to . . . our Christian libertie'.[71] In the Puritan Revolution, advocates of the separation of Church and state, or of the abolition of tithes, or of worshipping 'beyond parish bounds', would proclaim the incompatibility of existing practices with 'Christian liberty' or 'Christian liberties'.[72] Even the intolerant Presbyterian William Prynne could acknowledge in 1644 that the excessive use of excommunication, or of suspension from the sacrament, could constitute 'an arbitrary, papall, tyrannical domineering over . . . Christian liberties'.[73]

Our linguistic survey concludes with another phrase, which was widely associated with 'Christian liberty' and was often equated with it: 'liberty of conscience'. This term, too, had a double meaning, and here too there were pressures towards conflation. First, almost synonymously with the first meaning of 'Christian liberty',

---

[67] Henry Bullinger, *A Confutation of the Popes Bull* (1572), sig. K3ᵛ.

[68] See e.g. Christopher Goodman, *How Superior Powers Oght to be Obeyd* (1558), p. 223; George Abbot, *The Reasons which Doctour Hill Hath Brought, for the Upholding of Papistry* (1604), p. 353; Hopfl, *Christian Polity of John Calvin*, p. 37.

[69] Hastings Robinson, ed., *The Zurich Letters*, 2 vols (Parker Society, Cambridge, 1842), i. 153.

[70] William Haller, ed., *Tracts on Liberty in the Puritan Revolution*, 3 vols (repr. New York, 1979), ii. 114; Abraham Boun, *The Pride and Avarice of the Clergy* (1650), p. 104.

[71] Henry Barrow, *A Collection of Certaine Sclaunderous Articles* (1590), sig. F4; see too Tyacke, 'Puritan Paradigm', p. 531.

[72] *CPW*, vii. 307; Ellis Bradshaw, *An Husbandmans Harrow* (1649), p. 22; cf. Thomas Edwards, *The Third Part of Gangraena* (1646), p. 236.

[73] William Prynne, *A Vindication of Foure Serious Questions . . . both in the Pulpit . . . and in the Presse* (1645), p. 2.

liberty of conscience meant the spiritual freedom brought to the conscience by Christ's redemption. 'The libertie which Christ hath procured for us', explained Perkins, 'is libertie of conscience.'[74] The second meaning, though it differed from the second meaning of 'Christian liberty', sometimes overlapped it. It too was a practical meaning, and it too was conventionally taken to be an incommensurately lower one. For it too described a liberty derived not (or not directly) from God but from arrangements among men. In that usage, 'liberty of conscience', or 'liberty of tender consciences' or 'ease to' them, was a 'gift', or 'indulgence', or 'connivance', 'permitted' or 'conceded' by the civil power in the interests of prudence or charity or necessity—though rulers might sometimes be persuaded that faith itself would or might benefit from it.[75] Charles II's decision to 'declare a liberty to tender consciences' at Breda in 1660[76] rested on an assumption about the powers of princes that was shared by Elizabeth I, James I, Charles I, Oliver Cromwell, James II, and then William III, under whom the 'Toleration Act' of 1689 granted 'some ease to scrupulous consciences'.[77] But readers were reminded that the kind of 'liberty of conscience' which 'men may give to men' was 'below the true Christian liberty', which is 'merely spiritual'.[78]

Until the civil wars the pressures on conventional thinking to merge the higher and lower concepts both of Christian liberty and of liberty of conscience were more or less withstood. During them the distinctions broke down. The fragmentation of the Puritan movement, and the debates over ecclesiology and religious compulsion, brought a new urgency to the practical dimensions of the liberty of the spirit and conscience. To many minds the liberty of Christians in Christ, and the liberty they might enjoy in their ecclesiastical arrangements, became ever harder to distinguish. The coalescence was never complete, and there were many to protest against it. The concept of Christian liberty as liberty of the soul did not pass away. Within individual minds it merged or jostled or stood in tension with new emphases. Nonetheless, 'liberty' in religion was increasingly taken to involve the freedom to believe or worship as the 'conscience' prescribed. It was in that sense that the idea of religious liberty made common cause with that of civil liberty; and it was as a result of that alliance that the phrase 'civil and religious liberty' came into being.

---

[74] Perkins, *Godlie and Learned Exposition*, p. 77; cf. John Brinsley, *The Healing of Israels Breaches* (1642), p. 105. Catholics had their own approving conception of freedom of conscience, a virtue to which, according to Cardinal Reginald Pole, Mary Tudor's adviser, the Reformation had put an end: Eamon Duffy, *Fires of Faith: Catholic England under Mary Tudor* (2009), p. 44.

[75] See e.g. McMichael and Taft, *Writings of William Walwyn*, p. 57; *GD*, p. 327 (cf. pp. 416, 454–5); *CH*, ii. 232–23, 277; Sir John Birkenhead, *A Mystery of Godlinesse* (1663), p. 18; W. K. Jordan, *The Development of Religious Toleration in England*, 4 vols (1932–40), i. 207, ii. 68.

[76] *GD*, p. 466.

[77] W. C. Costin and J. S. Watson, eds, *The Law and Working of the Constitution: Documents 1660–1914*, 2 vols (1961 edn), i. 63.

[78] John Saltmarsh, *Sparkles of Glory* (1647), p. 117. In its practical form, at least, the concept of 'liberty of conscience' seems to have emerged in the sixteenth century (Philip Benedict, '*Un Roi, Une Loi, Deux Fois*: Parameters for the History of the Catholic-Reformed Co-Existence in France, 1555–1685', in Ole Peter Grell and Bob Scribner, eds, *Tolerance and Intolerance in the European Reformation* (Cambridge, 1996), pp. 67–8.

By 1660 the phrase was at least as widespread as it would be after 1688. If there had seemed no connection between the two spheres of liberty before the civil wars, by 1661 the lawyer and author Peter Pett could speak of the 'natural connexion of civil and religious liberty'.[79] In the next year, however, the Act of Uniformity changed the political and ecclesiological climate. Though 'civil and religious liberty' would be frequently invoked through the reigns of Charles II and James II, the reaction against Puritan rule, and the reassertion of monarchical authority, limited the scope of the phrase in that era. It was after 1688 that the currency broadened again, this time enduringly. By the eighteenth century, appeals to 'civil and religious liberty' were backed by the assumption that 'we cannot be deprived of one, without loseing both, nor be secure of one without retaining the other also'.[80] The interdependence of 'ecclesiastical tyranny' and 'civil bondage', or of 'civil and religious oppression', was now held to be innate or 'eternal'.[81] The 'conjunction', in Italian city-states, of 'temporal liberty' with 'spiritual tyranny' was declared 'unnatural'.[82] While everyone who paused to compare civil with religious liberty remembered to say that the second was the more important, there was a sense, explained the Dissenter Richard Price in 1776, in which the two were 'on the same footing'.[83] For religious liberty had become, no less than civil liberty, a human entitlement. 'Religious liberty' came generally to signify a right to freedom of worship and belief which properly accompanies the liberty that in civil affairs we derive, or ought to derive, from the law or the constitution or else from universal rights. Though God-given—as civil liberty, at least in some ultimate sense, was agreed to be—religious liberty incorporated values and practices of men.

We should not simplify that process. The question whether the mental rules and categories appropriate to civil society, or to the human sphere, could be applied to religion, God's sphere, remained complex and problematical. Usually the phrase 'civil and religious liberty' papered over it. It is easy, and it may be correct, to describe the shift, over a long term, from a God-centred conception of liberty in religion to a man-centred one as a process of secularization. Yet the story is one not of the retreat, or not only of the retreat, of Christianity, but of its adjustment and revision.[84] It was from within Puritanism, not in reaction against it, that the civil wars produced demands for 'civil and religious liberty'.

How then did the Puritan Revolution come to align liberty in the state with liberty in religion? That historical question was raised in the middle third of the twentieth century. It was studied not in Britain but in North America, where the

---

[79] Peter Pett, *A Discourse concerning Liberty of Conscience* (1661), p. 20. For Pett's outlook see Mark Goldie, 'Sir Peter Pett, Sceptical Toryism and the Science of Toleration in the 1680s', *Studies in Church History* 21 (1984), 247–73.

[80] Samuel Bradford, *The Reasonableness of Standing Fast in English and in Christian Liberty* (1713), p. 4; cf. John Brown, *The Mutual Connexion between Religious Truth and Civil Freedom* (n.d.: 1746?).

[81] Seed, *Dissenting Histories*, p. 119; cf. Catharine Macaulay, *History of England*, iv. 254.

[82] Wawrzyniec Goslicki, *The Accomplished Senator* (1733), preface (by William Oldisworth), p. ix.

[83] Richard Price, *Observations on the Nature of Civil Liberty* (1776), p. 32.

[84] Blair Worden, 'The Problem of Secularization', in Alan Houston and Steve Pincus, eds, *A Nation Transformed: England after the Restoration* (Cambridge, 2001), pp. 20–40; above, pp. 89–90.

Whig tradition lived on.[85] The relationship of the Puritan Revolution to the emergence of modern ideas of liberty engaged the minds of Wallace Notestein, A. S. P. Woodhouse, William Haller, Don Wolfe, Wilbur Jordan, Jack Hexter, and others. Haller's Introduction to his edition of *Tracts on Liberty in the Puritan Revolution* (1934), Woodhouse's Introduction to his collection of documents *Puritanism and Liberty* (1938), and Haller's book *Liberty and Reformation in the Puritan Revolution* (1955), offered sophisticated and lastingly instructive accounts of what they took to be the debt of liberal ideas to Puritan doctrine. 'Liberty', thought Haller, 'was first conceived as religious', but 'the argument that began as a plea for religious liberty and reform of Church government rapidly extended itself', as the debate became 'increasingly rationalistic' and 'secular', 'to include civil liberty and political revolution'.[86] Woodhouse's interpretation was more or less in line with Haller's.

Their perspective is now out of favour.[87] It had its shortcomings. Haller and Woodhouse had difficulty both in demonstrating and in explaining the advances of secular and rational thinking within the Puritan Revolution. Theirs was an over-simple thesis, which belied the subtlety of its authors' own narratives. An illuminating essay of 1992 by J. C. Davis, protesting at Haller's and Woodhouse's conclusions, brought to the religious history of the Puritan Revolution a scepticism about Whig perspectives, and about the hazards of Whig anachronism, that mirrors criticisms made by other historians in the field of political history. Puritans, insisted Davis, sought godliness, not—or rather, not in modern understandings of the word—liberty.[88] Haller and Woodhouse nonetheless identified a development of which we have lost sight to our cost, and which the emergence of the vocabulary studied in this chapter reflects. I hope to show that Davis's approach can be brought together with the one he opposes.

The association of civil with religious liberty during the Puritan Revolution evolved, we can broadly say, in five stages. The first belongs to the years 1641–2. In that time the intensity of a conflict which more or less united parliament against both the Laudian Church and absolutist monarchy produced novel pairings of concepts of liberty. The spur was the imposition of the 'etcetera oath' by the Laudian canons of 1640. The measure struck both at the conscience and, because the canons threatened to extend the powers of Church and state alike, at the liberty of the subject. 'If our goods and persons be free', protested the MP Sir Simonds Dewes in a debate on the oath early in the Long Parliament, 'much moore

---

[85] We see the contrast when we look at discussions in the two countries of the Levellers, who were hailed in England as proto-socialists, in America as spokesmen for individual liberty. Blair Worden, 'The Levellers in History and Memory, c. 1660–1960', in Michael Mendle, ed., *The Putney Debates of 1647* (Cambridge, 2001), pp. 277–80.

[86] Haller, *Tracts on Liberty*, i. 4.

[87] The failure of Hexter's Center for the History of Freedom at Washington University, St Louis, to put down lasting roots in the 1990s signalled the demise of the approach. Hexter's project in any case struggled to come to terms with religion.

[88] J. C. Davis, 'Religion and the Struggle for Freedom in the English Revolution', *Historical Journal* 35 (1992), pp. 507–30. See too D. B. Robertson's pioneering and still instructive study *The Religious Foundations of Leveller Democracy* (New York, 1951).

our soules and an oath ensnares them.'[89] In 1641 the preacher Jeremiah Bur-roughs reminded the House of Commons of the oath and other 'sinfull' recent deeds of 'conscience-oppression', whose perpetrators would not 'suffer men to enjoy Church or civill liberties'.[90] Next year another preacher urged the Com-mons to 'secure to us not onely liberty of person and estate, but also liberty of conscience from Church tyranny, that we be not pinched with ensnaring oaths, multiplied subscriptions'.[91] Those momentary couplings of the two spheres of liberty were tentative. We might almost describe them as a straining for literary effect through unfamiliar juxtapositions. It may be that the old conception of ecclesiastical liberty, as the immunity of the Church from state control, lies below their surface.[92] Insofar as they anticipate the couplings to which we are about to come, they seem inhibited by the difference of scale between the spiritual and secular spheres.[93]

It is the second stage that introduces a substantial mental shift. Now the spur was not the division between Crown and parliament that had brought the war, but the divisions within the parliamentarian cause during it. The second stage arose from the debate, which began in 1643–4 and tore the Puritan cause apart, over liberty of conscience. The recruitment of the word liberty by the movement of the 1640s in favour of diversity of worship and doctrine had formidable obstacles to overcome. Guardians of Presbyterian orthodoxy, who knew the wickedness of heresy and insisted on the duty of magistracy and ministry to impose a uniformity of religious belief, were shocked by demands for freedom for sectaries, who spoke 'as if it were a part of Christs legacy and his peoples liberty to be of what religion they will'.[94] Mainstream Puritanism had always believed uniformity of religious profession to be an essential bulwark against 'liberty of erring', 'that liberty of believing what men will'.[95] Calvin's lieutenant Theodore Beza had called '*liberté aux consciences*' a 'thoroughly diabolical dogma'.[96] In England's civil wars, Presbyterian divines queued to condemn the call for liberty of conscience as a 'pretence' or 'cloak' for the same goals of political or social subversion that had allegedly induced earlier radicals to misuse the doctrine of Christian liberty. Liberty of conscience, it was claimed, would soon lead to 'liberty of estates' or 'liberty of wives',[97] and a return to the communism of John à Leyden. That was the kind of thing, observed the Presbyterian minister Stephen Marshall in 1647, that happened when 'liberty of conscience' was aligned with the very different sphere of 'civil liberty'.[98] Marshall's

---

[89] Wallace Notestein, ed., *The Journal of Sir Simonds D'Ewes* (New Haven, 1923), p. 162.
[90] Jeremiah Burroughs, *Sions Joy* (1642), p. 28.
[91] Thomas Hill, *The Trade of Truth Advanced* (1642), p. 33.
[92] Cf. below, n. 105.
[93] Cf. Robert Sanderson, *Two Sermons* (1635), p. 11; and the alignment of the concepts of temporal and spiritual liberation in the French treatise of 1579, well known in England, the *Vindiciae, Contra Tyrannos*, ed. Garnett, p. 178.
[94] Cornelius Burgess, *The Second Sermon Preached to the Honourable House of Commons* (1645), p. 51.
[95] Matthew Newcomen, *A Sermon, tending to set forth the Right Vse of the Disasters that befall our Armies* (1644), p. 36.
[96] Benedict, '*Un Roi*', p. 68.
[97] Thomas Case, *Spirituall Whoredome Discovered* (1647), p. 34.
[98] Marshall, *An Expedient to Preserve Peace and Amity* (1647), pp. 13, 32.

words were an alarm signal against the trend of the decade. The alarm was wide and deep. In many contexts the very word 'liberty' carried connotations, on which the enemies of liberty of conscience played, of looseness, self-indulgence, lawlessness, 'libertinism'. Such was the liberty that had swollen when 'there was no king in Israel: every man did that which was right in his own eyes'.[99] Friends of religious diversity felt obliged to disparage 'liberty' of that kind, indeed were often wary in advancing their own language of liberty.[100] Most of them condemned claims made by the ungodly to liberty of religious conduct. Hostility to the 'liberty for the Mass' sought by Catholics,[101] or to 'that sinfull liberty on the Lords Day' for which the Book of Sports had provided,[102] prevailed almost across the Puritan spectrum.

Nonetheless, the two conceptions of 'liberty of conscience' came together. Liberty of worship or faith or conscience came to be thought of as the practical fulfilment of the liberty of the soul in Christ. In the years 1643 and 1644 the equation of 'Christian liberty' with freedom of religious association or profession became widespread. It may have been the Congregationalist minister John Goodwin who, in a tract of 1644 that pleaded for '(not loose, but) Christian libertie', pronounced that 'the liberties' bought 'by Christ's blood' included 'the RIGHTS', promised by the Gospel, of autonomous 'congregations'.[103] In the next year Goodwin called for 'the spirituall liberties of the congregations', for their 'exemption and immunity in their spirituall affairs'.[104] At first sight he may seem merely to have been claiming for Congregationalism the equation between Christian liberty and ecclesiastical immunity that English Protestants resented when it was deployed by Catholics. It had also been adopted, to English dismay, by Scottish Presbyterians.[105] Yet

---

[99] Deuteronomy 12:8; Judges 17:6 and 21:25. Such phrases as 'taking liberties' and 'What a liberty' are a modern residue of that thinking.

[100] Woodhouse, pp. 403, 409; John Cook, *What the Independents Would Have* (1647), p. 5.

[101] John Coffey, *Persecution and Toleration in Protestant England 1558–1689* (Harlow, 2000), p. 140; Abbott, ii. 201.

[102] John Greene, *Nehemiah's Teares and Prayers* (1644), p. 19.

[103] *A Paraenetick, or, Humble Addresse to the Parliament and Assembly for (not loose, but) Christian Libertie* (1644), p. 5. For the authorship see John Coffey, *John Goodwin and the English Revolution* (Woodbridge, 2006), p. 311.

[104] *Innocency and Truth Triumphing Together* (1645), p. 38.

[105] In Scotland the social and political power of the Kirk had allowed the language of civil and religious liberty to develop earlier than in England, with a different meaning. There the phrase brought the liberty of subjects together, not with freedom of worship or faith, but with the immunity of the Church. Thus in 1638 the Covenanter movement which resisted Charles I had spoken for 'our liberty, both Christian and civill': 'a strange phrase', replied the king, 'to proceed from dutifull or loyall hearted subjects'. Balcanquhall, *Large Declaration*, pp. 282, 366. For Scottish usage see also *Ane Shorte and Generall Confession of the Trewe Christiane Fayth and Religion* (1581), p. 1; David Calderwood, *An Exhortation of the Particular Kirks of Christ* (1624), p. 16; Alexander Henderson, *The Answeres of Some Brethren of the Ministrie* (1638), unpag. ('To the second'); *CH*, i. 204. In medieval England, in the same way, the actions of kings who allegedly invaded both the Church's independence and the people's rights could make 'ecclesiastical liberties' and 'the common liberties of England' a common cause (e.g. Nathaniel Bacon, *An Historical and Political Discourse* (1760 edn), [part] i. 131); but the convergence forged in mid-seventeenth-century England was of a different kind. In seventeenth-century Massachusetts, whose Congregationalism was as doctrinally unyielding as Britain's Presbyterianism, the authors of the *Body of Liberties* of 1641 had a traditional conception of ecclesiastical liberty in mind when they codified 'rights, freedoms, immunities, authorities and priviledges, both civil and ecclesiastical': Witte, *Reformation of Rights*, p. 286. Useful as Witte's book is, its readers will recognize

Congregationalists, and separatists with them, went beyond Catholic or Presbyterian usages. To them liberty in religion implied the freedom not merely of
ecclesiastical institutions but of the individuals whose consent alone could validate
them: individuals who, on the less fundamental matters of doctrine, might legitimately disagree among themselves or err on the path to truth, and with whose
relationships with Christ men must not interfere. From that perspective, the
practical liberty of the individual conscience was essential to salvation. The protest
of the Congregationalist divine Jeremiah Burroughs in 1641 against the invasion of
'Church . . . liberties' had been directed at persecution for 'differences in opinion,
(not fundamental, but) in things doubtfull, or indifferent', for 'wee must cast out
none, but whom Christ casts out before us'.[106] From 1643 the perception of
ecclesiastical liberty towards which Burroughs's words had pointed found many
adherents.

To Presbyterians there could be no such liberty. Faith, in their eyes, allowed no
place for individual judgement, which would unavoidably lead to heresy and blasphemy. In 1649 the Scottish Presbyterian Samuel Rutherford explained that the
allowance of 'many religions', and the dissemination of 'blasphemies in the name of
the Lord', were 'contrary to the true religious liberty'.[107] English Presbyterians, too,
felt compelled to deny that the imposition of true doctrine, which to them was
likewise an indispensable instrument of 'Christian liberty', was 'against' it.[108] Congregationalist and separatist thinking, by contrast, had long taken 'Christ's ecclesiastical government', and its 'liberty and power', to be 'not only tied to the publike
notions of the whole congregations, but extended to everie action of every Christian',
so that 'everie member thereof' had a 'right' in it.[109] Before the civil wars, such
perceptions had been confined to the periphery of Puritanism. During them, Congregationalism and separatism became widespread enough, and, through the support
of Oliver Cromwell and others in high places, powerful enough, to reshape the
vocabulary of religious liberty. In 1652 the Congregationalist John Owen, Cromwell's principal ecclesiastical adviser, who in the same year became his Vice-Chancellor at Oxford, conjoined the 'undoubted right of the Gospel' to 'have free passage into
all nations' with the 'right and interest in it' of 'persons of Christ's good-will'.[110]

That right came from Christ, not from man, and was due to men only as subjects
of Christ. Once the claims of liberty in religion had been made for individual
believers, however, parallels with the liberties of the subject came into view. The
alignment of the two spheres in the 1640s began not among the theologically more
orthodox of the Congregationalist divines such as Owen, whose conversion to

---

my disagreements with it. The terminology of civil and religious liberty may also have appeared in Ireland
before its rise in England: John Bramhall, *The Serpent Salve* (1643), p. 194.

[106] Burroughs, *Sions Joy*, p. 28.

[107] Samuel Rutherford, *A Free Disputation against Pretended Liberty of Conscience* (1649), p. 268; cf.
Rutherford's *The True Primitive State of Civil and Ecclesiastical Government* (1649), p. 5.

[108] Thomas Edwards, *Antapologia* (1644), p. 301; cf. Richard Baxter, *Two Treatises* (1696), p. 107.

[109] Leland H. Carlson, ed., *The Writings of Henry Barrow, 1587–1590* (1962), p. 609; Winship,
'Freeborn (Puritan) Englishmen', p. 1063.

[110] Owen, *Works*, viii. 390.

liberty of religious profession was gradual and partial, but among doctrinally more experimental Congregationalists and (more often) separatists, who were ready to question or repudiate the Calvinist doctrine of predestination. Chief among them were Goodwin and John Milton and the Levellers William Walwyn and Richard Overton. On those names the explanations of Haller and Woodhouse for the conjunction of liberty of conscience and liberty of the subject largely, and rightly, centred. It was through those men and their allies that liberty of religious profession became linked to 'other' liberties, which belonged to the civil sphere. By 1643 Walwyn was explaining that little could be done for 'common freedom' 'unlesse liberty of conscience be allowed for every man'.[111] In 1644 Goodwin spoke for 'liberty' both 'of the kingdome' and 'of the conscience', and asked how it was that ecclesiastical dissenters remained subject to punishment at a time when 'all other liberties' were being 'vindicated'.[112] In the same year a tract that seems to have emanated from Goodwin's circle linked the 'spirituall libertie' of 'the saints' with their 'state priviledges'.[113] Early in 1645 Goodwin connected 'Christian liberties of the Gospel' with the 'common priviledges of nature'.[114]

It was early in 1645, too, that Milton, whose plea for liberty of religious expression, *Areopagitica*, had appeared a few months earlier, lamented that 'in this age many are so opposite both to human and to Christian liberty'.[115] In the same year Overton asserted that, where there was 'persecution' in religion, 'the liberty of the subject (now in controversie) cannot be setled in this land', so that there could be 'no freedome, rights, or liberty either civil or spirituall'.[116] Overton is thought to have been the author of a tract of March 1646 which proclaimed that, if believers 'cannot be free to worship God…according to their particular consciences, all liberty to them is taken away: for what is all other liberty, where that is not?'[117] In the same year Walwyn described 'liberty of conscience' as 'the principall branch' of the people's 'safety and freedome'.[118] In 1647 he asserted that 'the liberty of my native country, and the freedome of all conscientious people hath been, and still is precious in my esteeme'.[119] Exponents of Christian liberty had often stated that the transitory liberties of this world were dispensable in the attainment or preservation of Christian liberty. In the civil wars a less submissive perspective asserted itself. If a man is 'abridge[d]…of his liberty of worshipping

---

[111] McMichael and Taft, *Writings of William Walwyn*, p. 102. Cf. the outlook in the same year of the Congregationalist Sir Cheney Culpepper: M. J. Braddick and M. Greengrass, eds, 'The Letters of Sir Cheney Culpepper (1641–1657)', *Camden Miscellany* 33 (Cambridge, 1996), pp. 137–41, 176–7.

[112] *Paraenetick*, p. 2; Coffey, *John Goodwin*, pp. 117–18.

[113] *Certain Briefe Observations and Antiquaeries* (1644), p. 5.

[114] John Goodwin, *A Short Answer to A.S.* (1645), p. 3.

[115] *CPW*, ii. 587.

[116] Haller, *Tracts on Liberty*, iii. 236; cf. iii. 245.

[117] *The Last Warning to all the Inhabitants of London* (1646), p. 4. Cf. William Dell, *Right Reformation* (1646), p. 24; McMichael and Taft, *Writings of William Walwyn*, p. 169; William Haller and Godfrey Davies, eds, *The Leveller Tracts 1647–1653* (New York, 1944), pp. 454–5; Marchamont Nedham, *Interest will not Lie* (1659), p. 23.

[118] McMichael and Taft, *Writings of William Walwyn*, p. 172.

[119] Ibid., p. 273; cf. Woodhouse, pp. 355–6.

God according to his conscience', declared Walwyn in 1646, 'his life in an instant becomes burthensome to him, his other contentments are of no esteeme, and you bring his gray hairs with extreame sorrow to the grave: for of all liberty liberty of conscience is the greatest: and where that is not: a true Christian findeth none'.[120] 'Who can be at rest', Milton would ask in 1660, 'who can enjoy any thing in this world with contentment, who hath not libertie to serve God and to save his own soul, according to the best light which God hath planted in him to that purpose?'[121]

How, in the 1640s, had liberty of the subject and liberty of conscience come together? Behind the convergence there lay the spread, in politics and religion alike, of the principle of consent. In the previous two chapters we witnessed the potency of the principle of political consent in the civil sphere of the Puritan Revolution. Here we see the impact of a parallel conviction in the religious history of the period. The debt of the Leveller movement to the Baptist one, which insisted on adult choice as the basis of Church membership, is one symptom of that development, which however extended across a broader spectrum of opinion than either the Baptists or the Levellers commanded. There was also, as we shall see, the 'Arminianism of the Left', whose conceptions of free will, of reason, and of the universal hope of salvation were more readily aligned with notions of civil liberty than Calvinist predestinarianism could be. Yet if the two spheres of liberty became linked, the connection was not spelled out or systematically explained. It was as much felt as thought. As often happens in the history of ideas that find political application, changes of perception were indebted not only to cerebral exploration but to pressures, practical and emotional, of events. Men who in the civil war fought and suffered for a cause that was both political and religious found a unifying bond in the conjunction of the two kinds of liberty. The conviction arose that liberty of conscience had been, or at least ought to have been, an initial war aim of the parliamentarians, alongside their demands for liberty of the subject. The 'liberty' of Independent congregations, Goodwin told parliament in 1644, was the 'expectation' in which 'wee have fought, and adventured purse and person'.[122]

Five years later Walwyn claimed that when in 1642 parliament had invited men 'to fight for the maintenance of the true Protestant religion, the libertyes of the people, and priviledges of parliament', 'many', hearing their cause defined in those 'generall terms', 'did believe the parliament under the notion of religion, intended to free the nation from all compulsion in matters of religion'.[123] The contribution of the 'saints', and especially of sectaries and separatists, to parliament's successes on the battlefield inspired the feeling that liberty of conscience should be among the fruits of victory. Here, to Cromwell, was the lesson of Naseby. As he wrote to the Commons after the victory, a soldier who 'ventures his life for the liberty of his

[120] McMichael and Taft, *Writings of William Walwyn*, p. 192.
[121] *CPW*, vii. 379.
[122] *Paraenetick*, p. 5.
[123] McMichael and Taft, *Writings of William Walwyn*, p. 298. Cf. pp. 94, 169, 207; Haller, *Tracts on Liberty*, iii. 249; Woodhouse, p. 459; *LP*, pp. 177–8.

country' should be rewarded with 'the liberty of his conscience'.[124] In time Cromwell would be viewed as an enemy of *Walwyn's* circle and with suspicion or hostility by countless sectaries, but those conflicts lay ahead.[125]

The afflictions which the saints sustained in God's cause intensified the sentiment to which Cromwell's letter gave voice. The godly ventured to compare the deaths of their fellows in battle with the death of the Redeemer. 'Christ bought our liberties with his blood,' Goodwin told parliament in 1644, and 'wee have bought them over again at your hands with our own blood'. Men who had suffered for 'liberty, first of the kingdome, then of the conscience', he avowed, 'should not be inslav'd in either'.[126] The contribution of the saints to the nation's deliverance from oppression in both politics and religion heightened indignation against the punishment, or the threat of punishment, of religious dissenters by parliament or the courts 'for exercising their consciences'.[127] Why, asked aggrieved soldiers in 1647, should men who had 'engaged their lives' for 'our country's liberties and freedom' be 'abridged' of the 'freedom to serve God according to our proportion of faith, and [be] like to be imprisoned, yea, beaten and persecuted, to enforce us to a human conformity never enjoined by Christ'?[128] Similar thinking was prompted by the exclusion of religious dissenters, on the grounds of their religion, from the holding of secular offices.[129]

Over the twentieth century the phrase 'civil and religious liberty' receded because, or partly because, the distinction between the two faded. Freedom of religious association and belief has itself come to be adjudged a 'civil liberty'.[130] No one in the seventeenth century would have defined it merely as a civil liberty, but the civil wars produced indications that it could be thought of as one. In the army's debates at Whitehall in 1648 we find John Goodwin suggesting that liberty of conscience might itself be a 'civil right', and Henry Ireton affirming, as 'a common right and freedom', the principle that 'any man submitting to the civil government of the nation should have liberty to serve God according to his conscience'.[131] By that year, as we shall soon see, connections between civil and religious liberty were being more boldly conceived and asserted. Even so, Goodwin's and Ireton's statements appear to have had a muffled reception. Insofar as they were noticed, they seem to have induced, not hostility, but conceptual puzzlement. For the movement that juxtaposed the two kinds of liberty could not proceed straightforwardly. The enduring potency of the conception of Christian liberty as liberty in Christ is illustrated in the minds of sectaries who were among the keenest champions of liberty of religious profession, and whose arguments often rested, not on the common

---

[124] Abbott, i. 360.

[125] McMichael and Taft, *Writings of William Walwyn*, p. 169.

[126] *Paraenetick*, pp. 2–9; Coffey, *John Goodwin*, pp. 117–18.

[127] McMichael and Taft, *Writings of William Walwyn*, p. 123.

[128] Woodhouse, p. 399.

[129] McMichael and Taft, *Writings of William Walwyn*, p. 282. Cf. Woodhouse, p. 409; *GD*, p. 455.

[130] e.g. Helen Fenwick, *Civil Liberties* (1998 edn), ch. 5 and pp. 574–6. Few are the modern advocates or analysts of 'civil liberties', or of 'human rights', who show an interest in the historical evolution of those terms.

[131] Woodhouse, pp. 126–7, 141, 143.

interests of secular and religious freedoms, but on the separation of the spheres of nature and grace, of the kingdom of Christ and the kingdoms of the world.[132] It was the complaint of Roger Williams and John Milton, those ardent advocates of the division of Church from state and of freedom of belief and worship, that compulsion in faith 'confounds' the 'civil' with the 'religious' or 'spiritual' sphere, which are properly 'sever[ed]'.[133] Williams insisted that 'a civil state and a spiritual' are 'of different natures and considerations, as far differing as spirit from flesh'.[134]

No one would charge Williams or Milton with having renounced the world or of indifference to its civil improvement. To both men 'civility', or 'civil virtue', was properly the partner of 'Christianity'.[135] So was it to the antinomian preacher John Saltmarsh, who, in a work of 1646 that he dedicated to the Roundhead grandee Lord Saye and Sele and to Oliver Cromwell, urged believers to 'assist the publike' on 'civill, natural, temporal, spiritual' fronts and to combat 'malignity in state, in Church'. Saltmarsh's premise was that 'the liberty of the subject is that of soul as well as body'. Yet the two kinds of freedom remained very different in his mind. He urged believers to look above their temporal concerns to the 'more dear, precious, glorious' liberty 'wherein Christ hath made us free', and to remember the differences and distance between 'civils' and 'spirituals'. Saltmarsh feared lest the hunger for liberty of conscience become a pretext for political disobedience. Not only was 'the liberty of the outward man', he thought, inferior to 'the true Christian liberty', but the army had 'managed' the 'glorious principle of Christian liberty ... too much in the flesh'.[136] Others asked whether the liberty of Christ's spirit, which 'bloweth where it listeth' (John 3:8), really required the aid of men. Though 'it cannot but be well taken', acknowledged the new model chaplain Joshua Sprigge in December 1648, that the army aimed 'to promote the spiritual liberties of the saints, as well as the civil liberties of men', the fact was that Christ's kingdom stood in no need of 'any power of man', for 'Christ will grow up in the world, let all powers whatsoever combine never so much against him'.[137]

Sprigge was speaking in a debate on the Levellers' claim, which had been enshrined in their *Agreement of the People* in 1647, that liberty of conscience was 'a native right', to be protected alongside native freedoms in civil life. Yet the Levellers' position, like Goodwin's and Ireton's, seems to have wrought perplexity if not incomprehension in the army.[138] For whereas the exercise of other native rights could be held to lie in men's free choices, or could be voluntarily entrusted by them

---

[132] See ibid., 'Introduction'.
[133] Ibid., p. 266; WJM, i. 65.
[134] Woodhouse, pp. 274, 282; cf. p. 267.
[135] Ibid., p. 266; *LP*, p. 162.
[136] John Saltmarsh, *The Smoke in the Temple* (1646), pp. 68–9; idem, *Sparkles of Glory*, pp. 116–17; Woodhouse, p. 438.
[137] Woodhouse, p. 135. From a very different angle, Scottish Presbyterians protested against the incorporation of Scotland with England after the battle of Worcester because 'it will be a means of mingling their civil liberties with their religion': C. S. Terry, *The Cromwellian Union* (Edinburgh, 1902), p. 9. From another angle still, John Wildman argued that 'the word of God' has nothing to tell us about 'what is fit to be done in civil matters': Firth, *Clarke Papers*, i. 384.
[138] Woodhouse, pp. 125 ff.

to the civil power, the *Agreement* acknowledged that in religion men have no such power of choice, since what they properly believe is what 'their consciences dictate to be the mind of God'.[139] The Levellers reaffirmed the old principle that 'the inward man is God's prerogative, the outward man is man's prerogative'.[140] On that point they would have agreed with Milton, in whose mind God has willed 'that the inviolable right and power of conscience are in his possession alone'.[141] Leveller thought, though rooted in religious dissent, can look a secularizing force in the later 1640s. We watch the movement of their ideas towards concrete social and political reforms, and their conflict with those Congregationalists and separatists who put religious reform before the liberty of the subject.[142] Lilburne, who in 1647 proclaimed his own 'civill liberties and freedoms',[143] had come a long way since the years before the war. Then he had, conventionally, identified Christian liberty with liberty of the soul, and had disowned any thought of disobedience in 'temporall things'. He had subsequently found, it has been observed, 'that religious principles could not be separated from political life'.[144] Yet that shift was a revision of, not a movement away from, his religious preoccupations. It reflected a growing conviction among the Levellers of the social or communal or charitable or 'practical' responsibilities of the Christian.[145] Those obligations included the promotion of 'common justice', and opposition to 'tyranny' of all forms that 'usurped' the sovereignty of God, who 'ALONE . . . is to reign'.[146] Inhibitions on the alliance of civil and religious liberty remained to be overcome.

The third stage emerged from the second civil war of 1648. Its source was the fury of the new model army and its supporters at the prospect of a treaty between Charles I and the Presbyterians at Westminster that would betray the cause, political and religious, to which the army was committed. In July a petition to parliament, presented on behalf of 'divers' magistrates, ministers, and inhabitants of London, warned against the 'invasions . . . intended upon our religious and civil liberties' by the promoters of the prospective 'personall treaty' between king and parliament.[147] According to the London book-collector George Thomason, the

---

[139] *GD*, 334–5; cf. Davis, 'Religion and the Struggle for Freedom', p. 515.

[140] Wolfe, *Leveller Manifestoes*, p. 181.

[141] *CPW*, v. 686.

[142] Murray Tolmie, *The Triumph of the Saints: The Separate Churches of London* (Cambridge, 1977), chs 7–8.

[143] John Lilburne, *The Resolved Mans Resolution* (1647), p. 1.

[144] Ibid., p. 7; Robertson, *Religious Foundations of Leveller Democracy*, pp. 6, 14–16.

[145] Lilburne, *Resolved Mans Resolution*, pp. 6–7; McMichael and Taft, *Writings of William Walwyn*, pp. 178, 356; Wolfe, *Leveller Manifestoes*, p. 393 (cf. p. 135); Haller and Davies, *Leveller Tracts*, pp. 272 (cf. pp. 290, 345); and see J. C. Davis, 'The Levellers and Christianity', in Brian Manning, ed., *Politics, Religion and the English Civil War* (1973), pp. 225–50.

[146] Robertson, *Religious Foundations of Leveller Thought*, p. 91; Davis, 'Religion and the Struggle for Freedom', p. 527.

[147] BL, Thomason Tracts, 669 f. 12 [63]: *To The Right Honourable the Lords and Commons*.

document was penned by the Congregationalist divine Philip Nye, an ally of the army leadership.[148] In November the army declared to the kingdom that Charles's re-enthronement would bring a return to 'the same principles and affections, both as to civil and religious interests, from which he hath acted the past evils'.[149] It was in the army's debates of the following month, after it had purged parliament in order to break the treaty and bring the king to justice, that Ireton and John Goodwin broached the notion that liberty of religious profession was a civil right, and that Joshua Sprigge acknowledged the attention being given by the new model both to 'civil liberties' and to 'spiritual liberties'. In March 1649 the parliamentary *Declaration* vindicating the abolition of kingship argued that it would produce 'a just freedom of . . . consciences, persons and estates'.[150] In 1650 the Rump remembered Charles I's 'opposition to all Christian as well as civil liberty'.[151]

The execution of the king in January 1649 saw off the Presbyterian-royalist threat. Yet among supporters of the regicide it heightened an awareness of the interdependence of civil and religious thraldom. Alertness to their entanglement was not new. But by now a relationship which in the early 1640s had looked merely a product of historical contingency was being viewed as intrinsic. The two kinds of grievance were presented, in heady language, as the products of a single and ubiquitous instinct of oppression, from which the parliamentarian cause was a struggle for deliverance. In the civil war Sir Cheney Culpepper, yearning for 'spiritual and civil truth', had looked forward to the end of the 'civil popery' in which the people had been 'educated' and to the 'downfall of civil and ecclesiastical Babylon', which 'as they have grown so will they fall together'.[152] Such perceptions grew in frequency and intensity in 1648–9. John Owen told the Rump in April 1649 that 'the peculiar light of this generation is that discovery which the Lord hath made to his people, of the mystery of civill and ecclesiasticall tyranny. The opening, unravelling, and revealing the Antichristian interest, interwoven, and coupled together in civill, and spirituall things, . . . is the great discovery of these days.'[153] Owen's words voiced an exultant mood in and near his circle in the period around the regicide. The mood was heightened by the news of revolutions or rebellions in the popish lands of France and Catalonia, which added to the European convulsions of the decade and in which the same cosmic movement was discerned. 'Who almost is there', Owen asked,

> who doth not evidently see, that for many generations, the western nations have been juggled into spiritual and civil slavery, by the legerdemain of the Whore, and the

---

[148] If Nye, who—at least by this time—was orthodox in his theology, was indeed the author, then he was following where those doctrinally unorthodox figures Goodwin and the Levellers had led.

[149] *OPH*, xviii. 187.

[150] Ibid., xx. 73.

[151] Ibid., xx. 361; cf. xx. 359.

[152] Braddick and Greengrass, 'Letters of Sir Cheney Culpepper', pp. 137, 173–4, 176, 184, 186, 207, 217, 271, 273–4, 291.

[153] Owen, *Shaking and Translation of Heaven and Earth*, p. 35. Cf. the statement of John Cook quoted by Davis, 'Religion and the Struggle for Freedom', p. 521; *Mercurius Politicus* 8 September 1653, p. 2708.

potentates of the earth. . . . [and see] how the whole earth hath been rolled in confusion, and the saints hurried out of the world, to give way to their combined interest? . . . .Is it not evident . . . that the whole present constitution of the governments of
the nations, is so cemented with Antichristian mortar from the very top to the bottom,
that without a thorough shaking they cannot be cleansed?[154]

'The particular light of this generation' was reaching Owen's allies. The army's
Remonstrance of November 1648, which announced the impending moves to bring
the king to justice, remembered that before the wars 'the generality of the people',
by 'means' of 'the corrupted forms of an outside religion and church-government',
had been 'held in darkness, superstition, and a blind reverence of persons and
outward things, fit for popery and slavery', 'fit subjects for ecclesiastical and civil
tyranny'. To counter that dual slavery, maintained the *Remonstrance*, the parliamentarians had fought for 'the increasing and spreading of light amongst men'.[155]
In January 1650 Cromwell told the 'deluded and seduced' Catholics of Ireland:

> Arbitrary power men begin to be weary of, in kings and churchmen; their juggle
> between them mutually to uphold civil and ecclesiastical tyranny begins to be trans-
> parent. Some have cast off both, and hope by the grace of God to keep so. Others are at
> it! Many thoughts are laid up about it, which will have their issue and vent. This
> principle, that people are for kings and churches, and saints for the pope or churchmen
> (as you call them), begins to be exploded. . . . [156]

Milton, like John Owen, saw an inherent 'interweaving' of civil and religious
oppression. Writing in defence of the regicide in 1649, he looked back on Charles's
reign and concluded that those 'twisted scorpions', 'temporal and spiritual tyranny',
those 'two burd'ns, the one of prelatical superstition, the other of civil tyrannie',
had 'very dark roots' which 'twine and interweave'.[157] Remembering the popular
support for the restoration of the king in the previous year, he reflected on the
proneness of the people 'not to a religious onely, but to a civil kinde of idolatry'.[158]
Previously, despite his readiness to use the phrase, 'civil liberty' had been a low
priority to Milton.[159] Now he had revised his estimate. Early in 1651 he declared
that civil and spiritual tyranny had a common source, 'the assigning of infallibility
and omnipotency to man'. Ready, here as elsewhere from the time of the regicide,
to find bold political lessons in the New Testament,[160] he decided that Paul's
injunction to us not to be 'servants of men' was an endorsement 'not only
of evangelical liberty but also of civil liberty' ('*non solum de evangelica solum, sed
de civile libertate*').[161]

---

[154] Owen, *Shaking and Translating*, pp. 35–6.   [155] *OPH*, xviii. 179–80.
[156] Abbott, ii. 200.   [157] *CPW*, iii. 446, 509, 549, 570.
[158] Ibid., iii. 343.   [159] *LP*, pp. 160–1.   [160] Ibid., pp. 43–4.
[161] *WJM*, vii. 145, 155–7, 211 (cf. viii. 131, 135); Blair Hoxby, '*Areopagitica* and Liberty',
in Nicholas McDowell and Nigel Smith, eds, *The Oxford Handbook of Milton* (Oxford, 2009),
pp. 225–6. Milton's position is nonetheless another warning against the interpretation of the new
language of civil and religious liberty simply as a secularizing force. His political interpretation of Paul's
injunction did not replace or reduce his commitment to the traditional understanding of Christian
liberty as liberty in Christ and liberty from sin. He did not want to see the 'divine and spiritual
kingdom' of Christ 'degrade[d] . . . to a kingdom of this world'. *CPW*, vi. 537, vii. 256, 258.

*

It was one thing for the alliance of civil and religious liberty to be taken up by sectaries and regicides. It was another for the alliance to enter the mainstream of political argument. Despite Milton's assertions, the association of civil and religious liberty in public debate did not much develop in the years 1649–53.[162] The government of the Rump over that time was generally taken to be an affront to civil conceptions of liberty. Though its rulers, in defending their rule, vigorously denied that charge, they were thrown back on de facto justificiations of their authority which appeared to validate the accusation.[163] The military coups of 1648–9—Pride's Purge and the regicide—that brought the Rump to power had won support from a number of people who were ready to see the liberty of the subject suspended or overridden in a religious cause. Yet the regime's provisions for liberty of conscience proved to be grudging and limited and were ungratefully received by their beneficiaries.[164]

The fourth stage began only in 1653–4, when Cromwell, with a politician's gift for semantic redirection, adopted the language of civil and religious liberty and brought it to the front of the political stage. At the outset of his rule his entourage asserted that the protectorate would best serve 'the liberties of the people both as men and Christians, the true ends whereupon the great controversie hath been stated.'[165] Liberty of conscience had always mattered to him much more than civil liberty, which he had been ready to confound in religion's cause. Freedom of religious profession was to him a means to the advancement of godliness, not, as Whig thinking would make it, a human right. His goal was liberty for the godly, not—unless, by fortifying his regime, it helped the godly to obtain it—for the rest.[166] When he did argue for civil liberty, his words could let slip that here too it was on the liberty of the godly that his heart was fixed, not on that of the nation in whose 'midst' the saints lived as 'the apple of God's eye'.[167] The military genesis of his rule, no less than of the Rump's, contradicted most perceptions of civil liberty. His elevation, no less than the revolution of 1648–9, was supported by many seekers of liberty of conscience who were willing to sacrifice civil liberty for it. There were ironies in the impact of his adoption of the language of civil and religious

---

[162] Whitelocke (*Memorials*, iii. 374, 472; cf. ii. 548) would remember after the Restoration that in discussions with Oliver Cromwell in 1651–2 he had expressed a commitment to 'our civil and spiritual liberties', but I suspect that his memory was distorted by the subsequent spread of the phrase. Cf. Blair Worden, 'The "Diary" of Bulstrode Whitelocke', *English Historical Review* 108 (1993), pp. 122–34. But Whitelocke's fellow lawyer and fellow rumper Nathaniel Bacon, writing from an Erastian perspective, did make a connection between 'liberty of conscience' and 'liberty of estates' in a work published in 1651 and perhaps written in the later 1640s: Bacon, *Historical and Political Discourse*, ii. 124.

[163] Quentin Skinner, 'Conquest and Consent: Thomas Hobbes and the Engagement Controversy', in G. E. Aylmer, ed., *The Interregnum: The Quest for Settlement* (Houndmills, 1972), pp. 79–98.

[164] Blair Worden, *The Rump Parliament 1648–1653* (Cambridge, repr. 1977), pp. 238–9, 294–7.

[165] E223[20], pp. 3565–6; E999[12], pp. 4, 6.

[166] Above, Chapter 3.

[167] Abbott, iii. 583, iv. 389.

liberty. In the short term it would hand a weapon to opponents who learned to use the phrase against him. In the long run it would nourish a Whig tradition which eschewed the vision of a godly commonwealth that had been the guiding ideal of his life.

But Cromwell was not only the head of the godly party. He was the ruler of England, who wanted as broad a power base as he could get. He knew he could not hope to win the nation to his cause of liberty of conscience unless that goal were made to seem the partner of civil liberty. 'I hope', he told MPs in 1657, 'I shall never be found to be one of them that go about to rob the nation of' its 'civil rights and liberties'. On the contrary he would do what he could 'to the attaining of them'.[168] He also saw that the seemingly immoveable political prominence that had been secured by his military and sectarian supporters would be intolerable to mainstream opinion unless they committed themselves to civil as well as religious liberty. The thinking of his son-in-law Charles Fleetwood had moved in the same direction, to his own surprise. In July 1654 Fleetwood told John Thurloe of his subscription to the principle of 'liberty, take it in either sense, as well civill as spirituall. The truth is, thos two interests are so intermixed in this day, that we canot sever them; and that will be found more than a phansy, when thoroughly discussed.'[169] Through the alignment of civil and religious liberty Cromwell aspired to merge what he too called two 'interests': 'the interest of Christians' and 'the interest of Englishmen'. From 1653 he helped to shape the future of political language by his determination to equate 'the cause of Christ', or the concerns of the 'people of God', with 'the good' of 'the nation' (or, when his thoughts extended to the newly conquered Ireland and Scotland, 'the nations') or of 'the whole people' or of 'men as men'.[170] Since, in his own mind, the cause of Christ was of so much the greater import, his assertions that the two 'interests' belonged beside each other had their uncomfortable moments.[171] Nonetheless he protested at the 'pitiful fancy', 'wild and ignorant', 'that the interest of God's people and the civil interest' were 'inconsistent'. Rather, 'he sings sweetly that sings a song of reconciliation betwixt' 'the liberty of the people of God and of the nation'.[172]

Civil and religious liberty became, in Cromwell's speeches to the protectoral parliaments, the issue over which the civil war had been fought: the 'cause', the 'quarrel . . . that was at the first'.[173] It had, he claimed, been his own cause too. 'If I were to give an account before a higher tribunal than any that's earthly, why I engaged in the late wars, I could give no account but it would be wicked, if it did not comprehend these two ends' of 'civil liberty' and 'the liberty of men professing godliness'.[174] His opening statements to the first parliament of the protectorate in

[168] Ibid., iv. 513.
[169] *TSP*, ii. 493.
[170] Abbott, iii. 59, 61; and see Austin Woolrych, 'The Cromwellian Protectorate: A Military Dictatorship?', *History* 75 (1990), pp. 230–1.
[171] Abbott, iv. 260–1, 276, 389, 445.
[172] Ibid., iv. 490.
[173] Ibid., iv. 705.
[174] Ibid., iv. 445.

1654 proclaimed that 'the ground of our first undertaking' the civil war had been 'to oppose that usurpation and tyranny that was upon us, both in civils and spirituals'. For 'liberty of conscience and liberty of subjects' were 'two as glorious things to be contended for as any God hath given us'. The protectorate, he recalled, had delivered the nation from the rule of Barebone's, when 'both' principles had been 'abused' by sectaries. Sects, while demanding liberty of conscience for themselves, had 'imposed' on men who 'with their blood' had earned 'civil liberty, and religious also'.[175] He told the same parliament that the outcome of the civil war had revealed God's intention to provide for 'a liberty of worship with the freedom of . . . consciences. . . . and freedom . . . in estates and persons'; and that he himself would not want to remain protector 'an hour longer than I may preserve England in its just rights, and may protect the people of God in . . . a just liberty of their consciences'.[176] After the dissolution of the parliament the government's printers published at his instigation a tract accusing the Presbyterians of seeking to 'deprive' 'dissenting Christians' 'of their civil and spiritual liberties'.[177]

In stressing the connection of the two the protector found assistance, as so often, from the government's house journalist Marchamont Nedham. Nedham's hand is visible in the declaration which justified Cromwell's forcible expulsion of the Rump in April 1653, and which complained of the parliament's failure 'to settle a due liberty both in reference to civil and spiritual things'.[178] It was in addressing Barebone's in July of the same year that Cromwell revealed his commitment to the merging of Christ's and the nation's causes.[179] Yet only under the protectorate did he and Nedham develop the language of civil and religious liberty. Two months after the inauguration of the regime, in writing for the government a tract that Cromwell would himself cite in expounding the principle of civil and religious liberty,[180] Nedham exploited the reaction against the rule of Barebone's Parliament, as Cromwell would do and as much of the early propaganda of the protectorate did. Barebone's, declared Nedham, 'would have utterly confounded the whole course of natural and civil right, which is the only basis or foundation of government in this world'. Under the protectorate, by contrast, 'the rights and liberties of the people' would be provided for on that 'basis', both in 'all the principal points of civil interest and freedom' and in 'the liberty of tender consciences', so that 'men may live in a plenary enjoyment of their liberty as Christians, and their rights as men'.[181] In the month following the appearance of Nedham's tract the government ordered a public 'day of humiliation'. The first of the prevalent 'sins' to be contemplated by

---

[175] Ibid., iii. 434, 436–7; *True State of the Case of Liberty of Conscience*, p. 1.
[176] *TSP*, iii. 583, 587.
[177] E828[8] (untitled), p. 15; *True State of the Case of Liberty of Conscience*, p. 1.
[178] *GD*, p. 400; *LP*, pp. 305–6; cf. Nedham's *Mercurius Politicus* 8 September 1653, p. 2708.
[179] Abbott, iii. 59, 61.
[180] Ibid., iii. 587.
[181] Nedham, *A True State of the Case of the Commonwealth* (1654), pp. 18, 40–1, 51.

the nation was the 'want', 'notwithstanding the just liberty spirituall and civill God hath procured by his own people', 'of humble walking in the vertues of Christ, or to communicate that liberty one to another'.[182]

In September 1654, echoing Nedham's phrase, Cromwell told the Commons, what he is unlikely to have worked out for himself, that 'liberty of conscience is a natural right'.[183] In defending the Instrument of Government before the same parliament the protector insisted that it 'provided for' 'a just liberty to the people of God, and the just rights of the people in these nations'.[184] Yet by February 1657 he had concluded that, as he then told the army officers, the Instrument would 'neither preserve our religious or civill rights'. The army itself, he told it, was too ready to 'grow upon the civill liberties' by purging parliaments, while parliaments themselves, as the recent treatment of the Quaker James Nayler had demonstrated, were prone 'to grow upon your liberty in religion'.[185] So he exchanged the Instrument for the Humble Petition and Advice, which, as he repeatedly proclaimed, would at last 'accomplish the end of our fighting' by supplying a 'settlement' which would 'give' the nation 'the greatest provision that ever was made' for 'liberty . . . civil and spiritual', for 'civil and religious liberties'.[186] MPs eager for Cromwell to accept the Humble Petition knew what language to speak to him. The new constitution hailed the nation's deliverance through the civil wars from 'tyranny and bondage, both in our spiritual and civil concernments', and promised 'the settling and securing our liberties as we are men and Christians'.[187] The members of the parliamentary delegation which negotiated with him over its terms lined up to emphasize the provision made by the new constitution 'both for spiritual and civil liberties'.[188]

---

[182] *Severall Proceedings of State Affaires* 23 March 1654, p. 3721.

[183] Abbott, iii. 459 (cf. iv. 513). Was that the first time that claim was unambiguously made? The Levellers are sometimes said to have embraced it elsewhere, but the statements of theirs that are pertinent are—unless, perhaps, we count their appeal to 'native rights'—gingerly (cf. Joseph Frank, *The Levellers* [Cambridge, Mass., 1955], p. 6). An early seventeenth-century Lutheran assertion that natural law requires freedom of conscience is quoted by Robert von Friedeburg and Michael J. Seidler, 'The Holy Roman Empire of the German Nation', in Howell A. Lloyd, Glenn Burgess, and Simon Hodson, eds, *European Political Thought 1450–1700* (New Haven, 2007), p. 147; see too the interpretation of the writings of Johannes Althusius by Witte, *Reformation of Rights*, ch. 3. In the England of the 1640s John Goodwin and others had brought ideas of natural law to bear on the matter of liberty of conscience (Coffey, *John Goodwin*, pp. 120–1). Yet it does not look as if the ideas of natural right and natural law that prevailed before and during the mid-seventeenth century (complex ideas, which had religious as well as secular components) were then widely adopted as arguments for liberty of conscience. It is notable, nonetheless, that in England the notion of natural rights as inalienable individual ones seems to have begun in 1644, the time when the claims of individual believers to liberty of conscience became widespread and when the alliance of the claims of civil and religious liberty was taking off: Richard Tuck, *Natural Rights Theories* (Cambridge, 1979), p. 148; see too John Bramhall, *A Just Vindication of the Church of England* (1654), pp. 114, 147.

[184] Abbott, iii. 587.

[185] Ibid., iv. 418–19.

[186] Ibid., iv. 454, 472, 485, 490, 512–13, 706, 708, 720; cf. *A Declaration of his Highness for a Day of Solemn Fasting & Humiliation* (1658).

[187] GD, pp. 447–8.

[188] *Somers Tracts*, vi. 355, 362, 364, 366, 376, 385.

*

It is in the final year of Cromwell's life, 1658, that we reach the last of our five stages. It was now that 'civil and religious liberty' became more than a familiar concept. It became a slogan. The more widely it was used, the more various the usages were. In his speeches of January and February 1658 to the brief second session of the parliament that had passed the Humble Petition the previous summer, Cromwell insistently reiterated his claim that the new constitution provided for civil and religious liberty.[189] Nathaniel Fiennes, addressing the assembly on the government's behalf, declared that the Humble Petition provided for 'liberties, both civil and Christian', 'both our spiritual and civil liberties'.[190]

In the last chapter we saw how the crisis of the protectorate that was produced by the breakdown of the same session of parliament early in 1658 was the moment when demands for the restoration of 'a commonwealth' began to supply a powerful basis of cooperation and common purpose among opponents of the protectorate. The same moment brought a parallel development in the language of civil and religious liberty. The same people were involved: the leading rumper Thomas Scot, and the army officer William Packer, whose Baptist tenets Cromwell had memorably defended against Presbyterians in 1644, but whom he now dismissed from the army, together with five other officers, for their resistance to the Humble Petition.[191] The dissolution of the parliament in early February was prompted by discontent, both in the public and among the soldiery, at the monarchical trend of the protectorate. 'We all know', Scot told the Commons, 'the state of our affairs under former powers of this [monarchical] kind; what encroachments upon both our civil and spiritual liberties'.[192] Packer and his sympathizers, a newswriter reported, 'begin to see that', in supporting Cromwell's rule, 'they have bin fooled under the specious pretence of liberty of conscience to betray the civill liberties of theyr owne native country'. One of them 'told' Cromwell 'to his head that if he could not have [the one] without the other, he would adventure or seeke it elsewhere'.[193]

Most of the soldiers stayed loyal to the protector. A series of dutiful army declarations in the wake of the dissolution reminded the nation of the cause for which (as the documents maintained) the soldiers had fought, and of which Cromwell had been the instrument: 'our civil and spiritual liberty', 'that precious prize of liberty, religious and civil'.[194] Yet subtle variations of wording in the declarations illustrate the struggle between two competing tendencies within Cromwellian politics, which by the time of his death had brought policy-making to a standstill. On one hand there were the men, largely civilians (though they had their military allies), who supported the Humble Petition and Advice, the document through

[189] Abbott, iv. 706, 708, 720.
[190] *CJ* 25 January 1658.
[191] C. H. Firth and Godfrey Davies, *The Regimental History of Cromwell's Army*, 2 vols (Oxford, repr. 1940), i. 35–6, 72–3.
[192] *Burton*, ii. 382. Scot's close ally Sir Arthur Hesilrige would take up the point in parliament a year later: ibid., iii. 189.
[193] C. H. Firth, ed., 'Letters Concerning the Dissolution of Cromwell's Last Parliament', *English Historical Review* 7 (1892), p. 110; cf. BL Add. MS 5138, pp. 152–3.
[194] *Mercurius Politicus* 1 April 1658, p. 420; 15 July 1658, p. 658. Cf. 8 April 1658, p. 432; 15 April 1658, p. 455.

which parliament hoped to restore something like the ancient constitution and make Cromwell king. On the other were those, the army officers Charles Fleet-wood and John Desborough at their head, who had been uneasy at Cromwell's elevation and who, though most of them accepted the Humble Petition, resisted the monarchical tendency of the regime. In the coded language of late protectoral politics, the two parties offered rival intimations that civil and religious liberty was safe with them and only with them. The army's call in March 1658, under Fleetwood's management, for the 'settlement' of 'our civill and spiritual liberty', which 'we hope' the Humble Petition has 'already in good measure provided for',[195] stands in contrast to the statement to Richard Cromwell's parliament by his prominent civilian adviser Nathaniel Fiennes that 'both our civil and spiritual liberties have been squared, stated and defined' in the Petition, 'with a great deal of care and exactness'.[196]

Cromwell's deployment of the language of civil and religious liberty had altered the vocabulary of political debate. Unfortunately for him, the language could work against the government as well as for it. Sectaries and champions of parliamentary sovereignty strove, as he had done, to build a power base on the joint claims of civil and religious liberty. Their efforts took time to take off. Yet it was probably as early as the autumn of 1654 that a 'well-wisher' of Fleetwood, who wanted him to break with the protectorate, told him that the Instrument of Government left 'our natural and civill rightes in our persons and estates . . . at the pleasure' of the protector, 'and the liberty of our faith in Christ and his worship . . . no lesse' so.[197] Early in 1655 John Wildman drew up an indictment of Cromwell's tyranny and pleaded for 'the liberties due unto us as men and Christians'.[198] In 1656 Sir Henry Vane made the same case, in an attack on the protectorate which earned him imprisonment. No less than Cromwell, Vane saw in the notion of civil and religious liberty a means of bringing political groups together. His tract commended 'desirers and lovers of true freedom, either in civils or in spirituals, or in both'. Vane proposed the restoration to the people of 'their just natural rights in civil things, and true freedome in matters of conscience'. Both goals, he averred, could be claimed 'upon the grounds of natural right', even if the second, 'the purchase of Christ's blood', 'respects a more heavenly and excellent object'.[199]

It was only in 1659, however, that men who had broken with Cromwell during the decade became widely addicted to the language of civil and religious freedom. In Richard Cromwell's parliament William Packer, who in the previous year had charged the protectorate with sacrificing civil liberty, ruefully remembered, in a powerful speech, his own endorsement of Cromwell's elevation. He had supported

---

[195] Ibid., 1 April 1658, p. 420. Cf. 8 April 1658, p. 432; 15 April 1658, p. 455; 24 June 1658, p. 623.
[196] *OPH*, xxi. 273.
[197] *TSP*, vi. 246. For the date of the letter cf. the reference to a speech by Cromwell to parliament on ibid., vi. 244 with Abbott, iii. 455.
[198] Whitelocke, *Memorials*, iv. 186.
[199] Sir Henry Vane, *A Healing Question Propounded* (1660), pp. 3, 5.

it, he recalled, because of the Long Parliament's failure to provide 'liberty or freedom of conscience', and in the hope that Cromwell would supply it. But now, he said, those 'good people of this nation' who had earlier been antagonized by the parliament's 'severity in that point' had come to understand the congruence of 'the two great interests of religious and civil liberty', which, Packer hoped, 'shall never be parted'.[200] Milton underwent a similar change of allegiance. He had served the Rump, but had subsequently disowned its memory. In 1653–4, despite his earlier pronouncements on the interdependence of civil and religious liberty, he had committed himself, albeit with inner doubts, to the protectorate, hoping that it would fulfil his hopes, as the Rump had not, of liberty of conscience. In 1659 he renounced the protectorate in favour of the cause of parliamentary supremacy. Like Packer he accordingly revised his estimate of the Long Parliament. Its members, he now decided, had been 'the authors and best patrons of religious and civil libertie, that ever these lands brought forth'.[201] His writings of 1659–60 are pervaded by the conviction that 'the whole freedom of man consists either in spiritual or civill libertie'.[202] In the same year the pamphleteer William Sprigge, arguing for a 'free-state', proclaimed that 'our civil liberties, as men' and 'our spiritual liberties as Christians' 'seem so link'd and twisted to each other, that what conduces to the security of one, hath no small tendency to the establishing of the other also'.[203]

In Chapter 7 we noticed the novel appearance of the term 'commonwealths-man', in its political meaning, in titles of tracts of 1659.[204] 'Civil and religious liberties' (or 'rights') appeared in titles for the first time in the same year.[205] The phrase had been adopted and adapted to serve a wide range of anti-Cromwellian opinion. It was adaptable because, in the way of slogans, it was imprecise. It had become a substitute for practical commitments and explanations. Under Oliver Cromwell, an array of critics of his regime had sought to unite themselves beneath the banner of 'the good old cause'. Cromwell complained that they would never tell him what the 'good old cause' consisted of.[206] Now, with parallel vagueness, the 'good old cause' was itself proclaimed to be the pursuit of 'civil and religious liberty'.[207] 'Ye know (friends)', declared the commonwealthsman George Bishop in 1659, 'that the good old cause was (chiefly) liberty of conscience . . . and the liberties of the nation, which with the liberty of conscience were bound up, and joined together, as two lovely twins that cannot be divided, but with the

---

[200] *Burton*, iii. 159; cf. E999[12], pp. 54–5.
[201] *CPW*, vii. 274; cf. vii. 318.
[202] Ibid., vii. 379.
[203] William Sprigge, *A Modest Plea, for an Equal Common-wealth* (1659), p. 23.
[204] Above, p. 308.
[205] *A Declaration of the Christian Free-Born Subjects . . . making out the Principles relating both to their Spiritual and Civil Liberties* (1659); *The Good Old Cause Explained, Revived, and Asserted . . . For the Settling and Securing of our Civil and Spiritual Rights* (1659).
[206] C. H. Firth, *The Last Years of the Protectorate*, 2 vols (1909), ii. 45.
[207] *OPH*, xxi. 342, 400, xxii. 94; *CJ* 9 May 1659; Henry Stubbe, *An Essay in Defence of the Good Old Cause* (1659), preface. Cf. *The Parliamentary Intelligencer* 27 February 1660, pp. 136–7; Ann Hughes, *Politics, Society and Civil War in Warwickshire* (Cambridge, 1987), p. 313.

mutual suffering, if not the dissolution of each other.'[208] The claim that the civil wars had been fought on behalf of 'civil and religious liberty', and that its friends had suffered in its cause, had become a mantra.[209]

Yet in bringing the two liberties together the anti-Cromwellians, no less than Cromwell himself before them, had political and conceptual difficulties to overcome. His opponents all took his elevation to have been an invasion of civil liberty. But not all of them were instinctive friends to liberty of conscience. Advocates of parliamentary supremacy did have wide support among sectaries who believed the liberty of religious profession achieved by Cromwell to have been insufficient. Even so, there were sectaries who feared, as their forebears of the 1640s had sometimes done, lest the new language might usurp or devalue the higher meaning of religious liberty. A pamphleteer of March 1659, lamenting the decay of the godly cause, acknowledged that the civil wars had been fought for 'a double cause' of 'spiritual' and 'civil liberties', but feared that the juxtaposition had obscured the 'subserviency' of earthly to heavenly goals. Thanks to it, 'the true liberty of the creature' in Christ had been subordinated to a man-centred preoccupation with 'outward and visible' liberty of religious profession, which was a mere 'natural right'.[210] Many devotees of liberty of religious profession found it easier, as Cromwell himself did, to plead for the civil and religious liberties of the 'saints' or the 'godly' or 'God's people' than for the nation at large, from which they held their own experience of the higher religious liberty to distinguish them.[211]

Between Cromwell's death and the Restoration, the claims of 'civil and religious liberty' were invoked by every parliamentarian group. They were used both to justify and to oppose each of the successive coups of the late Interregnum. On the accession of Richard Cromwell a series of addresses from the shires, orchestrated by Marchamont Nedham,[212] recalled (to the disgust of William Packer) Oliver's commitment to the principle and urged Richard to sustain 'the just liberty of the people of this nation, both religious and civil', 'our just rights and liberties in our spirituals and civils', and so on.[213] Richard himself, following the practice of his father, told the parliament he summoned that he had 'nothing in my design, but the maintenance of the peace, laws, liberties, both civil and Christian, of these

---

[208] George Bishop, *Mene Tekel* (1659), p. 4; Cf. *Good Old Cause Explained*.

[209] *OPH*, xxi. 340–1, xxii. 11; *The Army's Plea for their Present Practice* (1659), p. 6; *Parliamentary Intelligencer* 27 February 1660, p. 136; *A Brief Account of the Behaviour, &c.* (n.d.: 1660), p. 26; *Ludlow's Memoirs*, ii. 240 n.; Barry Reay, *The Quakers and the English Revolution* (1985), p. 19.

[210] *The Cause of God, and These Nations* (1659), pp. 29–30; cf. John Canne, *A Seasonable Word* (1659), p. 35.

[211] *Army's Plea*, pp. 6–7; *Mercurius Politicus* 28 July 1659, p. 623. Other groups, in pitching appeals to the saints in the language of civil and religious liberty, learned to play on that priority: Firth, *Clarke Papers*, iv. 192.

[212] *A True Catalogue, or, An Account of the Several Places . . . where . . . Richard Cromwell was Proclaimed* (1659), pp. 53–4, 75–6.

[213] Ibid., pp. 20, 30, 33; *Mercurius Politicus* 23 September 1658, pp. 845, 846; 5 November 1658, p. 21; *Burton*, iii. 162–3 (for Packer).

nations, which I shall always make the measure and rule of my government'.[214] During the revolution that produced the overthrow of Richard and the restoration of the Rump in the late spring of 1659, politicians and soldiers bombarded each other, and the nation, with pledges to 'just rights and liberties, civil and religious',[215] to both 'Christian and civil rights',[216] to 'the civil and religious rights and liberties of these nations',[217] to 'that righteous cause, wherein the civil and religious liberties of these nations were involved'; and so on.[218] In May 1659 the restored Rump promised to secure 'the liberties of the people, in reference unto all, both as men, and as Christians'.[219] Supporters and opponents of John Lambert's political manoeuvres in the autumn of 1659 joined the chorus. So did champions of the restored Rump after its second deposition. So did its antagonists on the committee of safety and among the army officers.[220] The same language entered the currency of negotiation and manoeuvre between George Monck and the contending parties during the moves that preceded the Restoration: 'the liberties, civil and spiritual, of the people',[221] 'our dear-purchased liberties, both spiritual and civil', etc.[222] In 1660, as the tide advanced in favour of the king's return, Milton's friend Robert Overton was one of many who feared 'the ruine of our civil and religious rights'.[223]

What is liberty to one man is tyranny to another. In the last two years of the Puritan Revolution the vocabulary of civil and religious liberty became common-place not only among the various groups which had ruled since 1649 and their supporters, but elsewhere. Conservative forces within the Puritan cause followed where the MPs who commended the provision for civil and religious liberty in the Humble Petition in 1657 had pointed. So did politically neutral opinion. To posterity the drive towards the return of monarchy in 1660 may look a reactionary and therefore illiberal force, but to a high proportion of its protagonists it seemed a movement for the return of liberty and the end of military and sectarian tyranny. In the language of civil and religious liberty such men found a ready-made instrument. Their adoption of it was already well under way under Richard Cromwell.[224] Although some Presbyterians protested against the vocabulary of civil and religious liberty,[225] it was more common for Presbyterians to appropriate it to their own ends. They asserted that the way to attain or secure 'the just liberty of the people of

---

[214] Quoted by Patrick Little and Richard Smith, *Parliaments and Politics during the Cromwellian Protectorate* (Cambridge, 2007), p. 138.

[215] *OPH*, xxi. 340–1.

[216] Ibid., xxi. 416.

[217] Ibid., xxi. 345.

[218] Ibid., xxi. 400.

[219] Ibid., xxi. 380.

[220] Ibid., xxi. 462, xxii. 15; Ruth Spalding, ed., *The Diary of Bulstrode Whitelocke* (Oxford, 1990), p. 549.

[221] *OPH*, xxii. 51.

[222] Ibid., xxii. 171

[223] *Parliamentary Intelligencer* 12 March 1660, p. 183.

[224] *Mercurius Politicus* 30 December 1658, p. 311; 27 January 1659, p. 187; 28 July 1659, p. 623.

[225] e.g. *Englands Settlement Mistaken, or, A Short Survay of a Pamphlet called England's Settlement upon the two Solid Foundations of Civil and Religious Liberties* (1660), esp. pp. 7–10.

this nation, both religious and civil', or 'our just rights and liberties in our spirituals and temporals', was to restore order in Church and state alike—a process that, Presbyterians hoped, would extinguish the very religious diversity for which other users of the vocabulary had pleaded. Presbyterians portrayed radical uses of the language as a perversion of it—as eighteenth-century defenders of the political establishment would do. Presbyterian supporters of the rising of Sir George Booth in August 1659 demanded 'the settlement of sacre[d] and civill rights'.[226] In the last months of the Puritan Revolution, when rumpers and soldiers and their allies protested that the 'specious pretence' of the demand for a 'free-parliament'—the movement that would soon restore the monarchy—was endangering 'the liberties of all good people, civil, and religious',[227] a host of Presbyterian petitions called for a 'free parliament' as a means to 'a firm, free, and legal settlement of our rights, civil and religious', to 'civil or Christian liberty', to 'all our civil and religious rights and liberties'.[228] Among the rulers of the disintegrating English regime in Ireland, advocates of kingless rule vied with Presbyterians for control of the same language.[229] Even Charles II and his advisers recognized its appeal and saw the need to take account of it.[230] As a rule, however, royalists, who had been ready to speak parliament's language of 'religion' and 'liberty' in the 1640s, were more likely to mock, or take issue with, the new slogan.[231] Under the Restoration it would generally belong to the language of opposition and protest.

The spread of two other ways of thinking lay behind the alliance of civil and religious liberty in the later 1650s. First there was the argument, which can loosely be called Erastian, that the Church should be subordinated to the state. The principle had drawn widening support from the divisions and chaos of the civil wars, when religion escaped the state's control, and from the reaction against the Presbyterian clericalism that was strident in the 1640s and remained vocal thereafter. Erastianism could be inimical to freedom of religious profession. Milton associated Erastus's name with 'state-tyranie over the Church'.[232] But there was a broad tolerant strain to Erastianism too. One of its representatives, whose writings achieved wide influence in 1659–60, was James Harrington. Whereas the alignment of civil and religious liberty by others was mostly more polemical than analytical, he appealed to logic in arguing that the two, being both matters for the jurisdiction of the civil power, were inseparable. As he tirelessly explained from 1656, 'Where there is no liberty of conscience there can be no civil liberty; and

[226] G. F. Warner, ed., *The Nicholas Papers*, 4 vols (Camden Society, 1886–1930), iv. 177.
[227] *Parliamentary Intelligencer* 26 December 1659, p. 6.
[228] See e.g. Thomas Fuller, *A Happy Handfull* (1660), pp. 20, 37, 49; cf. William Prynne, *The First and Second Part of the Signal Loyalty* (1660), pp. 45–6.
[229] Fuller, *Happy Handfull*, p. 57; *Parliamentary Intelligencer* 16 January 1660, p. 34; *The Declaration of Sir Charls Coot* (1660), p. 3.
[230] Warner, *Nicholas Papers*, iv. 135, 177, 180.
[231] Peter Heylin, *A Short View of the Life and Reign of King Charles* (1658), p. 71; and see Roger L'Estrange, *L'Estrange his Apology* (1660), p. 91; *To the Supreme Authority of the Nation: An Humble Petition on the behalf of Many Thousands of Quakers* (1660)—though also Bramhall, *Just Vindication*, pp. 114, 147.
[232] *CPW*, vii. 252.

where there is no civil liberty, there can be no liberty of conscience.' So the 'distinction of liberty into civil and spiritual' was false.[233]

Harrington is a key figure, too, in the second approach. The impact of his writings in 1659–60 owed much to his perception that the myriad competing groups, both religious and political, into which the nation had disintegrated could be brought together only when their 'interests' were understood and balanced. Other writers of the last phase of the Puritan Revolution took up the point.[234] So did George Monck. The civil wars, he declared, had 'given birth and growth to several interests both in Church and state heretofore not known', and no government could endure which did not accommodate 'all the former interests both civill and spiritual'.[235] So prudence as well as conviction brought the two spheres together.

Like most outcomes of the Puritan Revolution, the conjunction of civil and religious conceptions of liberty was remote from the original goals of the parliamentarians. Its durability after the Restoration, no less than its emergence before it, was indebted to changes within the Puritan movement. Having occupied power, Puritanism now had to learn to survive under it, as 'Nonconformity' or 'Dissent'. Whatever hunger it might retain for the enforcement of a national reformation of religion, the legal restrictions on its own profession of faith, and the public hostility to it, were of more immediate concern. Admittedly the common interests of civil and religious liberty, which had often been asserted hazily during the Puritan Revolution, did not become clear-cut after them. Just as, under Cromwell, a number of Puritans had accepted military rule, and pledged their obedience to it, as a means to secure liberty of conscience, so under Charles II and James II many Dissenters were tempted by offers of 'indulgence' that were designed to strengthen the royal prerogative. Even so, the polarization of the nation in the civil wars, which had joined Puritanism to parliamentarianism, and royalism to Anglicanism, had left its mark. Shared political and religious allegiances of public life were generally more lasting and more explicit after the civil wars than they had been over the generations before them. Under Charles II and James II, and then after 1688, Whigs and Dissenters combined in seeing 'popery' and 'arbitrary government' as common if not inseparable impulses. Against that common threat, it came to seem

[233] J. G. A. Pocock, ed., *The Political Works of James Harrington* (Cambridge, 1977), pp. 647, 703, 749–50, 751, 798, 844, 846; cf. p. 186. Harrington's assertion is illuminated by Eric Nelson, *The Hebrew Republic* (Cambridge, Mass., 2010), ch. 3. Nelson quotes (p. 131) Spinoza's attack on 'those who wish to separate secular rights from spiritual rights'.

[234] Nedham, *Interest Will Not Lie*; John Fell, *The Interest of England Stated* (1659); J. A. W. Gunn, *Politics and the Public Interest in the Seventeenth Century* (Toronto, 1969), pp. 51–3.

[235] *Collection of Several Letters and Declarations, sent by General Monck* (1660), pp. 13, 14; cf. *OPH*, xxii. 48. Monck's debt to the Harringtonian movement is evident in his statement of February 1660 (though he would soon put it behind him) that 'the old foundations' of monarchy were 'broken': *OPH*, xxii. 141.

almost self-evident 'that men ought to enjoy the same propriety and protection in their consciences, which they have in their lives, liberties, and estates'.[236]

Another development in the relationship of politics to religion fortified the conjunction. The fragmentation of religious allegiances during the Puritan Revolution, and the inability or unwillingness of successive Puritan regimes to withstand it, had brought diversity of Protestant belief to stay. Rulers had earlier been implacably against that prospect. From the Declaration of Breda onwards they accepted it, however grimly, as a fact of life. They might proscribe or persecute Dissent and seek to confine its influence, but they did not expect to suppress it. When in power, the Puritans, even a high proportion of those of them who pleaded for liberty of conscience, had sought to impose, through legislation, boundaries outside which doctrines should be forbidden.[237] The Restoration in effect abandoned the state's ambition to regulate the conscience, whose privacy and autonomy, which had sometimes been claimed or recognized in earlier times, were acknowledged with increasing candour.[238] What the state required of Dissenters was not internal conviction but submission to, and participation in, the external worship and observances of the Church of England. The same might be said of the Laudian regime. Again, however, the polarization effected by the civil wars had changed the mental map. More deeply and persistently than before the wars, outward conformity in religion was a test of political loyalty. Bishops, in the aggrieved words of John Goodwin in 1663, taught 'the importune doctrine of blind obedience to superiours, both ecclesiastical and civil'.[239] In response, civil and religious protest became hard to tell apart—especially in the opposition to James II's Catholicism.[240] Gilbert Burnet, as he prepared to join the fleet of William of Orange in 1688 in order to help overthrow 'popery and tyranny', argued that since Protestantism was the religion established by law, 'the right of professing' it 'comes to be one of the civil liberties'.[241] The 'Toleration Act' of 1689 provided a statutory basis not only for orthodox Protestantism but for Dissent, and thus made choice and liberty of religious profession, at least in one sense, a civil right. Yet what the law made it could at any time unmake. Dissenters strove to establish a more fundamental right to toleration, one based not merely on statute but on ideas: on the universal rights of 'mankind' or on universal limits to the entitlement of civil powers to intervene in religion. In the developments that made claims of civil and

---

[236] *State Tracts* (1689), p. 80.

[237] Chapter 3, above.

[238] An extreme but instructive illustration of that alteration is *A Reproof to The Rehearsal Tranprosed* (1673) by the future bishop Samuel Parker, which bluntly adopts arguments and language that in the Puritan Revolution had been used in the cause of liberty of conscience by Congregationalists and sectaries, but which confines that liberty to inner belief and sharply denies the right of Dissenters to outward nonconformity. For the background to the tract see Jon Parkin, 'Liberty *Transpros'd*: Andrew Marvell and Samuel Parker', in Warren Chernaik and Martin Dzelzainis, eds, *Marvell and Liberty* (Basingstoke, 1999), 269–89.

[239] Coffey, *John Goodwin*, p. 277.

[240] Steve Pincus, *1688. The First Modern Revolution* (New Haven, 2009), esp. ch. 7.

[241] H. C. Foxcroft, ed., *A Supplement to Burnet's History of My Own Time* (Oxford, 1902), p. 522; Pincus, *1688*, p. 415.

religious liberty ubiquitous after 1688, political and constitutional pressures mingled with mental or philosophical ones.

That story extends far outside the history of Puritanism. It belongs to the discovery, or reappraisal, of 'rights' by the Enlightenment, a movement that reacted against what it saw as the fanaticism of Dissent or at least of Dissent's Puritan past. Even so, Dissenters made an unrivalled contribution to the language of civil and religious liberty; and developments within Dissent are a mirror, and to a degree were even a cause, of wider changes in the thinking of society. Calvinist theology modified itself. In old Calvinist orthodoxy, the liberty won by Christ's redemption was the liberty of the saved, of the elect. In the civil wars, that assumption was made by many who argued for freedom of religious profession, and who aimed to restrict it to the godly, or at least to people who accepted the 'fundamentals' of Calvinist faith. By contrast the liberty of the subject, belonging to men as men, was agreed to belong to all men. Yet Calvinist exclusiveness was subjected both to refinement and to revolt during the Puritan Revolution. Thus William Walwyn claimed that 'liberty of conscience' should 'be allowed for every man' (even though it was the freedom of 'conscientious people', not of the rest, that preoccupied him).[242] It was within Roundhead Arminianism that civil and religious conceptions of liberty came together in the 1640s. Calvinists caught up with the convergence and, in the 1650s, made every political use of it, but they did not bring to it the sense of fresh intellectual or spiritual discovery visible among the pioneers of the movement. By the eighteenth century, Calvinism had adjusted to the Arminian challenge. It had also learned to think of religious liberty, as of civil liberty, as a human entitlement. Dissenters could now take it for granted that liberty of profession was 'every man's right', not merely the right of the godly.[243] They proclaimed religious liberty as a 'natural right' or the right of 'mankind', or anyway the right of 'a free people' or of 'all Englishmen'.[244] Arminianism, whether Anglican or Puritan, also betokened another change, a shift of emphasis from the primacy of Christian faith towards the primacy, if only as an expression of that faith, of Christian conduct—which must operate in the civil sphere, where questions of civil liberty arise.

The reaction against predestination in the civil wars was part of a larger challenge to Calvinist pessimism. Calvinists of the Puritan Revolution who were alarmed by the movement for 'liberty of conscience' explained that the conscience was too flawed, too prone to pride and wilfulness and self-centredness and self-deception, to arrive at spiritual or doctrinal truth without institutional direction or compulsion. Their

---

[242] McMichael and Taft, *Writings of William Walwyn*, pp. 102, 273.

[243] Seed, *Dissenting Histories*, p. 58.

[244] Ibid., pp. 7, 158, 50. If it can broadly be said that the Enlightenment gave 'rights' their modern meaning, then Dissent absorbed that development. Yet the process, again, was not a simple story of secularization. Inside and outside Dissent, the notion that religious liberty was an 'inalienable right' for long remained tied, as the Leveller perception of liberty of conscience as a 'native right' had been, to the supposition that the ordering of the conscience, being God's prerogative, was beyond man's: e.g. *The Case of Toleration Recogniz'd* (1702), p. 2; Ellis Sandoz, ed., *Political Sermons of the American Founding Era*, 2 vols (Indianapolis, Ind., 1998), i. 86.

critics had more confidence in the conscience, indeed in humanity. Again Dissent caught up, again with consequences for the relationship of ideas of civil and religious liberty. William Perkins's instruction to 'detest whatsoever is of our selves' can be contrasted with the approving observation of Richard Price, nearly two centuries later, that 'one general idea ... runs through' both 'civil liberty' and 'religious liberty': 'I mean, the idea of self-direction, or self-government'.[245]

Essential to self-government, in eighteenth-century eyes, was the cultivation of 'reason', a commodity in which hard-line Calvinism had had such limited faith, but to whose operation the conscience itself was increasingly held to be tied.[246] In the eighteenth century's confidence in reason there lies another echo of the anti-Calvinism within the Puritan Revolution. Where Calvinists traditionally emphasized the depravity and feebleness of the intellect, their Roundhead adversaries saluted its capacities. So, from a different perspective, did Anglicans and royalists; but non-Calvinist parliamentarians had their own contribution to make. Truth, they asserted, would be attained not by external imposition but by individual exploration, by 'the Scripture liberty of proving and trying all things'.[247] 'Every Christian', they urged, should have 'his right of free, yet modest, judging and accepting what he holds'.[248] The Cromwellian councillor Sir Charles Wolseley, author of *The Reasonableness of Scripture-Belief* (1672) and an adversary of Calvinist intolerance, wrote that to refuse a man the scope to 'judge for himself' in matters of religion is to 'change him from a rational creature to a bruit'.[249] Dissenters of later generations would take 'religious liberty' to signify 'the power of exercising, without molestation, that mode of religion which we think best'.[250] The 'Christian liberty' purchased by Christ's blood now meant, or included, 'a liberty to think for ourselves',[251] or 'judging according to my reason'.[252] Those who argued for the right of free judgement in religion were liable to claim it in the civil sphere too.

Reason would allow the conscience to tell different people different things. The mainstream of seventeenth-century opinion had proscribed that view,[253] but

---

[245] Price, *Observations on the Nature of Civil Liberty*, pp. 4–5.

[246] In time, 'reason' would declare its independence of God and of theology, but once more secularization was a complex process, for only slowly did the divine properties of reason decline. John Spurr, '"The Strongest Bond of Conscience": Oaths and the Limits of Tolerance in Early Modern England', in Harald Braun and Edward Vallance, eds, *Contexts of Conscience in Early Modern Europe, 1550–1700* (Houndmills, 2004), pp. 151–65; Isabel Rivers, *Reason, Grace and Sentiment*, 2 vols (Cambridge, 1991–2000), i. 63–6, 186–8.

[247] John Saltmarsh, *Groanes for Liberty* (1647), p. 32; cf. Woodhouse, p. 459.

[248] Woodhouse, p. 247; cf. McMichael and Taft, *Writings of William Walwyn*, p. 103.

[249] Quoted by Gary S. de Krey, 'Radicals, Reformers and Republicans: Academic Language and Political Discourse in Restoration London', in Houston and Pincus, *Nation Transformed*, p. 81. De Krey's article offers a number of insights into thinking about religious liberty in the later seventeenth century. For Wolseley see also above, pp. 89–90.

[250] Price, *Observations on the Nature of Civil Liberty*, p. 4; cf. John Jackson, *Christian Liberty Asserted* (1734), p. 24.

[251] *Christian Liberty: A Sermon, on the History and Principles of the Nonconformists* (1800), pp. 5–6.

[252] *Christian Liberty Asserted* (1719), p. 11.

[253] Keith Thomas, 'Cases of Conscience in Seventeenth-Century England', in John Morrill, Paul Slack, and Daniel Woolf, eds, *Public Duty and Private Conscience in Seventeenth-Century England* (Oxford, 1993), p. 30.

outside the mainstream there had been writers ready to espouse it. To the most eloquent Puritan adversary of Calvinist orthodoxy, John Milton, godliness was indissolubly connected to 'reason', which 'also is choice' or 'is but choosing'.[254] It was bound to the free exercise of 'the minde', to 'philosophic freedom'.[255] A free mind may be owned and illuminated by God, but he trusts its direction to human reason, which needs human protection. In 1644 William Walwyn indicated that a man has 'just liberty' if he 'may freely enjoy his minde, and exercise his conscience'.[256] It was apparently Walwyn who two years earlier had remonstrated against 'the fitting of our minds' for 'slavery' by court sermons which had preached up the prerogative.[257] The higher the claims made for the mind or reason in religion, and the closer the alliance between reason and faith grew, the stronger became the recognition of the religious function of what the Anglican the Earl of Clarendon called 'the liberty of thinking',[258] or what in the next century Thomas Gordon called 'the liberty of the mind', which Gordon judged 'preferable to the liberty of the body'.[259] Within such perspectives, freedom of faith partnered freedom of thought. In 1785 the philosopher and theologian William Paley could write for 'the general cause of intellectual and religious liberty'.[260] If the theological inheritance which had been received by the seventeenth century had separated the two kingdoms of God and the world, and thus the rules of politics from those of religion, 'the mind' now placed 'civil' and 'religious' contemplation on a common intellectual basis.

If the mind were to be free, so must the instruments of its persuasion be. Friends to liberty of conscience in the Puritan Revolution had called for 'liberty of free disquisition', or 'liberty of writing', or 'liberty of discourse', as a necessary vehicle of truth.[261] 'Give me the liberty', called Milton, 'to know, to utter and to argue freely according to conscience, above all other liberties', for 'without this freedom, we are still enslaved'.[262] Those had been pioneering sentiments. By the later eighteenth century the dependence of liberty of religious profession on 'freedom of speech', on the individual's freedom to 'speak his mind', was widely assumed.[263] Milton's goal in demanding free speech had been the open passage of religious truth, but in time civil liberty was taken to be dependent on it too.

---

[254] *CPW*, ii. 527; *Paradise Lost* III. 108. The adjustment of Calvinism to such thinking is intimated by John Owen's statement of 1667—made even as he distinguished between the rules of 'civil' and 'religious' obligation—that 'religion . . . is the choice of men, and he that chooseth not his religion hath none': Owen, *Works*, xiii. 531–2.

[255] *CPW*, i. 853, 925, ii. 537, 599, vi. 118.

[256] McMichael and Taft, *Writings of William Walwyn*, p. 140.

[257] Ibid., pp. 72–3.

[258] *CT*, p. 255.

[259] Thomas Gordon, *Priestianity* (1720), p. xiv. Gordon's and John Trenchard's widely read work *Cato's Letters*, first published in 1721, was subtitled *Essays on Liberty, Civil and Religious*. . . .

[260] William Paley, *The Principles of Moral and Political Philosophy* (1785), p. vi.

[261] Woodhouse, pp. 259, 340; McMichael and Taft, *Writings of William Walwyn*, p. 262.

[262] *CPW*, ii. 560, vi. 122.

[263] John Seed, 'The Spectre of Puritanism: Forgetting the Seventeenth Century in David Hume's *History of England*', *Social History* 30 (2005), p. 458 n.; Richard Price, *Britain's Happiness* (1791), p. 15.

At the end of the seventeenth century the two most famous writers of the 1650s to have espoused the cause of 'civil and religious liberty', Milton and Harrington, found a posthumous disciple in the deist and republican John Toland, another ardent advocate of freedom of the 'mind'. Toland saw in the forces of clerical intolerance and authoritarianism the enemy of 'civil and religious liberty'.[264] His own 'unalterable and indispensable' principles, he declared, were 'civil liberty, religious toleration, and the Protestant succession'.[265] Following in Milton's footsteps, he explained that 'when men are once enslaved in their understandings, it's scarce possible to preserve any other liberty'.[266] Comparing Protestant intellectual light to Catholic intellectual darkness, he proclaimed that 'liberty civil and religious is the cause of our knowledge, as their tyranny and inquisition is that of their ignorance'.[267] Silently Toland appropriated Harrington's statement that 'where there is no liberty of conscience, there can be no civil liberty', and expanded it so as to make it a plea for 'the liberty of the understanding', for 'men's freely informing themselves'.[268] In Toland's time such statements, at least in his provocative hands, remained controversial. Over the eighteenth century they became commonplaces.

In other ways, too, 'rational Dissent' adjusted and contributed to the new mental environment. The implacable, confrontational, and divisive deity of the Puritans became, in the Dissenting thought of later generations, a gentler, kinder, more nearly consensual God—and one more interested in civil liberty. Dissenters, even as they recalled the contribution of their Puritan 'ancestors' to 'the cause of civil and religious liberty',[269] now looked askance at what they took to have been the insufficiently 'enlarged' notions of liberty[270] to which those predecessors had subscribed. In the 1730s the Dissenter Daniel Neal's *History of the Puritans* regretted the 'passions and infirmities' of the Presbyterians of Elizabeth's reign, whose 'zeal for their platform of discipline would, I fear, have betrayed them into the imposition of it upon others. . . . Their notions of the civil and religious rights of mankind were dark and confused, and derived too much from the theocracy of the Jews'.[271] Neal's *History*

---

[264] John Toland, *Nazarenus*, ed. Justin Champion (Oxford, 1999), p. 212; cf. Toland, *Tetradymus* (1720), pp. 176, 223.

[265] *A Collection of Several Pieces of Mr John Toland*, 2 vols (1726), ii. 226–7. The presence of the phrase in Edmund Ludlow's *Memoirs* of 1698 (*Ludlow's Memoirs*, i. 347) may be indebted to Toland's editing (cf. Worden, *Roundhead Reputations*, pp. 54–63), though Ludlow, like other hard-line Calvinists, had himself come to adopt the new language (Ludlow, *Voyce*, p. 297; Worden, *Roundhead Reputations*, p. 119). His fellow exile of the 1660s, Algernon Sidney, used it too: Sidney, *Court Maxims*, ed. Hans W. Blom and Eco Haitsma Mulier (Cambridge, 1996), p. 176.

[266] *A Letter to a Member of Parliament* (1698), p. 22.

[267] *Collection of Several Pieces of Mr John Toland*, ii. 3.

[268] John Toland, *Anglia Libera* (1701), p. 100. Toland's preoccupation with the freedom of the mind is brought out by Justin Champion, *Republican Learning: John Toland and the Crisis of Christian Culture, 1696–1722* (Manchester, 2003).

[269] Edmund Calamy, *A Continuation of the Account*, 2 vols (1727), i. 317; Seed, *Dissenting Histories*, pp. 129, 132–3.

[270] *Christian Liberty: A Sermon*, pp. 14, 21–3.

[271] Daniel Neal, *The History of the Puritans*, 4 vols (1732–8), i. 596. Cf. John Aikin, *General Biography*, 10 vols (1799–1815), iv. 371; William Godwin, *History of the Commonwealth of England*, 4 vols (1824–8), ii. 48.

was revised late in the century by the grandfather of the Joshua Toulmin Smith whom we found saluting in 1848 his family's tradition of commitment to civil and religious liberty. Neal's book, declared the grandfather, 'has, on the whole, a liberal cast; it is on the side of civil and religious liberty'.[272]

In 1713 the Whig and low-Church bishop Samuel Bradford, whom William III had made a royal chaplain, published a sermon which he had delivered, in the teeth of the Tory reaction of the last years of Queen Anne, to the rulers and citizens of London in St Paul's Cathedral. He entitled it *The Reasonableness of Standing Fast in English and in Christian Liberty*. His sermon candidly applied to current events Galatians 5:1, 'Stand fast . . . in the liberty wherewith Christ hath made us free', the text which to orthodox Protestants had so long indicated the unbridgeable gap between the eternal and the temporal, between Christian and civil liberty. The liberty that is Christ's gift had been won, Bradford explained, not only on the Cross but in 1688, when our Saviour had 'made us free' both from the 'bondage of popery' and from 'illegal and arbitrary power, preserving to us our happy constitution'. It was in adherence to 'those principles upon which our liberty both spiritual and civil is founded', and in opposition to the enemies of the Revolution, that Bradford urged his hearers to 'stand fast'.[273] Not many eighteenth-century preachers, perhaps, would have drawn so bluntly political an inference from Bradford's text. Yet no preacher in the sixteenth or earlier seventeenth century, maybe even in the mid- or later seventeenth century, could have conceived of one.

The distance travelled from the Reformation to the eighteenth century is likewise indicated by the title given to a collection published in 1758 of the sermons of the Edwardian divine and Marian martyr Hugh Latimer: *The Sermons of . . . Hugh Latimer, on the Religious and Civil Liberties of Englishmen*. The phrase would have passed Latimer's comprehension. The same distance is evident if we set Calvin's statement that 'spiritual liberty may very well agree with civil bondage' beside a sermon by the President of Princeton in 1776, John Witherspoon, on a fast day appointed by the United States Congress. Explaining that 'our civil and religious liberties, and consequently in a great measure the temporal and eternal happiness of us and our posterity', were at stake in the American crisis, he declared that there was 'not a single instance in history in which civil liberty was lost, and religious liberty preserved entire. If therefore we yield up our temporal property, we at the same time deliver the conscience into bondage.'[274] In the process signalled by such contrasts the Puritan Revolution had played a critical part. We may or may not agree with, or warm to, the congratulatory declaration by the late

---

[272] Daniel Neal, *The History of the Puritans*, 5 vols (1793–7), iv. xiv.
[273] Bradford, *Reasonableness of Standing Fast*, pp. 4, 7, 14, 17, 28.
[274] Sandoz, *Political Sermons*, i. 549, 558. The passage is quoted, and the contrast with Calvin drawn, by Coffey, 'Civil Liberty'.

Victorian historian Lord Acton that the struggle within Puritanism for liberty of conscience had been the genesis of developments that had made England 'the foremost of the free'. Yet a significant historical development is missed if we bypass the perception on which his eulogy rested: that the bond between 'religious liberty' and 'civil liberty' was 'a discovery reserved for the seventeenth century'.[275]

---

[275] Lord Acton, *The History of Freedom and Other Essays* (1907), p. 52.

9

John Milton: Life and Writing

Upon the return of Charles II to the English throne in 1660, John Milton went into hiding. His treatises *Eikonoklastes* (1649) and *Defensio* (1651) were officially condemned for their 'sundry treasonous passages . . . and most impious endeavours to justifie the horrid and unmatchable murther' of Charles I, and were publicly burned.[1] He faced the prospect of public execution by hanging, drawing, and quartering, the fate of a number of those who had endorsed the king's execution in 1649, though in the event he escaped with a brief imprisonment. Yet three-quarters of a century later the writer who had been vilified on account of his political polemic was embraced in public memory on account of his verse, which since his lifetime had risen high in England's favour. In 1737 a bust of Milton was placed in Westminster Abbey, where it can be visited among the monuments to the nation's poets.

The distance between the two Miltons, the polemicist and the poet, has persisted in the public mind. The second has had the weight of national opinion and affection on its side. The late seventeenth century and the eighteenth celebrated the 'sublimity' of his poetry. They separated his verse from the memory of the Puritan Revolution, whose record of political and ecclesiastical destruction, and of military and republican and sectarian rule, was so widely denounced.[2] In the account of him in Dr Johnson's *Lives of the English Poets*, the greatness of *Paradise Lost* is proclaimed even as Milton's politics are detested. Since the late nineteenth century the emergence of literary criticism as an autonomous academic discipline has brought fresh conviction to the preference for Milton the poet. The co-authors of the standard recent biography of him rejoice in the achievement of his 'poetic genius' in 'surviving political engagement', and declare the reason why 'Milton still matters' to be 'almost too obvious to be given: it is because he wrote *Paradise Lost*'.[3]

Yet there has been a minority tradition too. While devoted to Milton's verse, it has regretted the neglect, sometimes relative, sometimes absolute, of his prose, a deficiency it has blamed on Tory and Anglican prejudice and propaganda. The tradition developed in the wake of the Revolution of 1688–9, which deposed Charles II's brother James II. Supporters of the coup, then and later, commended

---

[1] Barbara Lewalski, *The Life of John Milton: A Critical Biography* (Oxford, 2000), p. 401.

[2] Nicholas von Maltzahn, 'The Whig Milton, 1667–1700', in David Armitage, Armand Himy, and Quentin Skinner, eds, *Milton and Republicanism* (Cambridge, 1995), pp. 229–53.

[3] Gordon Campbell and Thomas F. Corns, 'Milton and his Biographers', in Paul Hammond and Blair Worden, eds, *John Milton: Life, Writing, Reputation* (Oxford, 2010), pp. 187, 201.

its moderation, which they contrasted with the violence and anarchy of the mid-century. In the 1690s, protests against that interpretation were raised by radical Whigs, of whom the most conspicuous was Milton's biographer the deist John Toland. They viewed 1688–9 as a missed opportunity to return to the principles of 1649. In support of their case they revived Milton's prose works and advertised his support for the execution of the king.[4] From the 1750s the leading publicists of another generation of anti-establishment Whigs, Richard Baron and Thomas Hollis, likewise republished Milton's prose. They celebrated its contribution to that 'good old cause' which, they remembered, had fought tyranny in the seventeenth century and to which they looked for national redemption now.[5] Their sentiments were sometimes echoed in the Romantic era and through the nineteenth century. The Victorian Nonconformist George Dawson praised Milton for having 'left his poetry' during the Puritan Revolution and having 'plunged into the mud, the mire, the dirt, the storm of politics'.[6] The conflict between the two traditions has persisted into modern times. In the academic world it has found an added dimension in rival suppositions about the pertinence or impertinence of biographical contexts to literary inspiration and aesthetic achievement. If *Paradise Lost* is why Milton still matters, will our understanding or appreciation of it be enhanced by a knowledge of his prose and of the career in which he wrote it?

My concern here is Milton's own literary purposes and priorities. It is a subject on which he has much to tell us. His most familiar pronouncement appears in his tract of 1642, *The Reason of Church Government*, his penultimate contribution to the campaign for the abolition of bishops. There the little-known writer, aged thirty-three, explains that considerations of 'duty' and 'conscience' have compelled him to join the attack, at a cost to the literary career he has envisaged. He tells us that his long and strenuous preparation for that career is incomplete, and that he has planned it with aims other than pamphleteering. It would have been in his interest, he says, to bring himself to public attention not in a hurried controversial tract but in a work that 'might be delayd at pleasure', with 'time enough to pencill it over with all the curious touches of art'. Besides, he has written against the bishops 'but of the left hand', in 'the cool element of prose', a 'manner of writing wherein [I know] my self inferior to my self'. He wants the nation—and potential patrons?—to learn of his vocation in poetry, towards which he has as yet taken only small steps. It is his hope that, through his verse, 'what the greatest and choycest wits of Athens, Rome, or modern Italy, and those Hebrews of old did for their country, I in my proportion with this over and above of being a Christian, might doe for mine'.[7]

If his prose was intended to be a mere aside from that aspiration, it became something much larger. The Puritan Revolution of 1641 to 1660 transformed his career. There are three phases in his life and in his writing. The first, the years of his

---

[4] Blair Worden, *Roundhead Reputations: The English Civil Wars and the Passions of Posterity* (2001), esp. chs 3–4.

[5] See the Introduction to my forthcoming edition of Marchamont Nedham, *The Excellencie of a Free-State*, to be published by Liberty Fund in 2012.

[6] George Dawson, *Biographical Letters* (1888), p. 87.

[7] *WJM*, i. 234–6.

London upbringing in a well-to-do citizen household, of his education at St Paul's School and at Cambridge, of his private studies in his family's homes in Hammersmith and Buckinghamshire, and of his journey to Italy, ends with the collapse of the rule of Charles I in 1641. Before that year, when Milton's attack on the bishops began, he was a writer mostly of poetry. He produced, to name only the poems that are perhaps best known, 'On The Morning of Christ's Nativity', 'L'Allegro' and 'Il Penseroso', *A Maske* (the work familiarly known as 'Comus'), and 'Lycidas'. In the second phase, from 1641 to 1660, the decades, roughly, of his thirties and forties, he mainly wrote prose. In the third phase, from 1660, he again mostly wrote poetry. It was then that his poems of surpassing fame, *Paradise Lost* and *Samson Agonistes* and *Paradise Regain'd*, were composed or completed. He did write verse during the Puritan Revolution. Almost the only evidence that we have about the dates of the composition of *Paradise Lost* plausibly indicates that he began it in 1658 (and completed it in or around 1663).[8] Over the 1640s and 1650s he wrote a number of short poems, among them some famous sonnets. Yet he produced them at a rate that makes the most famously exiguous poet of recent England, Philip Larkin, look prolific. It may be that Milton, who in his prose often reworked material over many years, drew in the late poems on drafts composed earlier. For all we know he may have attempted, and discarded, other ambitious verse during the revolution. Yet a reader who in 1660 had come across Milton's autobiographical reflections of 1642 would have wondered what had become of the ambition he had then announced.

We can expect to learn only so much about the inner struggles that determine an author's choices of direction. The immediately obvious explanation of his poetic infertility through most of the revolution is that the crisis of 1641–2, which at the time seemed temporary, proved merely the prelude to a far profounder convulsion, so that the prior claim of prose proved enduring. Yet that cannot be a complete answer, for he published no prose between 1645 and 1649 and next to none between 1655 and 1659. An alternative suggestion is that Milton, who liked to write in tranquillity, found the disorder of the revolution—of 'this damnable civil war' which, he complained, had rendered the muses 'homeless'[9]—inimical to the sustained writing of poetry.[10] That too would have to be an incomplete answer, at least if he was writing *Paradise Lost* during the particularly turbulent period of 1659–60, when he produced a series of urgent polemical pamphlets.

Like most people's, Milton's autobiographical accounts have to be viewed warily. It may be that his declaration of his priorities in 1642 can be taken at face value. There is nonetheless a striking contrast between it and the more rounded passage of personal recollection that is to be found in his Latin prose work of 1654, *Defensio Secunda*, his 'second defence' of 'the people of England', in whose name Charles I had been executed. Vindicating his own character from the charges levelled at it as a

---

[8] Helen Darbishire, ed., *The Early Lives of Milton* (1932), p. 13.
[9] *WJM*, i. 316.
[10] *LP*, p. 168.

result of his first *Defensio*, published in 1651, he decides to 'make known' the story of his life. His account offers no indication that he has ever written poetry or ever will. Instead the centre of his autobiographical attention is now the writing, with his failing eyes and against medical advice, of the first *Defensio*. He decided, explains the now blind writer, 'that, as the use of light would be allowed me for so short a time, it ought to be employed with the greatest possible utility to the public': in defence, that is, of the punishment of Charles I.[11] The sonnet which, perhaps in the mid-1650s, he addressed to his friend Cyriack Skinner dwells on the same achievement. 'What supports me' in blindness is the 'conscience' to have 'lost' his eyes because they had been 'overply'd | In libertyes defence, my noble task, | Of which all Europe talks from side to side'.[12] The exaggeration was pardonable. In his lifetime it was the first *Defensio*, not *Paradise Lost* or his other verse, that made him famous, and for which he was taken to matter.

It seems that in the later 1640s a part of Milton's mind turned not only away from poetry but against it; and that for a time his high poetic ambitions were not so much forgotten as renounced. *Eikonoklastes*, among other sallies against the muses,[13] spurns that 'vain amatorious poem', 'no serious book', the *Arcadia* of Sir Philip Sidney.[14] Earlier he had saluted the instructive power of the *Arcadia* and had embraced Sidney's ideal of teaching by the 'delight' of poetry.[15] Then, too, he had declared that one of the functions of poetry is 'to deplore the general relapses of kingdoms and states from justice and Gods true worship'.[16] Yet when, in the later 1640s and again in the mid-1650s, he arduously explored such 'relapses' in his own country, he did so not in verse but in his prose *History of Britain*. The *History*, which would be published only after the Restoration, was the most ambitious of his known undertakings of the 1640s.[17] It emerged from a radical reorientation of his literary methods. In 1641–2, in line with conventional opinion, he had seen poetry and the prose of history as allied literary forms. He had looked to the second as to the first to instruct readers by affording them 'delight', and by calming the perturbation of mind that can impede their reception of truth. He had taken history and poetry to share the techniques and goals of oratory and eloquence.[18] Just as poetry can impart virtue 'through the charm and smoothness of the sounds',[19] so Milton's prose of the earlier 1640s draws on 'true eloquence the daughter of vertue' to 'charme the multitude into the love of that which is really good'.[20] Yet in the later 1640s, in the *History of Britain*, he shuns the resources both of poetry and of eloquence. He eschews the customary device—a poet's device—of inventing speeches for his historical characters, that 'abuse of posteritie' which 'rais[es], in them that read, other conceptions of those times and places than

[11] *WJM*, viii. 71, 119–39.   [12] Ibid., i. 68.   [13] *LP*, pp. 51–2.
[14] *WJM*, v. 86.
[15] *CPW*, i. 371, 372, 463, 464; *WJM*, v. 238–9.
[16] *WJM*, v. 238–9.
[17] The essential guide to it is Nicholas von Maltzahn's *Milton's 'History of Britain': Republican Historiography in the English Revolution* (Oxford, 1991). I have proposed modifications on the periphery of his argument in *LP*.
[18] *LP*, pp. 389–90.   [19] *CPW*, i. 382.   [20] *WJM*, iii. 181.

were true'.[21] Now he told 'the truth naked, though as lean as a plain journal', even if the result 'may seem a calendar rather than a history'.[22] In the *History* his search for factual instruction had superseded the journey of his imagination. In 1642 he had contemplated a poem, set 'before the [Norman] conquest', that would place the Christian heroism of a 'k[ing] or knight' in a fictional or semi-fictional chivalric setting.[23] The *History*, which traces the history of Britain up to the Conquest, adopts instead a tone of frank realism. When he eventually found his way back to his quest for poetic immortality, it was after renouncing the theme of 'fabl'd knights | In battels feign'd', and after finding 'higher argument',[24] where the 'art' that he had set aside in 1641 was an adornment of, not an alternative to, what he took to be historical fact.

If the autobiographical reflections of 1642 and 1654 offer contrasting perceptions of his priorities, they have a point of concurrence. In both passages he presents himself, as he always does, as a man of learning, whose existence centres on his 'studies'.[25] His contemporaries portrayed him in the same way; even a royalist called him 'the most able and acute scholar living'.[26] Milton takes 'labour and intent study' to be 'my portion in this life', a life 'wholly dedicated to studious labours',[27] for 'books' are 'my true life'.[28] It is the interruption of his 'studies' by the revolution that dismays him.[29] By learning he means not crabbed or pedantic enquiry, with its 'marginal stuffings' and 'scholastical trash',[30] but the learning that equips us to think and live. Poets were expected to be learned. Without learning they could not master language or languages or come to know, as writers in the lifeblood of civilization must, the minds and writings of earlier ages and other lands. It was through his own studies that Milton had prepared himself to write poetry. Yet poetry was but one of learning's branches. He did not need the revolution to excite his interest in the subjects of his prose treatises on theology, history, grammar, and logic. His poetry and prose share not only language and imagery but the educative purpose which is the guiding and unifying mission of his life, and of which his writing is the instrument. It is a God-given purpose. The 'inward prompting' that, in 1642, has informed him of his immortal gifts as a poet has its counterpart in the 'divin[e] monitor within' that inspires him to the composition of the first *Defensio*.[31] His appeal, at the outset of *Paradise Lost*,[32] to his 'heav'nly muse' to empower him to justify God's ways to men is matched by his plea, at the start of the *History of Britain*, for 'divine assistance' in aid of God's glory.[33] Let us, from the range of his compositions, piece together—with inevitable concessions to compression and simplification—the lessons that his prose and poetry seek to teach.

In 1642 he recalls that he planned to enter the ministry—a frequent course among seventeenth-century poets—but felt unable to accept ordination under

---

[21] Ibid., x. 68.   [22] Ibid., x. 179–80.   [23] Ibid., iii. 237.
[24] *Paradise Lost* X. 68.   [25] *WJM*, i 234, 241, viii. 127.   [26] *CPW*, vii. 200.
[27] *WJM*, iii. 236, iv. 296.   [28] Ibid., i. 171; cf. Darbishire, *Early Lives of Milton*, p. 68.
[29] *CPW*, ii. 764, 772.   [30] *WJM*, iii. 241, vi. 95.   [31] Ibid., iii. 236, viii. 69.
[32] I. 6.   [33] *WJM*, x. 3.

the idolatrous Church of Charles I and Archbishop Laud. Those rulers had not only set their minds against Puritan reform: they had steered the Church back towards popery (a theme Milton had already broached in the verse of 'Lycidas'[34]). His prose gives us a number of glimpses of the work of enlightenment and correction that he believes to be a minister's function, and of the 'spiritual knowledge and sanctitie of life'[35] that it requires. Having been 'Church-outed' by the bishops, he turned to poetry, which shares its divine power with 'the office of a pulpit'. Not only can poetry glorify God and his works: it can 'inbreed and cherish in a great people the seeds of vertu, and public civility'.[36] For in Milton's mind religion is always the ally of 'civility' and 'civil life'.[37] They are qualities that encompass sociability; artistic achievement; the human merits perceptible in the literature and politics of classical antiquity; and the prudent debate and management of public affairs. Yet if religion partners the virtues of the world, it simultaneously soars above its vices and above the degradation of the human senses.

Through his writing there runs a conception of liberty. It is consistent at its core, though some of its dimensions and implications emerged only during the revolution or developed in it. 'True liberty', or 'real and substantial liberty', is for him a state of mind or soul.[38] It reproduces, in a distinctive form, the long-established ideal of 'Christian liberty', which frees its adherents from the bondage of sin. To Milton 'liberty' is indissolubly tied to, and can be synonymous with, virtue, for 'none can love freedom heartily, but good men';[39] 'to be free is precisely the same thing as to be pious, wise, just and temperate';[40] liberty is the handmaid of 'innocence of life and sanctity of manners',[41] of 'the just regulation and... proper conduct of life'.[42] The opposite of liberty is 'licence', the self-indulgence of the depraved which enslaves them to passion and lust, though they confuse liberty with the freedom to behave as they wish: 'Licence they mean when they cry libertie; | For who loves that, must first be wise and good.'[43]

The means to liberty and virtue, he insists, is the unfettered exercise of choice. This is the side of Milton that has attracted liberals of later centuries, even if the choices he mostly has in mind, having to do with man's relationship to Christ, are remote from the customary preoccupations of liberalism. First of all, the worship of God, which honours the wonder of the creation of the world and of mankind, is empty, and thus unacceptable to our maker, if it is involuntary. The fate of our souls lies in our choices too. The 'great argument' of *Paradise Lost*, which is spelled out by God the Father early in Book III and which, when grasped, 'justifi[es] the wayes of God to men',[44] is our freedom of will in the matter of our salvation. Milton had announced the argument in 1644, in his prose work *Areopagitica*. There as in *Paradise Lost* he repudiated the Calvinist doctrine of predestination, to which conventional opinion among his fellow opponents of the Laudian regime subscribed. If predestination were true—if the fate of our souls were predetermined,

[34] Ibid., i. 80–1. [35] Ibid., vi. 98. [36] Ibid., iii. 238, 242.
[37] *LP*, pp. 161–2. [38] *WJM*, viii. 9, 131. [39] Ibid., v. 1.
[40] Ibid., viii. 249–51. [41] Ibid., viii. 9. [42] Ibid., viii. 131.
[43] Ibid., i. 63. [44] I. 24–6, III. 80–134.

irrespective of our own exertions of mind and spirit—it would follow both that God is a tyrant and that he is the author of our sins. In Milton's scheme God has bestowed on us, in conjunction with the freedom of our wills, the freedom of our 'reason' or 'understanding'. Those nouns conveyed something more than the ratiocination that is their modern signification. They encompassed the remnant of divinity within us which has survived the Fall, and through which we can subdue our errant and debasing passions. They are innate to our freedom. God trusts man, reveals *Areopagitica*, 'with the gift of reason to be his own chooser'.[45] 'Reason', confirms *Paradise Lost*, 'also is choice', for 'what obeyes reason, is free'.[46] It is true that the will and the understanding, which before the Fall were 'naturally free', are free now 'only as they are regenerat and wrought on by' the 'divine grace' owed to Christ's redemption.[47] Yet if we obey reason we shall find 'libertie' to be the 'consort' of that 'grace'.[48]

Man-made restrictions on our choices corrupt and perplex our earthly pilgrimage. What humanity has done to Christianity, from early in its history, is to entangle it with the pressures of earthly power and of what he insistently calls 'lucre'.[49] Only when the Gospel is emancipated from worldly inducements can its truths, which Christ made intelligible to the poor and simple but which churchmen have embroiled in needless and agitating uncertainties, be readily perceived. By the early 1650s Milton favoured something close to the complete separation of Church and state. Most writers and preachers who addressed that subject maintained that, if Church and state were divided, heresy and blasphemy would escape control and destroy souls and society. Milton by contrast blamed the convulsions of his time on the corruption of truth by the pressures of the world, and insisted on the harmony that would ensue if the freedom of the soul to find its own path to God were secured.

What compulsion produces is not truth but 'a muddy pool of conformity and tradition'.[50] Men 'beleev[e] only as the Church beleevs' or 'as the state beleevs',[51] a perilous course even if the doctrines they hold are true, for a man may thus be 'a heretick in the truth'.[52] The ubiquitous adversary of truth is 'custom', by which our eyes are 'blear'd and dimm'd'.[53] Three of Milton's tracts—*The Doctrine and Discipline of Divorce*; *Tetrachordon*; *The Tenure of Kings and Magistrates*—open with meditations on the tyranny of custom.[54] In confronting it we have two principal weapons. The first is learning—the application of our reason to study—which enables us to scan the errors of inherited thought and recover ancient truths or even discover new ones. The second is courage: courage of the mind and where necessary of the body. Through it we can overcome 'the cowardice of doing wrong' and defeat the 'servile, and thrallike fear', the 'slavish fear', that makes conformists of us.[55] If we yield to fear and servility we become, in Milton's recurrent vocabulary, timorous, slothful,

[45] *WJM*, iv. 310.   [46] III. 108, IX. 351–2.   [47] *WJM*, vi. 21, xvi. 5.
[48] *Paradise Lost* XII. 525–6.
[49] *WJM*, iii. 56, 161, 162, 170, 274, 360, iv. 323, vi. 67; *Paradise Lost* XII. 511.
[50] *WJM*, iv. 333.   [51] Ibid., vi. 6.   [52] Ibid., iv. 333.   [53] Ibid., iv. 350.
[54] Ibid., iii. 367, iv. 63, v. 3.   [55] Ibid., iii. 3, 261.

lazy, sluggish, cold, dull, spiritless, effeminate, whereas Christians who overcome them are bold, active, cheerful, manly.

In this fallen world our attainment of truth and virtue will be a struggle, one always beset by our flaws and errors, towards spiritual adulthood. Good and evil will compete within us. *Areopagitica*, again anticipating *Paradise Lost*, explains that the eating of the apple has given us, in place of perfection, the knowledge of evil alongside the knowledge of good, and has made the contention between them the centre of human experience. Since the Fall, goodness has been definable and achievable only when set against its opposite. So there can be no 'wisdom . . . to choose', and 'no 'continence to forbeare', unless in combat with evil. He commends the 'Christian' who 'can apprehend and consider vice with all her baits . . . and yet abstain'. Milton 'cannot praise a fugitive and cloister'd vertue, unexercis'd & unbreath'd, that never sallies out and sees her adversary'.[56]

Areopagitica adds that, in the strife between good and evil, 'that which purifies us is trial'.[57] The theme of 'trial', and of its companion 'temptation', is another recurrent preoccupation of Milton's writing: the temptation to weak or wrong choice. The defeat of temptation is decisive in our spiritual advance,[58] whereas its victory disrupts or terminates it. In Milton's poetry there is the temptation of the lady in 'A Maske', where, as elsewhere in his writing, liberty is the partner of chastity. *Paradise Lost* and *Paradise Regain'd* turn respectively on Satan's successful temptation of Eve, which leads to the expulsion of mankind from Eden, and on his unsuccessful temptation of Christ, who 'by vanquishing | Temptation, hast regain'd lost Paradise'.[59] Samson brings disaster on the Israelite nation by yielding to the temptation of Dalila, but then delivers it after withstanding her second attempt. There are trial and temptation in the political prose too. In *Defensio Secunda* the fate of liberty and virtue depends on the character and conduct of Oliver Cromwell, who was lord protector when the treatise appeared. The burden of office, Milton tells him, will 'try you thoroughly; it will search you through and through, and lay open your inmost soul'.[60] The outcome depends no less on the English people themselves. Their liberators, the men who brought the king to justice, have prevailed in the 'trial of virtue fair and glorious' that the overthrow of tyranny entails.[61] But will the nation grasp, or will it miss, the opportunity that that feat has brought it?

Love of his nation, and fear for its fate, are abiding preoccupations of Milton, in whose writing the service of God and the service of country are joint aspirations. In the pamphlets against bishops he voices the hope that God has chosen England for a second Reformation, which will disclose new truths and may even prepare the way for the second coming of Christ. Then and later Milton looks to godly and virtuous leaders to reform the nation and equip it for its God-given responsibilities. Yet what a task lies before them, as they confront a people whose failings, which the 'infusion of servility' by the bishops has afforded,[62] have left them so sunk in 'corruption', so 'blin[d] in religion', so prone to 'whordoms and adulteries' and

---

[56] Ibid., iv. 311.   [57] Ibid., iv. 311.   [58] Ibid., xv. 87–91.
[59] *Paradise Regain'd* IV. 607–8.   [60] *WJM*, viii. 227.   [61] Ibid., viii. 7.
[62] Ibid., v. 69.

'unbounded licence', and whose 'spirit' has been reduced to a condition so 'degenerat and fal'n . . . from the apprehension of native liberty, and true manliness'.[63] The optimistic moments of *Areopagitica*, when he hopes that his 'noble and puissant nation' is casting off 'corruption' and 'entering the glorious waies of truth and prosperous vertue',[64] move against the melancholy grain of his thought.

Once war had broken out in 1642, Milton's polemic took an eccentric course. The issue of the bishops had been near the centre of the nation's attention. In 1643–5, however, he chose subjects that to most of his contemporaries would have seemed peripheral if not irrelevant to the civil war and to the debates between the two sides. After the controversy over the bishops in 1641–2 the leading religious question among the parliamentarians was liberty of conscience. No theme was of more central or lasting concern to Milton. Yet in the mountainous pamphlet debate which confronted that issue head-on, and which involved the kind of scholarly engagement with the Bible which he relished, he played only a brief and oblique part. Liberty of conscience is the underlying purpose of *Areopagitica*, but is not its principal subject matter, which is freedom of the press, a topic to which only a few other writers related it. The year 1644 also produced his tract *Of Education*, a topic still more distant than freedom of the press from the centre of civil-war controversy. More distant still were his pleas for freedom of divorce over the years 1643–5, his main literary preoccupation during the war.

Why did he take that unusual path? Until reforms had been accomplished in the fields on which he concentrated, alterations on other fronts would, he believed, prove fruitless.[65] He followed, and gave a Christian application to, the classical principle that the state is an extension of the ethical qualities of its citizens. 'A commonwealth', he explained, adapting Aristotle, in 1641, 'ought to be but as one huge Christian personage . . . for looke what the grounds, and causes are of single happines to one man, the same yee shall find them to a whole state'.[66] True liberty, lying as it does within the soul, is internal liberty, 'to be sought not from without, but within' ourselves.[67] If we can find it there, the outward forms of liberty will follow. For once the 'minds and spirits of a nation' are freed by truth 'from the thraldom of sin and superstition', 'all honest and legal freedom of civil life cannot be long absent'.[68] An unfettered press is one means to that freedom. Another is educational reform, 'for the want whereof this nation perishes'.[69] Milton's interest in freedom of divorce derives from his own matrimonial experience, but here too the reform and liberty of the nation are at stake. Since the household, of which the state is again an extension, is its own community of souls, parliament's political aims will hardly be worth attaining if the English do not grasp 'the most important freedom that God and nature hath givn us in the family'.[70] It is the chains of loveless matrimony that make men 'unactive to all public service' and 'unserviceable and

[63] Ibid., iii. 372.   [64] Ibid., iv. 344.

[65] A fine essay by Martin Dzelzainis is pertinent here: 'Milton's Classical Republicanism', in Armitage, *Milton and Republicanism*, pp. 3–24.

[66] *WJM*, iii. 38.   [67] Ibid., viii. 131.   [68] Ibid., iii. 272.

[69] Ibid., iv. 275.   [70] Ibid., iv. 18.

spiritlesse to the commonwealth'.[71] So 'farewell all hope of true reformation in the state' so long as the 'houshold unhappines' enforced by the divorce laws persists.[72] 'It is to little purpose', he would add in *Defensio Secunda*, for a man 'in bondage to an inferior'—his wife—'at home' to 'make a noise about liberty in the legislative assemblies'.[73]

During the civil war Milton showed next to no interest in parliament's military fortunes. His vague and momentary congratulations on its victories, offered in prose that sought its support for his programme of reform, could not decently or prudently have said less. His one poem on the military conflict was a lament at the prospect of the destruction of his house by soldiers.[74] What gladdened him was not the war effort but the simultaneous quest for spiritual truth by men 'whose life, learning, faith and pure intent | Would have been held in high esteem with Paul'.[75] Among his fellow Londoners he rejoiced to find writers 'sitting by their studious lamps, musing, searching, revolving new notions and idea's wherewith to present, as with their homage and their fealty the approaching reformation', and readers 'trying all things, assenting to the force of reason and convincement'.[76]

Over their efforts there hung a new threat of religious persecution, this one from the side not of the king but of parliament, which proposed to replace the rule of the bishops by Presbyterianism, the Calvinist system of ecclesiastical government. In 1641 Milton had looked to Presbyterianism to replace the bishops. Expecting the rescue of truth from the Laudians to be followed by its free promulgation, he had not anticipated the zealous intolerance of the Presbyterians. Now, fearing 'new fetters and captivity after all our hopes and labours lost',[77] he judged 'new presbyter' to be 'but old priest writ large'.[78] If Presbyterianism prevailed, could the civil war be worth winning? And what was to be hoped from a nation that, with the prospect of liberty before it, was bringing fresh persecution upon itself? Parliament's victory, which was achieved in 1646, brought him no cheer. In the years ahead he knew that, without the attainment of internal liberty, external slavery would reimpose itself. For men who are 'slaves within' strive 'to have the public state conformably govern'd to the inward vitious rule, by which they govern themselves'.[79] Charles I might be overcome, but unless the English reformed themselves, he told them, 'the tyrant, whom you imagined was to be sought abroad, and in the field, you will find…within,…in your own breasts'.[80] In *Paradise Regain'd* Christ would scorn Satan's invitation to deliver a depraved people from oppression, for who 'could of inward slaves make outward free'?[81]

After the civil war Milton turned his mind to his *History of Britain*. A nation's character, like that of an individual or household, must be candidly examined, for if a wise man is 'a true knower of himself', 'much more' is it 'a high point of

---

[71] Ibid., iii. 129, 501.   [72] Ibid., iii. 375.   [73] Ibid., viii. 133.

[74] On it see Gordon Campbell and Thomas N. Corns. *John Milton: Life, Work, and Thought* (Oxford, 2008), pp. 155–6.

[75] *WJM*, i. 71.   [76] Ibid., iv. 341.   [77] Ibid., iv. 61.   [78] Ibid., i. 71.

[79] Ibid., v. 1.   [80] Ibid., viii. 241.   [81] Ibid., iv. 145.

wisdom . . . in a nation to know it self'.[82] Like most historians of the era who wrote with an eye on current events, Milton explores correspondences between past and present.[83] In the 1640s, he observed, God drew 'so neare a parallel' between the state of the Britons upon the removal of the ancient Romans 'and ours in the late commotions'.[84] Now as then, deliverance from oppression offered one of those rare moments in history when the chance of true liberty is seized or missed, with lasting consequences for posterity. Now as then the nation and its leaders are found wanting in virtue and wisdom, and prove unable to create 'a just and well-amended common-wealth'.[85] Now as then the corruption of the Church has cowed and debauched the natives.

Written in the wake of parliament's victory in the civil war, the *History* is a work of profound pessimism. The territory of the English past that it covered was also analysed in a work the first half of which appeared during Milton's preparation or composition of the *History*: Nathaniel Bacon's *An Historicall Discourse of the Uniformity of the Government of England*. Bacon's treatise justifies, by historical analogy, the constitutional positions on which the Long Parliament had taken its stand against Charles I. Milton's treatise shows no interest in such matters or in the merits of the parliamentarian cause. Like the Britons before them, he reflects, the parliamentarians have won military victories, but like them they are unequal to the subsequent challenge of peace. The triumph, 'so fair a victory', over the Anglo-Saxon invaders at Mons Badonicus 'came to nothing':[86] in contemplating the England of 1646 Milton lamented 'all this wast of wealth, and loss of blood'.[87] In his thinking the support for Presbyterianism in parliament belonged to a larger dereliction of duty and public spirit by MPs. Persecution became the partner of venality, for power and money are ready allies in politics no less than in religion. MPs and their employees 'fell to hucster the commonwealth'; 'justice' was 'delai'd and . . . denyed'; 'faction' throve, and with it 'wrong and oppression' and 'the ravning seisure of innumerable theeves in office'.[88] When the brief second civil war arrived in 1648, Milton feared that it would be no more fruitful than the first. 'For what', he now asked in a sonnet on parliament's lord general Thomas Fairfax, 'can warr, but endless warr still breed, | Till truth, & right from violence be freed' and 'the shamefull brand | Of publick fraud' cleared? 'In vain doth valour bleed | While avarice, & rapine share the land'.[89]

Among the main themes of Milton's writing before 1649, one subject is conspicuous by its absence: politics. He was well read in political history. In 1642 he expressed his support for 'civil liberty'.[90] Yet he touched only briefly on it and did not explore its meaning. It was of secondary significance, for the scope of the civil

---

[82] Ibid., iii. 186, x. 103.

[83] He spells them out, not in the main text of the *History*, but in the 'Digression' from it, the composition of which is very hard to date. Most authorities place it in the late 1640s, though for my part I think that it was written, or revised, after the Restoration (*LP*, pp. 410–26). At all events it reproduces sentiments that we know Milton to have held in the earlier of those periods, and for simplicity I here quote it to illustrate his thinking during it.

[84] *CPW*, v. 441. [85] Ibid., v. 441. [86] *WJM*, x. 136. [87] Ibid., i. 63.

[88] Ibid., v. 443–5. [89] Ibid., i. 64. [90] Ibid., iii. 246.

ruler or 'magistrate' properly extends to the correction only of the 'outward' part of man, not of the 'inward' part which is God's treasure.[91] Laws and constitutions, which God has left mutable, can be altered in pragmatic ways and at a pragmatic pace, but the purification of religion must never wait upon 'state businesse'.[92] In 1641–2 it was in the prospective reform of the Church that he exulted. He mustered little enthusiasm for parliament's pursuit of constitutional and legal rights. As in the divorce tracts, so in the pamphlets against the bishops, he knows that political alteration can achieve nothing unless preceded by reform within. If the end of the bishops achieves that reform, however, the political problems will solve themselves.[93] During the war he was not impressed by people whose motive for fighting the king was a dislike of illegal taxation, for though 'I dispraise not the defence of just immunities, yet love my peace better, if that were all. Give me the liberty to know, to utter, and to argue freely according to conscience, above all liberties.'[94]

Yet in 1649 he became a political writer. It was not for his political prose alone that he suffered vilification in his own time or would attract it in posterity. His arguments for divorce, and for the division between Church and state, drew opprobrium too, but his prose of 1649–51 in defence of the king's execution provoked a wider and deeper animus. To him 1649 was what 1641 had been, a moment of miraculous 'deliverance'. He exulted in Pride's Purge in December 1648, that forcible expulsion of the Presbyterian majority in parliament which paved the way for the king's trial and execution the following month. He would remember that before the purge, when the Presbyterians were proposing to restore the king, the nation 'was tottering and almost quite reduced to slavery and utter ruin'.[95] The conjunction of Presbyterianism and royalism, the two main parties in the state, both of them allies of religious intolerance, seems to have persuaded Milton that political action could no longer wait on religious and ethical reform. Though he had long ago observed the tendency of tyranny in the state and superstition in religion to assist each other, it was the royalist revival of the late 1640s, and then the craven cult of the dead Charles I in 1649, that brought their proclivity to 'twine and interweave'[96] to the forefront of his mind.[97]

Besides, he had at last found political heroes. The new model army, the godly army that carried out Pride's Purge and led the movement to try the king, had brought into the public realm the quest for divine truth that he had applauded during the first civil war, but which he had not then associated with a political programme. 'A small handfull of men', 'partakers of the light of the Gospel', who were 'defame[d] and sp[a]t at with all the odious names of schism and sectarism', had rescued both the Church and the state by 'those actions . . . by which their faith assures them they . . . are had in remembrance before the throne of God'.[98] Characteristically, Milton's praise of them aligned their holiness with the virtues of classical antiquity. The king's execution, 'that impartiall and noble peece of

[91] Ibid., iii. 255–6.   [92] Ibid., iii. 225.   [93] *LP*, pp. 159–60.
[94] *WJM*, iv. 346.   [95] Ibid., vii. 511.   [96] Ibid., v. 226.
[97] Ibid., v. 226; above, p. 336.   [98] Ibid., v. 73, vii. 67.

justice',[99] 'an action . . . so worthy of heroic ages',[100] reminded him that 'the Greeks and Romans' had hailed tyrannicide as 'a glorious and heroic deed, rewarded publicly with statues and garlands'.[101]

The opening passage of the first of his political tracts, *The Tenure of Kings and Magistrates*, a work written in the weeks on either side of the execution of the king, resumes the theme of internal liberty that had preoccupied him in the civil war. Then the character of the pamphlet changes. Milton, for the first time, writes not as a petitioner to power but as an apologist for it. Five years later, emphasizing his superiority to worldly advancement, he allowed his readers to understand that *The Tenure* had been written on his own initiative and had been meant only as an aside from his studies. Having completed it, he recalled, he worked privately on his *History of Britain* for six weeks, until the council of state, the executive arm of the new republic, unexpectedly offered him the office, which he would hold for ten years, of Latin Secretary, or Secretary of Foreign Tongues: a post that primarily involved the preparation or translation of diplomatic documents. In reality he is likely to have had unofficial encouragement from on high to write *The Tenure*.[102] Whether he did or not, the two substantial works that followed, *Eikonoklastes* and the first *Defensio*, were commissioned by the new regime. Writers in seventeenth-century England habitually longed to be employed by governments and to write for them, though few of the able ones seem to have shared Milton's desire to write for the Commonwealth, whose illegality was so widely condemned and derided. He involved himself in the composition of the government's main newsbook, *Mercurius Politicus*, edited by his close friend the journalist Marchamont Nedham. He participated, with Nedham, in the darker arts of government propaganda.[103] His English prose for the republic, like almost all his English prose writings after the first civil war, kept rhetoric in check. Yet in the Latin *Defensio* rhetoric returned, in prose that dazzled even contemporaries who were shocked by its arguments, though a modern audience, which meets its scurrilously abusive assaults on his adversaries only in translation, can be puzzled to learn of its contemporary impact.

In writing for the republic he wrote particularly for a party within it: the party in which his friend John Bradshaw, who had presided over the trial of the king and was now president of the council of state, was a prominent figure. The majority of the members of the Rump had been dismayed by the king's trial. They hoped to reconstruct the broad parliamentarian cause of the 1640s, and to confine the memory of the purge and execution, which had broken it in two, to the past. Milton had no more admiration for those MPs now than he had had before the purge. He supported the political radicals, Bradshaw among them, who wanted to honour the memory of the king's trial and to confine power to men who had enacted or endorsed it.[104] It was they who resisted concessions to royalist and Presbyterian sentiment and to its intolerance. Glad as he was of their political stance, religion remained his priority. It was in the cause of liberating religion from worldly compulsion and inducement that, after four years apparently of poetic

---

[99] Ibid., vi. 251–2. [100] Ibid., vii. 51. [101] Ibid., v. 19.
[102] *LP*, p. 157–8. [103] Ibid., ch. 9. [104] Ibid., ch. 8.

silence, he returned to the writing of poetry, the brief poetry of his sonnets to Oliver Cromwell and Sir Henry Vane, in 1652—just as, seven years later, he would end four years of near-silence in prose by writing pamphlets that amplified the pleas of those two poems.

Even as he delighted in the deed that had brought the republic to power, Milton retained his doubts about both the nation and its leaders. The purge and execution had been achieved, he proclaimed, by a virtuous 'few', whose courage in defying the opinion of the many had itself been proof of their virtue. But if they could create the opportunity of liberty, it would be taken only if the many followed their lead. Early in 1660 Milton declared that 'a free commonwealth without a single person or House of Lords', the system of rule that had been established, albeit in imperfect form, in 1649, 'is by far the best government, if it can be had'.[105] Christianity, he now argued, is the natural ally of kingless rule, for republics observe the 'precept of Christ' that forbids lordliness among men.[106] He looked back to the glory of the Roman republic and bemoaned its tyrannical destruction. But could such a 'commonwealth ... be had'? Republics, he observed at the same time, 'have bin ever counted fittest and properest for civil, vertuous and industrious nations, abounding with prudent men worthie to govern'.[107] But what of a people that sighs, as Milton watched the English doing at the end of the Interregnum, for the Egyptian bondage from which it has been delivered? Might not his countrymen suffer the fate of ancient Rome, whose own heroic tyrannicides, Brutus and Cassius, 'felt themselves of spirit to free a nation but consider'd not that the nation was not fit to be free'? Their error demonstrated that 'libertie sought out of season in a corrupt and degenerate age' can bring nations 'into further slaverie'.[108]

Milton's unambiguous commitment to kingless rule in 1659–60 was new. Until then he was (normally) hostile, not to kingship, but to bad kings or tyrants. Between kings and tyrants, he explained, 'I make the widest difference',[109] for 'look how great a good and happiness a just king is, so great a mischiefe is a tyrant'.[110] Most kings, admittedly, were bad or weak kings; and Milton knew from Aristotle that it is iniquitous for men of superior virtue to be ruled by inferiors. Yet Aristotle had likewise taught that a supremely virtuous or heroic figure deserves to rule. Might not such a man, if he could be found, supply the unitive capacity and the reforming leadership that parliamentary rule, before and after the king's execution, had failed to provide?[111]

For a time Milton thought, or half-thought, that he had found such a figure. Through the 1650s his engagement with politics turned on his feelings, sometimes awed and reverential, sometimes ambivalent, but in time bitterly and implacably hostile, towards Oliver Cromwell.[112] Cromwell returned to Westminster in 1651 after his victorious campaigns in Ireland and Scotland over the previous two years. In 1652 Milton's sonnet to him hailed 'Cromwell, our cheif of men'[113] and urged the cause of religious liberty on him. For by now a fresh threat to freedom of

[105] *WJM*, vi. 124.   [106] Ibid., vi. 119–20, vii. 155.   [107] Ibid., vi. 160.
[108] *CPW*, i. 420, v. 449.   [109] *WJM*, viii. 25.   [110] Ibid., v. 19.
[111] *LP*, pp. 231–2.   [112] Ibid., chs 11–14.   [113] *WJM*, i. 65.

conscience had succeeded to the Anglican and Presbyterian ones. The Congregationalist divines who had the ear of the regime were pressing parliament to curb the growth of sectarian heresy. One of their targets was the most daring theological deviation of the seventeenth century, the rejection of the doctrine of the Trinity. Milton subscribed to that heresy, and had quietly given practical aid to its abettors.[114] His anti-Trinitarianism would reappear in *Paradise Lost*. It would also reappear, in a more candid form and together with a number of other adventurous heresies, in his ambitious manuscript work *De Doctrina Christiana*, 'my best and richest possession',[115] which sets out in prose his radically unconventional theological system.

Liberty of conscience was the abiding principle of Oliver Cromwell's career. Yet he drew the line at extreme departures from Calvinist orthodoxy. He also believed that the state, far from leaving the Church to itself, should deploy its own powers and resources to promote its teaching and improve the quality of the ministry. The Congregationalists who urged the state to restrict liberty of conscience in 1652 were his own ecclesiastical advisers and allies. There is consequently an ambiguity in Milton's sonnet to him, where praise mingles with warning, hope with fear. Milton's own position was far closer to that of another leading MP, Sir Henry Vane, whose convictions and character he saluted, unambiguously, in his other sonnet of 1652.[116] Milton had other anxieties about Cromwell. Though Cromwell had orchestrated the trial and execution of the king, he wanted to heal the national wounds it had opened. In that pursuit he came into conflict with Milton's patron and hero John Bradshaw, whose star waned after Cromwell's return to Westminster, as did the regime's favour to Milton.[117] With many others Milton suspected Cromwell of personal ambition and feared that he would sacrifice the cause of liberty to it. Hence Milton's reminder to him that power would 'search you through and through'.

Even so, Milton supported the military coup of April 1653 in which Cromwell, earlier the remover of the king, removed the parliament that had fought him. Milton likewise endorsed Cromwell's ensuing decision to summon the assembly, nominated by the army officers, which posterity knows as Barebone's Parliament. It embarked on radical reforms of the Church, of a kind to which Milton might have been expected to bring a warm welcome, and on equally radical reforms of the administration of the law, a course for which he also hoped. Yet he gave public endorsement to the dissolution of Barebone's in December 1653, again at the army's hands, and to Cromwell's elevation to the office of lord protector, a move which terminated five years of rule by a sovereign House of Commons and restored that of a 'single person'. In welcoming the two coups of 1653 Milton parted company with his friends Bradshaw and Vane. He remained in his official post until the collapse of the protectorate in 1659, when Oliver's son Richard, who had succeeded his father as protector on Oliver's death the previous year, was deposed. Employment by the state was compatible, however, with despair at its conduct. Milton's approval of the

---

[114] *LP*, pp. 240–3. [115] *WJM*, xiv. 9.
[116] *LP*, pp. 243–4. [117] Ibid., pp. 196–9; above, pp. 109–10.

protectorate, hesitant from the start, soon yielded to barely concealed antagonism. Cromwell, when 'searched through and through', was found wanting. Such hopes of radical reform as Milton may have entertained of the regime were dispelled as Cromwell wooed Presbyterians and even former royalists, and as a stately court grew up around him. By the twilight of Cromwellian rule Milton was ready to signal his renewed commitment to the principle, which he had shed in 1653, of sovereign rule by the Commons. After the fall of Richard and the restoration of the republic he denounced the protectorate as a 'scandalous' usurpation.[118] 'Ambitious leaders of armies', he decided, had shattered the cause to which most of his adulthood had been devoted.[119]

Could that cause now be rescued? As the revolution disintegrated in 1659–60, and as the succession of coups and of competing Puritan regimes provoked a fresh reaction in favour of the Stuart monarchy, Milton produced a series of warnings against that catastrophe. No longer writing as an employee of power, he returned to his petitionary prose of the first half of the 1640s. The pamphlets he now wrote were those of an increasingly solitary voice, who cries, as a prophet in the wilderness, against the nation's new self-enslavement. In the fullest and most defiant of them, *The Readie and Easie Way to Establish a Free Commonwealth*, published in two editions in the expiring months of the republic, his eloquence in English returned. What he could not supply, as he tried to envisage stopgap measures to prevent the Restoration, were plausible proposals for the preservation of his cause. That was partly because of his impatience with constitutional formulae and his inaptitude for designing them. As he had explained in 1641, 'piety, and justice, . . . are our foundresses; they stoop not, neither change colour for aristocracy, democraty, or monarchy', for they are 'farre above the taking notice of these inferior niceties'.[120] If the spirit were right the forms would look after themselves.

There was another obstacle. In politics as in religion Milton declared a commitment to the principle of free choice. For 'whoso takes from a people their power to choose what government they wish takes that indeed in which all civil liberty is rooted'.[121] When, at the end of the poem, Adam and Eve descend from Paradise, 'The world was all before them, where to choose | Their place of rest':[122] the *History* tells us that Milton's contemporaries have had 'set before them civil government in all her formes'. For like Adam, and like Adam's heirs in relation to God, nations are 'masters of their own choise'.[123] Yet how reluctant Milton was to convert the principle of political consent into political practice! For how could a nation unfit for liberty be entrusted with the selection of its rulers? One of his grounds for supporting the expulsion of parliament in April 1653 was its intention to hold elections.[124] In 1660 he dreaded 'the noise and shouting of a rude multitude' that elections would bring,[125] and feared the electorate's choices still more. Instead he urged what survived of the parliament of the 1640s to sit in perpetuity.

*

---

[118] *WJM*, vi. 43.   [119] Ibid., vi. 125; *LP*, ch. 14.   [120] *WJM*, iii. 69.
[121] Ibid., vii. 93.   [122] XII. 646–7.   [123] *CPW*, v. 441.
[124] *LP*, pp. 281–4.   [125] *WJM*, vi. 131.

Milton's most ambitious poetry, the eventual fulfilment of his early ambition, arose from political defeat. He apparently began *Paradise Lost* when he had lost hope of the protectorate, and when, in spite of his official duties, he retained 'very few intimacies with men of influence' and lived 'shut up at home…as I prefer to be'.[126] *Samson Agonistes*, which can be most probably dated to the earlier 1660s, is suffused by the experience of the Restoration and of the humiliation of God's servants at it, and by reflection on the duty that awaits them under renewed oppression.[127] Autobiographical as the poem is, and as passages of *Paradise Lost* are, those works dwarf the circumstances of their composition, which is why they speak, as his prose does much less often or readily, to people who know little if anything of the seventeenth century. There is next to no evidence to help us reconstruct the processes of mind and spirit and imagination that led him to that achievement. In guessing at them it may be a mistake to assume that even when, in *Paradise Lost*, he 'soar[s] | Above th' *Aonian* Mount',[128] and his muse 'Visit'st my slumbers nightly', literary preoccupations have supplanted political ones.[129] In and after 1660 he could not dare to draw attention to the revolutionary prose of his past or repeat its arguments. If the events of 1641 had led him from verse to prose, perhaps the constraints of publication from 1660 gave verse a renewed priority.

A decade after the Restoration, when cracks had appeared within the regime and there seemed some hope that more forgiving official attitudes to the memory of Puritan rule might emerge, he did return to the publication of prose. In the winter of 1670–1 he published the *History of Britain*, on which he had continued to work in the 1660s. He could risk its publication because the book, even though its author had championed the coup of 1649, did not allude to that event. In the same winter he felt able to publish *Samson Agonistes* and *Paradise Regain'd*. *Paradise Lost* had been published, apparently about four years after its completion, in 1667, at another moment when it seemed that the repression of Puritan ideals might ease. It was his first publication since the Restoration. There would be further prose publications in 1673–4, the last two years of his life. In producing a new edition of his poems of 1645 he added to it a reprint of his tract *Of Education*. More daringly he published a new work, *Of True Religion*, a warning against the growth of 'popery' and against the national sinfulness on which it throve. The popish threat acquired a new dimension in 1673, when the conversion of the future James II to Catholicism became public knowledge and when his Catholic marriage promised a succession of Catholic heirs. It was to counter that prospect that Milton produced, in his final months, a translation of an account of the recent election of a new King of Poland. The publication was an ingeniously covert plea for the replacement of hereditary by elective monarchy in England.[130]

In prose and verse alike he retained his instructive or didactic purpose after 1660. Our rare clues to the initial reception of his Restoration writings indicate that the purpose was noticed. A reader of *Paradise Lost* saw the poem as a bulwark against

---

[126] Ibid., xii. 103.   [127] *LP*, ch. 15.
[128] I. 14–15.   [129] VII. 28–9.
[130] Von Maltzahn, 'Whig Milton', p. 231.

the 'wickedness' of the court and nation. The acceptability of that lesson even to an audience hostile to the memory of 1649 is indicated by the same reader's description of Milton's tracts as 'criminal' and by his observation that Milton 'writes so good verse that 'tis pity he ever wrote prose'.[131] An early reader of *Samson Agonistes* wrote the words 'Englands case' beside Samson's complaint that 'Nations grown corrupt, | And by their vices brought to servitude', prefer 'Bondage with ease' to 'strenuous liberty.'[132] Milton's Restoration prose confronted wickedness too. Upon the publications of the winter of 1670–1 another reader reported that 'Milton is alive again, in prose and verse'. It was on the instructive properties not of the new poems, but of the *History*, that the same commentator remarked: 'we needed all . . . his sharp checks and sour instructions. For we must be a lost people if we are not speedily reclaimed.'[133] Milton's prose and verse alike were written to reclaim them.

---

[131] Nicholas von Maltzahn, 'The First Reception of Paradise Lost (1667)', *Review of English Studies* 47 (1996), 400–3.

[132] Laura Lunger Knoppers, ed., *The 1671 Poems: Paradise Regain'd and Samson Agonistes* (*The Complete Works of John Milton*, ii [Oxford, 2008]), p. lxx.

[133] Nicholas von Maltzahn, 'Laureate, Republican, Calvinist: An Early Response to Milton and *Paradise Lost*', *Milton Studies* 29 (1992), p. 191.

10
Clarendon: History, Religion, Politics

Even in an age of crowded centennial commemorations, Edward Hyde, who was created Earl of Clarendon in 1661, has in one respect a unique claim, at least within English history, to the recognition of posterity.[1] It lies in the combination of his political and his literary stature. He was either the Crown's leading minister, or as leading a minister as any, for sixteen years, from the aftermath of the battle of Worcester in 1651 to his fall in 1667: years when royal choices, first in exile, then in power, might determine the future of the monarchy and Church. And he wrote a book, *The History of the Rebellion*, which places him, as Leopold von Ranke said, among 'those who have essentially fixed the circle of ideas for the English nation'.[2] Other Lord Chancellors, Thomas More and Francis Bacon, have been famous statesmen and writers, but neither of them matched his ascendancy in the first field or has equalled the breadth of his influence in the second.[3]

Clarendon's writings would seem voluminous even if a full-time author had written them. Most of his writing was composed in periods of enforced leisure, of what he called 'vacations and retreats', or 'recesses or acquiescences', from an indefatigable public life.[4] They occurred in exile. He was in exile for twenty-one years: first those spent in royal service from 1646 to 1660, then the last seven years of his life after his fall from power in 1667. The 'vacations' arose from two extended periods of royal

---

[1] This chapter is based on a lecture given in 2009 to mark the four hundredth anniversary of Clarendon's birth.

[2] Leopold von Ranke, *A History of England*, 6 vols (1875), vi. 29.

[3] Clarendon has attracted distinguished writing. T. H. Lister, *Life and Administration of Edward, First Earl of Clarendon*, 3 vols (1837–8), which rose above the historiographical level of its time, established the shape of his career, and remains worth consulting. B. H. G. Wormald's *Clarendon: Politics, History, and Religion* (Cambridge, 1951) transformed perceptions of his thought and action in the 1640s. Martine Brownley's *Clarendon and the Rhetoric of Historical Form* (Philadelphia, 1985) is an acute and informative exploration of his literary characteristics. Richard Ollard's *Clarendon and his Friends* (1987) is a shrewd and sympathetic biographical account. There is a masterly study of Clarendon's role in Restoration politics by Paul Seaward, to whom I am indebted for discussions of Clarendon, in Seaward's *The Cavalier Parliament and the Reconstruction of the Old Regime, 1661–1667* (Cambridge, 1989). The insights of C. H. Firth's lecture on the three hundredth anniversary of Clarendon's birth in 1909 (in Firth, *Essays Historical and Literary* [Oxford, 1938], pp. 103–28), and of Hugh Trevor-Roper's on the three hundredth anniversary of his death in 1974 (in his *From Counter-Reformation to Glorious Revolution* [1992], pp. 173–94), endure. Graham Roebuck, *Clarendon and Cultural Continuity: A Bibliographical Study* (New York, 1981) is a valuable guide to works by and about Clarendon.

[4] *CL*, iii 973. (The first of the three volumes of this publication prints Clarendon's 'Life' to 1660; the other two reproduce the 'continuation' of it from the Restoration. The second and third volumes are continuously paginated.)

disfavour: first the late 1640s and early 1650s, and then the last years. Exile produced his *History*; his autobiography; and writings which can be seen as the philosophical and ethical sub-texts of those works, though they are little read or studied: the *Reflections (or Essays) upon Several Christian Duties, Divine and Moral, by way of Essays*; and the *Contemplations and Reflections upon the Psalms*.[5] The late exile also yielded his attacks on Hobbes's *Leviathan* and the Catholic convert Hugh Cressy and, at the end of Clarendon's life, the substantial history, entitled *Religion and Policy*, of papal usurpations of the rights of sovereigns. From other periods there is a series of works of propaganda, among them the dextrous declarations in the king's name that defined the royal cause in 1642 and some nimble forgeries designed to sow discord among parliamentarians.[6] There are also thousands of his letters, and there are writings that have not survived.

The *History of the Rebellion* is the towering work. It was the one, he tells us, that 'his heart was most set upon'.[7] It rises like a mountain from the hills of Renaissance and seventeenth-century writing on English history. There is nothing in other contemporary accounts of the civil wars, most of them either memoirs or two-dimensional chronicles, that begins to equal its vividness, its verisimilitude, its reflective power, or its breadth of vision. It is the only compelling long narrative of the whole conflict to have been written. We read its sole rival in scale, S. R. Gardiner's late Victorian *History*, for use, not for pleasure. The status of Clarendon's book has risen and fallen with the tides of political sympathy. The first edition, published in Tory Oxford with Tory prefaces early in Queen Anne's reign, countered the vindications of the parliamentarian cause in a recent spate of Whig publications.[8] Frequently republished in subsequent decades, the *History* was caught up in the long revenge for the regicide and for the destruction of the Church. Yet so powerful and persuasive was the story it told, and so much more so than its Whig rivals, that writers without royalist sympathies were almost as likely to appropriate Clarendon's writing and character as to criticize them. Eighteenth-century voices recognized his stances against arbitrary power in 1641 and again in the 1660s, and contrasted his high-minded tenure of office in the Restoration with the degeneration of public life after his fall. The tide turned in the nineteenth century, in the decades around the passage of the Great Reform Act of 1832. Hallam, Macaulay, and other Whig historians viewed the *History* as the product of a reactionary mind which, during its author's exercise of power, had impeded liberty and constitutional progress.

Later in the century Gardiner was troubled by Clarendon's royalist sympathies. He also, with his pupil C. H. Firth, exposed manifold inaccuracies in the *History*. The errors arose from conflations and distortions of memory; from Clarendon's geographical distance from people and papers that would have put him right; from

---

[5] The last two are published in *CT*.

[6] Oxford University Press has commissioned an edition of Clarendon's works under the general editorship of Martin Dzelzainis and Paul Seaward.

[7] *CL*, iii. 992.

[8] Blair Worden, *Roundhead Reputations: The English Civil Wars and the Passions of Posterity* (2001), chs 2–4.

his retrospective imposition of interpretative patterns; and from the distorting power of his indignation.[9] It is no use going to Clarendon for a reliable chronology. Twentieth-century scholarship, following Gardiner and Firth in giving priority to exactly contemporary sources, gave ever less esteem to all retrospective accounts of the civil wars. Modern political sympathies have also worked against him, for we can enter his thinking, and, with it, substantial dimensions of the mental world of his time, only by acclimatizing to premises that seem remote to a post-monarchical and post-Anglican age.

If the *History* has become undervalued, Clarendon himself bears some of the responsibility. Weakly structured, uneven in its coverage, it is a mongrel work, a mixture of history and autobiography. He began it, and took the story up to 1644, during his period, in practice one of exile, on the Scillies and in Jersey from 1646 to 1648, in the dusk and then defeat of the royalist resistance. He returned to it only a quarter of a century later, in France. There, cut off from his papers, he wrote his autobiography, from memory. When, in 1671, the unfinished manuscript of the *History* was shipped out to him, he decided to merge the two works. Large passages of the autobiography were spliced into the parts of the *History* he had already written, or were added to it to bring the *History* down to 1660, where it concludes. Even readers attentive to the footnotes of W. D. Macray's indispensable edition of 1888 can struggle to know which passages originated as history and which as autobiography, and to tell which were written in, and from the perspective of, the 1640s and which belong to the late years. Clarendon's own presence in the *History* is at once the strength and limitation of the work, for the book's hold on the reader is roughly proportionate to his own proximity to the events he describes. Clarendon subscribed to the view, which is or ought to be troubling to academic historians, that the worthwhile works of history, in both the ancient and the modern world, have been written by people with experience of 'courts' and of public 'business', which has qualified them to get inside events not only in their own time but in others.[10] Yet his own explorations of periods in which he had not lived lack the vitality of the contemporary history he wrote.

When the *History* has been read in modern times, it has usually been in one of the single volumes of extracts that have been made from it. They serve a purpose.[11] Yet the greatness of the *History* lies in an achievement which no selection can convey. In the range and sweep of the work Clarendon achieves a magnitude proportionate to his subject. We watch the unfolding of events beyond the intentions and horizons of their instigators; the evolving interaction of circumstance and character; the convulsion of a nation and a generation. For all the differences between factual and fictional writing, the work has something of the quality of the great sprawling novels of the nineteenth century. As the Renaissance

---

[9] S. R. Gardiner, *History of the Great Civil War*, 4 vols (1897–8 edn), i. 217, iii. 121–1; Ollard, *Clarendon*, p. 49 n. Clarendon's prejudices and methods are censured by Ronald Hutton, 'Clarendon's History of the Rebellion', *English Historical Review* 97 (1982), pp. 70–88.

[10] *CT*, p. 180.

[11] The best of them is Edward Hyde, Earl of Clarendon, *The History of the Rebellion: A New Selection*, ed. Paul Seaward (Oxford World's Classics, 2009).

and the seventeenth century understood, the representation of events we know to have happened can command its own emotional power. There may be nothing in the *History* that affects us in quite the same way as, say, the death of Vronsky's horse in *Anna Karenina*. Yet the account in the *History* of the death of Hyde's beloved friend Lord Falkland, from wounds sustained on horseback at the battle of Newbury in 1643, makes its own claim to symbolic import as it summons the waste and destruction of 'this odious and accursed civil war'.[12] Other literary associations, which remind us that Hyde's youth had been steeped in poetry and the discussion of it,[13] press on the reader's mind, whether or not they are in the author's own thoughts. During the onsets of melancholy or despair in the king's entourage in 1642, at Windsor or when the royal standard is raised in a disconsolate scene at Nottingham,[14] we might be among the followers whom Richard II invites to sit upon the ground, or Antony's sad captains.

The imaginative reach of the *History* is the more remarkable when we recognize its determinedly prosaic features, and acknowledge the absence from it of literary self-aggrandizement. Clarendon's mode is realism—often an informal realism—which shuns rhetorical embellishment. Like Milton, whose *History of Britain* was written intermittently over almost exactly the same long period, Clarendon reacts against what he calls the 'mixture of oratory and rhetorick with history'.[15] We could not conceive of him adopting the classical device of inventing speeches for his characters, an instrument which Milton, no less indebted to classical history but no less insistent on a realism that departs from it, eschewed in his own study of his nation's past.[16] Clarendon's *History* does bear the stamp of its author's lifelong love of Roman history and literature,[17] a world never far below its surface. In 1647, while writing the early parts, he 'read over Livy and Tacitus' and most of Cicero.[18] Quotations from and allusions to Roman writers give to the contemporary events he describes a historical and reflective framework. They also add emotional depth to the story. Tacitus was always somewhere in his mind, even though Clarendon's own prose could not have been more different from his. He had him in mind, not least, on Jersey, where so much of the *History* was written, and where his classical reading helped him to find the sense of perspective on recent events that his own hectic immersion in them had earlier denied him.[19] In a letter to his friend John Earles in 1647 he half-compared his own enterprise to that of Tacitus. Yet in the same breath he half-discouraged, with at least as much true modesty as false, so lofty a perception of his purposes.[20] It is sometimes said or implied that history was Clarendon's 'vocation', and that he saw in his subject an opportunity to

---

[12] *CH*, iii. 179.
[13] Roebuck, *Clarendon and Cultural Continuity*, pp. ix–xiv; Brownley, *Clarendon*, pp. 112–24, 126–7.
[14] *CH*, i. 524, ii. 290–1, 302.
[15] *CT*, p. 220; Brownley, *Clarendon*, p. 39.
[16] Above, pp. 358–9.
[17] *CL*, i. 9.
[18] *SPC*, ii. 375, 386.
[19] Ibid., ii. 386; *CL*, iii. 977–8.
[20] *SPC*, ii. 386.

be England's Thucydides.[21] Certainly he knew that historical writing must transcend its time. He knew history to need dignity and irony of expression and 'the beauty of a st[y]le'.[22] Gardiner himself acknowledged the *History* to be 'one of the masterpieces of English prose'.[23] In those winding, labyrinthine sentences, nuance rises upon nuance as one insight builds on or balances another. It is a style suited to convey the irreducible complexity of historical or biographical experience. Yet how artless it is, and how understandable is his readiness for the work to be posthumously corrected and reshaped. Occasionally haze settles over his successions of subordinate clauses or parentheses; or his syntax gets lost as Clarendon, who as he said wrote 'apace'[24] (and in a 'vile hand'[25]), presses on.[26]

The ambition that impels him is not literary but argumentative and didactic. For him as for Milton, who has different lessons to impart but the same eagerness to teach them, history is not for display but for practical application. Clarendon's narrative is always subordinated to analysis. Episodes are related not for their dramatic power but for their significance. He makes few appeals to the reader's visual sense, and shows little interest in describing the physically concrete.[27] Events that offer scope for epic description—the execution of the Earl of Strafford; the attempted arrest of the 'five members'; the great battles; the trial and death of the king; Cromwell's expulsion of the Long Parliament; the landing of Charles II at Dover—are swiftly and undemonstratively covered. He will interrupt his narrative voice to insert long contemporary documents that support his case; or will silently borrow, with only superficial literary improvements, commonplace reports written by others; or will omit an episode on the ground that another royalist work has already said what he would say. He thinks of the book more as 'memorials of passages' than as 'a digested history'.[28]

He has two principal purposes. The first, common among Renaissance and seventeenth-century historians, is counsel, and the persuasion that is counsel's instrument. He hopes to inform the king, whether Charles I or Charles II or some future successor, and his advisers of the errors of policy and conduct that have exposed the Crown to destruction. Like other literary counsellors before him, he has to move between a known audience and an unknowable one, and between a present-day readership and a future one. He cannot tell when, and cannot even be sure whether, prudence will warrant the circulation of the work within, let alone

---

[21] Philip Hicks, *Neoclassical History and English Culture: From Clarendon to Hume* (1996), pp. 3, 48–9, 56–7, 78–80, 209, 230; Simon Hornblower, *Thucydidean Themes* (Oxford, 2011), ch. 17; but cf. Brownley, *Clarendon*, p. 136.

[22] *CL*, i. 31.

[23] Gardiner, *Great Civil War*, iii. 121.

[24] *SPC*, ii. 289.

[25] Quoted by Brownley, *Clarendon*, p. 88.

[26] The spontaneity of the *History* is the more striking when we compare it with the stiff artifice of the early work of his that would be published in 1706 as *The Characters of Robert Earl of Essex and . . . G. Duke of Buckingham*.

[27] On this and other aspects of Clarendon's writing I am indebted to the penetrating discussion in Brownley, *Clarendon*, ch. 2.

[28] *SPC*, ii. 357.

beyond, a courtly circle. Secondly, he passes judgement on his generation and invites 'posterity' to emulate the virtues and shun the vices he sets before its eyes. That dimension of the *History* may have had a present as well as future intent. When from Jersey he lets other royalists know that he is writing the book, he offers them an inducement to future conduct that will earn the plaudits or escape the censure of aftertimes.

For to Clarendon, history is made by human choices. His narrative is famed for its character-portraits, those onion-peeling assessments of courtiers and noblemen and politicians which Ranke judged 'unequalled in the English language'.[29] There is no mistaking Clarendon's relish for the depiction of character.[30] Sometimes feline, occasionally embittered, the portraits are more generally characterized by a magnanimity, even to people he had reason to detest, that heightens, by the contrast with it, his injustices, which are occasionally severe. The sketches have often been excerpted, as flowers are brought in from a garden, but that is to cut them from their explanatory purpose. Clarendon is the great historian of the contingent, to whom everything in the civil wars might have happened differently. Has any historian used the word 'if' more often? He knows 'from how small springs great rivers may arise',[31] 'from how little accidents and small circumstances . . . the greatest matters followed'.[32] The *History* is full of 'accidents' or stray occurrences. Yet 'accidents', for him, always have 'causes'.[33] Chance may divert or complicate human purposes, but the accidents signify because they arise from those purposes, or else because they prompt them. Thus to understand the events we need to know the people, who are what interest him.

If they in turn are to be comprehended, the historian has to supply 'a lively representation of persons and actions, which makes the reader present at all they say or do'.[34] So Clarendon writes history, in ways that were beyond the other historians of his time, 'to the life'.[35] His characters are most tellingly glimpsed not on grand public stages but in close-up, in intimate conversation. He does relate some debates in parliament, but with less colour than he brings to what MPs say away from them, in private discourse as they leave the chamber or take walks or rides together. Character is disclosed by a blush or smile, or the absence of a smile.[36] Or people reveal themselves hugger-mugger, as when the king, secretly wooing Hyde to the royal cause early in 1642, summons him to the backstairs at Greenwich and conspiratorially locks the door of the privy gallery to keep his own courtiers in ignorance;[37] or when, in an interval of the peace negotiations in the extreme cold at Uxbridge early in 1645, a royalist

---

[29] Leopold von Ranke, *A History of England, principally in the Seventeenth Century*, 6 vols (1875), vi. 28.
[30] See especially his account, a high point of seventeenth-century biographical writing, of George, Lord Digby, printed in Richard Ollard, ed., *Clarendon's Four Portraits* (1988), pp. 51–105.
[31] *CL*, i. 14.
[32] *CH*, i. 322.
[33] Ibid., iv. 2.
[34] *CT*, p. 181.
[35] *CH*, i. 215.
[36] e.g. ibid., ii. 280, iv. 60, 503, v. 54, 93, 121, 319, 320.
[37] *CL*, i. 106–8.

commissioner and a parliamentarian one, whose 'familiarity' the war has sundered, whisper as they huddle by the fire.[38]

If we need to grasp the 'character' of 'the persons', he tells us, so must we the 'character' of 'the times', which is 'no less a part of history, and more useful to posterity'.[39] The times have their own 'spirit' or 'temper' or 'face' or 'disposition',[40] which makes intelligible the actions of people who would have behaved differently in periods with different features. 'There must', he reflected, 'be the spirit of the tyme considered in all ... instances of actions, as well as in expression and words, many things beinge fitt in one tyme to be sayd or done, which in another would be justly censured or reprehended.'[41] He has a sharp sense of the way his own unusual times have shaped his own life and character.[42] He knows, too, that an understanding of the 'time', and a capacity to sense what courses or policies it will and will not tolerate, is a qualification of statesmanship.[43] His alertness to the distinctive pressures of mood and circumstance makes him wary of the practice, favoured by Machiavelli (much as Clarendon learned from him) and other Renaissance historians, of deducing universal rules from the variety of historical experience.[44] To explain events we must recover that distinctiveness.

The fatal spirit of his own time was the 'drowsy and unactive genius of the kingdom', which was 'contracted by long ease and quiet':[45] by the peace and prosperity of what, when war came, seemed to have been halcyon days. The public spirit of men of natural good nature and integrity had been sapped by that era. Here is the basic answer to the great question the *History* poses. He unequivocally believed the rebellion to have been a triumph of wickedness and dissimulation, led by men aiming to ruin a Crown to which the nation was basically loyal. Why then had it not been successfully resisted? He seeks to understand how a 'handful of men', the 'contrivers' or 'great managers',[46] who 'might in the beginning have been easily crushed',[47] succeeded in bamboozling parliament by their avowals of allegiance to the king; and how it was that they encountered such abject resistance from the courtiers and councillors whose duty it was to articulate and defend the principles of monarchy.

Clarendon acknowledges that there were legitimate grievances in 1640–1. He had feelingly voiced some of them himself. He had been close to the 'contrivers', whose destructive intent he discerned only when they moved from reform to subversion, from outward loyalty to the sedition which, it turned out, they had

---

[38] *CH*, iii. 485.

[39] Ibid., iii. 232.

[40] Ibid., i. 10, 42, 51, 55, ii. 244, iii. 128; Clarendon, *Characters of ... Essex and ... Buckingham*, pp. 3, 7–8, 10, 21–3; *CL*, ii. 7, 39; *CT*, p. 203; *RP*, pp. 200, 319. (The last work, in two volumes, is continuously paginated.)

[41] Bodl., Clarendon MS 126, fo. 54ᵛ.

[42] e.g. *CL*, i. 97; and cf. Clarendon, *Characters*, pp. 21–3 with *CL*, i. 8–9.

[43] e.g. *CL*, ii. 254.

[44] Ollard, *Clarendon*, p. 112.

[45] *CH*, ii. 182.

[46] Ibid., ii. 191.

[47] Ibid., i. 429, ii. 192.

secretly harboured. Why, in the face of that development, had so many of his contemporaries been 'possessed by laziness and sleep', or allowed 'supine laziness, negligence', 'incogitancy', 'weariness', to keep them away from decisive debates, on the Grand Remonstrance or the status of episcopacy, in which their voices and votes could have stemmed the tide?[48] How had they been persuaded by the linguistic manufactures which the contrivers and 'the Calvinian faction' had imposed on those who resisted their designs: by the iniquitous or 'senseless' 'appellations' of 'papist', 'malignant', 'delinquent', 'scandalous clergy', 'enemies to the commonwealth'?[49] How had they been brought to wink at the legislative and procedural steps of 1641–2 that destroyed the constitution under the pretence of rescuing Charles I from 'evil counsellors' and making him 'a glorious king'?[50]

Those failings would have mattered less, indeed might never have been exposed, had not the same spirit of abdication corrupted the court. Courageous counsel and firm resolve, he believes, could at a number of points have stopped rebellion in its tracks, first in Scotland, then in England. The problem went back to the early years of the reign, when 'much the greater part' of the king's English courtiers and councillors lacked 'resolution and courage', being 'wholly intent upon their own accommodations in their fortunes . . . and in their ease and pleasure . . . having . . . no other consideration of the public than that no disturbance therein might interrupt their own quiet'.[51] Repeatedly during the prelude to the war in 1640–2, when the king needed firm and fearless advice that would embolden him to take firm and fearless decisions, few or 'none about him' had the 'courage', or 'durst', to act or speak as conscience demanded.[52] The consequent failures of resistance to the contrivers were the little accidents from which the greatest matters followed. Every misguided concession to them illustrated a rule: 'yield to one thing, and you justify the demand of another'.[53] It is a logical inference from Clarendon's narrative that the pains of hellfire awaited the contrivers. Yet it is not they whom the book counsels. The people whose consciences he tells us will have to answer to their maker are the royal advisers who either went over to the contrivers or, succumbing to the mood of *sauve qui peut* as the court disintegrated, shirked their duty of unflinching advice in favour of their own survival, so that a deserted king had to build, in 1642, a new party, 'unacquainted with the mysteries and necessary policy of government'.[54]

Legitimate authority having failed to exert or defend itself, its determined opponents penetrated the vacuum. They had the dexterity, the commitment, and the industry that the king's followers lacked, a contrast that would also be found between the war efforts of the two sides.[55] The faults of the royal entourage were

[48] Ibid., i. 363, 429, ii. 192.
[49] Ibid., i. 120, 201, 264, 365 (cf. i. 254).
[50] *CL*, ii. 14; *CH*, ii. 279.
[51] *CH*, i. 83.
[52] Ibid., i. 277, 340, ii. 7, 300–1.
[53] *SPC*, iii. 2.
[54] *CH*, i. 427–9, ii. 250.
[55] Ibid., ii. 192, 471–2, iii. 222.

aggravated by the moral indiscipline of wartime and by the humiliation of defeat. The royal council had 'a wonderful indisposition...to fighting or any other fatigue'.[56] 'Negligence, laziness, inadvertency and dejection of spirit' prevailed even among men 'who pretended most public-heartedness', and who 'did really wish the king all the greatness he desired', but who sacrificed 'the public peace and the security of their master to their own passions and appetites, to their ambition and animosities against each other'.[57] The court was torn by 'discomposures, jealousies, and disgusts' and by 'the poison of envy'.[58] The royal cause sank in a sea of disloyalty, quarrels, drink, egoism, 'atheism',[59] 'gross folly and madness'.[60] Nothing improved in the years of exile, when 'corruption' and 'so universal a licence and appetite to envy, malice and all uncharitableness' persisted at court.[61] If divine providence deployed a 'chain of miracles' to bring the king back in 1660, that was because the royalists themselves had been politically and ethically so unequal to that task.[62] There is nothing triumphalist in Clarendon's account of the Restoration. He knew what royalist divisions and weaknesses were obscured by the ephemeral rejoicing of 1660, and watched them bring the monarchy into renewed peril in the years thereafter.

In his late exile he described that process in a *Continuation* of his life of himself. There, too, history and autobiography merge. Yet as an autobiographer Clarendon is most forthcoming about those periods when he is out of politics, and when his career and character are accordingly addressed not in the course of a political narrative but in asides from it. His self-representation has, it is true, its seductive aspects. So often are his own words, whether in letters or in his retrospective narratives, our best or only source for the events that involved him that we may too readily take him at his own estimation, which was not low, and which could exasperate or antagonize men of lesser rectitude whom he felt obliged to inform of their deficiencies.[63] Even when he acknowledges shortcomings in himself, such as his being 'too proud of a good conscience',[64] he allows us to indulge them as forgivable accompaniments of strenuous merit. Nonetheless we can identify a set of convictions which held his life and thought together. They underlay his every choice and policy and his unshakeable commitment, in the blackest times, to a cause to all appearances doomed. Clarendon was a politician. He knew that even a virtuous cause will call on those subtle political 'arts, which must be indulged in the

[56] Ibid., iv. 490.
[57] Ibid., iv. 1–2.
[58] Ibid., ii. 222, 223.
[59] Quoted by Wormald, *Clarendon*, pp. 170–1.
[60] *SPC*, ii. 284.
[61] Ibid., ii. 108–9, iii. 59; *CL*, ii. 35–8.
[62] *CT*, p. 371.
[63] Some readers detect smugness in Clarendon's representation of himself. The impression may derive from a misjudgement of tone on his part (or from what to a different age may seem one): one comparable to, if less debilitating than, the straining for a humorous or anecdotal lightness of touch in the autobiographical recollections of his friend Bulstrode Whitelocke: Blair Worden, 'The "Diary" of Bulstrode Whitelocke', *English Historical Review* 108 (1993), pp. 133–4. Few readers can want Clarendon to tell them quite so often of the things he was 'wont to say' or 'often' said.
[64] *CL*, iii. 812.

transactions of human affairs'.[65] He despaired at the naiveté of royalist politicians who spurned the 'arts' exploited by the parliamentarians, who had to be beaten at their own game.[66] He knew that concessions and compromises, and disingenuous offers of them, are inherent in the political process. He recognized the need for ruthlessness when work to save the kingdom could not be 'done by halves'.[67] But to him political engagement was always the servant of conviction. There were principles he would never soften or betray.

His autobiographical asides cover four periods. All but the first were years of exile, when his beliefs were tested and deepened. But the first, the time of his early life, is instructively related too. Alongside the account of his upbringing in a family of lawyer-gentry in Wiltshire and of his swift rise as a professional lawyer, the career he sacrificed to politics from 1640, we have his description of the youthful friendships that, he says, transformed his career, brought focus to his life, and tamed his inclination to 'passion' and his 'humour between wrangling, and disputing, very troublesome'.[68] To Clarendon friendship has a sacramental quality.[69] True friends raise each other, by example and counsel, in virtue. Because they trust each other, the counsel can be candid. Friendship and counsel are almost synonymous to him, for 'without faithful counsel the tribute of friendship can never be given'.[70] The combination of the two is essential in the political world, where statesmen need friends to counsel them into prudence. The 'single misfortune' of the Duke of Buckingham in the 1620s, 'which indeed was productive of many greater', was 'that he never made a noble and a worthy friendship with a man so near his equal that he would frankly advise him, for his honour and true interest, against the current, or rather the torrent, of his impetuous passions'.[71] Friendship and counsel are linked to another word, 'conversation',[72] by which Clarendon means the improving and socializing interchange of humanity. 'Conversation', 'open and liberal-minded conversation', 'with wise and good men cannot be over-valued; it forms the mind and understanding'.[73]

The early friendships of Hyde that have attracted most attention—very rewarding attention—are those now associated with the theological discussions at Falkland's house at Great Tew in north Oxfordshire.[74] But those connections were part of a wider affinity, whose character was metropolitan as well as rural, literary as well as theological. The friend to whom the autobiography gives pride of place is the ageing

---

[65] *CH*, iii. 181.

[66] Ibid., i. 4, 82, 416, 464, 481, ii. 419 (cf. ii. 494), iii. 181, 183–5, 289; Edward Hyde, Earl of Clarendon, *A Full Answer to an Infamous and Trayterous Pamphlet* (1648), p. 80.

[67] Ibid., v. 376; cf. iv. 490.

[68] *CL*, i. 69.

[69] *CT*, p. 133.

[70] Ibid., p. 132.

[71] *CH*, i. 142.

[72] *CT*, pp. 130–9.

[73] Ibid., p. 103.

[74] See especially Hugh Trevor-Roper, *Catholics, Anglicans and Puritans* (1987), ch. 4.

Ben Jonson,[75] who was the presiding genius of Hyde's younger friends, and whose influence, from beyond the grave, would permeate the cultural dimension of royalism. One poem of Jonson takes us, as much as any other, into the values Hyde shares with him: 'Inviting a Friend to Supper'.[76] At the meal, where Virgil or Tacitus or Livy or the Bible will be read to the company, there will come together the pleasures of friendship, trust, 'innocence' (a favourite word of Clarendon's), openness, hospitality, cheer. At dinners attended by the young Hyde himself, the company 'enjoyed themselves with great delight, and publick reputation, for the innocence, and sharpness, and learning of their conversation'.[77] Clarendon's moralism is sometimes so strict that we can be surprised to discover his insistence on 'chearful' demeanour and on the jollity and merriment that, at least in fit season, become a guiltless heart, and his dislike of the 'sourness', 'sullenness', and 'morosity' that betray a guilty one. He was, as John Evelyn said, 'of a jolly temper, after the old English fashion'.[78]

Jonson's poem promises jollity at his 'mirthfull board'. Jonson, who had endured surveillance from brutal agents of the Crown under Elizabeth, assures us that the conviviality will be uninhibited, for there will be no spies present to impair the 'liberty that we'll enjoy tonight'. In his Roman play *Sejanus his Fall* Jonson repeatedly departed from the sources to which he was normally faithful to have the tyrannical regime place spies at the dinners of its antagonists.[79] Jonson's spirit unexpectedly surfaces in a declaration written by Hyde on the king's behalf in 1642, where Hyde breaks from tit-for-tat allegations about the issues of dispute between Crown and parliament to accuse the contrivers of 'examining' 'the discourses at tables', and of violating 'the laws of hospitality and civility . . . , the freedom and liberty of conversation (the pleasure and delight of life)'.[80] The *History* tells us of the hope, in the following year, that a truce in the war would 'give an opportunity of charitable intercourse, and revive that freedom of conversation which would rectify the understanding of many' who had been 'misled' into fighting the king.[81] Hating war, and civil war most of all,[82] Hyde was distressed not only by the waste of blood and the physical destruction but by the ruin of trust and charity and neighbourliness, and by the 'barbarous and bloody fierceness and savageness' which 'extinguished all relations'[83] and which produced in households a 'defection' of 'kindnesse and affectionate inclinations'.[84] He looked to the values,

---

[75] *CL*, i. 30. I plan to explore the relationship of the two men elsewhere.
[76] Epigram 101.
[77] *CL*, i. 27–8.
[78] E. S. de Beer, ed., *The Diary of John Evelyn*, 6 vols (Oxford, 1955), iv. 339.
[79] Blair Worden, 'Ben Jonson and the Monarchy', in Robin Headlam Wells, Glenn Burgess, and Rowland Wymer, eds, *Neo-Historicism* (Cambridge, 2000), p. 76.
[80] *CH*, ii 280; cf. i. 555.
[81] Ibid., ii. 499. Though Hyde was drawn to the sentiment, his hostility to negotiations overruled it.
[82] Edward Hyde, Earl of Clarendon, *A Brief View and Survey of . . . Mr. Hobbes's Book, entitled Leviathan* (1676), p. 22; *CT*, pp. 205–9.
[83] *CL*, iii. 978.
[84] Clarendon, *Full Answer*, p. 154.

and to the political, religious, and social institutions, that create and sustain peace, harmony, civility.

Until the early death of his elder brother, Hyde seems to have been intended for ordination. Thereafter, first training for the law and then practising it, he wondered how much time to give to his profession, how much to his friendships and the 'polite learning' that animated them. The law won out, not only because he was good at it and well paid for it but because it was central to his political and social thinking, which placed law, and the order and harmony it creates and protects, at the heart of political and social well-being. It was his incandescence at the government's manipulation of the judiciary, especially in the ship money case, and still more at the readiness of the judges to 'assist in' that and other 'acts of power', that made him an ally of the contrivers of 1641. Alas, the 'contempt' for the law that arose from 'the scandal of that judgement' enabled the contrivers themselves to play fast and loose with it.[85] That was the development that in turn moved Hyde to enter the king's service in the winter of 1641–2. He believed he had succeeded, though alas only temporarily, in winning the king to his view. 'And the truth is, (which I speak knowingly), . . . the king's resolution' in March 1642

> was to shelter himself wholly under the law, to grant any thing that by the law he was obliged to grant, and to deny what by the law was in his own power and which he found inconvenient to consent to, and to oppose and punish any extravagant attempt by the force and power of the law; presuming that the king and the law together would have been strong enough for any encounter that could happen; and that the law was so sensible a thing that the people would easily perceive who endeavoured to preserve and who to suppress it, and dispose themselves accordingly.[86]

Clarendon's mind would return to that moment in an apologia compiled after his fall, where his account of his service of Charles II lays out the connecting principle of his political career:

> I always endeavoured to imprint in his majesty's mind an affection, esteem and reverence for the laws of the land: without the trampling of which under foot himself could not have been oppress'd; and by the vindication and support of them, he could only hope and expect honour and security to the Crown. Upon this foundation and declared judgement, I came into the service of his father . . . and I never swerved from that rule in my advice and counsel to him or his son.[87]

In 1663 Clarendon risked his standing with Charles II by protesting against the 'wildness and illimitedness' of a court-sponsored bill, a 'ship money in religion' as he heatedly called it,[88] to enable the Crown to bypass the Act of Uniformity.

Yet if, under Charles I, there were lawyers ready to endorse arbitrary power, there were also members of the profession who challenged the Crown's legitimate powers by 'prostituting the dignity and learning of their profession, to the cheap and vile

---

[85] *CH*, i. 88–9, 230; Clarendon, *Brief View and Survey*, p. 54.
[86] *CH*, ii. 7.
[87] *CT*, p. 5.
[88] *CL*, ii. 472–3.

affection of popular applause'.[89] There was something he thought he noticed about them. Whereas 'liberal-minded' men were generally faithful to the Crown,[90] the thoughts of the 'popular' lawyers were 'contracted to the narrow limits of the few books of that profession'.[91] They were pedants, interested, as he alleged, in law but not in justice, the sacred principle the law serves. In the 1630s he had to work with such men, but avoided eating with them. Instead he took his meals with lawyers of broader interests,[92] who like him mingled in the world of poets and playwrights and scholars around the Inns of Court.

In exile, retrospect cast sunshine on those early years. Many seventeenth-century figures turned in adversity to the principles of stoicism, but whose commitment to them was more radically searched and proved? His is not a passive or 'sullen' stoicism, an outlook he abhors.[93] He has no time for inert virtue or for the purely contemplative life. There is, he maintains, no political predicament, not even that of the exiled royalists, so black as to warrant the withdrawal from public engagement that he sometimes privately craves. 'Let the world be as vayne and as bad as it can be,' he declares, 'good men will be able to doe some good in it.'[94] Yet nothing can be more restorative to an active man than the meditation induced by involuntary inactivity, and the sense of proportion it imposes on the favours and disfavours of fortune. In his enforced 'vacations and retreats' he learned to 'repair the breaches in his own mind' which the agitation and absorption of politics had opened.[95] For 'there is so transcendent a joy and delight in that well chosen and well instructed solitude' wherein a man 'enjoys a second fruition of whatsoever was agreeable to him in the active part of his life . . . by a sober recollection'.[96] Jonson, in lines that the young Hyde echoed in verse of his own on the death of John Donne, commended the ideal of the 'gathered self'.[97] Hyde gathered himself in his 'vacations', when he read as extensively as he wrote.

The first of them, on the islands that had become almost the last refuge of the king's cause, impelled him to a fundamental political reappraisal, in which the motives and conduct of the parliamentarians with whom he had worked in the early stages of the Long Parliament appeared in a new and unforgiving light. He would remember it in terms which intimate how close he had been to the contrivers before his breach with them in the winter of 1641–2, and how plausible he had found their professions of upright intent. In that first exile he

---

[89] *CH*, i. 404.
[90] Ibid., i. 429–30.
[91] Ibid., i. 406; cf. *CT*, p. 102.
[92] *CL*, i. 60.
[93] *CT*, p. 96; *CH*, iii. 183, 224; Clarendon, *Characters of . . . Essex and . . . Buckingham*, p. 5.
[94] Quoted by Brownley, *Clarendon*, p. 101.
[95] Ibid., iii. 973.
[96] *CT*, p. 203.
[97] Jonson, Epigram 98, lines 9–12 (and the concluding four lines of Jonson's play *Catiline his Conspiracy*); John Donne, *Poems* (1633), p. 377, lines 15–16.

had now time to mend his understanding...by the observation of and reflections upon the grounds and successes of those counsels he had been privy to.... He had originally in his nature so great a tenderness and love towards mankind, that he did...really believe that all men were such as they...appeared to be; that they had the same justice and candour and goodness in their nature, that they professed to have.... But now, upon the observation and experience he had in the parliament... he reformed all those mistakes.... He had seen those there, upon whose ingenuity and probity he would willingly have deposited all his concernments of this world, behave themselves with that signal uningenuity and improbity that must pull up all confidence by the roots; men of the most unsuspected integrity, and of the greatest eminence for their piety and devotion, most industrious to impose upon and to cozen men of weaker parts and understanding.... He saw the most inhuman and bloody rebellion contrived by them who were generally believed to be the most solicitous and zealous for the peace and prosperity of the kingdom, with such art and subtlety, and so great pretences to religion, that it looked like illnature to believe that such sanctified persons could entertain any but holy purposes.[98]

On Jersey he knew he might soon be captured and, as one of the royalists whom parliament, in all its propositions for a negotiated settlement with the king, had excluded from any future consideration of pardon,[99] face execution. Yet he found 'great tranquillity of spirit' there.[100] It was a time of self-renewal, when 'a mind so wasted and weakened as mine' had the opportunity 'to refresh and strengthen itself with sitting still, and resolving past omissions and mistakes, and forming and making up a resolution and constancy...to bear chearfully the worst that can happen by the malice or calumny or tyranny of the time'.[101] Yet it was not enough. The execution of the king in 1649, 'that unparalleled and stupendious wickednesse', moved him to bottomless anger at 'the most barefaced avowed rebellion, that hath bene known in any age', and at 'the pryde, malice, and ambition of sacrilegious, bloody, mischievous traytors'.[102] The crisis of the months around the regicide 'disturbed and distracted his understanding, and broke his mind'. He realized that in Jersey 'he had not fortified himself enough against future assaults, nor laid in ballast enough to be prepared to ride out the storms and tempests that he was like to be engaged in'.[103] On the doomed embassy to Madrid in 1650–1, his second 'vacancy', he 'recollect[ed] and compose[d] his broken thoughts'.[104] Not only was the royal cause now shattered. So—permanently, it perhaps seemed—was his own capacity to influence a court now set on what he took to be the fatally self-destructive policies favoured by his long rival in the counsels of the two kings he served, Henrietta Maria. The defeat at Worcester in 1651 discredited the queen mother's strategy and raised Hyde to eminence. But it did not spare him, in the

---

[98] *CL*, iii. 976–7. For Hyde's closeness to the 'contrivers' see Ollard, *Clarendon and his Friends*, pp. 57–8; *CH*, i. 334; *SPC*, iii. 435.
[99] Ollard, *Clarendon and his Friends*, p. 74.
[100] *CL*, i. 202, iii. 976.
[101] *SPC*, ii. 241.
[102] Bodl., Clarendon MS 39, fos 49ᵛ–50.
[103] *CL*, iii. 983–4, 984.
[104] Ibid., iii. 990.

years ahead, from the periods of penury and of hunger in unheated rooms, the hatred of his rivals in the demoralized vagrant court, or the crushing disappointments brought by the reluctance of Europe's kings to aid the Stuart cause and by the failures of royalist conspiracy in England.

In 1660 fortune's wheel abruptly turned. Only months after General Monck's march south had seemed to the despairing exiles to have given new life to the rule of the English traitors, Hyde was raised to the heights of power and prosperity. In 1667 came a turn no less abrupt. Now the object of public detestation and ridicule, blamed for disasters beyond his control and policies he had not favoured, charged with malpractices he had not committed, abandoned by the king he had served for more than twenty years, he fled abroad from impeachment. He would not see his country again. In his extremities of gout or arthritis it now took two men to carry his pain-racked, corpulent body. At Evreux in Normandy he was beaten within an inch of his life by an aggrieved and drunken gang of English sailors. Only eventually was Louis XIV persuaded to permit him to stay in France, where Clarendon found a succession of homes. Yet this last of his 'vacations', the most productive for his prose, was also, he recorded, the 'most blessed' of them.[105] Driven into 'such a solitariness and desertion, as must reduce my giddy and wandring soul to some recollection and steddiness', he 'recovered . . . a marvellous tranquillity and serenity of mind, by making a strict review and recollection into all the actions, all the faults and follies' of the 'continued fatigue' of the long years of business since his elevation after the battle of Worcester.[106] He reflected on the errors of his 'too great prosperity'[107] since the Restoration, when he had forgotten the stoical vows of his previous exile and, 'carried away with the ambition and vanity of the world',[108] had plunged into the shameful 'folly' and ruinous expense of building Clarendon House in the Strand.[109] Now he resumed the meditations on the Psalms on which he had worked in the previous two exiles, and which were perhaps his strongest comfort in adversity. The sense of inner equability that pervades his late writing was born of his hard-won assurance, at once stoic and Christian, that if we do our 'duty without hesitation', and 'leave all the rest to the disposition of providence', no tribulation that God allows to visit us will do us any harm that matters.[110]

To Clarendon the civil wars were a national fit, an aberration. He did not think that they had long-term causes, or that the world had been moved on by them. In 1660 he hoped that the damage could be rectified by a return to the nation's 'old good humour and its old good nature'.[111] It was not that he lacked a sense of historical development or a capacity to welcome change. On the contrary. He approvingly

---

[105] *CH*, iii. 991.
[106] *CT*, p. 373; *CL*, iii. 991–2.
[107] *CT*, p. 373.
[108] Ibid., p. 770.
[109] *CL*, iii. 971–2.
[110] Ibid., iii. 984–5; *CH*, iii. 227–8.
[111] *CJ* 13 September 1660.

traced processes of evolution in the histories of the Church and of parliament and of ideas. He believed recent generations to have attained, in the teeth of those deplorable European ideological conflicts against which so much of his thought was a reaction, great advances in 'learning', 'knowledge', 'piety', 'wisdom', and 'good manners'.[112]

That progress had been made possible, he believed, by two interconnected blessings: freedom of enquiry, and a readiness to confront inherited suppositions. In the spirit of Great Tew he pleaded for liberty for the 'natural doubts or discourses which cannot but arise among learned men'. Without them, not only is a nation's 'mind' 'shackled' but its 'spirits and courage' will be 'broken'.[113] There is 'no greater obstruction in the investigation of truth, or the improvement of knowledge', than a 'supine' or 'stupid resignation of the understanding' to 'authority' or 'old dictates' or 'tradition' (that 'rope of sand'), or a readiness to 'dote' on the 'wrinkled face' of 'antiquity'. It was absurd of the papacy to refuse 'the mention of any thing that is new' in either 'science' or 'divinity', for 'religion . . . hath received great benefit' from 'improvement' in 'arts and sciences, and in all human literature'.[114] Yet when it comes to politics and to the institutions of society a quite different tone prevails. His heart sinks to contemplate Charles II's taste for 'novelty' and 'innovation', which are 'ever attended by mischiefs unforeseen', and the king's lack of 'reverence' for 'antiquity' and for 'old orders, forms and institutions'.[115]

That word 'reverence' runs through Clarendon's writings and binds their preoccupations. Reverence sustains and dignifies the framework of moral agreement and political security within which peace, virtue, piety, learning, and sociability can flourish. 'Reverence' is, with 'honour' and 'reputation', 'the life itself of princes' and 'the best support of . . . royalty'.[116] The veneration of kings is a manifestation not, as Milton would have said, of idolatry, but of civility,

> it being the most miraculous act, not only of God's kindness but of his power, to produce such a harmony of obedience out of such a discord of affections, that the pride, and passions, and humours, and interests, and ambitions of a whole nation, should be wrapt up and kneaded into a joint and universal submission to the dictates and order of one man, whom much the major part never saw.[117]

If a king oppresses us we must not 'so much as murmur in private' against him, 'much less traduce him to others', for there is no telling what 'pernicious and destructive conspiracies may be effects of those reproaches'.[118]

A chain of duty and civility links a good man's devotion to his king to an esteem for religion and the Church, for law, for country, for heads of households. 'The progress is very natural', Clarendon warns, from a want of respect for the Church to

---

[112] *CT*, p. 236; *RP*, pp. 306, 417.
[113] *RP*, pp. 373–4.
[114] *CT*, pp. 196–7, 582–3; *RP*, pp. 373–4.
[115] *CL*, ii. 188, iii. 596, 605.
[116] *CH*, i. 260; *CL*, iii. 676.
[117] *CT*, p. 419.
[118] Ibid., p. 555.

'an equal irreverence to the government of the state'.[119] So 'there cannot be too intent a care in kings and princes to preserve and maintain all decent forms and ceremonies both in Church and state, which keeps up the veneration and reverence due to religion and the Church of Christ'.[120] 'Reverence' for the law and judges and 'reverence' for the Crown likewise sustain each other.[121] Then there was the duty of respect within the family. In the civil war, he alleged, the mentality of disobedience had spread not only through the political nation but into family life, where it induced the insubordination of children and servants.[122] Then too there were the bonds of 'king and country'.[123] Nature commands us to reverence our 'country' as we do our parents. Its 'benefit' is, alongside 'the service of God' and our 'own salvation', one of 'the three peculiar ends of man's creation', and is to be sought as industriously as the other two. So 'they who have not a very strong affection for their country, cannot love any other thing, hardly God himself'. The assault by Puritan rule on the nation's laws and religion makes larger claims on our feeling than do our own 'particular sufferings' under it.[124] Our obligations to our native land are inseparable from those to its institutions, for 'the Patria, which is the object of our reverence and veneration, is to be understood of, or with the form, frame, and constitution of government to which all men owe their safety and subsistence'.[125]

Clarendon tells us, what his writings confirm, that he has 'taken more pains' than most men 'in the examination of religion'.[126] It is sometimes suggested that religion was secondary to politics in his mind, or that his attitude to the Church was the 'secular and constitutional' position of a man who never 'felt drawn to godliness'.[127] After all, he held that 'the intermixture' of 'ecclesiastical government with the civil state' required 'the government of the Church' to be directed 'by the rules of human policy'.[128] He thought of episcopacy as 'a part of the government of England',[129] and in defending the bishops took his stand not on their religious functions but on their right to sit in the House of Lords. He regarded their exclusion in 1642 as 'the removing a landmark; and the shaking the very foundation of government; and therefore he always opposed, upon the impulsion of conscience, all mutations in the Church'.[130] He himself was puzzled to find that to 'mention', 'seriously', 'the policy of religion, and religion of state' was to incur

[119] *CH*, i. 265–6.
[120] Edward Hyde, Earl of Clarendon, *Animadversions upon a Book* (1673), p. 140.
[121] *CH*, i. 88–9.
[122] Hyde, *Full Answer*, p. 154.
[123] *CT*, p. 370.
[124] Ibid., pp. 189, 340, 745.
[125] *SPC*, ii. 340.
[126] *CL*, i. 96.
[127] David L. Smith, *Constitutional Royalism and the Search for Settlement, c. 1640–1649* (Cambridge, 1994), p. 53. But Smith has excellent material on Clarendon's political world.
[128] *CH*, ii. 513.
[129] *SPC*, iii. 3.
[130] *CL*, i. 96–7.

'the censure of being without religion'.[131] We in turn may be surprised by his invocation, on such a front, of 'conscience'. For we tend instinctively to equate Erastianism, which subordinates, as he did, the Church to the state, with cool scepticism. In his case nothing could be further from the truth. Religion was no less broad or deep a foundation of his life than it was of the conduct of his Puritan opponents.[132]

His faith and mentality were far removed from theirs, or at least from what he took theirs to be. 'Very merry men', he told parliament in 1660 in urging the nation to turn its back on the Puritan years, 'have been very godly men.'[133] There is, he wrote elsewhere, 'nothing more acceptable to God' than 'mirth', 'joy', and 'jollity' in his worship, those 'chearful breathings of the soul'.[134] He rebukes 'sowre and severe moroseness' in religion, whose practitioners behave 'as if our thoughts ought to be so entirely engrossed and disposed to the contemplation of heaven, that we ought to have no taste and relish in the matters of this life'. For 'God hath made this world, not only for us to live in, but to take pleasure and delight in'. Clarendon did not, with the Puritans, insist on the chasm between God's perfection and man's helpless sinfulness, or suppose God to be offended by accommodations between his decrees and the frailties of the human heart and mind. Doctrinal 'errors have always been' and always will be;[135] 'no reformation is worth . . . a civil war';[136] and 'there are very few errors or corruptions in Christian religion, that are not in themselves more innocent, or less mischievous, than the course that is taken for the removal and extirpation of them'.[137]

No incomprehensible or intimidating distance separates man from God or this world from the next. 'We cannot represent a more lively image' of the 'glory' of heaven than by imagining, in manifestations 'more sublime and delicate, more ravishing, and more comforting', 'the most beautiful and heightened satisfaction in all the pleasures this good world can yield'. After all, 'it would be no commendation of the beauty and delicacy of a palace, or of the healthy air in which it is situated, that we found a sudden refreshment and delight by coming into it, out of some noisome dungeon in which we had been very long imprisoned'.[138] Hell, too, has its earthly correspondences: 'we cannot make a more lively representation and emblem to our selves of hell, than by the view of a kingdom in war'.[139]

He scarcely mentions the Fall. He tells us that a man who is unaware of 'the dignity of our creation', and who does not see 'how near he is of kin to God himself', will slip into shameful conduct, having 'too little reverence for himself'.

---

[131] *CT*, p. 255.
[132] Wormald, *Clarendon*, gives a stronger sense of what Hyde's religion was not than of what it was. Wormald's difficulty in thinking of his subject's Erastian Anglicanism as religious can be deduced from Michael Bentley, *The Life and Thought of Herbert Butterfield* (Cambridge, 2011), p. 278.
[133] *CJ*, 13 September 1660.
[134] *CT*, pp. 535, 745.
[135] Ibid., p. 271.
[136] Hyde, *Animadversions*, p. 136; cf. *SPC*, iii. 2.
[137] *CT*, p. 242.
[138] Ibid., pp. 760–1.
[139] Ibid., p. 211.

Through 'reason' and the other 'noble faculties' of man which God has created in his own image, we can, with 'firm and magnanimous resolution', reform 'our greatest infirmities and disorders'.[140] In the great controversy between Calvinism and Arminianism over predestination and free will, Clarendon takes the Arminians to have reason and learning on their side. No less than Milton, to whose words on the subject in *Areopagitica* his own come close,[141] he takes freedom of the will and of choice to be essential properties both of virtue and of the mind's enquiries. But he does not go into the theological controversy. Again in the spirit of Great Tew, he dislikes 'unnecessary' doctrinal disputes and 'questions'.[142] The Synod of Dort, which had met in 1618 to resolve the Calvinist-Arminian contest, 'hath given the world so much occasion since for uncharitable disputations which they were called together to prevent'.[143] We should not 'perplex ourselves' with those 'hard words' of theological contention, so important to Puritans, 'justification and merit, which signify no more, or less, than they who use them intend they should'.[144] The truths essential for salvation, concisely defined by the primitive Church, are few. No good man could reject them, but beyond them it is not what we 'think' that matters but what we 'do'.[145] The 'very life of religion', which struggles to survive 'the bitterness and uncharitableness of contention in matters of opinion', lies in its 'practice' and its 'practical duties',[146] a view to which others of his generation were coming round.[147] He shared it with 'my very good friend' Henry Hammond,[148] who in the civil wars set about the reconstruction of Anglican theology on the same premise. Clarendon reminds us 'how little pains our Saviour took ... to explain any doctrinal parts, or indeed to institute anything of speculative doctrine, in his Sermon on the Mount, which comprehends all Christianity'. Instead Christ had 'resolved all into practice'.[149] What God will judge at our entry to the next world is our use of the time he has allotted us to improve this one by an active and virtuous life.

Hyde ties his ideals of law, peace, harmony, and security to the precepts of Christianity. Since it is the rule of sovereigns that sustains those blessings, God entrusts the management of religion to them. Accordingly the boundaries of churches are those of kingdoms. National churches should live in dialogue and charity with each other, and pursue ecumenical initiatives that might reconcile Protestant and Catholic, western Christianity and Greek. But the same churches are to respect each other's independence. God expects the government of churches, as of states, to vary in their 'forms and customs', those 'superstructures for the exercise and practice of religion' that are to suit 'the nature, temper and inclinations of the people'. The raiser and preserver of the superstructures is to be the sovereign. To authorize and assist him, the Apostles had commended obedience to rulers as a 'vital' part of religion.[150] Yet how heavy are the obligations which that

---

[140] *CT*, pp. 99, 102; Hyde, *Brief View and Survey*, pp. 27, 29.
[141] *CT*, pp. 190–1 (cf. p. 199); *RP*, p. 374; *WJM*, iv. 311.
[142] *CT*, p. 561.   [143] *CH*, i. 81.   [144] *CT*, p. 414.   [145] Ibid., p. 261.
[146] *CH*, ii. 419; *CT*, pp. 212, 229.
[147] Above, pp. 88, 334.   [148] *CT*, p. 381.   [149] Ibid., p. 248.
[150] Ibid., p. 221.

subordination lays on princes, and how 'odious and inexcusable' in rulers is 'indevotion and coldness in religion', which 'takes away all lustre and beauty in them'.[151] Clarendon took the political health of kingdoms to depend on the ethical examples of kings. He went further. Since God judges us by our conduct, the 'decent and pious examples' of princes, and their discountenance of vice, can be the 'means' of their subjects' 'salvation'.[152]

Clarendon, he tells us, was 'one of those who do really believe the Church of England to be the best constituted ... of any that is now in the Christian world', 'the most exactly formed and framed for the encouragement and advancement of learning and piety, and for the preservation of peace'.[153] 'It enjoins nothing to be believed or practised which excludes salvation, nor inhibits any thing that is necessary to it.'[154] Alone among the substantial states of the sixteenth century, England had achieved its Reformation through its rightful instruments, the Crown and the law. In the civil wars the preservation of episcopacy was essential, not because as a form of church government it had any divine sanction, but because it was 'as much fenced and secured by the laws, as monarchy itself'.[155] He could not warm to the Calvinist churches abroad, which had established and sullied themselves by war and revolution. The Church of England had another immeasurable advantage. It was a ceremonial Church. A devotee of 'the beauty of holiness',[156] but not of 'gaudry and pomp' which got separated from 'the inward operation and effect of religion', he maintained that 'inward sanctity' appears 'the more beautiful, for the outward decency and lustre that attends it'.[157] He dismissed as 'fantastick madness' the notion that God is no more 'present and propitious to our devotion in churches, than in any other places'.[158] Ceremony of worship can bring this world closer to the next, for 'in churches decently kept, and beautified as they ought to be ... we have even a sight of God', and our collective prayers and praises are a 'lively representation upon earth' of 'the court and company of heaven'.[159]

England's 'blessed time' since the Reformation, he declared, was 'not to be paralleled in any nation under heaven'. The Church had come to 'flourish with learned and extraordinary men'.[160] Yet in the early seventeenth century disaster had struck, with the appointment to the see of Canterbury, on 'the never enough lamented death' of Richard Bancroft, that vigilant corrector of nonconformity, of George Abbot, the friend of the 'Calvinian party', 'a man of very morose manners and a very sour aspect, which in that time was called gravity'. His reign had 'profaned' the Church and sanctioned 'a negligence that gave great scandal to it'. Churches fell into disrepair; their insides were kept 'indecently and slovenly'; the sacraments were casually administered. So when William Laud, whose devoted friend and follower Hyde would soon become, replaced Abbot he had 'a very difficult work to do, to reform and reduce' the Church 'into order'.[161] Though Clarendon believed that Laud and his followers made disastrous mistakes of tactics and tone—for

---

[151] Ibid., p. 444.   [152] Ibid., pp. 567–9, 572, 647.
[153] Ibid., p. 271; *CL*, i. 96.   [154] *CT*, p. 244.   [155] *SPC*, ii. 308.
[156] *CH*, i. 110.   [157] *CT*, p. 489.   [158] Ibid., p. 574.   [159] Ibid., p. 607.
[160] *CH*, i. 95.   [161] Ibid., i. 118–19, 126.

'clergymen . . . understand the least, and take the worst measure of human affairs, of all mankind, that can write, and read'—he applauded their goals.[162] Historians like to contrast the liberalism of Great Tew with the Laudian drive for uniformity, but in Hyde's mind intellectual freedom and institutional compulsion were allied virtues. In line with Great Tew he balked at the notion 'that all men must think the same thing', a condition that would 'obstruct all growth of knowledge and improvement of virtue'.[163] But as in politics, so in religion, intellectual enquiry was one thing, challenges to institutional authority another. The conformity demanded of us, being only to 'the superstructures of religion', cannot imperil our salvation. In the 1630s Hyde was appalled by the 'exorbitances' and 'extraordinary courses' of the Court of Star Chamber in 'vindicating illegal commissions'.[164] Yet he roundly welcomed the same court's severe punishment of those nonconformist insulters of Church and state, William Prynne, John Bastwick, and Henry Burton.[165]

Hyde is contemptuous of the ostensibly religious basis of the parliamentarian cause. The invocation of 'conscience' to sanction the withdrawal of allegiance from princes is always a 'pretence',[166] for Scripture, which is the rule of conscience, enjoins nothing more unambiguously than obedience to them. A long tradition of exegetical debate is brushed aside by his assertion that 'rebellion never did, never can take deep root, while the Scripture is hearkened to, and the priests . . . enforce the true sense' of the Bible on the subject.[167] What then could be said for the parliamentarian preachers, who, 'by their function being messengers of peace, are the only trumpets of war and incendiaries towards rebellion', and who make Christ, 'that is all mercy and peace', 'the argument for the most bloody, cruel and unnatural wars'?[168] And how could anyone with any 'knowledge or science' be taken in by the claims of parliamentarians that their successes showed God to be on their side?[169] The revolution, in Hyde's judgement, had no roots in true religion. Episcopacy and the Prayer Book and liturgy had commanded wide public support until 1641–2, when the manipulation of hysterical fears of popery by the contrivers undermined it. His detestation of Presbyterians was lifelong. If he offered them temporary concessions in the Restoration, it was in the hope that accommodation might soften their asperity, and that the Church might 'by degrees recover what cannot be had at once'.[170] One cannot make a moderate of Clarendon, though many have tried.

Although the Puritan upheaval was the central event of his life, his observations on Puritans (a word he uses sparingly) are mostly confined to sharp glances. He wrote much more about Catholicism: not about Catholic theology, but about the claims of the papacy to an allegiance incompatible with loyalty to prince and state. That was to him the basic sickness of Europe, now as for ages past. It was the subject he addressed, with urgency and wide learning, right at the end of his life, in

[162] *CL*, i. 66.   [163] *CT*, p. 267.   [164] *CH*, i. 374.
[165] Ibid., i. 266–9.   [166] *CT*, pp. 162, 250; Hyde, *Brief View and Survey*, p. 165.
[167] *CT*, p. 564.   [168] *CH*, ii. 321; *CT*, p. 487.
[169] *CH*, iii. 302; cf. above, p. 61.   [170] *SPC*, iii. 732.

his long book *Religion and Policy*. He acknowledged that there were 'good Catho-lics',[171] 'pious and sober Catholics', 'very many learned and pious Catholics'.[172] Since the Reformation 'good Catholic families' in England, 'of ancient extraction', had served the Crown without 'blemish'.[173] He memorialized the Catholics who hid and helped Charles II in his flight from Worcester,[174] though by the same token he was unforgiving of those of their co-religionists who had 'very unreason-ably' failed to rally to the Crown in 1642.[175] What he could not stomach was the ardour of converts to Catholicism, who tended to 'contract a wonderful warmth and zeal for the religion they are newly acquainted with, and an equal fierceness and animosity against that which they are departed from'. How could they have brought themselves to change the religion 'in which they have been born and bred'?[176] He likewise asked how Puritans could reject 'a faith and a form of worship in which they had been educated from their cradle'.[177] As so often, his values are Ben Jonson's. In Jonson's poem 'To Penshurst' we are told nothing of the content of the faith of the Sidney family which owns the house, only of its place in the social harmony and stability for which the house stands.[178] The children 'are and have been taught religion; that thence | Their gentle spirits may suck innocence'. Jonson, who renounced Catholicism in favour of the religion of his country, had himself wrestled with the problem of allegiance which Clarendon extensively addresses, and had come out on what to Clarendon was unanswerably the right side.

Clarendon is distressed to think that there are people among 'my countrymen the Roman Catholics' who have brought themselves to 'disobey and condemn the laws of their country, upon pretence of religion'.[179] Thus did they, and those who submitted to papal allegiance on the Continent,

> distinguish themselves from their fellow subjects, by acknowledging but half that obedience to their prince which the other half pays, and in that part which relates merely and purely to the peace and security of their common country, and not at all to the exercise of their religion; and thereby to force and compel their sovereign princes, who should be common fathers to their subjects, to give but a half protection to them who will pay but half obedience; and to make the strictest laws to disenable those from doing hurt by their depraved affections to their king and country, by taking those lawful oaths which are the common bonds of all subjects within the same dominions, and which have as well to do with the illimited fancies of the brain, as the dutiful affections of the heart; and though men cannot reasonably be tied to think what others think, they may be ready to do what others do.[180]

If Catholics would only renounce the papal claims, their errors of doctrine—for Clarendon was sure they were errors—would prove 'not dangerous to the state'.[181] Like the Presbyterian fallacies, they could be expected to wither once the political passions that had entrenched them had subsided. *Religion and Policy* advises 'Catholic princes' to heed his teaching about allegiance.[182] But it is the English

---

[171] *RP*, p. 491.   [172] Ibid., p. 490.   [173] Ibid., p. 561; *CL*, ii. 561.
[174] *CH*, v. 194–214.   [175] Ibid, ii. 276–7; cf. RP, pp. 657–8.   [176] *RP*, pp. 85–6.
[177] *CH*, iii. 484.   [178] 'The Forest', no. 2.   [179] *CT*, p. 343; *RP*, p. 667.
[180] *RP*, p. 666.   [181] Ibid., p. 707.   [182] Ibid., pp. 141–2.

king he has at the front of his mind. Perhaps hoping, even to the end, that Charles II might recall him, or at least take notice of his advice, he counsels against the 'mistaken charity' of the king's plans for the 'indulgence' of Catholics who have not renounced the pope.[183]

If the papacy should respect the sovereignty of kings, so must kings respect the sovereignty of each other. It is perhaps surprising to find a Protestant writer remembering how Gustavus Adolphus 'covered all Germany with blood and slaughter' by his barbaric invasion of the territory of the Catholic Emperor.[184] Kings who wage unjust wars, 'as if the religion of princes were nothing but policy enough to make all other kingdoms but their own miserable',[185] 'should wisely remember and foresee' that the afterlife will 'inevitably' bring them before 'a high court of justice . . . where the perjury of princes will be so much more severely punished than that of private men, by how much it is always attended with a train of blood and rapine, which the other is not guilty of'.[186] He longed to see Europe's kings, especially the present rulers of France and Spain who had plunged their countries into so unwarrantable and hideous a war against each other, 'awake' to the obligations of amity among princes, which are as holy as the ties of king and subject. The concluding sentence of the *History* voices its author's enduring anger at the 'machinations' of the leading ministers of France and Spain. Instead of uniting on behalf of their fellow prince Charles II against the regicides, 'against whom', he tells us elsewhere, 'all the kings of the earth ought to have denounced fire and sword, and extirpation',[187] they had turned his plight to their own unscrupulous diplomatic purposes.[188]

Clarendon is sometimes called a 'constitutional monarchist' or 'constitutional royalist', but that depends what one means.[189] His thought was 'constitutional' in the sense that he believed the Crown's powers to be defined by law and that he insisted on its observance. He did not think that kingship, any more than episcopacy, was enjoined by divine right. In their political no less than their ecclesiastical organization, countries may go their own way, though in England it would be 'sinful', at least in disordered circumstances, to abolish either monarchy or episcopacy, rooted as they were in law and time.[190] He wrote of his own 'reverence' for the nation's 'equally poised' system of government, and recalled that he had been 'as much troubled

---

[183] Ibid., p. 706.
[184] Ibid., p. 555. Where Puritans lamented the failure of the expedition to the Ile de Ré in 1627 on behalf of the Huguenots' struggle against the Catholic monarchy of France, Clarendon called it a 'provocation': *CH*, iv. 159.
[185] *SPC*, ii. 318; *CH*, ii. 420.
[186] *CT*, p. 142.
[187] Ibid., p. 370.
[188] *CH*, vi. 234.
[189] The notion of 'constitutional royalism' is critically scrutinized by David Scott, 'Rethinking Royal Politics, 1642–9', in John Adamson, ed., *The English Civil War* (Houndmills, 2009), pp. 36–60.
[190] *SPC*, ii. 308; cf. Hyde, *Brief View and Survey*, p. 99. He did think of the King of England as God's 'own vicegerent': Bodl., Clarendon MS 39, fo. 49ᵛ.

when the Crown exceeded its just limits' as by incursions upon the prerogative. But that was because the prerogative had been 'hurt' by attempts to extend it and by the 'damage and mischief' they had brought on the monarchy. He himself, as he warrantably recalled, 'never consented to any diminution of the king's authority'.[191] He maintained (as did other royalists) that over time the Crown, in order to enhance its authority in its subjects' minds, had by 'voluntary abatements' imposed restraints of statute and custom on itself.[192] He had no time for the idea of mixed monarchy, even when Falkland espoused it.[193] He thought that some of his fellow royalists exaggerated the constitutional status of parliament. Charles I is sometimes charged with stubbornness of political principle, but Clarendon thinks it was his 'softness', his failure to supply the smack of firm government or to insist on those ancient premises and practices of government which the Long Parliament invaded, that undid him.[194] When Hyde countenanced insubstantial concessions on the constitution during the peace talks of the 1640s it was solely with the purpose of dividing the king's enemies.

In his mind it is not constitutional mechanisms that create the conditions of good kingship. It is wise counsel. That is the function of the privy council, to Hyde an integral feature of the constitution. The diminution of the 'reverence' for it, he thinks, was fatal to Charles. One problem was the poor quality of its members. Another was its surrender, through the collapse of the principles of confidentiality and collective responsibility, of its capacity for 'freedom' of advice.[195] Counsellors must speak truth to power; and Hyde spoke it. We might question his retrospective accounts of his directness if his own letters from the time did not confirm it. It was a quality respected by Henrietta Maria, who told her attendants 'she did verily believe, that if he thought her a whore he would tell her of it': a statement which got back to him and 'of which he used to speak often, and looked upon as a great honour to him'.[196] At least until late in his career, his advice to princes and their close advisers contrived with singular delicacy to preserve the obligatory rules of courtesy and tenderness while submitting unambiguous assertions of unwelcome realities. It was a combination true to the ideal of counsel he had formed in his own friendships. In his last years of power, peremptoriness may have set in. By temperament and inclination never a courtier, always a man of business, he could never have participated in what he contemptuously called 'the evening conversation' of the Restoration court,[197] where the insinuations of his enemies were so damaging and provoking to him.

The *History*, that work of counsel, passes—after the king's death—'such reflections' on the reign of Charles I, on the king's 'mistakes and weaknesses', 'as shall

---

[191] *CL*, i. 96; *CH*, i. 88; cf. *CT*, p. 372.
[192] Hyde, *Brief View and Survey*, pp. 45, 71, 89–90; cf. Janelle Greenberg, *The Radical Face of the English Constitution* (Cambridge, 2001), p. 191.
[193] *CL*, i. 97, 130–2.
[194] e.g. *CH*, ii. 287–8, iv. 490.
[195] Ibid., i. 90, 257–62.
[196] Ibid., v. 66–7.
[197] *CL*, ii. 321, 324.

seem to call both his wisdom and his courage into question'.[198] None of the king's errors was greater than his readiness, which was nurtured by his queen and which shocked Hyde to the core, to make allies of enemies of the Church and Crown, whether Catholic or Presbyterian or a foreign power. Whatever conditions of alliance might be extracted from them they would remain enemies still. The terms negotiated with the Irish Catholics by the Earl of Glamorgan in 1645 were 'inexcusable to justice, piety, and prudence'.[199] When in 1646, against the 'fundamental rules of policy',[200] Charles I had the Prince of Wales sent from Jersey to his mother in Paris, Hyde, who had carefully built his trust with the king, risked all by refusing to accompany the prince, the decision which gave Hyde the leisure to write the *History*. He despaired at the 'wilderness of prudential motives, and expedients'[201] that in due course produced Charles II's humiliating submission to the Scottish Presbyterians—and despaired the more, as he admitted in the most euphemistic of his many euphemisms, because he himself 'was not without some natural prejudice to the ingenuity and sincerity of that nation'.[202] Even if such policies succeeded, a king restored by foreign or Catholic or Presbyterian conquest would be deservedly hated, and the Crown would deservedly await a second destruction.[203]

If present circumstances precluded the friends of king and Church from acting effectively, it would be best for Charles II to 'sit still' and hope for a more favourable conjuncture of international alliances or for the disintegration of the republic, which, since any league of wickedness will destroy itself, was sooner or later inevitable. From the end of the civil war Hyde's mind was clear. The Crown could be lastingly restored only 'upon the old foundation of the established government, and the good known laws in Church and state'.[204] From 1649 that was a hard stance to sustain among exiles impatient for action and for home, who reasonably asked how a monarchy which had been so wholly crushed and so devastatingly punished could hope for restoration other than on negotiated terms and with limited powers. Hyde's 'fixing upon honest principles' and his 'sober reliance upon God's providence' earned him, he acknowledged, derision for his 'senseless expectation of miracles'.[205] If the king adhered to Hyde's advice, might not the royal party melt away in discouragement? Hyde's fury at *Leviathan*, the work of 1651 by his old friend Thomas Hobbes, arose not only from the influence of what seemed to him its religious and ethical bankruptcy but from the encouragement he believed the book to have given to royalists to submit to the rebels.[206]

What was it that, amid the gloom and prevarications of the exiled court, enabled his 'principles' to remain 'fixed'? It was not any disdain for political calculation or for the art of the possible. But calculation, he believed, must start

[198] *CH*, iv. 2–4.
[199] *SPC*, ii. 337.
[200] *CH*, iv. 202.
[201] *SPC*, ii. 459.
[202] *CH*, v. 241.
[203] Wormald, *Clarendon*, p. 173.
[204] *SPC*, ii. 233, 459.
[205] Ibid., ii. 28, 326, 333.
[206] Hobbes, *Brief View and Survey*, pp. 168–9, 306–7.

with the moral truths that make or break political designs. The unyielding policies he favoured through the 1640s and 1650s were the practical expression of a philosophy of public virtue, in which, no less than in Milton's mind, Christian precepts merged with classical teaching. No one can be against virtue, but the Renaissance and post-Renaissance ideal of it was no mere platitude. It was a system of ideas, meant for use. This was the virtue whose 'sound' Sir Philip Sidney had looked to poetry to sing,[207] and which echoes through the politics and literature of the era. Like the no less far-reaching doctrine of divine providence, the principle is too pervasive for instances of it to surprise us, and suffers historical neglect through its very familiarity.

In essence the philosophy was classical, though Christianity had partially absorbed it. Its premise was that politics are an outward projection of the conflict within each mind for the sovereignty of reason and virtue. In the seventeenth century that philosophy came under challenge. There was the growing preoccupation with men as they are, not as they ought to be; and there was the insistence that political stability depends less on virtue than on reason of state or on the balancing of men's interests. Clarendon learned from those developments. A part of him was receptive to Machiavelli's teaching on statecraft and to other modern trends of historical realism.[208] Yet—like Milton, another student of Machiavelli whose mind nonetheless adhered to a classical scheme of virtue—he assimilated the lessons of 'politic history' into the ethical framework that Machiavellianism questioned.[209]

Within that framework it is virtue, fortified by prudence and resolve, that brings kings the moral authority that is the durable basis of power. The breaches of promise, and the cynical concessions to enemies, on which the Crown embarked in its negotiations with Presbyterians and Catholics could only diminish its reputation. If only Charles I, instead of taking himself to the Scots after the first civil war, had stayed in Oxford and, in captivity, 'relied upon his own virtue'![210] Here is the old call, which Sidney had made in a different political cause, for rulers to 'stand' on their virtue and to shun 'causeless yieldings' to pressures of appeasement and self-betrayal.[211] In Hyde's mind 'the virtue and vivacity of the king' was indispensable to political health.[212] In words that might almost have been Sidney's he counselled Charles I 'never to depart from his own virtue, upon which his own fate depended', and told him 'that if he forsook himself, he had no reason to depend upon the constancy of any other man'.[213] Charles II would thrive, wrote Clarendon after the regicide, only if he had 'courage and resolution to do according to his own judgement', and if he convinced the world that he was 'guided by his own

[207] Blair Worden, *The Sound of Virtue: Philip Sidney's 'Arcadia' and Elizabethan Politics* (1996).
[208] Paul Seward, 'Clarendon, Tacitism, and the Civil Wars of Europe', in Paulina Kewes, ed., *The Uses of History in Early Modern England, Huntington Library Quarterly* 68 (2005), pp. 289–311; Brownley, *Clarendon*, p. 19.
[209] *CH*, ii. 85, 546.
[210] *SPC*, ii. 338.
[211] Worden, *Sound of Virtue*, chs 7, 19.
[212] *CH*, i. 261.
[213] *CL*, i. 181.

virtue'.[214] 'There was in no conjunction more need' than at the Restoration 'that the virtue and industry of a prince should be evident'.[215]

What brings a sense of tragedy to Clarendon's narrative, and summons Shakespearian echoes, is the cease of majesty. The weaknesses of two kings who have virtue in their hearts and intentions cost the Crown its 'reverence'. Posterity has so often sanctified or vilified Charles I that Clarendon's three-dimensional portrait is unexpected. We might take his statement that he had 'a very particular devotion and passion for the person of the king'[216] to be the hyperbole of an instinctive monarchist, until we remember John Aubrey's recollection that his own close friend the republican theorist James Harrington, who was sent by parliament to serve in the royal bedchamber in the last phase of the king's life and was as afflicted as Hyde by the regicide, voiced the same ardour of affection.[217] The royal martyrdom of 1649 may have brought a heightened intensity to Hyde's love for the king and to his admiration for his better sides, but the sentiments ran deep.[218] In Clarendon's account, Charles believed all the right things about Church and state and the duty of kings. He chose wise courses—at least when Hyde's influence over him prevailed—and meant to stick to them. Time and again Clarendon tells us of the disasters for the royal cause that might have been averted 'if his majesty had continued his resolution' to pursue a particular course, 'if this resolution had been pursued', 'if this counsel had been pursued steadily and resolutely'.[219] Too often the king allowed himself to be overborne by pernicious or imprudent advisers. He was 'not confident' enough of his own 'excellent understanding', and 'trusted less to his own judgement, than he ought to have done; which rarely deceived him so much as that of other men'.[220]

Clarendon's affection for Charles II is manifest too, even if it ran less deep. In the 1650s, hoping that time would cure the king of the natural follies of youth, he coached him in the principles of pious and energetic leadership. At the Restoration he believed the king's mind, or a part of it, to be resolved on them.[221] Alas, like father like son. Delicately Clarendon indicates the difference between the chaste tone of the father's court and the promiscuity of the son's.[222] Yet behind the contrast of personal morality there lay a debilitating resemblance of temperament. Clarendon uses the same phrase of both kings: they were 'too irresolute'.[223] The son's 'resolutions' of virtuous kingship 'vanished and expired' in the jollity of the Restoration. He too was 'apt to be shaken in those counsels which with the greatest deliberation he had concluded'. He had 'that unfixedness and irresolution of judgement that was natural to all his family of the male line', 'the unhappy fate

[214] *SPC*, ii. 518.
[215] *CL*, ii. 7.
[216] Ibid., i. 96.
[217] John Aubrey, *Brief Lives*, ed. A. Clark, 2 vols (1898), i. 288–9.
[218] See especially *CH*, iv. 74, 453–5.
[219] Ibid., ii. 220–2, 388, iii. 344; cf. ii. 7, iv. 2.
[220] Ibid., iii. 344, iv. 490.
[221] *CL*, ii. 8, 45, 88 (cf. ii. 311, iii. 675).
[222] *CH*, iv. 489.
[223] Ibid., iv. 72–3; *CL*, ii. 300.

and constitution of that family' to be talked out of their disposition to 'virtue and justice' by advisers of inferior worth and perception.[224] Again we learn of the problems that would have been avoided 'if' the king had kept his 'resolutions'.[225]

Clarendon's readers watch the opportunity to renew the health of the monarchy slip away in the years from 1660. The king 'by degrees unbent his mind' from business and took refuge in laziness and licence.[226] Like his father he was betrayed by the timidity of his councillors, 'few' of whom did not 'lament' the excesses, but 'few' of whom had 'the courage' to confront him.[227] Clarendon had the courage, and paid the price for it. Charles, having heard one too many lecture from him on his extra-marital misconduct, protested that the Chancellor's condescension had become 'insupportable', and surrendered him to the earl's enemies in court and parliament. So it was that in 1667 Clarendon, who seven years earlier had landed in state with the royal party at Dover, had to embark secretly at night on a small boat for France, as regicides had done in 1660. There, in every outward respect broken and humiliated, he began that final gathering of the self in which his great collection of writings was brought together. To his completion of them we owe the supreme history of his time. We also owe a royalist record, as rounded and imposing as the surviving documentary witnesses to the lives and hearts of Cromwell, Milton, or others from the more familiar world of Puritanism, of that inherent yet to posterity permanently intractable feature of the age, the synthesis of religious and political aspiration.

---

[224] *CL*, ii. 300, 643, 687; cf. *SPC*, ii. 518.
[225] *CL*, ii. 250.
[226] Ibid., ii. 38–9, 45–8, 88.
[227] Ibid., iii. 676.

Index

OC = Oliver Cromwell